Unit 5 • Communities across Time

Program Authors

Carl Bereiter
Andrew Biemiller
Joe Campione
Iva Carruthers
Doug Fuchs
Lynn Fuchs
Steve Graham
Karen Harris
Jan Hirshberg
Anne McKeough
Peter Pannell
Marsha Roit
Marlene Scardamalia
Marcy Stein
Gerald H. Treadway Jr.
Michael Pressley

Level 3

Columbus, OH

Acknowledgments
Grateful acknowledgment is given to the following publishers and copyright owners for permissions granted to reprint selections from their publications. All possible care has been taken to trace ownership and secure permission for each selection included. In case of any errors or omissions, the Publisher will be pleased to make suitable acknowledgments in future editions.

READ ALOUD
A RIVER RAN WILD, copyright © 1992 by Lynne Cherry, reprinted by permission of Harcourt, Inc. This material may not be reproduced in any form or by any means without the prior written permission of the publisher.

STUDENT READER
THE HOUSE ON MAPLE STREET by Bonnie Pryor, illustrated by Beth Peck. Copyright © 1987. Used by permission of HarperCollins Publishers.

From: ARCHAEOLOGISTS: LIFE DIGGING UP ARTIFACTS by Holly Cefrey. Copyright © 2004 by the Rosen Publishing Group, Inc.

From EARTHQUAKE! THE 1906 SAN FRANCISCO NIGHTMARE. Reprinted with permission of Bearport Publishing Co., Inc.

The Disappearing Island Text Copyright © 2000 by Corinne Demas. Reprinted with permission of McIntosh & Otis, Inc. Illustrations used with the permission of Ted Lewin.

WHAT EVER HAPPENED TO THE BAXTER PLACE? Story by Pat Ross. By permission of Jeanne C. Duvoisin, trustee, Roger Duvoisin, "Whatever Happened to the Baxter Place?" 1976. Text copyright © 1976 by Pat Ross. Illustrations copyright © 1976 by Roger Duvoisin. Reprinted by arrangement with Jeanne C. Duvoisin, trustee.

"Early Explorers" From FOOTPRINTS ON THE ROOF: POEMS ABOUT THE EARTH by Marilyn Singer and illustrated by Meilo So, copyright © 2002 by Marilyn Singer. Illustrations copyright © 2002 by Meilo So. Used by permission of Alfred A. Knopf, an imprint of Random House Children's Books, a division of Random House, Inc.

"Caring for the World." "A Sreen Prayer" by Jane Whittle (original title). Used by permission of the author.

SRAonline.com

SRA

Printed in the United States of America.

Send all inquiries to this address:
SRA/McGraw-Hill
4400 Easton Commons
Columbus, OH 43219

ISBN: 978-0-07-616482-0
MHID: 0-07-616482-9

3 4 5 6 7 8 9 WEB 15 14 13 12 11 10 09 08

The McGraw·Hill Companies

National Advisory Board

Patricia Appell
Instructional Interventionist
Annapolis, MD

Christine P. Collins
Former Assistant Superintendent for Instruction and Curriculum
Weymouth, MA

Betsy Degen
Curriculum Director
Shawnee Mission, KS

Bryan Ertsgaard
Teacher
Dayton, OH

James T. Garvin
Assistant Principal
Charlotte, NC

Patsy M. Hall
Title I Professional Development Coordinator
Indianapolis, IN

Michelle L. King
Reading Enhancement Coach
Indianapolis, IN

Deb Owen
Assistant Superintendent for Curriculum and Instruction
Effingham, IL

Patricia Schmella
Curriculum Director
Toppenish, WA

JoAnn Schweda
Teacher
Worley, ID

Sylvia Teahan
Teacher
Medford Lakes, NJ

Joseph Turner
Assistant Principal
Indianapolis, IN

Sue Wennerberg
Teacher
Oak Park, IL

Contributing Author

Michael Milone
Assessment Specialist
Placitas, NM

Literature Consultant

Dr. Laura Apol
Professor, Michigan State University
East Lansing, MI

Program Reviewers

Noemi Arteaga-Gonzales
Teacher
San Antonio, TX

Susan Beede
Consulting Teacher
Nampa, ID

Lisa Beringer
Teacher
Bonita Springs, FL

Paula Bleakley
Teacher
Leesburg, FL

Lisa Bohanan
Instructional Specialist
Pflugerville, TX

Judi Braxton
Reading Coach
Marianna, FL

Benjamin Broadwater
Teacher
Fort Worth, TX

Jodie Broussard
Reading Coach
Pensacola, FL

Jennifer Brown-Mendoza
Reading First Coach
Hominy, OK

Kristine Cain
Teacher
Pensacola, FL

Kellie Campbell
Teacher
Cocoa, FL

Caroline Carithers
Reading Resource Teacher
Pensacola, FL

Jenny Cronan
Literacy Coach
Pittsburg, CA

Margo DiBasio
Reading Specialist
Chelsea, MA

Jennie Eddy
Title I Literacy Coach
Moore, OK

Bryan Ertsgaard
Teacher
Dayton, OH

Tami Ethridge
Instructional Coach
Lancaster, SC

Pamela C. Fendrick
Reading Coach
Tallahassee, FL

Melanie Flores
Teacher
Austin, TX

Tim Francisco
Teacher
Colorado Springs, CO

Kari Franklin
Reading Coach
Pensacola, FL

Rosa Elia Garcia
Reading Specialist
San Antonio, TX

Ashley Garrett
Teacher
Austin, TX

James T. Garvin
Assistant Principal
Charlotte, NC

Dr. Marsha R. Glover
Elementary Reading and Language Arts Developer
Tallahassee, FL

Elaine M. Grohol
Elementary Instructional Specialist
Kissimmee, FL

Patricia Ingles
Teacher
Laguna Niguel, CA

Sarah Jordan
Literacy Specialist
Longview, WA

Cindy Kearney
Teacher
Tulsa, OK

Kim Kempa
Teacher
Santa Ana, CA

Kathy Kindelan
Reading Specialist
Winter Haven, FL

Michelle L. King
Reading Enhancement Coach
Indianapolis, IN

Linda Ann Kosinski
Reading First Coordinator
La Quinta, CA

Sheryl Kurtin
Elementary Specialist, Curriculum and Instruction
Sarasota, FL

Teresa Lopez
Supervisor, Academic Achievement and Accountability
Bakersfield, CA

Jan Maglione
Teacher
Upton, MA

Barbara Maspero
Teacher
San Antonio, TX

Chaitra S. McGrew
Teacher
Austin, TX

Kathy McGuire
Instructional Coach
Roseburg, OR

Becky McPherson
Literacy Coach
Cuthbert, GA

Sheila Menning
Teacher
Largo, FL

Tamarah Michalek
Teacher
Roseburg, OR

Michele Mower
Director of Professional Development
Fontana, CA

Pamela W. Patterson
Instructional Specialist
East Point, GA

Susan Patterson
Reading Coach
Charlotte, NC

Angela Pilcher
Teacher
Stockton, CA

Dr. Jan Rauth
Educational Consultant
Longview, WA

Carlotta Ruiz
Reading Coach
Elk Grove, CA

Dr. Lynda Samons
Curriculum Director
Magnet Cove, AR

Jake Schweikhard
Teacher
Tulsa, OK

Nancy Snyder
Reading Coach
Spring Hill, FL

Dyan Wagner
District Reading Specialist and Intervention Coordinator
Milwaukee, WI

Darlene Watson
Instructional Lead Teacher
Valdosta, GA

Linda Webb
LA Program Specialist
Stockton, CA

Sue Wennerberg
Teacher
Oak Park, IL

Gayle Wilson
Preprimary Department Head
Jacksonville, FL

Linda Wiltz
Instructional Support Teacher
Orlando, FL

Meet the SRA Imagine It! Authors

Carl Bereiter, Ph.D.

A professor emeritus and special advisor on learning technology at the Ontario Institute for Studies in Education, University of Toronto, Dr. Bereiter also invented Computer Supported Intentional Learning Environments, the first networked system for collaborative learning, with Dr. Marlene Scardamalia.

Andrew Biemiller, Ph.D.

A coordinator of elementary teacher education programs at the University of Toronto for thirty-six years, Dr. Biemiller's research on vocabulary development and instruction has had a significant effect on the shape of vocabulary instruction for elementary education in the twenty-first century.

Joe Campione, Ph.D.

A leading researcher on cognitive development, individual differences, assessment, and the design of innovative learning environments, Dr. Campione is a professor emeritus in the School of Education at University of California, Berkeley.

Iva Carruthers, Ph.D.

Equipped with both hands-on and academic experience, Dr. Carruthers serves as a consultant and lecturer in educational technology and matters of multicultural inclusion.

Doug Fuchs, Ph.D.

Dr. Fuchs, the Nicholas Hobbs Professor of Special Education and Human Development at Vanderbilt University, has conducted programmatic research on response-to-intervention as a method for preventing and identifying children with learning disabilities and on reading instructional methods for improving outcomes for students with learning disabilities.

Lynn Fuchs, Ph.D.

A co-director of the Kennedy Center Reading clinic at Vanderbilt University, Dr. Fuchs also conducted research on assessment methods for enhancing instructional planning and instructional methods for improving reading and math outcomes for students with learning disabilities.

Steve Graham, Ph.D.

A professor of literacy at Vanderbilt University, Dr. Graham's research focuses on identifying the factors that contribute to writing development and writing difficulties.

Karen Harris, Ph.D.

The Currey-Ingram Professor of Special Education and Literacy at Vanderbilt University, Dr. Harris's research focuses on theoretical and intervention issues in the development of academic and self-regulation strategies among students who are at risk.

Jan Hirshberg, Ed.D.

Focusing on how children learn to read and write and the logistics of teaching reading and writing in the early grades, Dr. Hirshberg works as a language arts resource coordinator and consultant in Alexandria, Virginia.

Anne McKeough, Ph.D.

A professor in the Division of Applied Psychology at the University of Calgary, Dr. McKeough teaches graduate courses in cognitive development and educational assessment, as well as teacher preparation courses to undergraduates.

Peter Pannell, MA
Principal of Longfellow Elementary School in Pasadena, California, Mr. Pannell has worked to develop the literacy of countless students. To help accomplish this goal, he wrote and implemented a writing project that allowed his students to make great strides in their writing performance.

Marsha Roit, Ed.D.
The Director of Professional Development for SRA/McGraw-Hill, Dr. Roit spends considerable time in classrooms developing reading curricula and working with teachers and administrators in effective instructional practices.

Marlene Scardamalia, Ph.D.
Dr. Scardamalia is the Presidents' Chair in Education and Knowledge Technologies at the University of Toronto and is also the Director of the Institute for Knowledge Innovation and Technology. She received the 2006 World Award of Education from the World Cultural Council for outstanding work in education.

Marcy Stein, Ph.D.
Professor and founding faculty member of the education program at the University of Washington, Tacoma, Dr. Stein teaches At-Risk and Special Education graduate and teacher certification programs.

Gerald H. Treadway Jr., Ph.D.
Chair of the Literacy Education Program and professor of education at San Diego State University, Dr. Treadway teaches classes on reading methods, English Language Learner methods, balanced reading programs, assessment, and reading comprehension. He is also a consultant for the California Reading and Literature Project.

In memoriam

Michael Pressley, Ph.D.
1951–2006
Dr. Pressley was a tireless supporter of education. He championed the rights of all children to a quality education, made seminal contributions in research and practice, and nurtured the development of a host of beginning teachers, young scholars, and editors. While his work and spirit lives on in those he influenced and inspired, there is no substitute for the real thing. We will all miss his wisdom and friendship every day.

Unit 5

Communities across Time

Table of Contents

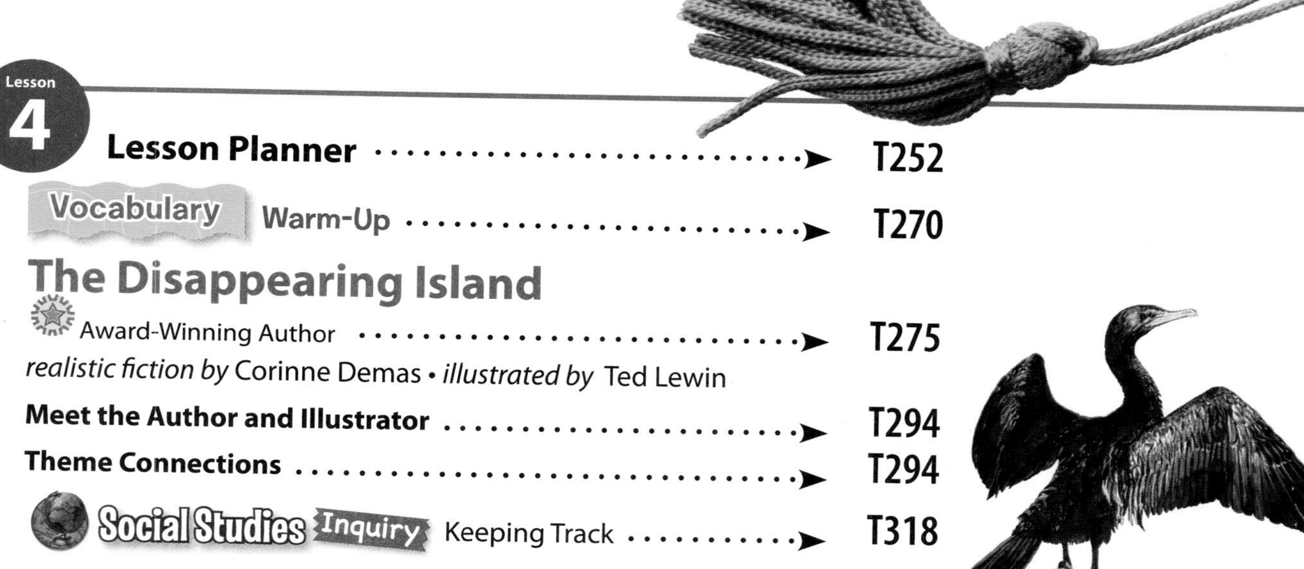

Additional Reading

You may wish to provide the following titles to students for additional theme-related reading.

In My Own Backyard by Judi Kurjian

A City Album by Peter and Connie Roop

Everglades by Jean Craighead George

Hottest, Coldest, Highest, Deepest by Steve Jenkins

Where People Live by Angela Royston

Archaeologists Dig for Clues by Kate Duke

If You're Not from the Prairie . . . by David Bouchard

Heartland by Diane Siebert

Note: You should preview any trade books and videos for appropriateness in your classroom before recommending them to students.

Unit 5

Communities across Time

OVERVIEW

What do you think of when you hear the word *community*? A community can be a geographic location, such as a town or a city. A community also can be the group of people who live within the town or city. Where is your community? What was it like twenty, one hundred, or even 1,000 years ago? How has your community changed since its beginning? Let's find out how our communities came to be, how human beings affect the land where we live and work, and how the land affects us!

Theme Connection

Look at the illustration. How many time periods do you see? How has this community changed through the years? What has changed and what has not changed?

BIG Idea

How has my community changed over time?

Unit 5

Launching the Theme

Setting Up the Theme

Each community has its own conventions, but one thing communities across the world share is history. All communities have a history, and their history is directly connected to Earth's history. In this unit, students will read about archaeology and how artifacts are studied to understand past cultures. They will read about how communities change over time and continue to progress. This unit teaches students the impact land has on people, and the impact people have on land.

To excite students about the theme Communities across Time, try some of the following ideas:

- Explore books about the history of your community. When was it established? Who discovered it? What was the chief industry? What is distinctive about its culture? How has it changed over the years?
- Discuss how artifacts can tell us things about the past and present. Display examples of artifacts. Have students bring in examples of artifacts from where they live.
- Discuss how natural occurrences such as earthquakes, hurricanes, and erosion have affected communities.
- Discuss the positive and negative impacts humans have had on the land through the years. How can human beings today save and restore the land?
- Show students the Unit 5 ***eBackground Builder*** video "Communities across Time."

Students will begin a unit investigation about communities across time and will continue this investigation during the next six weeks. At the end of the unit, students will publish the results of their investigations.

Concept/Question Board

Throughout the unit, students can share their ideas, experiences, and questions by posting them on the **Concept/Question Board**. This will allow the class to become a knowledge-building community in which questioning and learning are cooperative.

The **Concept/Question Board** can be displayed on a wall, a dry-erase board, or a large poster board. It should be easy for students to access, and they should be given ownership of the board. Consider making teams of students responsible for its maintenance.

Use some of the following materials to generate interest and encourage students to post their ideas and questions on the **Concept/Question Board**:

- Magazines for students to cut
- Construction paper and markers
- Books about past and present communities

After discussing the Big Idea question, ask students to share any stories they might know about communities and the land.

Using the Inquiry Planner

Students will research the theme Communities across Time using the steps below.

How has my community changed over time?

Read the Big Idea question to students. Then discuss how all communities had a beginning. Discuss how communities change and progress with the times. Students might point out some things they know about the community where they live.

	Steps	Models
Week 1	**Step 1** Generate ideas and questions for the **Concept/Question Board.**	**Model 1** *How can a community support so many people? What may happen to the land, the people, and the wildlife? How can nature and people live in harmony?*
Week 2	**Step 2** Decide on a problem or question to research.	**Model 2** *How can our community avoid expanding too much and destroying valuable countryside?*
Week 3	**Step 3** Formulate an idea or a conjecture about the problem or question.	**Model 3** *Some land should be set aside for nature parks and protected wildlife sanctuaries.*
	Step 4 Identify needs and make plans.	**Model 4** *I need information about nature parks and wildlife sanctuaries. I will search the library and Internet for books, articles, and Web pages. I also will interview a park ranger or urban planner.*
Week 4	**Step 5** Collect facts and use new information to reevaluate the problem or question.	**Model 5** *The best land for nature parks is already privately owned.*
Week 5	**Step 6** Continue collecting facts and confirm or revise the conjecture.	**Model 6** *Our community has to find a way to buy the right land for nature parks, or it has to convince people to stop developing all of the countryside.*
Week 6	**Step 7** Create a presentation and share information.	**Model 7** *I will give an oral presentation using maps to show good places for nature parks.*
	Step 8 Identify new questions.	**Model 8** *How can our community acquire countryside land to prevent it from being developed? How long can our city keep expanding? Why do so many people want to live on newly developed land? How were national parks created?*

Unit 5

Unit Skills

Week 1

Preparing to Read

Word Structure ★
Prefixes *re-*, *un-*, *pre-*, and *mis-*

Reading and Responding

Comprehension ★

Strategies
- Adjusting Reading Speed
- Visualizing

Skills
- ✓ Fact and Opinion
- ✓ Classify and Categorize
- ✓ Author's Purpose

Fluency ★
Leveled Reader

✓ **Selection Vocabulary** ★

Inquiry

Language Arts

Writing
Persuasive Paragraph

Spelling
✓ Prefixes *re-*, *un-*, *pre-*, and *mis-*

Penmanship
Cursive *N* and *M*

Grammar, Usage, and Mechanics
✓ Verb Tense

Study Skills
Conducting an Internet Search

Listening/Speaking/Viewing
Group Discussion

Week 2

Preparing to Read

Word Structure ★
Prefixes *bi-*, *mid-*, *dis-*, and *auto-*

Reading and Responding

Comprehension ★

Strategies
- Asking Questions
- Clarifying
- Summarizing

Skills
✓ Drawing Conclusions

Fluency ★
Leveled Reader

✓ **Selection Vocabulary** ★

Inquiry

Language Arts

Writing
Persuasive Letter

Spelling
✓ Prefixes *bi-*, *mid-*, *dis-*, and *auto-*

Penmanship
Cursive *P* and *R*

Grammar, Usage, and Mechanics
✓ Prepositions and Prepositional Phrases

Study Skills
Interviews

Listening/Speaking/Viewing
Following Directions

Week 3

Preparing to Read

Word Structure ★
- Affixes as Syllables
- Affixes used to change word meaning

Reading and Responding

Comprehension ★

Strategies
- Making Connections
- Visualizing

Skills
- ✓ Fact and Opinion
- ✓ Drawing Conclusions
- ✓ Cause and Effect

Fluency ★
Leveled Reader

✓ **Selection Vocabulary** ★

Inquiry

Language Arts

Writing
Business Letter

Spelling
✓ Affixes used to change word meaning

Penmanship
Cursive *S, G, N, M, P* and *R*

Grammar, Usage, and Mechanics
✓ Sentence Tense

Study Skills
Maps

Listening/Speaking/Viewing
Effective Voice and Word Choice

Week 4

Preparing to Read

Word Structure ★
- Word Families
- Multisyllabic Words
- Silent Consonants

Reading and Responding

Comprehension ★

Strategies
- Clarifying
- Summarizing

Skills
- ✓ Cause and Effect
- ✓ Author's Purpose

Fluency ★

Leveled Reader

✓ **Selection Vocabulary** ★

Inquiry

Language Arts

Writing
Directions

Spelling
- Word Families
- Multisyllabic Words
- Silent Consonants

Penmanship
Cursive *D* and *B*

Grammar, Usage, and Mechanics
✓ Verb *to be* and Irregular Verbs

Study Skills
Calendars

Listening/Speaking/Viewing
Using Multimedia

Week 5

Preparing to Read

Word Structure ★
- Prefixes *re-*, *un-*, *pre-*, and *mis-*
- Prefixes *bi-*, *mid-*, *dis-*, and *auto-*
- Affixes as Syllables
- Affixes used to change word meaning

Reading and Responding

Comprehension ★

Strategies
- Asking Questions
- Making Connections
- Predicting

Skills
- ✓ Author's Point of View
- ✓ Main Idea and Details

Fluency ★

Leveled Reader

✓ **Selection Vocabulary** ★

Inquiry

Language Arts

Writing
Play

Spelling
- ✓ Prefixes *re-*, *un-*, *pre-*, and *mis-*
- ✓ Prefixes *bi-*, *mid-*, *dis-*, and *auto-*
- ✓ Affixes as Syllables
- ✓ Affixes used to change word meaning
- ✓ Word Families

Penmanship
Cursive *Q* and *F*

Grammar, Usage, and Mechanics
✓ Complex Sentences

Study Skills
Story Maps and Character Webs

Listening/Speaking/Viewing
Descriptive Presentations

Week 6

Preparing to Read

Word Structure ★
Unit Review

Reading and Responding

B ✓ **Vocabulary** ★

Reading with a Writer's Eye
Unit Review

B **Comprehension** ★

Strategies
Unit Review

✓ **Skills**
Unit Review

B **Fluency** ★

✓ **Test Strategy**
Referring to a Story to Answer Questions

Inquiry

Language Arts

Writing
Play

Penmanship
Cursive *H* and *K*

Key: ★ = five components of Reading ✓ = Lesson Assessment B = Benchmark Assessment

Assessment Plan for Making AYP

is an ongoing cycle.

1 Screen

Administer the initial Benchmark Assessment as a screener to target students who are at risk for failing end of year measures.

Diagnose students' strengths and weaknesses, and differentiate instruction according to their abilities.

2 Diagnose and Differentiate

Diagnosing, differentiating instruction, and monitoring progress is an ongoing cycle.

3 Monitor Progress

Monitor progress weekly, monthly, or any time as needed with both formal and informal assessments.

4 Measure Outcomes

Administer summative Assessments such as Lesson, Benchmark, or state assessments to measure student outcomes.

1 Screen

For students entering class after the school year has begun, administer ***Benchmark Assessment,*** Benchmark 1, to target students at risk for reading failure.

2 Diagnose and Differentiate

Use the results from the Lesson Assessments, ***Benchmark Assessments,*** and informal observation measures to diagnose students' strengths and weaknesses and to differentiate instructions individually and in small groups.

	Approaching Level	On Level	English Learner	Above Level
Leveled Practice	• ***Reteach*** • ***Workshop Kit*** - Activities - Games • ***Intervention Guide*** • ***Curriculum Connections***	• ***Skills Practice 2*** • ***Workshop Kit*** - Activities - Games • ***Intervention Guide*** • ***Curriculum Connections***	• ***English Learner Support Activities*** • ***Workshop Kit*** - Activities - Games	• ***Challenge Activities*** • ***Workshop Kit*** - Activities - Games
 Leveled Readers	• ***Leveled Readers*** • ***Leveled Social Studies Readers***	• ***Leveled Readers*** • ***Leveled Social Studies Readers***	• ***Leveled Readers*** • ***Leveled Social Studies Readers***	• ***Leveled Readers*** • ***Leveled Social Studies Readers***
 Technology	• ***eSkills***	• ***eSkills***	• ***eSkills***	

Monitor Progress

Between ***Benchmark Assessments,*** use the following to monitor student progress. Regroup student daily or as needed, based on these formative assessment results.

Monitor Progress ✔

Formal Assessment

- Comprehension Rubrics
- Writing Rubrics
- Lesson Assessments
- Oral Fluency Assessments
- ***eAssess***
- Comprehension Observation Logs
- ***Skills Practice 2***
- Research Rubrics

Measure Outcomes

Assess student understanding and mastery of skills by using the Lesson Assessments or ***Benchmark Assessments.***

Resources to Monitor Progress

	Week 1	Week 2
Skills Practice 2	Word Structure, pp. 85–88 Vocabulary, pp. 89–90 Comprehension, pp. 91–92 Inquiry, pp. 93–94 Writing, pp. 95–96 Spelling, pp. 97–98 Grammar, pp. 99–100 Study Skills, pp. 101–102	Word Structure, pp. 103–106 Vocabulary, pp. 107–108 Inquiry, pp. 109–110 Writing, pp. 111–112 Spelling, pp. 113–114 Grammar, pp. 115–116 Study Skills, pp. 117–118
Decodable Stories		
Leveled Readers	"Aunt Jade Comes to Visit" "After the Hurricane" "We Can Rebuild" "Leon's Treasure Chest"	"Aunt Jade Comes to Visit" "After the Hurricane" "We Can Rebuild" "Leon's Treasure Chest"
Lesson Assessments	Lesson 1, pp. 43–50	Lesson 2, pp. 51–58
Benchmark Assessments		
Technology e-Suite		
Skills & eGames	Skills: Unit 5 Phonics Games: Greek and Latin Roots	Skills: Unit 5 Phonics Unit 5 Writing Games: Suffixes, Prefixes, and Word Endings
Decodable Stories		
Fluency	Approaching Level: "Aunt Jade Comes to Visit" On Level: "After the Hurricane" English Learner: "We Can Rebuild" Above Level: "Leon's Treasure Chest"	Approaching Level: "Aunt Jade Comes to Visit" On Level: "After the Hurricane" English Learner: "We Can Rebuild" Above Level: "Leon's Treasure Chest"
Assess	***Lesson Assessment 2,*** Unit 5, Lesson 1	***Lesson Assessment 2,*** Unit 5, Lesson 2

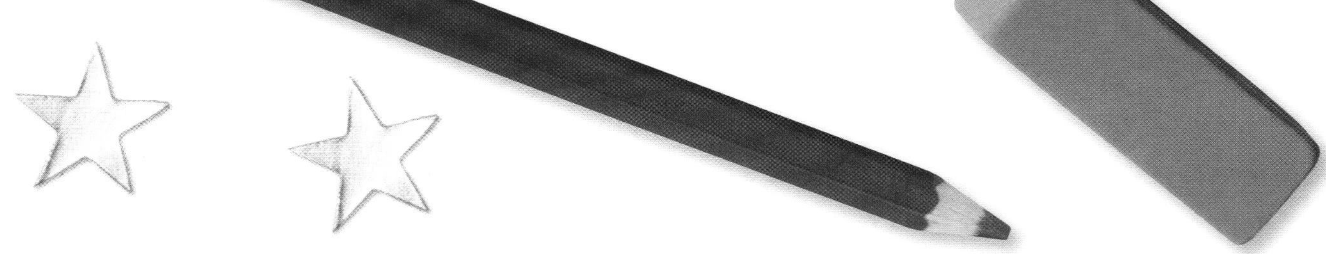

Week 3	Week 4	Week 5	Week 6
Word Structure, pp. 119–122 Vocabulary, pp. 123–124 Comprehension, pp. 125–126 Inquiry, pp. 127–128 Writing, pp. 129–130 Spelling, pp. 131–132 Grammar, pp. 133–134 Study Skills, pp. 135–136	Word Structure, pp. 137–140 Vocabulary, pp. 141–142 Comprehension, pp. 143–144 Inquiry, pp. 145–146 Writing, pp. 147–148 Spelling, pp. 149–150 Grammar, pp. 151–152 Study Skills, pp. 153–154	Word Structure, pp. 155–158 Vocabulary, pp. 159–160 Comprehension, pp. 161–162 Writing, pp. 163–164 Spelling, pp. 165–166 Grammar, pp. 167–168 Study Skills, pp. 169–170	
"Plymouth Colony" "Native Americans Live with the Land" "Living with the Land" "Planning the Capital"	"Plymouth Colony" "Native Americans Live with the Land" "Living with the Land" "Planning the Capital"	"The Oldest City in Our Country" "Life on the Prairie" "The Prairie" "The History of New York City"	"The Oldest City in Our Country" "Life on the Prairie" "The Prairie" "The History of New York City"
Lesson 3, pp. 59–66	Lesson 4, pp. 67–74	Lesson 5, pp. 75–82	End of Unit Writing Prompt, pp. 83–84
			Unit 5, Benchmark 6
Skills: Unit 5 Spelling Unit 5 Vocabulary Unit 5 Writing Games: Suffixes, Prefixes, and Word Endings	Games: Suffixes, Prefixes, and Word Endings	Skills: Unit 5 Spelling Unit 5 Vocabulary Games: Greek and Latin Roots Suffixes and Prefixes	Skills: Unit 5 Spelling Unit 5 Vocabulary Games: Unit 5 Spelling Words
Approaching Level: "Plymouth Colony" On Level: Native "Americans Live with the Land" English Learner: "Living with the Land" Above Level: "Planning the Capital"	Approaching Level: "Plymouth Colony" On Level: Native "Americans Live with the Land" English Learner: "Living with the Land" Above Level: "Planning the Capital"	Approaching Level: "The Oldest City in Our Country" On Level: "Life on the Prairie" English Learner: "The Prairie" Above Level: "The History of New York City"	Approaching Level: "The Oldest City in Our Country" On Level: "Life on the Prairie" English Learner: "The Prairie" Above Level: "The History of New York City"
Lesson Assessment 2, Unit 5, Lesson 3	***Lesson Assessment 2,*** Unit 5, Lesson 4	***Lesson Assessment 2,*** Unit 5, Lesson 5	

Lesson Planner

Preparing to Read

MATERIALS

- ***Transparencies*** 130, 133
- ***Skills Practice 2,*** pp. 85–88
- Routine 10

Day 1

Daily News, p. T26
Word Structure
Prefixes *re-* and *un-*, pp. T26–T27

Day 2

Daily News, p. T40
Word Structure, p. T41
Developing Oral Language, p. T41

Reading and Responding

MATERIALS

- ***Student Reader,*** Book 2, pp. 126–147
- ***Transparencies*** 5, 15, 132
- ***Home Connection,*** pp. 49–52
- Routines 11, 12, 14, A
- ***Skills Practice 2,*** pp. 89–94
- ***Listening Library CD***
- Writer's Notebook
- ***Leveled Reader***
- ***Lesson Assessment Book 2***

Day 1

Read Aloud, pp. T28–T33
Inquiry, pp. T34–T35

Day 2

Build Background, p. T42
Preview and Prepare, p. T43
Selection Vocabulary, pp. T44–T45
Reading the Selection, pp. T46–T49

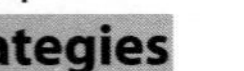

Comprehension Strategies
- Visualizing, pp. T47, T50–T51, T53
- Adjusting Reading Speed, pp. T47, T51–T52

Comprehension Skill
☆ Author's Purpose, p. T48

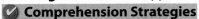

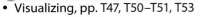

Language Arts

MATERIALS

- ***Language Arts Handbook,*** pp. 172–175, 324–325
- ***Student Reader,*** Book 2, pp. 130–143
- ***Skills Practice 2,*** pp. 95–102
- ***Transparencies*** 17, 17A, 33, 33A, 121, 131
- Routines 15, 16, 17
- ***Lesson Assessment Book 2,*** pp. 43–50

Day 1

Writing
Prewriting, pp. T36–T37
Spelling Pretest, p. T37
Penmanship
Cursive Letters *N* and *M*, p. T38

Day 2

Writing, Drafting, pp. T54–T55
Spelling, p. T55
Grammar, Usage, and Mechanics
Verb Tenses, pp. T56–T57

Monitor Progress

✓ = **Formal Assessment**

Day 1

- **Word Structure, p. T27**
- **Spelling Pretest, p. T37**

Day 2

- **Word Structure, p. T41**
- **Comprehension Strategy, p. T46**
- **Comprehension Skill, p. T47**
- **Grammar, Usage, and Mechanics, p. T57**

Literature Overview

Read Aloud

A River Ran Wild
by Lynne Cherry

Student Reader

The House on Maple Street
by Bonnie Pryor
illustrated by Beth Peck

Social Studies Inquiry

Home Tour Celebrates Spanish Heritage

SRA
Imagine It!

★ Phonics ★ Fluency ★ Vocabulary ★ Comprehension

Day 3

Daily News, p. T58
Word Structure
Prefixes *pre-* and *mis-*, pp. T58–T59

Comprehension Strategies
- Adjusting Reading Speed, pp. T60, T62
- Visualizing, pp. T60, T61, T63

Discussing the Selection, p. T64
Review Selection Vocabulary, p. T65
Fluency, p. T65
Theme Connections, p. T66

Writing, Revising, p. T68
Spelling, p. T69
Study Skills
Conducting an Internet Search, p. T70
Grammar, Usage, and Mechanics, p. T71

Word Structure, p. T59
Selection Vocabulary, p. T65
Fluency, p. T65
Spelling, p. T69
Study Skills, p. T70

Day 4

Daily News, p. T72
Word Structure, p. T73
Developing Oral Language, p. T73

2nd READ

Comprehension Skills
- Classify and Categorize, p. T74
- Fact and Opinion, pp. T76, T80

☆ Author's Purpose, p. T78

Reading with a Writer's Eye, pp. T75, T77, T79
Supporting the Reading
☆ Comprehension Skill:
Author's Purpose, p. T82
Fluency, p. T83
Social Studies Inquiry, pp. T84–T85
Inquiry, pp. T86–T87

Writing, Editing/Proofreading, pp. T88–T89
Spelling, p. T89
Study Skills, p. T90
Listening/Speaking/Viewing
Group Discussion, p. T91

Word Structure, p. T73
Comprehension Skill, p. T82
Fluency, p. T83
Writing, p. T89

Day 5 Review

Word Structure, p. T92

Selection Vocabulary, p. T93
Comprehension Strategies
- Adjusting Reading Speed, p. T94
- Visualizing, p. T94

Comprehension Skills
☆ Author's Purpose, p. T94
- Classify and Categorize, p. T94
- Fact and Opinion, p. T94

Reading with a Writer's Eye, p. T95
Fluency, p. T95

Writing, Publishing, p. T96
Spelling Test, p. T97
Penmanship, p. T97
Study Skills, p. T98
Listening/Speaking/Viewing, p. T98
Grammar, Usage, and Mechanics, p. T99

Spelling Posttest, p. T97
***Lesson Assessment Book 2,* pp. 43–50**

Student Resources

Genre

Realistic Fiction involves stories about people and events that are true to life and that could really happen.

Comprehension Skill

Author's Purpose
The author's purpose can be to inform, to explain, to entertain, or to persuade. As you read, think about why the author wrote this story.

The House on Maple Street

by Bonnie Pryor
illustrated by Beth Peck

Focus Questions

What do you think your neighborhood looked like several hundred years ago? How has the town or city you live in changed over time?

128 129

Student Reader, Book 2, pp. 128–145

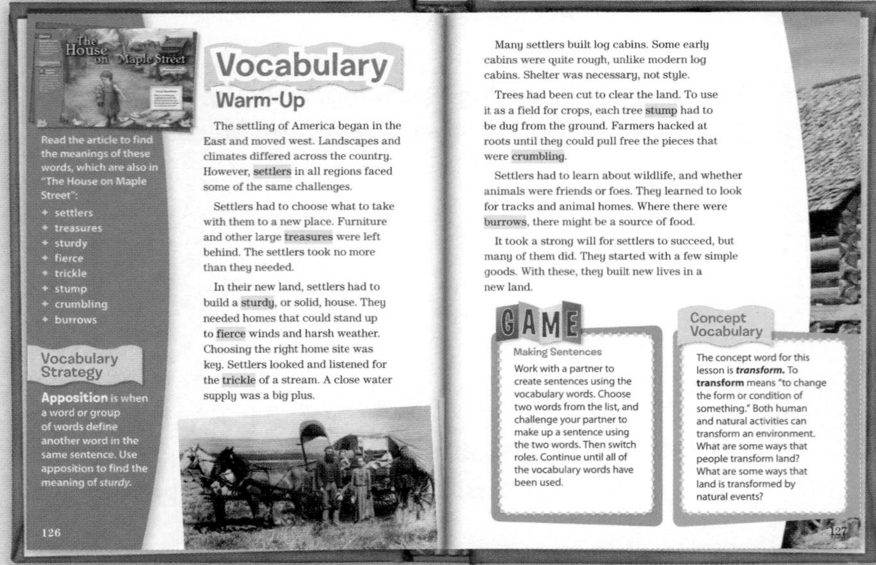

Vocabulary Warm-Up

Read the article to find the meanings of these words, which are also in "The House on Maple Street":

- settlers
- treasures
- sturdy
- fierce
- trickle
- stump
- crumbling
- burrows

Vocabulary Strategy

Apposition is when a word or group of words define another word in the same sentence. Use apposition to find the meaning of *sturdy*.

The settling of America began in the East and moved west. Landscapes and climates differed across the country. However, settlers in all regions faced some of the same challenges.

Settlers had to choose what to take with them to a new place. Furniture and other large treasures were left behind. The settlers took no more than they needed.

In their new land, settlers had to build a sturdy, or solid, house. They needed homes that could stand up to fierce winds and harsh weather. Choosing the right home site was key. Settlers looked and listened for the trickle of a stream. A close water supply was a big plus.

Many settlers built log cabins. Some early cabins were quite rough, unlike modern log cabins. Shelter was necessary, not style.

Trees had been cut to clear the land. To use it as a field for crops, each tree stump had to be dug from the ground. Farmers hacked at roots until they could pull free the pieces that were crumbling.

Settlers had to learn about wildlife, and whether animals were friends or foes. They learned to look for tracks and animal homes. Where there were burrows, there might be a source of food.

It took a strong will for settlers to succeed, but many of them did. They started with a few simple goods. With these, they built new lives in a new land.

GAME

Making Sentences

Work with a partner to create sentences using the vocabulary words. Choose two words from the list, and challenge your partner to make up a sentence using the two words. Then switch roles. Continue until all of the vocabulary words have been used.

Concept Vocabulary

The concept word for this lesson is ***transform.*** To **transform** means "to change the form or condition of something." Both human and natural activities can transform an environment. What are some ways that people transform land? What are some ways that land is transformed by natural events?

126 127

Student Reader, Book 2, pp. 126–127

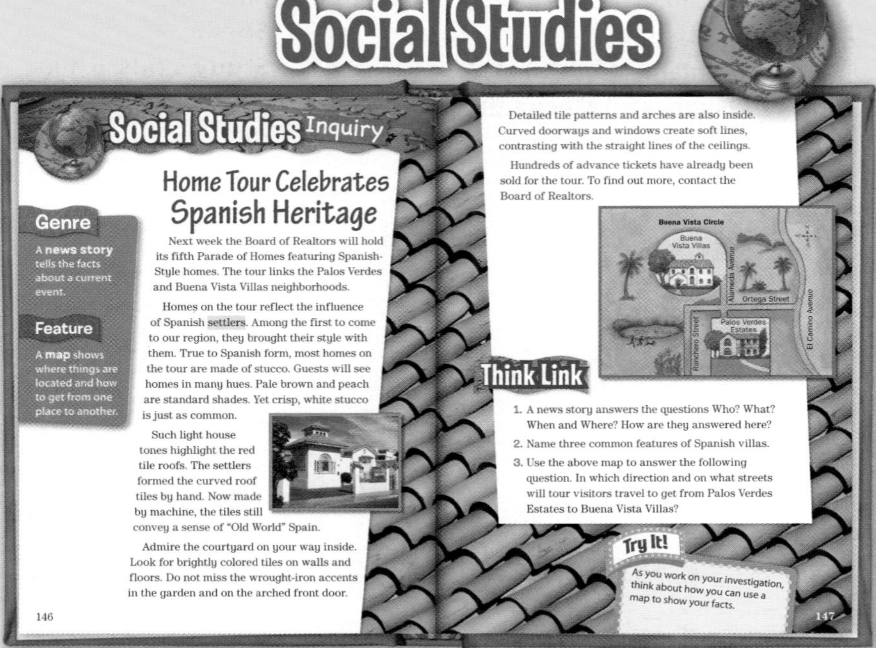

Social Studies

Social Studies Inquiry

Home Tour Celebrates Spanish Heritage

Genre

A **news story** tells the facts about a current event.

Feature

A **map** shows where things are located and how to get from one place to another.

Next week the Board of Realtors will hold its fifth Parade of Homes featuring Spanish-Style homes. The tour links the Palos Verdes and Buena Vista Villas neighborhoods.

Homes on the tour reflect the influence of Spanish settlers. Among the first to come to our region, they brought their style with them. True to Spanish form, most homes on the tour are made of stucco. Guests will see homes in many hues. Pale brown and peach are standard shades. Yet crisp, white stucco is just as common.

Such light house tones highlight the red tile roofs. The settlers formed the curved roof tiles by hand. Now made by machine, the tiles still convey a sense of "Old World" Spain.

Admire the courtyard on your way inside. Look for brightly colored tiles on walls and floors. Do not miss the wrought-iron accents in the garden and on the arched front door.

Detailed tile patterns and arches are also inside. Curved doorways and windows create soft lines, contrasting with the straight lines of the ceilings.

Hundreds of advance tickets have already been sold for the tour. To find out more, contact the Board of Realtors.

Think Link

1. A news story answers the questions Who? What? When and Where? How are they answered here?
2. Name three common features of Spanish villas.
3. Use the above map to answer the following question. In which direction and on what streets will tour visitors travel to get from Palos Verdes Estates to Buena Vista Villas?

Try It!

As you work on your investigation, think about how you can use a map to show your facts.

146 147

Student Reader, Book 2, pp. 146–147

Cross-Curricular Resources

Curriculum Connections

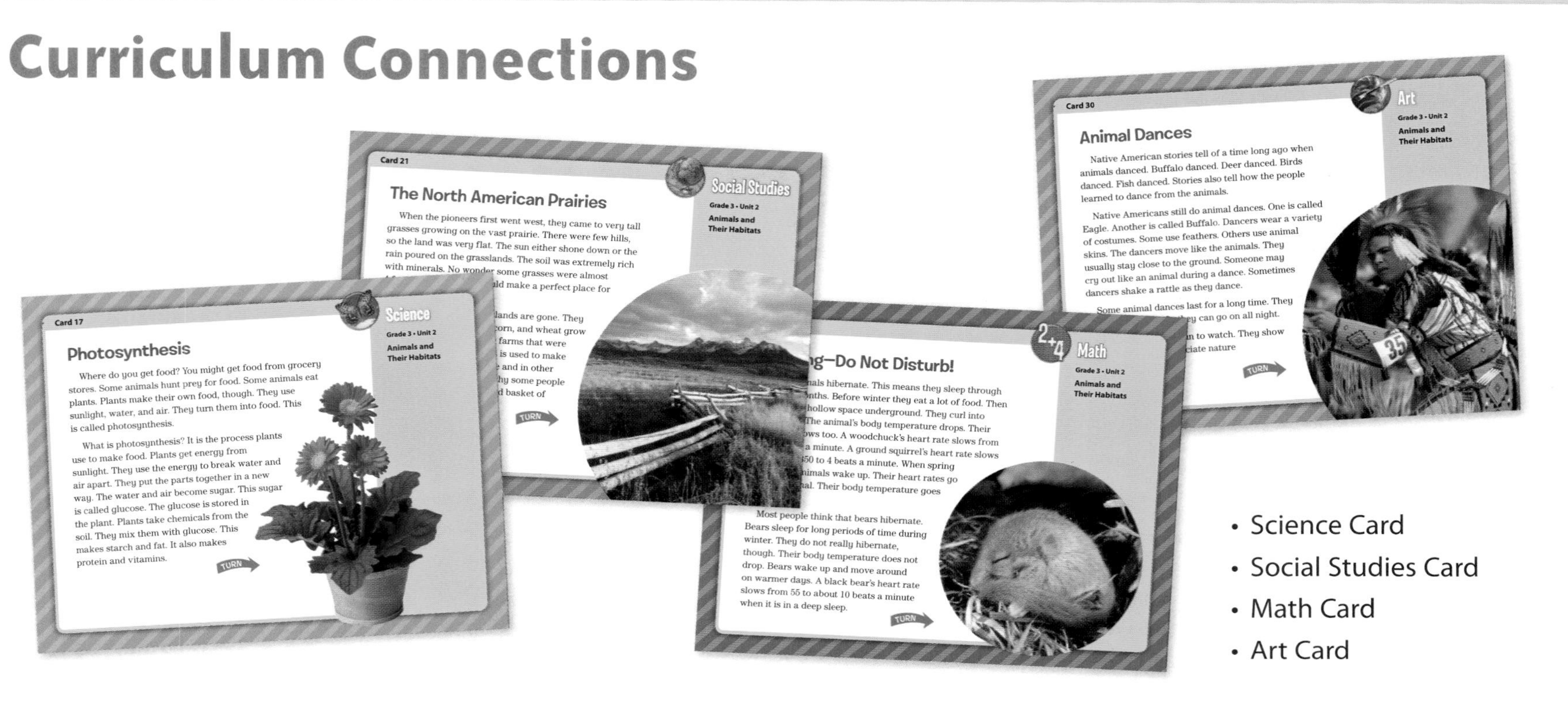

Card 21
Social Studies
Grade 3 • Unit 2
Animals and Their Habitats
The North American Prairies
When the pioneers first went west, they came to very tall grasses growing on the vast prairie. There were few hills, so the land was very flat. The sun either shone down or the rain poured on the grasslands. The soil was extremely rich with minerals.
Card 17
Science
Grade 3 • Unit 2
Animals and Their Habitats
Photosynthesis
Where do you get food? You might get food from grocery stores. Some animals hunt prey for food. Some animals eat plants. Plants make their own food, though. They use sunlight, water, and air. They turn them into food. This is called photosynthesis.
What is photosynthesis? It is the process plants use to make food. Plants get energy from sunlight. They use the energy to break water and air apart. They put the parts together in a new way. The water and air become sugar. This sugar is called glucose. The glucose is stored in the plant. Plants take chemicals from the soil. They mix them with glucose. This makes starch and fat. It also makes protein and vitamins.
TURN
Math
Grade 3 • Unit 2
Animals and Their Habitats
Most people think that bears hibernate. Bears sleep for long periods of time during winter. They do not really hibernate, though. Their body temperature does not drop. Bears wake up and move around on warmer days. A black bear's heart rate slows from 55 to about 10 beats a minute when it is in a deep sleep.
TURN
Card 30
Art
Grade 3 • Unit 2
Animals and Their Habitats
Animal Dances
Native American stories tell of a time long ago when animals danced. Buffalo danced. Deer danced. Birds danced. Fish danced. Stories also tell how the people learned to dance from the animals.
Native Americans still do animal dances. One is called Eagle. Another is called Buffalo. Dancers wear a variety of costumes. Some use feathers. Others use animal skins. The dancers move like the animals. They usually stay close to the ground. Someone may cry out like an animal during a dance. Sometimes dancers shake a rattle as they dance.
TURN

- Science Card
- Social Studies Card
- Math Card
- Art Card

Leveled Readers for Social Studies

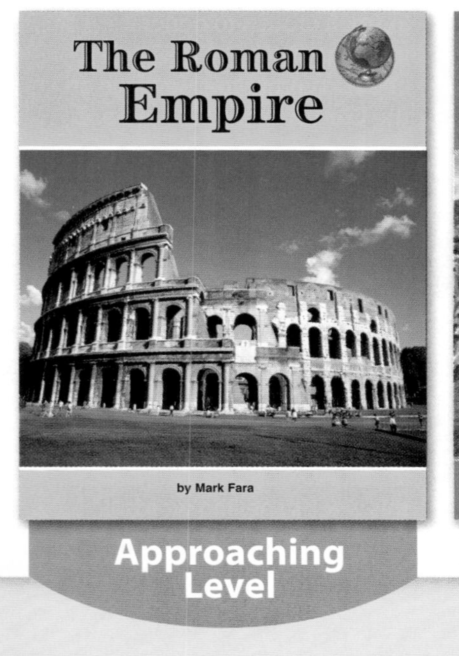

Approaching Level

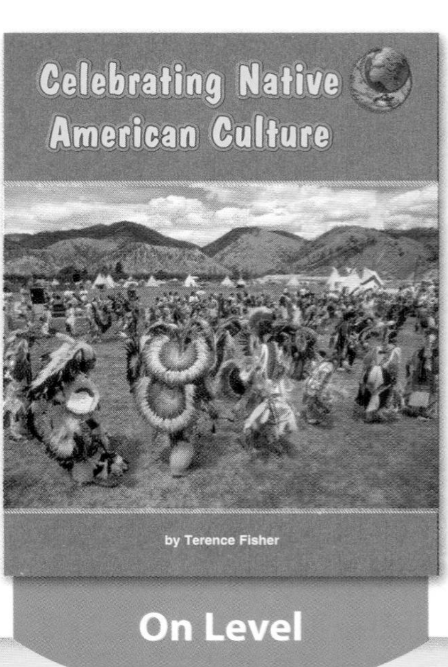

On Level

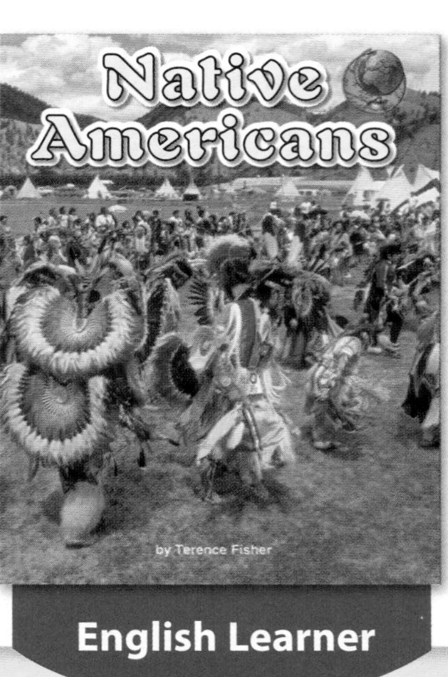

English Learner

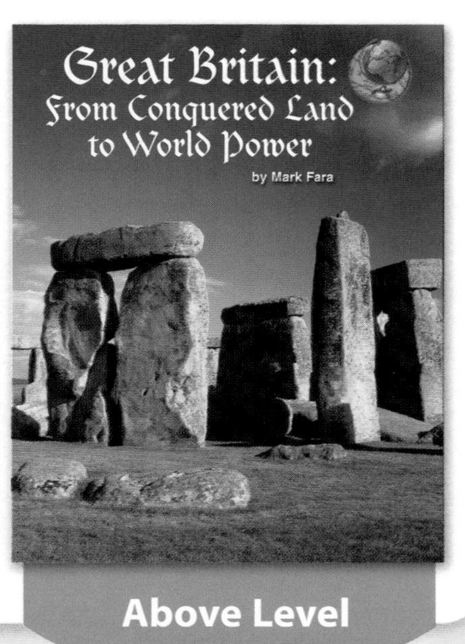

Great Britain: From Conquered Land to World Power
by Mark Fara

Above Level

Lesson 1 Overview

Differentiating Instruction
for Workshop

Day 1

	Approaching Level	On Level	English Learner	Above Level
Preparing to Read	**Word Structure:** Have students form small groups, and help them complete ***Reteach*** page 123, or work with them on the word structure activities in the ***Intervention Guide,*** Unit 5, Lesson 1.	**Word Structure:** Have students make lists of words to add to the word lines.	**Word Structure:** Review the word lines. Then use the ***English Learner Support Guide*** for additional word structure instruction.	**Word Structure:** Have students complete ***Challenge Activities*** page 112. Then have students make lists of words to add to the word lines.
Reading and Responding	**Vocabulary:** Have students add interesting words from "A River Ran Wild" to their Writer's Notebooks. Have students find the definitions to these words in a dictionary. **Comprehension:** Have students write a journal entry about a personal connection they can make to "A River Ran Wild." **Inquiry:** Have students work in small groups to generate ideas, questions, and pictures about communities to place on the **Concept/Question Board.**	**Vocabulary:** Have students add words from "A River Ran Wild" that relate to the unit theme to their Writer's Notebooks. **Comprehension:** Assign students an article or poem about Communities across Time. Have student read and discuss passages with a partner. **Inquiry:** Have students work in small groups to generate ideas, questions, and pictures about communities to place on the **Concept/Question Board.**	**Vocabulary:** Have students add words from "A River Ran Wild" to their Writer's Notebooks. Have students begin a picture dictionary by drawing small illustrations to help them remember the meaning of the words. **Comprehension:** Give students an article or poem about Communities across Time. Pair English learners with native English speakers, and have them read together. **Inquiry:** Have students work in small groups to generate ideas, questions, and pictures about communities to place on the **Concept/Question Board.**	**Vocabulary:** Have students add words from "A River Ran Wild" that relate to the unit theme to the Word Bank. **Comprehension:** Give students an article or poem about Communities across Time. Have students read to each other in small groups and discuss how the material applies to the unit theme. **Inquiry:** Have students work in small groups to generate ideas, questions, and pictures about communities to place on the **Concept/Question Board.**
Language Arts	**Writing:** Have students organize their ideas according to fact and opinion. **Spelling:** Have students divide three spelling words into separate syllables then try to spell each syllable.	**Writing:** Have students use a thesaurus to look up new words as they organize their writing. **Spelling:** Have students create flash cards to review this lesson's spelling words.	**Writing:** Have students use a dictionary as they generate and organize ideas. **Spelling:** Have students create flash cards to review this lesson's spelling words.	**Writing:** Have students research facts to present in their persuasive paragraphs. **Spelling:** Have students work in pairs to quiz one another on this week's spelling words.

Day 2

Approaching Level	On Level	English Learner	Above Level
Preparing to Read			
Word Structure: Review the word lines. Then have students write sentences using words on the word lines.	**Word Structure:** Have students make lists of base words and practice adding the prefixes *re-* and *un-* to them.	**Word Structure:** Review the word lines. Then have students write sentences using words on the word lines.	**Word Structure:** Have students write paragraphs using words from the word lines.
Reading and Responding			
Vocabulary: Have students create illustrations for the selection vocabulary words. **Comprehension:** Have students share any questions they have about "The House on Maple Street" with the rest of the class. Add these questions to the **Concept/Question Board.**	**Vocabulary:** Have students think of examples for each of the selection vocabulary words. **Comprehension:** Have students keep track of their visualizations in a journal or a notebook.	**Vocabulary:** Use ***English Learner Support Guide,*** Unit 5, Lesson 1 to review vocabulary. **Comprehension:** Read some passages aloud using different reading speeds to students. Have students raise their hands when you begin to read a passage that should be read at a slower pace. Discuss how adjusting the reading speed helps them better understand the text.	**Vocabulary:** Have students use a thesaurus to find words that are related to the selection vocabulary words. **Comprehension:** Have students find a passage or idea they can visualize. Have students create illustrations using their visualizations.
Language Arts			
Writing: Have students discuss their ideas and individual goals. **Spelling:** Have students write five spelling words on a piece of paper, leaving one letter blank. Then have them exchange papers with a partner to fill in the blanks. **Grammar, Usage, and Mechanics:** Have students complete ***Reteach*** page 129.	**Writing:** Have students find facts to add to their persuasive paragraphs. **Spelling:** Have students think of four words that rhyme with spelling words and spell them on a sheet of paper. **Grammar, Usage, and Mechanics:** Have students work with ***Workshop Kit.***	**Writing:** Have students use a thesaurus or dictionary as they draft their persuasive paragraphs. **Spelling:** Have students slowly read aloud four spelling words, carefully pronouncing each letter or sound spelling in the word. **Grammar, Usage, and Mechanics:** Refer to the ***English Learner Support Guide*** for support activities.	**Writing:** Have students directly quote a passage from a primary source. **Spelling:** Have students find a partner, slowly read two lines of this week's selection aloud, and have the partner write the sentence on a piece of paper. **Grammar, Usage, and Mechanics:** Have students complete ***Challenge Activities*** page 117.

Lesson 1 Overview

Differentiating Instruction for Workshop

Day 3

	Approaching Level	On Level	English Learner	Above Level
Preparing to Read	**Word Structure:** Review the word lines with the prefixes *pre-* and *mis-*. Then have students complete ***Reteach*** page 124, or work with them on the word structure activities in the ***Intervention Guide,*** Unit 5, Lesson 1.	**Word Structure:** Have students make lists of words to add to the word lines.	**Word Structure:** Review the word lines with the prefixes *pre-* and *mis-*. Use the ***English Learner Support Guide*** for additional word structure instruction.	**Word Structure:** Have students complete ***Challenge Activities*** page 113.
Reading and Responding	**Vocabulary:** Have students use ***Reteach*** page 125. **Comprehension:** Have students find a passage where they adjusted their reading speed while reading. Have students share with the class what they learned after adjusting their reading speed. **Fluency:** Have students reread a passage from the story with a partner or individually.	**Vocabulary:** Have students complete a game in the ***Workshop Kit.*** **Comprehension:** Have students identify passages where they adjusted their reading speed to understand the story better. **Fluency:** Have students read into a tape recorder at the beginning and end of the week. Have them listen to themselves at the end of the week so they can hear their progress.	**Vocabulary:** Help students create flash cards for the selection vocabulary words. Have students test themselves with the cards and allow them to use the cards to quiz a partner. **Comprehension:** Have students create an illustration for the story by drawing one of their visualizations. **Fluency:** Have students engage in echo reading with passages from the story.	**Vocabulary:** Have students complete ***Challenge Activities*** page 114. **Comprehension:** Have students read fiction and nonfiction texts and compare how often they adjusted their reading speed. Have students say whether one genre is easier to read than another and explain why. **Fluency:** Have students choose a text that applies to Communities across Time to read silently.
Language Arts	**Writing:** Have students continue to revise their persuasive paragraphs. **Spelling:** Have students complete ***Reteach*** page 128. **Grammar, Usage, and Mechanics:** Have students check their writing for correct verb tenses.	**Writing:** Have students revise and edit and proofread their persuasive paragraphs. **Spelling:** Have students write two more words for each prefix that were not included in this week's lesson on a separate sheet of paper. **Grammar, Usage, and Mechanics:** Have students look for errors in verb tense in another writing piece.	**Writing:** Have students work with a peer to revise their persuasive paragraphs. **Spelling:** Have students write two more words for each prefix that were not included in this week's lesson on a separate sheet of paper. **Grammar, Usage, and Mechanics:** Have students look for verb tense errors in their persuasive paragraphs.	**Writing:** Have students separate their ideas and facts into paragraphs. **Spelling:** Have students complete ***Challenge Activities*** page 116. **Grammar, Usage, and Mechanics:** Have students use a consistent verb tense in their persuasive papers.

Day 4

	Approaching Level	On Level	English Learner	Above Level
Preparing to Read	**Word Structure:** Have students make flash cards with the prefixes *re-*, *un-*, *pre-* and *mis-* on one side and their definitions and examples on the other side.	**Word Structure:** Have students use words from the word lines in sentences.	**Word Structure:** Have students make flash cards with the prefixes *re-*, *un-*, *pre-* and *mis-* on one side and their definitions and examples on the other side.	**Word Structure:** Have students make lists of words with the prefixes *pre-* and *mis-* to add to the word lines. Then have students write paragraphs using words from their lists.
Reading and Responding	**Vocabulary:** Have students find additional words in the story that can be applied to the Word Bank. **Comprehension:** Have students visualize the setting of "The House on Maple Street" using clues given by the author. Have students create illustrations of the setting using the clues. **Fluency:** Have students review fluency by using ***Leveled Readers.*** **Inquiry:** Have students share ideas and questions about the unit theme to generate possible investigation questions.	**Vocabulary:** Have students write riddles for the vocabulary words. **Comprehension:** Have students discuss the author's purpose of the story. Have students discuss how this purpose helps the author support the theme Communities across Time. **Fluency:** Have students whisper read along with you as you reread passages from the text. **Inquiry:** Have students share ideas and questions about the unit theme to generate possible investigation questions.	**Vocabulary:** Have students write sentences using the selection vocabulary words. **Comprehension:** Have students use a Venn diagram to illustrate the similarities and differences between the past and the present homes on Maple Street. **Fluency:** Have students reread passages from the story to a partner. **Inquiry:** Have students share ideas and questions about the unit theme to generate possible investigation questions.	**Vocabulary:** Have students write their own functional definitions for the expanding vocabulary words. **Comprehension:** Have students write a short paragraph explaining how "The House on Maple Street" would be different if it had been written as another genre, such as biography, fairy tale, or folktale. **Fluency:** Have students use vocabulary from the ***Leveled Readers*** in their writing. **Inquiry:** Have students share ideas and questions about the unit theme to generate possible investigation questions.
Language Arts	**Writing:** Have students edit and proofread their persuasive paragraphs. **Spelling:** Have students find a partner, and tell them to help each other correctly spell the spelling words.	**Writing:** Have students work on their final drafts after they edit and proofread their persuasive paragraphs. **Spelling:** Have students carefully proofread their writing activity for spelling errors.	**Writing:** Have students work with a peer to edit persuasive paragraphs. **Spelling:** Have students review this week's spelling words using the flash cards they made.	**Writing:** Have students assess their writing for strengths and weaknesses. **Spelling:** Have students write a sentence with at least four spelling words on a piece of paper.

Lesson 1 Overview

Differentiating Instruction for Workshop

Day 5

	Approaching Level	On Level	English Learner	Above Level
Preparing to Read	**Word Structure:** Review the word lines with the prefixes *re-*, *un-*, *pre-*, and *mis-*. Then have students write sentences using the words on the word lines.	**Word Structure:** Have pairs of students write clues for words on the word lines.	**Word Structure:** Review the word lines with the prefixes *re-*, *un-*, *pre-*, and *mis-*. Then have students practice adding these prefixes to other words.	**Word Structure:** Have students play word detective, looking for other words with the prefixes *re-*, *un-*, *pre-*, and *mis-*.
Reading and Responding	**Vocabulary:** Have students find words in the story that are unfamiliar, find the meaning in the glossary, and use the words in sentences. **Comprehension:** Have students summarize the story. **Fluency:** Have students write answers to comprehension questions from the ***Leveled Readers.***	**Vocabulary:** Have students read texts about communities and find additional concept vocabulary words. **Comprehension:** Have students write a summary of "The House on Maple Street." **Fluency:** Have students review fluency by using ***eFluency.***	**Vocabulary:** Assign students a partner, and have the pairs write and perform a vocabulary playlet for the class. **Comprehension:** Have students write a summary of "The House on Maple Street." Have students discuss which part of the story they enjoyed the most. **Fluency:** Have students use vocabulary from the ***Leveled Readers*** in extended sentences.	**Vocabulary:** Have students write a story using the selection vocabulary words. **Comprehension:** Have students summarize "The House on Maple Street." **Fluency:** Have students reread passages from the story to each other.
Language Arts	**Writing:** Have students reflect upon their writing. **Spelling:** Have students think of four new words with the prefixes from this lesson and write them on a piece of paper.	**Writing:** Have students discuss what they have learned with a partner. **Spelling:** Have students write an imaginary newspaper headline using as many spelling words as possible.	**Writing:** Have students proofread and publish their persuasive paragraphs. **Spelling:** Have students practice spelling by reading each spelling word aloud to a partner and writing the words as they are heard.	**Writing:** Have students share their persuasive papers outside the classroom. **Spelling:** Have students write two sentences using three spelling words each on a piece of paper.

Resources for

Differentiating Instruction 

Leveled Readers

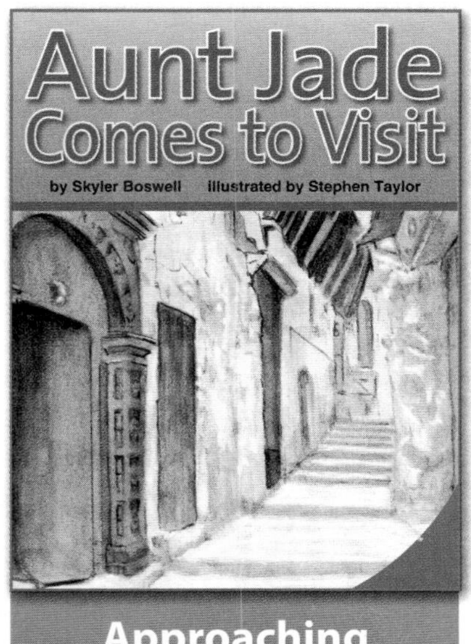

Aunt Jade
Comes to Visit
by Skyler Boswell illustrated by Stephen Taylor

Approaching Level

After the
Hurricane
by Sydney Ethan
illustrated by Debby Fisher

On Level

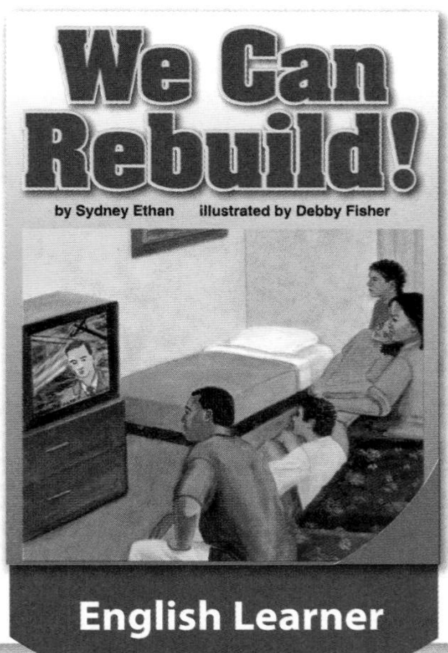

English Learner

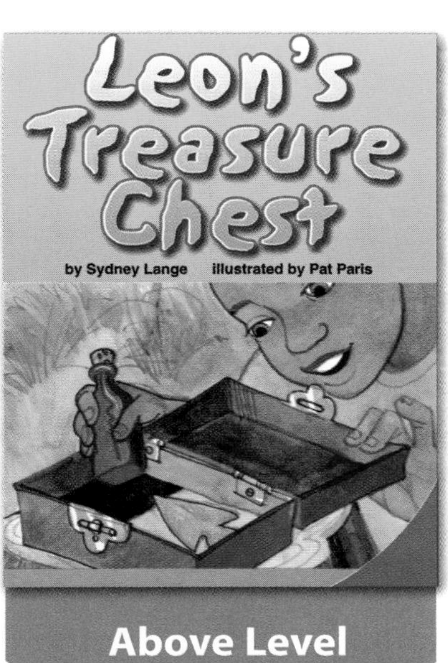

Leon's
Treasure
Chest
by Sydney Lange illustrated by Pat Paris

Above Level

Additional Skills Practice

Approaching Level

Reteach

- Prefixes, p. 123
- Prefixes, p. 124
- Vocabulary, p. 125
- Author's Purpose, pp. 126–127
- Spelling, p. 128
- Verb Tenses, p. 129

On Level

Skills Practice 2

- Prefixes, pp. 85–86
- Prefixes, pp. 87–88
- Vocabulary, pp. 89–90
- Author's Purpose, pp. 91–92
- Inquiry, pp. 93–94
- Writing a Persuasive Paragraph, pp. 95–96
- Spelling, pp. 97–98
- Verb Tenses, pp. 99–100

English Learner

English Learner Support Activities

English Learner Support Activities, Unit 5, Lesson 1

Above Level

Challenge Activities

- Prefixes, p. 112
- Prefixes, p. 113
- Vocabulary, p. 114
- Author's Purpose, p. 115
- Spelling, p. 116
- Verb Tenses, p. 117

Additional Resources for Differentiating Instruction

Workshop Kit

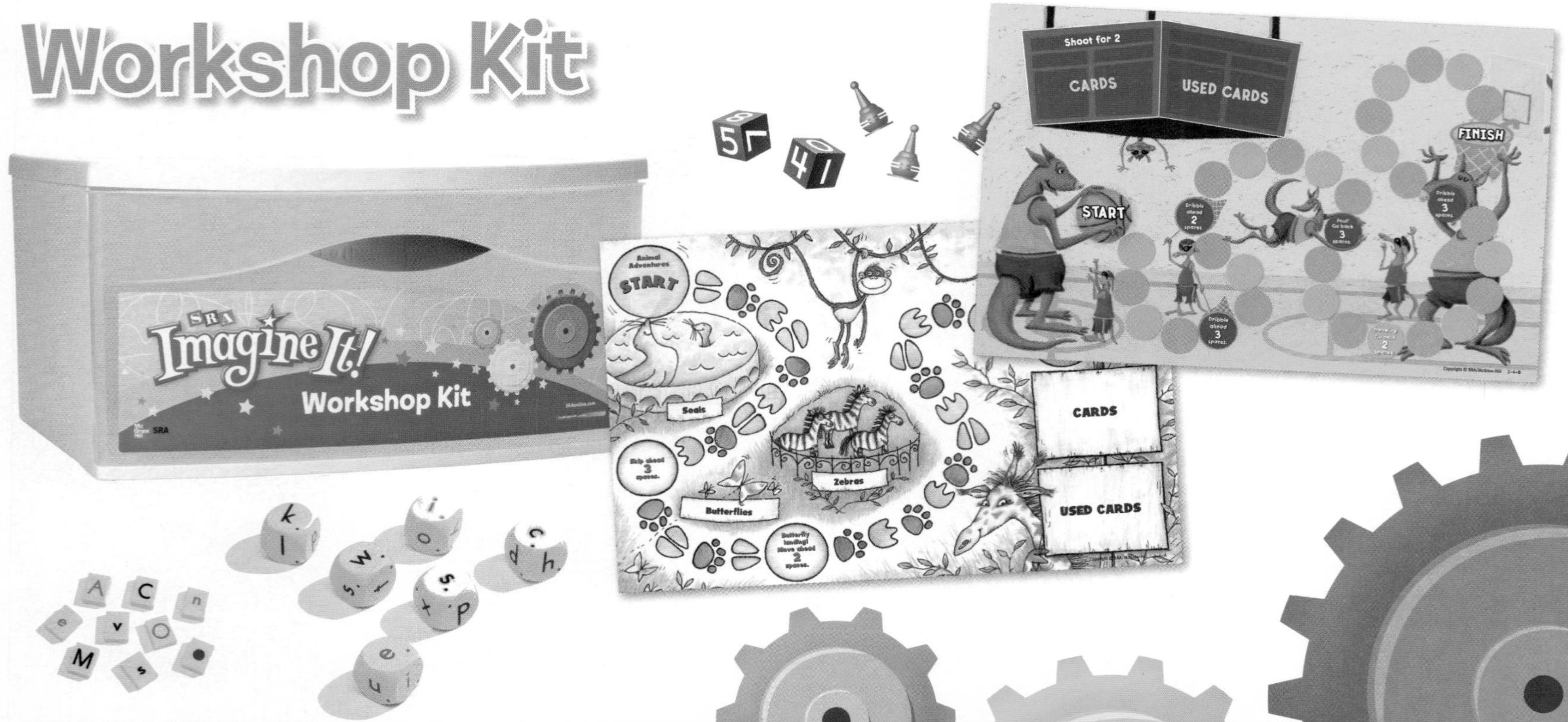

Technology

The following electronic resources are available for students:

- ***eStudent Reader***
- ***eSkills & eGames***
- ***Listening Library CD***

Electronic resources for the teacher include:

- ***ePlanner***
- ***eTeacher's Edition***
- ***eAssess***
- ***ePresentation***

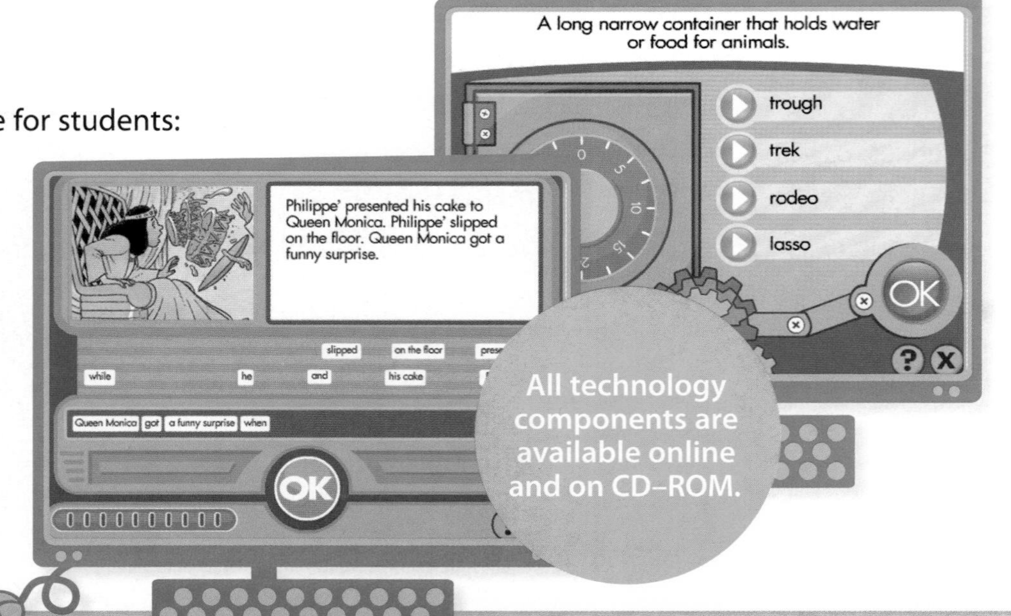

English Learner

Leveled Reader

English Learner Support Activities, Lesson 1

Listening Library CD Unit 5

English Learner Support Guide, Lesson 1

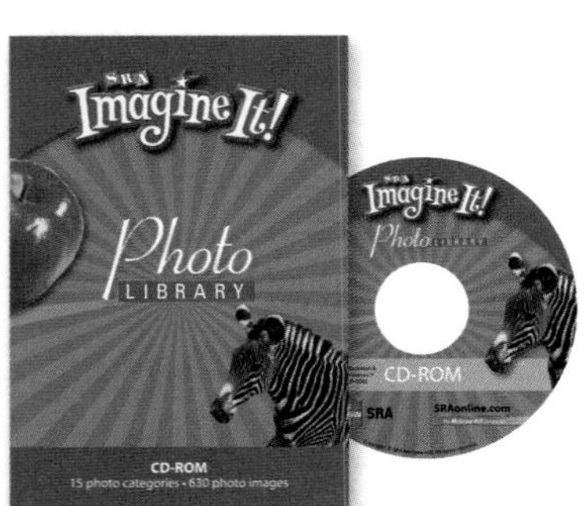

Photo Library CD

Approaching Level

Intervention

Intervention Workbook

Intervention Guide

Lesson 1 Overview

Lesson Assessment

Monitor Progress to Differentiate Instruction

Comprehension Strategies Rubrics

Use the Comprehension Strategies Rubrics to determine whether a student is using the strategies.

- ✦ Visualizing, p. T47
- ✦ Adjusting Reading Speed, p. T47

Inquiry Rubrics

Use the Inquiry Rubrics to assess a student's performance throughout the stages of the investigation for each unit. In addition, at the end of the unit you can use the rubrics to assess the groups' collaborative work as well as an individual's participation in that group.

- ✦ Generating Ideas and Questions, p. T87

Writing Rubrics

Use the writing rubrics in the Level Appendix to evaluate each student's persuasive paragraph.

- ✦ Genre
- ✦ Writing Process
- ✦ Writing Traits

Lesson Assessments

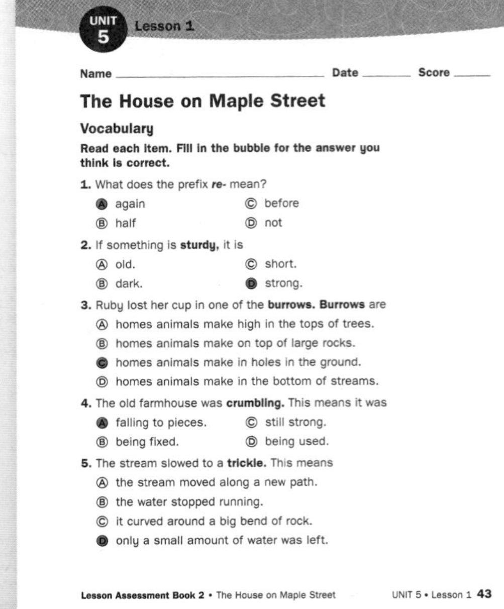

UNIT 5 Lesson 1

Name ______ Date ______ Score ______

The House on Maple Street

Vocabulary

Read each item. Fill in the bubble for the answer you think is correct.

1. What does the prefix *re-* mean?
   - Ⓐ again
   - Ⓑ half
   - Ⓒ before
   - Ⓓ not
2. If something is **sturdy**, it is
   - Ⓐ old.
   - Ⓑ dark.
   - Ⓒ short.
   - Ⓓ strong.
3. Ruby lost her cup in one of the **burrows. Burrows** are
   - Ⓐ homes animals make high in the tops of trees.
   - Ⓑ homes animals make on top of large rocks.
   - Ⓒ homes animals make in holes in the ground.
   - Ⓓ homes animals make in the bottom of streams.
4. The old farmhouse was **crumbling.** This means it was
   - Ⓐ falling to pieces.
   - Ⓑ being fixed.
   - Ⓒ still strong.
   - Ⓓ being used.
5. The stream slowed to a **trickle.** This means
   - Ⓐ the stream moved along a new path.
   - Ⓑ the water stopped running.
   - Ⓒ it curved around a big bend of rock.
   - Ⓓ only a small amount of water was left.

Lesson Assessment Book 2 • The House on Maple Street UNIT 5 • Lesson 1 43

Lesson Assessment Book 2, p. 43

UNIT 5 Lesson 1

The House on Maple Street (continued)

Comprehension

Read the following questions carefully. Then completely fill in the bubble of each correct answer. You may look back at the selection to find the answer to each of the questions.

1. Which of these happened first?
   - Ⓐ People set up tepees near the stream.
   - Ⓑ Ruby played with her china dishes.
   - Ⓒ The woods caught fire.
   - Ⓓ The schoolteacher sold some of the land.
2. Who lost the arrowhead?
   - Ⓐ a great hunter
   - Ⓑ a young boy
   - Ⓒ the boy's friend
   - Ⓓ the father

44 UNIT 5 • Lesson 1 The House on Maple Street • Lesson Assessment Book 2

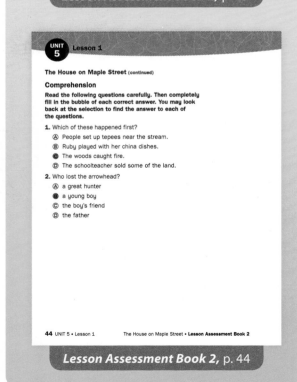

Lesson Assessment Book 2, p. 44

Formal Assessment 

Use these summative assessments along with your informal observations to assess student mastery.

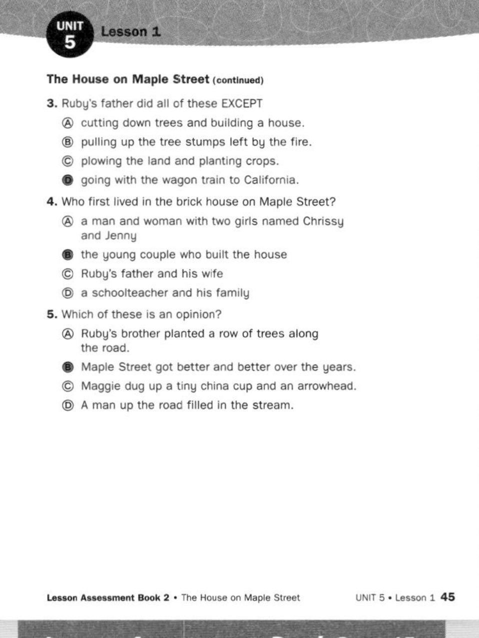

UNIT 5 Lesson 1

The House on Maple Street (continued)

3. Ruby's father did all of these EXCEPT
- Ⓐ cutting down trees and building a house.
- Ⓑ pulling up the tree stumps left by the fire.
- Ⓒ plowing the land and planting crops.
- ● going with the wagon train to California.

4. Who first lived in the brick house on Maple Street?
- Ⓐ a man and woman with two girls named Chrissy and Jenny
- ● the young couple who built the house
- Ⓒ Ruby's father and his wife
- Ⓓ a schoolteacher and his family

5. Which of these is an opinion?
- Ⓐ Ruby's brother planted a row of trees along the road.
- ● Maple Street got better and better over the years.
- Ⓒ Maggie dug up a tiny china cup and an arrowhead.
- Ⓓ A man up the road filled in the stream.

Lesson Assessment Book 2 • The House on Maple Street UNIT 5 • Lesson 1 **45**

Lesson Assessment Book 2, p. 45

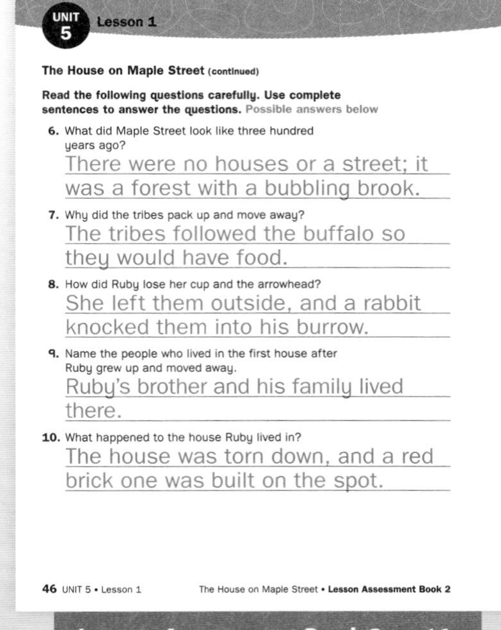

UNIT 5 Lesson 1

The House on Maple Street (continued)

Read the following questions carefully. Use complete sentences to answer the questions. Possible answers below

6. What did Maple Street look like three hundred years ago?
There were no houses or a street; it was a forest with a bubbling brook.

7. Why did the tribes pack up and move away?
The tribes followed the buffalo so they would have food.

8. How did Ruby lose her cup and the arrowhead?
She left them outside, and a rabbit knocked them into his burrow.

9. Name the people who lived in the first house after Ruby grew up and moved away.
Ruby's brother and his family lived there.

10. What happened to the house Ruby lived in?
The house was torn down, and a red brick one was built on the spot.

46 UNIT 5 • Lesson 1 The House on Maple Street • Lesson Assessment Book 2

Lesson Assessment Book 2, p. 46

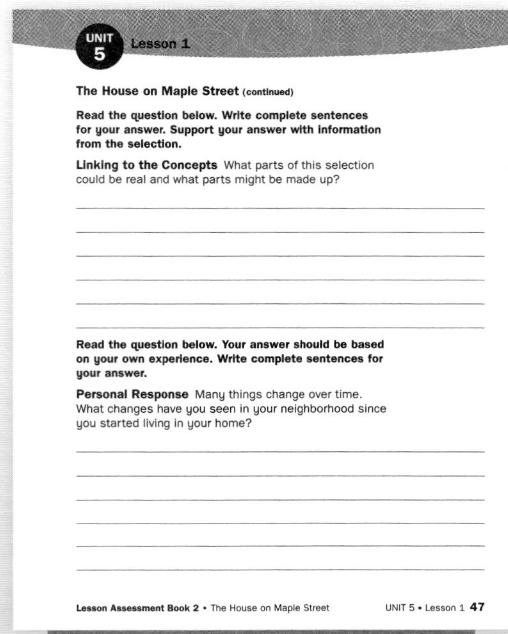

UNIT 5 Lesson 1

The House on Maple Street (continued)

Read the question below. Write complete sentences for your answer. Support your answer with information from the selection.

Linking to the Concepts What parts of this selection could be real and what parts might be made up?

Read the question below. Your answer should be based on your own experience. Write complete sentences for your answer.

Personal Response Many things change over time. What changes have you seen in your neighborhood since you started living in your home?

Lesson Assessment Book 2 • The House on Maple Street UNIT 5 • Lesson 1 **47**

Lesson Assessment Book 2, p. 47

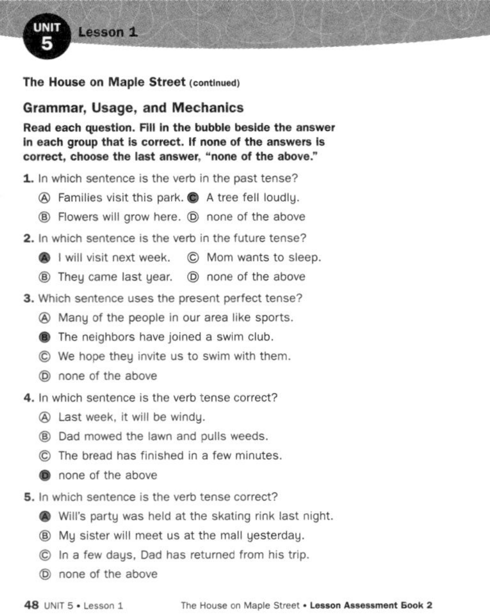

UNIT 5 Lesson 1

The House on Maple Street (continued)

Grammar, Usage, and Mechanics

Read each question. Fill in the bubble beside the answer in each group that is correct. If none of the answers is correct, choose the last answer, "none of the above."

1. In which sentence is the verb in the past tense?
- Ⓐ Families visit this park.
- ● A tree fell loudly.
- Ⓑ Flowers will grow here.
- Ⓓ none of the above

2. In which sentence is the verb in the future tense?
- ● I will visit next week.
- Ⓒ Mom wants to sleep.
- Ⓑ They came last year.
- Ⓓ none of the above

3. Which sentence uses the present perfect tense?
- Ⓐ Many of the people in our area like sports.
- ● The neighbors have joined a swim club.
- Ⓒ We hope they invite us to swim with them.
- Ⓓ none of the above

4. In which sentence is the verb tense correct?
- Ⓐ Last week, it will be windy.
- Ⓑ Dad mowed the lawn and pulls weeds.
- Ⓒ The bread has finished in a few minutes.
- ● none of the above

5. In which sentence is the verb tense correct?
- ● Will's party was held at the skating rink last night.
- Ⓑ My sister will meet us at the mall yesterday.
- Ⓒ In a few days, Dad has returned from his trip.
- Ⓓ none of the above

48 UNIT 5 • Lesson 1 The House on Maple Street • Lesson Assessment Book 2

Lesson Assessment Book 2, p. 48

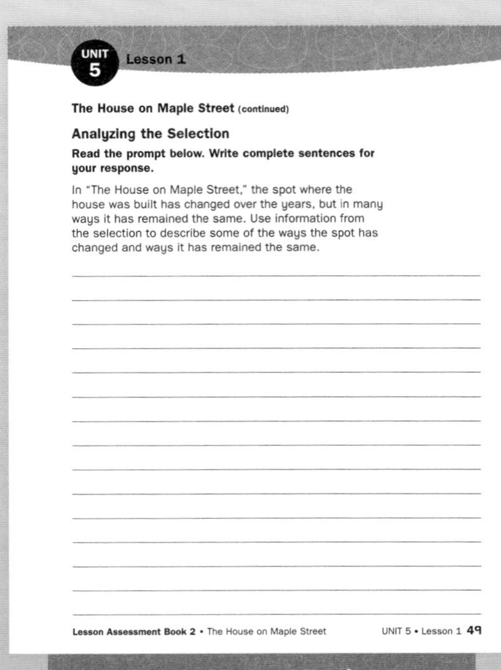

UNIT 5 Lesson 1

The House on Maple Street (continued)

Analyzing the Selection

Read the prompt below. Write complete sentences for your response.

In "The House on Maple Street," the spot where the house was built has changed over the years, but in many ways it has remained the same. Use information from the selection to describe some of the ways the spot has changed and ways it has remained the same.

Lesson Assessment Book 2 • The House on Maple Street UNIT 5 • Lesson 1 **49**

Lesson Assessment Book 2, p. 49

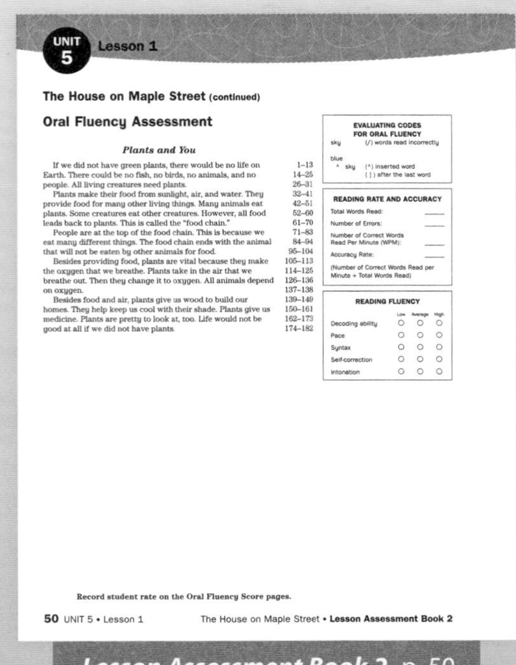

UNIT 5 Lesson 1

The House on Maple Street (continued)

Oral Fluency Assessment

Plants and You

If we did not have green plants, there would be no life on 1–13
Earth. There could be no fish, no birds, no animals, and no 14–25
people. All living creatures need plants. 26–31
Plants make their food from sunlight, air, and water. They 32–41
provide food for many other living things. Many animals eat 42–51
plants. Some creatures eat other creatures. However, all food 52–60
leads back to plants. This is called the "food chain." 61–70
People are at the top of the food chain. This is because we 71–83
eat many different things. The food chain ends with the animal 84–94
that will not be eaten by other animals for food. 95–104
Besides providing food, plants are vital because they make 105–113
the oxygen that we breathe. Plants take in the air that we 114–125
breathe out. Then they change it to oxygen. All animals depend 126–136
on oxygen. 137–138
Besides food and air, plants give us wood to build our 139–149
homes. They help keep us cool with their shade. Plants give us 150–161
medicine. Plants are pretty to look at, too. Life would not be 162–173
good at all if we did not have plants. 174–182

EVALUATING CODES FOR ORAL FLUENCY

sky (/) words read incorrectly

blue
^ sky (^) inserted word
( ]) after the last word

READING RATE AND ACCURACY

Total Words Read: ____

Number of Errors: ____

Number of Correct Words Read Per Minute (WPM): ____

Accuracy Rate: ____

(Number of Correct Words Read per Minute ÷ Total Words Read)

READING FLUENCY

	Low	Average	High
Decoding ability	○	○	○
Pace	○	○	○
Syntax	○	○	○
Self-correction	○	○	○
Intonation	○	○	○

Record student rate on the Oral Fluency Score pages.

50 UNIT 5 • Lesson 1 The House on Maple Street • Lesson Assessment Book 2

Lesson Assessment Book 2, p. 50

Day 1 **Preparing to Read**

OBJECTIVES

Students will
- identify and know the meanings of the prefixes *re-* and *un-*.
- build fluency.

MATERIALS
- ***Transparency*** 130
- Routine 10
- ***Skills Practice 2,*** pp. 85–86

Daily Oral Practice

Daily News

Today!

The pretty river outside my house runs swiftly. Many fish swim quickly through the clean water. The trees lining the river are home to many birds who happily fly from branch to branch. I hope the friendly flowing river stays the way it is. I'll do all I can to make sure it does.

- Write the daily news on the board or on chart paper. Then have students read the daily news in unison to practice fluency.
- As a word structure review from Unit 4, ask a volunteer to identify any words in the message with the suffixes *-ly* or *-y. swiftly, quickly, happily, friendly; pretty*

Word Structure

ROUTINE 10

The Prefixes *re-* and *un-*

- Write these word lines on the board or use ***Transparency*** 130. They will also be used the next day.

Line 1	make	remake	play	replay
Line 2	read	reread	start	restart
Line 3	happy	unhappy	lucky	unlucky
Line 4	tie	untie	wrap	unwrap

Differentiating Instruction **English Learner**

IF . . . students are native speakers of Spanish, **THEN . . .** point out to them that many adverbs in English that end in *-ly*, such as *swiftly*, end in *-mente* (*rápidamente*) in Spanish. Other adverbs include *easily (fácilmente)* and *happily (felizmente).*

Teacher Tip

SELF-CORRECTING Each day as students read the daily news and the word lines, have them correct themselves when they notice that the way they pronounced the words doesn't make sense. When they pronounce words incorrectly, have them correct their mistakes by rereading.

Teacher Tip

SYLLABICATION To help students blend words and build fluency, demonstrate syllabication using the decodable, multisyllabic words in the word lines.

re • make	re • play
re • read	re • start
un • hap • py	un • luck • y
un • tie	un • wrap

Lines 1–2 The Prefix *re-*

Use Rountine 10 for words with prefixes and suffixes to teach today's prefixes. Explain to students that prefixes are letters that are added to the beginning of base words. The prefix *re-* can be added to base verbs or action words. For example, the prefix *re-* can be added to the base verb *write* to make the new verb *rewrite*. Explain that the prefix *re-* means "again," and that adding it to a base verb or action word changes the meaning of the verb. The verb *rewrite* means "write again."

As you point to each word in Lines 1–2, have students read the word aloud in unison. Have students identify the base verbs in Lines 1–2. *make, play, read, start* Then have students define each word that has the prefix *re-*.

Lines 3–4 The Prefix *un-*

Explain to students that the prefix *un-* can be added to base words that are either adjectives or verbs. For example, the prefix *un-* can be added to the adjective *safe* to make the new adjective *unsafe*. Explain that the prefix *un-* means "not," and that adding it to a base word changes it to the opposite of the base word. The adjective *unsafe* means "not safe," which is the opposite of *safe*.

- Point out that the words on Line 3 are adjectives. Have students read the words on Line 3 in unison. Have students identify the base adjectives on Line 3. *happy, lucky* Then have students define each adjective with the prefix *un-*.
- Point out that the words on Line 4 are verbs. When the prefix *un-* is added to verbs or actions, the action becomes the opposite. For example, the verb or action word *unbutton* is the opposite of *button*. Have students read the words on Line 4 in unison. Have students identify the base verbs on Line 4. *tie, wrap* Then have students define each verb with the prefix *un-*.
- Help students start the word structure activities on ***Skills Practice 2*** pages 85–86. Read the Focus box with them, and help them with the first few questions. Then have them complete the pages on their own.

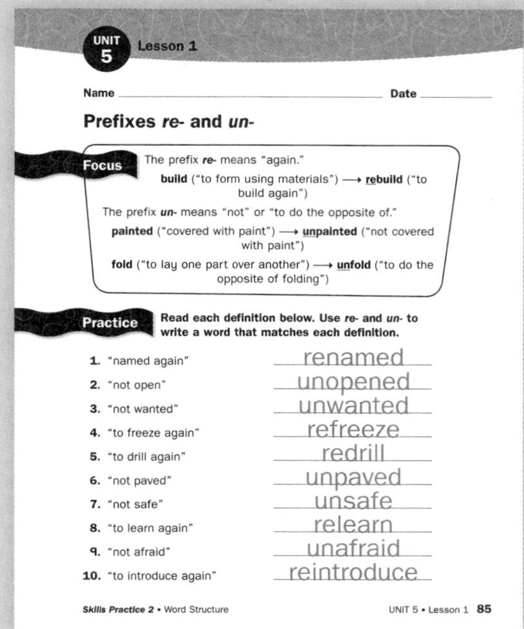

UNIT 5 Lesson 1

Name ____ Date ____

Prefixes *re-* and *un-*

Focus The prefix *re-* means "again."
build ("to form using materials") → **rebuild** ("to build again")
The prefix *un-* means "not" or "to do the opposite of."
painted ("covered with paint") → **unpainted** ("not covered with paint")
fold ("to lay one part over another") → **unfold** ("to do the opposite of folding")

Practice **Read each definition below. Use *re-* and *un-* to write a word that matches each definition.**

1. "named again" renamed
2. "not open" unopened
3. "not wanted" unwanted
4. "to freeze again" refreeze
5. "to drill again" redrill
6. "not paved" unpaved
7. "not safe" unsafe
8. "to learn again" relearn
9. "not afraid" unafraid
10. "to introduce again" reintroduce

Skills Practice 2 • Word Structure UNIT 5 • Lesson 1 85

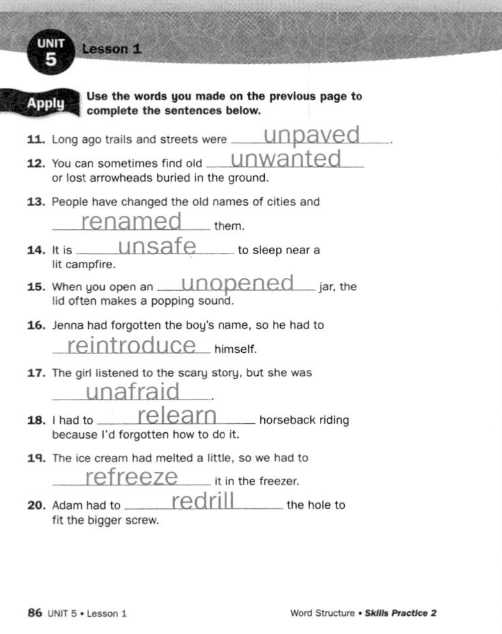

UNIT 5 Lesson 1

Apply **Use the words you made on the previous page to complete the sentences below.**

11. Long ago trails and streets were unpaved.
12. You can sometimes find old unwanted or lost arrowheads buried in the ground.
13. People have changed the old names of cities and renamed them.
14. It is unsafe to sleep near a lit campfire.
15. When you open an unopened jar, the lid often makes a popping sound.
16. Jenna had forgotten the boy's name, so he had to reintroduce himself.
17. The girl listened to the scary story, but she was unafraid.
18. I had to relearn horseback riding because I'd forgotten how to do it.
19. The ice cream had melted a little, so we had to refreeze it in the freezer.
20. Adam had to redrill the hole to fit the bigger screw.

86 UNIT 5 • Lesson 1 Word Structure • *Skills Practice 2*

Skills Practice 2, pp. 85–86

Monitor Progress to Differentiate Instruction

Formal Assessment 

Word Structure During the word structure activity, note how well students understand the prefixes *re-* and *un-*.

APPROACHING LEVEL	**IF . . .** students need practice with the prefixes *re-* and *un-*,	**THEN . . .** work with them in small groups on the word structure activities on ***Reteach*** page 123 during Workshop.
	IF . . . students need extra practice with the prefixes *re-* and *un-*,	**THEN . . .** work with them in small groups on the word structure activities for Unit 5 Lesson 1 in the ***Intervention Guide*** during Workshop.
ON LEVEL	**IF . . .** students understand the prefixes *re-* and *un-*,	**THEN . . .** have them make lists of words to add to the word lines during Workshop.
ABOVE LEVEL	**IF . . .** students are ready for a challenge with the prefixes *re-* and *un-*,	**THEN . . .** have them complete the word structure activities on ***Challenge Activities*** page 112 during Workshop.

Reading and Responding

OBJECTIVES

Students will

- ✦ relate prior knowledge to the unit theme Communities across Time.
- ✦ listen attentively.
- ✦ build vocabulary.

MATERIALS

- ✦ ***Home Connection,*** pp. 49–50
- ✦ ***Skills Practice 2,*** p. 93

Vocabulary Tip

Before reading aloud *A River Ran Wild*, introduce the following vocabulary words to students. Say each word and its definition. Then use the word in a sentence.

- ✦ **quench** (kwench) *adv.* to satisfy one's thirst
- ✦ **migration** (mī • grā' • shun) *n.* the act of moving from one place to another
- ✦ **grist** (grist) *n.* grain that is ready to be crushed

Teacher Tip

BUILDING BACKGROUND Before reading the story, use a map to show students where the Nashua River is located. Explain to students that the story about the Nashua River is true, and that the author wrote the story to inspire children to respect Earth.

Read Aloud

Activate Prior Knowledge

- ✦ Tell students that in this unit they will read and learn about communities across time. Ask students the following questions:
  - *What does the word* community *mean?*
  - *What do you know about the community where you live?*
  - *How are communities formed?*
  - *What was the land like before communities were built?*
  - *Have you ever found an artifact?*
  - *How does finding artifacts teach us about the past, the present, and the future?*
- ✦ Share with students your own ideas of communities across time.

Genre

A River Ran Wild is narrative nonfiction. Explain that in narrative nonfiction, elements of fiction are blended with elements of nonfiction to make a more exciting story.

Comprehension Strategies

It is important to model the comprehension strategies. Modeling is a powerful way to get students to use the comprehension strategies. Keep the following in mind when reading:

- **Adjusting Reading Speed** helps when you encounter difficult words or passages. Let students see how slowing down and rereading helps you comprehend.

Set Purposes

As students listen to *A River Ran Wild*, have them think about how people have different beliefs about the land. Have them think about how people can have a tremendous effect on the natural world and how harming the land will eventually harm all those who live on it. Encourage them to think about what this story teaches them about communities across time and what the characters in the story believe about the land. Then read the Focus Questions, and have students suggest possible answers.

Focus Questions How can actions from the past affect other communities later in time? What can you do to help protect the area you live in for people in the future?

A River Ran Wild

by Lynne Cherry

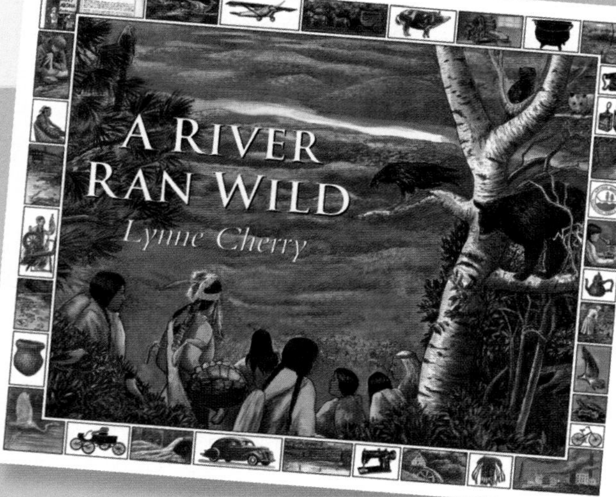

Long ago a river ran wild through a land of towering forests. Bears, moose, and herds of deer, hawks and owls all made their homes in the peaceful river valley. Geese paused on their long migration and rested on its banks. Beavers, turtles, and schools of fish swam in its clear waters.

One day a group of native people, searching for a place to settle, came upon the river valley. From atop the highest mountain, known today as Mt. Wachusett, they saw the river nestled in its valley, a silver sliver in the sun.

They came down from the mountain, and at the river's edge they knelt to quench their thirst with its clear water. Pebbles shone up from the bottom.

"Let us settle by this river," said the chief of the native people. He named the river Nash-a-way—River with the Pebbled Bottom.

By the Nash-a-way, Chief Weeawa's people built a village. They gathered cattails from the riverbanks to thatch their dwellings. In the forest they set fires to clear brush from the forest floor. In these clearings they planted corn and squash for eating. They made arrows for hunting and canoes for river travel.

When the Indians hunted in the forest or caught salmon in the river, they killed only what they needed for themselves for food and clothing. They asked all the forest creatures that they killed to please forgive them.

The Nashua people saw a rhythm in their lives and in the seasons. The river, land, and forest provided all they needed.

The Nashua had lived for generations by the clear, clean, flowing river when one day a pale-skinned trader came with a boatload full of treasures. He brought shiny metal knives, colored beads, and cooking kettles, mirrors, tools, and bolts of bright cloth. His wares seemed like magic. The Nashua welcomed him, traded furs, and soon a trading post was built.

Reading and Responding Read Aloud

In the many years that followed, the settlers' village and others like it grew and the Nash-a-way became the Nashua. The settlers worked together to clear land by cutting down the forests, which they thought were full of danger—wilderness that they would conquer. They hunted wolves and beaver, killing much more than they needed. Extra pelts were sent to England in return for goods and money.

The settlers built sawmills along the river, which the Nashua's current powered. They built dams to make the millponds that were used to store the water. They cut down the towering forest and floated tree trunks down the river. The logs were cut up into lumber, which was used for building houses.

The settlers built fences for their pastures, plowed the fields, and planted crops. They called the land their own and told the Indians not to trespass. Hunting land disappeared as the settlers cleared the forest. Indian fishing rights vanished as the settlers claimed the river.

The Indians' ways were disrupted and they began to fight the settlers. The wars raged for many years but the Indians' bows and arrows were no match against gunpowder, and so the settlers' rifles drove the Indians from the land.

Through a hundred years of fighting, the Nashua was a healthy river, sometimes dammed for grist and sawmills, but still flowing wild and free. Muskrats, fish, and turtles still swam from bank to bank. Deer still came to drink from the river, and owls, raccoons, and beaver fed there.

At the start of the new century, an industrial revolution came to the Nashua's banks and waters. Many new machines were invented. Some spun thread from wool and cotton. Others wove the thread into cloth. Some machines turned wood to pulp, and others made the pulp into paper. Leftover pulp and dye and fiber was dumped into the Nashua River, whose swiftly flowing current washed away the waste.

These were times of much excitement, times of "progress" and "invention." Factories along the Nashua River made new things of new materials. Telephones and radios and other things were made of plastics. Chemicals and plastic waste were also dumped into the river. Soon the Nashua's fish and wildlife grew sick from this pollution.

The paper mills continued to pollute the Nashua's waters. Every day for many decades pulp was dumped into the Nashua, and as the pulp clogged up the river, it began to run more slowly.

As the pulp decomposed, bad smells welled up from the river. People who lived near the river smelled its stench and stayed far from it. Each day as the mills dyed paper red, green, blue, and yellow, the Nashua ran whatever color the paper was dyed.

Soon no fish lived in the river. No birds stopped on their migration. No one could see pebbles shining up through murky water. The Nashua was dark and dirty. The Nashua was slowly dying.

One night Oweana, a descendant of Weeawa who still lived by the Nashua, had a dream so vivid that he awoke in wide-eyed wonder. In his dream Chief Weeawa's spirit returned to the river and saw it as it was now—still and deadly.

Chief Weeawa mourned for the Nash-a-way, but where his tears fell upon the dirty waters, the waters were cleansed until the river once again flowed freely.

The next morning Oweana went to speak to his friend Marion. When he told her of his dream, she said, "I had this dream also! River with the Pebbled Bottom is the name Weeawa gave it, but today no pebbles shine up through the Nashua River's waters." Together they decided something must be done.

Marion traveled to each town along the Nashua. She spoke of the river's history and of her vision to restore it. "No longer do we have a river—it's a stinking, smelly sewer. But it wasn't always this way."

People listened and imagined a sparkling river, full of fish. They imagined pebbles shining up through clear waters. They signed petitions and sent letters. They protested to politicians and showed them jars of dirty water. They convinced the paper mills to build a plant to process the waste. They persuaded the factories to stop dumping. Finally, new laws were passed and the factories stopped polluting.

Slowly, slowly, the Nashua's current began to clean its water. Year by year the river carried away the dyes and fiber to the ocean. Marion and Oweana thanked the people who had helped to clean the Nashua.

Through the meadows, towns, and cities, the Nashua once again flows freely. Paper pulp no longer clogs it. Chemicals no longer foul it.

Now we walk along its banks and row upon its fragrant waters. We can set our boats upon it and with its current, drift downstream.

Once again the river runs wild through a towering forest greenway. Red-tailed hawks and barred owls live here. Geese pause from their long migration and rest on the river banks. Deer come to drink from the river's waters. We, too, have settled by this river. Pebbles shine up through clear waters. Nashua is what we call it—River with the Pebbled Bottom.

Reading and Responding

Discussing the Read Aloud

✦ Review the Focus Questions with students: *How can actions from the past affect other communities later in time? What can you do to help protect the area you live in for people in the future?*

✦ Lead students in a discussion about what they learned about the theme Communities across Time. Ask them the following questions regarding the theme:

- *How does A River Ran Wild relate to the theme Communities across Time?* **Possible Answer** *A River Ran Wild shows what can happen to an area if it becomes overdeveloped and polluted. The story also shows that people can make a difference in their communities by demanding change, which can lead to a better, cleaner community.*
- *What did you learn about communities across time?* **Possible Answer** *I learned that people's attitudes can have a great effect on their communities. I also learned that with work, a polluted area can become beautiful again.*
- *How do you feel about the land and how it is used and treated?* **Possible Answer** *I feel that the land is very important and should be treated with respect.*

✦ Create a Word Bank for students to organize the vocabulary for this unit. Organize the Word Bank by parts of speech: nouns, verbs, adjectives, and adverbs. Write the words or have students write the words on cards and then place them under the appropriate part of speech on the Word Bank. Encourage students to find other words related to the unit theme Communities across Time and add them to the Word Bank. You might also want to encourage students to find synonyms, antonyms, words with Greek roots, and words with Latin roots for the Word Bank and add them as well.

Concept/Question Board

- Remind students the **Concept/Question Board** will help them explore the theme Communities across Time. To get the Board started, have students write what they know about communities, how we can learn about them, and how they can change and post the information on the board.
- Brainstorm with students things that would be appropriate to post on the Communities across Time **Concept/Question Board.** Suggestions include the following about our land, archaeology, the environment, or communities:
  - Short stories, poems, or songs
  - Magazine or newspaper articles
  - Photographs or illustrations
  - Television programs or movies
- Remind students that they
  - may post a question, comment, note, word, illustration, or object related to the theme Communities across Time any time.
  - should feel free to write an answer or a note on someone else's question.
  - can read and listen to stories about the theme Communities across Time at home.

Concept/Question Board

To get the **Concept/Question Board** started for this unit, bring in one or two items, such as a newspaper or magazine article related to a community, its history, and how it has developed and changed. Post theme items on the **Concept/Question Board.**

Distribute page 49 of ***Home Connection.*** Students can read books and articles about communities across time with their families. This ***Home Connection*** is also available in Spanish on page 50.

Lesson 1 Inquiry Planner

STEP 1: Generating Ideas and Questions

Day 1 Students will share stories, ideas, and questions about communities. They will also discuss ideas about the theme in *A River Ran Wild.*

Day 2 Students will continue generating ideas and questions they have related to the theme.

Day 3 In small groups, have students discuss ideas about the theme in the Read Aloud and "The House on Maple Street."

Day 4 Students will discuss ideas about the theme in "The House on Maple Street." Groups will generate potential investigation questions and topics.

Day 5 Students can work in small groups to generate questions and investigation topics that interest them.

Teacher Tip

GENERATING IDEAS To assist students in early investigations, provide support by modeling the procedure step-by-step. At this point, students should be involved in discussions that help them to identify a question or idea that they wonder about and wish to better understand.

To help students support their knowledge of a topic, have them read the ***Leveled Social Studies Readers.*** If students are working in a group, encourage them to share their information with their group members. Use each student's Oral Fluency Assessment score from the Benchmark Assessment to diagnose the appropriate ***Leveled Social Studies Reader.***

Inquiry Process

Step 1—Generating Ideas and Questions

Whole-Group Time

Whole Group

Explain to students the goals of the unit investigation. For this unit, student groups will create their own questions to investigate and will research ideas related to the theme Communities across Time. At the end of the unit, groups will present what they learned from their investigations.

- To get students thinking about the theme, have students discuss what they know about communities and the things they find interesting about their community. Students may want to share personal stories about their own experience in their community, how they think or know their community has changed over time, or what they think communities were like in previous generations. Students may also be interested in how people change the land and how land can change life in a community. Students' initial stories and interests should help them generate good investigation questions. During this discussion, take note of students' interests to help organize them into small groups with similar interests.
- The ideas or stories that students share might cause them to wonder about new things and ask new questions about communities. Model how discussion can raise questions. For example, you might tell a story about a community that became overpopulated, which caused the city to expand into the country and tear down valuable forests and disrupt animals' habitats. This might raise such questions as *How did this community get so big? Why were there so many people moving there? How can a community support so many people? What's going to happen to the land, the people, and the wildlife? How can nature and people live in harmony?* As you model, encourage students to ask questions and add to your ideas. Remember that any questions you propose are only intended to model for students. Students should pursue their own interests in the theme.
- Ask students if the Read Aloud, *A River Ran Wild,* gives them any new ideas about communities. Encourage discussion of this selection and how communities can both change nature and be changed by it. Have students take notes about *A River Ran Wild* in their Writer's Notebooks.

Small-Group Time

- ✦ In small groups, have students continue discussing the questions and ideas that were started in the whole-group discussion. Remind them to pursue the ideas and questions that interest and excite them, because these should lead to a question they will investigate further.
- ✦ Allow students to exchange ideas and stories they have about communities, reminding them that the ideas and stories they share can lead to questions they want to research. As students exchange ideas and stories, have them ask each other questions about the ideas they share.
- ✦ Have students complete ***Skills Practice 2*** page 93 to help them start thinking about things in their community that interest them.

Concept/Question Board

Have students write information, opinions, ideas, or questions on the **Concept/Question Board.** Students might also

- post magazine or newspaper articles about their community.
- post short stories, paragraphs, or poems about our land, natural disasters, the environment, or communities.
- post photographs or illustrations of our land, archaeology, natural disasters, the environment, and/or communities.
- listen to songs about the land, the environment, or the communities we live in that students bring in. Post the song or CD cover on the Board.
- list television programs or movies that deal with our land, archaeology, natural disasters, the environment, or communities.

Teacher Tip

COMMUNITIES It can be hard to define just what a community is. To allow students to pursue their own interests, accept a broad interpretation of what counts as a community. You may want to explain the concept of sub-communities, smaller communities that exist within larger ones.

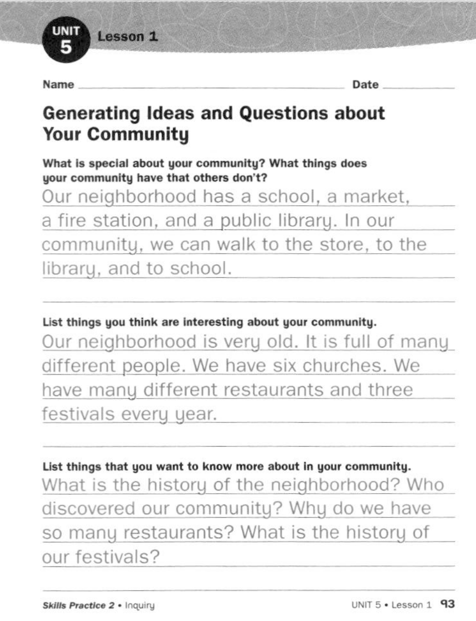

UNIT 5 Lesson 1

Name ______ Date ______

Generating Ideas and Questions about Your Community

What is special about your community? What things does your community have that others don't?

Our neighborhood has a school, a market, a fire station, and a public library. In our community, we can walk to the store, to the library, and to school.

List things you think are interesting about your community.

Our neighborhood is very old. It is full of many different people. We have six churches. We have many different restaurants and three festivals every year.

List things that you want to know more about in your community.

What is the history of the neighborhood? Who discovered our community? Why do we have so many restaurants? What is the history of our festivals?

Skills Practice 2 • Inquiry UNIT 5 • Lesson 1 93

Skills Practice 2, p. 93

OBJECTIVES

Students will
- take the spelling pretest.
- practice cursive *N* and *M*.
- prewrite persuasive paragraphs.

MATERIALS

- ***Language Arts Handbook,*** pp. 172–175
- ***Transparencies*** 121, 131
- ***Skills Practice 2,*** p. 95
- Routines 15 and 16

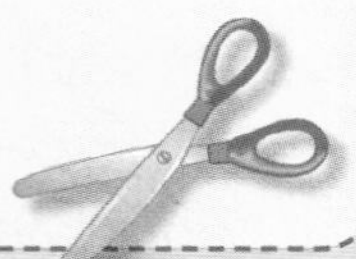

Traits of Good Writing

IDEAS AND ORGANIZATION The writer generates and organizes ideas to create elements of persuasion.

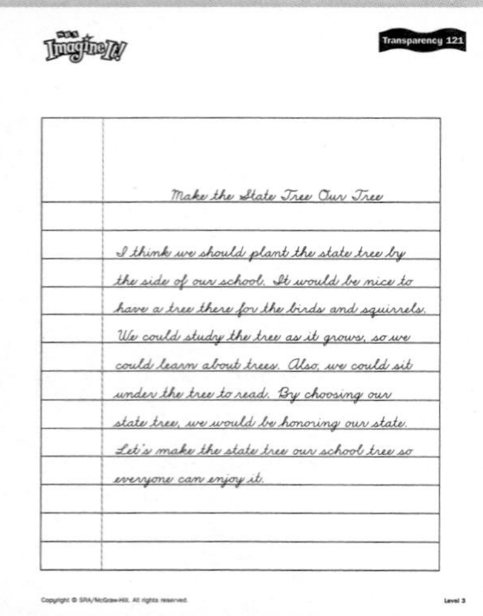

Imagine It! Transparency 121

Make the State Tree Our Tree

I think we should plant the state tree by the side of our school. It would be nice to have a tree there for the birds and squirrels. We could study the tree as it grows, so we could learn about trees. Also, we could sit under the tree to read. By choosing our state tree, we would be honoring our state. Let's make the state tree our school tree so everyone can enjoy it.

 Level 3

Transparency 121

Teacher Tip

ASSESSMENT You will use the Writing Rubrics found in the Level Appendix to evaluate students' persuasive paragraphs. You may use any of the rubrics for Genre, Writing Process, and Writing Traits. Share with students what you will be looking for when assessing their persuasive paragraphs.

Writing Persuasive Paragraph

Prewriting

ROUTINE 15 ROUTINE 16

Teach—Generating and Organizing Ideas

- Have students discuss the topics of the persuasive paragraphs they wrote in Unit 4 Lesson 4. Have them discuss why they chose those topics. Tell students they are going to write another persuasive paragraph. If necessary, remind students they should feel strongly about the topic of their persuasive text.
- Remind students that in persuasive writing it is the writer's job to get the readers to think, feel, or act in a certain way. Writers can change a reader's mind with persuasive writing.
- Tell students that the beginning of a piece of persuasive writing should grab the reader's attention, tell what the subject of the writing is, and tell how the writer feels about it. The ending of a piece of persuasive writing should summarize the reasons given and suggest that the readers take action or accept the writer's opinion.
- Explain to students that there are two ways in which writers can persuade readers: give facts and good reasons or tell readers how they feel about the subject.
- Refer to ***Language Arts Handbook*** pages 172–175 for information on persuasive paragraphs.
- Display ***Transparency*** 121 and discuss the parts of a persuasive paragraph. Explain that persuasive paragraphs have three parts: the topic sentence; the body, which contains facts and examples; and the closing sentence.
  - The topic sentence tells the reader what the subject of the paragraph is as well as the writer's viewpoint on the subject.
  - The body gives the reasons or facts that support the writer's viewpoint.
  - The closing sentence summarizes the writer's reasons and suggests that readers take action or accept the writer's viewpoint on the subject.

Writing, continued

Guided Practice

- ✦ Use Routine 15 to model the writing and Routine 16 to model filling out the graphic organizer. Brainstorm a list of topics for persuasive paragraphs with students. Write the list on the board.
- ✦ Have students turn to ***Skills Practice 2*** page 95. Read and discuss the Think section about audience and purpose for writing a persuasive paragraph.
- ✦ Create a graphic organizer on the board or chart paper like the one on ***Skills Practice 2*** page 95 to model inserting information based on a topic you select. For example, if you would like to persuade the school board to start a recycling program, you would put Starting a Recycling Program in the School District in the Main Idea circle. Tell students that this is your main idea. You will write facts, reasons, or feelings in each of the Detail circles. Write To Save Trees in one of the circles.

Apply

Composing — Prewriting Have students complete their graphic organizers on page 95 in ***Skills Practice 2*** based on the topic and the audience they selected during brainstorming.

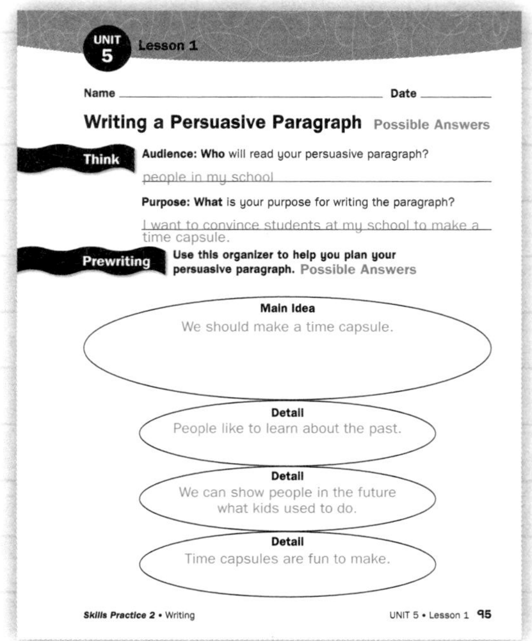
UNIT 5 Lesson 1

Name ______ Date ______

Writing a Persuasive Paragraph Possible Answers

Think **Audience:** Who will read your persuasive paragraph?
people in my school

Purpose: What is your purpose for writing the paragraph?
I want to convince students at my school to make a time capsule.

Prewriting **Use this organizer to help you plan your persuasive paragraph.** Possible Answers

Main Idea: We should make a time capsule.

Detail: People like to learn about the past.

Detail: We can show people in the future what kids used to do.

Detail: Time capsules are fun to make.

Skills Practice 2 • Writing UNIT 5 • Lesson 1 95

Skills Practice 2, p. 95

Spelling

Prefixes *re-, un-, pre-, mis-* Pretest

Teach

Say the sentences below aloud. Have students write the spelling words on a separate sheet of paper. When they are finished, have them correct any misspelled words.

Pretest Sentences

1. I like to **mismatch** my socks.
2. The directions are **unclear.**
3. The teacher asked us to **reread** the article.
4. My mom got a **refund** for the broken radio.
5. When it gets warmer, I'll **unzip** my jacket.
6. There was a **misprint** in the newspaper.
7. **Unload** the groceries on the kitchen counter.
8. The guide did not intend to **mislead** the hikers.
9. **Preheat** the oven before baking the cookies.
10. If you have problems, **restart** the computer.
11. The **prefix** changes the meaning of the word.
12. The fans thought the call was **unfair.**
13. The voters demanded a **recount.**
14. I don't want to **misplace** my homework again.
15. Dorene enjoyed the **preview** of the movie.

Challenge Sentences

16. Charlie's brother starts **preschool** this year.
17. The dog was totally **unaware** of the cat.

Diagnose any misspellings by determining whether students misspelled the prefixes or some other part of the word. Then have students use the pretest as a take-home list to study the spellings of these words with prefixes.

Penmanship

Cursive Letters *N* and *M*

Teach

✦ Introduce capital cursive *N* and *M* as curve forward letters.

✦ Display ***Transparency*** 131. Using a pointer, trace the letters while saying the formations aloud.

- **Letter *N*** Starting point, undercurve
  Slant down
  Retrace up slant
  Overcurve down into undercurve:
  capital *N*
- **Letter *M*** Starting point, undercurve
  Slant down
  Retrace up slant, overcurve
  Slant down, retrace up slant
  Overcurve down into undercurve:
  capital *M*

✦ On the board, write capital cursive letters *N* and *M* saying the strokes aloud as you form the letters.

Guided Practice

Ask a volunteer to write the letters on the board while saying the strokes aloud. Guide the student as he or she writes.

Apply

Have students practice writing each of the letters four times. Ask students to circle the best formation of each of their letters.

Teacher Tips

CONNECTING *N* Show how to connect cursive *N* to other letters.

PENMANSHIP If students are having problems with letters that float between the lines, then review proper paper positioning and check to make sure students are holding their pencils correctly.

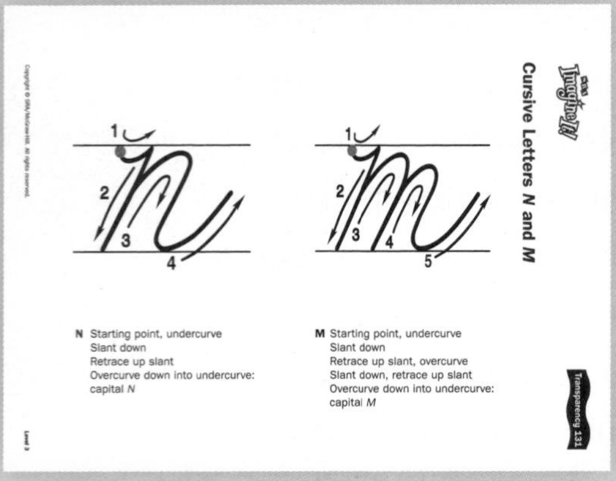

Transparency 131

Differentiating Instruction **English Learner**

IF . . . students have difficulty following your directions for handwriting, **THEN . . .** review words such as undercurve, overcurve, downcurve, slant and loop. Say and demonstrate each word, having students mimic both your words and movements.

Lesson 1

Skills Traces

Preparing to Read

Word Structure: Prefix *re-*

Grade 3
Introduced: Unit 5, Lesson 1
Practiced: Unit 5, Lesson 5
Assessed: ***Lesson Assessment Book 2,*** p. 43

Reviewed in Grade 4, Unit 1, Lesson 2

Word Structure: Prefixes *un-, pre-, and mis-*

Introduced in Grade 2, Unit 4, Lesson 3

Grade 3
Reviewed: Unit 5, Lesson 1
Practiced: Unit 5, Lesson 5

Reviewed in Grade 4, Unit 4, Lesson 2

Reading and Responding

Comprehension Skill: Classify and Categorize

Reviewed in Grade 2, Unit 2, Lesson 5

Grade 3
Reviewed: Unit 2, Lesson 5
Practiced: Unit 5, Lesson 1
Assessed: ***Lesson Assessment Book 2,*** pp. 44–46

Reviewed in Grade 4, Unit 2, Lesson 5

Comprehension Skill: Fact and Opinion

Reviewed in Grade 2, Unit 2, Lesson 5

Grade 3
Reviewed: Unit 1, Lesson 1
Practiced: Unit 5, Lesson 1
Assessed: ***Lesson Assessment Book 2,*** pp. 44–46

Reviewed in Grade 4, Unit 2, Lesson 4

Comprehension Strategy: Adjusting Reading Speed

Introduced in Grade 2, Unit 1, Lesson 4

Grade 3
Reviewed: Unit 1, Lesson 2
Practiced: Unit 5, Lesson 1
Assessed: Unit 5, Lesson 1, p. T47

Reviewed in Grade 4, Unit 1, Lesson 4

Comprehension Strategy: Visualizing

Reviewed in Grade 2, Unit 1, Lesson 4

Grade 3
Reviewed: Unit 1, Lesson 4
Practiced: Unit 5, Lesson 1
Assessed: Unit 1, Lesson 1, p. T47

Reviewed in Grade 4, Unit 1, Lesson 1

Language Arts

Writing: Persuasive Writing

Reviewed in Grade 2, Unit 3, Lesson 5

Grade 3
Reviewed: Unit 5, Lesson 1
Assessed: Refer to Unit 5, Lesson 2 Assessment

Reviewed in Grade 4, Unit 2, Lesson 5

Grammar, Usage, and Mechanics: Tense

Reviewed in Grade 2, Unit 5, Lesson 5

Grade 3
Reviewed: Unit 5, Lesson 1
Practiced: Unit 6, Lesson 5
Assessed: ***Lesson Assessment Book 2,*** p. 48

Reviewed in Grade 4, Unit 4, Lesson 5

Preparing to Read

OBJECTIVES

Students will

- ✦ identify and know the meanings of the prefixes *re-* and *un-*.
- ✦ build fluency.

MATERIALS

- ✦ ***Transparency*** 130
- ✦ Routine 10

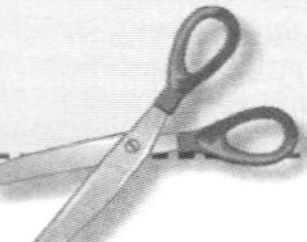

Daily Oral Practice

Differentiating Instruction **English Learner**

IF . . . students have limited vocabulary and don't understand the word *artifact*,
THEN . . . explain that an artifact is a tool or object made by humans many years ago that is of historical interest.

Daily News

Today!

What's that sticking up in the dirt? It's small, yellow, and pointy. Maybe it's the bone from an unlucky dinosaur. Finding an artifact is like unwrapping a birthday present! I wonder how many people have stood on this land through the years and never seen this tiny artifact.

- ✦ Write the daily news on the board or on chart paper. Then have the girls read the daily news in unison to practice fluency.
- ✦ As a review of yesterday's word structure lesson, ask a volunteer to identify any words in the message with the prefix *un-*. *unlucky, unwrapping*

Word Structure 

ROUTINE 10

The Prefixes *re-* and *un-*

✦ Use ***Transparency*** 130 word lines from Day 1.

Line 1	make	remake	play	replay
Line 2	read	reread	start	restart
Line 3	happy	unhappy	lucky	unlucky
Line 4	tie	untie	wrap	unwrap

✦ Use Routine 10 to review the prefixes *re-* and *un-*. If necessary, remind students that the prefix *re-* means "again," and *un-* means "not."

Developing Oral Language

Use any or all of the following activities to help students practice reading the words from the word lines.

- Have a student choose a word from the word lines and use it in a sentence. **Possible Answer** *I want to* unwrap *my present.* Have another student create a new sentence using the original word, plus a new word from the list. **Possible Answer** *I want to* unwrap *my present, because I know it will make me* happy.
- Have students point to and say a word in the word lines. Have them choose a volunteer to use the word in a sentence and extend the sentence. Encourage students to add information at the beginning and end of the sentence.
- Ask a volunteer to choose a base word from the word lines and use it in a sentence. **Possible Answer** *I don't know how to* tie *a bow.* Then have that student choose another volunteer to use the other form of that word in a different sentence. **Possible Answer** *But I know how to* untie *a bow.*
- Choose a word from the word lines with the prefix *re-* or *un-*. Have a student give a definition for that word. Then ask the class if the definition is correct. If the definition needs to be modified, have volunteers offer suggestions. Repeat for all the words with suffixes on the lines.

Differentiating Instruction **English Learner**

IF . . . students have difficulty with negative prefixes, **THEN . . .** emphasize that *un-, in-, ir-, im-,* and *non-* all have the same meaning. Refer to the ***English Learner Support Guide*** for additional instruction for new English learners.

Monitor Progress 

to Differentiate Instruction
Formal Assessment

Word Structure During the word structure activity, note how well students understand the words.

APPROACHING LEVEL

IF . . . students do not understand the words on the word lines, **THEN . . .** use pictures, photos, objects, stick drawings, or pantomime to help them visualize the words.

ON LEVEL

IF . . . students need practice with the words on the word lines, **THEN . . .** have them write sentences using the same words on the lines.

ABOVE LEVEL

IF . . . students understand the words on the word lines, **THEN . . .** have them make a list of other words with the prefixes *re-* and *un-* and use them in sentences.

Reading and Responding

OBJECTIVES

Students will
- ✦ activate prior knowledge by discussing the theme Communities across Time.
- ✦ learn selection vocabulary.
- ✦ review the elements of realistic fiction.
- ✦ use the comprehension strategies Visualizing and Adjusting Reading Speed.

MATERIALS

- ✦ Routines 11, 12, 14
- ✦ ***Transparencies*** 5, 132
- ✦ ***Student Reader,*** Book 2, pp. 126–137
- ✦ ***Home Connection,*** pp. 51–52
- ✦ ***Lesson Assessment Book 2***

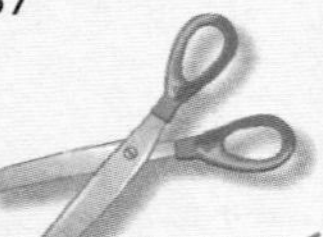

Build Background

Activate Prior Knowledge

- ✦ Discuss with students what they know about how communities were formed.
- ✦ Ask students what they learned about how land changes over time in *A River Ran Wild*.
- ✦ Ask students if they have ever found an artifact. Ask students if they have ever investigated the history of their town or city.
- ✦ Encourage students to make connections to books, articles, or programs they have read or seen about communities and how they change over time.

Background Information

The following information might help students understand the story they are about to read:

- Long before there were cars and houses, the land was wilderness. Wildlife roamed freely, partaking of the fruits and water that the land provided.
- The Native Americans were the first to settle on patches of land. Pioneers followed with more building and trading. The land started changing form.
- New industry developed along with more homes and forms of transportation.
- One piece of land looked quite different hundreds of years ago.

Preview and Prepare

Browse

Use Routine 12, the clues, problems, and wonderings routine, to help students identify what they know before reading, what problems they may encounter while reading, and set their purposes for reading. Students will chart these on a transparency.

Have students read the title, and take a few minutes to browse the first few pages of the story. Have students use features such as the story's title and illustrations to predict what this story might have to do with communities across time.

Encourage students to look for interesting words or ideas they might come across. They may note that the story starts in what looks like modern times and then shifts to the past.

Use ***Transparency*** 5 to model browsing for students. For example, point out that the title "The House on Maple Street" might be a Clue to where the story takes place. Under Problems, write *fierce* as an unfamiliar word. Write *What happens at the house on Maple Street?* under Wonderings. Record students' observations on the transparency as they browse the story.

Set Purposes

Encourage students to set their own purposes for reading the story. Remind students to set purposes by picking up clues from the title, illustrations, and genre of the text they are going to read. If students are having trouble determining purpose, suggest that as they read, they learn about how people change the land over time.

How has my community changed over time?

Before reading the story, read the Big Idea question. Tell students to keep this question in mind when reading the story.

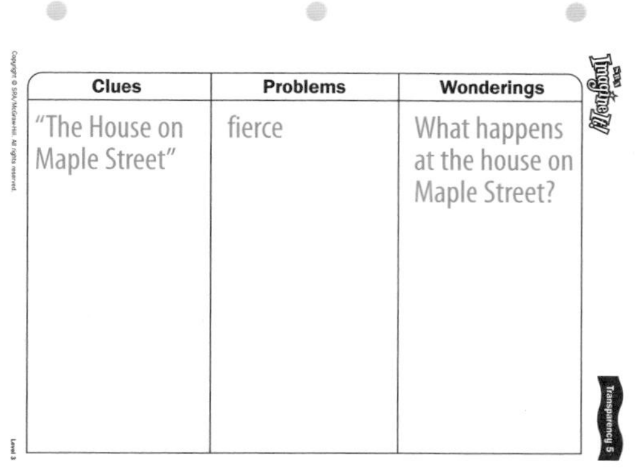

Clues	Problems	Wonderings
"The House on Maple Street"	fierce	What happens at the house on Maple Street?

Transparency 5

Give each student a copy of ***Home Connection*** page 51. Encourage students to discuss "The House on Maple Street" with their families and complete the activity provided. The same information is also available in Spanish on ***Home Connection*** page 52.

Differentiating Instruction — **English Learner**

IF . . . students have limited proficiency,
THEN . . . pair them with proficient English speakers and have the pair browse the story together.

Selection Vocabulary

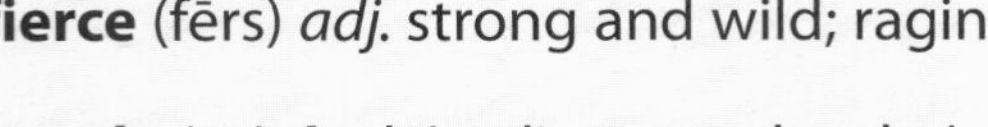

fierce (fērs) *adj.* strong and wild; raging (page 131)

sturdy (stûr´ • dē) *adj.* strong; hardy (page 131)

stump (stump) *n.* part of tree left over after cutting away at the trunk (page 134)

settlers (set´ • tlûrz) *n.* plural form of **settler:** a person who makes a new home in a new land or country (page 135)

burrows (bûr´ • rowz) *n.* plural form of **burrow:** a hole in the ground where some animals live (page 135)

trickle (trik´ • əl) *n.* a small amount (page 140)

crumbling (krum´ • bəl • ing) *v.* a form of the verb **crumble:** to fall to pieces (page 141)

treasures (trezh´ • ûrz) *n.* plural form of **treasure:** something special; a keepsake (page 143)

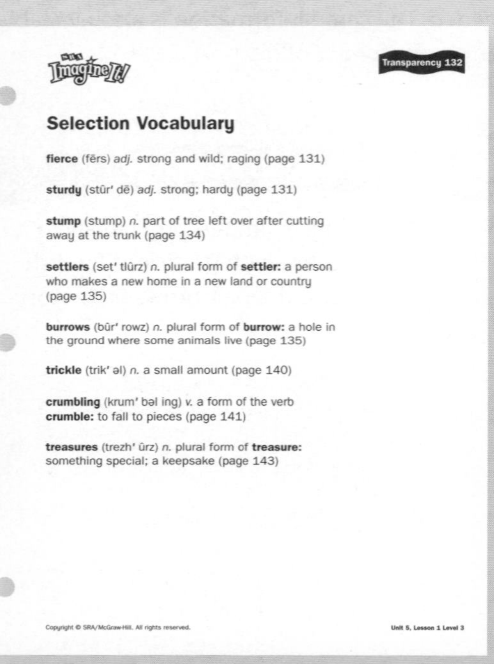

Imagine It! Transparency 132

Selection Vocabulary

fierce (fērs) *adj.* strong and wild; raging (page 131)

sturdy (stûr' dē) *adj.* strong; hardy (page 131)

stump (stump) *n.* part of tree left over after cutting away at the trunk (page 134)

settlers (set' tlûrz) *n.* plural form of **settler:** a person who makes a new home in a new land or country (page 135)

burrows (bûr' rowz) *n.* plural form of **burrow:** a hole in the ground where some animals live (page 135)

trickle (trik' əl) *n.* a small amount (page 140)

crumbling (krum' bəl ing) *v.* a form of the verb **crumble:** to fall to pieces (page 141)

treasures (trezh' ûrz) *n.* plural form of **treasure:** something special; a keepsake (page 143)

 Unit 5, Lesson 1 Level 3

Transparency 132

Writer's Notebook

Have students copy the vocabulary words and definitions into the vocabulary section of their Writer's Notebooks.

Building Vocabulary

ROUTINE 11

Using Routine 11, the selection vocabulary process, have students read aloud the Vocabulary Warm-Up on ***Student Reader,*** Book 2 pages 126–127.

As students read, have them stop to blend any difficult or unfamiliar words. Provide students with the pronunciation of words that are not decodable or that they cannot read automatically or fluently.

Guided Vocabulary Practice

Ask students to identify the highlighted vocabulary words they figured out using the vocabulary strategy Apposition. **Possible Answer** *sturdy* Have students explain how they figured out the meaning of the other vocabulary words as they read the Vocabulary Warm-Up.

Display ***Transparency*** 132, and have students read the words and definitions. Return to the Vocabulary Warm-Up, and read the sentences containing the vocabulary words with students. Then, if necessary, provide a brief in-context explanation of the words.

Read the article to find the meanings of these words, which are also in "The House on Maple Street":

- settlers
- treasures
- sturdy
- fierce
- trickle
- stump
- crumbling
- burrows

Vocabulary Strategy

Apposition is when a word or group of words define another word in the same sentence. Use apposition to find the meaning of *sturdy*.

Vocabulary Warm-Up

The settling of America began in the East and moved west. Landscapes and climates differed across the country. However, settlers in all regions faced some of the same challenges.

Settlers had to choose what to take with them to a new place. Furniture and other large treasures were left behind. The settlers took no more than they needed.

In their new land, settlers had to build a sturdy, or solid, house. They needed homes that could stand up to fierce winds and harsh weather. Choosing the right home site was key. Settlers looked and listened for the trickle of a stream. A close water supply was a big plus.

126

Many settlers built log cabins. Some early cabins were quite rough, unlike modern log cabins. Shelter was necessary, not style.

Trees had been cut to clear the land. To use it as a field for crops, each tree stump had to be dug from the ground. Farmers hacked at roots until they could pull free the pieces that were crumbling.

Settlers had to learn about wildlife, and whether animals were friends or foes. They learned to look for tracks and animal homes. Where there were burrows, there might be a source of food.

It took a strong will for settlers to succeed, but many of them did. They started with a few simple goods. With these, they built new lives in a new land.

GAME

Making Sentences

Work with a partner to create sentences using the vocabulary words. Choose two words from the list, and challenge your partner to make up a sentence using the two words. Then switch roles. Continue until all of the vocabulary words have been used.

Concept Vocabulary

The concept word for this lesson is ***transform.*** To **transform** means "to change the form or condition of something." Both human and natural activities can transform an environment. What are some ways that people transform land? What are some ways that land is transformed by natural events?

127

Use the vocabulary words on ***Transparency*** 132 to create fill-in-the-blank sentences. Have students fill in the appropriate vocabulary words. For example, "The __________ traveled hundreds of miles to find new homes for their families." *settlers*

Discuss the concept vocabulary word *transform* with students. Ask students how they think the word *transform* relates to the theme Communities across Time. As students read the selections in this unit, encourage them to think about other words that relate to the theme. Students can record these words in the vocabulary section of their Writer's Notebooks.

GAME

Have students play the Making Sentences Game during Small-Group Time.

Differentiating Instruction English Learner

IF . . . students have limited vocabulary,
THEN . . . explain that a *pioneer* is a person who is the first to explore or settle a new area.

Concept/Question Board

As students read "The House on Maple Street" encourage them to post questions, answers, comments, or other items related to Communities across Time on the **Concept/Question Board.**

Monitor Progress

Formal Assessment

Comprehension Observation Log Observe individual students as they read, and use the Comprehension Observation Log, located in ***Lesson Assessment Book 2,*** to record anecdotal information about each student's strengths and weaknesses.

Reading the Selection

Genre Realistic Fiction

Have students identify the genre of "The House on Maple Street." *realistic fiction* If necessary, remind students of the following elements of realistic fiction:

- The characters behave as people do in real life.
- The setting of the story is a real place or could be a real place.
- The events in the story could happen in real life.

Silent Reading

This realistic fiction story lends itself to silent reading because it is short and will cause few problems for students. You might want to stop periodically or wait until students have finished the story to discuss the reading strategies. Have students practice reading on their own for at least 10 minutes at a time. Preview the strategies below with students, and have them use the strategies to understand the story. For example, have them visualize the scenery in the text whenever they can, or slow down their reading when they reach confusing words or ideas. As they become better readers, students will be able to read silently with increasing ease over longer periods of time.

Comprehension Strategies

Prompt the use of the following comprehension strategies during the first reading of "The House on Maple Street":

- Visualizing
- Adjusting Reading Speed

Comprehension Strategies Rubrics

Use the Informal Comprehension Strategies Rubrics to determine whether a student is using any of the strategies listed below. Note the strategies a student is using, instead of the degree to which a student might be using any particular strategy. In addition, encourage the student to tell of any strategies other than the ones being taught that he or she is using.

Visualizing

- ✦ The student recognizes appropriate places in the text to stop and visualize.
- ✦ The student visualizes literal ideas or scenes described by the author.
- ✦ The student makes inferences while visualizing to show understanding of characters' feelings, mood, and setting. The visualizations go beyond the author's literal words.
- ✦ The student uses visualizing differently depending on the type of text (for example, characters, setting, and actions in narratives or a process description in nonfiction).

Adjusting Reading Speed

- ✦ The student knows the text is not making sense and stops to reread.
- ✦ The student identifies the specific part of the text that is not making sense and rereads only that part.
- ✦ The student changes reading speed in reaction to the demands of the text.
- ✦ The student adjusts reading rate to skim or scan for specific information.

Monitor Progress to Differentiate Instruction

Formal Assessment

Comprehension Skill Note students' understanding of the comprehension skill Author's Purpose as they read.

APPROACHING LEVEL

IF . . .	THEN . . .
IF . . . students are having difficulty understanding author's purpose as they read,	**THEN . . .** work with them independently, giving examples of different purposes and pointing them out in different texts.

ON LEVEL

IF . . .	THEN . . .
IF . . . students are gaining an understanding of author's purpose as they read,	**THEN . . .** have them read three separate articles on the same subject, identifying the purpose in each.

ABOVE LEVEL

IF . . .	THEN . . .
IF . . . students are demonstrating an understanding of author's purpose as they read,	**THEN . . .** have them write three short paragraphs on similar subjects, choosing a different purpose for writing in each paragraph.

Technology

eSTUDENT READER Students can access ***SRA Imagine It! Student Reader*** electronically by using the ***eStudent Reader*** online or on CD-ROM.

Comprehension Skills

Reread "The House on Maple Street" using the following comprehension skills:

- Classify and Categorize
- Fact and Opinion
- Author's Purpose

Research in Action

Students who do not seem to be using the reading strategies on their own should be given some prompting to think about, choose, and use strategies as they read. They should listen as classmates who use strategies read the text aloud and discuss strategies during the lesson. Students will probably notice that reading strategies, once learned, come naturally and enhance the meaning and enjoyment of a selection. *(Jan Hirshberg)*

Reading with a Writer's Eye

When rereading "The House on Maple Street" explain the following literary elements:

- Plot
- Setting

Focus Questions

Have students read aloud the Focus Questions on page 129 of the ***Student Reader,*** Book 2. Encourage students to think about the Focus Questions as they read "The House on Maple Street."

Reading Recommendation

Silent Reading

Use Routine 14, the reading the selection routine, as you read the story. While reading, model strategies and stop to ask and answer questions. Point out how the pictures reflect the story. Share the images that pop up in your mind as you read and how points in the reading relate to ideas you already know. Reread the text by applying comprehension skills. After reading, be sure to discuss the story using the handing-off procedure, and have students discuss new information they have learned.

The simple language and style of this story make it ideal for silent reading.

Genre

Realistic Fiction involves stories about people and events that are true to life and that could really happen.

Comprehension Skill

Author's Purpose
The author's purpose can be to inform, to explain, to entertain, or to persuade. As you read, think about why the author wrote this story.

The House on Maple Street

by Bonnie Pryor
illustrated by Beth Peck

Focus Questions

What do you think your neighborhood looked like several hundred years ago? How has the town or city you live in changed over time?

128 129

Students will read the story twice over a three-day period.

Day 2 **SILENT READ** Have students read the first half of the story. Tell students to use the comprehension strategies.

Day 3 **SILENT READ** Have students finish reading the story. Remind students to use the comprehension strategies.

Day 4 **SILENT READ** Have students reread the story silently or orally. Have students focus on comprehension skills and Reading with a Writer's Eye.

Technology

Have students listen to "The House on Maple Street" on the ***Listening Library CD.*** After students have listened, have them discuss what other things, such as poetry, songs, or nonfiction, they prefer to listen to on the radio or on CDs.

Reading and Responding

This is 107 Maple Street. Chrissy and Jenny live here with their mother and father, a dog named Maggie, and a fat cat named Sally.

Three hundred years ago there was no house here or even a street. There was only a forest and a bubbling spring where the animals came to drink. 1

130

One day a fierce storm roared across the forest. The sky rolled with thunder, and lighting crashed into a tree. A deer sniffed the air in alarm. Soon the woods were ablaze. 2

The next spring a few sturdy flowers poked through the ashes, and by the year after that the land was covered with grass. Some wildflowers grew at the edge of the stream where the deer had returned to drink.

131

1st READ

Comprehension Strategies

This story is broken into two parts. On the first day, read pages 130–137. On the second day, read pages 138–143.

1 **Visualizing** Teacher Prompt: *Remember to visualize what you are reading to help it seem more real. Would anyone like to share their visualizations with the class?* **Possible Student Response** *I can picture both scenes in my head: the house on Maple Street with the family and the forest with the bubbling spring and all of the animals who wander over the land.*

2 **Visualizing** Teacher Prompt: *This is another good section to visualize. Who wants to share what they can see in this section?* **Possible Student Response** *I can see the deer sniffing the air. He is probably frightened by what he smells. I can see the fire. And then, after time, the flowers poke back up through the ashes. The woods become lively again.*

Teacher Tip

WORKSHOP During Workshop have students find multisyllabic words in the story and list them under columns for two- or three-syllable words. Have them underline the vowel spellings.

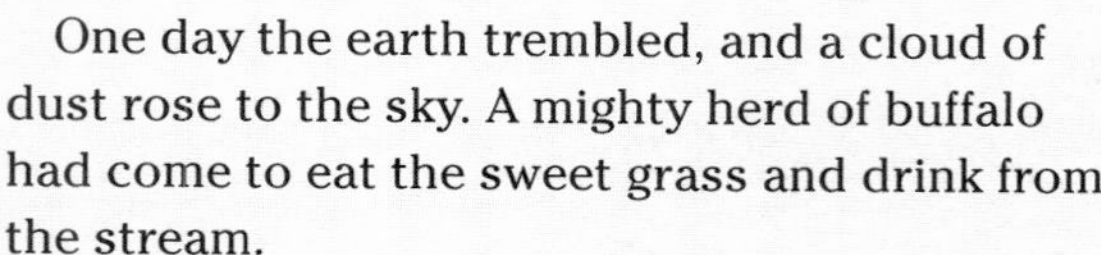

One day the earth trembled, and a cloud of dust rose to the sky. A mighty herd of buffalo had come to eat the sweet grass and drink from the stream. ❸

People came, following the buffalo herd. They set up their tepees near the stream, and because they liked it so much, they stayed for the whole summer.

One boy longed to be a great hunter like his father, but for now he could only pretend with his friends. In their games, one boy was chosen to be the buffalo.

132

His father taught the boy how to make an arrowhead and smooth it just so, the way his father had taught him. But the boy was young, and the day was hot.

He ran off to play with his friends and left the arrowhead on a rock. When he came back later to get it, he could not find it. ❹

133

❸ **Adjusting Reading Speed** Teacher Prompt: *Who can explain how adjusting our reading speed can help us understand this paragraph?* **Possible Student Response** *When I first read this paragraph, I didn't understand what was happening. The first sentence says that the "earth trembled." I thought there was going to be another storm. I slowed down my reading speed and reread the first paragraph. Now I understand that the trembling was caused by a herd of buffalo stamping across the land.*

❹ **Visualizing** Teacher Prompt: *Who would like to share their visualizations?* **Possible Student Response** *I can picture the boy coming back to the rock and looking all around for his arrowhead. He was probably surprised that it had disappeared.*

Comprehension Check

How did a natural event affect the land? **Possible Answer** *A storm came through and started a fire, but some flowers survived and the grass and wildflowers came back.*

Word Structure

In this lesson, students will review the suffixes ***-ful*** and inflectional endings ***-ed*** and ***-ing.***

Inflectional ending *-ed:* trembled, liked, stayed, longed

Reading and Responding

The buffalo moved on, searching for new grass, and the people packed up their tepees and followed.

For a long time the land was quiet. Some rabbits made their home in the stump of a burned tree, and a fox made a den in some rocks.

134

One day there was a new sound. The fox looked up. A wagon train passed by, heading for California. The settlers stopped beside the stream for a night. But they dreamed of gold and places far away and were gone the next morning. 5

Other wagons came, following the tracks of the first. The fox family moved into the woods, but the rabbits stayed snug in their burrows until the people had gone.

135

Word Structure

Inflectional ending *-ed:* packed, burned, stopped, dreamed

Inflectional ending *-ing:* searching, heading

Teacher Tip

COMPREHENSION STRATEGIES If students have difficulty identifying or modeling a strategy, review the steps in the strategy process with them.

5 Adjusting Reading Speed Teacher Prompt: *It looks as if something new is about to happen. Who can tell us what they learned by adjusting their reading speed?* **Possible Student Response** *The people following the buffalo seemed to like the spot where they lived, but it says that the people in the wagons stayed for only a night and were gone the next morning. I'm going to slow down and reread this paragraph to see if I can figure out why the people in the wagons did not want to stay. Oh, I see. It says that they were heading for California and that they dreamed of gold. I guess because there wasn't any gold at this place, they wanted to keep moving.*

Comprehension Check

Why did the man and the woman think this spot would make a good home? **Possible Answer** *This spot of land had a stream, trees, flowers, and grass. It probably seemed like a place where things lived and thrived.*

Soon after, a man and a woman camped along the stream. They were heading west, but the woman would soon have a child. They looked around them and knew it was a good place to stay. The man cut down trees and made a house.

He pulled up the tree stumps left from the fire and planted his crops. The child was a girl, and they named her Ruby and called her their little jewel.

136

Ruby had a set of china dishes that she played with every day. One day when she was making a mudpie on the banks of the stream, she found an arrowhead buried deep in the ground. She put it in a cup to show her father when he came in from the fields.

Ruby's mother called her to watch the new baby. While she was gone, a rabbit sniffed at the 6 cup and knocked it off the rock. It fell into the tunnel to his burrow, and the rabbit moved away to a new home under the roots of a tree.

137

6 **Visualizing** Teacher Prompt: *Here is another good place to visualize what is happening in the story. Who would like to share their visualizations with the class?*
Possible Student Response *I can see the rabbit sniffing at the cup, probably wondering what it was and where it came from. And then the cup tumbles to the ground and into the tunnel. Ruby is going to be surprised when she gets back, just as the boy with the arrowhead was.*

Teacher Tip

COMPREHENSION Ask students the following questions to make sure they understand the story:

- *Can you summarize what you have read?*
- *Does what you are reading make sense?*

Vocabulary Tip

Point out the word *settlers* on page 135. Ask students how knowing that *settle* means "to come to rest" and that the suffix -*er* means "one who" helps them figure out that *settlers* means "one who comes to rest." Point out the word *burrows* on page 135. Ask students how reading that the burrow belonged to the rabbit, and then he found a new home, helps them remember the meaning of the word *burrows*.

STOP You have read the first half of the story. Continue the story tomorrow on page T60.

Language Arts

OBJECTIVES

Students will

- draft persuasive paragraphs.
- learn to spell words with prefixes *re-*, *un-*, *mis-*, and *pre-*.
- learn verb tenses.

MATERIALS

- ***Transparency*** 121
- ***Skills Practice 2,*** pp. 95 and 99–100
- ***Language Arts Handbook,*** pp. 324–325

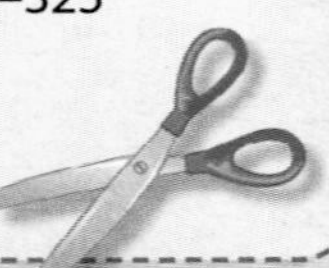

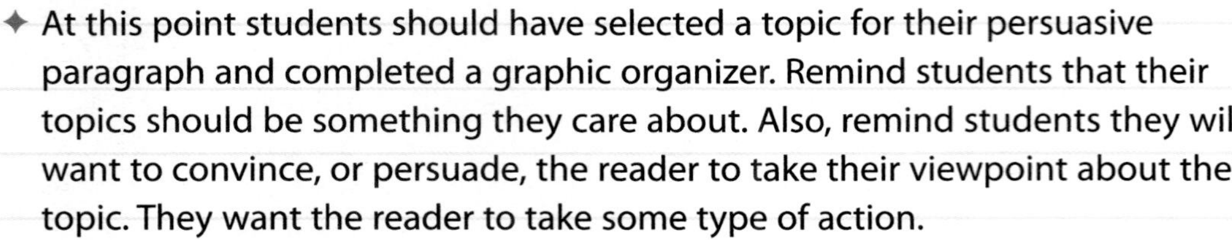

Writing Persuasive Paragraph

Drafting

Teach

- At this point students should have selected a topic for their persuasive paragraph and completed a graphic organizer. Remind students that their topics should be something they care about. Also, remind students they will want to convince, or persuade, the reader to take their viewpoint about the topic. They want the reader to take some type of action.
- Tell students they will write a draft of their persuasive paragraphs. Review the parts of a paragraph, and remind students to concentrate only on putting ideas on paper at this stage.
- Tell students that when drafting their persuasive paragraphs, they should write using the correct verb tense and connect their ideas with valid and appropriate reasons. They should write a conclusion that summarizes all of their reasons.
- Explain to students that the completed web will provide a structure for their written drafts, showing them what to include in their paragraphs. Tell students that as they draft, they should concentrate on making their reasons clear so readers understand what the writer wants them to do and why. They can revise and edit/proofread later.

Guided Practice

- Review the three parts of the persuasive paragraph using ***Transparency*** 121. Explain to students that they should include all three parts in their drafts.
- Using the graphic organizer you created, model creating a draft of your persuasive paragraph. Have students help you draft sentences. Highlight the reasons and the particular words you used to persuade as you write. Allow students to help you write the draft. If ideas or reasons are not in a logical order, you can model organizing information during revision.

Research in Action

Writing is a recursive process as authors move back and forth through writing activities—from planning to drafting to revising and back—to create their final pieces. It is a process of thinking, experimenting, and evaluating.
(Steve Graham and Karen Harris)

Teacher Tip

VERB TENSE Remind students to use the appropriate verb tenses in their paragraphs.

Writing, continued

Apply

Composing—Drafting Have students write a draft of their persuasive paragraphs. Remind students to use the reasons and examples in their graphic organizers on page 95 in ***Skills Practice 2.***

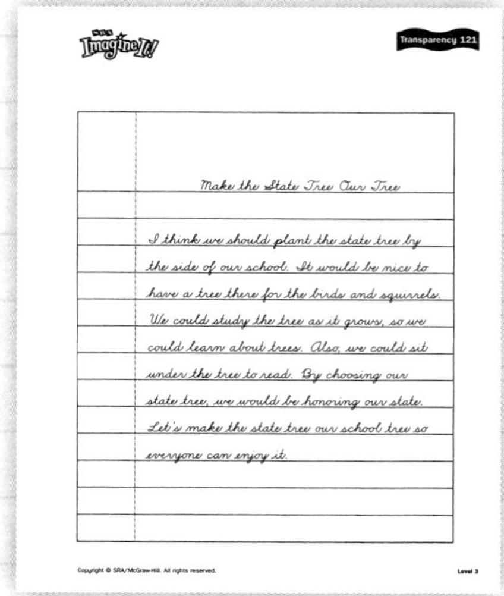

Imagine It! Transparency 121

Make the State Tree Our Tree

I think we should plant the state tree by the side of our school. It would be nice to have a tree there for the birds and squirrels. We could study the tree as it grows, so we could learn about trees. Also, we could sit under the tree to read. By choosing our state tree, we would be honoring our state. Let's make the state tree our school tree so everyone can enjoy it.

 Level 3

Transparency 121

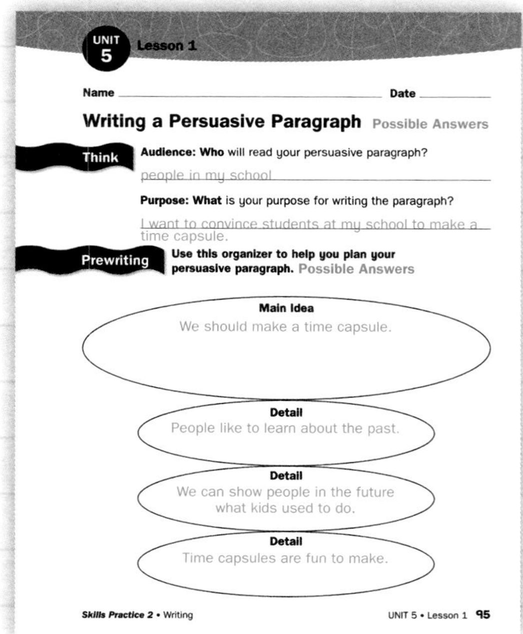

UNIT 5 Lesson 1

Name ______ Date ______

Writing a Persuasive Paragraph Possible Answers

Think

Audience: Who will read your persuasive paragraph?

people in my school

Purpose: What is your purpose for writing the paragraph?

I want to convince students at my school to make a time capsule.

Prewriting

Use this organizer to help you plan your persuasive paragraph. Possible Answers

Main Idea
We should make a time capsule.

Detail
People like to learn about the past.

Detail
We can show people in the future what kids used to do.

Detail
Time capsules are fun to make.

Skills Practice 2 • Writing UNIT 5 • Lesson 1 95

Skills Practice 2, p. 95

Spelling

Prefixes *re-, un-, pre-, mis-*

Teach

Use a word sort to teach words with the prefixes *re-, un-, pre-,* and *mis-*.

Guided Practice

Write the following headings on the board: *re-, un-, pre-,* and *mis-*. Then write the following word list: *mismatch, unclear, reread, refund, unzip, misprint, unload, mislead, preheat, restart, prefix, unfair, recount, misplace,* and *review.* Have volunteers write the words under the correct heading. After all the spelling words have been used, ask for students to come to the board and underline the part of each word that reflects the category in which it was placed.

Word Sort Answers

Words with the Prefix *re-: reread, refund, restart, recount*

Words with the Prefix *un-: unclear, unzip, unload, unfair*

Words with the Prefix *pre-: preheat, prefix, preview*

Words with the Prefix *mis-: mismatch, misprint, mislead, misplace*

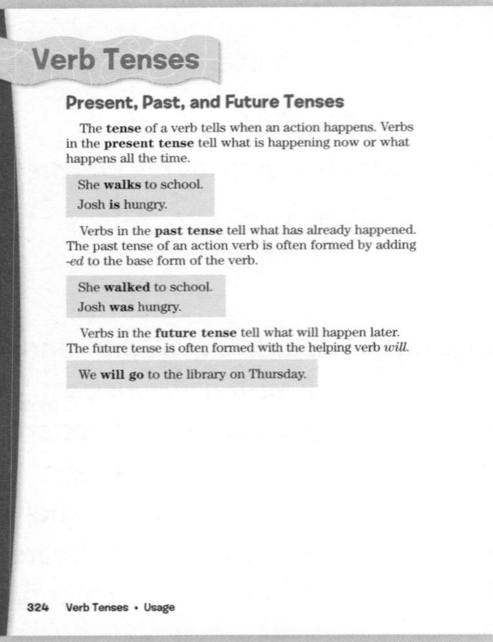

Verb Tenses

Present, Past, and Future Tenses

The **tense** of a verb tells when an action happens. Verbs in the **present tense** tell what is happening now or what happens all the time.

She **walks** to school.
Josh **is** hungry.

Verbs in the **past tense** tell what has already happened. The past tense of an action verb is often formed by adding *-ed* to the base form of the verb.

She **walked** to school.
Josh **was** hungry.

Verbs in the **future tense** tell what will happen later. The future tense is often formed with the helping verb *will.*

We **will go** to the library on Thursday.

324 Verb Tenses • Usage

Language Arts Handbook, p. 324

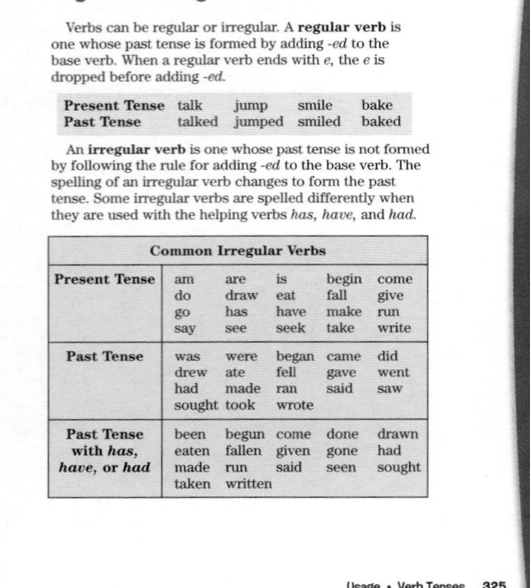

Regular and Irregular Verbs

Verbs can be regular or irregular. A **regular verb** is one whose past tense is formed by adding *-ed* to the base verb. When a regular verb ends with *e*, the *e* is dropped before adding *-ed.*

Present Tense	talk	jump	smile	bake
Past Tense	talked	jumped	smiled	baked

An **irregular verb** is one whose past tense is not formed by following the rule for adding *-ed* to the base verb. The spelling of an irregular verb changes to form the past tense. Some irregular verbs are spelled differently when they are used with the helping verbs *has, have,* and *had.*

Common Irregular Verbs					
Present Tense	am	are	is	begin	come
	do	draw	eat	fall	give
	go	has	have	make	run
	say	see	seek	take	write
Past Tense	was	were	began	came	did
	drew	ate	fell	gave	went
	had	made	ran	said	saw
	sought	took	wrote		
Past Tense with *has, have,* or *had*	been	begun	come	done	drawn
	eaten	fallen	given	gone	had
	made	run	said	seen	sought
	taken	written			

Usage • Verb Tenses 325

Language Arts Handbook, p. 325

Differentiating Instruction

English Learner

IF . . . students would benefit from additional practice with the past tense of verbs, **THEN . . .** ask them to go through and find all the past tense verbs used in the first half of the story.

Grammar, Usage, and Mechanics 

Verb Tenses

Teach

- Select a topic, and ask students to generate a sentence about that topic. Write the sentence on the board. Ask students to identify the verb or action of the sentence. Underline the verb. Explain that the tense of the verb tells when an action happens. Ask students when the action of the sentence on the board happens.
- Explain these rules about verb tenses.
  - The present tense tells what is happening now or what happens all the time.
  - The past tense tells what has already happened. The past tense of a verb is often formed by adding *-ed* to the base word. Some verbs are irregular and their past tense spellings must be memorized.
  - The future tense tells what will happen later. The future tense is often formed with the helping verb *will.*
- Use ***Language Arts Handbook*** pages 324–325 for rules and examples of verbs and verb tenses.

Guided Practice

- Write *jog, jogged,* and *will jog* on the board. Have students generate a sentence for each of the words. Write the sentences on the board, and then have students identify past, present, or future tense.
- Tell students that other words in the sentence can sometimes give an indication of the tense of the verbs. Discuss words such as *yesterday, today, tomorrow, now,* and *later* with students.
- Have students list three or four verbs and then generate sentences for present, past, and future tense for each verb.
- Have students turn to ***Skills Practice 2*** page 99. Have a student read the directions aloud. Help students begin the Practice section.

Apply

Have students complete ***Skills Practice 2*** pages 99–100 to practice using correct verb tenses.

Formal Assessment

to Differentiate Instruction

Verb Tense Note whether students use correct verb tenses.

APPROACHING LEVEL

IF . . . students need to practice verb tenses,	**THEN . . .** have them complete ***Reteach*** page 129 during Workshop.
IF . . . students need more practice with verbs tenses,	**THEN . . .** refer to Unit 5 Lesson 1 of the ***Intervention Guide*** for intervention activities.

ON LEVEL

IF . . . students have an understanding of verb tenses,	**THEN . . .** have them work on ***Workshop Kit*** activities during Workshop.

ABOVE LEVEL

IF . . . students need a challenge,	**THEN . . .** have them complete ***Challenge Activities*** page 117 during Workshop.

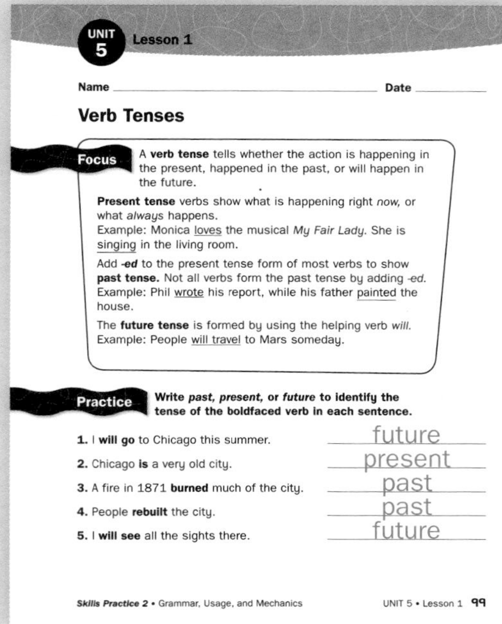

UNIT 5 Lesson 1

Name ______________________ Date __________

Verb Tenses

Focus A **verb tense** tells whether the action is happening in the present, happened in the past, or will happen in the future.

Present tense verbs show what is happening right *now,* or what *always* happens.
Example: Monica loves the musical *My Fair Lady.* She is singing in the living room.

Add ***-ed*** to the present tense form of most verbs to show **past tense.** Not all verbs form the past tense by adding *-ed.*
Example: Phil wrote his report, while his father painted the house.

The **future tense** is formed by using the helping verb *will.*
Example: People will travel to Mars someday.

Practice **Write *past, present,* or *future* to identify the tense of the boldfaced verb in each sentence.**

1. I **will go** to Chicago this summer. future
2. Chicago **is** a very old city. present
3. A fire in 1871 **burned** much of the city. past
4. People **rebuilt** the city. past
5. I **will see** all the sights there. future

Skills Practice 2 • Grammar, Usage, and Mechanics UNIT 5 • Lesson 1 99

Skills Practice 2, p. 99

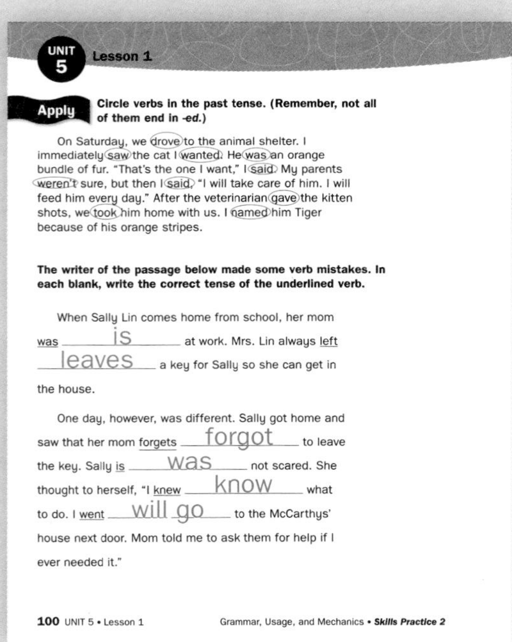

UNIT 5 Lesson 1

Apply **Circle verbs in the past tense. (Remember, not all of them end in *-ed.*)**

On Saturday, we drove to the animal shelter. I immediately saw the cat I wanted. He was an orange bundle of fur. "That's the one I want," I said. My parents weren't sure, but then I said, "I will take care of him. I will feed him every day." After the veterinarian gave the kitten shots, we took him home with us. I named him Tiger because of his orange stripes.

The writer of the passage below made some verb mistakes. In each blank, write the correct tense of the underlined verb.

When Sally Lin comes home from school, her mom was ___is___ at work. Mrs. Lin always left ___leaves___ a key for Sally so she can get in the house.

One day, however, was different. Sally got home and saw that her mom forgets ___forgot___ to leave the key. Sally is ___was___ not scared. She thought to herself, "I knew ___know___ what to do. I went ___will go___ to the McCarthys' house next door. Mom told me to ask them for help if I ever needed it."

100 UNIT 5 • Lesson 1 Grammar, Usage, and Mechanics • *Skills Practice 2*

Skills Practice 2, p. 100

Preparing to Read

OBJECTIVES

Students will

- identify and know the meanings of the prefixes *pre-* and *mis-*.
- build fluency.

MATERIALS

- ***Transparency*** 133
- Routine 10
- ***Skills Practice 2,*** pp. 87–88

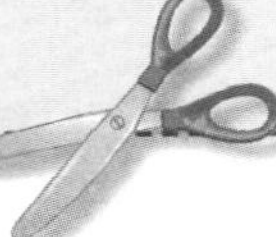

Daily Oral Practice

Daily News

I keep marbles in a big glass jar on my dresser. I think I'll put some in a pouch with a drawstring and bury them in my backyard. Maybe someday someone will uncover the pouch, untie the drawstring, and find my marbles. It is fun to think about what his or her reaction would be.

- Write the daily news on the board or on chart paper. Then have the boys read the daily news in unison to practice fluency.
- As a review of yesterday's word structure lesson, ask a volunteer to identify any words in the message with the prefix *un-*. *uncover, untie*

Differentiating Instruction — English Learner

IF... students are native speakers of Spanish, **THEN...** they may pronounce *i* in the prefix *mis-* with /ē/, like the vowel sound in *feet.* Provide students with extra practice associating *i* with the short *i* sound in English words such as *tip, fin, bin, hit,* and *win.*

Word Structure

ROUTINE 10

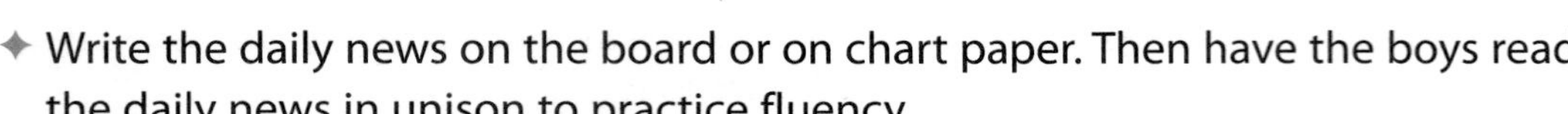

The Prefixes *pre-* and *mis-*

- Write these word lines on the board or use ***Transparency*** 133. The word in boldface is in "The House on Maple Street."

Line 1	pay	prepay	heat	preheat
Line 2	school	preschool	view	preview
Line 3	count	miscount	behave	misbehave
Line 4	place	misplace	spell	misspell

Teacher Tip

SYLLABICATION To help students blend words and build fluency, demonstrate syllabication using the decodable, multisyllabic words in the word lines.

pre • pay	pre • heat
pre • school	pre • view
mis • count	be • have
mis • be • have	mis • place
mis • spell	

Lines 1–2 The Prefix *pre-*

Use Routine 10 for words with prefixes and suffixes to teach today's prefixes. Remind students that prefixes are letters added to the beginning of a word that change the meaning of the word. Explain that the prefix *pre-* means "before." For example, adding the prefix *pre-* to the verb *write* makes the new verb *prewrite*. The verb or action *prewrite* is something you do before you write.

Point out that adding the syllable *pre-* to a word adds a syllable to it. As you point to each word in Lines 1–2, have students read it aloud in unison. Then have students identify the base words in Lines 1–2. *pay, heat, school, view* Have students define each word that has the prefix *pre-*. Have students use a dictionary if necessary.

Lines 3–4 The Prefix *mis-*

Explain that the prefix *mis-* can be added to verbs and means "wrong" or "bad." For example, adding the prefix *mis-* to the verb *lead* makes the new verb *mislead*. The verb *mislead* means "to lead someone badly or in the wrong direction."

- Point out that adding the prefix *mis-* to a word adds a syllable to it. As you point to each word in Lines 3–4, have students read it aloud. Have students identify the base verbs in Lines 3–4. *count, behave, place, spell* Then have students define each word that has the prefix *mis-*. Have students use a dictionary if necessary.
- Help students start the word structure activities on ***Skills Practice 2*** pages 87–88. Read the Focus box with them and help them with the first few questions. Then have students complete the pages on their own.

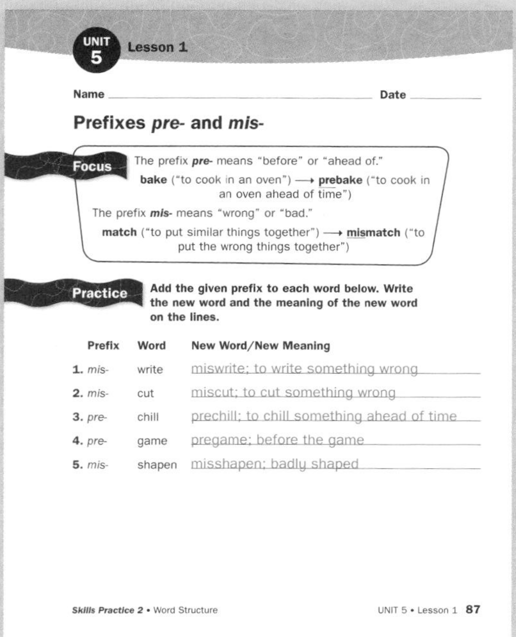
UNIT 5 Lesson 1

Name ____________ Date ______

Prefixes *pre-* and *mis-*

Focus The prefix *pre-* means "before" or "ahead of."
bake ("to cook in an oven") → **prebake** ("to cook in an oven ahead of time")
The prefix *mis-* means "wrong" or "bad."
match ("to put similar things together") → **mismatch** ("to put the wrong things together")

Practice Add the given prefix to each word below. Write the new word and the meaning of the new word on the lines.

	Prefix	Word	New Word/New Meaning
1.	mis-	write	miswrite; to write something wrong
2.	mis-	cut	miscut; to cut something wrong
3.	pre-	chill	prechill; to chill something ahead of time
4.	pre-	game	pregame; before the game
5.	mis-	shapen	misshapen; badly shaped

Skills Practice 2 • Word Structure UNIT 5 • Lesson 1 87

UNIT 5 Lesson 1

Apply Write sentences using two of the words you made on the previous page. Possible Answers

6. We had a pregame party.
7. I miscut the shape of my picture.

Circle the word that correctly completes each sentence below.

8. Abby had one red and one blue sock on because she had ______ her socks.
(a.) mismatched b. premade

9. The oven was already hot because it was ______.
a. prefrozen (b.) preheated

10. I rinse and ______ the dishes before putting them in the dishwasher.
a. prewrap (b.) prewash

11. Sonja called the wrong phone number because she ______.
(a.) misdialed b. pretaped

12. The boys got lost because they ______ their walk.
a. preplanned (b.) misplanned

88 UNIT 5 • Lesson 1 Word Structure • *Skills Practice 2*

Skills Practice 2, pp. 87–88

Monitor Progress to Differentiate Instruction

Formal Assessment 

Word Structure During the word structure activity, note how well students understand the prefixes *pre-* and *mis-*.

Level	IF . . .	THEN . . .
APPROACHING LEVEL	IF . . . students need practice with the prefixes *pre-* and *mis-*,	THEN . . . work with them in small groups on the word structure activities on ***Reteach*** page 124 during Workshop.
	IF . . . students need extra practice with the prefixes *pre-* and *mis-*,	THEN . . . work with them in small groups on the word structure activities for Unit 5 Lesson 1 in the ***Intervention Guide*** during Workshop.
ON LEVEL	IF . . . students understand the prefixes *pre-* and *mis-*,	THEN . . . have them make lists of words to add to the word lines during Workshop.
ABOVE LEVEL	IF . . . students are ready for a challenge with the prefixes *pre-* and *mis-*,	THEN . . . have them complete the word structure activities on ***Challenge Activities*** page 113 during Workshop.

Ruby grew up and moved away, but her brother stayed on the farm. By now there were other people nearby, and he married a girl from another farm. They had six children, and he built a larger house so they would all fit.

Now the old wagon trail was used as a road, and the dust got into the house. When his wife complained, Ruby's brother planted a row of maple trees along the road to keep out the dust and shade the house. After the children were grown, he and his wife moved away, but one of their daughters stayed on the farm with her husband and children. 7

138

One day the children's great-aunt Ruby came for a visit. She was an old lady with snow-white hair. The children loved to hear her stories of long ago. She told them about the cup and arrowhead she had lost when she was a girl.

After she left, the children looked and looked. But they never found them, though they searched for days. 8

139

OBJECTIVES

Students will

- use the comprehension strategies Adjusting Reading Speed and Visualizing.
- discuss the story using the handing-off process.
- review vocabulary, genre, and fluency.

MATERIALS

- ***Student Reader,*** Book 2, pp. 138–145
- Routine A
- ***Skills Practice 2,*** pp. 89–90
- ***Transparencies*** 5, 132

Comprehension Strategies

7 Adjusting Reading Speed Teacher Prompt: *It seems as if a lot of time has passed here. What can we learn by slowing our reading speed down?* **Possible Student Response** *I'm going to slow down my reading and reread this section to make sure I know exactly what's going on. Ruby, the little girl who lost the arrowhead and the cup, has now grown up and moved away. Her brother stayed on the land and built a house and had a family, and then his children grew up. Many people have lived out their lives on this one piece of land.*

8 Visualizing Teacher Prompt: *Who would like to share any visualizations they have with the class?* **Possible Student Response** *Once again, children are searching for the arrowhead and the cup. I can see them looking all over the yard, day after day.*

The town had grown nearly to the edge of the farm, and another man up the road filled in the stream and changed its course. For a while there was a trickle of water in the spring when the snow melted, but weeds and dirt filled in the bed, until hardly anyone remembered a stream had ever been there.

New people lived on the farm. It was the schoolteacher and his family, and they sold much of the land to others. The road was paved with bricks, so there was no longer any dust, but the maple trees remained. The branches hung down over the road, making it shady and cool. People called it Maple Street. Automobiles drove on the road, along with carts and wagons, and there were many new houses.

140

The house was crumbling and old, and one day some men tore it down. For a while again, the land was bare. The rabbits lived comfortably, with only an occasional owl or fox to chase them. But one day a young couple came walking along and stopped to admire the trees.

"What a wonderful place for a home," said the young woman. So they hired carpenters and masons to build a cozy house of red bricks with white trim. 9

The young couple lived happily in the house for several years. The young man got a job in another town, and they had to move.

141

9 Visualizing Teacher Prompt: *These pages are very descriptive. Who would like to share their visualizations with the class?* **Possible Student Response** *I can visualize many of the scenes on these pages. I can see the little trickle of water running from the spring. I can see and almost feel the branches of the maple trees hanging over the road. I can see the old house that had been there for so long it crumbled. And then I can also see the brand new house with red bricks standing under the branches of the maple trees.*

Comprehension Check

Why did the man fill in the stream? **Possible Answer** *The town was growing farther out into the woods near the stream. He probably thought land would be more useful than the stream.* *Why did the people in the town name the road "Maple Street?"* **Possible Answer** *The branches of the maple trees hung down over the road, making the street shady and cool.*

Word Structure

Inflectional ending *-ed*: married, used, stayed, loved, looked

Differentiating Instruction **English Learner**

IF . . . students are not familiar with the expression *snow-white* on page 139,
THEN . . . explain that snow is considered to be pure white in color. When something is referred to as *snow-white*, it means that it is very white.

Reading and Responding

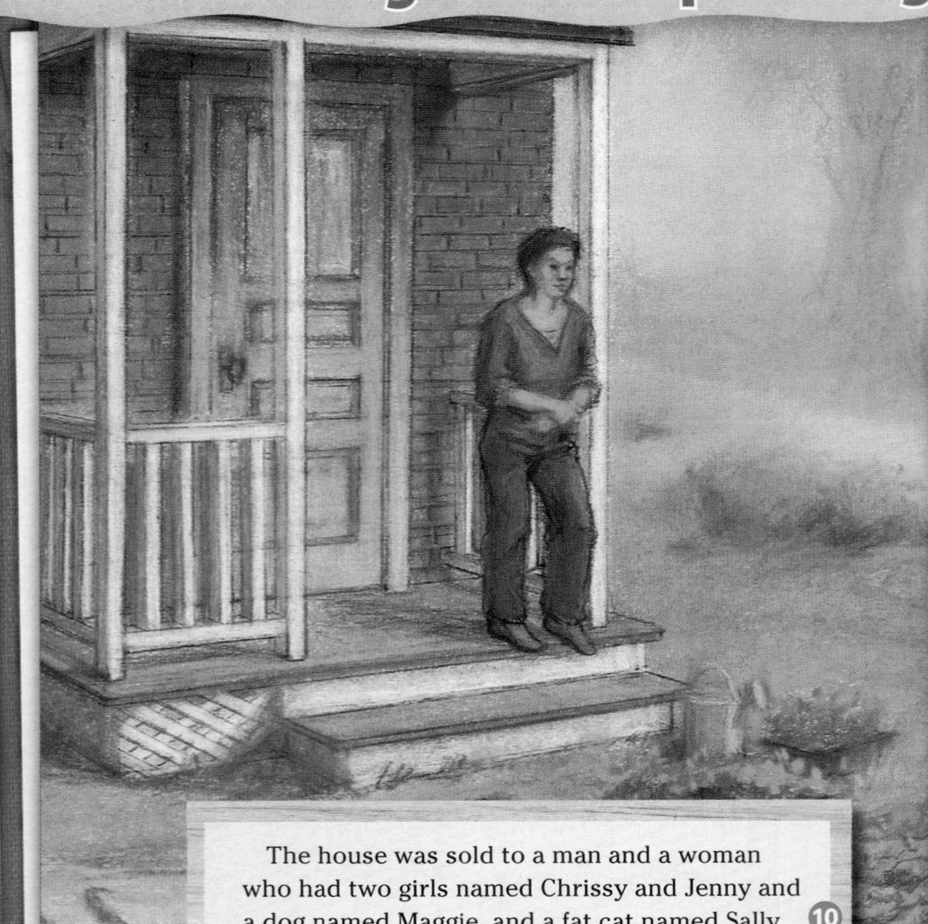

The house was sold to a man and a woman who had two girls named Chrissy and Jenny and a dog named Maggie, and a fat cat named Sally. 10

The girls helped their father dig up a spot of ground for a garden, but it was Maggie the dog who dug up something white in the soft spring earth.

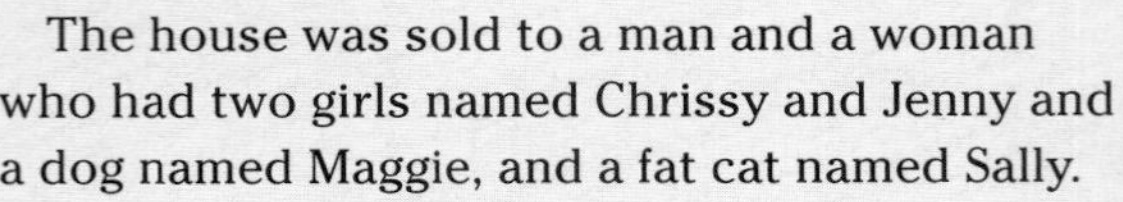

142

"Stop," cried Chrissy, and she picked up the tiny cup made of china. Inside was the arrowhead found and lost so long ago.

"Who lost these?" the girls wondered. Chrissy and Jenny put the cup and arrowhead on a shelf for others to see. Someday perhaps their children will play with the tiny treasures and wonder about them, too. But the cup and arrowhead will forever keep their secrets, and the children can only dream. 11

143

Word Structure

Suffix *-ful:* wonderful
Infectional ending *-ed:* named, helped, cried, picked, wondered

Teacher Tip

ADJUSTING READING SPEED Remind students to slow down and reread passages whenever they are confused or need clarification.

10 **Adjusting Reading Speed** *Teacher Prompt: Why do you think we should slow down as we read this page?* **Possible Student Response** *Once again, I'm going to slow down and reread this part so I can figure this out. That's right, these are the same names from the beginning of the story. We're back to where we started at the house on Maple Street.*

Comprehension Check

What do you think Maggie has unearthed? **Possible Answer** *the arrowhead and cup* *What do you think the house on Maple Street symbolizes?* **Possible Answer** *It symbolizes how the people changed the land as time passed. It represents all of the people who lived on that one piece of land.*

⑪ **Visualizing** *Teacher Prompt: What can we visualize on the last page of the story?* **Possible Student Response** *In all of the other scenes with the arrowhead and the cup I was visualizing the confused and disappointed looks on the faces of the children when they found their items missing. Now in this scene I can picture the faces of Chrissy and Jenny when they discover the arrowhead and the cup. They have looks of surprise and wonder.*

Vocabulary Tip

Point out the words *trickle* on page 140 and *crumbling* on page 141. Ask students how the words "water in the spring" helps them remember the meaning of the word *trickle*. Ask students how knowing that the house was old helps them remember the meaning of the word *crumbling*.

Clues	Problems	Wonderings
"The House on Maple Street"	fierce	What happens at the house on Maple Street?

Transparency 5

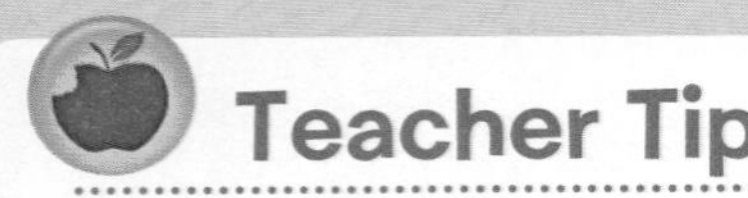

Teacher Tip

COMPREHENSION STRATEGIES Ask students about the comprehension strategies they used to understand the selection they read silently. If they used strategies besides the ones listed for the selection, have them give examples of how they employed the strategies.

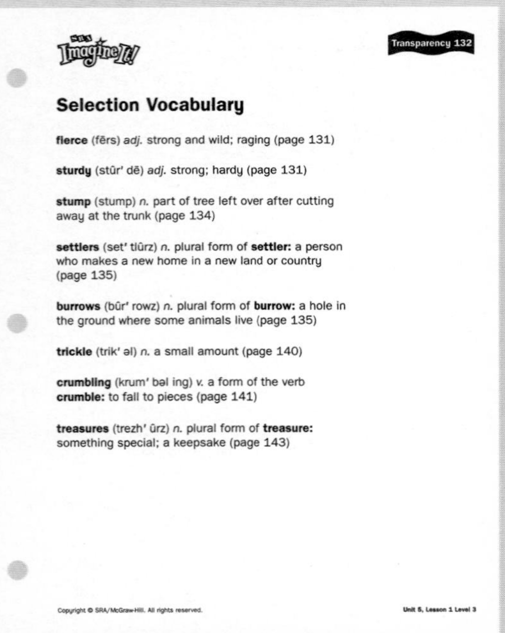

Transparency 132

Selection Vocabulary

fierce (fērs) *adj.* strong and wild; raging (page 131)

sturdy (stûr' dē) *adj.* strong; hardy (page 131)

stump (stump) *n.* part of tree left over after cutting away at the trunk (page 134)

settlers (set' tlûrz) *n.* plural form of **settler:** a person who makes a new home in a new land or country (page 135)

burrows (bûr' rowz) *n.* plural form of **burrow:** a hole in the ground where some animals live (page 135)

trickle (trik' əl) *n.* a small amount (page 140)

crumbling (krum' bəl ing) *v.* a form of the verb **crumble:** to fall to pieces (page 141)

treasures (trezh' ûrz) *n.* plural form of **treasure:** something special; a keepsake (page 143)

Transparency 132

Discussing the Selection

✦ It is important for students to see you as a contributing member of the group. Use Routine A, handing-off, to emphasize that you are part of the group. Actively participate in handing-off by raising your hand to be called on by the last speaker when you have a contribution to make. Point out unusual and interesting insights verbalized by students so these insights are recognized and discussed.

✦ Engage students in a discussion using handing-off to determine whether they have grasped the following ideas:

- Chrissy and Jenny found the arrowhead and the cup that belonged to people who lived on the same land years and years before.
- They will always be curious about the history and the secrets of the arrowhead and the cup.

✦ Ask students how the story demonstrates the following key concepts:

- As more people settled the land, the more the land changed.
- The arrowhead and the cup represent the people who lived on one piece of land through many years.

✦ Return to the Clues, Problems, and Wonderings chart on ***Transparency*** 5. Have students discuss which clues were useful, how they resolved their problems, and how they answered their questions. Also ask students if the predictions they made while browsing the story were confirmed or not confirmed.

✦ Have students return to the Focus Questions on ***Student Reader,*** Book 2 page 129. Select a student to read the questions aloud, and have students answer and discuss the questions. Have them return to the text as necessary.

Genre Review

Review the elements of realistic fiction with students on page T46. Then ask students how they know "The House on Maple Street" is realistic fiction.

How has my community changed over time?

After reading the story, read the Big Idea question. Discuss with students how the story helps answer this question.

Vocabulary Review

Review with students the selection vocabulary words and definitions they wrote in the vocabulary section of their Writer's Notebooks. Then refer students to ***Skills Practice 2,*** pages 89–90. Help students complete the first two questions. Then have students complete the rest on their own. Also, review the concept vocabulary word *transform*. Ask students if they can think of other words related to the theme Communities across Time. **Possible Answers** *change, land, civilizations, cultures, development, environment*

Fluency

- When modeling fluency, practice pace. Pace, or reading with appropriate speed, is essential to fluency. Tell students that reading with appropriate pace makes the reading sound natural. Unnatural, forced reading is difficult for readers and listeners to understand.
- Read aloud pages 130–131 of "The House on Maple Street." Model pace for students. For example, after reading *Chrissy and Jenny live here with their mother and father, a dog named Maggie, and a fat cat named Sally,* point out how, when read at an appropriate pace, the text sounds like the author is talking to the reader. Tell students that when reading, it is important to pay attention to end punctuation and commas. Have students follow along in ***Student Reader,*** Book 2 and tell them to raise their hands when you pause. Tell students that as they reread, they should practice pausing after commas.

Monitor Progress to Differentiate Instruction

Informal Assessment 

Selection Vocabulary Observe students' understanding of the vocabulary words and their definitions.

APPROACHING LEVEL

IF . . .	THEN . . .
IF . . . students need extra help with the selection vocabulary,	**THEN . . .** refer to ***Intervention Guide*** Unit 5 Lesson 1.
IF . . . students need extra help with the selection vocabulary,	**THEN . . .** use ***Reteach*** page 125.

ON LEVEL

IF . . .	THEN . . .
IF . . . students need practice using the selection vocabulary words,	**THEN . . .** have students write sentences using the selection vocabulary words.

ABOVE LEVEL

IF . . .	THEN . . .
IF . . . students understand the selection vocabulary,	**THEN . . .** use ***Challenge Activities*** page 114.

Teacher Tips

FLUENCY By this time in Grade 3, good readers should be reading approximately 137 words per minute with fluency and expression. The only way to gain this fluency is with practice. Have students reread the story to you and to each other during Workshop to help build fluency. As students read, you may notice that some need work in building fluency. During Workshop, have these students choose a section of the selection (a minimum of 160 words) to read aloud several times to build fluency.

WORD BANK Review the Word Bank with students. Encourage students to add words to the Word Bank. You may also want to encourage students to add synonyms and antonyms to the Word Bank as well.

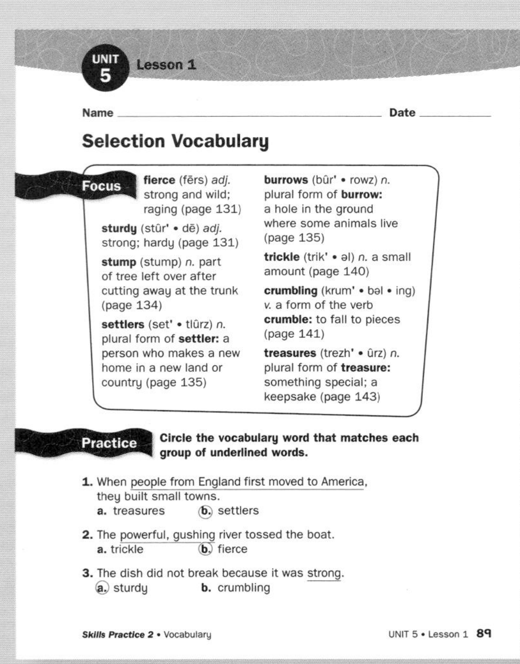
UNIT 5 Lesson 1

Name ______ Date ______

Selection Vocabulary

Focus

fierce (fērs) *adj.* strong and wild; raging (page 131)

sturdy (stûr' • dē) *adj.* strong; hardy (page 131)

stump (stump) *n.* part of tree left over after cutting away at the trunk (page 134)

settlers (set' • tlûrz) *n.* plural form of **settler:** a person who makes a new home in a new land or country (page 135)

burrows (bûr' • rowz) *n.* plural form of **burrow:** a hole in the ground where some animals live (page 135)

trickle (trik' • əl) *n.* a small amount (page 140)

crumbling (krum' • bəl • ing) *v.* a form of the verb **crumble:** to fall to pieces (page 141)

treasures (trezh' • ûrz) *n.* plural form of **treasure:** something special; a keepsake (page 143)

Practice **Circle the vocabulary word that matches each group of underlined words.**

1. When people from England first moved to America, they built small towns.
   a. treasures (**b.**) settlers
2. The powerful, gushing river tossed the boat.
   a. trickle (**b.**) fierce
3. The dish did not break because it was strong.
   (**a.**) sturdy **b.** crumbling

Skills Practice 2 • Vocabulary UNIT 5 • Lesson 1 89

Skills Practice 2, pp. 89 –90

Teacher Tips

WORKSHOP During Workshop, have students listen to "The House on Maple Street" for a model of oral reading. While students listen, have them keep an ongoing list in their Writer's Notebooks of any new or unfamiliar words they encounter, and instruct them to check the words using a dictionary or glossary. Also, instruct students to listen for the lesson's vocabulary words and to check that the words make sense within the reading.

WRITE ABOUT IT! Have students write a news story about an old tree near their home or school in their Writer's Notebooks.

BEYOND THE SELECTION Have students summarize what they have learned and tell how they might use this information in further investigations.

Writer's Notebook

- Have students use their Writer's Notebooks to list other fiction selections they have read in class or on their own.
- Have students compare the elements found in each selection.

Meet the Author and Illustrator

After students read the information about the author and illustrator, discuss the following questions with them.

- *Why do you think Pryor decided to become an author?* **Possible Answer** *She loved to read when she was a child, and so she decided to write books for children.*
- *Why do you think Peck studied in three different art schools?* **Possible Answer** *She wanted to be the best she could be at art and design.*

Theme Connections

Within the Selection

1. How do you think the street where you live was named? **Possible Answer** *I think my street was named after a kind of tree, because I live on Elm Street.*
2. What kind of changes have taken place in your neighborhood since you have lived there? **Possible Answer** *Three new houses have been built.*

Beyond the Selection

3. What are some things you can usually find in a community? **Possible Answers** *parks, community recreation centers, pools, and so on*
4. How do you feel about being part of a community? **Possible Answer** *I like knowing all of the kids on my block, and I have a lot of friends to play with.*

Meet the Author

Bonnie Pryor
Books and reading have always been important to Bonnie Pryor. As a child, she sometimes got into trouble for reading when she was supposed to be helping around the house or when she was supposed to be sleeping late at night. Pryor says her six children often appear in her stories. She and her husband now live in the country where they care for horses, rabbits, cats, and a dog.

Meet the Illustrator

Beth Peck
Beth Peck studied art at the Rhode Island School of Design, the Art Students League, and the National Academy of Design. Her favorite books to illustrate are those about people from all over the world. She has lived in Wisconsin and New York City. She lives with her husband and a few cats.

144

Communities across Time

Theme Connections

Within the Selection

1. How do you think the street where you live was named?
2. What kind of changes have taken place in your neighborhood since you have lived there?

Beyond the Selection

3. What are some things you can usually find in a community?
4. How do you feel about being part of a community?

Write about It!
Write a news story about an old tree near your home or school.

Remember to look for newspaper articles about historic sites in your town to add to the Concept/Question Board.

145

Concept/Question Board

As students discuss "The House on Maple Street" encourage them to post questions, answers, comments, or other items related to Communities across Time on the **Concept/Question Board.**

✦ Encourage students to
- post articles from magazines.
- bring objects from home that relate to the theme Communities across Time.
- draw pictures that support the theme.
- post poems that connect with the theme.

OBJECTIVES

Students will
- ✦ revise persuasive paragraphs.
- ✦ practice spelling words with prefixes *pre-*, *un-*, *mis-*, and *re-*.
- ✦ conduct an Internet search.
- ✦ practice verb tenses.

MATERIALS

- ✦ ***Skills Practice 2,*** pp. 96–98 and 101–102
- ✦ Routine 16

Writing Persuasive Paragraph

Revising

ROUTINE 16

Teach

- ✦ Students will use the drafts they have written to revise their persuasive paragraphs.
- ✦ Use Routine 16, and emphasize to students the need to make sure they have correctly organized their paragraphs in the following manner:
  - The topic sentence comes first.
  - The body containing the facts, reasons, or feelings is in the middle.
  - A closing sentence ends the paragraph.
- ✦ Remind students of the purpose of a persuasive paragraph. As students revise their paragraphs, have them ask the following questions: is the reasoning clear? Is there a strong voice? Can readers tell that the writer believes in what he or she has written? Does the argument sound convincing?

Guided Practice

- ✦ Using the draft you created earlier, have students help you revise the draft to organize information to create clarity and meaning and to create a strong persuasive voice.
- ✦ Have students turn to ***Skills Practice 2*** page 96 to read and discuss the revising checklist.

Apply

Composing—Revising Have students refer to page 96 in ***Skills Practice 2*** as they revise their persuasive paragraphs. Assist students as necessary with questions they have about the revising stage of the writing process.

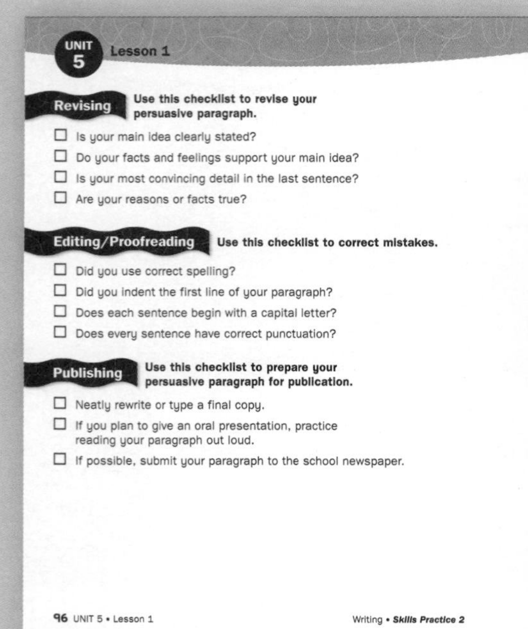

UNIT 5 Lesson 1

Revising Use this checklist to revise your persuasive paragraph.

- ☐ Is your main idea clearly stated?
- ☐ Do your facts and feelings support your main idea?
- ☐ Is your most convincing detail in the last sentence?
- ☐ Are your reasons or facts true?

Editing/Proofreading Use this checklist to correct mistakes.

- ☐ Did you use correct spelling?
- ☐ Did you indent the first line of your paragraph?
- ☐ Does each sentence begin with a capital letter?
- ☐ Does every sentence have correct punctuation?

Publishing Use this checklist to prepare your persuasive paragraph for publication.

- ☐ Neatly rewrite or type a final copy.
- ☐ If you plan to give an oral presentation, practice reading your paragraph out loud.
- ☐ If possible, submit your paragraph to the school newspaper.

96 UNIT 5 • Lesson 1 Writing • *Skills Practice 2*

Skills Practice 2, p. 96

Spelling

Prefixes *re-, un-, pre-, mis-*

Teach

- Tell students that prefixes are added to the beginning of words to change the meaning of the words.
- Tell students that the prefix *re-* means "again," the prefix *un-* means "not" or "opposite of," the prefix *pre-* means "before," and the prefix *mis-* means "wrong" or "wrongly."
- Write the word list on the board: *mismatch, unclear, reread, refund, unzip, misprint, unload, mislead, preheat, restart, prefix, unfair, recount, misplace,* and *preview.* Have volunteers come to the board and choose a word. Have them say the word, circle the prefix, and use the word in a sentence. Continue until all the words have been used.

Guided Practice

Have students turn to ***Skills Practice 2*** page 97. Read the instructions with them, and complete the first two questions as a class.

Apply

Have students complete ***Skills Practice 2*** pages 97–98 on their own. Remind students that challenge words are not used in ***Skills Practice*** exercises.

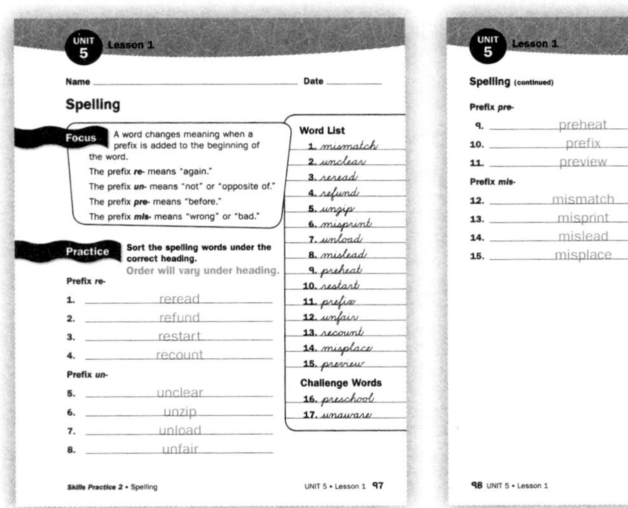

UNIT 5 Lesson 1

Name ______ Date ______

Spelling

Focus A word changes meaning when a prefix is added to the beginning of the word.
The prefix *re-* means "again."
The prefix *un-* means "not" or "opposite of."
The prefix *pre-* means "before."
The prefix *mis-* means "wrong" or "bad."

Practice Sort the spelling words under the correct heading.
Order will vary under heading.

Prefix *re-*
1. reread
2. refund
3. restart
4. recount

Prefix *un-*
5. unclear
6. unzip
7. unload
8. unfair

Word List
1. mismatch
2. unclear
3. reread
4. refund
5. unzip
6. misprint
7. unload
8. mislead
9. preheat
10. restart
11. prefix
12. unfair
13. recount
14. misplace
15. preview

Challenge Words
16. preschool
17. unaware

Skills Practice 2 • Spelling UNIT 5 • Lesson 1 97

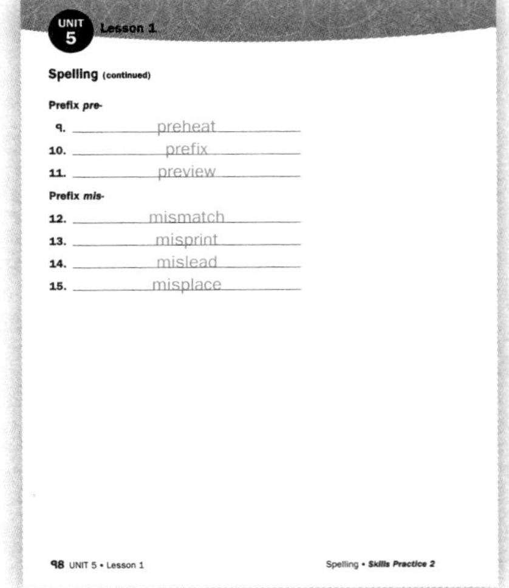

UNIT 5 Lesson 1

Spelling (continued)

Prefix *pre-*
9. preheat
10. prefix
11. preview

Prefix *mis-*
12. mismatch
13. misprint
14. mislead
15. misplace

98 UNIT 5 • Lesson 1 Spelling • Skills Practice 2

Skills Practice 2, pp. 97–98

Monitor Progress 

to Differentiate Instruction
Formal Assessment

Spelling Note whether students are able to spell the lesson words correctly.

APPROACHING LEVEL

IF . . . students need to practice spelling this week's words, **THEN . . .** have them complete ***Reteach*** page 128.

ON LEVEL

IF . . . students can spell this week's spelling words, **THEN . . .** have them think of two more words for each prefix that were not included in this week's lesson. Then have them write the eight words on a separate sheet of paper.

ABOVE LEVEL

IF . . . students are ready for a challenge, **THEN . . .** have them complete ***Challenge Activities*** page 116.

Teacher Tip

PLAN AHEAD You may want to plan to conduct this lesson in the library, computer lab, or by classroom computers, depending on the school resources.

Monitor Progress

to Differentiate Instruction
Formal Assessment

Conducting Internet Searches Note whether students are using keywords during Internet searches.

APPROACHING LEVEL

IF . . . students need to practice conducting Internet searches,	**THEN . . .** have them look up vocabulary word definitions on the Internet during Workshop.

ON LEVEL

IF . . . students have an understanding of conducting Internet searches,	**THEN . . .** have them look for supporting facts for their persuasive paragraphs during Workshop.

ABOVE LEVEL

IF . . . students need a challenge,	**THEN . . .** have them help another student conduct research for either their unit investigation or persuasive paragraph during Workshop.

Study Skills

Conducting an Internet Search

Teach

Ask students what they know about conducting Internet searches. If necessary, give them the following information.

- When searching for information on the Internet, you must first select a search engine. Search engines exist to help students locate age-appropriate materials. Direct students to these search engines.
- Next, students need to select keywords that are most likely to lead them to useful information. For example, to look up ancient cultures that lived in California, students can select the keywords *ancient, cultures,* and *California.* Explain that sometimes students will find they must experiment with several terms to get exactly the type of information they want. They should keep trying and not get discouraged.
- Tell students they will need to decide how to combine the terms to get the kind of information they seek. To do this they can use logical operators, which are special keywords or characters that tell the search engines how to use the keywords. The most common ones are the words *and* or *or* and using quotation marks.

Guided Practice

- Have students turn to ***Skills Practice 2*** page 101. Have a student read the directions aloud. Complete the first two questions as a class.

Apply

Have students complete ***Skills Practice 2*** pages 101–102.

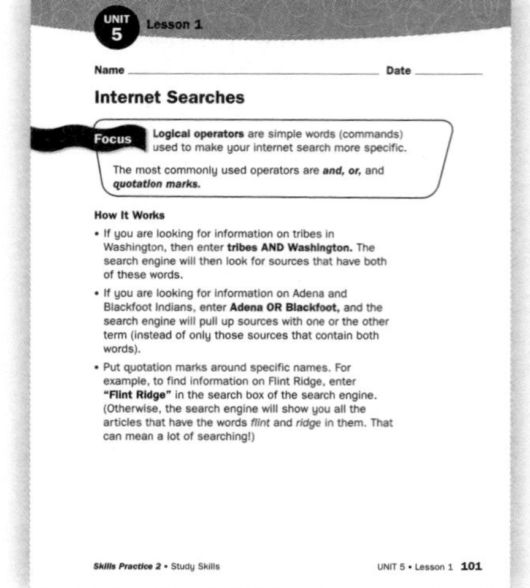

UNIT 5 Lesson 1

Name ______________________ Date __________

Internet Searches

Focus **Logical operators** are simple words (commands) used to make your internet search more specific.

The most commonly used operators are ***and, or,*** and ***quotation marks.***

How It Works

- If you are looking for information on tribes in Washington, then enter **tribes AND Washington.** The search engine will then look for sources that have both of these words.
- If you are looking for information on Adena and Blackfoot Indians, enter **Adena OR Blackfoot,** and the search engine will pull up sources with one or the other term (instead of only those sources that contain both words).
- Put quotation marks around specific names. For example, to find information on Flint Ridge, enter **"Flint Ridge"** in the search box of the search engine. (Otherwise, the search engine will show you all the articles that have the words *flint* and *ridge* in them. That can mean a lot of searching!)

Skills Practice 2 • Study Skills UNIT 5 • Lesson 1 **101**

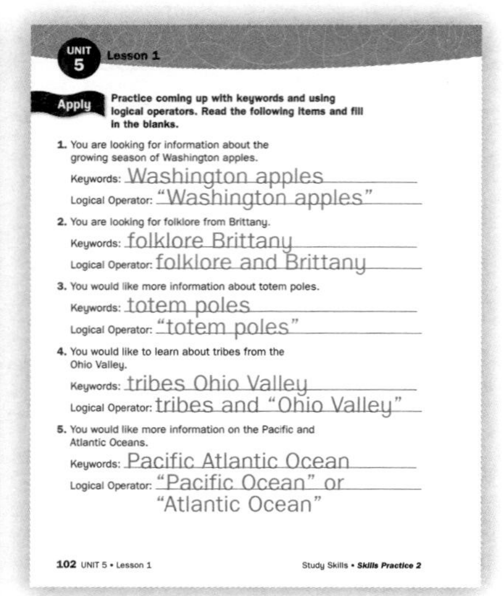

UNIT 5 Lesson 1

Apply **Practice coming up with keywords and using logical operators. Read the following items and fill in the blanks.**

1. You are looking for information about the growing season of Washington apples.
   Keywords: Washington apples
   Logical Operator: "Washington apples"
2. You are looking for folklore from Brittany.
   Keywords: folklore Brittany
   Logical Operator: folklore and Brittany
3. You would like more information about totem poles.
   Keywords: totem poles
   Logical Operator: "totem poles"
4. You would like to learn about tribes from the Ohio Valley.
   Keywords: tribes Ohio Valley
   Logical Operator: tribes and "Ohio Valley"
5. You would like more information on the Pacific and Atlantic Oceans.
   Keywords: Pacific Atlantic Ocean
   Logical Operator: "Pacific Ocean" or "Atlantic Ocean"

102 UNIT 5 • Lesson 1 Study Skills • ***Skills Practice 2***

Skills Practice 2, pp. 101–102

Grammar, Usage, and Mechanics

Verb Tenses

Teach

- Remind students that the tense of a verb tells when an action happens. A verb can express past, present, or future time.
- Write the following sentences on the board, and ask students to fill in the blank with a verb in its correct form. Possible answers follow.
  - I __________ on the phone every day with my sister. *talk*
  - We __________ for several minutes yesterday. *talked*
  - I'm sure I __________ to her again tomorrow. *will talk*
- You might want to bring in other literature to show students examples of verb tenses. A good example might be a short story.

Guided Practice

Write three or four verbs on the board and have students generate sentences for each tense for each verb.

Apply

Have students write a brief summary of the story "The House on Maple Street." Have them underline the subject or subjects of each sentence and circle the corresponding verbs. Have students write the verb tense after each verb.

Differentiating Instruction — English Learner

IF . . . students need extra help with verb tenses, **THEN . . .** refer to Unit 5 Lesson 1 in the ***English Learner Support Guide*** for support activities.

IF . . . students cannot generate their own sentences, **THEN . . .** have them copy sentences from the selection and then underline the subject and circle the verb in those sentences.

Preparing to Read

OBJECTIVES

Students will

- identify and know the meanings of the prefixes *pre-* and *mis-*.
- build fluency.

MATERIALS

- ***Transparency*** 133
- Routine 10

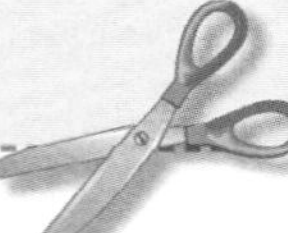

Daily Oral Practice

Daily News

I wonder who lived in my house before I did. They preserved the land well; they must have cared for it. I wonder what roamed the land before the house was here—maybe huge dinosaurs that predate humans! Many kinds of animals lived here before humans finally did.

- Write the daily news on the board or on chart paper. Then have students read the daily news in unison to practice fluency.
- As a review of yesterday's word structure lesson, ask a volunteer to identify any words in the message with the prefix *pre-*. *preserved, predate*

Technology

WORD STRUCTURE Have students review compound words and contractions using ***eSkills & eGames.***

Word Structure 

ROUTINE 10

The Prefixes *pre-* and *mis-*

✦ Use ***Transparency*** 133 with these word lines from Day 3.

Line 1	pay	prepay	heat	preheat
Line 2	school	preschool	view	preview
Line 3	count	miscount	behave	misbehave
Line 4	place	misplace	spell	misspell

✦ Use Routine 10 to review the meaning of the prefixes *pre-* and *mis-*. If necessary, remind students that *pre-* means "before," and *mis-* means "wrong" or "bad."

Developing Oral Language

Use any of these activities to help students practice reading the words.

- Randomly point to a word in one of the word lines and have the class say the word. Ask a student to use the word in a sentence. **Possible Answer** *When you bake cookies, you have to* preheat *the oven.* Call on another student to use the same word in another sentence. **Possible Answer** *If you use a microwave, you don't have to* preheat *it.* Repeat for all the words on the word lines.
- Invite a student to choose one of the base words from the word lines and use it in a sentence. **Possible Answer** *Sometimes I* misplace *my book bag.* Then have that student choose a volunteer to use the other form of the word in a sentence. **Possible Answer** *Maybe if you put your bag in the same* place *every time, you won't lose it.* Continue for all of the words on the word lines.
- Write on the board more examples of words with the prefixes *pre-* and *mis-* such as *prejudge, preslice, prewash, preplan, mistake, misinform, mismatch,* and *mispronounce*. For each example you give, have volunteers come to the board, underline the prefix, and give a definition for the word. Then have the class decide whether each definition is accurate. Help the class modify each definition as necessary.

Monitor Progress 

to Differentiate Instruction
Formal Assessment

Word Structure During the word structure activity, note how well students understand the words.

APPROACHING LEVEL

IF . . . students do not understand the words on the word lines, **THEN . . .** use pictures, photos, objects, stick drawings, or pantomime to help them visualize the words.

ON LEVEL

IF . . . students need practice with the words on the word lines, **THEN . . .** have them write sentences using the words on the lines.

ABOVE LEVEL

IF . . . students understand the words on the word lines, **THEN . . .** have them make a list of other words with the prefixes *pre-* and *mis-* and use them in sentences.

Reading and Responding

This is 107 Maple Street. Chrissy and Jenny live here with their mother and father, a dog named Maggie, and a fat cat named Sally.

Three hundred years ago there was no house here or even a street. There was only a forest and a bubbling spring where the animals came to drink.

130

One day a fierce storm roared across the forest. The sky rolled with thunder, and lighting crashed into a tree. A deer sniffed the air in alarm. Soon the woods were ablaze.

The next spring a few sturdy flowers poked through the ashes, and by the year after that the land was covered with grass. Some wildflowers grew at the edge of the stream where the deer had returned to drink.

131

OBJECTIVES

Students will

- use the comprehension skills Classify and Categorize, Fact and Opinion, and Author's Purpose.
- review fluency.
- investigate the theme Communities across Time using the Inquiry process.

MATERIALS

- ***Student Reader,*** Book 2, pp. 130–147
- ***Skills Practice 2,*** pp. 91–92, 94
- ***Transparency*** 15

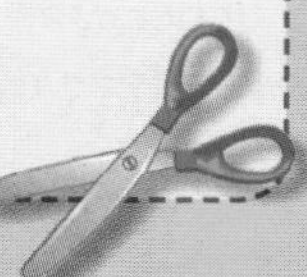

2nd READ

Comprehension Skill

Reread the story using the comprehension skills Classify and Categorize, Fact and Opinion, Author's Purpose and Reading with a Writer's Eye.

Classify and Categorize

Remind students that putting things that are in some way alike into groups is called *classifying* or *categorizing*. Using this skill can help readers understand and remember the information they read in a story. Have students search for items on page 130 of the text that can be classified under the headings *Maple Street Today* and *Maple Street 300 Years Ago* in the story.

Maple Street Today	Maple Street 300 Years Ago
house at 107 Maple Street	forest
a family lives in the house	bubbling spring

One day the earth <u>trembled</u>, and a cloud of dust rose to the sky. A mighty herd of buffalo had come to eat the sweet grass and drink from the stream.

People came, following the buffalo herd. They set up their <u>tepees</u> near the stream, and because they liked it so much, they stayed for the whole summer.

One boy longed to be a great hunter like his father, but for now he could only pretend with his friends. In their games, one boy was chosen to be the buffalo.

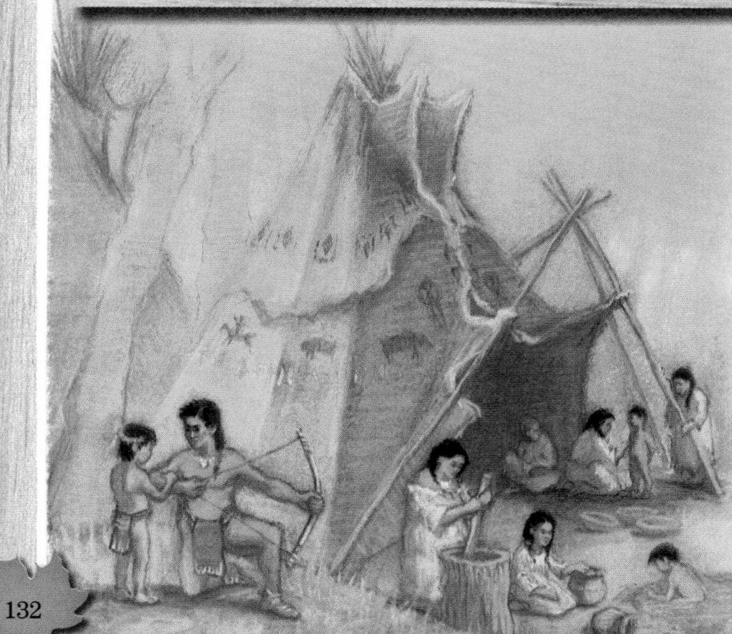

132

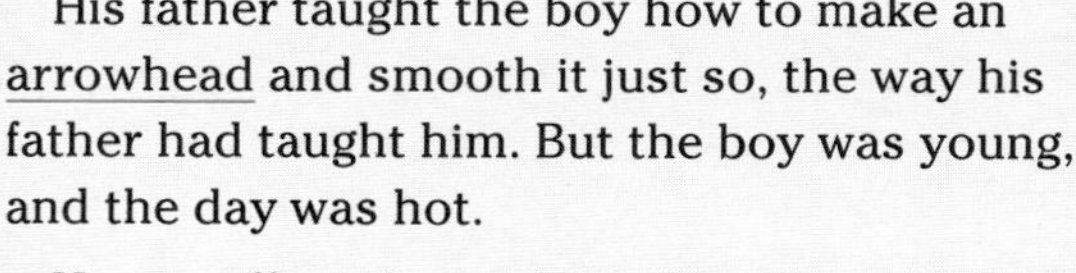

His father taught the boy how to make an <u>arrowhead</u> and smooth it just so, the way his father had taught him. But the boy was young, and the day was hot.

He ran off to play with his friends and left the arrowhead on a rock. When he came back later to get it, he could not find it.

133

Reading with a Writer's Eye

Plot

Remind students that the plot of the story is the events that occur, including a desire or goal that is attained or a problem that is solved. The author of this story, Bonnie Pryor, sets a similar goal for all of her characters. Story plots also contain a sequence of events that helps readers understand what is happening. Ask students the following questions:

- *What is the goal of the people in the story so far?* **Possible Answer** *They want to settle on land that they like and will support them. The boy in the story wants to be a great hunter like his father.*
- *Is there a problem in the story so far?* **Possible Answer** *The boy left his arrowhead on a rock, and it has disappeared.*

Expanding Vocabulary

alarm (əl • ärm′) *n.* a sudden fear of danger (page 131)

The people felt a sense of *alarm* when the storm roared through the town.

trembled (trem′ • bəld) *v.* past tense of **tremble:** to shake (page 132)

The actor was so nervous that his hands *trembled* as he took the stage.

tepees (tē′ • pēz) *n.* plural form of **tepee:** a portable house used by Native Americans (page 132)

Sometimes we go camping and stay all night in *tepees* by the lake.

arrowhead (âr′ • rō • hed) *v.* the tip of an arrow (page 133)

I found an ancient *arrowhead* buried in a hillside.

The buffalo moved on, searching for new grass, and the people packed up their tepees and followed.

For a long time the land was quiet. Some rabbits made their home in the stump of a burned tree, and a fox made a den in some rocks.

134

One day there was a new sound. The fox looked up. A wagon train passed by, heading for California. The settlers stopped beside the stream for a night. But they dreamed of gold and places far away and were gone the next morning.

Other wagons came, following the tracks of the first. The fox family moved into the woods, but the rabbits stayed snug in their burrows until the people had gone.

135

Expanding Vocabulary

den (den) *n.* a place where wild animals rest or sleep (page 134)

The four foxes huddled together in the warmth of their *den*.

Comprehension Skill

Fact and Opinion

Remind students that writers use both facts, which can be verified, and opinions, which are ideas which might be supported but not proven. "The House on Maple Street" is a realistic fiction story. The characters and events are made up, but they could have really happened. The author presents some information as facts and some as opinions. Ask students to find these examples:

- *Find an example of a fact on page 134.* **Possible Answer** *The buffalo moved off the land. Why is this a fact?* **Possible Answer** *It can be verified that the buffalo moved from place to place across the land.*
- *Find an example of an opinion on page 135.* **Possible Answer** *The people in the wagons didn't stay because they wanted to find gold in California. Why is this an opinion?* **Possible Answer** *It was their opinion that the land was not right for them. They had a different opinion than the people before them about what they wanted from the land.*

Soon after, a man and a woman camped along the stream. They were heading west, but the woman would soon have a child. They looked around them and knew it was a good place to stay. The man cut down trees and made a house.

He pulled up the tree stumps left from the fire and planted his crops. The child was a girl, and they named her Ruby and called her their little jewel.

136

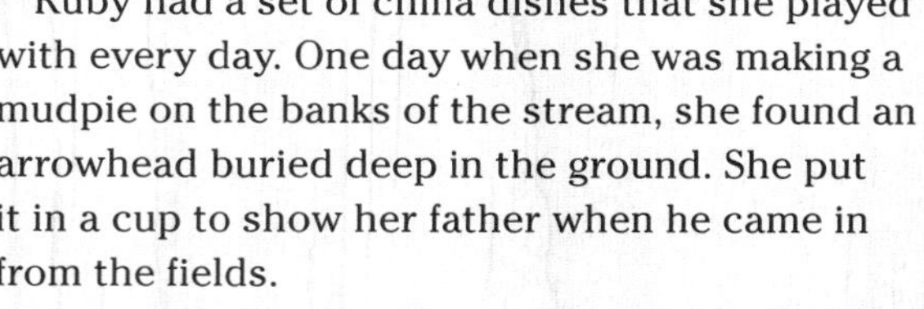

Ruby had a set of china dishes that she played with every day. One day when she was making a mudpie on the banks of the stream, she found an arrowhead buried deep in the ground. She put it in a cup to show her father when he came in from the fields.

Ruby's mother called her to watch the new baby. While she was gone, a rabbit sniffed at the cup and knocked it off the rock. It fell into the tunnel to his burrow, and the rabbit moved away to a new home under the roots of a tree.

137

Reading with a Writer's Eye

Setting

Remind students that the setting of the story is where it takes place. The setting is important in this story. Pryor uses the setting in her title: "The House on Maple Street." Ask students to identify the story's setting. If necessary, tell students that the setting of the story is the land where the house on Maple Street is. We have learned what this land was like 300 years ago, the animals and people who have lived on it, and the first house that was built on it. Ask students the following question:

What clue does Bonnie Pryor give us on page 137 to indicate that all of these changes have occurred on one piece of land? **Possible Answer** *Ruby finds the arrowhead that the little boy lost years before.*

Teacher Tip

SETTING Ask students to name one of the settings they have encountered in other selections they have read. How were the settings important in those stories? How do settings differ in realistic fiction stories from those in fantasy stories?

Word Structure

Inflectional ending *-ed:* camped, pulled, sniffed, knocked

Inflectional ending *-ing:* heading, making

Day 4

Reading and Responding

Ruby grew up and moved away, but her brother stayed on the farm. By now there were other people nearby, and he married a girl from another farm. They had six children, and he built a larger house so they would all fit.

Now the old wagon trail was used as a road, and the dust got into the house. When his wife complained, Ruby's brother planted a row of maple trees along the road to keep out the dust and shade the house. After the children were grown, he and his wife moved away, but one of their daughters stayed on the farm with her husband and children.

138

One day the children's great-aunt Ruby came for a visit. She was an old lady with snow-white hair. The children loved to hear her stories of long ago. She told them about the cup and arrowhead she had lost when she was a girl.

After she left, the children looked and looked. But they never found them, though they searched for days.

139

Teacher Tips

PLOT Have students follow the plot of a story as it develops by completing a story map graphic organizer as they read along. Encourage them to use graphic organizers when they write their own stories.

AUTHOR'S PURPOSE Remind students that authors can have more than one purpose for writing. For example, in "The House on Maple Street," the author probably wanted to tell an entertaining story that readers would enjoy. The writer probably also wanted to inform readers about the effects that people and natural occurrences have on our land.

Comprehension Skill

Author's Purpose

Remind students that paying attention to details in a story can help them discover the author's purpose. When readers understand an author's purpose for writing, they can better understand the text, identify important details, and know what to expect. As students continue to read "The House on Maple Street," ask them to look for clues to the author's purpose. Ask students the following question:

Are there any clues on pages 138–139 that might indicate the author's purpose?

Possible Answer *The author tells about the many people who lived on the farm and the changes to the farm. The trail turned into a road, and more trees were planted. The author's purpose is to tell a story about all of the changes that can happen to one area of land.*

The town had grown nearly to the edge of the farm, and another man up the road filled in the stream and changed its course. For a while there was a trickle of water in the spring when the snow melted, but weeds and dirt filled in the bed, until hardly anyone remembered a stream had ever been there.

New people lived on the farm. It was the schoolteacher and his family, and they sold much of the land to others. The road was paved with bricks, so there was no longer any dust, but the maple trees remained. The branches hung down over the road, making it shady and cool. People called it Maple Street. Automobiles drove on the road, along with carts and wagons, and there were many new houses.

140

The house was crumbling and old, and one day some men tore it down. For a while again, the land was bare. The rabbits lived comfortably, with only an occasional owl or fox to chase them. But one day a young couple came walking along and stopped to admire the trees.

"What a wonderful place for a home," said the young woman. So they hired carpenters and masons to build a cozy house of red bricks with white trim.

The young couple lived happily in the house for several years. The young man got a job in another town, and they had to move.

141

Reading with a Writer's Eye

Plot

The plot in Pryor's story is quickly evolving. Much time has passed since the days the buffalo roamed the land. Sometimes writers slowly progress through time in their stories, sometimes time passes at what seems like normal speed, and sometimes it passes quickly, as in this story. Ask students the following question:

- *Why do you think the writer of "The House on Maple Street" has time pass so quickly?* **Possible Answer** *She wants to show all of the changes and developments to the same piece of land over time. It's important to the story to show all of the different people who lived on the land and how that changed it.*

Expanding Vocabulary

remained (rə • mānd′) *v.* past tense of **remain:** to stay (page 140)

Some of the students got off of the bus, but the ones who had to go farther *remained*.

admire (əd • mīr′) *v.* to look at with pleasure (page 141)

The students were treated to a visitor and person they *admire*: a local firefighter.

carpenters (kär′ • pən • dûrz′) *n.* plural form of **carpenter:** a person who builds and repairs houses and other things made of wood (page 141)

Carpenters helped my dad and mom build a kitchen table.

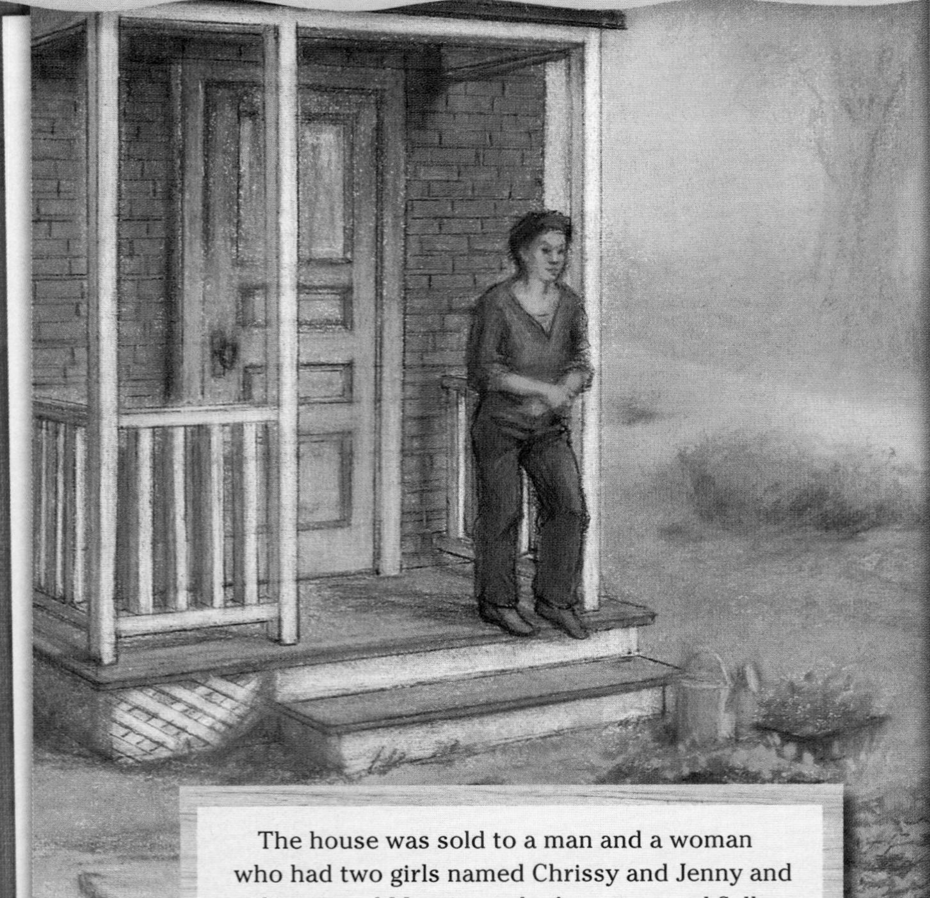

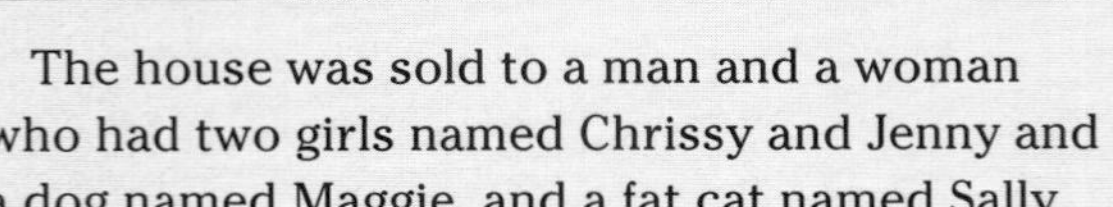

The house was sold to a man and a woman who had two girls named Chrissy and Jenny and a dog named Maggie, and a fat cat named Sally.

The girls helped their father dig up a spot of ground for a garden, but it was Maggie the dog who dug up something white in the soft spring earth.

142

"Stop," cried Chrissy, and she picked up the tiny cup made of china. Inside was the arrowhead found and lost so long ago.

"Who lost these?" the girls wondered. Chrissy and Jenny put the cup and arrowhead on a shelf for others to see. Someday perhaps their children will play with the tiny treasures and wonder about them, too. But the cup and arrowhead will forever keep their secrets, and the children can only dream.

143

Comprehension Skill

Fact and Opinion

Encourage students to look for facts and opinions as they read. So far, most of this story has been presented with factual information. Ask students the following questions:

- *Are facts or opinions found on page 142?* **Possible Answer** *This page gives facts. The house was sold to a man and woman with two daughters, a dog, and a cat. While digging in the garden, Maggie, the dog, dug something up.*
- *If you were a writer and wanted to add an opinion to this page, how would you do it?* **Possible Answers** *The family really liked the house. The father really enjoyed working in the garden.*

Teacher Tip

COMPREHENSION SKILLS As an extended activity, you may want to have students classify and categorize the facts and opinions in this story or other stories you have read or are reading. This will provide them with additional practice with the comprehension skills Classify and Categorize and Fact and Opinion.

Checking Comprehension

Ask students the following questions to check their comprehension of the story:

- *What was 107 Maple Street like 300 years ago?* **Possible Answer** *It was a wilderness forest and stream.*
- *How did natural events change the land?* **Possible Answer** *A storm and fire destroyed the land, and then it rebuilt itself.*
- *How did people change the land?* **Possible Answer** *As more people settled on the land, trees and the stream were cleared away. More space was needed for roads and houses.*
- *How did the children who lived at 107 Maple Street find a link to the past?* **Possible Answer** *They found the arrowhead and china cup from years before.*

Word Structure

Inflectional ending *-ed:* named, helped, cried, picked

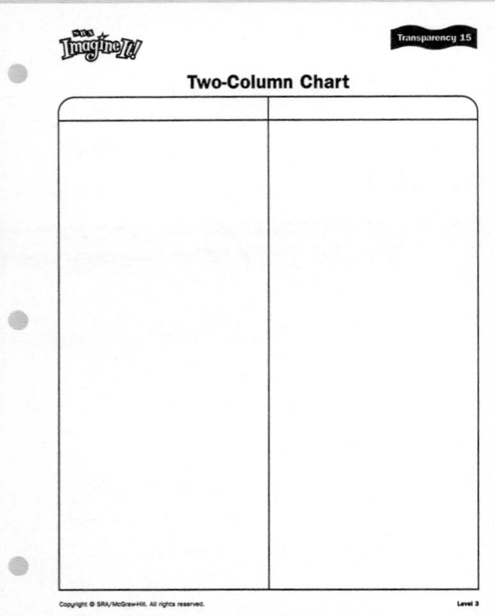

Transparency 15

Supporting the Reading

Comprehension Skill: Author's Purpose

Teach

Remind students that understanding an author's purpose helps readers identify important details in a text and helps them know what they can expect to find in it. Additionally, paying attention to details in a text can help readers discover the author's purpose. This will make reading more meaningful and enjoyable.

Guided Practice

Bring in a short story to read aloud to the class. After you have read the story, ask students what they think the author's purpose was for writing the story. Remind them that an author's purpose could be to entertain, to inform, to teach a lesson, to persuade, to explain a process, or a combination of reasons. Ask students what details in the article reflected the author's purpose and led them to their choice. Record students' answers in a two-column chart on ***Transparency*** 15. You can use the following as an example for students to follow.

Author's Purpose	Supporting Details
to explain	Author gives step-by-step instructions.

Apply

Have students turn to pages 91–92 in their ***Skills Practice 2.*** Have students read aloud the Focus section of the lesson. Work through the Practice section of the lesson with students. Have them look in the story "The House on Maple Street" to find examples of the author's purpose. Then have them complete the Practice and Apply sections of the lesson. Explain to students that determining author's purpose is a skill on which all readers and writers rely. Remind students to always keep their purposes in mind as they draft their persuasive paragraphs.

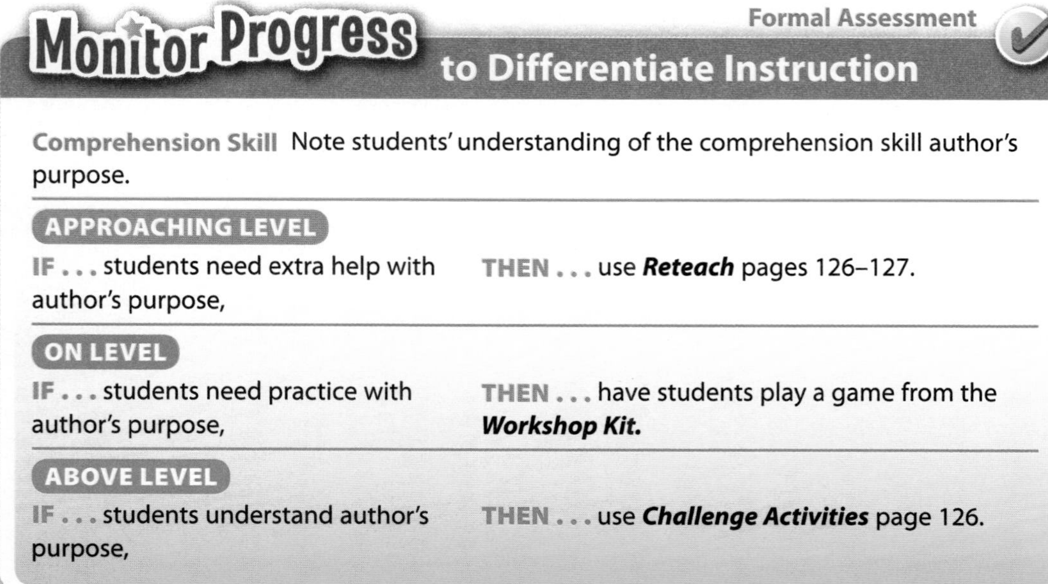

Monitor Progress to Differentiate Instruction

Formal Assessment

Comprehension Skill Note students' understanding of the comprehension skill author's purpose.

APPROACHING LEVEL

IF . . .	THEN . . .
IF . . . students need extra help with author's purpose,	THEN . . . use ***Reteach*** pages 126–127.

ON LEVEL

IF . . .	THEN . . .
IF . . . students need practice with author's purpose,	THEN . . . have students play a game from the ***Workshop Kit.***

ABOVE LEVEL

IF . . .	THEN . . .
IF . . . students understand author's purpose,	THEN . . . use ***Challenge Activities*** page 126.

Fluency

The simple and straightforward style of "The House on Maple Street" should not pose a problem for students to read. If necessary, review pronunciations and meanings of selection vocabulary words, additional vocabulary words, or any other words unfamiliar to students.

- Model fluent reading by reading pages 138–139 from "The House on Maple Street." Have students follow along in the **Student Reader,** Book 2.
- After you have read through the passage, call on a volunteer to read the first couple of paragraphs. Before the student begins, make sure the student understands how the text moves readers forward quickly in time.
- After the volunteer has finished, have all students chorally read aloud the passage several times until they can read it naturally with good phrasing.
- For additional practice, have students work in pairs reading different passages from this story to each other. Monitor them to make sure they are reading the passage fluently.

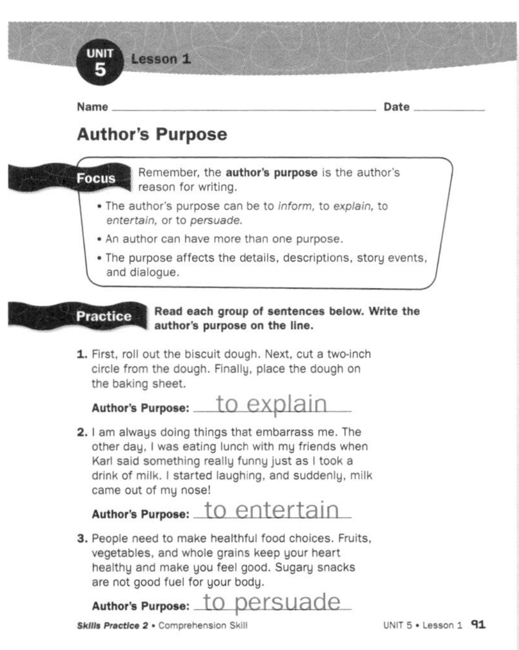

UNIT 5 Lesson 1

Name ____________ Date ________

Author's Purpose

Focus Remember, the **author's purpose** is the author's reason for writing.

- The author's purpose can be to *inform,* to *explain,* to *entertain,* or to *persuade.*
- An author can have more than one purpose.
- The purpose affects the details, descriptions, story events, and dialogue.

Practice **Read each group of sentences below. Write the author's purpose on the line.**

1. First, roll out the biscuit dough. Next, cut a two-inch circle from the dough. Finally, place the dough on the baking sheet.

   Author's Purpose: to explain

2. I am always doing things that embarrass me. The other day, I was eating lunch with my friends when Karl said something really funny just as I took a drink of milk. I started laughing, and suddenly, milk came out of my nose!

   Author's Purpose: to entertain

3. People need to make healthful food choices. Fruits, vegetables, and whole grains keep your heart healthy and make you feel good. Sugary snacks are not good fuel for your body.

   Author's Purpose: to persuade

Skills Practice 2 • Comprehension Skill UNIT 5 • Lesson 1 91

Skills Practice 2, p. 91

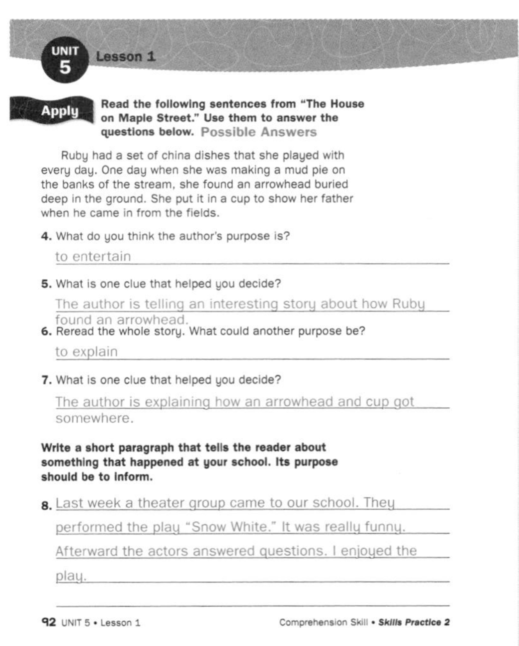

UNIT 5 Lesson 1

Apply **Read the following sentences from "The House on Maple Street." Use them to answer the questions below.** Possible Answers

Ruby had a set of china dishes that she played with every day. One day when she was making a mud pie on the banks of the stream, she found an arrowhead buried deep in the ground. She put it in a cup to show her father when he came in from the fields.

4. What do you think the author's purpose is?

   to entertain

5. What is one clue that helped you decide?

   The author is telling an interesting story about how Ruby found an arrowhead.

6. Reread the whole story. What could another purpose be?

   to explain

7. What is one clue that helped you decide?

   The author is explaining how an arrowhead and cup got somewhere.

Write a short paragraph that tells the reader about something that happened at your school. Its purpose should be to inform.

8. Last week a theater group came to our school. They performed the play "Snow White." It was really funny. Afterward the actors answered questions. I enjoyed the play.

92 UNIT 5 • Lesson 1 Comprehension Skill • ***Skills Practice 2***

Skills Practice 2, p. 92

To help students build fluency and strengthen their vocabulary and comprehension skills, have them read the ***Leveled Readers*** for this unit. Use each student's Oral Fluency Assessment score from the previous ***Lesson Assessment*** to diagnose the appropriate ***Leveled Reader.***

Fluency Tip

FLUENCY For additional fluency practice, have students practice reading this story in small groups.

Research in Action

While reading decodable text gives students the opportunity to develop two of the three elements of fluency — accuracy and automaticity — students also need to learn about the third critical element — prosody. Prosody includes the rhythmic and tonal aspects of oral language: making reading sound natural like spoken language; using appropriate intonation; using appropriate expression; and pausing appropriately at phrase boundaries. Beginning readers are introduced to prosody as they listen to their teacher read with expression and intonation. Once students are able to decode and read with accuracy, however, prosodic elements should be taught.

(Marsha Roit)

Social Studies Inquiry

Genre: News Story 

A news story tells the facts about a current event.

Feature: Map

Tell students that maps show where things are located and how to get from one place to another.

Ask students to point to the map in the "Home Tour Celebrates Spanish Heritage." Ask students how they think the map might be useful.

Reading "Home Tour Celebrates Spanish Heritage"

Have students take turns reading aloud "Home Tour Celebrates Spanish Heritage." Encourage students to think about how homes, such as the one on Maple Street in the selection, have a heritage, or something that is handed down through the generations.

Think Link

1. A news story answers the questions *Who? What? When?* and *Where?* How are they answered here? **Possible Answer** *Who? the Board of Realtors, What? the Parade of Homes; When? next week; Where? Palos Verdes and Buena Vista Villas.*
2. Name three common features of Spanish villas. **Possible Answer** *they are made of stucco, use light tones, and have courtyards outside*
3. Use the above map to answer the following question. In which direction and on what streets will tour visitors travel to get from Palos Verdes Estates to Buena Vista Villas? *Tour visitors will travel north on Alameda Avenue, which will lead to Buena Vista Villas.*

Teacher Tip

SELECTION VOCABULARY Review the meaning of the highlighted selection vocabulary word *settlers* in "Home Tour Celebrates Spanish Heritage."

Social Studies Inquiry

Genre

A **news story** tells the facts about a current event.

Feature

A **map** shows where things are located and how to get from one place to another.

Home Tour Celebrates Spanish Heritage

Next week the Board of Realtors will hold its fifth Parade of Homes featuring Spanish-style homes. The tour links the Palos Verdes and Buena Vista Villas neighborhoods.

Homes on the tour reflect the influence of Spanish settlers. Among the first to come to our region, they brought their style with them. True to Spanish form, most homes on the tour are made of stucco. Guests will see homes in many hues. Pale brown and peach are standard shades. Yet crisp, white stucco is just as common.

Such light house tones highlight the red tile roofs. The settlers formed the curved roof tiles by hand. Now made by machine, the tiles still convey a sense of "Old World" Spain.

Admire the courtyard on your way inside. Look for brightly colored tiles on walls and floors. Do not miss the wrought-iron accents in the garden and on the arched front door.

Detailed tile patterns and arches are also inside. Curved doorways and windows create soft lines, contrasting with the straight lines of the ceilings.

Hundreds of advance tickets have already been sold for the tour. To find out more, contact the Board of Realtors.

Think Link

1. A news story answers the questions Who? What? When? and Where? How are they answered here?
2. Name three common features of Spanish villas.
3. Use the above map to answer the following question. In which direction and on what streets will tour visitors travel to get from Palos Verdes Estates to Buena Vista Villas?

Try It!

As you work on your investigation, think about how you can use a map to show your facts.

Inquiry Connection

Have students discuss ways in which maps might be helpful in their investigations. For example, if students are investigating how one piece of land has changed over time, they could use a topographical map to show the changes. If they are investigating how one group of people or animals moved across the land, they could use a map to show the different places they traveled and how they got from one place to another.

Teacher Tip

INVESTIGATION TOPICS Students will likely be interested in things relevant to their own communities. Encourage interested groups to pursue investigation topics that concern their own communities or subcommunities.

Inquiry Process

Step 1—Generating Ideas and Questions

Whole-Group Time

Whole Group

- Remind students that they can post questions and ideas about unit selections on the **Concept/Question Board.** They should feel free to respond to others' questions as well.
- Discuss with students what they learned about how the land and communities change over time from reading the selection, "The House on Maple Street." What new things did they learn? What did they find most interesting? Did they change the way they think about the land and past communities? Write their answers on the board or on chart paper, and have students take notes in their Writer's Notebooks. Make sure that the group discusses the idea that communities are constantly changing the land on which they live.
- To help students get ideas for possible investigation topics, conduct a brainstorming session with the class to generate ideas, questions, and topics related to the theme Communities across Time. Students might want to discuss things currently happening in their community, the history of their community, or how the land on which their community lives has changed over time. If they have questions about any of these topics, encourage students to pursue them. Ask students to help write their ideas, questions, and topics on the board. Also have them write any new interests they have about the theme in their Writer's Notebooks.

Small-Group Time

Small Group

- Have students break into their small groups. Have students post some of the ideas they have shared on the **Concept/Question Board.** Remind them that any stories, ideas, and questions they share might give people new questions or ideas about the theme.
- Using the brainstorming ideas on the board, other notes they may have taken, and ideas about the theme that they took from "A River Ran Wild" and "The House on Maple Street," groups should start formulating potential investigation questions.
- To help groups continue to generate questions and ideas that interest them, have them complete ***Skills Practice 2*** page 94 in their small groups.
- As you circulate among the groups, continue to model initial questions such as these: *How is our community different now than it was 100 years ago? How long have people lived in our area? How did the people who first settled here live, and what were they like? What would the perfect community be like? Why did our community pollute our river? How can communities protect the natural world? What is unique about how our community uses its land? How should our community change? Why do communities change?* Suggest these questions to get groups started in their thinking, but allow them to choose questions that interest them.

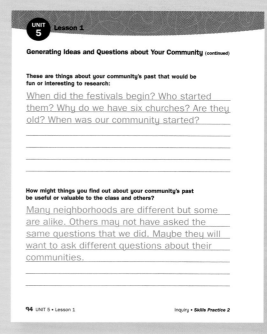

UNIT 5 Lesson 1

Generating Ideas and Questions about Your Community (continued)

These are things about your community's past that would be fun or interesting to research:

When did the festivals begin? Who started them? Why do we have six churches? Are they old? When was our community started?

How might things you find out about your community's past be useful or valuable to the class and others?

Many neighborhoods are different but some are alike. Others may not have asked the same questions that we did. Maybe they will want to ask different questions about their communities.

94 UNIT 5 • Lesson 1 Inquiry • *Skills Practice 2*

Skills Practice 2, p. 94

Concept/Question Board

Continue to encourage use of the **Concept/Question Board** by recognizing and thanking students for their contributions. Incorporate discussion of those items into classroom discussions whenever possible. Remember to also model by posting your own questions and ideas.

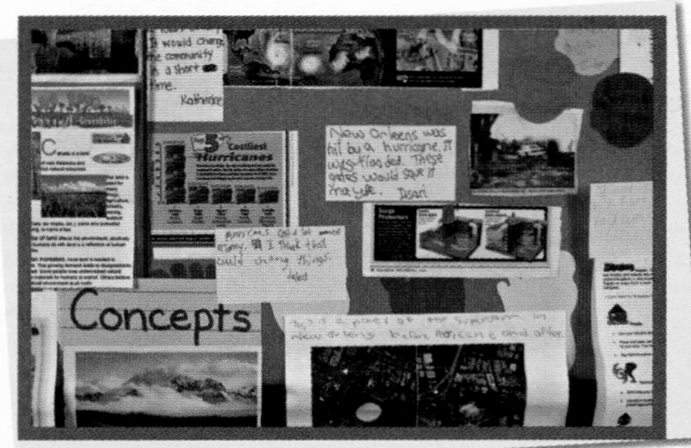

Inquiry Rubric

To assess Generating Ideas and Questions, see the Inquiry Rubrics in the Level Appendix.

Day 4 Language Arts

OBJECTIVES

Students will
- ✦ edit/proofread persuasive paragraphs.
- ✦ review spelling words.
- ✦ conduct an Internet search.
- ✦ conduct group discussions.

MATERIALS
- ✦ ***Transparencies*** 33, 33A, 17
- ✦ ***Skills Practice 2,*** p. 96
- ✦ Routine 16

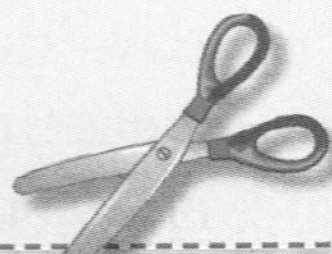

UNIT 5 Lesson 1

Revising Use this checklist to revise your persuasive paragraph.
- ☐ Is your main idea clearly stated?
- ☐ Do your facts and feelings support your main idea?
- ☐ Is your most convincing detail in the last sentence?
- ☐ Are your reasons or facts true?

Editing/Proofreading Use this checklist to correct mistakes.
- ☐ Did you use correct spelling?
- ☐ Did you indent the first line of your paragraph?
- ☐ Does each sentence begin with a capital letter?
- ☐ Does every sentence have correct punctuation?

Publishing Use this checklist to prepare your persuasive paragraph for publication.
- ☐ Neatly rewrite or type a final copy.
- ☐ If you plan to give an oral presentation, practice reading your paragraph out loud.
- ☐ If possible, submit your paragraph to the school newspaper.

96 UNIT 5 • Lesson 1 Writing • *Skills Practice 2*

Skills Practice 2, p. 96

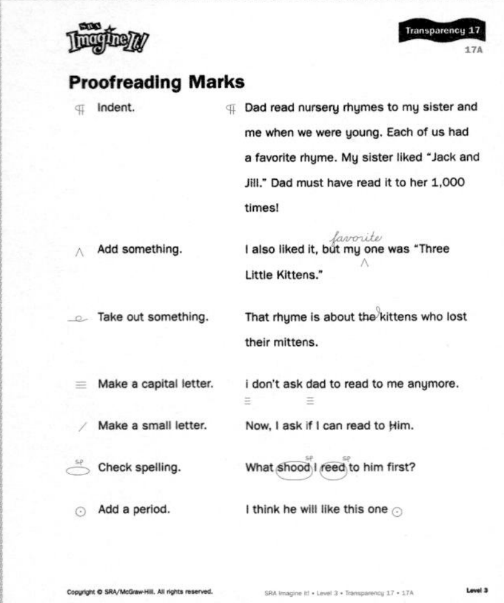

Imagine It! Transparency 17 17A

Proofreading Marks

¶ Indent.	¶ Dad read nursery rhymes to my sister and me when we were young. Each of us had a favorite rhyme. My sister liked "Jack and Jill." Dad must have read it to her 1,000 times!
^ Add something.	I also liked it, but my ^favorite one was "Three Little Kittens."
Take out something.	That rhyme is about the kittens who lost their mittens.
≡ Make a capital letter.	i don't ask dad to read to me anymore.
/ Make a small letter.	Now, I ask if I can read to Him.
Check spelling.	What shood I reed to him first?
⊙ Add a period.	I think he will like this one ⊙

Copyright © SRA/McGraw-Hill. All rights reserved. SRA Imagine It! • Level 3 • Transparency 17 • 17A Level 3

Transparency 17

Writing Persuasive Paragraph

Editing/Proofreading

ROUTINE 16

Teach

- ✦ Remind students of the proofreading marks they are to use by displaying ***Transparency*** 17.
- ✦ Use Routine 16. Tell students it is time to edit/proofread their persuasive paragraphs.
- ✦ Remind students that when editing, they will be making corrections to spelling, punctuation, capitalization, and grammar.
- ✦ Encourage students to review verb choices and tense. Tell students that the verb tense should be the same throughout their paragraphs.

Guided Practice

- ✦ Model editing and proofreading grammar with ***Transparencies*** 33 and 33A, or by using the persuasive paragraph you created earlier.
- ✦ Have students turn to ***Skills Practice 2*** page 96 to read and discuss the editing/proofreading checklist.

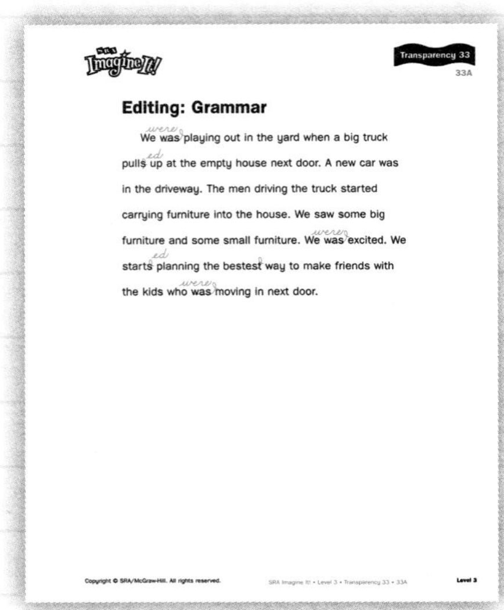

Imagine It! Transparency 33 33A

Editing: Grammar

We was playing out in the yard when a big truck pulls up at the empty house next door. A new car was in the driveway. The men driving the truck started carrying furniture into the house. We saw some big furniture and some small furniture. We was excited. We starts planning the bestest way to make friends with the kids who was moving in next door.

Copyright © SRA/McGraw-Hill. All rights reserved. SRA Imagine It! • Level 3 • Transparency 33 • 33A Level 3

Transparencies 33, 33A

Writing, continued

Apply

- **Composing—Editing/Proofreading** Have students edit/proofread their persuasive paragraphs. Remind them to refer to the checklist on page 96 in ***Skills Practice 2.***
- After students have finished editing/proofreading, encourage them to begin the final drafts of their persuasive paragraphs.

Monitor Progress to Differentiate Instruction

Formal Assessment

Editing/Proofreading Note whether students catch and correct errors in grammar.

APPROACHING LEVEL

IF . . . students need to practice editing for grammar,	**THEN . . .** have them work with a partner on editing for grammar during Workshop.

ON LEVEL

IF . . . students have an understanding of editing/proofreading,	**THEN . . .** have them complete their edits and begin their final drafts during Workshop.

ABOVE LEVEL

IF . . . students need a challenge,	**THEN . . .** have them check for verb tense errors and then write their final drafts during Workshop.

Spelling

Prefixes *re-, un-, pre-, mis-*

Teach

Conventions Strategy Tell students that they can use their knowledge of the rules for adding prefixes to words to determine how to change the meaning of new words by adding prefixes that they already know.

Guided Practice

Write the following columns on the board. Then have volunteers come to the board to add the prefix to the base word to create a new word.

re	+	read	=	________ *reread*
un	+	load	=	________ *unload*
mis	+	place	=	________ *misplace*
pre	+	shrunk	=	________ *preshrunk*
mis	+	spell	=	________ *misspell*

Study Skills

Conducting an Internet Search

Teach

- ✦ Remind students that it is important to know how to use search engines when conducting an Internet search. Choosing specific words carefully will help narrow the research criteria. This helps researchers find the information they need more quickly.
- ✦ Remind students that it is also important to use special keywords and characters, such as *and, or,* and quotation marks, to help narrow their search.

Guided Practice

Write this sentence on the board: *I want to learn more about Everglades National Park in Florida*. Ask students what words and characters they would use in a search engine to find the best information about the topic. **Possible Answer** *Everglades National Park*

Apply

Using the unit theme, Communities across Time, have students conduct an Internet search about their hometown or another location in which they are interested. Remind them to use keywords and characters. Tell them they can look up information about when their town was first settled, when it became a town or a city, or what it was like during a certain period in history.

Differentiating Instruction **English Learner**

IF . . . students need to develop vocabulary related to computer technology **THEN . . .** ask a proficient English speaker to teach this vocabulary by pointing and demonstrating.

Listening/Speaking/Viewing

Group Discussions

Teach

- Have students discuss the proper way to conduct a class discussion. Remind students that interacting with others involves two steps: listening and speaking. We take turns listening and speaking to one another, sharing information, acquiring information, and reacting to one another's thoughts or comments.
- Ask students how imagination plays a part in conversations. *We can use our imaginations to discuss any topic.*
- Remind students that nonverbal cues are also very important when communicating with others.

Guided Practice

Ask students to imagine what Chrissy and Jenny in "The House on Maple Street" might have discussed and thought about the arrowhead and china tea cup. Ask students to share a time they found something and wondered who had lost it or where it had come from.

Apply

- In small groups, have students share a time when they found an object. Did they wonder where it had been and who had lost it? What kind of object was it? Have students discuss what kinds of objects they would like to find. Have they ever looked for objects in their backyards, in a park, or on a beach? Remind students to take turns speaking and listening and to be considerate of one another.
- Remind the groups to make an effort to include each member in the conversation and to use verbal and nonverbal cues. Nonverbal cues sometimes signal to other members of the group when one person is finished speaking, or they may signal whose turn is next. Tell students that each person in the group should have the opportunity to vocalize his or her ideas.

Differentiating Instruction **English Learner**

IF . . . students are hesitant to participate in small groups, **THEN . . .** encourage proficient English-speaking group members to invite English Learners to participate. You may wish to assign one proficient English speaker to be the partner of each English Learner and to help the English Learner participate.

Preparing to Read

Review

OBJECTIVES

Students will

- review the prefixes *re-*, *un-*, *pre-*, and *mis-*.
- build fluency.

MATERIALS

Transparencies 130 and 133

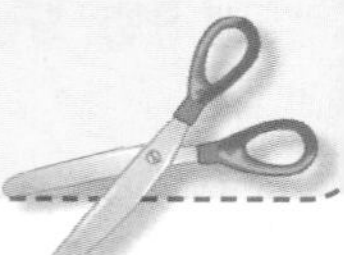

Word Structure

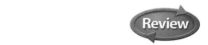

Use ***Transparency*** 130 with the word lines from Days 1 and 2 to review the prefixes *re-* and *un-*. Have students read the words on the word lines. Then have volunteers define each word and use it in a sentence.

Line 1	make	remake	play	replay
Line 2	read	reread	start	restart
Line 3	happy	unhappy	lucky	unlucky
Line 4	tie	untie	wrap	unwrap

Word Structure

Use ***Transparency*** 133 with the word lines from Days 3 and 4 to review the prefixes *pre-* and *mis-*. Have students read the words on the word lines. Then have students define each word and use it in a sentence.

Line 1	pay	prepay	heat	preheat
Line 2	school	preschool	view	preview
Line 3	count	miscount	behave	misbehave
Line 4	place	misplace	spell	misspell

OBJECTIVES

Students will

- review selection vocabulary.
- review the comprehension strategies Adjusting Reading Speed and Visualizing.
- review the comprehension skills Author's Purpose, Classify and Categorize, and Fact and Opinion.
- review fluency.

MATERIALS

- ***Student Reader,*** Book 2, pp. 128–145
- ***Transparency*** 132

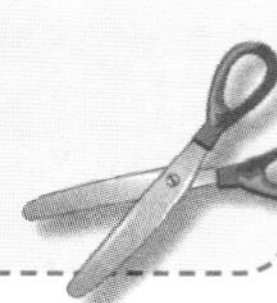

Selection Vocabulary

To review the selection vocabulary with students, organize them into small groups of three or four. Give each group two or three words. Ask each group to write a definition for each vocabulary word in their own words. When they are finished, have a volunteer from each group share their definitions with the class.

Selection Vocabulary

fierce (fērs) *adj.* strong and wild; raging (page 131)

sturdy (stûr´• dē) *adj.* strong; hardy (page 131)

stump (stump) *n.* part of tree left over after cutting away at the trunk (page 134)

settlers (set´• tlûrz) *n.* plural form of **settler:** a person who makes a new home in a new land or country (page 135)

burrows (bûr´• rowz) *n.* plural form of **burrow:** a hole in the ground where some animals live (page 135)

trickle (trik´• əl) *n.* a small amount (page 140)

crumbling (krum´• bəl • ing) *v.* a form of the verb **crumble:** to fall to pieces (page 141)

treasures (trezh´• ûrz) *n.* plural form of **treasure:** something special; a keepsake (page 143)

Comprehension Strategies 

Review the following comprehension strategies with students:

- **Adjusting Reading Speed** helps readers slow down and reread to obtain all the information in a text. Ask students to review "The House on Maple Street" and find passages where this strategy helped them read certain sections of this story more easily and fluently.
- **Visualizing** requires readers to mentally picture the events or characters in a story, resulting in a more vivid and imaginative understanding of the story. Ask students to revisit the text and share a visualization they made about the story with the class. Have students explain how visualizing helped them better understand "The House on Maple Street."

Comprehension Skills   

Review the following comprehension skills with students:

- **Classify and Categorize** helps readers put similar things or ideas together to make new information easier to understand and remember. Have students review "The House on Maple Street," and explain how this strategy helps them better understand the story.
- **Fact and Opinion** is the reader's understanding of the difference between facts, which can be verified or tested, and opinions, which are judgments that cannot be tested and that may vary between sources. Ask students to find examples of facts and opinions in "The House on Maple Street." Have students explain how they know what information is fact and what information is opinion.
- **Author's Purpose** allows readers to determine the purpose the author had for writing the text. Readers can then sort out what is important in a text from what is less important. Knowing the author's purpose also gives readers an idea of what they can expect to find in the text. Review the author's purpose of "The House on Maple Street." Have students find examples in the story that support their ideas about the author's purpose.

Reading with a Writer's Eye

Review

Review the following literary elements with students:

- **Plot** is a sequence of events that happen in a story. It explains a goal and whether it was attained or a problem and whether it was solved. Have students find the sequence of events in the story "The House on Maple Street." As students locate the sequence of events, write their responses on a time line on the board. Have students explain how the sequence is important in the telling of the story.
- **Setting** is the time and place or places where the story takes place. Ask students to review the setting in "The House on Maple Street." Have students explain why setting is important to the story.

Fluency

Review fluency by modeling pace for students. Remind students that pace, or reading with an appropriate speed, adds to the meaning of text by making it easier to comprehend and enjoy. Read aloud a passage from pages 140–143 from "The House on Maple Street." Make sure that the passage totals at least 160 words to ensure an appropriate practice length.

Have students read the passage chorally. Remind students to pay attention to the pace of their reading. Also remind students to pause after commas and end punctuation.

OBJECTIVES

Students will
- publish persuasive writing.
- take the spelling posttest.
- practice cursive *N* and *M*.

MATERIALS

- ***Skills Practice 2,*** p. 96
- ***Transparency*** 131
- Routine 17

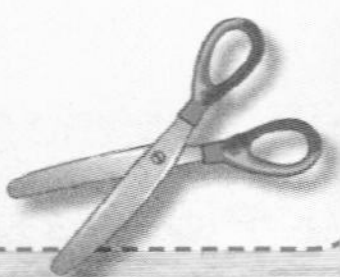

Writing Persuasive Paragraph

Publishing

ROUTINE 17

Teach

- Use Routine 17 as a model for publishing. Because other people will be reading their persuasive paragraphs and each student has a paragraph to share, have students create a class newspaper so other students in the school can read the paragraphs.
- Encourage students to add artwork, such as illustrations or photographs, to the newspaper to help illustrate their ideas.

Guided Practice

- Display an example of a class or school newspaper. Show students how to cut and paste their paragraphs onto chart paper in order to make a class newspaper. Provide examples of topics and how to organize their paragraphs into topics in a newspaper. You may want to use the students' paragraphs as examples of topics.
- Have students turn to ***Skills Practice 2*** page 96, and have a student read the publishing checklist aloud.

Apply

- **Composing—Publishing** Students should use page 96 in ***Skills Practice 2*** as a guide to publishing their persuasive paragraphs. Encourage students as a class to organize their persuasive paragraphs by topic before placing them in the newspaper. Have them choose headings for each topic and a title for the newspaper. After students have assembled their newspaper, have them take turns reading their persuasive paragraphs to the class.
- Have volunteers discuss whether the paragraphs were persuasive and convinced them to feel or believe the way the writer intended. Ask students if they were persuaded to take action.

Teacher Tip

ASSESSMENT Use the Writing Rubrics found in the Level Appendix to evaluate students' persuasive paragraphs. You may use any of the rubrics for Genre, Writing Process, and Writing Traits.

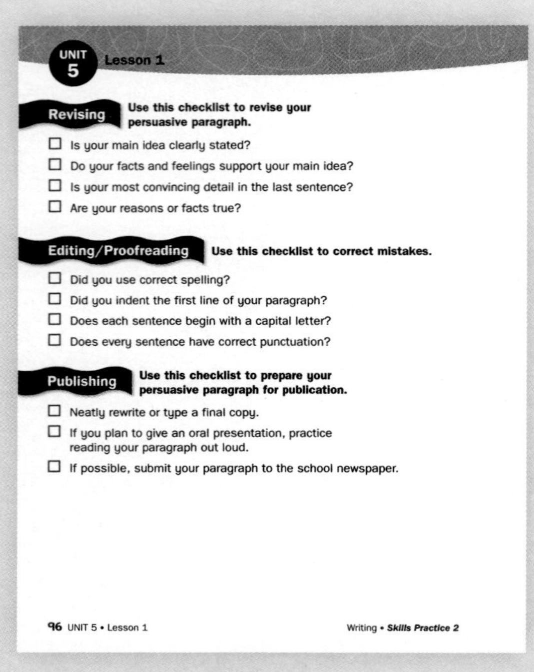

UNIT 5 Lesson 1

Revising Use this checklist to revise your persuasive paragraph.

- ☐ Is your main idea clearly stated?
- ☐ Do your facts and feelings support your main idea?
- ☐ Is your most convincing detail in the last sentence?
- ☐ Are your reasons or facts true?

Editing/Proofreading Use this checklist to correct mistakes.

- ☐ Did you use correct spelling?
- ☐ Did you indent the first line of your paragraph?
- ☐ Does each sentence begin with a capital letter?
- ☐ Does every sentence have correct punctuation?

Publishing Use this checklist to prepare your persuasive paragraph for publication.

- ☐ Neatly rewrite or type a final copy.
- ☐ If you plan to give an oral presentation, practice reading your paragraph out loud.
- ☐ If possible, submit your paragraph to the school newspaper.

96 UNIT 5 • Lesson 1 Writing • *Skills Practice 2*

Skills Practice 2, p. 96

Spelling

Prefixes *re-, un-, pre-, mis-*

Teach

Ask students to write *Spelling* and their names in the top margin of a clean piece of paper. Have them number the first fifteen lines 1–15, then skip a line and number the next two lines 1–2. Read each word, use it in a sentence, and give students time to spell it correctly. Encourage students to try to spell the challenge words, but assure them that misspelling a challenge word will not affect their test scores.

Spelling Words		**Challenge Words**
mismatch	preheat	preschool
unclear	restart	unaware
reread	prefix	
refund	unfair	
unzip	recount	
misprint	misplace	
unload	preview	
mislead		

Guided Practice

✦ Have students proofread for any mistakes they made on the post-test. Tell them to categorize the mistakes as
- careless errors.
- errors in spelling words with the prefix *re-, un-, pre-,* or *mis-*.

✦ Make certain students are spelling words with the prefixes *re-, un-, pre-,* and *mis-* correctly.

Penmanship

Cursive Letters *N* and *M*

Teach

✦ Review cursive *N* and cursive *M* with students, using ***Transparency*** 131 if necessary.

- **Letter *N*** Starting point, undercurve
Slant down
Retrace up slant
Overcurve down into undercurve:
capital *N*
- **Letter *M*** Starting point, undercurve
Slant down
Retrace up slant, overcurve
Slant down, retrace up slant
Overcurve down into undercurve:
capital *M*

✦ To model proper letter formation, write the following sentence on the board: *Nancy and Miguel live in New Mexico.*

Guided Practice

Ask a volunteer to write the sentence on the board. Assist the student as needed.

Apply

After reviewing the sentence that you wrote on the board, have students practice writing the sentence on a separate piece of paper. Ask students to circle their best sentence based on the correct formation of *N* and *M*.

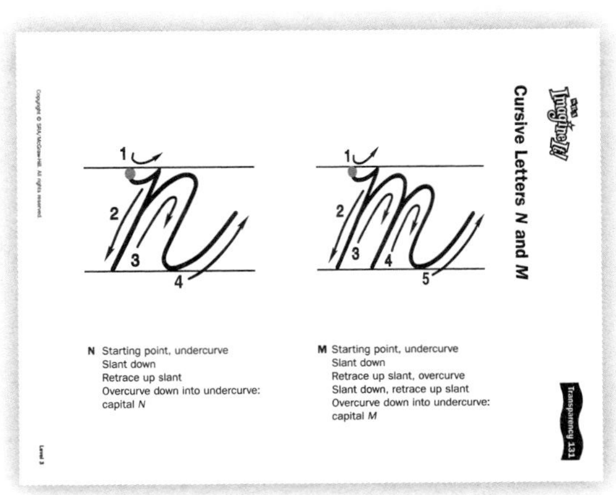

Transparency 131

Language Arts Review

OBJECTIVES

Students will

- review conducting Internet searches.
- review the importance of participating in group discussions.
- review sentence tense.

MATERIALS

Lesson Assessment Book 2, pp. 43–50

Study Skills

Conducting an Internet Search

- Remind students that successfully conducting Internet searches will be useful for unit investigations and other assignments.
- Ask students in what subjects they might conduct Internet searches. *science assignment, social studies assignment, writing assignment, and so on*
- Ask students what it means to conduct a keyword search. **Possible Answer** *using the main words with "and" or "or" to conduct a search on the Internet*
- Ask students to discuss what they learned about their hometown or the town or city they researched on the Internet. Ask them what they found most interesting.

Listening/Speaking/Viewing

Group Discussions

Remind students that when engaged in a group discussion, it is important to both listen attentively and speak clearly.

- Organize students into small groups.
- Have students discuss what they learned from "The House on Maple Street." Have them talk about how they might use this information in their unit investigations. Have students also discuss what the enjoyed about the story.
- Remind students that everyone in the group should have a chance to speak and be heard.

Grammar, Usage, and Mechanics

Verb Tenses

Write the following sentences on the board. Have students fill in the blank with the correct tense of an appropriate verb. Possible answers follow.

- Mieko, Kanera, Barb, and Lyndy ________ together every day. *play*
- Mieko, Kanera, Barb, and Lyndy ________ until dusk last evening. *played*
- Mieko, Kanera, Barb, and Lyndy ________ together every day this coming summer. *will play*

Have students select a previous writing piece from their writing portfolios. You may want to suggest one of the creative pieces. Have students edit their writing for correct verb tense. Remind students that if the plot of the story is happening in the past, the verbs will be in the past tense. If the plot is happening in the future, the verbs will be in the future tense.

Monitor Progress
Formal Assessment

Use pages 43–50 in ***Lesson Assessment Book 2*** to assess students' understanding of the skills taught in this lesson. Intervene with ***Reteach, Challenge Activities, Intervention Guide, eSkills & eGames, Leveled Readers,*** or activities in the ***Workshop Kit*** as needed.

Lesson Planner

	Day 1	Day 2
Preparing to Read MATERIALS ✦ ***Transparencies*** 134, 138 ✦ Routine 10 ✦ ***Skills Practice 2,*** pp. 103–106	**Daily News,** p. T114 **Word Structure** Prefixes *bi-* and *mid-*, pp. T114–T115	**Daily News,** p. T132 **Word Structure,** p. T133 **Developing Oral Language,** p. T133
Reading and Responding MATERIALS ✦ ***Student Reader,*** Book 2, pp. 148–163 ✦ ***Transparencies*** 15, 35, 135 ✦ ***Home Connection,*** pp. 53–54 ✦ Routines 11, 13, 14, A ✦ ***Skills Practice 2,*** pp. 93–94, 107–110 ✦ ***Listening Library CD*** ✦ Writer's Notebook ✦ ***Leveled Readers*** ✦ ***Lesson Assessment Book 2***	**Build Background,** p. T116 **Preview and Prepare,** p. T117 **Selection Vocabulary,** pp. T118–T119 **Reading the Selection,** pp. T120–T123 1st READ **Comprehension Strategies** ☆ Asking Questions, pp. T120, T124, T125 • Clarifying, pp. T121, T124 • Summarizing, pp. T121, T125 **Inquiry,** pp. T126–T127	**Comprehension Strategies** ☆ Asking Questions, p. T134 • Clarifying, pp. T134, T135 • Summarizing, p. T135 **Discussing the Selection,** p. T136 **Review Selection Vocabulary,** p. T137 **Fluency,** p. T137 **Theme Connections,** pp. T138–T139
Language Arts MATERIALS ✦ ***Transparencies*** 136, 137, 139, 139A ✦ ***Skills Practice 2,*** pp. 111–118 ✦ ***Language Arts Handbook,*** pp. 168–170, 312 ✦ Routines 15, 16, 17 ✦ ***Lesson Assessment Book 2,*** pp. 51–58	**Writing** Prewriting, pp. T128–T129 **Spelling Pretest,** p. T129 **Penmanship,** Cursive letters *P* and *R*, p. T130	**Writing** Drafting, pp. T140–T141 **Spelling,** p. T141 **Grammar, Usage, and Mechanics** Prepositions and Prepositional Phrases, pp. T142–T143
Monitor Progress ✓ = Formal Assessment	✓ **Word Structure, p. T115** ✓ **Comprehension Strategy, p. T121** ✓ **Spelling Pretest, p. T129**	✓ **Word Structure, p. T133** ✓ **Selection Vocabulary, p. T137** **Fluency, p. T137** ✓ **Grammar, Usage, and Mechanics, p. T143**

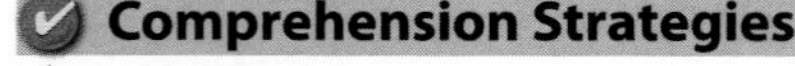

Literature Overview

Student Reader

Days of Digging

from Archaeologists: Life Digging Up Artifacts

by Holly Cefrey

Social Studies Inquiry

John Muir: Mountain Man

SRA
Imagine It!

★ Phonics ★ Fluency ★ Vocabulary ★ Comprehension

Day 3

Daily News, p. T144
Word Structure
Prefixes *dis-* and *auto-*, pp. T144–T145

Comprehension Skill
- Drawing Conclusions, p. T146

2nd READ

Reading with a Writer's Eye, p. T147
Supporting the Reading
Comprehension Strategy: Asking Questions, p. T148
Fluency, p. T149
Inquiry, p. T149

Writing
Revising, p. T150
Spelling, p. T151
Study Skills
Interviews, p. T152
Grammar, Usage, and Mechanics, pp. T153

Word Structure, p. T145
Comprehension Strategy, p. T148
Fluency, p. T149
Spelling, p. T151
Study Skills, p. T152

Day 4

Daily News, p. T154
Word Structure, p. T155
Developing Oral Language, p. T155

Comprehension Skill
- Drawing Conclusions, pp. T156

Social Studies Inquiry, pp. T158–T159
Inquiry, pp. T160–T161

Writing
Editing/Proofreading, pp. T162–T163
Spelling, p. T163
Study Skills, p. T164
Listening/Speaking/Viewing
Following Directions, p. T165

Word Structure, p. T155
Writing, p. T163

Day 5 Review

Word Structure, p. T166

Selection Vocabulary, p. T167
Comprehension Strategies
Asking Questions, p. T168
- Clarifying, p. T168
- Summarizing, p. T168

Comprehension Skill
Drawing Conclusions, p. T168
Reading with a Writer's Eye, p. T169
Fluency, p. T169

Writing
Publishing, p. T170
Spelling Posttest, p. T171
Penmanship, p. T171
Study Skills, p. T172
Listening/Speaking/Viewing, p. T172
Grammar, Usage, and Mechanics, p. T173

Spelling Posttest, p. T171
***Lesson Assessment Book 2*, pp. 51–58**

Student Resources

Genre

Expository Text is nonfiction that is written to inform, to explain, or to persuade.

Comprehension Strategy

Asking Questions
As you read, ask yourself questions about things or ideas in the selection that you do not understand.

Days of Digging

by Holly Cefrey

Focus Questions

What are different ways you can find out about ancient cultures and civilizations? How have past and present cultures left their marks on your community?

150

151

Student Reader, Book 2, pp. 150–161

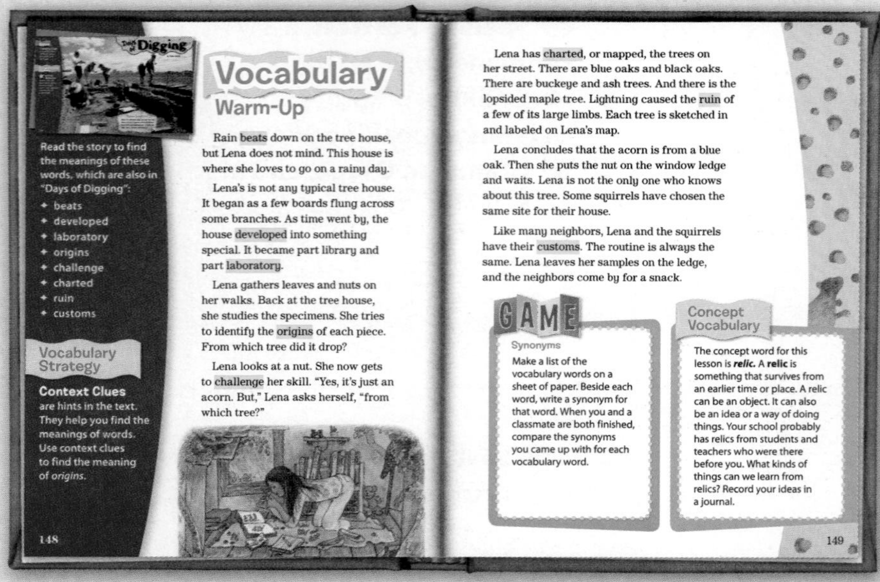

Vocabulary Warm-Up

Read the story to find the meanings of these words, which are also in "Days of Digging":

- beats
- developed
- laboratory
- origins
- challenge
- charted
- ruin
- customs

Vocabulary Strategy

Context Clues are hints in the text. They help you find the meanings of words. Use context clues to find the meaning of *origins*.

Rain beats down on the tree house, but Lena does not mind. This house is where she loves to go on a rainy day.

Lena's is not any typical tree house. It began as a few boards flung across some branches. As time went by, the house developed into something special. It became part library and part laboratory.

Lena gathers leaves and nuts on her walks. Back at the tree house, she studies the specimens. She tries to identify the origins of each piece. From which tree did it drop?

Lena looks at a nut. She now gets to challenge her skill. "Yes, it's just an acorn. But," Lena asks herself, "from which tree?"

148

Lena has charted, or mapped, the trees on her street. There are blue oaks and black oaks. There are buckeye and ash trees. And there is the lopsided maple tree. Lightning caused the ruin of a few of its large limbs. Each tree is sketched in and labeled on Lena's map.

Lena concludes that the acorn is from a blue oak. Then she puts the nut on the window ledge and waits. Lena is not the only one who knows about this tree. Some squirrels have chosen the same site for their house.

Like many neighbors, Lena and the squirrels have their customs. The routine is always the same. Lena leaves her samples on the ledge, and the neighbors come by for a snack.

GAME

Synonyms

Make a list of the vocabulary words on a sheet of paper. Beside each word, write a synonym for that word. When you and a classmate are both finished, compare the synonyms you came up with for each vocabulary word.

Concept Vocabulary

The concept word for this lesson is ***relic.*** A **relic** is something that survives from an earlier time or place. A relic can be an object. It can also be an idea or a way of doing things. Your school probably has relics from students and teachers who were there before you. What kinds of things can we learn from relics? Record your ideas in a journal.

149

Student Reader, Book 2, pp. 148–149

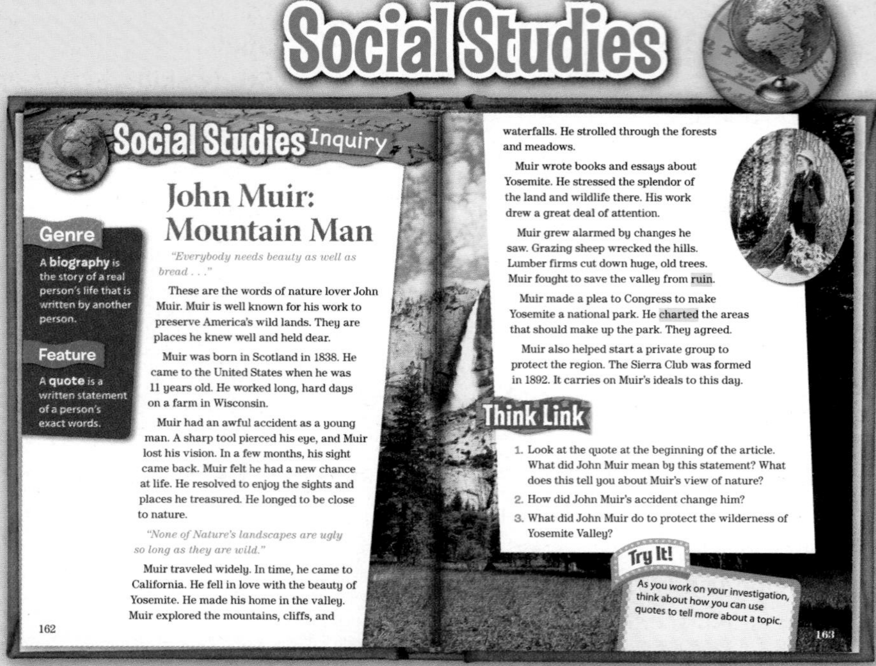

Social Studies

Social Studies Inquiry

John Muir: Mountain Man

Genre

A **biography** is the story of a real person's life that is written by another person.

Feature

A **quote** is a written statement of a person's exact words.

"Everybody needs beauty as well as bread . . ."

These are the words of nature lover John Muir. Muir is well known for his work to preserve America's wild lands. They are places he knew well and held dear.

Muir was born in Scotland in 1838. He came to the United States when he was 11 years old. He worked long, hard days on a farm in Wisconsin.

Muir had an awful accident as a young man. A sharp tool pierced his eye, and Muir lost his vision. In a few months, his sight came back. Muir felt he had a new chance at life. He resolved to enjoy the sights and places he treasured. He longed to be close to nature.

"None of Nature's landscapes are ugly so long as they are wild."

Muir traveled widely. In time, he came to California. He fell in love with the beauty of Yosemite. He made his home in the valley. Muir explored the mountains, cliffs, and waterfalls. He strolled through the forests and meadows.

162

Muir wrote books and essays about Yosemite. He stressed the splendor of the land and wildlife there. His work drew a great deal of attention.

Muir grew alarmed by changes he saw. Grazing sheep wrecked the hills. Lumber firms cut down huge, old trees. Muir fought to save the valley from ruin.

Muir made a plea to Congress to make Yosemite a national park. He charted the areas that should make up the park. They agreed.

Muir also helped start a private group to protect the region. The Sierra Club was formed in 1892. It carries on Muir's ideals to this day.

Think Link

1. Look at the quote at the beginning of the article. What did John Muir mean by this statement? What does this tell you about Muir's view of nature?
2. How did John Muir's accident change him?
3. What did John Muir do to protect the wilderness of Yosemite Valley?

Try It!

As you work on your investigation, think about how you can use quotes to tell more about a topic.

163

Student Reader, Book 2, pp. 162–163

Cross-Curricular Resources

Curriculum Connections

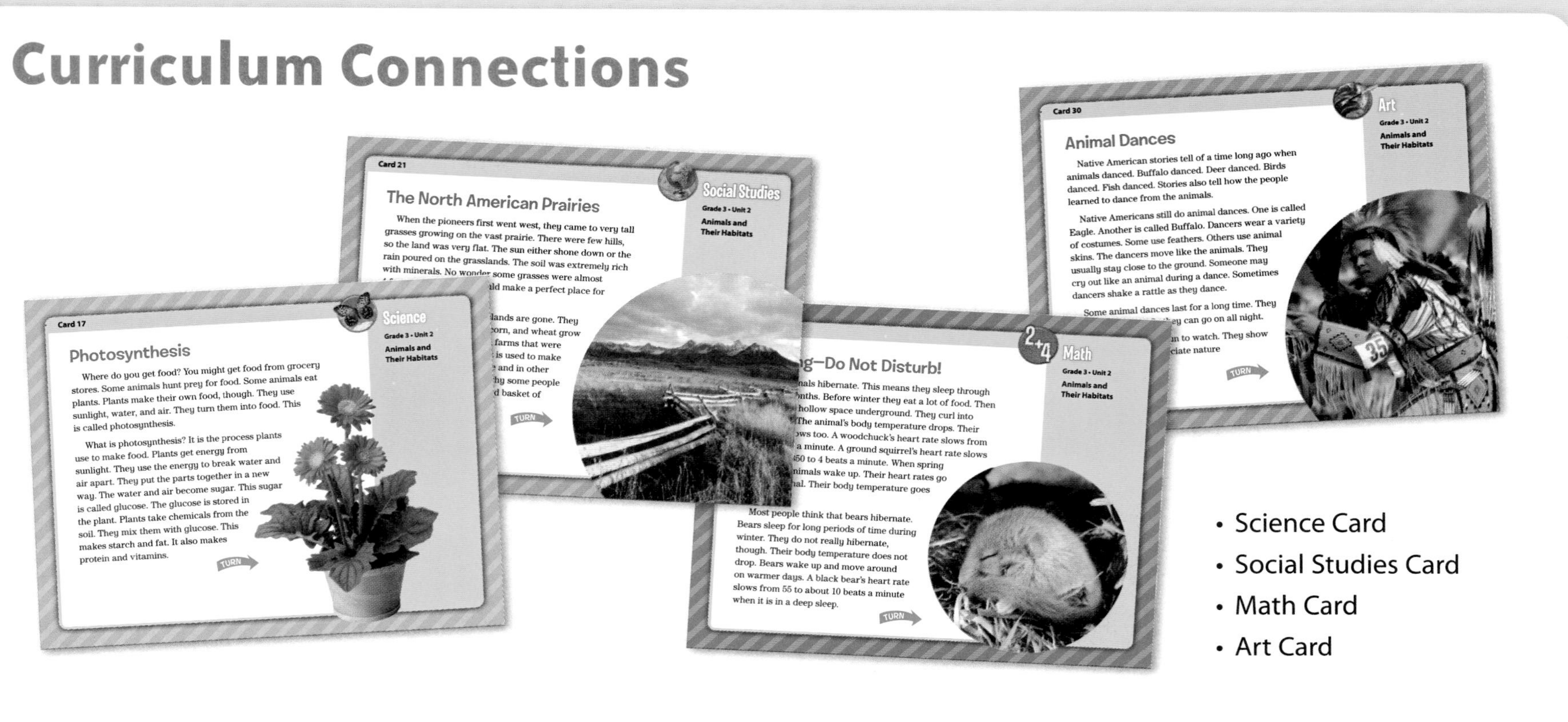

- Science Card
- Social Studies Card
- Math Card
- Art Card

Leveled Social Studies Readers

Approaching Level

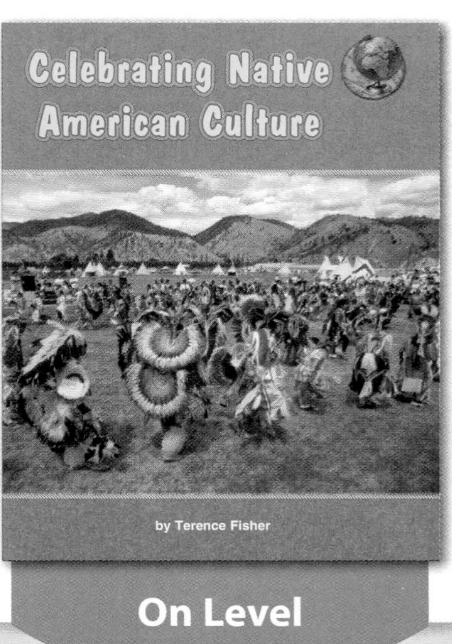

On Level

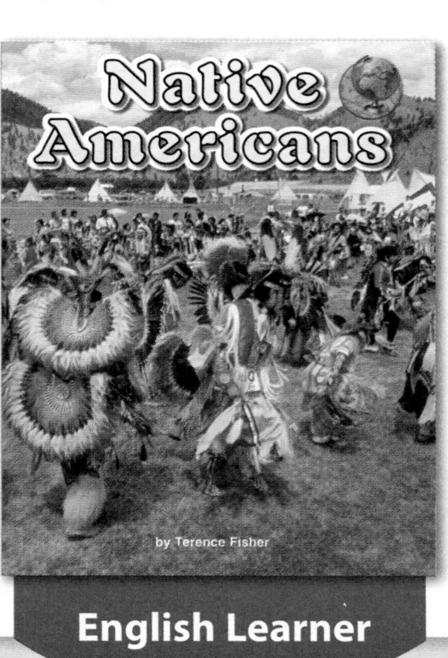

English Learner

Above Level

Lesson 2 Overview

Differentiating Instruction for Workshop

Day 1

	Approaching Level	On Level	English Learner	Above Level
Preparing to Read	**Word Structure:** Review the word lines with the prefixes *bi-* and *mid-*. Help small groups of students complete ***Reteach*** page 130, or work with them on the word structure activities in the ***Intervention Guide,*** Unit 5, Lesson 2.	**Word Structure:** Have students write lists of words with the prefixes *bi-* and *mid-* to add to the word lines.	**Word Structure:** Use the ***English Learner Support Guide*** for additional word structure instruction. Review the word lines with the prefixes *bi-* and *mid-*.	**Word Structure:** Have students complete ***Challenge Activities*** page 118. Students can then read other materials, looking for other words to add to the word lines.
Reading and Responding	**Vocabulary:** Have students create illustrations for the selection vocabulary words. **Comprehension:** Have students write possible answers to the Big Idea question. **Inquiry:** Have students work in groups to discuss questions about the communities that they would like to research.	**Vocabulary:** Have students use the selection vocabulary words to write sentences. **Comprehension:** Have students write a list of questions that they have about the story. **Inquiry:** Have students work in groups to discuss questions about the communities that they would like to research.	**Vocabulary:** Use ***English Learner Support Guide***, Unit 5, Lesson 2. **Comprehension:** Have students share a question they have about the selection with the class. Have students add their questions to the **Concept/Question Board**. **Inquiry:** Have students work in groups to discuss questions about the communities that they would like to research.	**Vocabulary:** Have students find similar words for the selection vocabulary words in a thesaurus. **Comprehension:** Have students begin a list of ideas about how this story relates to the unit theme. Place new ideas on the **Concept/Question Board.** **Inquiry:** Have students work in groups to discuss questions about the communities that they would like to research.
Language Arts	**Writing:** Have students create a two-column chart with what the reader does or feels on one side and the reasons on the other. **Spelling:** Have pairs of students study the spelling words in this lesson.	**Writing:** Have students work on ideas and graphic organizers. **Spelling:** Have students proofread their persuasive writing activity for spelling errors.	**Writing:** Have students read a speech that contains persuasion. **Spelling:** Have students rewrite one paragraph from their selections, spelling the words carefully.	**Writing:** Have students support their argument by adding researched facts and examples. **Spelling:** Have students pick five spelling words and use the letters from those words to correctly spell new words.

Day 2

	Approaching Level	On Level	English Learner	Above Level
Preparing to Read	**Word Structure:** Have students make flash cards for the prefixes *bi-* and *mid-*.	**Word Structure:** Have students write sentences using words from the word lines.	**Word Structure:** Have students make flash cards for the prefixes *bi-* and *mid-*. With a partner, have students write sentences using words from the word lines and read them aloud.	**Word Structure:** Have students write paragraphs using words from the word lines.
Reading and Responding	**Vocabulary:** Have students use ***Reteach*** page 132. **Comprehension:** Review any questions asked by students during the first day of reading. **Fluency:** Have students reread a passage from the story with a partner or individually.	**Vocabulary:** Have students complete a game in the ***Workshop Kit.*** **Comprehension:** Have students find a passage or idea they clarified while reading. Have students share with the class the method they used to clarify. **Fluency:** Have students read into a tape recorder at the beginning and end of the week. Have them listen to themselves at the end of the week so they can hear their progress.	**Vocabulary:** Help students find the selection vocabulary words in the story. Have students rewrite the sentences in the story using their own words. **Comprehension:** Have students summarize the selection. **Fluency:** Have students engage in echo reading with passages from the selection.	**Vocabulary:** Have students complete ***Challenge Activities*** page 120. **Comprehension:** Have students write a short summary of the selection so far. **Fluency:** Have students choose a text on their independent level to read silently.
Language Arts	**Writing:** Have students continue to draft their persuasive letters. **Spelling:** Have students work in groups to review this week's spelling word list. **Grammar, Usage, and Mechanics:** Have students complete ***Reteach*** page 134.	**Writing:** Have students conference with a partner. **Spelling:** Have students write on a piece of paper the meaning of each prefix in this lesson. **Grammar, Usage, and Mechanics:** Have students do a ***Workshop Kit*** activity.	**Writing:** Have students continue to draft their persuasive letters. **Spelling:** Have students work in pairs to brainstorm ideas to help them with their spelling. **Grammar, Usage, and Mechanics:** Refer to the ***English Learner Support Guide,*** Unit 5, Lesson 2.	**Writing:** Have students assess their writing and look for areas to revise. **Spelling:** Have students think of and spell four place words that were not in this lesson. **Grammar, Usage, and Mechanics:** Have students complete ***Challenge Activities*** page 122.

Lesson 2 Overview

Differentiating Instruction for Workshop

Day 3

	Approaching Level	On Level	English Learner	Above Level
Preparing to Read	**Word Structure:** Review the word lines. Then have students complete ***Reteach*** page 131, or work with them on the word structure activities in the ***Intervention Guide,*** Unit 5, Lesson 2**.**	**Word Structure:** Have students make lists of words with the prefixes *dis-* and *auto-* to add to the word lines.	**Word Structure:** Review the word lines and the instruction in the ***English Learner Support Guide,*** Unit 5, Lesson 2.	**Word Structure:** Have students complete ***Challenge Activities*** page 119. Then have students write short stories using words from the word lines.
Reading and Responding	**Vocabulary:** Have students write functional definitions for three of the selection vocabulary words. **Comprehension:** Have students review the elements of expository text. Ask students how this selection would be different if it had been written in another genre, such as narrative nonfiction, realistic fiction, or a biography. **Fluency:** Have students use ***Leveled Readers.***	**Vocabulary:** Have students find unfamiliar words and find the definitions in a dictionary. Have students use the words in their writing. **Comprehension:** Have students research archaeology using reference materials or the Internet. **Fluency:** Have students reread passages from the selection to a partner.	**Vocabulary:** Have students write three examples of three of the selection vocabulary words. **Comprehension:** Have students share stories of important artifacts that belong to their culture. For example, you could tell students that important artifacts that represent the United States are the Declaration of Independence, the Liberty Bell, and the Statue of Liberty. **Fluency:** Have students review fluency by using ***eFluency.***	**Vocabulary:** Have students design a board game that helps players learn the vocabulary words. **Comprehension:** Have students research important artifacts belonging to ancient cultures. For example, students might research ancient Roman, Egyptian, or Chinese artifacts. **Fluency:** Have students review fluency by using ***eFluency.***
Language Arts	**Writing:** Have students conference with a partner to help during revision. **Spelling:** Have students complete ***Reteach*** page 133. **Grammar, Usage, and Mechanics:** Have students add prepositional phrases to their persuasive paragraphs.	**Writing:** Have students revise their persuasive paragraphs. **Spelling:** Have students use five spelling words to write five sentences. In each sentence, have them spell the word incorrectly and trade sentences with a partner. Have each student correct the other's sentences. **Grammar, Usage, and Mechanics:** Have students add prepositional phrases to their writing.	**Writing:** Have students work with a partner to revise their persuasive letters. **Spelling:** Have students write *Place Words* and *Prefixes* on a separate sheet of paper and try to think of as many new words that fit under those headings as they can in one minute. **Grammar, Usage, and Mechanics:** Have student work with a partner to review prepositional phrases.	**Writing:** Have students conference with their peers. **Spelling:** Have students complete ***Challenge Activities*** page 121. **Grammar, Usage, and Mechanics:** Have students work with a less proficient student to complete grammar activities.

Day 4

	Approaching Level	On Level	English Learner	Above Level
Preparing to Read	**Word Structure:** Have students make flash cards for the prefixes *dis-* and *auto.*	**Word Structure:** Have pairs of students create clue sentences for the words on the word lines. Students can also use ***eSkills & eGames*** for practice with prefixes.	**Word Structure:** Have students make flash cards for the prefixes *dis-* and *auto-*. Then have students write sentences using words from the word lines.	**Word Structure:** Have pairs of students create clue sentences for the words on the word lines. Students also can use ***eSkills & eGames*** for practice with prefixes.
Reading and Responding	**Vocabulary:** Have students use the expanding vocabulary words in their writing. **Comprehension:** Have students write a journal entry explaining what archaeologists do. **Inquiry:** Have students read one of the ***Leveled Readers*** to get new ideas and raise new questions about the unit theme.	**Vocabulary:** Have students use a thesaurus to find related words to add to the Word Bank. **Comprehension:** Have students write a summary of "Days of Digging." **Inquiry:** Have students read one of the ***Leveled Readers*** to get new ideas and raise new questions about the unit theme.	**Vocabulary:** Have students find interesting words in the selection. Have them add the words and their meanings to their Writer's Notebooks. **Comprehension:** Have students research archaeology on the Internet. **Inquiry:** Have students read one of the ***Leveled Readers*** to get new ideas and raise new questions about the unit theme.	**Vocabulary:** Have students write a story using the selection vocabulary words. **Comprehension:** Have students research the Internet for information about careers in archaeology. **Inquiry:** Have students read one of the ***Leveled Readers*** to get new ideas and raise new questions about the unit theme.
Language Arts	**Writing:** Have students edit, proofread, and then begin the final draft of their persuasive letters. **Spelling:** Have students proofread their writing activity for spelling errors.	**Writing:** Have students search for graphics to accompany their final drafts. **Spelling:** Have students write five words that rhyme with spelling words on a piece of paper.	**Writing:** Have students work with peers to edit and proofread their persuasive letters. **Spelling:** Have students circle the spelling words with a prefix, underline the base word, and draw a box around the place words.	**Writing:** Have students use a word-processing program to complete the final draft of their persuasive letters. **Spelling:** Have students pick two spelling words and write four words each that rhyme with those words.

Lesson 2 Overview

Differentiating Instruction for Workshop

Day 5

	Approaching Level	On Level	English Learner	Above Level
Preparing to Read	**Word Structure:** Review the word lines. Then have students write sentences using words from the lines. Students can also use ***eSkills & eGames*** for practice with prefixes.	**Word Structure:** Have students play word detective by reading other materials while looking for words with the prefixes *bi-*, *mid-*, *dis-*, and *auto-*.	**Word Structure:** Review the word lines. Have pairs of students write sentences using words from the lines and read them aloud. Students also can use ***eSkills & eGames*** for practice with prefixes.	**Word Structure:** Have students play word detective by reading other materials while looking for words with the prefixes *bi-*, *mid-*, *dis-*, and *auto-*.
Reading and Responding	**Vocabulary:** Have students find additional archaeology-related words on the Internet or print reference materials. **Comprehension:** Have students create review questions for the story and then trade questions with a partner. **Fluency:** Have students write answers to comprehension questions from ***Leveled Readers.***	**Vocabulary:** Have students create riddles for three of the selection vocabulary words to share with the class. **Comprehension:** Have students review the **Concept/ Question Board.** Have students see whether any new information they learned after reading the selection can be applied to the Board. **Fluency:** Have students reread passages from the selection to a partner.	**Vocabulary:** Have students write extended sentences using the selection vocabulary. **Comprehension:** Have students discuss "Days of Digging." Have them write a short summary of the selection. **Fluency:** Have students use vocabulary from the ***Leveled Readers*** in extended sentences.	**Vocabulary:** Have students write a story using the selection vocabulary words. **Comprehension:** Have students discuss the elements of expository text in "Days of Digging." Have students discuss how the author's choice of genre contributes to the selection's meaning. **Fluency:** Have students read other articles about archaeology and artifacts.
Language Arts	**Writing:** Encourage students to share their persuasive letters. **Spelling:** Have students carefully rewrite a paragraph from their selection, while keeping an eye on spelling the words correctly.	**Writing:** Have students share their persuasive letters in a peer group before mailing them. **Spelling:** Have students make a list of five spelling words with one letter missing, trade papers with a partner, and fill in the blanks.	**Writing:** Encourage students to share their persuasive letters with others. **Spelling:** Have students choose five spelling words for a partner to spell on a piece of paper.	**Writing:** Encourage students to share their persuasive letter with other classes before mailing them. **Spelling:** Have students write an imaginary letter to someone using at least six spelling words.

Resources for

Differentiating Instruction 

Leveled Readers

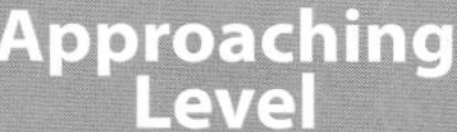

Approaching Level

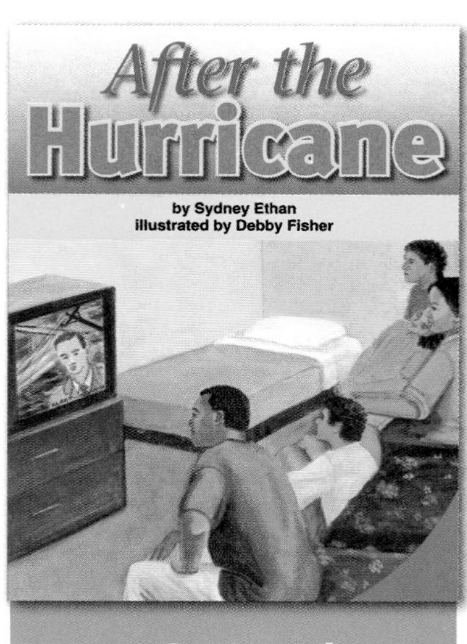

On Level

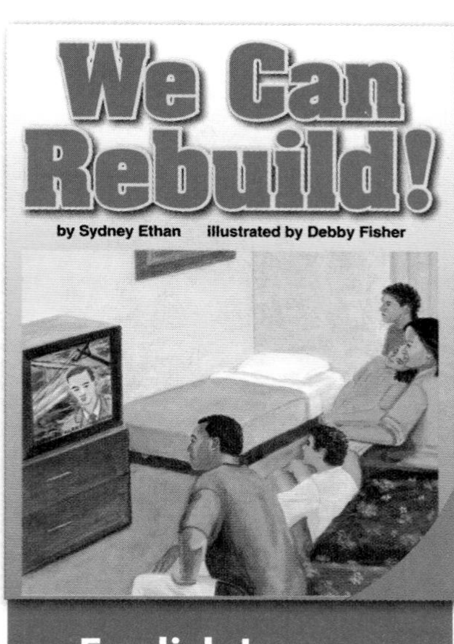

English Learner

Above Level

Additional Skills Practice

Approaching Level

Reteach

- Prefixes *bi-* and *mid-*, p. 130
- Prefixes *dis-* and *auto-*, p. 131
- Selection Vocabulary, p. 132
- Spelling, p. 133
- Prepositions and Prepositional Phrases, p. 134

On Level

Skills Practice 2

- Prefixes *bi-* and *mid-*, pp. 103–104
- Prefixes *dis-* and *auto-*, pp. 105–106
- Selection Vocabulary, pp. 107–108
- Writing a Persuasive Letter, pp. 111–112
- Spelling, pp. 113–114
- Prepositions and Prepositional Phrases, pp. 115–116

English Learner

English Learner Support Activities

Unit 5 Lesson 2

Above Level

Challenge Activities

- Prefixes *bi-* and *mid-*, p. 118
- Prefixes *dis-* and *auto-*, p. 119
- Selection Vocabulary, p. 120
- Spelling, p. 121
- Prepositions and Prepositional Phrases, p. 122

Additional Resources for Differentiating Instruction

Workshop Kit

Technology

The following electronic resources are available for students:

- ***eStudent Reader***
- ***eSkills & eGames***
- ***Listening Library CD***

Electronic resources for the teacher include:

- ***ePlanner***
- ***eTeacher's Edition***
- ***eAssess***
- ***ePresentation***

All technology components are available online and on CD-ROM.

English Learner

Leveled Reader

English Learner Support Activities, Lesson 2

Listening Library Unit 5

English Learner Support Guide, Lesson 2

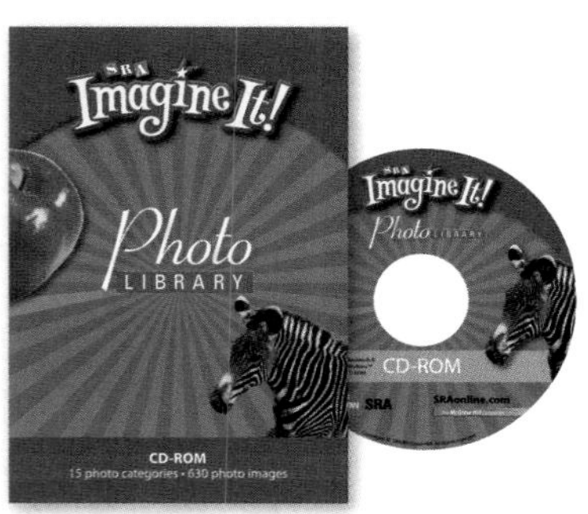

Photo Library

Approaching Level

Intervention

Intervention Workbook

Intervention Guide

Lesson 2 Overview

Lesson Assessment

Monitor Progress to Differentiate Instruction

Comprehension Strategies Rubrics

Use the Comprehension Strategies Rubrics to determine whether a student is using the strategies.

- Asking Questions, p. T120
- Clarifying, p. T121
- Summarizing, p. T121

Inquiry Rubrics

Use the Inquiry Rubrics to assess a student's performance throughout the stages of the investigation for each unit. In addition, at the end of the unit you can use the rubrics to assess the groups' collaborative work as well as an individual's participation in that group.

- Identifying a Question to Investigate, p. T161

Writing Rubrics

Use the writing rubrics in the Level Appendix to evaluate each student's persuasive letter.

- Genre
- Writing Process
- Writing Traits

Lesson Assessments

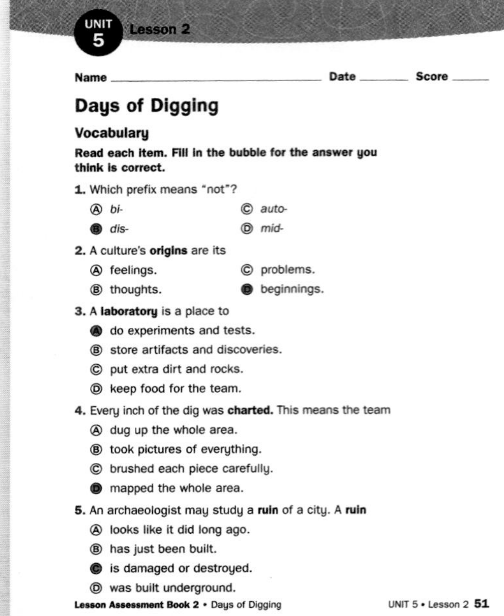

UNIT 5 Lesson 2

Name ____________ Date ______ Score ______

Days of Digging

Vocabulary

Read each item. Fill in the bubble for the answer you think is correct.

1. Which prefix means "not"?
   - Ⓐ *bi-*
   - ● *dis-*
   - Ⓒ *auto-*
   - Ⓓ *mid-*
2. A culture's **origins** are its
   - Ⓐ feelings.
   - Ⓑ thoughts.
   - Ⓒ problems.
   - ● beginnings.
3. A **laboratory** is a place to
   - ● do experiments and tests.
   - Ⓑ store artifacts and discoveries.
   - Ⓒ put extra dirt and rocks.
   - Ⓓ keep food for the team.
4. Every inch of the dig was **charted.** This means the team
   - Ⓐ dug up the whole area.
   - Ⓑ took pictures of everything.
   - Ⓒ brushed each piece carefully.
   - ● mapped the whole area.
5. An archaeologist may study a **ruin** of a city. A **ruin**
   - Ⓐ looks like it did long ago.
   - Ⓑ has just been built.
   - ● is damaged or destroyed.
   - Ⓓ was built underground.

Lesson Assessment Book 2 • Days of Digging UNIT 5 • Lesson 2 51

Lesson Assessment Book 2, p: 51

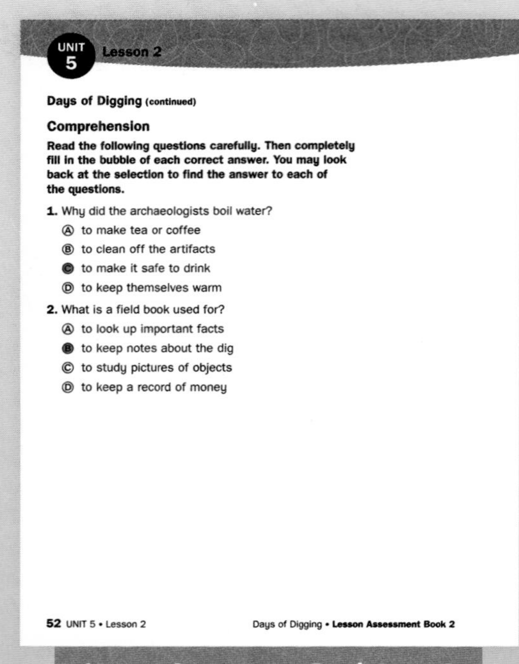

UNIT 5 Lesson 2

Days of Digging (continued)

Comprehension

Read the following questions carefully. Then completely fill in the bubble of each correct answer. You may look back at the selection to find the answer to each of the questions.

1. Why did the archaeologists boil water?
   - Ⓐ to make tea or coffee
   - Ⓑ to clean off the artifacts
   - ● to make it safe to drink
   - Ⓓ to keep themselves warm
2. What is a field book used for?
   - Ⓐ to look up important facts
   - ● to keep notes about the dig
   - Ⓒ to study pictures of objects
   - Ⓓ to keep a record of money

52 UNIT 5 • Lesson 2 Days of Digging • Lesson Assessment Book 2

Lesson Assessment Book 2, p. 52

Formal Assessment

Use these summative assessments along with your informal observations to assess student mastery.

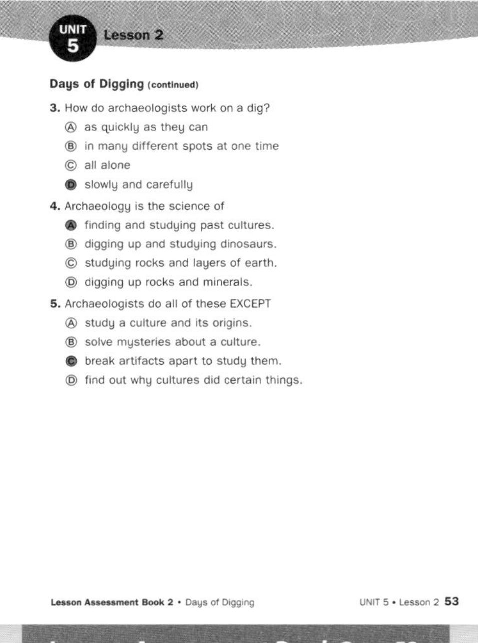

UNIT 5 Lesson 2

Days of Digging (continued)

3. How do archaeologists work on a dig?
   - Ⓐ as quickly as they can
   - Ⓑ in many different spots at one time
   - Ⓒ all alone
   - ● slowly and carefully
4. Archaeology is the science of
   - ● finding and studying past cultures.
   - Ⓑ digging up and studying dinosaurs.
   - Ⓒ studying rocks and layers of earth.
   - Ⓓ digging up rocks and minerals.
5. Archaeologists do all of these EXCEPT
   - Ⓐ study a culture and its origins.
   - Ⓑ solve mysteries about a culture.
   - ● break artifacts apart to study them.
   - Ⓓ find out why cultures did certain things.

Lesson Assessment Book 2 • Days of Digging UNIT 5 • Lesson 2 **53**

Lesson Assessment Book 2, p. 53

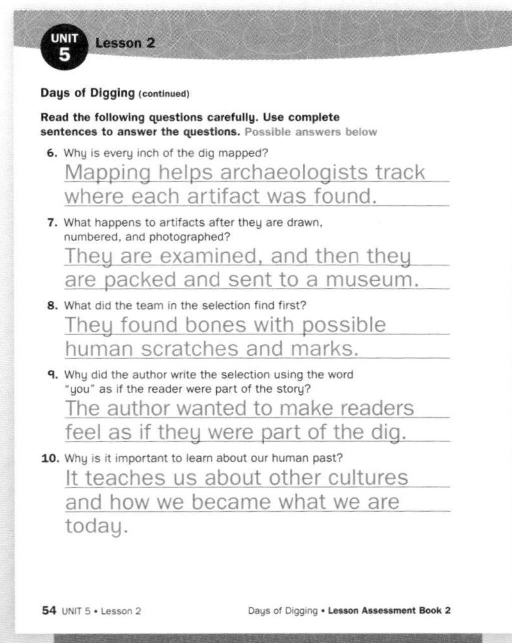

UNIT 5 Lesson 2

Days of Digging (continued)

Read the following questions carefully. Use complete sentences to answer the questions. Possible answers below

6. Why is every inch of the dig mapped?
   Mapping helps archaeologists track where each artifact was found.
7. What happens to artifacts after they are drawn, numbered, and photographed?
   They are examined, and then they are packed and sent to a museum.
8. What did the team in the selection find first?
   They found bones with possible human scratches and marks.
9. Why did the author write the selection using the word "you" as if the reader were part of the story?
   The author wanted to make readers feel as if they were part of the dig.
10. Why is it important to learn about our human past?
    It teaches us about other cultures and how we became what we are today.

54 UNIT 5 • Lesson 2 Days of Digging • **Lesson Assessment Book 2**

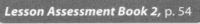

Lesson Assessment Book 2, p. 54

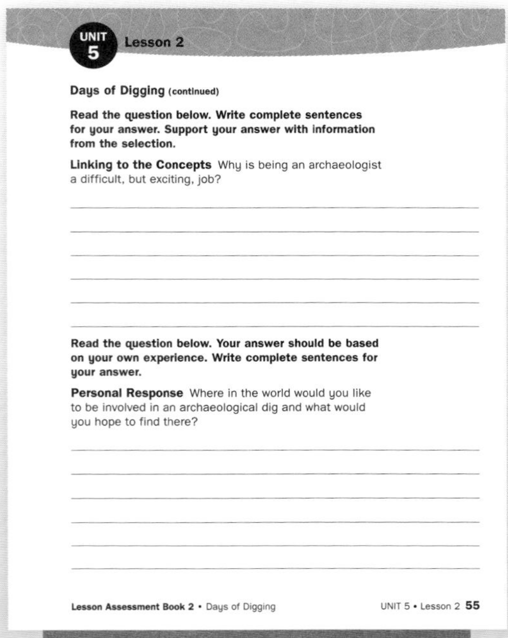

UNIT 5 Lesson 2

Days of Digging (continued)

Read the question below. Write complete sentences for your answer. Support your answer with information from the selection.

Linking to the Concepts Why is being an archaeologist a difficult, but exciting, job?

Read the question below. Your answer should be based on your own experience. Write complete sentences for your answer.

Personal Response Where in the world would you like to be involved in an archaeological dig and what would you hope to find there?

Lesson Assessment Book 2 • Days of Digging UNIT 5 • Lesson 2 **55**

Lesson Assessment Book 2, p. 55

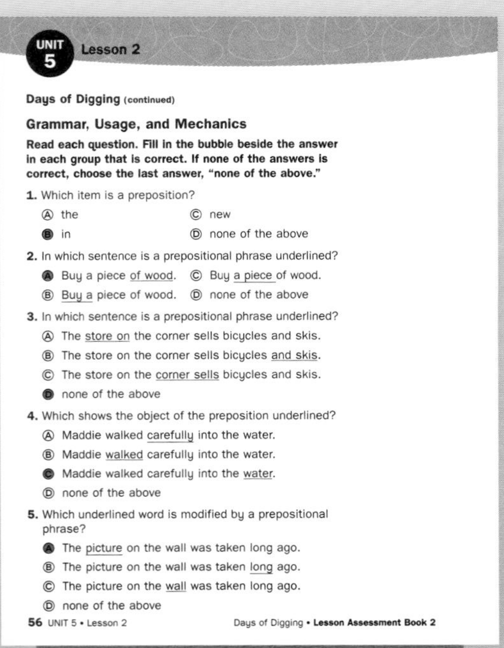

UNIT 5 Lesson 2

Days of Digging (continued)

Grammar, Usage, and Mechanics

Read each question. Fill in the bubble beside the answer in each group that is correct. If none of the answers is correct, choose the last answer, "none of the above."

1. Which item is a preposition?
   - Ⓐ the
   - Ⓒ new
   - ● in
   - Ⓓ none of the above
2. In which sentence is a prepositional phrase underlined?
   - ● Buy a piece <u>of wood</u>.
   - Ⓒ Buy <u>a piece</u> of wood.
   - Ⓑ <u>Buy a</u> piece of wood.
   - Ⓓ none of the above
3. In which sentence is a prepositional phrase underlined?
   - Ⓐ The <u>store on</u> the corner sells bicycles and skis.
   - Ⓑ The store on the corner sells bicycles <u>and skis</u>.
   - Ⓒ The store on the <u>corner sells</u> bicycles and skis.
   - ● none of the above
4. Which shows the object of the preposition underlined?
   - Ⓐ Maddie walked <u>carefully</u> into the water.
   - Ⓑ Maddie <u>walked</u> carefully into the water.
   - ● Maddie walked carefully into the <u>water</u>.
   - Ⓓ none of the above
5. Which underlined word is modified by a prepositional phrase?
   - ● The <u>picture</u> on the wall was taken long ago.
   - Ⓑ The picture on the wall was taken <u>long</u> ago.
   - Ⓒ The picture on the <u>wall</u> was taken long ago.
   - Ⓓ none of the above

56 UNIT 5 • Lesson 2 Days of Digging • **Lesson Assessment Book 2**

Lesson Assessment Book 2, p. 56

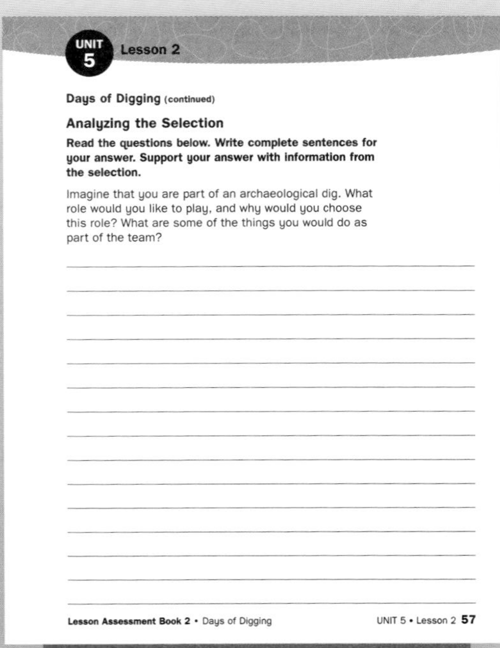

UNIT 5 Lesson 2

Days of Digging (continued)

Analyzing the Selection

Read the questions below. Write complete sentences for your answer. Support your answer with information from the selection.

Imagine that you are part of an archaeological dig. What role would you like to play, and why would you choose this role? What are some of the things you would do as part of the team?

Lesson Assessment Book 2 • Days of Digging UNIT 5 • Lesson 2 **57**

Lesson Assessment Book 2, p. 57

UNIT 5 Lesson 2

Days of Digging (continued)

Oral Fluency Assessment

Our National Bird

The bald eagle is one of the largest birds in America. It is 1–13
a beautiful bird. However, it is not bald. An eagle has white 14–25
feathers on its head. The eagle's name comes from an old word. 26–37
The word is *piebald*. It means "marked with white." 38–46
Most people do not know that eagles like to eat fish. This is 47–59
why they live near water. You can spot them at rivers, lakes, 60–71
and the ocean. 72–74
Bald eagles are rare. They are found only in America. That is 75–86
one reason why we made the bald eagle our national bird. 87–97
Many people like the eagle as a symbol for our country. 98–108
They like what the eagle stands for. It represents freedom and 109–119
strength for them. 120–122
Ben Franklin was not one of these people. He was not a fan 123–135
of the bald eagle. He once wrote a letter to his daughter. In it, 136–149
he said eagles robbed other birds. He also said eagles were not 150–161
brave. They flew away when small birds came after them. He 162–172
wanted the turkey to be the national bird. 173–180

EVALUATING CODES FOR ORAL FLUENCY

sky (/) words read incorrectly
blue ^ sky (^) inserted word
( ]) after the last word

READING RATE AND ACCURACY

Total Words Read: ____
Number of Errors: ____
Number of Correct Words Read Per Minute (WPM): ____
Accuracy Rate: ____
(Number of Correct Words Read per Minute ÷ Total Words Read)

READING FLUENCY

	Low	Average	High
Decoding ability	○	○	○
Pace	○	○	○
Syntax	○	○	○
Self-correction	○	○	○
Intonation	○	○	○

Record student rates on the Oral Fluency Scores pages.

58 UNIT 5 • Lesson 2 Days of Digging • **Lesson Assessment Book 2**

Lesson Assessment Book 2, p. 58

Day 1 **Preparing to Read**

OBJECTIVES

Students will
- ✦ identify and know the meanings of the prefixes *bi-* and *mid-*.
- ✦ build fluency.

MATERIALS

- ✦ ***Transparency*** 134
- ✦ Routine 10
- ✦ ***Skills Practice 2,*** pp. 103–104

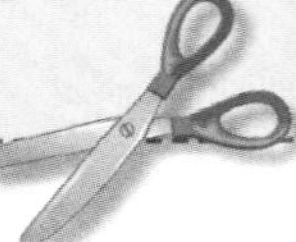

Daily Oral Practice

Daily News

Do you like digging in the dirt? Do you like making discoveries? Do you like science? If you answered "yes, yes, yes," then you should think about becoming an archaeologist. Archaeologists reconstruct the past to learn about its people and cultures.

- ✦ Write the daily news on the board or on chart paper. Then have students read the daily news in unison to practice fluency.
- ✦ As a word structure review from Lesson 1, ask a volunteer to identify any words in the message with the prefix *re-*. *reconstruct*

Differentiating Instruction **English Learner**

IF . . . students would benefit from practice with action verbs, **THEN . . .** ask them to identify all the action verbs in the daily news. *digging, making, answered, becoming, reconstruct*

Teacher Tips

DAILY NEWS The word *archaeologist* in the daily news will be hard for some students to prounounce. Before having students read the daily news, clearly pronounce *archaeologist* once for them, and have them repeat after you.

SYLLABICATION To help students blend words and build fluency, demonstrate syllabication using the decodable, multisyllabic words in the word lines.

cy • cle	bi • cy • cle
month • ly	bi • month • ly
bi • plane	week • ly
bi • week • ly	mid • day
mid • night	mid • point
sum • mer	mid • sum • mer

Word Structure

ROUTINE 10

The Prefixes *bi-* and *mid-*

- ✦ Write these word lines on the board or use ***Transparency*** 134. The words in boldface are in "Days of Digging."

Line 1	cycle	bicycle	monthly	bimonthly
Line 2	plane	biplane	weekly	biweekly
Line 3	**day**	midday	night	midnight
Line 4	point	midpoint	**summer**	midsummer

Lines 1–2 The Prefix *bi-*

Use Routine 10 for words with prefixes and suffixes to teach today's prefixes. Explain to students that the prefix *bi-* means "two," and that adding it to a base word changes the meaning of the base word. For example, adding the prefix *bi-* to the word *yearly* makes the new word *biyearly.* Explain that an event that occurs biyearly occurs once every two years.

Point out that adding the prefix *bi-* to a word adds a syllable to it. As you point to each word in Lines 1–2, have students read the word aloud in unison. Have students identify the base words in Lines 1–2. *cycle, month, plane, week* Have students identify which words in these lines have a suffix. *monthly, weekly* Then have students define each word that has the prefix *bi-*. Have them use a dictionary if necessary.

Lines 3–4 The Prefix *mid-*

Explain that the prefix *mid-* can be added to nouns. For example, the prefix *mid-* can be added to the noun *afternoon* to make the new noun *midafternoon.* Explain that the prefix *mid-* means "middle." Something that happens in the midafternoon happens in the middle of the afternoon.

- Have students read the words in Lines 3–4 in unison. Ask students to identify the base words in the lines. *day, night, point, summer* Then have students define each noun with the prefix *mid-*. Have students use a dictionary if necessary.
- Help students start the word structure activities on ***Skills Practice 2*** pages 103–104. Read the Focus box with them and help them with the first few questions. Then have students complete the pages on their own.

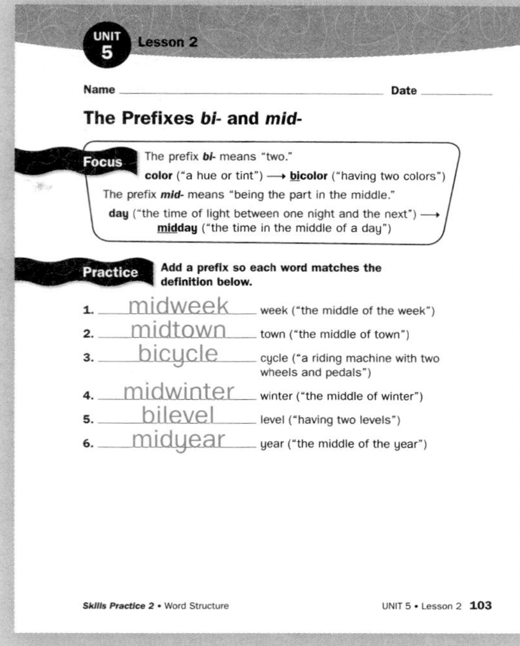

UNIT 5 Lesson 2

Name ______ Date ______

The Prefixes *bi-* and *mid-*

Focus The prefix *bi-* means "two."
color ("a hue or tint") → **bicolor** ("having two colors")
The prefix *mid-* means "being the part in the middle."
day ("the time of light between one night and the next") → **midday** ("the time in the middle of a day")

Practice Add a prefix so each word matches the definition below.

1. midweek week ("the middle of the week")
2. midtown town ("the middle of town")
3. bicycle cycle ("a riding machine with two wheels and pedals")
4. midwinter winter ("the middle of winter")
5. bilevel level ("having two levels")
6. midyear year ("the middle of the year")

Skills Practice 2 • Word Structure UNIT 5 • Lesson 2 103

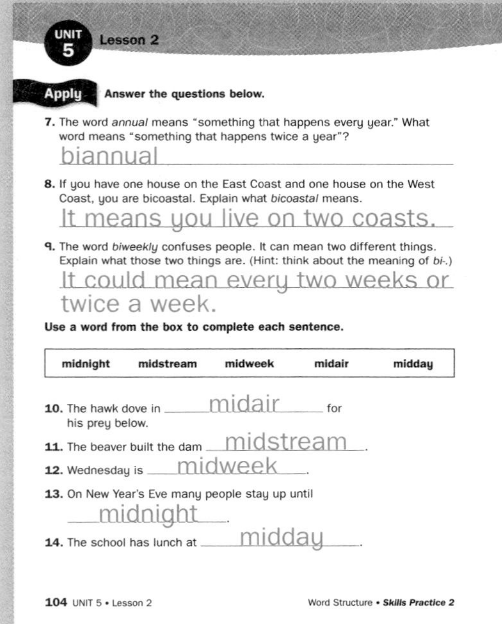

UNIT 5 Lesson 2

Apply Answer the questions below.

7. The word *annual* means "something that happens every year." What word means "something that happens twice a year"?
biannual
8. If you have one house on the East Coast and one house on the West Coast, you are bicoastal. Explain what *bicoastal* means.
It means you live on two coasts.
9. The word *biweekly* confuses people. It can mean two different things. Explain what those two things are. (Hint: think about the meaning of *bi-*.)
It could mean every two weeks or twice a week.

Use a word from the box to complete each sentence.

midnight	midstream	midweek	midair	midday

10. The hawk dove in midair for his prey below.
11. The beaver built the dam midstream.
12. Wednesday is midweek.
13. On New Year's Eve many people stay up until midnight.
14. The school has lunch at midday.

104 UNIT 5 • Lesson 2 Word Structure • *Skills Practice 2*

Skills Practice 2, pp. 103–104

Monitor Progress to Differentiate Instruction — Formal Assessment

Word Structure During the word structure activity, note how well students understand the prefixes *bi-* and *mid-*.

APPROACHING LEVEL	IF . . . students need practice with the prefixes *bi-* and *mid-*,	THEN . . . work with them in small groups on the word structure activities on ***Reteach*** page 130 during Workshop.
	IF . . . students need extra practice with the prefixes *bi-* and *mid-*,	THEN . . . work with them in small groups on the word structure activities for Unit 5 Lesson 2 in the ***Intervention Guide*** during Workshop.
ON LEVEL	IF . . . students understand the prefixes *bi-* and *mid-*,	THEN . . . have them make lists of words to add to the word lines during Workshop.
ABOVE LEVEL	IF . . . students are ready for a challenge with the prefixes *bi-* and *mid-*,	THEN . . . have them complete the word structure activities on ***Challenge Activities*** page 118 during Workshop.

Reading and Responding

OBJECTIVES

Students will
- activate prior knowledge to prepare to read the selection.
- learn selection vocabulary.
- review the elements of expository text.
- use the comprehension strategies Clarifying, Asking Questions, and Summarizing.
- investigate the theme Communities across Time using the Inquiry process.

MATERIALS

- ***Student Reader,*** Book 2, pp. 148–155
- Routines 11, 13, 14
- ***Skills Practice 2,*** pp. 93–94, 109
- ***Lesson Assessment Book 2***
- ***Home Connection,*** pp. 53–54
- ***Transparencies*** 35, 135

Build Background

Activate Prior Knowledge

- Ask students if they know what archaeology is. If necessary, tell students that archaeologists are people who study past cultures as it is shown by its tools, pottery, and other artifacts.
- Ask students if they know anyone who is an archaeologist. Ask them if they have read stories or articles about archaeology or careers in archaeology.
- Ask students if and how archaeology was studied in "The House on Maple Street." If necessary, remind them that Maggie dug up the old arrowhead and china cup. If Chrissy and Jenny were to study the objects and learn about their past, then they would be studying archaeology.

Background Information

The following information might help students understand the selection they are about to read:

- Point out to students that the selection they will be reading is expository text. It gives factual information.
- The text they will be reading, "Days of Digging," is from a larger piece called *Archaeologists: Life Digging Up Artifacts.*
- Students may want to read more from this book. The book explains about careers in archaeology and discusses the education, training, and on-the-job requirements that are necessary.

Preview and Prepare

ROUTINE 

Browse

Use Routine 13, the KWL routine, to help students identify what they know before reading, what they want to learn while reading, and any answers they might find.

Have students read the title and the name of the author, and then give them a few minutes to browse the selection. Have students use features such as the selection's title and illustrations to predict what this selection might have to do with the theme Communities across Time.

Tell students to look for interesting words or photographs they might come across. They may point out the word *pickax* or some of the photographs.

Use ***Transparency*** 35 to model browsing for students. For example, students will Know by reading the text that says "The team has been at the dig for three months." Under Want to Know, write *What are they digging?* Record students' observations on the transparency under Learn as they read the selection.

Set Purposes

Encourage students to set their own purposes for reading this selection. Remind students that readers can set purposes for reading by picking up clues from the title, illustrations, and genre of the text they are going to read. If students have trouble, suggest that as they read, they learn about archaeology, artifacts, and how studying artifacts can tell people about ancient cultures.

Before reading the selection, read the Big Idea question. Tell students to keep this question in mind as they read the selection.

How has my community changed over time?

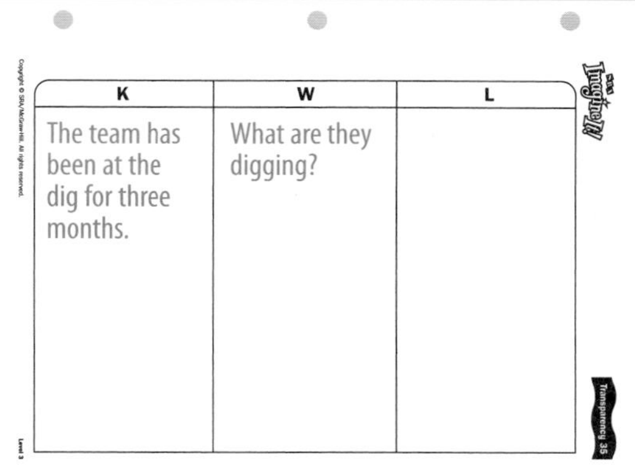

K
W
L
The team has been at the dig for three months.
What are they digging?

Transparency 35

Give each student a copy of ***Home Connection*** page 53. Encourage students to discuss "Days of Digging" with their families and complete the activity provided. The information is also available in Spanish on ***Home Connection*** page 54.

Differentiating Instruction **English Learner**

IF . . . students have limited proficiency, **THEN . . .** pair them with proficient English speakers and have the pair browse the selection together.

Selection Vocabulary

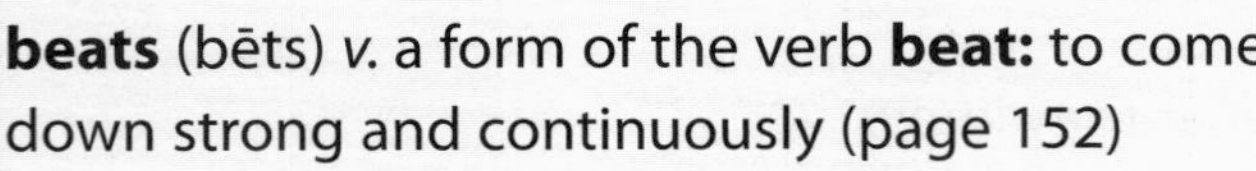

beats (bēts) *v.* a form of the verb **beat:** to come down strong and continuously (page 152)

charted (chärt´ • əd) *v.* a form of the verb **chart:** to map; to show information as a picture (page 153)

laboratory (la´ • brə • tor´ • ē) *n.* a room for science experiments and tests (page 153)

challenge (chal´ • lənj) *v.* to give the best of (page 156)

customs (kus´ • təmz) *n.* plural form of **custom:** a practice that has become accepted by many people; a tradition (page 157)

ruin (ro͞o´ • in) *n.* destruction, damage, or collapse (page 158)

origins (or´ • əg • ənz) *n.* plural form of **origin:** the cause or source of something; what something begins as or comes from (page 158)

developed (də • vel´ • əpd) *v.* past tense of **develop:** to grow; to change (page 157)

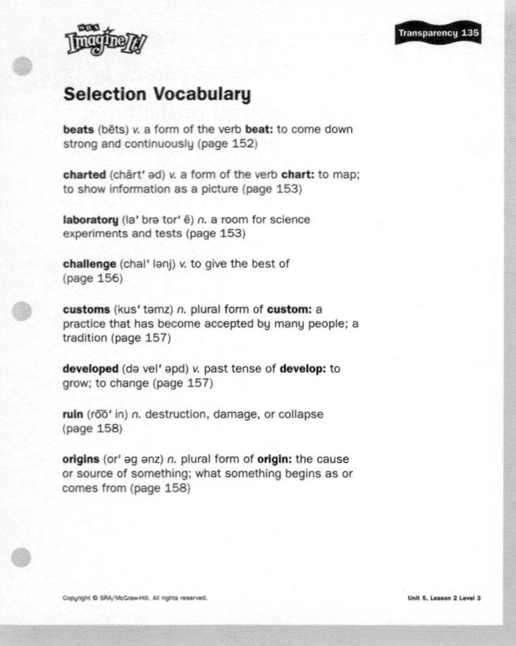

Transparency 135

Selection Vocabulary

beats (bēts) *v.* a form of the verb **beat:** to come down strong and continuously (page 152)

charted (chärt' əd) *v.* a form of the verb **chart:** to map; to show information as a picture (page 153)

laboratory (la' brə tor' ē) *n.* a room for science experiments and tests (page 153)

challenge (chal' lənj) *v.* to give the best of (page 156)

customs (kus' təmz) *n.* plural form of **custom:** a practice that has become accepted by many people; a tradition (page 157)

developed (də vel' əpd) *v.* past tense of **develop:** to grow; to change (page 157)

ruin (ro͞o' in) *n.* destruction, damage, or collapse (page 158)

origins (or' əg ənz) *n.* plural form of **origin:** the cause or source of something; what something begins as or comes from (page 158)

Unit 5, Lesson 2 Level 3

Transparency 135

Building Vocabulary

ROUTINE 11

Using Routine 11, the selection vocabulary process, have students read aloud the Vocabulary Warm-Up on ***Student Reader,*** Book 2 pages 148–149.

As students read, have them stop to blend any difficult or unfamiliar words. Provide students with the pronunciation of words that are not decodable or that they cannot read automatically or fluently.

Guided Vocabulary Practice

Ask students to identify the highlighted vocabulary words they figured out using the vocabulary strategy context clues. **Possible Answers** *beats, origins, challenge, ruin, customs* Have students explain how they figured out the meaning of the other vocabulary words as they read the Vocabulary Warm-Up.

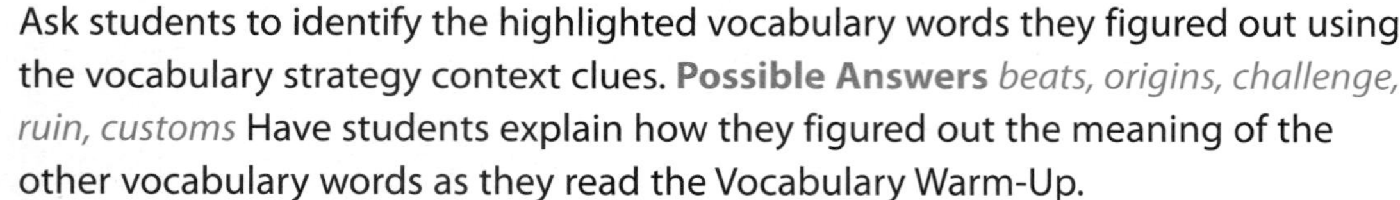

Display ***Transparency*** 135, and have students read the words and definitions. Return to the Vocabulary Warm-Up, and read the sentences containing the vocabulary words with students. Then, if necessary, provide a brief in-context explanation of the words.

Writer's Notebook

Have students copy the selection vocabulary and concept vocabulary words and definitions into the vocabulary section of their Writer's Notebooks. They can also include other words they think of that relate to the theme.

Read the story to find the meanings of these words, which are also in "Days of Digging":

- beats
- developed
- laboratory
- origins
- challenge
- charted
- ruin
- customs

Vocabulary Strategy

Context Clues are hints in the text. They help you find the meanings of words. Use context clues to find the meaning of *origins*.

Vocabulary Warm-Up

Rain beats down on the tree house, but Lena does not mind. This house is where she loves to go on a rainy day.

Lena's is not any typical tree house. It began as a few boards flung across some branches. As time went by, the house developed into something special. It became part library and part laboratory.

Lena gathers leaves and nuts on her walks. Back at the tree house, she studies the specimens. She tries to identify the origins of each piece. From which tree did it drop?

Lena looks at a nut. She now gets to challenge her skill. "Yes, it's just an acorn. But," Lena asks herself, "from which tree?"

Lena has charted, or mapped, the trees on her street. There are blue oaks and black oaks. There are buckeye and ash trees. And there is the lopsided maple tree. Lightning caused the ruin of a few of its large limbs. Each tree is sketched in and labeled on Lena's map.

Lena concludes that the acorn is from a blue oak. Then she puts the nut on the window ledge and waits. Lena is not the only one who knows about this tree. Some squirrels have chosen the same site for their house.

Like many neighbors, Lena and the squirrels have their customs. The routine is always the same. Lena leaves her samples on the ledge, and the neighbors come by for a snack.

GAME

Synonyms

Make a list of the vocabulary words on a sheet of paper. Beside each word, write a synonym for that word. When you and a classmate are both finished, compare the synonyms you came up with for each vocabulary word.

Concept Vocabulary

The concept word for this lesson is ***relic.*** A **relic** is something that survives from an earlier time or place. A relic can be an object. It can also be an idea or a way of doing things. Your school probably has relics from students and teachers who were there before you. What kinds of things can we learn from relics? Record your ideas in a journal.

Use the vocabulary words on ***Transparency*** 135 to create fill-in-the-blank sentences. Have students fill in the appropriate vocabulary words. For example, "When I researched dogs, I learned that a puppy's heart ________ 180 times per minute." *beats*

Discuss the concept vocabulary word *relic* with students. Ask students how they think the word *relic* relates to the theme Communities across Time. As students read the selections in this unit, encourage them to think about other words that relate to the theme. Students can record these words in the vocabulary section of their Writer's Notebooks.

GAME

Have students play the Synonyms game during Small-Group Time.

Differentiating Instruction: English Learner

IF . . . students have difficulty pronouncing the plural endings in the selection vocabulary words *customs* and *origins,* **THEN . . .** explain that in some words the plural *-s* has the /z/ sound.

Concept/Question Board

As students read "Days of Digging," encourage them to post questions, answers, comments, or other items related to communities across time on the **Concept/Question Board.**

Monitor Progress

Formal Assessment

Comprehension Observation Log Observe individual students as they read, and use the Comprehension Observation Log, located in ***Lesson Assessment Book 2,*** to record anecdotal information about each student's strengths and weaknesses.

Reading the Selection

Genre Expository Text

Have students identify the genre of "Days of Digging." *expository text* If necessary, remind students that expository text:

- gives information.
- uses facts about real events, people, or animals.
- presents information in a clear way.
- gives events in the order in which they happen.
- might be organized by topics.
- might contain diagrams, photographs, or other illustrations.
- contains information that can be checked in sources such as encyclopedias or newspapers.

Comprehension Strategies

Prompt the use of the following comprehension strategies during the first reading of "Days of Digging":

- Clarifying
- ☆ Asking Questions
- Summarizing

Comprehension Strategies Rubrics

Use the Informal Comprehension Strategies Rubrics to determine whether a student is using any of the strategies listed below. Note the strategies a student is using, instead of the degree to which a student might be using any particular strategy. In addition, encourage the student to tell of any strategies other than the ones being taught that he or she is using.

☆ Asking Questions

- ✦ The student stops to ask questions—any question.
- ✦ The student asks questions directly related to the text.
- ✦ The student asks *who, what, why, when, where,* or *how* questions as opposed to *yes* or *no* questions.
- ✦ The student asks questions that help clarify information in the text.

Clarifying

- ✦ The student recognizes when a word or idea is not making sense.
- ✦ The student uses decoding skills to read unfamiliar words.
- ✦ The student uses structural elements in words to read them.
- ✦ The student uses structural elements, context, and questioning to clarify the meanings of unfamiliar words.

Summarizing

- ✦ The student retells information from the story.
- ✦ The student paraphrases or puts the main ideas and details in his or her own words.
- ✦ The student gives a summary that includes only the important or main ideas.
- ✦ The student recognizes when the same ideas are included more than once in a summary and deletes them.

Monitor Progress to Differentiate Instruction

Formal Assessment 

Comprehension Strategy Note students' understanding of the comprehension strategy Asking Questions.

APPROACHING LEVEL

IF . . . students are having difficulty asking questions as they read,	**THEN . . .** model the strategy for students. Continue to model the strategy until students are able to use the strategy on their own.

ON LEVEL

IF . . . students are gaining an understanding of asking questions as they read,	**THEN . . .** have them come up with at least one question about events or characters per page of the text.

ABOVE LEVEL

IF . . . students are demonstrating an understanding of asking questions as they read,	**THEN . . .** have them read the first few pages of another theme-related selection and explain how asking questions about the story helps them find additional information about the theme Communities across Time. Have them post their discoveries on the **Concept/Question Board.**

Reading and Responding

Comprehension Skills

Reread "Days of Digging" using the following comprehension skill:

Drawing Conclusions

Reading with a Writer's Eye

During the rereading of "Days of Digging," explain the following literary element:

Genre Knowledge

Focus Questions

Have students read aloud the Focus Questions on page 151 of the ***Student Reader,*** Book 2. Encourage students to think about the Focus Questions as they read "Days of Digging."

Reading Recommendation

Oral Reading

Use Routine 14, the reading the selection routine, as you read the entire selection. As you read, stop to ask and answer questions. Point out how the pictures reflect the story. Share what images pop up in your mind as you read and how points in the reading relate ideas you already know.

This story is told from the second person point of view. Readers feel as if they are actually on the dig with the writer. For this reason, this selection is ideal for oral reading.

Research in Action

A good general approach to reading is to try to identify why the writer wrote the text the way he or she did. As young writers, students are learning to plan as they write. It follows, then, that figuring out the writer's plan will help them understand a text.

(Marlene Scardamalia)

Technology

eSTUDENT READER Students can access ***SRA Imagine It! Student Reader*** electronically by using the ***eStudent Reader*** online or on CD-ROM.

Genre

Expository Text is nonfiction that is written to inform, to explain, or to persuade.

Comprehension Strategy

Asking Questions
As you read, ask yourself questions about things or ideas in the selection that you do not understand.

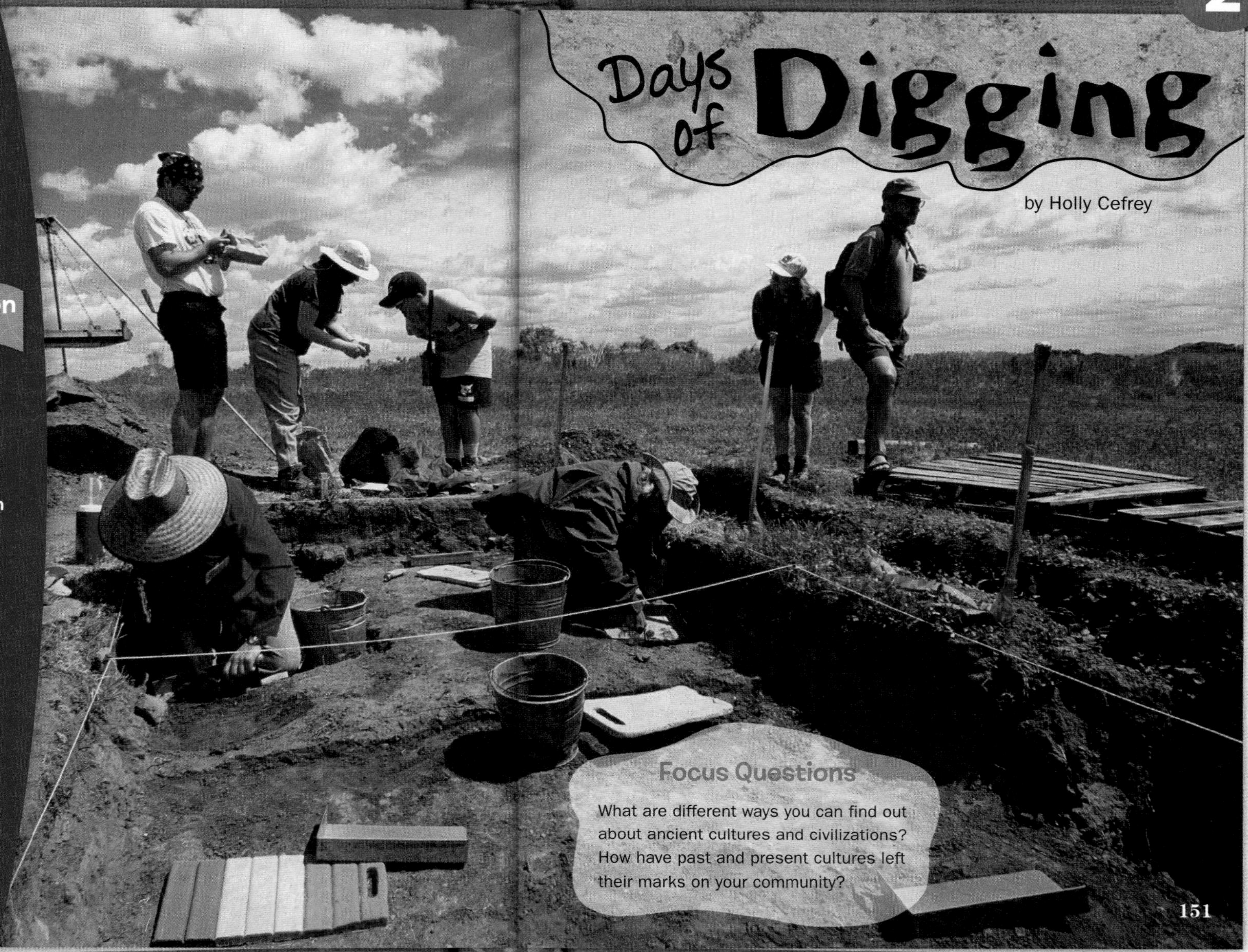

150

Days of Digging

by Holly Cefrey

Focus Questions

What are different ways you can find out about ancient cultures and civilizations? How have past and present cultures left their marks on your community?

151

Students will read the story twice over a four-day period.

Day 1 **ORAL READ** Have students read the first half of the selection. Prompt the use of the comprehension strategies.

Day 2 **ORAL READ** Have students finish reading the selection. Continue to prompt the comprehension strategies.

Day 3 **SILENT READ** Have students reread the selection silently. Have students focus on the comprehension skills and Reading with a Writer's Eye.

Day 4 **SILENT READ** Have students finish rereading the selection.

Technology

Have students listen to "Days of Digging" on the ***Listening Library CD.*** After students have listened, have them discuss what other things, such as poetry, songs, or nonfiction, they prefer to listen to on the radio or on CDs.

The summer sun beats down. You wipe the sweat from your forehead. The sound of a pickax hitting rock carries off into the distance. Your team has been at this dig for three months. Each day, it takes an hour by jeep to get to the site. The water that you drink has to be boiled so that you will not get sick. Within the month, you hope to be back at the museum. 1

152

You sit back for a moment, jotting notes in your field book. While you take a break, you watch as the twenty members of the team carry out the excavation. Slowly and carefully, layers of dirt are removed. Every inch of the dig is charted or mapped on paper. Objects are studied before they are removed from the ground. Artifacts are drawn, numbered, and photographed. The artifacts are then examined inside a tent—your makeshift laboratory. Then they are carefully packed so that they can be sent to the museum. 2

153

Vocabulary Tip

Point out the words *charted* and *laboratory* in the text. Ask students how they can use apposition to understand the meaning of the word *charted*. *the definition "mapped on paper" appears directly after the word charted* Ask students to identify any context that might help readers remember the meaning of *laboratory* *artifacts are then examined*

Comprehension Strategies

This selection is broken into two parts. On the first day, read pages 152–155. On the second day, read pages 156–159.

1 **Clarifying** Teacher Prompt: *Does anyone need to clarify anything?* **Possible Student Response** *I'm not sure what a pickax is. If I use context clues to figure it out, it is something that "hits rocks." I'm going to look it up in a dictionary to make sure I am correct. The dictionary says that a pickax is a tool used for breaking up dirt. That makes sense because the title of the selection is "Days of Digging."*

2 **Asking Questions** Teacher Prompt: *Would anyone like to ask a question?* **Possible Student Response** *The people are being careful with the objects they find. Why do they take such good care of these objects?*

Comprehension Check

This selection is written in the second-person point of view. How do you feel as the reader? **Possible Answer** *It makes you feel like you are on the dig with the writer.*

You put your field book down and return to your work. You use a fine brush to remove the loose dirt around something that you have found. So far, the team has found animal bones. The bones are thousands of years old. The bones have scratches and marks on them. Your team believes that humans made the marks. You hope to find the bones of the humans who you believe lived here long ago. 3

154

The piece that you are working on slowly comes loose. It is a small rock, but it is no ordinary rock. It has sharp edges, which were made by humans. You have found an ancient human tool. It may have even been the sharp tool that made marks on the animal bones. Your heart beats with excitement. Now you know that humans were here. 4

You tell the rest of your team. Everyone is excited. Within the next few weeks, your team discovers many more tools. Human bones are also found. Who were these people? What were they like? Your team has just begun to find out the history of these people of the past. 5

155

3 **Asking Questions** Teacher Prompt: *Does anyone have another question?* **Possible Student Response** *The team has found animal bones with marks and scratches on them. They think humans made these marks. How will they find out if humans made these marks? I'll keep reading to find out.*

4 **Answering Questions** Teacher Prompt: *Have anyone's questions about the selection been answered?* **Possible Student Response** *They found out that humans really did make the marks on the animal bones. An ancient human tool has been found that could have been used to make the marks and scratches on the animal bones. Now they know that humans were there.*

5 **Summarizing** Teacher Prompt: *Now that we are going to stop reading for the day, this is a good place to summarize what we have read. Who would like to summarize for us?* **Possible Student Response** *The readers of this story are on a dig. Artifacts are found which are then examined and charted. Human bones and tools are then discovered. This discovery leads to more questions as the journey continues.*

Teacher Tip

COMPREHENSION Ask students one or both of the following questions to make sure they understand the selection:

- *Can you summarize what you have read?*
- *Does what you are reading make sense?*

STOP You have read the first half of the story. Continue the story tomorrow on page T134.

Inquiry Process

Step 2—Identifying a Question to Investigate

Whole-Group Time

Whole Group

- By this point, students have formed groups and explored possible investigation questions and ideas.
- Remind students that the ideas and questions each group has may be helpful for the other groups. Ask students to share some of the ideas and questions they discussed in their small groups. Have students practice the skills they learned for having a group discussion with classmates. Remind them to listen to the person speaking and participate in the discussion by adding their own ideas about a topic. Have the students take notes about the ideas other students present in their Writer's Notebooks.
- Model how to choose good investigation questions. For example, return to the story you told previously about a community that became overpopulated and how people started destroying forests and disrupting wildlife. This led to the question *How can nature and people live in harmony?* Ask students to share any other questions or ideas they might have that are related to this question.
- Remind students that a good investigation question will not have a *yes* or *no* answer, and it might not even have just one correct answer. A good investigation question will require gathering information to learn new things about a topic and improve their understanding. The purpose of their investigation question is to allow them to explore something related to the theme that interests them.

Lesson 2

Inquiry Planner

STEP 2: Identifying a Question to Investigate

Day 1 With the whole group and in small-group discussions, students will generate possible investigation questions.

Day 2 Students will continue asking new questions about the theme and read "Days of Digging" for new ideas about the theme.

Day 3 With the whole group, discuss how "Days of Digging" relates to the unit theme.

Day 4 Groups will choose one question to research and investigate.

Day 5 Students can post and view items on the **Concept/Question Board** and continue thinking about their investigation topics and generating ideas.

Teacher Tip

CHOOSING AN INVESTIGATION QUESTION Some students may decide on their investigation question quickly. If so, have them start making conjectures. Because Inquiry is not a lock-step process, allow groups to progress through the steps of their investigations in the ways that are most effective for them.

Small-Group Time

Small Group

- Have students break into their groups. As students share stories and discuss ideas for their investigations, have them ask each other questions that their stories raise.
- Circulate among the groups, and continue modeling potential investigation topics and questions. You may want to suggest questions such as the following: *How were original communities formed? What does learning about the past teach us about the future? How have natural occurrences affected the land? How have people affected the land? How can land that has been damaged be saved? How will our communities continue to change? If archaeologists can study past cultures, how can we study the future?*
- Students should review the interesting ideas, facts, and questions about their communities that they recorded earlier in ***Skills Practice 2*** pages 93–94. Remind students that their interests can change, but they should develop a question or topic that they want to investigate. Have students record any new questions they have about the theme in their Writer's Notebooks.
- Help each group complete ***Skills Practice 2*** page 109 to help them generate possible investigation topics about past communities.

Concept/Question Board

Encourage students to write facts, opinions, ideas, or questions on the **Concept/Question Board.** Students might also

- post new ideas learned from whole-group or small-group discussions.
- post their short stories or poems about communities.
- post magazine or newspaper articles about important community issues.
- post photographs or illustrations of past, present, and future communities.
- list television programs or movies about communities or how people use land. Encourage students to write summaries of any programs they post.

Teacher Tip

CHOOSING A QUESTION As students begin selecting the question they want to investigate, remind them that it should relate to the theme Communities across Time. Explain that a good investigation will pose a question that can be researched. Questions about single facts, or questions with *yes* or *no* answers, should be made more open-ended.

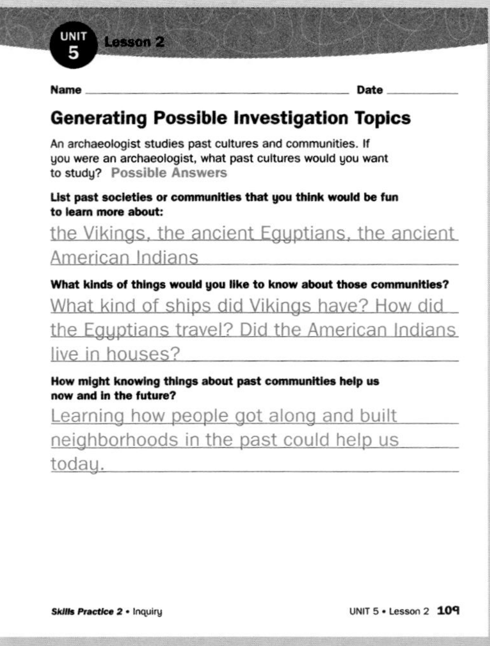
UNIT 5 Lesson 2

Name ______ Date ______

Generating Possible Investigation Topics

An archaeologist studies past cultures and communities. If you were an archaeologist, what past cultures would you want to study? Possible Answers

List past societies or communities that you think would be fun to learn more about:

the Vikings, the ancient Egyptians, the ancient American Indians

What kinds of things would you like to know about those communities?

What kind of ships did Vikings have? How did the Egyptians travel? Did the American Indians live in houses?

How might knowing things about past communities help us now and in the future?

Learning how people got along and built neighborhoods in the past could help us today.

Skills Practice 2 • Inquiry   UNIT 5 • Lesson 2 109

Skills Practice 2, p. 109

OBJECTIVES

Students will
- ✦ prewrite a persuasive letter.
- ✦ take the spelling pretest.
- ✦ practice cursive *P* and *R*.

MATERIALS

- ✦ ***Language Arts Handbook,*** pp. 168–170
- ✦ ***Transparencies*** 136, 137
- ✦ ***Skills Practice 2,*** p. 111
- ✦ Routines 15 and 16

UNIT 5 Lesson 2

Name ______________________ Date __________

Writing a Persuasive Letter

Think **Audience:** Who will read your letter?
Possible Answer The person I want to convince.
Purpose: What is your reason for writing the persuasive letter?
Possible Answer I want to convince my uncle to visit me.

Prewriting **Use this graphic organizer to plan your persuasive letter. Write reasons that support your topic on the lines.**

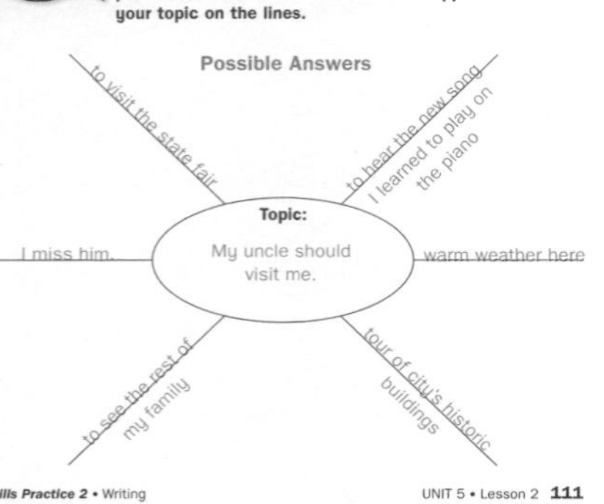
Possible Answers
Topic: My uncle should visit me.
to visit the state fair
to hear the new song I learned to play on the piano
I miss him.
warm weather here
to see the rest of my family
tour of city's historic buildings

Skills Practice 2 • Writing UNIT 5 • Lesson 2 111

Skills Practice 2, p. 111

Writing Persuasive Letter

Prewriting

Teach—Generating and Organizing Ideas

- ✦ Remind students of the persuasive paragraphs they have written, and ask them to discuss what methods they used to persuade their audiences. Remind students that persuasive writing tries to convince readers to take action or to believe the same way as the writer. If necessary, remind students that they used facts and examples as well as opinions in their previous writing activities.
- ✦ Use Routines 15 and 16. Tell students that instead of writing a paragraph as they did in the last lesson, they will be writing a letter. Explain that it is still the writer's job to grab the reader's attention, tell what the subject of the writing is, and communicate how the writer feels about it. Tell students that they will select a specific person or group of people to address as they write their letters.
- ✦ If necessary, review the rules for persuasive writing in ***Language Arts Handbook*** pages 168–170.

- ✦ Guide students through the parts of a persuasive letter by displaying ***Transparency*** 136. Read the letter aloud and point out each part. Explain that like the letters they have written before, persuasive letters should include the following elements:
  - Heading: your address and the date
  - Greeting: to whom the letter is addressed
  - Body: the subject of the letter (include facts, reasons, or beliefs about the subject and why you are trying to convince your reader to believe the same way)
  - Closing: *Yours truly, Sincerely*
  - Signature
- ✦ Tell students they should select a topic that is important to them. In the letter, they will ask the reader to take an action or to believe what they are saying.

Traits of Good Writing

Ideas and Organization The writer generates and organizes ideas to create elements of persuasion.

Writing, continued

Guided Practice

- Brainstorm with students to create a list of possible topics on the board. Remind students that their audiences are equally as important as the topic they choose.
- Have students turn to ***Skills Practice 2*** page 111. Have a student read aloud the Think section and fill in their responses.
- Create a web graphic organizer on the board or on chart paper like the one on ***Skills Practice 2*** page 111. Select a topic and an audience for your model. Have students help you insert information into your graphic organizer. If you do not have a specific fact to add to the organizer, tell students you will need to look up information to add to your persuasive letter to support your argument.

Apply

- Based on the topic students selected during brainstorming, have students complete the graphic organizer on page 111 in ***Skills Practice 2.*** Remind students to use facts, examples, and opinions.

Assessment

You will use the Writing Rubrics found in the Level Appendix to evaluate students' persuasive letters. You may use any of the rubrics for Genre, Writing Process, and Writing Traits. Share with students what you will be looking for when assessing their persuasive letters.

Differentiating Instruction **English Learner**

IF . . . students are just beginning to learn English, **THEN . . .** adjust the writing task to suit their abilities. For example, instead of writing an entire letter, have students write a persuasive note.

Spelling

Place Words and Prefixes *bi-*, *mid-*, *dis-*, and *auto-* Pretest

Teach

Say the sentences below aloud. Have students write the spelling words on a separate sheet of paper. When they are finished, have them correct any misspelled words.

Pretest Sentences

1. Can the scientist **disprove** the theory?
2. The **bifocal** glasses help me to see more clearly.
3. The plane flew on **autopilot.**
4. The bird landed **upon** the rock.
5. We will take a **midsummer** vacation this year.
6. The students **distrust** the facts in that movie.
7. My uncle flies a **biplane.**
8. Load the dishes into the **automatic** dishwasher.
9. The new **midtown** apartments are expensive.
10. The glasses are **within** reach.
11. Her uncle works at an **automobile** plant.
12. Set the sugar **near** the tea.
13. Our **midweek** review is due today.
14. The club will **disband** after this meeting.
15. Yoshi needs a new bell for his **bicycle.**

Challenge Sentences

16. The condo owners **disagree** with the rules.
17. His **autobiography** is very popular.

Diagnose any misspellings by determining whether students misspelled the prefixes or some other part of the word. Then have students use the pretest as a take-home list to study the spellings of these words with prefixes.

Teacher Tips

PENMANSHIP If students are having problems forming cursive *P* or *R,* or their letters are floating between the lines, then review proper paper position, check to make sure students are holding their pencils correctly, or review letter formation.

CONNECTING *R* Show how to connect cursive *R* to other letters.

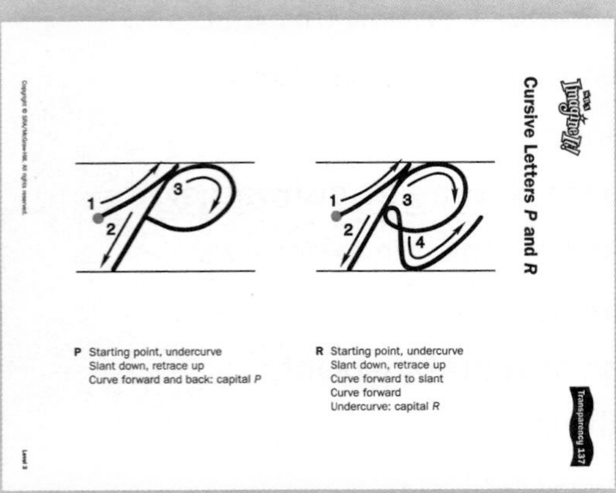

Transparency *137*

Differentiating Instruction English Learner

IF . . . students have difficulty following your directions for handwriting, **THEN . . .** introduce or review words such as *top, bottom, up, down, right, left, straight,* and *curve.* Say and demonstrate each word, having students mimic both your words and movements.

Penmanship

Cursive Letters *P* and *R*

Teach

- Introduce capital cursive *P* and *R* as undercurve slant letters.
- Display ***Transparency*** 137. Using a pointer, trace the letters while saying the formations aloud.
  - **Letter *P*** Starting point, undercurve
Slant down, retrace
Curve forward and back:
capital *P*
  - **Letter *R*** Starting point, undercurve
Slant down, retrace up
Curve forward to slant
Curve forward
Undercurve: capital *R*
- On the board, write capital cursive letters *P* and *R,* saying the strokes aloud as you form the letters.
- To model proper letter formation, write the following proper nouns on the board: *Peter Piper, Ronald Reagan,* and *Providence, Rhode Island.*

Guided Practice

- Tell students to hold their index fingers in the air in front of them. Say the strokes aloud as you trace the letters, and have students mimic your movements as if they were writing in the air. Ask students to say the strokes with you as you repeat the process.
- Have a volunteer write the proper nouns on the board. Assist the student with the formations as needed.

Apply

- Have students practice writing the letters four times. Ask them to circle the best formation for each of their letters.
- After reviewing the words you wrote on the board, set a timer for three minutes and have students practice writing each of the words. Ask them to circle the best formations for each of the words based on the correct formation of *P* and *R.*

Skills Traces

Preparing to Read

Word Structure: Prefix *dis-*

Introduced in Grade 2, Unit 4, Lesson 3

Grade 3
Reviewed: Unit 5, Lesson 2
Practiced: Unit 5, Lesson 5
Assessed: ***Lesson Assessment Book 2,*** p. 51

Reviewed in Grade 4, Unit 4, Lesson 2

Word Structure: Prefixes *bi-*, *mid,* and *auto-*

Introduced in Grade 2, Unit 4, Lesson 4

Grade 3
Reviewed: Unit 5, Lesson 2
Practiced: Unit 5, Lesson 5

Reading and Responding

Comprehension Skill: Drawing Conclusions

Reviewed in Grade 2, Unit 1, Lesson 2

Grade 3
Reviewed: Unit 1, Lesson 4
Practiced: Unit 5, Lesson 2
Assessed: ***Lesson Assessment Book 2,*** pp. 52–54

Reviewed in Grade 4, Unit 1, Lesson 2

Comprehension Strategy: Asking Questions

Reviewed in Grade 2, Unit 1, Lesson 1

Grade 3
Reviewed: Unit 1, Lesson 1
Practiced: Unit 5, Lesson 2
Assessed: Unit 5, Lesson 2, p. T120

Reviewed in Grade 4, Unit 1, Lesson 4

Comprehension Strategy: Clarifying

Reviewed in Grade 2, Unit 1, Lesson 3

Grade 3
Reviewed: Unit 1, Lesson 5
Practiced: Unit 5, Lesson 2
Assessed: Unit 5, Lesson 2, p. T121

Reviewed in Grade 4, Unit 1, Lesson 4

Comprehension Strategy: Summarizing

Reviewed in Grade 2, Unit 1, Lesson 2

Grade 3
Reviewed: Unit 1, Lesson 2
Practiced: Unit 5, Lesson 2
Assessed: Unit 5, Lesson 2, p. T121

Reviewed in Grade 4, Unit 1, Lesson 2

Language Arts

Writing: Persuasive Writing

Reviewed in Grade 2, Unit 4, Lesson 2

Grade 3
Reviewed: Unit 5, Lesson 1
Assessed: Unit 5, Lesson 2, p. T170

Reviewed in Grade 4, Unit 3, Lesson 4

Grammar, Usage, and Mechanics: Prepositions and Prepositional Phrases

Grade 3
Introduced: Unit 5, Lesson 2
Assessed: ***Lesson Assessment Book 2,*** p. 56

Reviewed in Grade 4, Unit 5, Lesson 1

Preparing to Read

OBJECTIVES

Students will
- identify and know the meanings of the prefixes *bi-* and *mid-*.
- build fluency.

MATERIALS
- ***Transparency*** 134
- Routine 10

Daily Oral Practice

Daily News

Today!

Last weekend, I was on a midafternoon bicycle ride when I found a ring. It looked really old. My mom said it was probably someone's family treasure. We put an ad in the paper to try to find the owner. I wonder what the people were like who used to own the ring. I'll try to find out.

- Write the daily news on the board or on chart paper. Then have the boys read the daily news in unison to practice fluency.
- As a review of yesterday's word structure lesson, ask a volunteer to identify any words in the message with the prefixes *bi-* and *mid-*. *bicycle; midafternoon*

Differentiating Instruction **English Learner**

IF . . . students would benefit from more practice with /s/ spelled *ce* or *ci_*, **THEN . . .** lead them to identify and correctly pronounce words in "Days of Digging" that contain these /s/ sound/spellings. Examples: *piece, excited* (p. 155), *place* (p. 156), *disappearance* (p. 158).

Research in Action

Fluency is the bridge between decoding and comprehension. Because fluent readers access words rapidly and cluster words into meaningful units automatically, they are free to focus their cognitive energies on the meaning of the text. Fluent readers are not engaged in reading at the word level, but are focused on figuring out the meaning of the text they are reading.
(Marsha Roit)

Word Structure

ROUTINE 10

The Prefixes *bi-* and *mid-*

✦ Use ***Transparency*** 134 with these word lines from Day 1.

Line 1	cycle	bicycle	monthly	bimonthly
Line 2	plane	biplane	weekly	biweekly
Line 3	day	midday	night	midnight
Line 4	point	midpoint	summer	midsummer

✦ Use Routine 10 to review the prefixes *bi-* and *mid-*. If necessary, remind students that the prefix *bi-* means "two," and *mid-* means "middle."

Developing Oral Language

Use any or all of the following activities to help students practice reading the words from the word lines.

✦ Have a volunteer choose one of the word lines. Then have the volunteer identify the two base words on the line, and use them in sentences. **Possible Answers** *The seasons change as part of a* cycle. *I make* monthly *visits to see my grandparents.* Then have another student use the two words from the line with the prefix. **Possible Answers** *They know how to ride a* bicycle. *I go to the dentist* bimonthly. Continue for all the word lines.

✦ Point to a pair of words on the word lines, and have a student give a definition for each word. **Possible Answers** Weekly *means something that happens once a week.* Biweekly *means something that happens once every two weeks.* Have the class decide whether the definitions are correct, and correct them as necessary. Continue for each pair of words. Help students define *cycle* and *biplane,* using a dictionary if necessary.

✦ Write sentences containing blanks for words on the word lines. Have students identify the word that belongs in each blank and cross out the words from the lines until all have been used. Examples: Because I get my allowance every other week, I get it ____________. The seasons of the year are part of a ____________. *biweekly; cycle*

Differentiating Instruction **English Learner**

IF . . . students have difficulty blending words, **THEN . . .** keep in mind that syllabication rules vary among languages. Provide English learners with extra practice breaking words into syllables and blending the syllables to decode words. Use the ***English Learner Support Guide*** for additional instruction for new English learners.

Monitor Progress

to Differentiate Instruction
Formal Assessment

Word Structure During the word structure activity, note how well students understand the words.

APPROACHING LEVEL

IF . . . students do not understand the words on the word lines,	**THEN . . .** use pictures, photos, objects, stick drawings, or pantomime to help them visualize the words.

ON LEVEL

IF . . . students need practice with the words on the word lines,	**THEN . . .** have them write sentences using the words on the lines.

ABOVE LEVEL

IF . . . students understand the words on the word lines,	**THEN . . .** have them make a list of other words with the prefixes *bi-* and *mid-* and use them in sentences.

Imagine being the first person to unearth an ancient city. Imagine finding the bones of an ancient warrior. Imagine solving the five-thousand-year-old mystery of what happened at a place where all the villagers died at once. Archaeologists get to challenge themselves with many thrilling possibilities of the past. 6

156

Archaeology (ancient study) is a science. The archaeologist discovers and studies past human cultures or societies. Each group that is studied has its own values, customs, and beliefs. An archaeologist does research about a culture. He or she studies the artifacts from that culture. He or she also tries to find out when and how the culture developed. This study can take an archaeologist to any place on the planet. 7

157

OBJECTIVES

Students will

- use the comprehension strategies Clarifying, Asking Questions, and Summarizing.
- discuss the selection using the handing-off process.
- review vocabulary, genre, and fluency.

MATERIALS

- ***Student Reader,*** Book 2, pp. 156–161
- Routine A
- ***Skills Practice 2,*** pp. 107–108
- ***Transparencies*** 35, 135

Comprehension Strategies

6 **Clarifying** Teacher Prompt: *A lot of information is given in this paragraph about what archaeology is and what archaeologists do. Who would like to clarify what exactly archaeology is for the class?* **Possible Student Response** *I'm going to reread this paragraph to make sure I understand. Archaeology is a science. Archaeologists discover and study ancient cultures by examining artifacts.*

7 **Answering Questions** Teacher Prompt: *Has anyone's questions been answered so far in the selection?* **Possible Student Response** *Earlier I asked why the diggers were being so careful with the objects they found. Now I understand. Archaeologists study these artifacts. They are too important to be lost or damaged.*

Comprehension Check

What qualities would it take to be a good archaeologist? **Possible Answer** *An archaeologist would need to like science, enjoy digging in the earth, and be interested in the customs of many different cultures.*

Some archaeologists try to solve puzzling issues. They may try to solve mysteries about a culture's ruin or disappearance. They may try to find out why a culture did certain things. They may try to find out why a culture changed dramatically from its origins. For example, an archaeologist would try to discover why a culture that fished developed into a culture that farmed. What caused the culture to stop fishing? What made them start farming? These questions may be answered through archaeology. 8

158

You may wonder why it is so important to learn about our human past. It is important because it teaches us about being human. It shows us how creative and resourceful humans really are—and have been. The past is important because it tells us how we became what we are today. It also explains how and why we have so many different cultures. It teaches us to respect those cultures, and our own. 9

159

8 Clarifying Teacher Prompt: *Is anyone having trouble understanding the sentence "They may try to find out why a culture changed dramatically from its origins." Who can help me clarify?* **Possible Student Response** *I'm going to keep reading and see if I can figure it out. After reading further in the paragraph, it makes sense. The author gives the example of a culture that used to fish and then changed to farming. It "originally" fished and then changed. Archaeologists want to know why it changed.*

9 Summarizing Teacher Prompt: *We have finished reading the selection; who would like to summarize it?* **Possible Student Response** *The author takes us on an archaeological dig. Everything that is discovered must be examined and charted. Animal bones are found that lead to discovering human bones. Archaeologists learn about ancient cultures and they study how and why they developed. Learning about ancient times teaches us respect for the many cultures of the past and the present.*

Vocabulary Tip

Point out the words *ruin, origins,* and *developed* in the text. Ask students how they can use apposition to figure out the meaning of the word *ruin.* *the words* or disappearance *immediately follow the word ruin.* Ask students how reading the example of how a fishing culture changed over time helps them remember the meaning of the word *origins.* Ask whether the same clues in the story help them understand the meaning of the word *developed.*

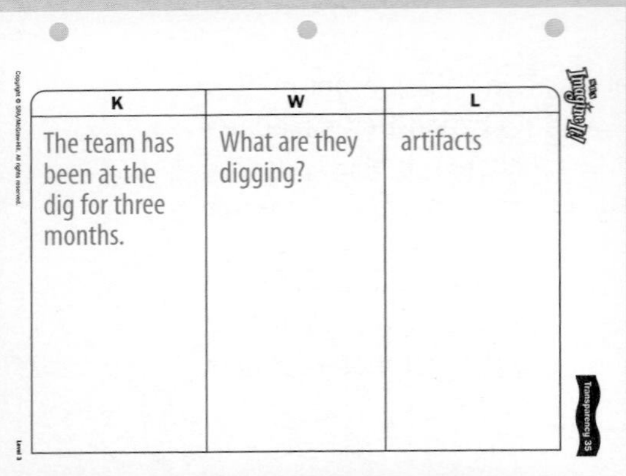

K	W	L
The team has been at the dig for three months.	What are they digging?	artifacts

Transparency 35

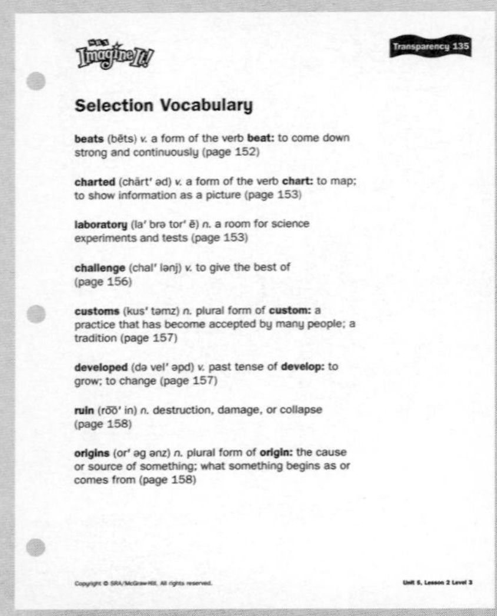

Transparency 135

Selection Vocabulary

beats (bēts) *v.* a form of the verb **beat:** to come down strong and continuously (page 152)

charted (chärt' əd) *v.* a form of the verb **chart:** to map; to show information as a picture (page 153)

laboratory (la' brə tor' ē) *n.* a room for science experiments and tests (page 153)

challenge (chal' lənj) *v.* to give the best of (page 156)

customs (kus' təmz) *n.* plural form of **custom:** a practice that has become accepted by many people; a tradition (page 157)

developed (də vel' əpd) *v.* past tense of **develop:** to grow; to change (page 157)

ruin (rōō' in) *n.* destruction, damage, or collapse (page 158)

origins (or' əg ənz) *n.* plural form of **origin:** the cause or source of something; what something begins as or comes from (page 158)

 Unit 5, Lesson 2 Level 3

Transparency 135

Differentiating Instruction English Learner

IF . . . students would benefit from practice with identifying facts, **THEN . . .** have them review "Days of Digging," and ask them to identify one fact on each page of the selection.

Discussing the Selection

ROUTINE

- It is important for students to see you as a contributing member of the group. Use Routine A, handing-off, to emphasize that you are part of the group. Actively participate in handing-off by raising your hand to be called on by the last speaker when you have a contribution to make. Point out unusual and interesting insights verbalized by students so that these insights are recognized and discussed.
- Engage students in a discussion using handing-off to determine whether they have grasped the following ideas:
  - Archaeologists must have patience and be dedicated to their work. They face many challenges, but also experience many exciting discoveries.
  - Archaeologists dig up artifacts, and they also research to understand how cultures changed and developed over time.
- Ask students how the selection demonstrates the following key concepts:
  - Learning about the past helps us understand the present. It helps us gain respect for cultures before us and how they helped us become who we are today.
  - Archaeologists have many questions. They find answers to their questions, which lead them to even more questions.
- Return to the KWL chart on ***Transparency*** 35. Have students discuss whether the selection provided enough information to tell them what they wanted to know, and also have them discuss what they learned by reading the selection. Ask students if the predictions they made while browsing the selection were confirmed or not confirmed.
- Have students return to the Focus Questions on page 151. Select a student to read the questions aloud, and have students answer and discuss the questions. Have them return to the text as necessary.

Genre Review

Review the elements of expository text on page T120 with students. Then ask students how they know "Days of Digging" is expository text.

How has my community changed over time?

After reading the selection, read the Big Idea question. Discuss with students how the selection helps answer this question.

Vocabulary Review

Review with students the selection vocabulary words and definitions they wrote in the vocabulary section of their Writer's Notebooks. Then refer students to ***Skills Practice 2*** pages 107–108. Help students complete the first two questions. Then have students complete the rest on their own. Also, review the concept vocabulary word *relic*. Ask students if they can think of other words related to the theme Communities across Time. **Possible Answers** *cultures, customs, beginnings, ancient, past, present, future*

Fluency

- Automaticity, or the ability to decode words spontaneously, is essential to fluency. Automaticity helps readers understand and enjoy the text that is being read.
- Read aloud pages 152–153 of "Days of Digging." Model fluent reading for students. For example, after reading *Artifacts are drawn, numbered, and photographed*, point out how your voice paused after each of the commas. Point out to students that to read with automaticity, sometimes a word or sentence must be reread. Tell students that when reading it is important to pay attention to end punctuation and commas. Have students follow along in the ***Student Reader,*** Book 2, and tell them to raise their hands when you pause. Tell students that as they reread, they should practice pausing after commas.

Monitor Progress to Differentiate Instruction

Formal Assessment 

Selection Vocabulary Observe students' understanding of the vocabulary words and their definitions.

APPROACHING LEVEL

IF . . . students need extra help with the selection vocabulary,	**THEN . . .** refer to ***Intervention Guide*** Unit 5, Lesson 2.
IF . . . students need extra help with the selection vocabulary,	**THEN . . .** use ***Reteach*** page 132.

ON LEVEL

IF . . . students need practice using the selection vocabulary words,	**THEN . . .** have students complete ***eSkills & eGames*** vocabulary activities.

ABOVE LEVEL

IF . . . students understand the selection vocabulary,	**THEN . . .** use ***Challenge Activities*** page 120.

Teacher Tips

FLUENCY By this time in Grade 3, good readers should be reading approximately 137 words per minute with fluency and expression. The only way to gain this fluency is through practice. Have students reread the selection to you and to each other during Workshop to help build fluency. As students read, you may notice that some need work in building fluency. During Workshop, have these students choose a section of the text (a minimum of 160 words) to read aloud several times to build fluency.

WORD BANK Review the Word Bank with students. Encourage students to add words to the Word Bank that are related to the unit theme Communities across Time. Encourage students to add synonyms and antonyms to the Word Bank as well.

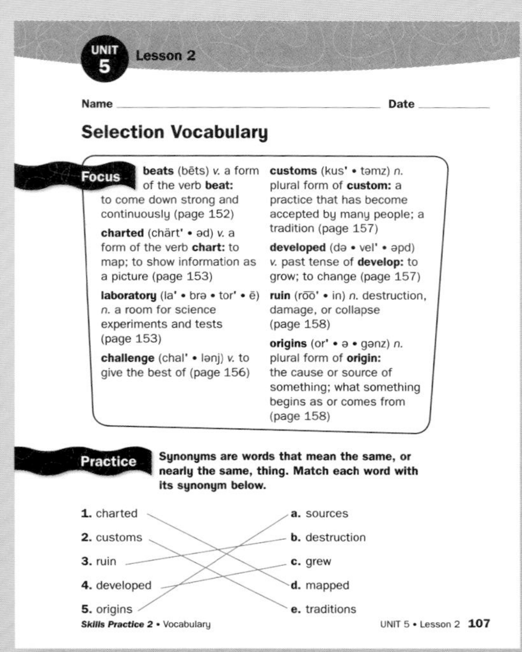

UNIT 5 Lesson 2

Name ______ Date ______

Selection Vocabulary

Focus

beats (bēts) *v.* a form of the verb **beat:** to come down strong and continuously (page 152)

charted (chärt' • əd) *v.* a form of the verb **chart:** to map; to show information as a picture (page 153)

laboratory (la' • brə • tor' • ē) *n.* a room for science experiments and tests (page 153)

challenge (chal' • lənj) *v.* to give the best of (page 156)

customs (kus' • təmz) *n.* plural form of **custom:** a practice that has become accepted by many people; a tradition (page 157)

developed (də • vel' • əpd) *v.* past tense of **develop:** to grow; to change (page 157)

ruin (rōō' • in) *n.* destruction, damage, or collapse (page 158)

origins (or' • ə • gənz) *n.* plural form of **origin:** the cause or source of something; what something begins as or comes from (page 158)

Practice **Synonyms are words that mean the same, or nearly the same, thing. Match each word with its synonym below.**

1. charted	**a.** sources
2. customs	**b.** destruction
3. ruin	**c.** grew
4. developed	**d.** mapped
5. origins	**e.** traditions

Skills Practice 2 • Vocabulary UNIT 5 • Lesson 2 **107**

Skills Practice 2, pp. 107–108

Reading and Responding

Teacher Tips

WORKSHOP During Workshop, have students listen to "Days of Digging" for a model of oral reading. While students listen, have them keep a list in their Writer's Notebooks of any new or unfamiliar words they encounter, and instruct them to check the words using a dictionary or glossary. Also, instruct students to listen for the lesson's vocabulary words and to check that the words make sense within the reading.

WRITE ABOUT IT! In their Writer's Notebooks, have students describe a modern tool as if it were an artifact discovered at a dig hundreds of years from now.

Writer's Notebook

- Have students use their Writer's Notebooks to list other nonfiction selections they have read in class or on their own.
- Have students compare the elements found in each selection.

Differentiating Instruction: English Learners

IF . . . students need help answering the Across Selections questions, **THEN . . .** allow them to review "The House on Maple Street" and "Days of Digging."

IF . . . students have not read any nonfiction selections in English, **THEN . . .** remind them that they can list nonfiction selections they have read in their native languages in their Writer's Notebooks.

IF . . . students need help contributing to the **Concept/Question Board, THEN . . .** remind them to post information in their native languages. Encourage them to convey the general idea of their postings to their English-speaking classmates.

Teacher Tip

BEYOND THE SELECTION Have students summarize what they have learned and tell how they might use this information in further investigations.

Meet the Author

After students read the information about the author, discuss the following questions with them.

- *Why do you think Cefrey writes nonfiction books?* **Possible Answers** *Cefrey wants to help children learn. Cefrey likes the subjects she writes about.*
- *Cefrey has won awards for her writing. Based on the selection you just read, why do you think she is successful?* **Possible Answer** *She writes about interesting topics and helps readers feel like they are a part of the text.*

Theme Connections 

Within the Selection

1. If you were an archaeologist, what culture would you like to study? Explain why. **Possible Answer** *I would like to study Ancient Egypt, because I am fascinated by the tombs, pyramids, and the way they preserved the dead.*

2. How is an archaeologist's work like putting together a jigsaw puzzle? **Possible Answer** *Archaeologists try to learn about people of the past by piecing together a picture of their lives with the artifacts they unearth.*

Across Selections

3. How are Chrissy and Jenny from "The House on Maple Street" like archaeologists? **Possible Answer** *They wonder about the person or people who lost the treasures so long ago.*

4. How are artifacts found in "The House on Maple Street" like those found in "Days of Digging"? **Possible Answer** *The artifacts give us a glimpse of people from long ago.*

Meet the Author

Holly Cefrey

As a freelance writer, Holly Cefrey writes for a variety of people and publishers. She is primarily known for writing informational books that help children learn about different subjects, such as science and health. Cefrey has won many awards for her writing.

Communities across Time

Theme Connections

Within the Selection

1. If you were an archaeologist, what culture would you like to study? Explain why.
2. How is an archaeologist's work like putting together a jigsaw puzzle?

Across Selections

3. How are Chrissy and Jenny from "The House on Maple Street" like archaeologists?
4. How are artifacts found in "The House on Maple Street" like those found in "Days of Digging"?

Beyond the Selection

5. What are some skills an archaeologist should have?
6. What other jobs involve studying the past?

Write about It!

Describe a modern tool as if it were an artifact discovered at a dig hundreds of years from now.

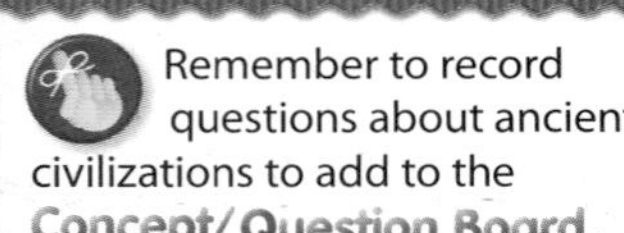

Remember to record questions about ancient civilizations to add to the **Concept/Question Board.**

Beyond the Selection

5. What are some skills an archaeologist should have? **Possible Answers** *They need to be patient; they need to be very careful in their work; they need to like to dig; they need to know an artifact when they uncover it; and so on.*

6. What other jobs involve studying the past? **Possible Answers** *History teachers, professors, art historians, anthropologists, and so on.*

Concept/Question Board

As students discuss "Days of Digging," encourage them to post questions, answers, comments, or other items related to communities across time on the **Concept/Question Board.**

OBJECTIVES

Students will

- ✦ draft persuasive letters.
- ✦ learn to spell place words and words with *bi-*, *mid-*, *dis-*, and *auto-* prefixes.
- ✦ learn prepositions and prepositional phrases.

MATERIALS

- ✦ ***Language Arts Handbook,*** p. 312
- ✦ ***Skills Practice 2,*** pp. 115–116
- ✦ ***Transparency*** 136

Writing Persuasive Letter

Drafting

Teach

- ✦ At this point, students should have selected a subject and an audience for their persuasive letters as well as completed the graphic organizer.
- ✦ Tell students they will begin drafting their letters. Remind students to make sure they include all five parts of a letter in their drafts.
- ✦ Tell students as they draft their persuasive letters, they should concentrate on creating the cause-and-effect relationship of their argument like they did when they wrote their persuasive paragraphs.
- ✦ Display ***Transparency*** 136 to review the parts of a letter.
- ✦ Using the web you created, review each part of the persuasive letter with students to make sure each is included.
- ✦ Remind students that they can go back to make corrections to spelling, grammar, punctuation, and capitalization during editing/proofreading. They should concentrate on getting all of their ideas on paper.
- ✦ Tell students that if they are using facts, they must make sure those facts could be proven accurate by using resource materials.

Guided Practice

- ✦ Using the topic you selected earlier and the graphic organizer, have students help you create your body paragraph by thinking of reasons why you want to persuade your audience to take your viewpoint or to act on your words. Encourage them to create sentences that show the cause-and-effect relationship in your argument.

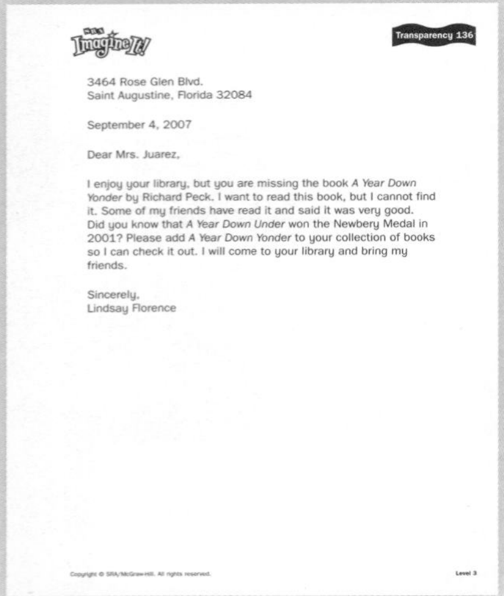

Imagine It! Transparency 136

3464 Rose Glen Blvd.
Saint Augustine, Florida 32084

September 4, 2007

Dear Mrs. Juarez,

I enjoy your library, but you are missing the book *A Year Down Yonder* by Richard Peck. I want to read this book, but I cannot find it. Some of my friends have read it and said it was very good. Did you know that *A Year Down Under* won the Newbery Medal in 2001? Please add *A Year Down Yonder* to your collection of books so I can check it out. I will come to your library and bring my friends.

Sincerely,
Lindsay Florence

Transparency 136

Apply

Composing — Drafting Students should use their graphic organizers to write the drafts of their persuasive letters. You may want to leave ***Transparency*** 136 visible so students can refer to it as they write their drafts.

Differentiating Instruction **English Learner**

IF . . . students are having difficulty drafting their persuasive letters, **THEN . . .** allow them to use words from their native languages for any English words they do not know. After they are finished revising their drafts, they can use a bilingual dictionary to find those unknown English words.

Spelling

Place Words, and Prefixes *bi-, mid-, dis-,* and *auto-*

Teach

Use a word sort to teach place words and words with the prefixes *bi-, mid-, dis-,* and *auto-*.

Guided Practice

Write the following headings on the board: *place words, bi-, mid-, dis-,* and *auto-*. Then write the following word list: *disprove, bifocal, autopilot, upon, midsummer, distrust, biplane, automatic, midtown, within, automobile, near, midweek, disband,* and *bicycle.* Have students sort words into place words and prefix groups. Have students circle the prefixes.

Word Sort Answers

Place Words: *upon, within, near*

Words with the Prefix *bi-: bifocal, biplane, bicycle*

Words with the Prefix *mid-: midsummer, midtown, midweek*

Words with the Prefix *dis-: disprove, distrust, disband*

Words with the Prefix *auto-: autopilot, automatic, automobile*

Grammar, Usage, and Mechanics 

Prepositions and Prepositional Phrases

Teach

- ✦ Write the word *cat* on the board. Ask students to describe things that cats do. Write some of the verbs. Next, ask students where cats sleep, sit, play, and so on, depending on the verbs written on the board. Write those answers on the board.
- ✦ Explain that a preposition is a word that tells about the position or direction of a noun or pronoun. Depending on student responses, write one complete sentence on the board and underline the prepositional phrase. For example, *My cat sleeps in my room.* Underline *in my room.*
- ✦ Write the following examples of common prepositions on the board: *above, across, after, at, before, behind, below, beside, between, by, for, from, in, of, on, to.*
- ✦ Explain that a prepositional phrase begins with a preposition and ends with a noun or pronoun. Tell students that articles and adjectives can be between the preposition and the noun.
- ✦ Use ***Language Arts Handbook*** page 312 for further information on prepositions and prepositional phrases.

Guided Practice

- ✦ Draw a mountain or a building on the board. Tell students that anywhere they go on the mountain is a preposition. For example, they can climb *over the mountain*. Write *over the mountain* on the board and have students point out the preposition *over,* the article *the,* and the noun *mountain.*
- ✦ Using the same example *over the mountain,* add an adjective before the noun: *over the high mountain,* and have students identify the word *high* as an adjective describing the word mountain.
- ✦ Have students take turns writing prepositional phrases using *around, in,* and *on* the mountain. Have students add adjectives to their prepositional phrases.
- ✦ After completing the activity, have students turn to ***Skills Practice 2*** page 115. Have a student read the directions aloud, and then help students with the first two questions in Practice.

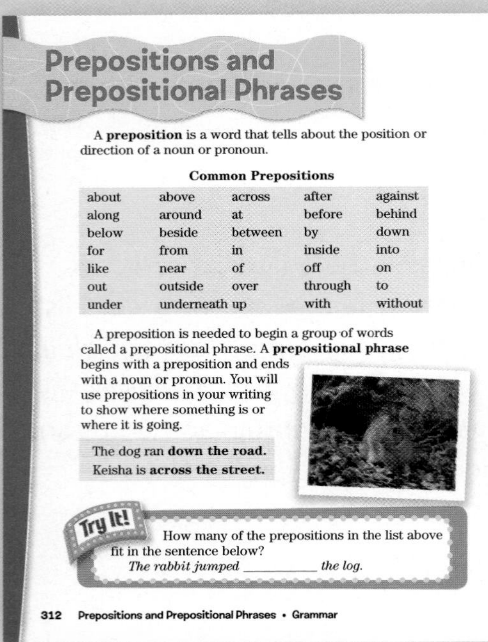

Prepositions and Prepositional Phrases

A **preposition** is a word that tells about the position or direction of a noun or pronoun.

Common Prepositions

about	above	across	after	against
along	around	at	before	behind
below	beside	between	by	down
for	from	in	inside	into
like	near	of	off	on
out	outside	over	through	to
under	underneath	up	with	without

A preposition is needed to begin a group of words called a prepositional phrase. A **prepositional phrase** begins with a preposition and ends with a noun or pronoun. You will use prepositions in your writing to show where something is or where it is going.

The dog ran **down the road.**
Keisha is **across the street.**

Try It! How many of the prepositions in the list above fit in the sentence below?
The rabbit jumped __________ the log.

312 Prepositions and Prepositional Phrases • Grammar

Language Arts Handbook, p. 312

Differentiating Instruction English Learner

IF . . . students need help understanding prepositions, **THEN . . .** use objects in the classroom and movement to demonstrate their meanings. For example, say *The chair rolls under the desk. I am walking around the table.*

Apply

Have students complete ***Skills Practice 2*** pages 115–116 for practice using prepositional phrases.

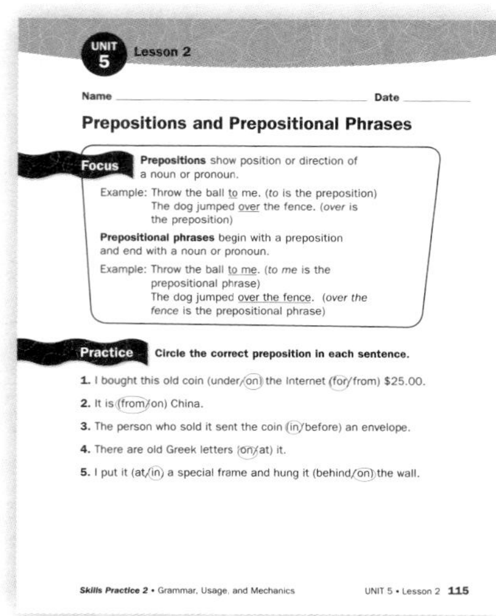

UNIT 5 Lesson 2

Name ______ Date ______

Prepositions and Prepositional Phrases

Focus **Prepositions** show position or direction of a noun or pronoun.

Example: Throw the ball to me. (*to* is the preposition)
The dog jumped over the fence. (*over* is the preposition)

Prepositional phrases begin with a preposition and end with a noun or pronoun.

Example: Throw the ball to me. (*to me* is the prepositional phrase)
The dog jumped over the fence. (*over the fence* is the prepositional phrase)

Practice **Circle the correct preposition in each sentence.**

1. I bought this old coin (under/on) the Internet (for/from) $25.00.
2. It is (from/on) China.
3. The person who sold it sent the coin (in/before) an envelope.
4. There are old Greek letters (on/at) it.
5. I put it (at/in) a special frame and hung it (behind/on) the wall.

Skills Practice 2 • Grammar, Usage, and Mechanics UNIT 5 • Lesson 2 115

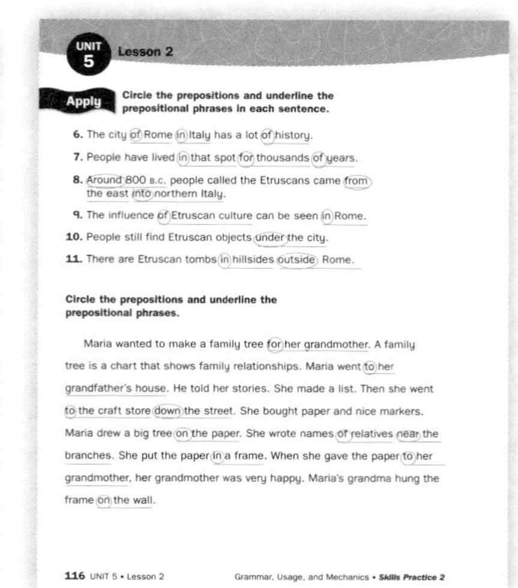

UNIT 5 Lesson 2

Apply **Circle the prepositions and underline the prepositional phrases in each sentence.**

6. The city of Rome in Italy has a lot of history.
7. People have lived in that spot for thousands of years.
8. Around 800 B.C. people called the Etruscans came from the east into northern Italy.
9. The influence of Etruscan culture can be seen in Rome.
10. People still find Etruscan objects under the city.
11. There are Etruscan tombs in hillsides outside Rome.

Circle the prepositions and underline the prepositional phrases.

Maria wanted to make a family tree for her grandmother. A family tree is a chart that shows family relationships. Maria went to her grandfather's house. He told her stories. She made a list. Then she went to the craft store down the street. She bought paper and nice markers. Maria drew a big tree on the paper. She wrote names of relatives near the branches. She put the paper in a frame. When she gave the paper to her grandmother, her grandmother was very happy. Maria's grandma hung the frame on the wall.

116 UNIT 5 • Lesson 2 Grammar, Usage, and Mechanics • *Skills Practice 2*

Skills Practice 2, pp. 115–116

Monitor Progress to Differentiate Instruction

Formal Assessment

Prepositional Phrases Note whether students are using prepositions and prepositional phrases correctly.

APPROACHING LEVEL

IF . . . students need to practice prepositional phrases,	**THEN . . .** have them complete ***Reteach*** page 134 during Workshop.
IF . . . students need more practice with prepositional phrases,	**THEN . . .** refer to the ***Intervention Guide.***

ON LEVEL

IF . . . students have an understanding of prepositional phrases,	**THEN . . .** have them complete ***Workshop Kit*** activities during Workshop.

ABOVE LEVEL

IF . . . students need a challenge,	**THEN . . .** have them complete ***Challenge Activities*** page 122 during Workshop.

Differentiating Instruction **English Learner**

IF . . . students have difficulty with prepositions and prepositional phrases, **THEN . . .** refer to Unit 5 Lesson 2 in the ***English Learner Support Guide.***

Day 3

Preparing to Read

OBJECTIVES

Students will

- identify and know the meanings of the prefixes *dis-* and *auto-*.
- build fluency.

MATERIALS

- ***Transparency*** 138
- Routine 10
- ***Skills Practice 2,*** pp. 105–106

Daily Oral Practice

Daily News Today!

My community is celebrating the anniversary of its bicentennial—that means it is 200 years old! We are going to study what life was like in our town 200 years ago. Our mayor is going to open a time capsule left by people living here 200 years ago. What do you think we will find?

- Write the daily news on the board or on chart paper. Then have the girls read the daily news in unison to practice fluency.
- As a review of yesterday's word structure lesson, ask a volunteer to identify any words in the message with the prefix *bi-*. *bicentennial*

Word Structure

ROUTINE 10

The Prefixes *dis-* and *auto-*

- Write these word lines on the board or use ***Transparency*** 138. The words in boldface are in "Days of Digging."

Line 1	agree	disagree	honest	dishonest
Line 2	cover	**discover**	appearance	**disappearance**
Line 3	graph	autograph	pilot	autopilot
Line 4	biography	autobiography	mobile	automobile

Teacher Tip

SYLLABICATION To help students blend words and build fluency, demonstrate syllabication using the decodable, multisyllabic words in the word lines.

a • gree	dis • a • gree
hon • est	dis • hon • est
cov • er	dis • cov • er
ap • pear • ance	dis • ap • pear • ance
au • to • graph	pi • lot
au • to • pi • lot	
bi • og • ra • phy	au • to • bi • og • ra • phy
mo • bile	au • to • mo • bile

Lines 1–2 The Prefix *dis-*

Use Routine 10 for words with prefixes and suffixes to teach today's prefixes. Explain to students that the prefix *dis-* means "opposite," and that adding it to a base word changes the meaning of the base word. For example, adding the prefix *dis-* to the word *like* makes the new word *dislike*. The word *dislike* means the opposite of the word *like*.

Point out that adding the prefix *dis-* to a word adds a syllable to it. As you point to each word in Lines 1–2, have students read the word aloud in unison. Point out that *ance* in the word *appearance* is a suffix. Have students identify the base words in Lines 1–2. *agree, honest, cover, appear* Then have students define each word that has the prefix *dis-*. Have students use a dictionary if necessary.

Lines 3–4 The Prefix *auto-*

Explain that the prefix *auto-* means "self." Point out the prefix *auto-* in the word *automatic*, and ask students to suggest the word's meaning. *something that works automatically works by itself*

- Point out that adding the prefix *auto-* to a word adds two syllables to it because *auto* has two vowel sounds. Have students read the words in Lines 3–4 in unison. Help students define each word, and discuss how the prefix *auto-* changes the definition of the words to which it's added. Have students use a dictionary if necessary.
- Help students start the word structure activities on ***Skills Practice 2*** pages 105–106. Read the Focus box with them and help them with the first few questions. Then have students complete the pages on their own.

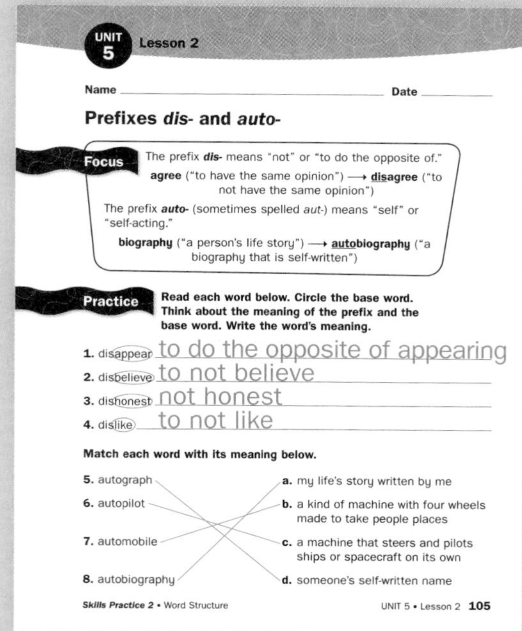

UNIT 5 Lesson 2

Name ____________ Date ______

Prefixes *dis-* and *auto-*

Focus The prefix ***dis-*** means "not" or "to do the opposite of."
agree ("to have the same opinion") → **disagree** ("to not have the same opinion")
The prefix ***auto-*** (sometimes spelled *aut-*) means "self" or "self-acting."
biography ("a person's life story") → **autobiography** ("a biography that is self-written")

Practice **Read each word below. Circle the base word. Think about the meaning of the prefix and the base word. Write the word's meaning.**

1. disappear to do the opposite of appearing
2. disbelieve to not believe
3. dishonest not honest
4. dislike to not like

Match each word with its meaning below.

5. autograph — a. my life's story written by me
6. autopilot — b. a kind of machine with four wheels made to take people places
7. automobile — c. a machine that steers and pilots ships or spacecraft on its own
8. autobiography — d. someone's self-written name

Skills Practice 2 • Word Structure UNIT 5 • Lesson 2 **105**

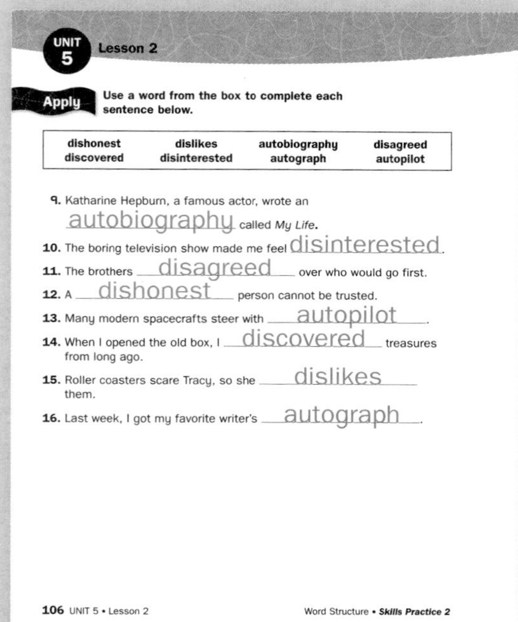

UNIT 5 Lesson 2

Apply **Use a word from the box to complete each sentence below.**

dishonest	dislikes	autobiography	disagreed
discovered	disinterested	autograph	autopilot

9. Katharine Hepburn, a famous actor, wrote an autobiography called *My Life*.
10. The boring television show made me feel disinterested.
11. The brothers disagreed over who would go first.
12. A dishonest person cannot be trusted.
13. Many modern spacecrafts steer with autopilot.
14. When I opened the old box, I discovered treasures from long ago.
15. Roller coasters scare Tracy, so she dislikes them.
16. Last week, I got my favorite writer's autograph.

106 UNIT 5 • Lesson 2 Word Structure • *Skills Practice 2*

Skills Practice 2, pp. 105–106

Monitor Progress to Differentiate Instruction — Formal Assessment

Word Structure During the word structure activity, note how well students understand the prefixes *dis-* and *auto-*.

APPROACHING LEVEL	**IF . . .** students need practice with the prefixes *dis-* and *auto-*,	**THEN . . .** work with them in small groups on the word structure activities on ***Reteach*** page 131 during Workshop.
	IF . . . students need extra practice with the prefixes *dis-* and *auto-*,	**THEN . . .** work with them in small groups on the word structure activities for Unit 5 Lesson 2 in the ***Intervention Guide*** during Workshop.
ON LEVEL	**IF . . .** students understand the prefixes *dis-* and *auto-*,	**THEN . . .** have them make lists of words to add to the word lines during Workshop.
ABOVE LEVEL	**IF . . .** students are ready for a challenge with the prefixes *dis-* and *auto-*,	**THEN . . .** have them complete the word structure activities on ***Challenge Activities*** page 119 during Workshop.

The summer sun beats down. You wipe the sweat from your forehead. The sound of a pickax hitting rock carries off into the distance. Your team has been at this dig for three months. Each day, it takes an hour by jeep to get to the site. The water that you drink has to be boiled so that you will not get sick. Within the month, you hope to be back at the museum.

152

You sit back for a moment, jotting notes in your field book. While you take a break, you watch as the twenty members of the team carry out the excavation. Slowly and carefully, layers of dirt are removed. Every inch of the dig is charted or mapped on paper. Objects are studied before they are removed from the ground. Artifacts are drawn, numbered, and photographed. The artifacts are then examined inside a tent—your makeshift laboratory. Then they are carefully packed so that they can be sent to the museum.

153

OBJECTIVES

Students will

- ✦ use the comprehension skill Drawing Conclusions.
- ✦ review fluency.
- ✦ investigate the theme Communities across Time using the Inquiry process.

MATERIALS

- ✦ ***Student Reader,*** Book 2, pp. 152–155
- ✦ ***Transparency*** 15

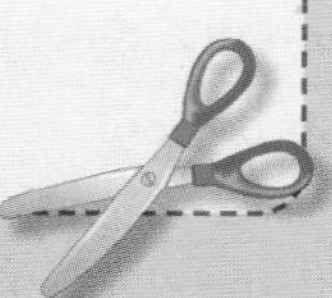

2nd READ

Comprehension Skill

Reread the selection using the comprehension skill Drawing Conclusions and Reading with a Writer's Eye.

Drawing Conclusions

Ask students to explain what it means to draw conclusions when reading. *To use information in a text to figure out things the author does not mention directly.* Ask students to use clues from the text to help them draw conclusions as they read. Ask students the following questions:

- *What conclusions can you draw on page 152?* **Possible Answer** *Even though the text does not say the setting is a hot desert, I believe that is the setting. The clues I found are: "sun beats down" and "it takes an hour by jeep to get to the site."*
- *What conclusions can you draw on page 153?* **Possible Answer** *The text doesn't say the writer is an archaeologist or scientist, but that is what I believe she is. The clues I found are: "jotting notes in your field book," "members of the team carry out the excavation," and "your makeshift laboratory."*

You put your field book down and return to your work. You use a fine brush to remove the loose dirt around something that you have found. So far, the team has found animal bones. The bones are thousands of years old. The bones have scratches and marks on them. Your team believes that humans made the marks. You hope to find the bones of the humans who you believe lived here long ago.

154

The piece that you are working on slowly comes loose. It is a small rock, but it is no ordinary rock. It has sharp edges, which were made by humans. You have found an ancient human tool. It may have even been the sharp tool that made marks on the animal bones. Your heart beats with excitement. Now you know that humans were here.

You tell the rest of your team. Everyone is excited. Within the next few weeks, your team discovers many more tools. Human bones are also found. Who were these people? What were they like? Your team has just begun to find out the history of these people of the past.

155

Reading with a Writer's Eye

Genre Knowledge

When writers want to tell a story, they have to decide what genre they are going to use to tell it. Will they write fiction, nonfiction, fantasy, or expository text? It usually depends on what type of story they want to tell. Holly Cefrey uses expository text to tell the story of who archaeologists are and what they do. Ask students the following questions:

- *What clues in this story tell you that this is expository text?* **Possible Answers** *The author uses facts and examples, such as the animal and human bones, to tell readers about what archaeologists discover and why their discoveries are important. She explains how the archaeologists go about trying to find out answers to questions.*
- *Why do you think she chose this genre for her story?* **Possible Answer** *She wants to present facts and examples in a straightforward way so readers understand her purpose for writing.*

Expanding Vocabulary

site (sīt) *n.* a location (page 152)
Let's meet at the *site* of the discovery.

boiled (boild) *v.* past tense of **boil:** to heat until steaming (page 152)
My dad made *boiled* potatoes for dinner.

excavation (eks´• kav • ā´• shən) *n.* a site created by digging. the process of creating the site (page 153)
Raj found an artifact at the *excavation* site.

artifacts (är´ • də • faks) *n.* plural form of **artifact:** an old tool, a weapon, or other thing made by people of the past (page 153)
The archaeologists dug up *artifacts*.

STOP You have reread the first half of the story. Continue the story tomorrow on page T156.

Teacher Tip

ASKING QUESTIONS Remind students of the questions the author asks in "Days of Digging" and how the archaeologists continue to search for the answers.

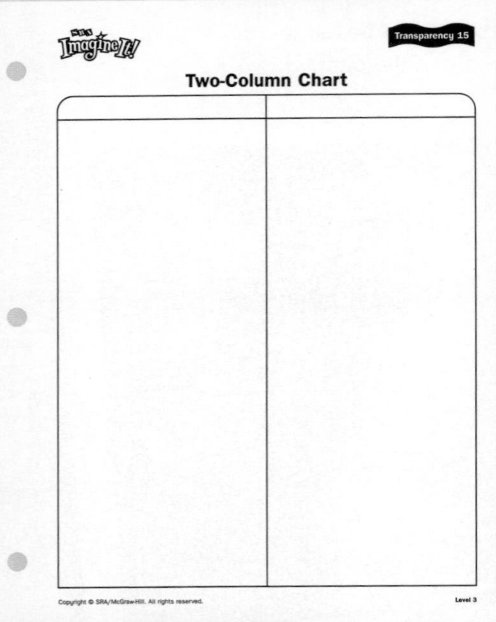

Transparency 15

Supporting the Reading

Comprehension Strategy: Asking Questions

Teach

Remind students that asking questions helps them focus their attention on important points in a selection. Students gain a better understanding of the text as they search for the answers.

Guided Practice

Read aloud a short expository article that is theme related. Tell students that as you read they are to raise their hands whenever they have a question. Use the first column of the two-column chart on ***Transparency*** 15 to record their questions. As you continue to read, encourage students to raise their hands when they think they have an answer to any of the questions on the transparency. Write their answers in the second column of the chart. Use the following as an example.

Questions	Answers
Why did the people of that culture move to another state?	The river dried up and the plants died after a drought. The people no longer had enough to eat.

Apply

Good readers ask questions when they are unclear about an event or a character, or when they wonder why an event is occurring. Have students look in the selection "Days of Digging" to find examples of questions they would ask an archaeologist about his or her job. Have students write short paragraphs asking these questions. Then have students respond to those questions by using the information in the story.

Fluency

The second person point of view may be unfamiliar for students. Remind them that the author is placing her readers in the story by using this point of view. When the story is read, it should be read with the same emotions as those in the story. By reading fluently and spontaneously, the enthusiasm and excitement of the selection will sound natural and not forced.

- Model fluent reading by reading aloud pages 156–157 from "Days of Digging." Have students follow along in ***Student Reader,*** Book 2. Read the passage with the same enthusiasm and excitement as the author presents.
- After you have read through the passage, call on a volunteer to read the first paragraph. Before the student begins, make sure he or she understands the emotion of the scene.
- After the volunteer has finished, have all students read the passage chorally several times until they can read it naturally with good phrasing.

Inquiry

Asking Questions and Generating Ideas

✦ Remind students that they will need to narrow their ideas and interests in the theme to one question or topic to investigate. The unit selections can help them get new ideas and questions to research.

✦ Discuss with students how "Days of Digging" relates to the unit theme. Students may want to talk about specific mysteries about past communities that an archeologist would try to solve. Encourage these interests as possible investigation topics.

✦ Encourage students to ask why and how our communities change over time. Why do different societies die out? How do communities change to avoid being destroyed? How can we learn from the mistakes of past communities? What can the past and present tell us about future communities?

LEVELED READERS To help students build fluency and strengthen their vocabulary and comprehension skills, have them read the ***Leveled Readers*** for this unit. Use each student's Oral Fluency Assessment score from the previous lesson assessment to diagnose the appropriate ***Leveled Reader.***

Fluency Tip

FLUENCY For additional fluency practice, students can read the passage aloud with a partner during Small-Group Time.

OBJECTIVES

Students will

- ✦ revise persuasive letters.
- ✦ practice spelling place words, and words with *bi-*, *mid-*, *dis-*, and *auto-* prefixes.
- ✦ review interviewing techniques.
- ✦ practice writing sentences with prepositions and prepositional phrases.

MATERIALS

- ✦ ***Skills Practice 2,*** pp. 112–114 and 117–118
- ✦ Routine 16

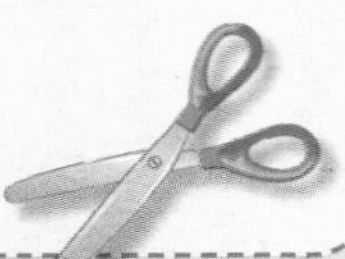

UNIT 5 Lesson 2

Revising Use this checklist to revise your persuasive letter.

- ☐ Did you write the reason for the persuasive letter?
- ☐ Did you include all of the parts of a letter?
- ☐ Did you use a variety of sentence types?
- ☐ Are the sentences in a clear order?
- ☐ Are there any words you have used too often?
- ☐ Did you use the best words to persuade?

Editing/Proofreading Use this checklist to correct mistakes.

- ☐ Did you indent your paragraphs?
- ☐ Did you use correct verb tenses?
- ☐ Did you use correct spellings?
- ☐ Did you capitalize the greeting and the closing?
- ☐ Did you capitalize proper nouns?
- ☐ Did you end each sentence with correct punctuation?

Publishing Use this checklist to get your persuasive letter ready to send.

- ☐ Neatly rewrite or type a final copy.
- ☐ Address an envelope.

112 UNIT 5 • Lesson 2 Writing • *Skills Practice 2*

Skills Practice 2, p. 112

Traits of Good Writing

Sentence Fluency The writer uses a variety of sentences.

Differentiating Instruction English Learner

IF . . . students have difficulty revising their Persuasive Letter, **THEN . . .** be sure to pair them with proficient English speakers for this.

Writing Persuasive Letter

ROUTINE 16

Revising

Teach—Varying Sentence Types

- ✦ Use Routine 16, and tell students that as they revise their persuasive letters, they are going to work on using a variety of sentence types to make the writing more interesting. For example, students might want to ask and then answer a question or they could make an imperative statement, such as "Pick up litter when you see it."
- ✦ Write the following reminders on the board. Tell students that as they revise they should make sure that
  - all parts of the letter are included.
  - their main idea is clear.
  - their facts, reasons, or feelings support the action they want their readers to support.
  - they have used a variety of sentence types.
  - they have used a variety of sentence lengths, including some longer and some shorter sentences, as well as combined sentences.
  - they have used the appropriate voice.

Guided Practice

- ✦ Using the draft you created, model revising your persuasive letter to create sentence variety.
- ✦ Have students help check this process.
- ✦ Have students turn to ***Skills Practice 2*** page 112. Have a student read aloud the revising checklist.

Apply

Composing — Revising Have students refer to the revising checklist on page 112 in ***Skills Practice 2*** as they revise their persuasive letters.

Spelling

Place Words and Prefixes *bi-*, *mid-*, *dis-*, and *auto-*

Teach

- Remind students that prefixes are added to the beginning of words to change the meanings of the words.
- Tell students that the prefix *bi-* means "every two" or "twice," the prefix *mid-* means "in the middle of," the prefix *dis-* means "not," and the prefix *auto-* means "self."
- Write the following word list on the board: *prove, focal, graph, summer, trust, plane, town, mobile, band,* and *cycle.* Have volunteers come to the board and choose a word to say aloud. Then have student use one of the four prefixes from this lesson to make the word into one of their spelling words.

Guided Practice

Have students turn to ***Skills Practice 2*** page 113. Read the instructions with them, and complete the first two questions as a class.

Apply

Have students complete ***Skills Practice 2*** pages 113–114 on their own. Remind students that challenge words are not used in ***Skills Practice*** exercises.

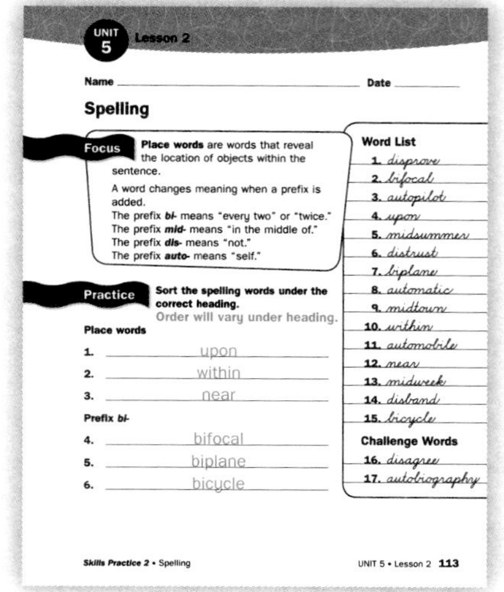

UNIT 5 Lesson 2

Name ____________ Date ______

Spelling

Focus **Place words** are words that reveal the location of objects within the sentence.

A word changes meaning when a prefix is added.
The prefix ***bi-*** means "every two" or "twice."
The prefix ***mid-*** means "in the middle of."
The prefix ***dis-*** means "not."
The prefix ***auto-*** means "self."

Word List
1. disprove
2. bifocal
3. autopilot
4. upon
5. midsummer
6. distrust
7. biplane
8. automatic
9. midtown
10. within
11. automobile
12. near
13. midweek
14. disband
15. bicycle

Challenge Words
16. disagree
17. autobiography

Practice **Sort the spelling words under the correct heading.**
Order will vary under heading.

Place words
1. upon
2. within
3. near

Prefix *bi-*
4. bifocal
5. biplane
6. bicycle

Skills Practice 2 • Spelling UNIT 5 • Lesson 2 **113**

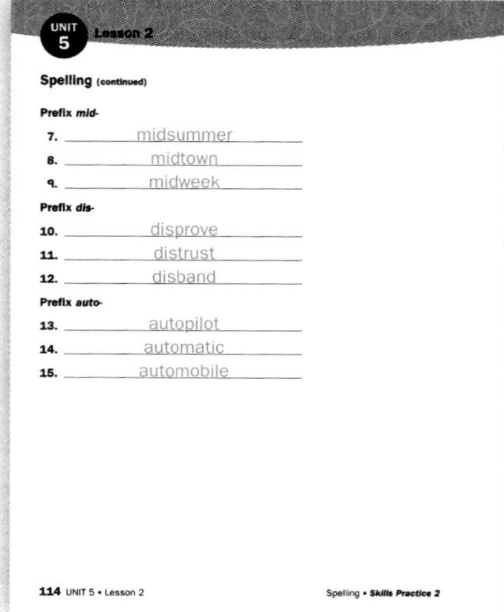

UNIT 5 Lesson 2

Spelling (continued)

Prefix *mid-*
7. midsummer
8. midtown
9. midweek

Prefix *dis-*
10. disprove
11. distrust
12. disband

Prefix *auto-*
13. autopilot
14. automatic
15. automobile

114 UNIT 5 • Lesson 2 Spelling • ***Skills Practice 2***

Skills Practice 2, pp. 113–114

Monitor Progress

to Differentiate Instruction
Formal Assessment

Spelling Note whether students are able to spell the lesson words correctly.

APPROACHING LEVEL

IF . . . students need to practice spelling this week's words, **THEN . . .** have them complete ***Reteach*** page 133.

ON LEVEL

IF . . . students can spell this week's spelling words, **THEN . . .** have them use five spelling words to write five sentences. Have them spell the spelling word incorrectly, and then trade sentences with a partner and have each student correct the other's sentences.

ABOVE LEVEL

IF . . . students are ready for a challenge, **THEN . . .** have them complete ***Challenge Activities*** page 121.

Monitor Progress

to Differentiate Instruction
Formal Assessment

Interviewing Note whether students create relevant questions for the theme Communities across Time.

APPROACHING LEVEL

IF . . . students need to practice interviewing skills,	**THEN . . .** have them practice interviewing a classmate during Workshop.

ON LEVEL

IF . . . students have an understanding of interviewing skills,	**THEN . . .** have them interview someone for their unit investigation during Workshop.

ABOVE LEVEL

IF . . . students need a challenge,	**THEN . . .** have them participate in a formal interview during Workshop.

Study Skills 

Interviews

Teach

- Have students discuss why conducting an interview is an important research tool.
- Remind students that an interviewer asks questions to obtain information about a subject or a feeling about the subject. In an interview, the interviewee is the source.
- If necessary, refer students to ***Skills Practice 1*** page 17 to review the interview guidelines.
- Display ***Transparency*** 9, which lists guidelines for conducting an interview.

Guided Practice

Have students turn to ***Skills Practice 2*** page 117. Read and discuss the Focus box. Have students begin the Practice activity as a class.

Apply

Have students complete ***Skills Practice 2*** pages 117–118.

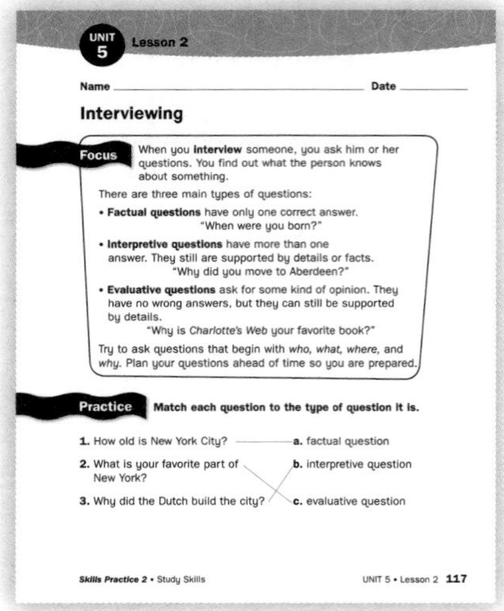

UNIT 5 Lesson 2

Name ______ Date ______

Interviewing

Focus When you **interview** someone, you ask him or her questions. You find out what the person knows about something.

There are three main types of questions:

- **Factual questions** have only one correct answer. "When were you born?"
- **Interpretive questions** have more than one answer. They still are supported by details or facts. "Why did you move to Aberdeen?"
- **Evaluative questions** ask for some kind of opinion. They have no wrong answers, but they can still be supported by details. "Why is *Charlotte's Web* your favorite book?"

Try to ask questions that begin with *who, what, where,* and *why.* Plan your questions ahead of time so you are prepared.

Practice **Match each question to the type of question it is.**

1. How old is New York City? — a. factual question
2. What is your favorite part of New York? — b. interpretive question
3. Why did the Dutch build the city? — c. evaluative question

Skills Practice 2 • Study Skills UNIT 5 • Lesson 2 **117**

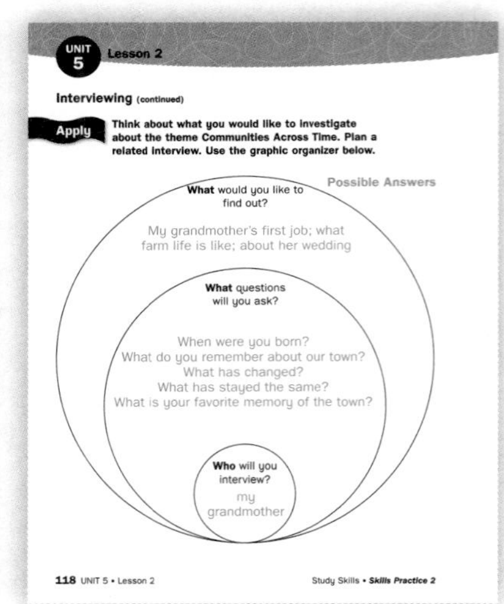

UNIT 5 Lesson 2

Interviewing (continued)

Apply **Think about what you would like to investigate about the theme Communities Across Time. Plan a related interview. Use the graphic organizer below.**

Possible Answers

What would you like to find out?

My grandmother's first job; what farm life is like; about her wedding

What questions will you ask?

When were you born?
What do you remember about our town?
What has changed?
What has stayed the same?
What is your favorite memory of the town?

Who will you interview?

my grandmother

118 UNIT 5 • Lesson 2 Study Skills • ***Skills Practice 2***

Skills Practice 2, pp. 117–118

Grammar, Usage, and Mechanics

Prepositions and Prepositional Phrases

Teach

- Ask for a volunteer to share a descriptive sentence with a prepositional phrase.
- Have students review the rules for prepositions and prepositional phrases. If necessary, remind students that a prepositional phrase always begins with a preposition and ends with a noun or pronoun.

Guided Practice

Write the following sentences on the board, and have students replace the existing prepositional phrase with a new prepositional phrase.

- The dog plays in his yard.
- Let's have soup for dinner.
- The athlete jumped over the hurdles.

Apply

Have students work individually on creating sentences with prepositional phrases. You may want to have students write three to five sentences about "Days of Digging," or have them write descriptive sentences about an event occurring in school. Have students save this work for the Review lesson.

APPLICATION Have students use prepositional phrases in their persuasive letters.

Preparing to Read

OBJECTIVES

Students will

- identify and know the meanings of the prefixes *dis-* and *auto-*.
- build fluency.

MATERIALS

- ***Transparency*** 138
- Routine 10

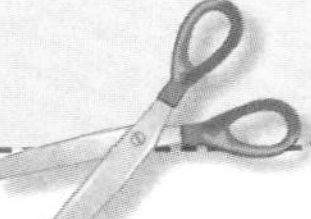

Daily Oral Practice

Daily News

Today!

I want to be an archaeologist. I love solving puzzles and making discoveries. Maybe I will make a big discovery someday, and I will be asked to write my autobiography. Until then, I will study hard in school, especially in science, and carry on my own investigations.

- Write the daily news on the board or on chart paper. Then have students read the daily news in unison to practice fluency.
- As a review of yesterday's word structure lesson, ask a volunteer to identify any words in the message with the prefixes *dis-* and *auto-*. *discoveries, discovery; autobiography*

Technology

WORD STRUCTURE Have students use the ***eSkills & eGames*** activity for this unit for practice with prefixes.

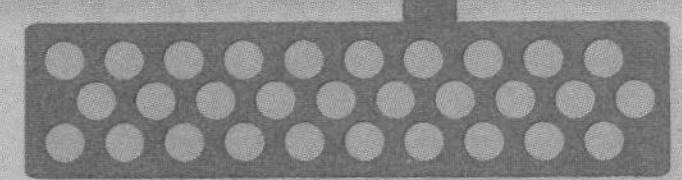

Word Structure

The Prefixes *dis-* and *auto-*

✦ Use ***Transparency*** 138 with these word lines from Day 3.

Line 1	agree	disagree	honest	dishonest
Line 2	cover	discover	appearance	disappearance
Line 3	graph	autograph	pilot	autopilot
Line 4	biography	autobiography	mobile	automobile

✦ Use Routine 10 to review the meanings of the prefixes *dis-* and *auto-*. If necessary, remind students that *dis-* means "opposite," and *auto-* means "self."

Developing Oral Language

Use any of the following activities to help students practice reading the words.

- Ask a student to find a word by naming its location in the word lines. For example, "Line 4, Word 2 is *autobiography*." Then ask the student to identify the word by reading it aloud and using it in a sentence. **Possible Answer** *Maybe I will turn my diary into an* autobiography. Ask the student to choose a volunteer to continue. Continue the activity until all words have been used.
- Have a volunteer select a base word and use it in a sentence. **Possible Answer** *The* pilot *of the plane needs to be very careful.* Then have that student select another volunteer to use the other form of the word in another sentence. **Possible Answer** *On long flights, sometimes the plane is on* autopilot. Continue until all of the words have been used.
- Ask a volunteer to choose a word and use it in a sentence to begin a story. Ask another volunteer to use a different word in a different sentence to continue the story started with the first sentence. Have volunteers continue to add to the story using words from the word lines until all words have been used.
- Have a volunteer choose a word from the word lines with the prefix *dis-* or *auto-*. Then have the student define the word based on the meaning of the prefix. Have the student use a dictionary if necessary. Continue for all the words with *dis-* or *auto-* on the word lines.

Monitor Progress

to Differentiate Instruction
Formal Assessment

Word Structure During the word structure activity, note how well students understand the words.

APPROACHING LEVEL

IF . . . students do not understand the words on the word lines, **THEN . . .** use pictures, photos, objects, stick drawings, or pantomime to help them visualize the words.

ON LEVEL

IF . . . students need practice with the words on the word lines, **THEN . . .** have them write sentences using the words on the lines.

ABOVE LEVEL

IF . . . students understand the words on the word lines, **THEN . . .** have them make a list of other words with the prefixes *dis-* and *auto-* and use them in sentences.

Imagine being the first person to unearth an ancient city. Imagine finding the bones of an ancient warrior. Imagine solving the five-thousand-year-old mystery of what happened at a place where all the villagers died at once. Archaeologists get to challenge themselves with many thrilling possibilities of the past.

156

Archaeology (ancient study) is a science. The archaeologist discovers and studies past human cultures or societies. Each group that is studied has its own values, customs, and beliefs. An archaeologist does research about a culture. He or she studies the artifacts from that culture. He or she also tries to find out when and how the culture developed. This study can take an archaeologist to any place on the planet.

157

OBJECTIVES

Students will

- use the comprehension skill Drawing Conclusions.
- check comprehension.
- investigate communities across time using the Inquiry Process.

MATERIALS

- ***Student Reader,*** Book 2, pp. 156–163
- ***Skills Practice 2,*** pp. 93–94, 109–110

Comprehension Skills

Drawing Conclusions

Continue to have students look for conclusions they can draw from clues given by the author. Ask students the following questions:

- *What conclusions can you draw from pages 156–157?* **Possible Answer** *The author asks the readers to imagine what it would be like to find an ancient city and people and solve ancient mysteries. Even though she doesn't tell readers how she feels about it, you can tell how excited she is about archaeology.*
- *What conclusions can you draw from page 157?* **Possible Answer** *When the author mentions that archaeologists could go anyplace on the planet to study, you can tell that she is excited about that and likes traveling to many places.*

Some archaeologists try to solve puzzling issues. They may try to solve mysteries about a culture's ruin or disappearance. They may try to find out why a culture did certain things. They may try to find out why a culture changed dramatically from its origins. For example, an archaeologist would try to discover why a culture that fished developed into a culture that farmed. What caused the culture to stop fishing? What made them start farming? These questions may be answered through archaeology.

158

You may wonder why it is so important to learn about our human past. It is important because it teaches us about being human. It shows us how creative and resourceful humans really are—and have been. The past is important because it tells us how we became what we are today. It also explains how and why we have so many different cultures. It teaches us to respect those cultures, and our own.

159

Checking Comprehension

Ask students the following questions to check their comprehension of the story.

- *What is the selection mainly about?* **Possible Answer** *It is about what it is like being an archaeologist.*
- *Why is studying and learning about our human past so important?* **Possible Answer** *It tells us about how we became what we are today, and it teaches us to respect the cultures of the past.*

Word Structure

Prefix *dis-*: discovers, disappearance

Expanding Vocabulary

thrilling (thril´• ing) *adj.* exciting (page 156) The roller coaster is a *thrilling* ride.

cultures (kəl´• chûrz) *n.* plural form of **culture:** the arts, beliefs, and customs that make up a way of life for a group of people at a certain time (page 157) We have studied several *cultures* in social studies class.

research (rē • sûrch´) *n.* a careful study to find and learn facts (page 157) To complete our assignment, we must conduct *research* about three different cultures.

creative (krē • āt´ • əv´) *adj.* able to make or invent new things (page 159) The artist is a very *creative* person.

Social Studies Inquiry

Genre Biography 

A biography is the story of a real person's life that is written by another person.

Feature Quote

Point to the quotes in "John Muir: Mountain Man." Tell students that a quote is a written statement of a person's exact words. Explain that quotes are often used in biographies and other expository texts.

Ask students to point to and read each quote in "John Muir: Mountain Man." Then ask students why they think the quotes are important.

Teacher Tip

SELECTION VOCABULARY Review the meaning of the highlighted selection vocabulary words *ruin* and *charted* in "John Muir: Mountain Man."

Reading "John Muir: Mountain Man"

Have students take turns reading aloud "John Muir: Mountain Man." Ask students how this biography relates to the theme Communities across Time. Make sure students read each quote and understand why it was used in the biography.

Think Link

1. Look at the quote at the beginning of the article. What did John Muir mean by this statement? What does this tell you about Muir's view of nature? **Possible Answer** *He meant that beauty is very important in life, just as important as food. He loved nature very much and it was probably the most important thing in his life.*
2. How did John Muir's accident change him? **Possible Answer** *He felt as if he had a second chance at life and he wanted to enjoy all of the sights and places around him.*
3. What did John Muir do to protect the wilderness of Yosemite Valley? **Possible Answer** *He protected the wilderness by convincing Congress to make Yosemite a national park.*

Social Studies Inquiry

John Muir: Mountain Man

Genre

A **biography** is the story of a real person's life that is written by another person.

Feature

A **quote** is a written statement of a person's exact words.

"Everybody needs beauty as well as bread . . ."

These are the words of nature lover John Muir. Muir is well known for his work to preserve America's wild lands. They are places he knew well and held dear.

Muir was born in Scotland in 1838. He came to the United States when he was 11 years old. He worked long, hard days on a farm in Wisconsin.

Muir had an awful accident as a young man. A sharp tool pierced his eye, and Muir lost his vision. In a few months, his sight came back. Muir felt he had a new chance at life. He resolved to enjoy the sights and places he treasured. He longed to be close to nature.

"None of Nature's landscapes are ugly so long as they are wild."

Muir traveled widely. In time, he came to California. He fell in love with the beauty of Yosemite. He made his home in the valley. Muir explored the mountains, cliffs, and

waterfalls. He strolled through the forests and meadows.

Muir wrote books and essays about Yosemite. He stressed the splendor of the land and wildlife there. His work drew a great deal of attention.

Muir grew alarmed by changes he saw. Grazing sheep wrecked the hills. Lumber firms cut down huge, old trees. Muir fought to save the valley from ruin.

Muir made a plea to Congress to make Yosemite a national park. He charted the areas that should make up the park. They agreed.

Muir also helped start a private group to protect the region. The Sierra Club was formed in 1892. It carries on Muir's ideals to this day.

Think Link

1. Look at the quote at the beginning of the article. What did John Muir mean by this statement? What does this tell you about Muir's view of nature?
2. How did John Muir's accident change him?
3. What did John Muir do to protect the wilderness of Yosemite Valley?

Try It!

As you work on your investigation, think about how you can use quotes to tell more about a topic.

Inquiry Connection

Have students discuss how quotes might be helpful in their investigations about the theme Communities across Time. For example, if students interview an archaeologist about a culture of the past, they would use quotes to make the writing more credible and more interesting.

Teacher Tip

INVESTIGATION TOPICS The more possibilities for investigation topics and questions students are presented with, the more likely they are to find a topic that keenly interests them. Offer students many possibilities, but allow them to choose their own investigation path.

Inquiry Process

Step 2—Identifying a Question to Investigate

Whole-Group Time

Whole Group

- ✦ So far in their investigations, students have formed groups and generated ideas and questions about past and present communities. Now they will choose one research question or topic that interests them.
- ✦ Explain that students can get ideas and new questions from the selections they read. Guide a discussion about how "Days of Digging" relates to the theme. For example, students might wonder about why communities from different times are so different. They might also wonder how and why communities form. Students interested in a present-day community might wonder what kind of changes that community will undergo. Allow students' particular interests in the theme to steer the group discussions, and encourage a wide variety of possible investigation topics.
- ✦ Model the process of choosing your own investigation question. Return to the topic you modeled earlier. For example, say something such as the following*: I was concerned about the community that became overpopulated and began destroying forests and animal habitats to make room for more people. This led me to ask the question* How can nature and people live in harmony? *Since I'm interested in helping the community and protecting natural habitats, I want to investigate something about this topic. My investigation question will be* How can our community avoid expanding too much and destroying valuable countryside? *By researching this question, I can learn a lot about how communities can change while still protecting people and nature.* Encourage students to offer relevant questions and comments about the question you modeled. Remind students that their investigations should focus on something important or interesting to them within the unit theme.
- ✦ To continue to make discoveries about this unit theme, students may want to invite an expert to the class. They may want to invite an archaeologist, a director of a museum on ancient civilizations, an environmental expert who deals with land management, the mayor of the city, or some other prominent community planner. Help students make the necessary arrangements for any class speakers.

Small-Group Time

Small Group

- Have students break into their investigation groups. Let students know that they can investigate the possibilities for future communities. To encourage interest in future communities, have students complete ***Skills Practice 2*** page 110.
- Before choosing their investigation questions, have students review all their notes from class discussions and unit selections, as well as ***Skills Practice 2*** pages 93–94 and 109–110. Have groups discuss which questions they are most interested in researching. Then have them select one group investigation question. When each group has selected its question, have them post their investigation question on the **Concept/Question Board.** Remind students that they can update or change their questions as they encounter new information.

Concept/Question Board

- Remind students that they can consult the **Concept/Question Board** for ideas to help them decide which question to investigate.
- Provide opportunities for students to read and comment on information posted on the Board.
- Ask students to think about what they can add to the **Concept/Question Board.** Continue to encourage use of the Board by recognizing and thanking students for their contributions. Incorporate discussion of those items into classroom discussions whenever possible. Remember to also model by posting your own questions and ideas.

Inquiry Rubric

To assess Identifying a Question to Investigate, see the Inquiry Rubrics in the Level Appendix.

Research in Action

Our teachers noted that all students, regardless of their ability levels, made progress in their abilities to communicate effectively about their investigations and to talk about their ideas. Some students who previously were not actively involved began to take leadership roles.

(McKeough, 2006)

UNIT 5 Lesson 2

Generating Possible Investigation Topics (continued)

We can't always perfectly predict the future, but it is fun to think about. Even though we can't know what the future will bring, we can investigate what it *might* bring.

How will communities ten years from now be different? What about 100 years from now? What about a trillion years from now?

Maybe communities will be in space. Maybe in 100 years people will stop fighting and live in peace together.

How might communities use land differently in the future?

Land may not be used at all. Maybe in the future, people will use the air and build floating farms.

What are some of the problems future communities might have? How might they be able to solve these problems?

Future communities might run out of land and need to use air space for farming and living.

110 UNIT 5 • Lesson 2 Inquiry • *Skills Practice 2*

Skills Practice 2, p. 110

OBJECTIVES

Students will
- ✦ edit/proofread persuasive letters.
- ✦ review spelling words.
- ✦ write a list of questions for an interview.
- ✦ learn how to follow a series of directions.

MATERIALS
- ✦ ***Transparencies*** 17, 17A, 139, 139A
- ✦ ***Skills Practice 2,*** p. 112
- ✦ Routine 16

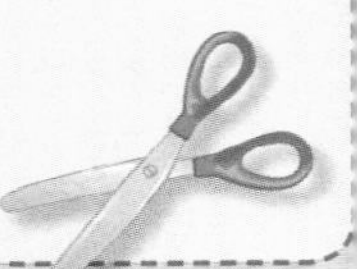

Imagine It! Transparency 139 139A

Revising: Varying Types of Sentences

I enjoy your library, but you are missing the book A Year Down Yonder by Richard Peck. I want to read this book, but I cannot find it. Some of my friends have read it, and they said it was very good. Did you know that it even won the Newbery Medal in 2001?

Transparencies 139, 139A

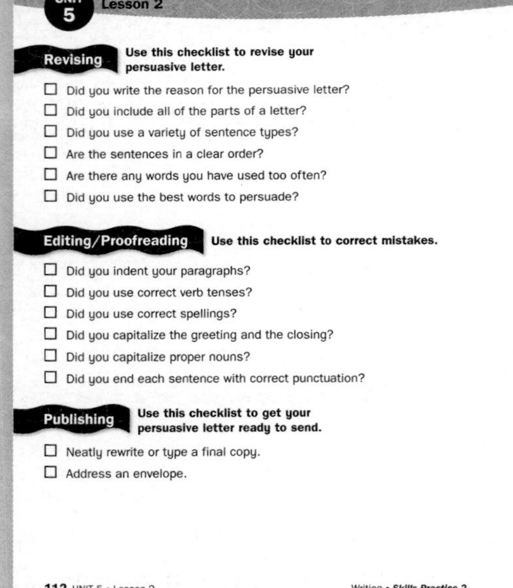

UNIT 5 Lesson 2

Revising Use this checklist to revise your persuasive letter.
- ☐ Did you write the reason for the persuasive letter?
- ☐ Did you include all of the parts of a letter?
- ☐ Did you use a variety of sentence types?
- ☐ Are the sentences in a clear order?
- ☐ Are there any words you have used too often?
- ☐ Did you use the best words to persuade?

Editing/Proofreading Use this checklist to correct mistakes.
- ☐ Did you indent your paragraphs?
- ☐ Did you use correct verb tenses?
- ☐ Did you use correct spellings?
- ☐ Did you capitalize the greeting and the closing?
- ☐ Did you capitalize proper nouns?
- ☐ Did you end each sentence with correct punctuation?

Publishing Use this checklist to get your persuasive letter ready to send.
- ☐ Neatly rewrite or type a final copy.
- ☐ Address an envelope.

112 UNIT 5 • Lesson 2 Writing • *Skills Practice 2*

Skills Practice 2, p. 112

Writing Persuasive Letter

ROUTINE 16

Editing/Proofreading

Teach

- ✦ Use Routine 16 as you model editing/proofreading.
- ✦ Remind students that when they are editing their letters, they will be making corrections in spelling, grammar, capitalization, and punctuation.
- ✦ Discuss some items students should pay particular attention to in letters.
  - Are names spelled correctly? Are correct titles used?
  - Are capital letters used in the heading, greeting, closing, and signature?
  - Are commas used correctly in the heading, greeting, and closing?
  - Tell students to add prepositional phrases for added description and to vary sentences.
  - Tell students to make sure they check to be sure they have correctly spelled the name of the recipient in the greeting. If necessary, remind students how to use periods for capitalization, abbreviations, and initials.
- ✦ Remind students of the proofreading marks they should use by displaying ***Transparencies*** 17, 17A.

Guided Practice

- ✦ Model editing and proofreading using ***Transparencies*** 139 and 139A. Display ***Transparency*** 139. Have a student read the paragraph aloud, and then have students discuss the edits they would make. You may want to write a list on the board. Next, display ***Transparency*** 139A, and have a student read the corrected information. Match the edits against the list students generated.
- ✦ Have students turn to ***Skills Practice 2*** page 112. Read and discuss the editing/proofreading checklist.

Writing, continued

Apply

Composing—Editing/Proofreading Have students edit their persuasive letters. Encourage them to refer to the checklist on page 112 in ***Skills Practice 2*** while they edit their letters. Tell students to proofread their letters with a partner.

Monitor Progress to Differentiate Instruction

Formal Assessment

Editing/Proofreading Note whether students catch and correct errors in grammar, spelling, capitalization, and punctuation.

APPROACHING LEVEL

IF . . . students need extra help editing/proofreading,	**THEN . . .** have them work with a peer to edit/proofread during Workshop.

ON LEVEL

IF . . . students have an understanding of editing/proofreading,	**THEN . . .** have them search for graphics to accompany their persuasive letters.

ABOVE LEVEL

IF . . . students need a challenge,	**THEN . . .** have them work on publishing their persuasive letters using a word processing program.

Spelling

Place Words and Prefixes *bi-, mid-, dis-,* and *auto-*

Teach

Meaning Strategy Tell students that when they use a word, it is important to make sure that the word is spelled correctly and that they are using the correct meaning.

Guided Practice

Write the correct spelling word next to its clue.

1. in, or into the interior of ________ *within*
2. operating by itself ________ *automatic*
3. in the middle of summer ________ *midsummer*
4. not to have trust in ________ *distrust*
5. an airplane with two sets of wings ________ *biplane*

Study Skills

Interviews

Teach

- Remind students that conducting an interview is another research tool. The interviewee is a source in an investigation.
- When conducting an interview, interviewers should always be prepared with questions. The questions should be relevant to the topic, and the interviewee should be an expert on the topic.

Guided Practice

Ask students to think of people they would like to interview while researching the theme Communities across Time. Write their ideas on the board. Ask why these people would be good choices and what they expect to learn from them. You may want to suggest grandparents as an important resource for explaining how their community has changed over time.

Apply

Have students write a list of questions to ask the person they selected to interview. Tell students the questions should relate to the theme Communities across Time.

Differentiating Instruction — English Learner

IF . . . students would benefit from additional support during Apply in Study Skills, **THEN . . .** be sure to pair them with proficient English speakers.

Listening/Speaking/Viewing

Following Directions

Teach

- Explain to students that many times throughout their lives they will be asked to listen to and follow directions. The directions may contain several steps.
- Emphasize the importance of listening carefully to be able to perform the steps correctly.
- As an example, ask students to think about a process they know how to perform and to consider what problems could occur if the steps of the process were not followed. Give students time to consider the idea and encourage them to share their thoughts.

Guided Practice

Create a set of how-to directions for a process that involves three to five steps. Possible ideas include a simple recipe, wrapping a gift, potting a plant, or making a simple craft. Give students the directions orally. Remind students to listen carefully. Ask students to write the directions, retell the directions, or complete the process.

Apply

- Have students work in groups to create a set of directions archaeologists would use for proper digging techniques based on "Days of Digging."
- Have the groups present their directions to the class.
- As a class, have the groups discuss why it would be important for an archaeologist to follow these directions completely and in the correct order.

Preparing to Read Review

OBJECTIVES

Students will
- review the prefixes *bi-*, *mid-*, *dis-*, and *auto-*.
- build fluency.

MATERIALS

Transparencies 134 and 138

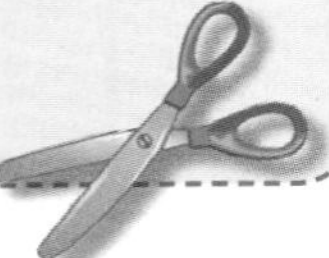

Word Structure

Use ***Transparency*** 134 with the word lines from Days 1 and 2 to review the prefixes *bi-* and *mid-*. Have students read the words on the word lines. Then have students use each word on the lines in a sentence.

Line 1	cycle	bicycle	monthly	bimonthly
Line 2	plane	biplane	weekly	biweekly
Line 3	day	midday	night	midnight
Line 4	point	midpoint	summer	midsummer

Word Structure

Use ***Transparency*** 138 with the word lines from Days 3 and 4 to review the prefixes *dis-* and *auto-*. Have students read the words on the word lines. Then have volunteers choose a pair of words from the lines and use them in sentences.

Line 1	agree	disagree	honest	dishonest
Line 2	cover	discover	appearance	disappearance
Line 3	graph	autograph	pilot	autopilot
Line 4	biography	autobiography	mobile	automobile

Reading and Responding

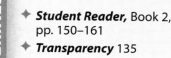

OBJECTIVES

Students will
- review selection vocabulary.
- review the comprehension strategies Asking Questions, Clarifying, and Summarizing.
- review the comprehension skill Drawing Conclusions.
- review fluency.

MATERIALS

- ***Student Reader,*** Book 2, pp. 150–161
- ***Transparency*** 135

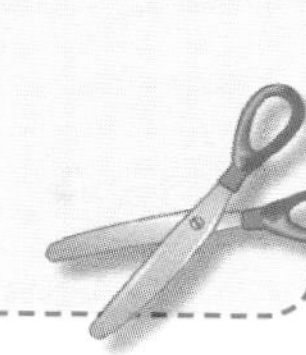

Selection Vocabulary

To review the selection vocabulary, organize students into small groups. Give each group a slip of paper with two of the selection vocabulary words written on it. Tell each group to develop clues that describe the meanings of their words. When students have written several clues for each word, bring them together and have them share their clues with the class. Have students guess which vocabulary word is being described.

Selection Vocabulary

beats (bēts) *v.* a form of the verb **beat:** to come down strong and continuously (page 152)

charted (chärt′• əd) *v.* a form of the verb **chart:** to map; to show information as a picture (page 153)

laboratory (la′• brə • tor′• ē) *n.* a room for science experiments and tests (page 153)

challenge (chal′• lənj) *n.* to give the best of (page 156)

customs (kus′• təmz) *n.* plural form of **custom:** a practice that has become accepted by many people; a tradition (page 157)

ruin (ro͞o′• in) *n.* destruction, damage, or collapse (page 158)

origins (or′• əg • ənz) *n.* plural form of **origin:** the cause or source of something; what something begins or comes from (page 158)

developed (də • vel′ • əpd) *v.* past tense of **develop:** to grow; to change. (page 157)

Day 5

Reading and Responding Review

Comprehension Strategies 

Review the following comprehension strategies with students:

- **Clarifying** is used by readers to figure out the meaning of words, passages, and difficult ideas. To review this strategy, have students find examples in the text of words, ideas, and passages that they clarified while reading. Have students discuss what strategies they used to clarify the words, passages, and ideas as they read "Days of Digging."
- **Asking Questions** helps readers focus attention on what they are reading by asking and finding the answers to questions they have about the text. Have students turn back to "Days of Digging" and share the questions they had about the selection with the class. Ask students how using this strategy helped them to understand this selection.
- **Summarizing** prompts readers to keep track of what they are reading and to focus their minds on important information. Have students write a short paragraph that summarizes "Days of Digging" and explain how summarizing helps them better understand the selection.

Comprehension Skill   

Review the following comprehension skill with students:

- **Drawing Conclusions** requires readers to find clues within the text to make their own conclusions, or judgments or opinions, about events or characters within the story. Ask students to review "Days of Digging," and discuss the conclusions they made while reading the selection. Ask students to explain how drawing their conclusions helped them better understand "Days of Digging."

Reading with a Writer's Eye 

Review the following literary element with students:

Genre Knowledge is a category or type of literature, such as realistic fiction, expository text, myth, biography, and so on. Review the genre of "Days of Digging" with students. *expository text* Have students review "Days of Digging," and find examples of expository text elements in the story.

Fluency

Review

Review fluency by reading aloud for students. Remind students that automaticity, or reading words spontaneously, adds to the meaning of text by making it easier to comprehend and enjoy. Read a passage from pages 156–159 from "Days of Digging." Make sure that the passage totals at least 160 words to ensure an appropriate practice length.

Have students read the passage chorally. Encourage students to use expression. Also remind students to pause after commas and end punctuation.

OBJECTIVES

Students will
- ✦ publish their persuasive letters.
- ✦ take the spelling posttest.
- ✦ review cursive *P* and *R*.

MATERIALS

- ✦ ***Skills Practice 2,*** p. 112
- ✦ ***Transparency*** 137
- ✦ Routine 17

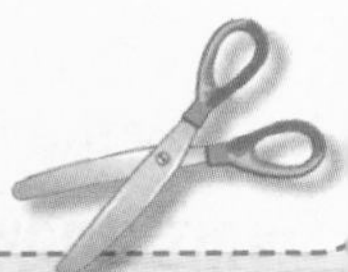

Writing Persuasive Letter

ROUTINE 17

Publishing

Teach

- ✦ Use Routine 17 and tell students they are at the final stage of the writing process: publishing. This means that they will be sharing and mailing their persuasive letters.
- ✦ Remind students that in addition to making clean, neat copies of their letters to send, they also need to address envelopes.
- ✦ Explain to students that because these letters are more formal and the main purpose is to convince readers to take action or to hold a specific belief, they should type the letters on plain paper or stationery. Photographs, diagrams, charts, or illustrations that serve as examples of the facts or reasons in the letters are acceptable for formal writing.
- ✦ Model inserting a photograph, diagram, or charts into the final copy of your persuasive letter.

Guided Practice

- ✦ Create a large rectangle on the board to show students how to address an envelope. Have students help you complete the sender and receiver information for your letter. Also indicate where the stamp should be placed.
- ✦ Have students turn to ***Skills Practice 2*** page 112 to read and discuss the publishing checklist.

Apply

- ✦ **Composing—Publishing** Students should type the final version of their persuasive letters. Have students refer to page 112 in ***Skills Practice 2*** as a guide to publishing with visual aids. Remind students to address an envelope so that the letter can be mailed.
- ✦ Have volunteers discuss whether the letters they read and heard were persuasive and actually convinced them to feel or believe in the writer's point of view. Ask volunteers whether they were persuaded to take action.

Teacher Tip

ASSESSMENT Use the Writing Rubrics found in the Level Appendix to evaluate students' persuasive paragraphs. You may use any of the rubrics for Genre, Writing Process, and Writing Traits.

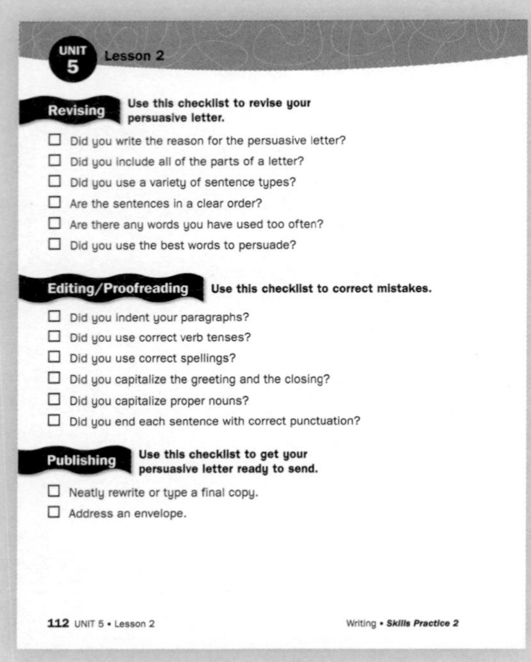

UNIT 5 Lesson 2

Revising Use this checklist to revise your persuasive letter.

- ☐ Did you write the reason for the persuasive letter?
- ☐ Did you include all of the parts of a letter?
- ☐ Did you use a variety of sentence types?
- ☐ Are the sentences in a clear order?
- ☐ Are there any words you have used too often?
- ☐ Did you use the best words to persuade?

Editing/Proofreading Use this checklist to correct mistakes.

- ☐ Did you indent your paragraphs?
- ☐ Did you use correct verb tenses?
- ☐ Did you use correct spellings?
- ☐ Did you capitalize the greeting and the closing?
- ☐ Did you capitalize proper nouns?
- ☐ Did you end each sentence with correct punctuation?

Publishing Use this checklist to get your persuasive letter ready to send.

- ☐ Neatly rewrite or type a final copy.
- ☐ Address an envelope.

112 UNIT 5 • Lesson 2 Writing • *Skills Practice 2*

Skills Practice 2, p. 112

Spelling

Place Words and Prefixes *bi-*, *mid-*, *dis-*, and *auto-*

Teach

Ask students to write *Spelling* and their names in the top margin of a clean piece of paper. Have them number the first fifteen lines 1–15, then skip a line and number the next two lines 1–2. Read each word, use it in a sentence, and give students time to spell it correctly. Encourage students to try to spell the challenge words, but assure them that misspelling a challenge word will not affect their test scores.

Spelling Words		**Challenge Words**
disprove	midtown	disagree
bifocal	within	autobiography
autopilot	automobile	
upon	near	
midsummer	midweek	
distrust	disband	
biplane	bicycle	
automatic		

Guided Practice

✦ Have students proofread for any mistakes they made on the posttest. Tell them to categorize the mistakes as
- careless errors.
- errors in spelling place words.
- errors in spelling words with the prefix *bi-*, *mid-*, *dis-*, or *auto-*.

✦ Make certain students are spelling place words, and words with the prefixes *bi-*, *mid-*, *dis-*, and *auto-* correctly.

Penmanship

Cursive Letters *P* and *R*

Teach

✦ Review cursive *P* and cursive *R* with students. Use ***Transparency*** 137 if necessary.
- **Letter *P*** Starting point, undercurve
  Slant down, retrace
  Curve forward and back: capital *P*
- **Letter *R*** Starting point, undercurve
  Slant down, retrace up
  Curve forward to slant
  Curve forward
  Undercurve: capital *R*

✦ To model proper letter formation, write the following sentence on the board: *Ramsis and Palesa live on Pike River Road.*

Guided Practice

Ask for a volunteer to write the sentence on the board. Guide the student while he or she makes the formations.

Apply

After reviewing the sentence you wrote on the board, have students practice writing the sentence on a separate piece of paper. Ask students to circle their best sentence based on the correct formation of *P* and *R*.

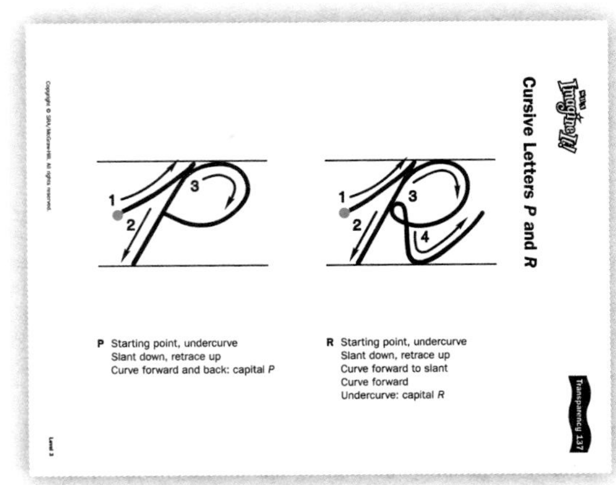

Transparency 137

Language Arts

OBJECTIVES

Students will

- review prepositions and prepositional phrases.
- discuss interviewing as a research tool.
- review the importance of following directions carefully.

MATERIALS

- ***Lesson Assessment Book 2,*** pp. 51–58

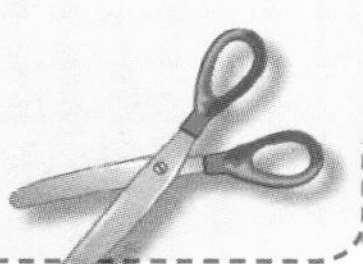

Study Skills

Interviews

Remind students that interviewing experts is an excellent source of information when conducting research.

Ask students what they must do to prepare to interview an expert. **Possible Answer** *They must have appropriate questions ready to ask.*

Have students create a list of questions to ask another student about changes that have happened recently in their communities.

Listening/Speaking/Viewing

Following Directions

Remind students of the importance of listening carefully when following directions.

- Have students work in pairs. Ask one student from each pair to give directions for a process of his or her choice. Then have the other student write or retell the directions. Have the first student take notes, making sure all of the steps were retold correctly and in the correct order.
- Have students switch roles, completing the same steps for a different process.

Grammar, Usage, and Mechanics

Prepositions and Prepositional Phrases

Write the following sentences on the board. Then have students circle the prepositions and underline the prepositional phrases.

- David likes climbing up mountains. *circle: up; underline: up mountains*
- The deer are moving through the woods. *circle: through; underline: through the woods*
- John and Doreen live across the street. *circle: across; underline: across the street*
- Theo sits between Donna and Will. *circle: between; underline: between Donna and Will*
- The nature book is on the bookshelf. *circle: on; underline: on the bookshelf*

Using the sentences students created earlier in the lesson, have them work with a partner to review their work. Tell students to make sure all their sentences have prepositional phrases. Also tell them to add an additional prepositional phrase to one of their sentences.

Monitor Progress

Formal Assessment

Use pages 51–58 in ***Lesson Assessment Book 2*** to assess students' understanding of the skills taught in this lesson. Intervene with ***Reteach, Challenge Activities, Intervention Guide, eSkills & eGames, Leveled Readers,*** or activities in the ***Workshop Kit*** as needed.

Lesson Planner

Preparing to Read

MATERIALS
- ***Transparencies*** 140, 143
- ***Skills Practice 2,*** pp. 119–122
- Routine 10

Day 1

Daily News, p. T188
Word Structure
Affixes as Syllables, pp. T188–T189

Day 2

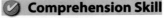

Daily News, p. T208
Word Structure
Developing Oral Language, p. T209

Reading and Responding

MATERIALS
- ***Student Reader,*** Book 2, pp. 164–183
- ***Transparencies*** 23, 35, 141
- Routines 11, 13, 14, A
- Writer's Notebook
- ***Skills Practice 2,*** pp. 123–128
- ***Home Connection,*** pp. 55–56
- ***Listening Library CDs***
- ***Leveled Reader***
- ***Lesson Assessment Book 2***

Day 1

Build Background, p. T190
Preview and Prepare, p. T191
Selection Vocabulary, pp. T192–T193
Reading the Selection, pp. T194–T197 (1st READ)
Comprehension Strategies
- Visualizing, pp. T194, T198–T201
- Making Connections, pp. T195, T199–T200

Comprehension Skill
☆ Fact and Opinion, p. T196
Inquiry, pp. T202–T203

Day 2

Comprehension Strategies
- Making Connections, pp. T210, T211
- Visualizing, p. T210

Discussing the Selection, p. T212
Review Selection Vocabulary, p. T213
Fluency, p. T213
Theme Connections, pp. T214–T215

Language Arts

MATERIALS
- ***Transparencies*** 17, 17A, 127, 131, 137, 139, 139A, 142
- ***Skills Practice 2,*** pp. 129–136
- ***Language Arts Handbook,*** pp. 72–77, 324–325
- Routines 16, 17
- ***Lesson Assessment Book 2,*** pp. 59–66

Day 1

Writing
Prewriting, pp. T204–T205
Spelling Pretest, p. T205
Penmanship, Cursive Letters *S, G, N, M, P* and *R*, p. T206

Day 2

Writing
Drafting, pp. T216–T217
Spelling, p. T217
Grammar, Usage, and Mechanics
Sentence Tense, pp. T218–T219

Monitor Progress

✓ = **Formal Assessment**

Day 1
- ✓ **Word Structure, p. T189**
- ✓ **Comprehension Strategy, p. T194**
- ✓ **Comprehension Skill, p. T195**
- ✓ **Spelling Pretest, p. T205**

Day 2
- ✓ **Word Structure, p. T209**
- ✓ **Selection Vocabulary, p. T213**
- **Fluency, p. T213**
- ✓ **Grammar, Usage, and Mechanics, p. T219**

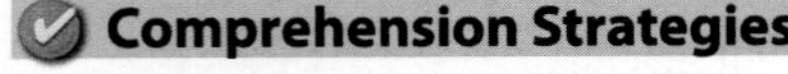

Literature Overview

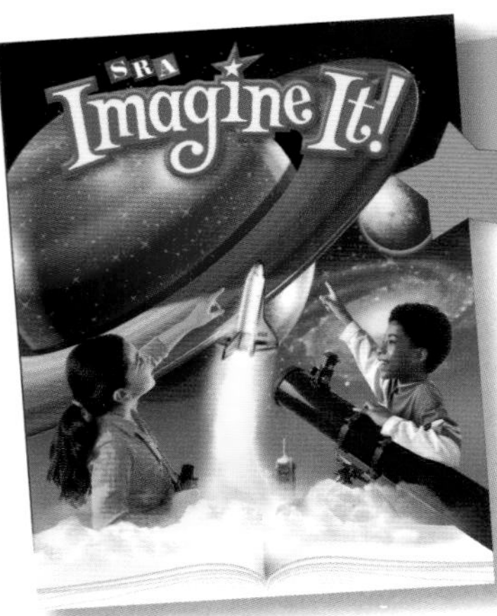

Student Reader

Earthquake! The 1906 San Francisco Nightmare

by Lynn Brunelle

Social Studies Inquiry

Shear Joy!

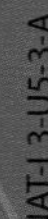

SRA
Imagine It!

Day 3

Daily News, p. T220
Word Structure
Affixes Used to Change Word Meaning, pp. T220–T221

Comprehension Skill
- Drawing Conclusions, p. T222
- Fact and Opinion, p. T223
- Cause and Effect, p. T224

Reading with a Writer's Eye, p. T225
Supporting the Reading
Comprehension Skill: Fact and Opinion, p. T226
Fluency, p. T227
Inquiry, p. T227

2nd READ

Writing
Revising, p. T228
Spelling, p. T229
Study Skills
Maps, p. T230
Grammar, Usage, and Mechanics, p. T231

Word Structure, p. T221
Comprehension Skill, p. T226
Fluency, p. T227
Spelling, p. T229
Study Skills, p. T230

Day 4

Daily News, p. T232
Word Structure, p. T233
Developing Oral Language, p. T233

Comprehension Skill
Fact and Opinion, p. T234
Social Studies Inquiry, pp. T236–T237
Inquiry, pp. T238–T239

Writing
Editing/Proofreading, pp. T240–T241
Spelling, p. T241
Study Skills, p. T242
Listening/Speaking/Viewing
Effective Voice and Word Choice, p. T243

Word Structure, p. T233
Writing, p. T240

Day 5 Review

Word Structure, p. T244

Selection Vocabulary, p. T245
Comprehension Strategies
- Making Connections, p. T246
- Visualizing, p. T246

Comprehension Skills
- Drawing Conclusions, p. T246
- Fact and Opinion, p. T246
- Cause and Effect, p. T246

Reading with a Writer's Eye, p. T247
Fluency, p. T247

Writing
Publishing, p. T248
Spelling Posttest, p. T249
Penmanship, p. T249
Study Skills, p. T250
Listening/Speaking/Viewing, p. T250
Grammar, Usage, and Mechanics, p. T251

Spelling Posttest, p. T249
Lesson Assessment Book 2, pp. 59–66

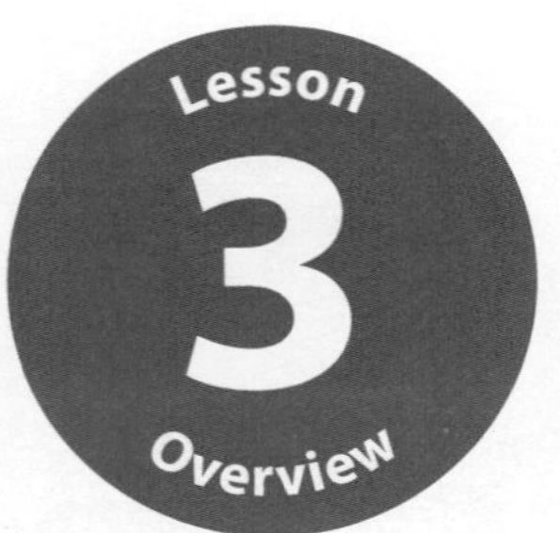

Student Resources

Genre

Expository Text is nonfiction that is written to inform, to explain, or to persuade.

Comprehension Skill

Fact and Opinion
As you read, identify facts and opinions within the selection.

166

Earthquake!

The 1906 San Francisco Nightmare

by Lynn Brunelle

Focus Questions

How do the weather and other environmental factors affect your community? How have communities around the United States handled different natural disasters?

167

Student Reader, Book 2, pp. 166–181

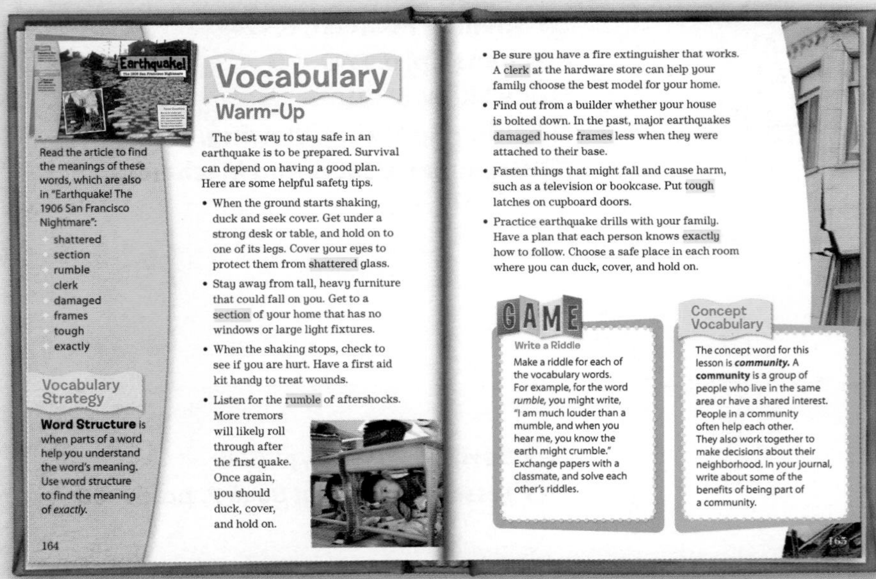

Read the article to find the meanings of these words, which are also in "Earthquake! The 1906 San Francisco Nightmare":

- shattered
- section
- rumble
- clerk
- damaged
- frames
- tough
- exactly

Vocabulary Strategy

Word Structure is when parts of a word help you understand the word's meaning. Use word structure to find the meaning of *exactly.*

Vocabulary Warm-Up

The best way to stay safe in an earthquake is to be prepared. Survival can depend on having a good plan. Here are some helpful safety tips.

- When the ground starts shaking, duck and seek cover. Get under a strong desk or table, and hold on to one of its legs. Cover your eyes to protect them from shattered glass.
- Stay away from tall, heavy furniture that could fall on you. Get to a section of your home that has no windows or large light fixtures.
- When the shaking stops, check to see if you are hurt. Have a first aid kit handy to treat wounds.
- Listen for the rumble of aftershocks. More tremors will likely roll through after the first quake. Once again, you should duck, cover, and hold on.
- Be sure you have a fire extinguisher that works. A clerk at the hardware store can help your family choose the best model for your home.
- Find out from a builder whether your house is bolted down. In the past, major earthquakes damaged house frames less when they were attached to their base.
- Fasten things that might fall and cause harm, such as a television or bookcase. Put tough latches on cupboard doors.
- Practice earthquake drills with your family. Have a plan that each person knows exactly how to follow. Choose a safe place in each room where you can duck, cover, and hold on.

GAME

Write a Riddle

Make a riddle for each of the vocabulary words. For example, for the word *rumble,* you might write, "I am much louder than a mumble, and when you hear me, you know the earth might crumble." Exchange papers with a classmate, and solve each other's riddles.

Concept Vocabulary

The concept word for this lesson is ***community.*** A **community** is a group of people who live in the same area or have a shared interest. People in a community often help each other. They also work together to make decisions about their neighborhood. In your journal, write about some of the benefits of being part of a community.

164

165

Student Reader, Book 2, pp. 164–165

Social Studies

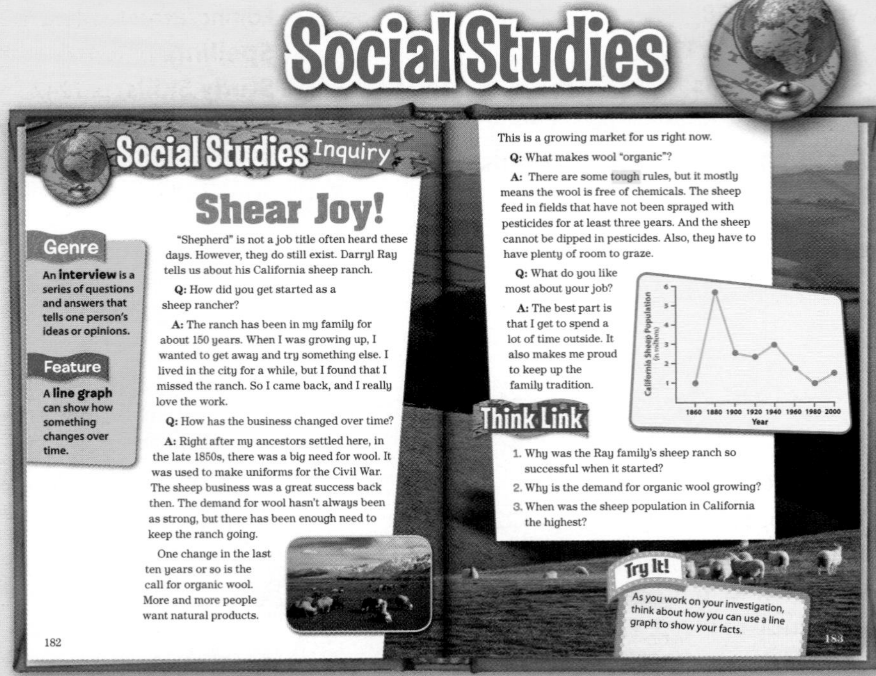

Social Studies Inquiry

Shear Joy!

Genre

An **interview** is a series of questions and answers that tells one person's ideas or opinions.

Feature

A **line graph** can show how something changes over time.

"Shepherd" is not a job title often heard these days. However, they do still exist. Darryl Ray tells us about his California sheep ranch.

Q: How did you get started as a sheep rancher?

A: The ranch has been in my family for about 150 years. When I was growing up, I wanted to get away and try something else. I lived in the city for a while, but I found that I missed the ranch. So I came back, and I really love the work.

Q: How has the business changed over time?

A: Right after my ancestors settled here, in the late 1850s, there was a big need for wool. It was used to make uniforms for the Civil War. The sheep business was a great success back then. The demand for wool hasn't always been as strong, but there has been enough need to keep the ranch going.

One change in the last ten years or so is the call for organic wool. More and more people want natural products. This is a growing market for us right now.

Q: What makes wool "organic"?

A: There are some tough rules, but it mostly means the wool is free of chemicals. The sheep feed in fields that have not been sprayed with pesticides for at least three years. And the sheep cannot be dipped in pesticides. Also, they have to have plenty of room to graze.

Q: What do you like most about your job?

A: The best part is that I get to spend a lot of time outside. It also makes me proud to keep up the family tradition.

Think Link

1. Why was the Ray family's sheep ranch so successful when it started?
2. Why is the demand for organic wool growing?
3. When was the sheep population in California the highest?

Try It!

As you work on your investigation, think about how you can use a line graph to show your facts.

182

183

Student Reader, Book 2, pp. 182–183

Cross-Curricular Resources

Curriculum Connections

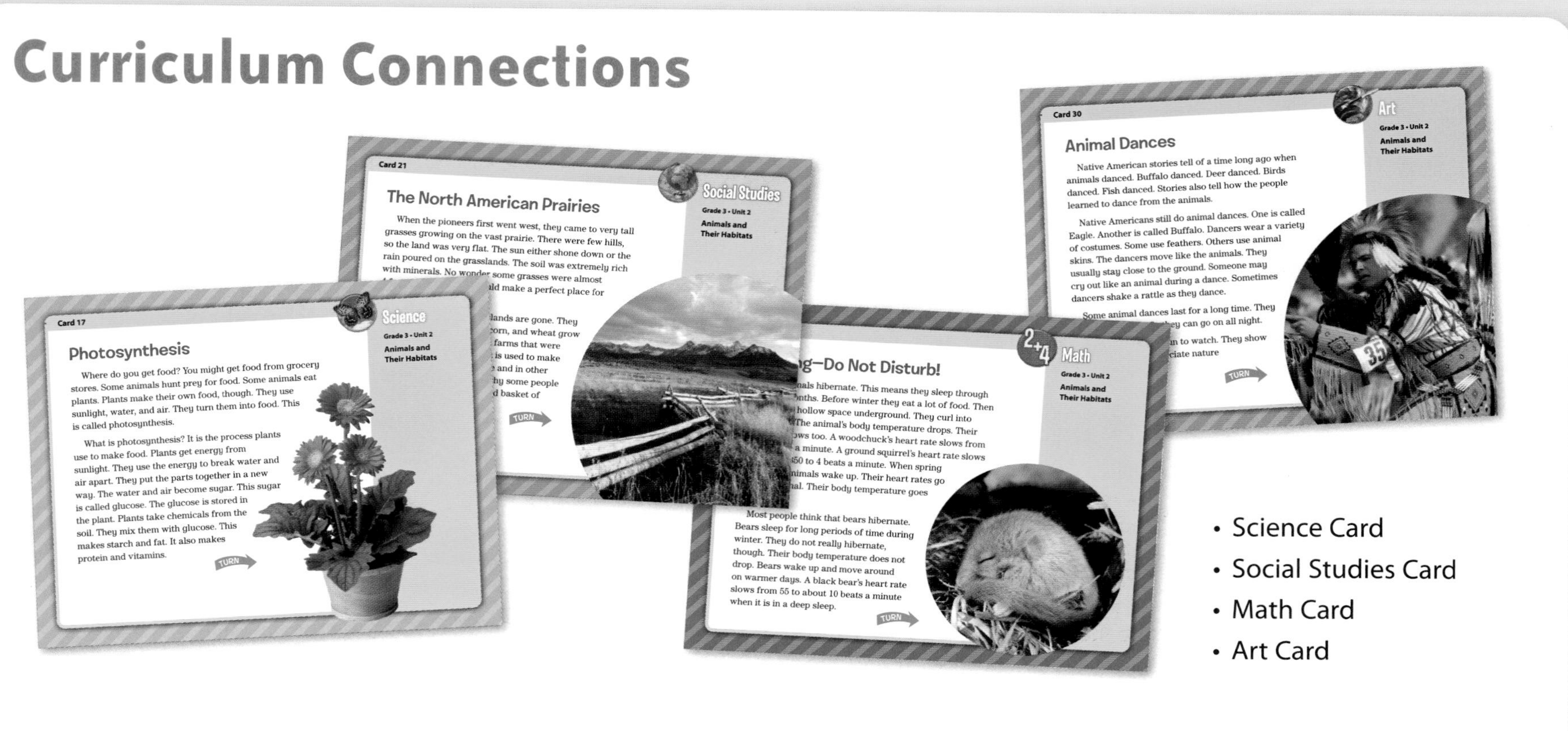

- Science Card
- Social Studies Card
- Math Card
- Art Card

Leveled Readers for Social Studies

Approaching Level

On Level

English Learner

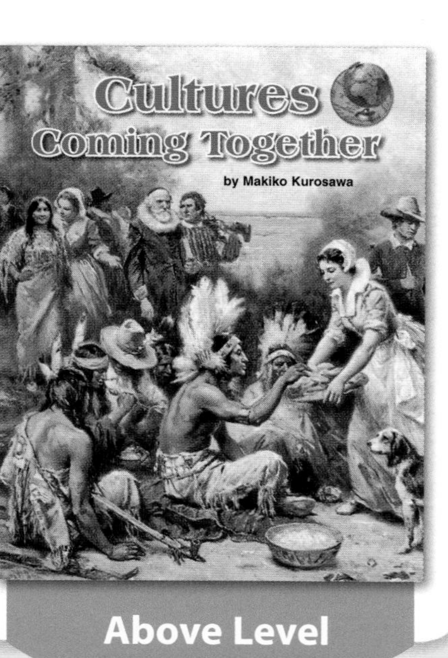

Above Level

Lesson 3 Overview

Differentiating Instruction for Workshop

Day 1

	Approaching Level	On Level	English Learner	Above Level
Preparing to Read	**Word Structure:** Review the word lines with affixes as syllables. Have students form small groups, and help them complete ***Reteach*** page 135, or work with them on the word structure activities in the ***Intervention Guide.***	**Word Structure:** Have students read other materials to look for words to add to the word lines.	**Word Structure:** Use the ***English Learner Support Guide*** for additional word structure instruction.	**Word Structure:** Have students complete ***Challenge Activities*** page 123. Then have students read other materials looking for words with affixes.
Reading and Responding	**Vocabulary:** Have students create a writing prompt using a selection vocabulary word. Have students write responses to their prompts in their Writer's Notebooks. **Comprehension:** Have students share their visualizations with the class. **Inquiry:** Have groups of students compare conjectures they made about their investigation questions.	**Vocabulary:** Have students use the selection vocabulary words to write riddles. **Comprehension:** Have students write a journal entry about a personal connection they can make to the selection. **Inquiry:** Have groups of students compare conjectures they made about their investigation questions.	**Vocabulary:** Use ***English Learner Support Guide,*** Unit 5, Lesson 3. **Comprehension:** Have students write a short paragraph about a personal connection they can make to the story. If students have difficulty expressing themselves, encourage them to illustrate their ideas. **Inquiry:** In groups, have students compare conjectures they made about their investigation question.	**Vocabulary:** Have students use the selection vocabulary words in a story. **Comprehension:** Have students write a journal entry about a connection they can make to the selection. **Inquiry:** Have groups of students compare conjectures they made about their investigation questions.
Language Arts	**Writing:** Have students complete their graphic organizers. **Spelling:** Have students complete the ***eSkills & eGames*** spelling activity.	**Writing:** Have students work independently on graphic organizers. **Spelling:** Have students proofread their persuasive letters for spelling errors.	**Writing:** Have students discuss reasons to write business letters with peers. **Spelling:** Have students work in small groups to scramble the spelling words, trade papers with another group, and unscramble the words.	**Writing:** Have students share their graphic organizers with classmates. **Spelling:** Have students write four spelling words on a piece of paper with their affixes and write the base word without the affix next to each.

Day 2

Approaching Level	On Level	English Learner	Above Level
Preparing to Read			
Word Structure: Have students write sentences using words from the word lines. Students also can play activities with prefixes or suffixes in the ***Workshop Kit.***	**Word Structure:** Students can write new sentences using words from the blending lines. Challenge them to write sentences about the theme Communities across Time.	**Word Structure:** Have students write sentences using words from the word lines. Students also can play activities with prefixes or suffixes in the ***Workshop Kit.***	**Word Structure:** Have students make lists of base words without affixes. Then have them practice adding different affixes to the base words.
Reading and Responding			
Vocabulary: Have students use ***Reteach*** page 137. **Comprehension:** Have students write a short summary about what they have learned in the selection so far. **Fluency:** Have students reread a passage from the selection with a partner or individually.	**Vocabulary:** Have students complete a game in the ***Workshop Kit.*** **Comprehension:** Have students make connections between the selection and other selections they have read. **Fluency:** Have students engage in echo reading with passages from the story.	**Vocabulary:** Help students create flash cards for the selection vocabulary words. **Comprehension:** Have students choose another selection from the unit and demonstrate the similarities and differences between the two texts by using a Venn diagram. **Fluency:** Have students read into a tape recorder at the beginning and end of the week. Have them listen to themselves at the end of the week so they can hear their progress.	**Vocabulary:** Have students complete ***Challenge Activities*** page 125. **Comprehension:** Have students create a chart that maps the main ideas of the selection so far. **Fluency:** Have students discuss the books they are reading independently in a book chat.
Language Arts			
Writing: Have students conference with peers. **Spelling:** Have students work in groups to review this week's spelling word list. **Grammar, Usage, and Mechanics:** Have students complete ***Reteach*** page 141.	**Writing:** Have students continue to draft their business letters. **Spelling:** Have students complete the ***eSkills & eGames*** spelling activity. **Grammar, Usage, and Mechanics:** Have students do an activity from the ***Workshop Kit.***	**Writing:** Have students work with a partner to help them choose words for their business letters. **Spelling:** Have students work in pairs to brainstorm ideas to help them with their spelling. **Grammar, Usage, and Mechanics:** Refer to the ***English Learner Support Guide,*** Unit 5, Lesson 3.	**Writing:** Have students pay attention to specific word usage as they draft their business letters. **Spelling:** Have students think of and spell two words other than spelling words that contain affixes. **Grammar, Usage, and Mechanics:** Have students complete ***Challenge Activities*** page 128.

Lesson 3 Overview

Differentiating Instruction for Workshop

Day 3

	Approaching Level	On Level	English Learner	Above Level
Preparing to Read	**Word Structure:** Review the word lines. Have small groups of students complete ***Reteach*** page 136, or work with them on the word structure activities in the ***Intervention Guide.***	**Word Structure:** Have students make lists of base words and practice adding different prefixes and suffixes to them.	**Word Structure:** Review the word lines. Then use the ***English Learner Support Guide*** for additional word structure instruction.	**Word Structure:** Have students complete ***Challenge Activities*** page 124. Then have students make lists of words with affixes that change word meaning to add to the word lines.
Reading and Responding	**Vocabulary:** Have students write functional definitions of three of the selection vocabulary words. **Comprehension:** Have students research a fact from the selection. Have students make notes about what they find, and remind them to note the sources they use for their information. **Fluency:** Have students read the ***Leveled Readers.***	**Vocabulary:** Have students research earthquakes adding new words they find that relate to earthquakes to the Word Bank. **Comprehension:** Have students create a list of questions beginning with *why* or *how.* Have students trade their questions with a partner and answer each other's questions. **Fluency:** Have students choose a text about the unit theme to read silently.	**Vocabulary:** Have students use an online thesaurus or dictionary to find additional words that are related to the concept vocabulary words. **Comprehension:** Have students write a summary of the main ideas learned after reading the selection. **Fluency:** Have students whisper read passages from the selection as you read aloud.	**Vocabulary:** Have students select a concept vocabulary word and write a journal entry explaining how it is related to the unit theme. **Comprehension:** Have students research facts found in the selection. Have students make notes about what they find, and remind them to note their sources. **Fluency:** Have students read the ***Leveled Readers.***
Language Arts	**Writing:** Have students work with a partner to help each other revise their drafts. **Spelling:** Have students complete ***Reteach*** page 140. **Grammar, Usage, and Mechanics:** Refer to the ***Intervention Guide,*** Unit 5, Lesson 3, for intervention activities.	**Writing:** Have students continue to revise their business letters. Have students conference with a peer. **Spelling:** Have students write each spelling word with an affix. Then have them write next to each affix whether it is used as a prefix or a suffix. **Grammar, Usage, and Mechanics:** Have students look for sentence-tense errors in their letters.	**Writing:** Have students read another student's revised business letter. **Spelling:** Have students complete the ***eSkills & eGames*** spelling activity. **Grammar, Usage, and Mechanics:** Have students refer to the ***English Learner Support Guide,*** Unit 5, Lesson 3.	**Writing:** Have students work on incorporating more sophisticated language into their business letters. **Spelling:** Have students complete ***Challenge Activities*** page 127. **Grammar, Usage, and Mechanics:** Have students proofread their work for sentence-tense errors.

Day 4

	Approaching Level	On Level	English Learner	Above Level
Preparing to Read	**Word Structure:** Have students review their prefix and suffix flash cards. Students also can play activities with prefixes or suffixes in the ***Workshop Kit.***	**Word Structure:** Have students create lists of words with affixes that change word meaning to add to the word lines. Students also can play activities with prefixes or suffixes in the ***Workshop Kit.***	**Word Structure:** Have students review their prefix and suffix flash cards. Students also can play activities with prefixes or suffixes in the ***Workshop Kit.***	**Word Structure:** Have students find a partner and write clue sentences for words on the word lines. Students also can play activities with prefixes or suffixes in the ***Workshop Kit.***
Reading and Responding	**Vocabulary:** Have students review the selection and find other related words to the unit theme that can be added to the Word Bank. **Comprehension:** Have students find examples in the text that show that this selection is expository text. **Inquiry:** Have students discuss with their groups how they will research their topic. Have them make a research plan based on their investigation needs.	**Vocabulary:** Have students write sentences using expanding vocabulary words. **Comprehension:** Have students read additional articles about earthquakes. Have them summarize the articles. **Inquiry:** Have students discuss with their groups how they will research their topic. Have them make a research plan based on their investigation needs.	**Vocabulary:** Have students create a question using each concept vocabulary word, and then trade questions with a partner. **Comprehension:** Have students read additional articles about earthquakes. Have students summarize the articles. **Inquiry:** Have students discuss with their groups how they will research their topic. Have them make a research plan based on their investigation needs.	**Vocabulary:** Have students write examples for three of the selection vocabulary words. **Comprehension:** Have students summarize the selection. **Inquiry:** Have students discuss with their groups how they will research their topic. Have them make a research plan based on their investigation needs.
Language Arts	**Writing:** Have students work with ***eSkills*** as a tool for developing editing skills. **Spelling:** Have students working in pairs to help each other study this week's spelling words.	**Writing:** Have students finish the editing and proofreading process and work on writing the final draft of their business letters. **Spelling:** Have students write five words that rhyme with each spelling word on a piece of paper.	**Writing:** Have students conference with a peer. **Spelling:** Have students take turns reading spelling words aloud to a partner while the partner spells the words on a sheet of paper.	**Writing:** Have students help others get their drafts ready to publish. **Spelling:** Have students complete the ***eSkills*** spelling activity.

Differentiating Instruction for Workshop

Day 5

	Approaching Level	On Level	English Learner	Above Level
Preparing to Read	**Word Structure:** Review the word lines. Then have students review their prefix and suffix flash cards with a partner.	**Word Structure:** Have students use ***eSkills & eGames*** for practice with prefixes and suffixes.	**Word Structure:** Have students review their prefix and suffix flash cards with a partner. Then students can use ***eSkills & eGames*** for practice with prefixes and suffixes.	**Word Structure:** Have students write short stories using words with affixes, or students can use ***eSkills & eGames*** for practice with prefixes and suffixes.
Reading and Responding	**Vocabulary:** Have students select a concept vocabulary word and write a journal entry explaining how it relates to the unit theme. **Comprehension:** Have students write review questions about the selection on flash cards. Have students quiz each other using their flash cards. **Fluency:** Have students write answers to comprehension questions from the ***Leveled Readers.***	**Vocabulary:** Have students use the selection vocabulary words in their writing. **Comprehension:** Have students write a summary of the selection. Encourage students to include illustrations if they have trouble expressing themselves. **Fluency:** Have students write a skit using the vocabulary words and then present them to the class.	**Vocabulary:** Have students use a thesaurus to find antonyms and synonyms for the selection vocabulary words. **Comprehension:** Have students write a summary of the selection. Encourage students to include illustrations if they have trouble expressing themselves. **Fluency:** Have students use vocabulary from the ***Leveled Readers*** in extended sentences.	**Vocabulary:** Have students write a story using the selection vocabulary words. **Comprehension:** Have students write a realistic fiction story using facts learned from the selection. **Fluency:** Have students reread passages from the selection to a partner.
Language Arts	**Writing:** Have students share their business letters. **Spelling:** Have students carefully rewrite a paragraph from their selection, while keeping an eye on spelling the words correctly.	**Writing:** Have students prepare an envelope to mail their business letters. **Spelling:** Have students write the spelling words into alphabetical order on a piece of paper.	**Writing:** Have students share their business letters with the class. **Spelling:** Have students choose five spelling words for a partner to spell on a piece of paper.	**Writing:** Have students send their business letters. **Spelling:** Have students write an imaginary letter to someone using at least six spelling words.

Resources for

Differentiating Instruction 

Leveled Readers

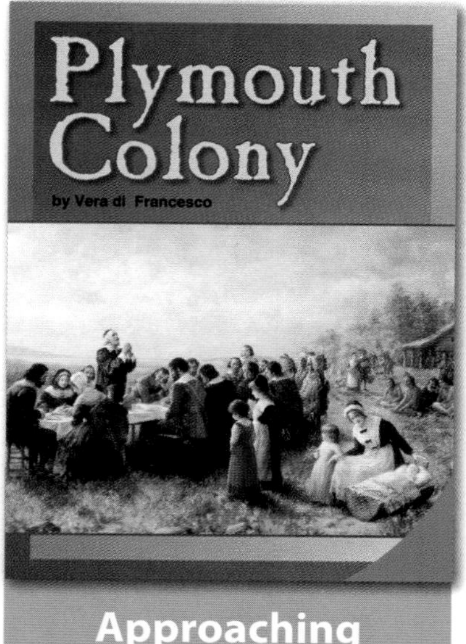

Approaching Level

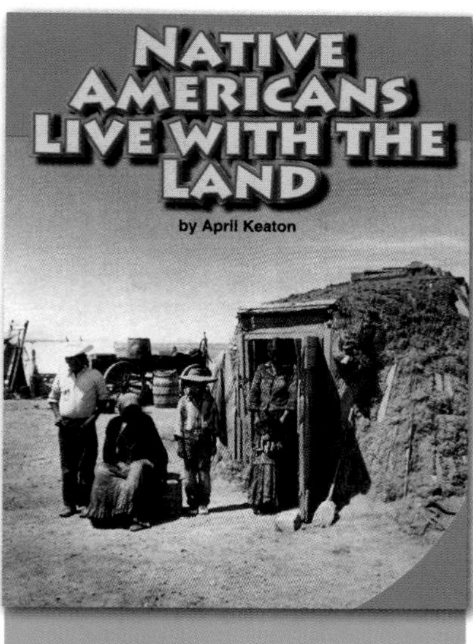

On Level

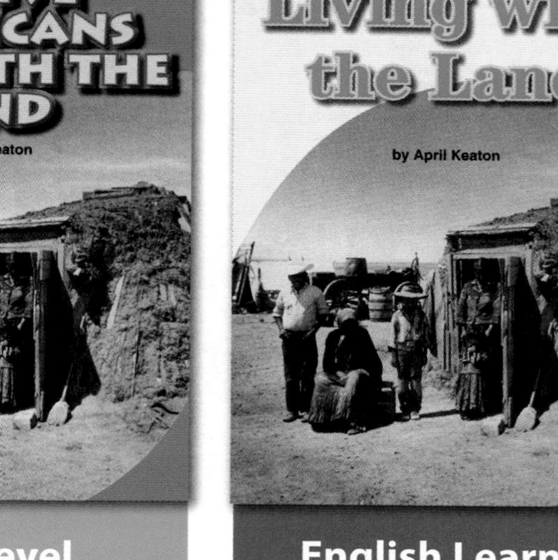

English Learner

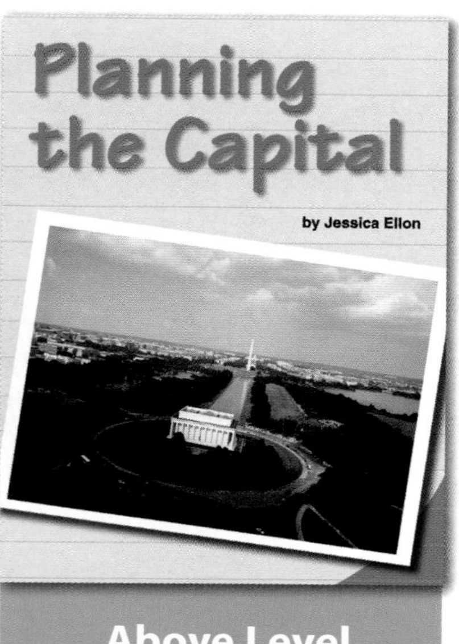

Above Level

Additional Skills Practice

Approaching Level

Reteach

- Affixes as Syllables, p. 135
- Affixes Used to Change Word Meaning, p. 136
- Vocabulary, p. 137
- Fact and Opinion, pp. 138–139
- Spelling, p. 140
- Subject and Verb Agreement, p. 141

On Level

Skills Practice 2

- Affixes, pp. 119–120
- Affixes, pp. 121–122
- Vocabulary, pp. 123–124
- Fact and Opinion, pp. 125–126
- Business Letter, pp. 129–130
- Spelling, pp. 131–132
- Subject and Verb Agreement, pp. 133–134

English Learner

English Learner Support Activities

Unit 5, Lesson 3

Above Level

Challenge Activities

- Affixes as Syllables, p. 123
- Affixes Used to Change Word Meaning, p. 124
- Vocabulary, p. 125
- Fact and Opinion, p. 126
- Spelling, p. 127
- Subject and Verb Agreement, p. 128

Additional Resources for Differentiating Instruction

Workshop Kit

Technology

The following electronic resources are available for students:

- ***eStudent Reader***
- ***eSkills & eGames***
- ***Listening Library CD***

Electronic resources for the teacher include:

- ***ePlanner***
- ***eTeacher's Edition***
- ***eAssess***
- ***ePresentation***

All technology components are available online and on CD–ROM.

English Learner

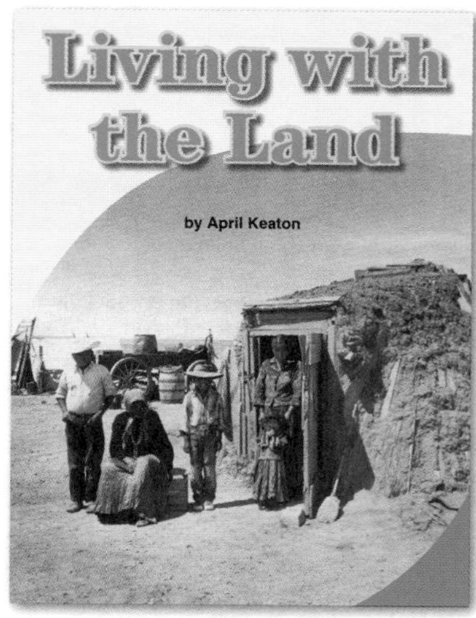

Leveled Reader

English Learner Support Activities, Lesson 3

Listening Library CD, Unit 5

English Learner Support Guide, Lesson 3

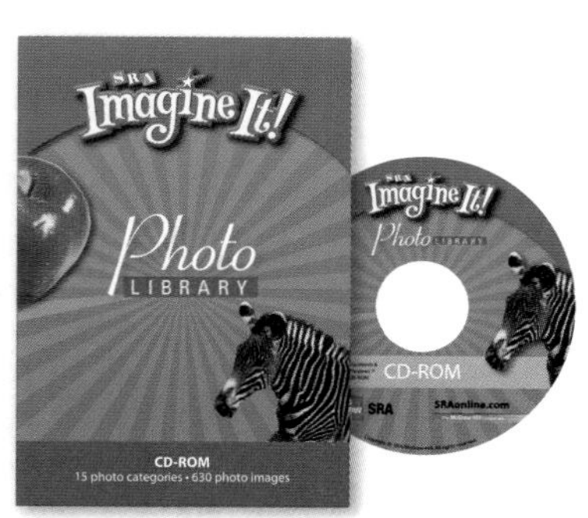

Photo Library CD

Approaching Level

Intervention

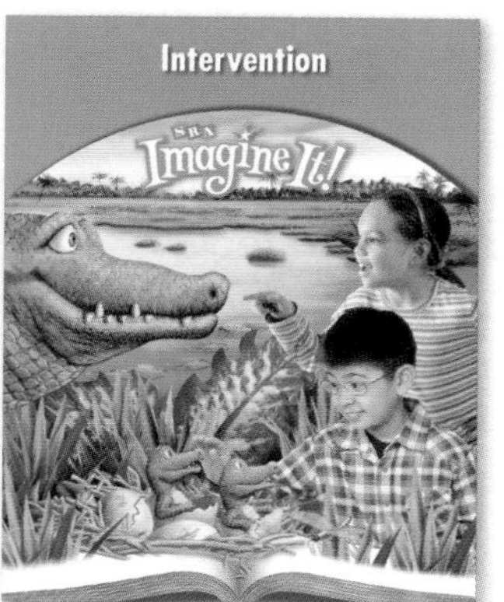

Intervention Workbook

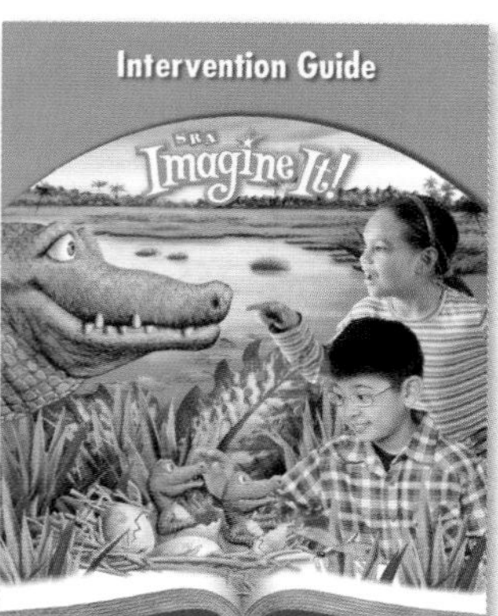

Intervention Guide

Lesson Assessment

Monitor Progress to Differentiate Instruction

Comprehension Strategies Rubrics

Use the Comprehension Strategies Rubrics to determine whether a student is using the strategies.

- ✦ Visualizing, p. T194
- ✦ Making Connections, p. T195

Inquiry Rubrics

Use the Inquiry Rubrics to assess a student's performance throughout the stages of the investigation for each unit. In addition, at the end of the unit you can use the rubrics to assess the groups' collaborative work as well as an individual's participation in that group.

- ✦ Making Conjectures, p. T203
- ✦ Identifying Information Needs, p. T239

Writing Rubrics

Use the writing rubrics in the Level Appendix to evaluate a student's business letter.

- ✦ Genre
- ✦ Writing Process
- ✦ Writing Traits

Lesson Assessments

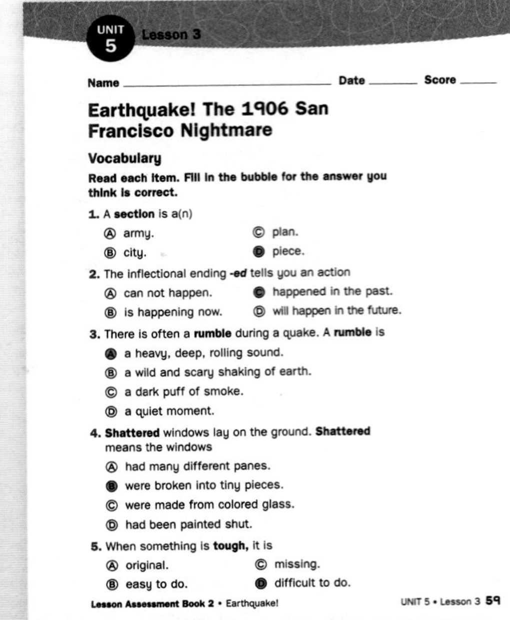
UNIT 5 Lesson 3

Name ______________ Date ______ Score ______

Earthquake! The 1906 San Francisco Nightmare

Vocabulary

Read each item. Fill in the bubble for the answer you think is correct.

1. A **section** is a(n)
   Ⓐ army. Ⓒ plan.
   Ⓑ city. ● piece.
2. The inflectional ending **-ed** tells you an action
   Ⓐ can not happen. ● happened in the past.
   Ⓑ is happening now. Ⓓ will happen in the future.
3. There is often a **rumble** during a quake. A **rumble** is
   ● a heavy, deep, rolling sound.
   Ⓑ a wild and scary shaking of earth.
   Ⓒ a dark puff of smoke.
   Ⓓ a quiet moment.
4. **Shattered** windows lay on the ground. **Shattered** means the windows
   Ⓐ had many different panes.
   ● were broken into tiny pieces.
   Ⓒ were made from colored glass.
   Ⓓ had been painted shut.
5. When something is **tough,** it is
   Ⓐ original. Ⓒ missing.
   Ⓑ easy to do. ● difficult to do.

Lesson Assessment Book 2 • Earthquake! UNIT 5 • Lesson 3 59

Lesson Assessment Book 2, p. 59

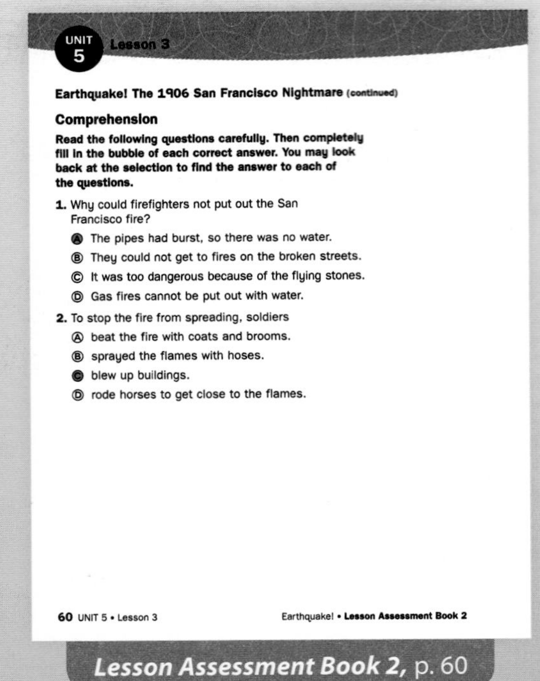
UNIT 5 Lesson 3

Earthquake! The 1906 San Francisco Nightmare (continued)

Comprehension

Read the following questions carefully. Then completely fill in the bubble of each correct answer. You may look back at the selection to find the answer to each of the questions.

1. Why could firefighters not put out the San Francisco fire?
   ● The pipes had burst, so there was no water.
   Ⓑ They could not get to fires on the broken streets.
   Ⓒ It was too dangerous because of the flying stones.
   Ⓓ Gas fires cannot be put out with water.
2. To stop the fire from spreading, soldiers
   Ⓐ beat the fire with coats and brooms.
   Ⓑ sprayed the flames with hoses.
   ● blew up buildings.
   Ⓓ rode horses to get close to the flames.

60 UNIT 5 • Lesson 3 Earthquake! • Lesson Assessment Book 2

Lesson Assessment Book 2, p. 60

Use these summative assessments along with your informal observations to assess student mastery.

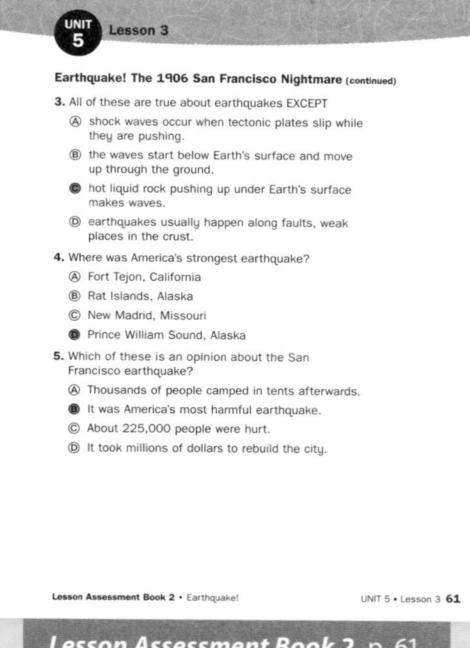
UNIT 5 Lesson 3

Earthquake! The 1906 San Francisco Nightmare (continued)

3. All of these are true about earthquakes EXCEPT
   - Ⓐ shock waves occur when tectonic plates slip while they are pushing.
   - Ⓑ the waves start below Earth's surface and move up through the ground.
   - ● hot liquid rock pushing up under Earth's surface makes waves.
   - Ⓓ earthquakes usually happen along faults, weak places in the crust.
4. Where was America's strongest earthquake?
   - Ⓐ Fort Tejon, California
   - Ⓑ Rat Islands, Alaska
   - Ⓒ New Madrid, Missouri
   - ● Prince William Sound, Alaska
5. Which of these is an opinion about the San Francisco earthquake?
   - Ⓐ Thousands of people camped in tents afterwards.
   - ● It was America's most harmful earthquake.
   - Ⓒ About 225,000 people were hurt.
   - Ⓓ It took millions of dollars to rebuild the city.

Lesson Assessment Book 2 • Earthquake! UNIT 5 • Lesson 3 61

Lesson Assessment Book 2, p. 61

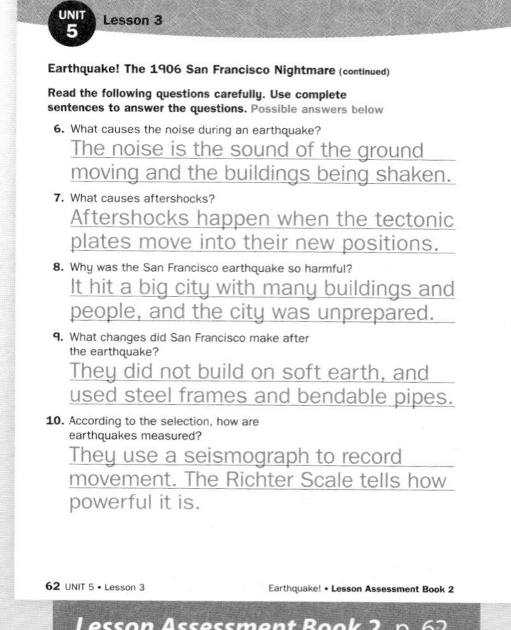
UNIT 5 Lesson 3

Earthquake! The 1906 San Francisco Nightmare (continued)

Read the following questions carefully. Use complete sentences to answer the questions. Possible answers below

6. What causes the noise during an earthquake?
   The noise is the sound of the ground moving and the buildings being shaken.
7. What causes aftershocks?
   Aftershocks happen when the tectonic plates move into their new positions.
8. Why was the San Francisco earthquake so harmful?
   It hit a big city with many buildings and people, and the city was unprepared.
9. What changes did San Francisco make after the earthquake?
   They did not build on soft earth, and used steel frames and bendable pipes.
10. According to the selection, how are earthquakes measured?
   They use a seismograph to record movement. The Richter Scale tells how powerful it is.

62 UNIT 5 • Lesson 3 Earthquake! • Lesson Assessment Book 2

Lesson Assessment Book 2, p. 62

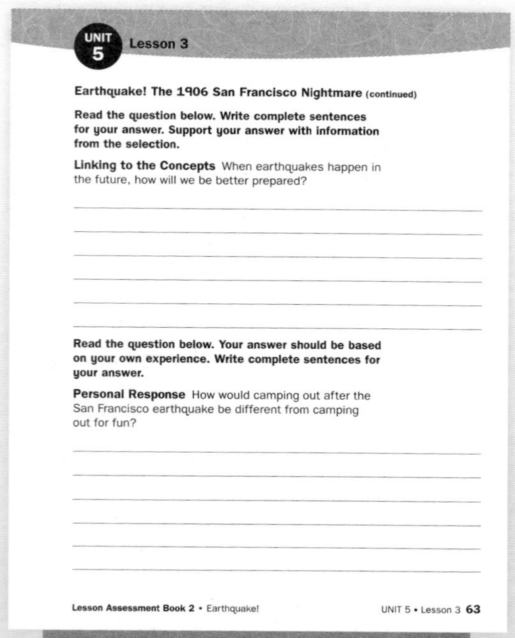
UNIT 5 Lesson 3

Earthquake! The 1906 San Francisco Nightmare (continued)

Read the question below. Write complete sentences for your answer. Support your answer with information from the selection.

Linking to the Concepts When earthquakes happen in the future, how will we be better prepared?

Read the question below. Your answer should be based on your own experience. Write complete sentences for your answer.

Personal Response How would camping out after the San Francisco earthquake be different from camping out for fun?

Lesson Assessment Book 2 • Earthquake! UNIT 5 • Lesson 3 63

Lesson Assessment Book 2, p. 63

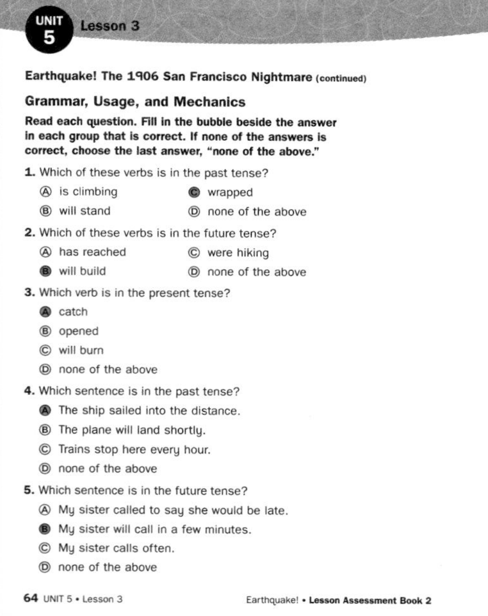
UNIT 5 Lesson 3

Earthquake! The 1906 San Francisco Nightmare (continued)

Grammar, Usage, and Mechanics

Read each question. Fill in the bubble beside the answer in each group that is correct. If none of the answers is correct, choose the last answer, "none of the above."

1. Which of these verbs is in the past tense?
   - Ⓐ is climbing
   - ● wrapped
   - Ⓑ will stand
   - Ⓓ none of the above
2. Which of these verbs is in the future tense?
   - Ⓐ has reached
   - Ⓒ were hiking
   - ● will build
   - Ⓓ none of the above
3. Which verb is in the present tense?
   - ● catch
   - Ⓑ opened
   - Ⓒ will burn
   - Ⓓ none of the above
4. Which sentence is in the past tense?
   - ● The ship sailed into the distance.
   - Ⓑ The plane will land shortly.
   - Ⓒ Trains stop here every hour.
   - Ⓓ none of the above
5. Which sentence is in the future tense?
   - Ⓐ My sister called to say she would be late.
   - ● My sister will call in a few minutes.
   - Ⓒ My sister calls often.
   - Ⓓ none of the above

64 UNIT 5 • Lesson 3 Earthquake! • Lesson Assessment Book 2

Lesson Assessment Book 2, p. 64

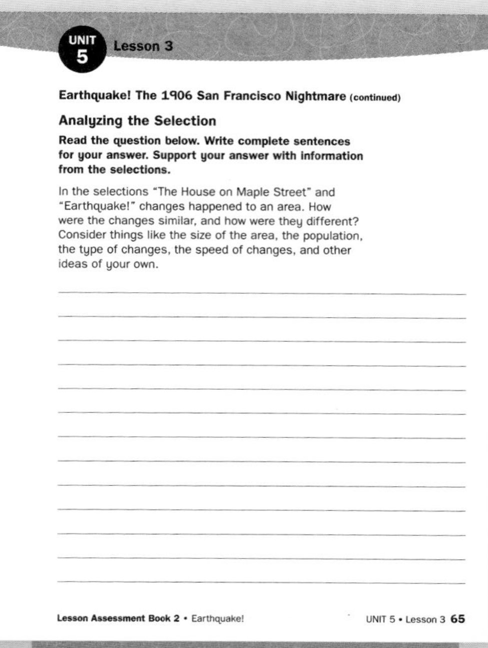
UNIT 5 Lesson 3

Earthquake! The 1906 San Francisco Nightmare (continued)

Analyzing the Selection

Read the question below. Write complete sentences for your answer. Support your answer with information from the selections.

In the selections "The House on Maple Street" and "Earthquake!" changes happened to an area. How were the changes similar, and how were they different? Consider things like the size of the area, the population, the type of changes, the speed of changes, and other ideas of your own.

Lesson Assessment Book 2 • Earthquake! UNIT 5 • Lesson 3 65

Lesson Assessment Book 2, p. 65

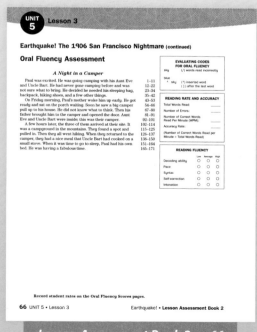

UNIT 5 Lesson 3

Earthquake! The 1906 San Francisco Nightmare (continued)

Oral Fluency Assessment

A Night in a Camper

Paul was excited. He was going camping with his Aunt Eve 1–11
and Uncle Bart. He had never gone camping before and was 12–22
not sure what to bring. He decided he needed his sleeping bag, 23–34
backpack, hiking shoes, and a few other things. 35–42
On Friday morning, Paul's mother woke him up early. He got 43–53
ready and sat on the porch waiting. Soon he saw a big camper 54–66
pull up to his house. He did not know what to think. Then his 67–80
father brought him to the camper and opened the door. Aunt 81–91
Eve and Uncle Bart were inside; this was their camper. 92–101
A few hours later, the three of them arrived at their site. It 102–114
was a campground in the mountains. They found a spot and 115–125
pulled in. Then they all went hiking. When they returned to the 126–137
camper, they had a nice meal that Uncle Bart had cooked on a 138–150
small stove. When it was time to go to sleep, Paul had his own 151–164
bed. He was having a fabulous time. 165–171

EVALUATING CODES FOR ORAL FLUENCY

sky (/) words read incorrectly

blue ^ sky (^) inserted word

( ]) after the last word

READING RATE AND ACCURACY

Total Words Read: ____

Number of Errors: ____

Number of Correct Words Read Per Minute (WPM): ____

Accuracy Rate: ____

(Number of Correct Words Read per Minute ÷ Total Words Read)

READING FLUENCY

	Low	Average	High
Decoding ability	○	○	○
Pace	○	○	○
Syntax	○	○	○
Self-correction	○	○	○
Intonation	○	○	○

Record student rates on the Oral Fluency Scores pages.

66 UNIT 5 • Lesson 3 Earthquake! • Lesson Assessment Book 2

Lesson Assessment Book 2, p. 66

Day 1 **Preparing to Read**

OBJECTIVES

Students will
- ✦ recognize affixes as syllables.
- ✦ build fluency.

MATERIALS

- ✦ ***Transparency*** 140
- ✦ ***Skills Practice 2,*** pp. 119–120

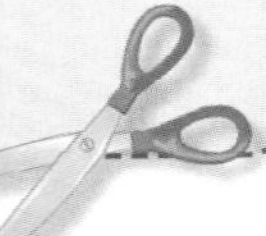

Daily Oral Practice

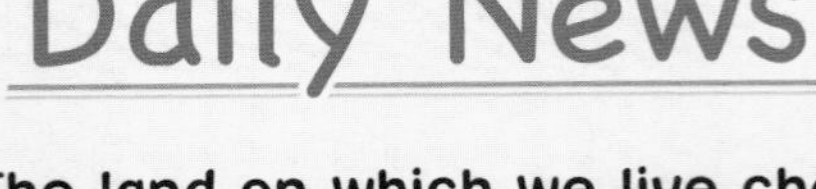

Daily News Today!

The land on which we live changes every day. Because seasons come and go, weather patterns shift and change. People can change the land too, but sometimes nature brings about some of the largest and most discomforting changes to our land.

- ✦ Write the daily news on the board or on chart paper. Then have a volunteer read the daily news aloud to practice fluency.
- ✦ As a word structure review from Lesson 2, ask a volunteer to identify any words in the message with the prefix *dis-*. *discomforting*

Differentiating Instruction **English Learner**

IF . . . students are native Spanish speakers, **THEN . . .** they may need extra help producing /w/ and associating it with the letter *w*. The letter *w* does not appear in Spanish words, although Spanish speakers use /w/ occasionally for words borrowed from other languages.

Word Structure

Affixes as Syllables

- ✦ Write these word lines on the board or use ***Transparency*** 140. The words in boldface are in "Earthquake! The 1906 San Francisco Nightmare."

Line 1	harm	**harmless**	main	mainly
Line 2	bend	**bendable**	thank	**thankful**
Line 3	build	**rebuild**	connect	disconnect
Line 4	treat	mistreat	helpful	unhelpful

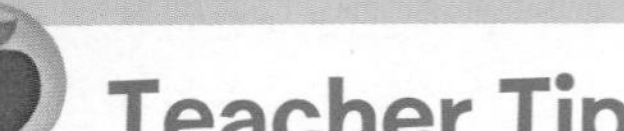

Teacher Tip

SYLLABICATION To help students blend words and build fluency, demonstrate syllabication using the decodable, multisyllabic words in the word lines.

harm • less	main • ly
bend • a • ble	thank • ful
re • build	con • nect
dis • con • nect	mis • treat
help • ful	un • help • ful

Lines 1–2 Suffixes as Syllables

Explain that affixes are letters, such as prefixes and suffixes, that are added to base words. Remind students that suffixes are affixes added to the end of base words. For example, the suffix *-ness* is added to base adjectives, such as *dark* or *hard*. Remind students that affixes also add syllables to base words. When *-ness* is added to the one syllable word *dark*, it becomes *darkness,* which has two syllables.

As you point to each word in Lines 1–2, have students read it aloud in unison. Then have students identify the suffixes in each word. -less *in* harmless; -ly *in* mainly; able *in* bendable; -ful *in* thankful Have students identify the suffix in these words that adds more than one syllable to the base word. *-able*

Lines 3–4 Prefixes as Syllables

Remind students that prefixes are affixes added to the beginning of base words. For example, the prefix *pre-* is added to the beginning of verbs or actions, such as *wash* or *heat*. Remind students that affixes add syllables to base words. When *pre-* is added to the one syllable word *wash,* it becomes *prewash,* which has two syllables.

✦ As you point to each word in Lines 3–4, have students read it aloud together. Then have students identify the prefixes in each word. re- *in* rebuild; dis- *in* disconnect; mis- *in* mistreat; un- *in* unhelpful Have students identify the word in these lines with more than one affix. *unhelpful* Then have students identify the prefix and suffix in this word. *the prefix* un-; *the suffix* -ful

✦ Help students start the word structure activities on ***Skills Practice 2*** pages 119–120. Read the Focus box with them and help them with the first few questions. Then have students complete the pages on their own.

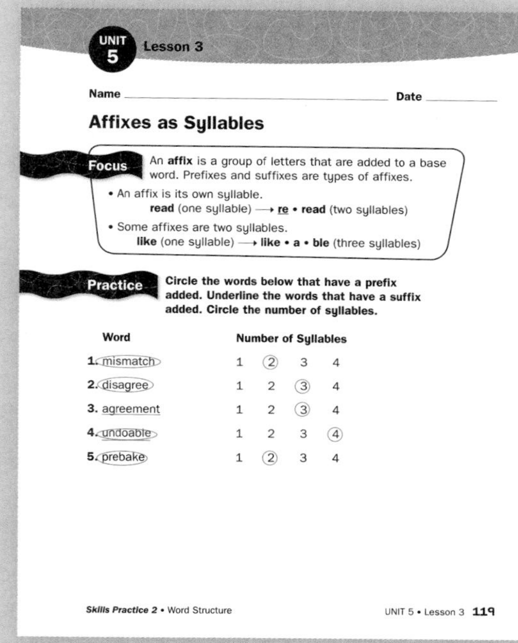

UNIT 5 Lesson 3

Name ______ Date ______

Affixes as Syllables

Focus An **affix** is a group of letters that are added to a base word. Prefixes and suffixes are types of affixes.

• An affix is its own syllable.
read (one syllable) → **re • read** (two syllables)

• Some affixes are two syllables.
like (one syllable) → **like • a • ble** (three syllables)

Practice **Circle the words below that have a prefix added. Underline the words that have a suffix added. Circle the number of syllables.**

Word	Number of Syllables			
1. mismatch	1	2	3	4
2. disagree	1	2	3	4
3. agreement	1	2	3	4
4. undoable	1	2	3	4
5. prebake	1	2	3	4

Skills Practice 2 • Word Structure UNIT 5 • Lesson 3 119

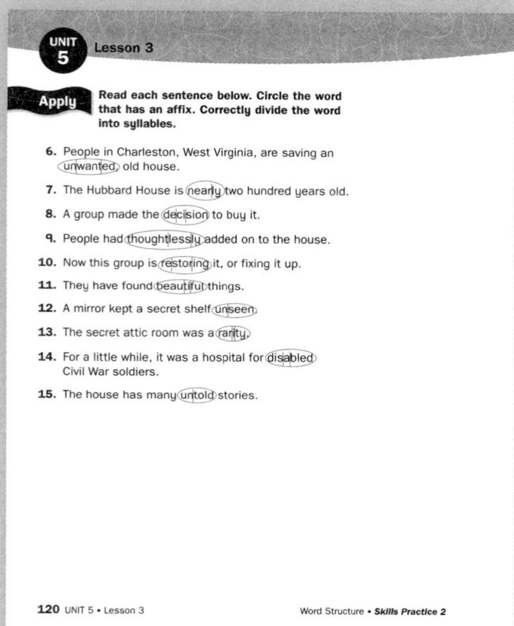

UNIT 5 Lesson 3

Apply **Read each sentence below. Circle the word that has an affix. Correctly divide the word into syllables.**

6. People in Charleston, West Virginia, are saving an unwanted old house.
7. The Hubbard House is nearly two hundred years old.
8. A group made the decision to buy it.
9. People had thoughtlessly added on to the house.
10. Now this group is restoring it, or fixing it up.
11. They have found beautiful things.
12. A mirror kept a secret shelf unseen.
13. The secret attic room was a rarity.
14. For a little while, it was a hospital for disabled Civil War soldiers.
15. The house has many untold stories.

120 UNIT 5 • Lesson 3 Word Structure • *Skills Practice 2*

Skills Practice 2, pp. 119–120

Monitor Progress to Differentiate Instruction

Formal Assessment

Word Structure During the word structure activity, note how well students recognize affixes as syllables.

APPROACHING LEVEL	IF . . . students need practice recognizing affixes as syllables,	THEN . . . work with them in small groups on the word structure activities on ***Reteach*** page 135 during Workshop.
	IF . . . students need extra practice recognizing affixes as syllables,	THEN . . . work with them in small groups on the word structure activities for Unit 5 Lesson 3 in the ***Intervention Guide*** during Workshop.
ON LEVEL	IF . . . students adequately recognize affixes as syllables,	THEN . . . have them read other materials to find words to add to the word lines during Workshop.
ABOVE LEVEL	IF . . . students are ready for a challenge with affixes as syllables,	THEN . . . have them complete the word structure activities on ***Challenge Activities*** page 123 during Workshop.

Reading and Responding

OBJECTIVES

Students will

- ✦ activate prior knowledge to prepare to read the selection.
- ✦ learn selection vocabulary.
- ✦ review the elements of expository text.
- ✦ use the comprehension strategies Visualizing and Making Connections.
- ✦ investigate the theme communities across time using the Inquiry process.

MATERIALS

- ✦ ***Student Reader,*** Book 2, pp. 164–175
- ✦ Routines 11, 13, 14
- ✦ ***Transparencies*** 35, 141
- ✦ ***Lesson Assessment Book 2***
- ✦ ***Home Connection,*** pp. 55–56

Differentiating Instruction **English Learner**

IF . . . students have intermediate or advanced English mastery, **THEN . . .** encourage them to tell something about natural disasters in their native countries.

Build Background

Activate Prior Knowledge

- ✦ Ask students if they have ever experienced a natural disaster, such as an earthquake. Ask students how it made them feel and how the people around them reacted.
- ✦ Ask students if their families and their schools have natural disaster plans and drills. Explain the importance of being prepared.
- ✦ Ask students how the land changed in *A River Ran Wild* and "The House on Maple Street." Explain that sometimes acts of nature change the land.

Background Information

The following information might help students understand the selection they are about to read:

- "Earthquake! The 1906 San Francisco Nightmare" is a true story.
- Earthquakes occur when rocks far below Earth's crust push against each other and slip. This causes shock waves to move the ground.
- Explain to students that people in the early 1900s were not as aware of safety precautions as we are today. Scientists now have special tools to predict earthquakes, and buildings are built in different ways in order to withstand earthquakes.

Preview and Prepare 

ROUTINE 13

Browse

Use Routine 13, the KWL routine, to help students identify what they know before reading, what they want to know while reading, and any answers they may find.

Have students read the title and the name of the author, and then give them a few minutes to browse the selection. Have students use features such as the selection's title and illustrations to predict what this selection might have to do with the theme Communities across Time.

Tell students to look for interesting words, ideas, or photographs as they browse. They may point out the old-looking photographs.

Use ***Transparency*** 35 to model browsing for students. For example, students will Know that the selection is about "Earthquake! The 1906 San Francisco Nightmare." Under Want to Know, write *I wonder what causes earthquakes.* Record students' observations on the transparency as they browse the selection.

Set Purposes

Encourage students to set their own purposes for reading this selection. Remind students that readers can set purposes for reading by picking up clues from the title, photographs, and genre of the text they are going to read. If students have trouble, suggest that as they read, they learn about what causes earthquakes, what happened in San Francisco in 1906, and how we are better prepared for natural disasters today.

BIG Idea

How has my community changed over time?

Before reading the selection, read the Big Idea question. Tell students to keep this question in mind as they read the selection.

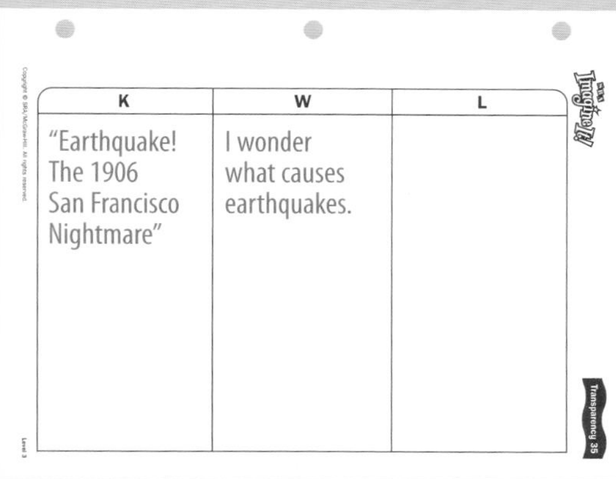

K	W	L
"Earthquake! The 1906 San Francisco Nightmare"	I wonder what causes earthquakes.	

Transparency 35

Give each student a copy of ***Home Connection*** page 55. Encourage students to discuss "Earthquake! The 1906 San Francisco Nightmare" with their families and complete the activity provided. The same information is also available in Spanish on ***Home Connection*** page 56.

Differentiating Instruction **English Learner**

IF . . . students have limited proficiency, **THEN . . .** pair them with proficient English speakers and have the pair browse the selection together.

Selection Vocabulary

clerk (klûrk) *n.* a person who sells goods or services to customers (page 168)

rumble (rum′• bəl) *n.* a heavy, deep, rolling sound (page 168)

shattered (shat′ • tərd) *adj.* destroyed completely (page 171)

exactly (eg • zakt′ • lē) *adv.* without any mistakes (page 174)

damaged (dam′ • ijd) *v.* past tense of **damage:** to make something less valuable or useful (page 176)

tough (tuf) *adj.* hard to deal with or do; demanding (page 177)

frames (frāmz) *n.* plural form of **frame:** the skeleton of a building (page 177)

section (sek′ • shən) *n.* part of something (page 178)

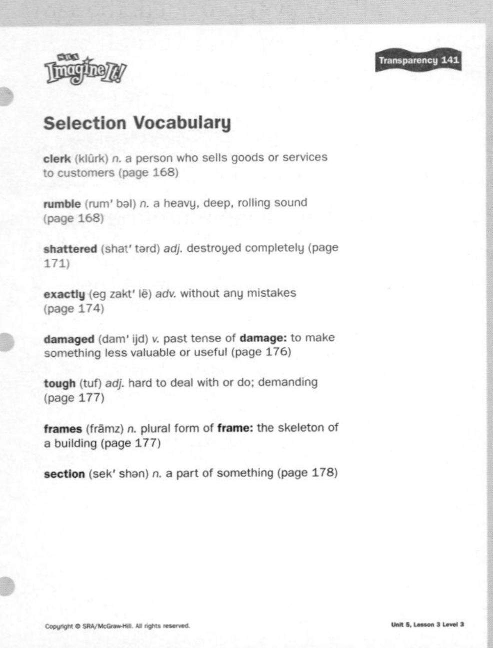
Imagine It! Transparency 141

Selection Vocabulary

clerk (klûrk) *n.* a person who sells goods or services to customers (page 168)

rumble (rum′ bəl) *n.* a heavy, deep, rolling sound (page 168)

shattered (shat′ tərd) *adj.* destroyed completely (page 171)

exactly (eg zakt′ lē) *adv.* without any mistakes (page 174)

damaged (dam′ ijd) *v.* past tense of **damage:** to make something less valuable or useful (page 176)

tough (tuf) *adj.* hard to deal with or do; demanding (page 177)

frames (frāmz) *n.* plural form of **frame:** the skeleton of a building (page 177)

section (sek′ shən) *n.* a part of something (page 178)

Copyright © SRA/McGraw-Hill. All rights reserved. Unit 5, Lesson 3 Level 3

Transparency 141

Differentiating Instruction **English Learner**

IF . . . students need extra help with selection vocabulary, **THEN . . .** see ***English Learner Support Guide*** Unit 5 Lesson 3 or use pictures, objects, drawings, or pantomime to help them visualize the words.

Building Vocabulary

Using Routine 11, the selection vocabulary process, have students read aloud the Vocabulary Warm-Up on ***Student Reader,*** Book 2 pages 164–165.

As students read, have them stop to blend any difficult or unfamiliar words. Provide students with the pronunciation of words that are not decodable or that they cannot read automatically or fluently.

Guided Vocabulary Practice

Ask students to identify the highlighted vocabulary words they figured out using the vocabulary strategy word structure. **Possible Answers** *shattered, damaged, exactly* Have students explain how they determined the meaning of the other vocabulary words as they read the Vocabulary Warm-Up.

Display ***Transparency*** 141, and have students read the words and definitions. Return to the Vocabulary Warm-Up, and read the sentences containing the vocabulary words with students. Then, if necessary, provide a brief in-context explanation of the words.

Read the article to find the meanings of these words, which are also in "Earthquake! The 1906 San Francisco Nightmare":

- shattered
- section
- rumble
- clerk
- damaged
- frames
- tough
- exactly

Vocabulary Strategy

Word Structure is when parts of a word help you understand the word's meaning. Use word structure to find the meaning of *exactly*.

164

Vocabulary

Warm-Up

The best way to stay safe in an earthquake is to be prepared. Survival can depend on having a good plan. Here are some helpful safety tips.

- When the ground starts shaking, duck and seek cover. Get under a strong desk or table, and hold on to one of its legs. Cover your eyes to protect them from shattered glass.
- Stay away from tall, heavy furniture that could fall on you. Get to a section of your home that has no windows or large light fixtures.
- When the shaking stops, check to see if you are hurt. Have a first aid kit handy to treat wounds.
- Listen for the rumble of aftershocks. More tremors will likely roll through after the first quake. Once again, you should duck, cover, and hold on.

- Be sure you have a fire extinguisher that works. A clerk at the hardware store can help your family choose the best model for your home.
- Find out from a builder whether your house is bolted down. In the past, major earthquakes damaged house frames less when they were attached to their base.
- Fasten things that might fall and cause harm, such as a television or bookcase. Put tough latches on cupboard doors.
- Practice earthquake drills with your family. Have a plan that each person knows exactly how to follow. Choose a safe place in each room where you can duck, cover, and hold on.

GAME

Write a Riddle

Make a riddle for each of the vocabulary words. For example, for the word *rumble,* you might write, "I am much louder than a mumble, and when you hear me, you know the earth might crumble." Exchange papers with a classmate, and solve each other's riddles.

Concept Vocabulary

The concept word for this lesson is ***community.*** A **community** is a group of people who live in the same area or have a shared interest. People in a community often help each other. They also work together to make decisions about their neighborhood. In your journal, write about some of the benefits of being part of a community.

165

Use the vocabulary words on ***Transparency*** 141 to create fill-in-the-blank sentences. Have students fill in the appropriate vocabulary words. For example, "The tree limb crashed into the window and ________ it during the storm." *shattered*

Discuss the concept vocabulary word *community* with students. Ask students how they think the word *community* relates to the theme Communities across Time. As students read the selections in this unit, encourage them to think about other words that relate to the theme. Students can record these words in the vocabulary section of their Writer's Notebooks.

GAME

Have students play the Write a Riddle game during Small-Group Time.

Differentiating Instruction: English Learner

IF . . . students have difficulty playing the game, **THEN . . .** be sure to pair each English Learner with a proficient English speaker.

Concept/Question Board

As students read "Earthquake! The 1906 San Francisco Nightmare," encourage them to post questions, answers, comments, or other items related to communities across time on the **Concept/Question Board.**

Monitor Progress

Formal Assessment

Comprehension Observation Log Observe individual students as they read, and use the Comprehension Observation Log, located in ***Lesson Assessment Book 2,*** to record anecdotal information about each student's strengths and weaknesses.

Research in Action

As they read, good readers envision the action being described in a text. This process heightens their enjoyment of the text and also improves comprehension and long-term memory. Many elementary readers do not visualize sufficiently. As a result, their comprehension suffers. The mental images created while visualizing are a form of interpretation. They reflect the interaction between what the reader receives from the text and what she or he brings to the reading of the text. These images are a type of nonverbal coding that is deeper and more meaningful than the verbal coding that follows from reading the words of the text.

(Michael Pressley)

Reading the Selection

Genre Expository Text

Have students identify the genre of "Earthquake! The 1906 San Francisco Nightmare." *expository text* If necessary, remind students that expository text

- gives information.
- uses facts about real events, people, or animals.
- presents information in a clear way.
- gives events in the order in which they happen.
- can be organized by topics.
- might contain diagrams, photographs, or other illustrations.
- contains information that can be checked in sources, such as encyclopedias or newspapers.

Comprehension Strategies

Prompt the use of the following comprehension strategies during the first reading of "Earthquake! The 1906 San Francisco Nightmare":

- Visualizing
- Making Connections

Comprehension Strategies Rubrics

Use the Informal Comprehension Strategies Rubrics to determine whether a student is using any of the strategies listed below. Note the strategies a student is using, instead of the degree to which a student might be using any particular strategy. In addition, encourage the student to tell of any strategies other than the ones being taught that he or she is using.

Visualizing

✦ The student recognizes appropriate places in the text to stop and visualize.

✦ The student visualizes literal ideas or scenes described by the author.

✦ The student makes inferences while visualizing to show understanding of characters' feelings, mood, and setting. The visualizations go beyond the author's literal words.

✦ The student uses visualizing differently depending on the type of text (for example, characters, setting, and actions in narratives or a process description in nonfiction).

Making Connections

- ✦ The student makes connections between prior knowledge and information in the text.
- ✦ The student makes connections between or relates personal experiences to what is read in the text (text-to-self connections).
- ✦ The student makes connections across or relates information from different selections (text-to-text connections).
- ✦ The student makes connections or relates information between what is happening in the text to what is happening in the world today (text-to-world connections).

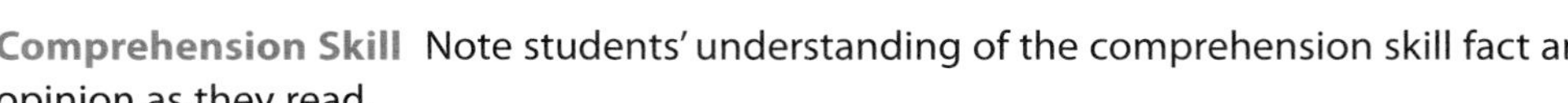

Formal Assessment

to Differentiate Instruction

Comprehension Skill Note students' understanding of the comprehension skill fact and opinion as they read.

APPROACHING LEVEL

IF . . . students are having difficulty understanding fact and opinion as they read,	**THEN . . .** have them practice identifying fact and opinion in all of their selections and reading assignments.

ON LEVEL

IF . . . students are gaining an understanding of fact and opinion as they read,	**THEN . . .** have students look for examples of facts and opinions in newspaper and magazine articles.

ABOVE LEVEL

IF . . . students are demonstrating an understanding of fact and opinion as they read,	**THEN . . .** have students research the unit theme Communities across Time and write a list of facts they discover about communities across time. Have students share the facts with the rest of the class.

Differentiating Instruction

English Learner

IF . . . students need help contributing to the Concept/Question Board, **THEN . . .** remind them to post questions, answers, comments, news articles, and other theme-related information in their native languages. Encourage them to convey the general idea of their postings to their English-speaking classmates.

IF . . . students would benefit from hearing "Earthquake! The 1906 San Francisco Nightmare" before it is read to the class, **THEN . . .** have them listen to the selection on ***Listening Library CDs*** during Workshop.

Comprehension Skills

Reread "Earthquake! The 1906 San Francisco Nightmare" using the following comprehension skills:

- Drawing Conclusions
- Fact and Opinion
- Cause and Effect

Reading with a Writer's Eye

During the rereading of "Earthquake! The 1906 San Francisco Nightmare," explain the following literary element:

Text Structures—Techniques

Focus Questions

Have students read aloud the Focus Questions on page 167 of the ***Student Reader,*** Book 2. Encourage students to think about the Focus Questions as they read "Earthquake! The 1906 San Francisco Nightmare."

Reading Recommendation

Oral Reading

Use Routine 14, the reading the selection routine, as you read the entire selection. As you read, stop to ask and answer questions. Point out how the pictures reflect the story. Share the images that pop up in your mind as you read and how points in the reading relate to ideas you already know.

Due to the amount of information being presented, the headings, and the captions, this selection is best suited for oral reading. Remind students that, due to the amount of information being provided by the author, they might want to adjust their reading speed in order to better comprehend and remember the information in the text.

Technology

eSTUDENT READER Students can access ***Imagine It! Student Reader*** electronically by using the ***eStudent Reader*** online or on CD-ROM.

Genre

Expository Text is nonfiction that is written to inform, to explain, or to persuade.

Comprehension Skill

Fact and Opinion
As you read, identify facts and opinions within the selection.

Earthquake!

The 1906 San Francisco Nightmare

by Lynn Brunelle

Focus Questions

How do the weather and other environmental factors affect your community? How have communities around the United States handled different natural disasters?

166 167

Students will read the story twice over a four-day period.

Day 1 **ORAL READ** Have students read the first half of the selection. Prompt the use of the comprehension strategies.

Day 2 **ORAL READ** Have students finish reading the selection. Continue to prompt the comprehension strategies.

Day 3 **SILENT READ** Have students reread the selection silently. Have students focus on the comprehension skills and Reading with a Writer's Eye.

Day 4 **SILENT READ** Have students finish rereading the selection.

Technology

Have students listen to "Earthquake! The 1906 San Francisco Nightmare" on the ***Listening Library CD.*** After students have listened, have them discuss what other things, such as poetry, songs, or nonfiction, they prefer to listen to on the radio or on CDs.

Shaking at Dawn

On April 18, 1906, the sun had just begun to rise in San Francisco, California. Most people were asleep. Others were getting ready for work.

Thomas Jefferson Chase was a ticket clerk on a ferryboat. As he walked to his job, the streets were empty and quiet. Suddenly, without warning, a loud roar and rumble filled the air. The ground shook so hard that Thomas was thrown flat on his face.

The ground kept shaking. Then it opened up around him. He couldn't stand up.

What was going on? A huge earthquake was happening. It would change San Francisco forever.

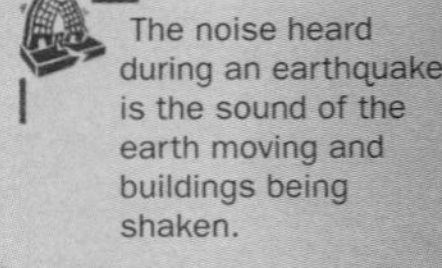

The noise heard during an earthquake is the sound of the earth moving and buildings being shaken.

168

Broken Windows, Broken Lives

Nearby, young Lloyd Head held onto his shaking bed so he wouldn't fall out. The house was rocking back and forth. When the shaking stopped, he ran to his parents' room. The whole family looked outside. 1

Buildings had fallen down. Windows were broken. There were huge holes in the earth. The sidewalks were cracked and bent. Water flowed from pipes that had burst. Crowds of people were on the streets.

Downtown, Lloyd could see a fire. He didn't know it, but gas was coming out of broken gas lines all over the city. The real terror was just starting.

San Francisco is in northern California. Earthquakes also occur in southern California. About 10,000 small earthquakes occur there each year.

169

Word Structure

Affixes as syllables: warning, shaking, going, happening, shaking, rocking, coming, starting

Comprehension Strategies

This selection is broken into two parts. On the first day, read pages 168–175. On the second day, read pages 176–179.

1 **Visualizing** Teacher Prompt: *Remember that visualizing what you are reading involves forming mental images of a story's characters and events. Who would like to share their visualizations with the class?* **Possible Student Response** *I can see the city and some of the buildings in the photographs, but I can also visualize the characters. I can imagine what Thomas Jefferson Chase and Lloyd Head might have looked like as the ground began to shake. They probably both looked surprised and scared.*

Fire!

Thomas Chase had stayed away from flying stones and sparking power lines to get to work. Now he helped people onto ferryboats. 2

The gas had caught fire and flames covered the city. Horses couldn't get through the broken streets. Firefighters had to get to the fires on foot. When they reached a fire there was no water to put it out. The pipes had burst.

Lloyd Head's mother sewed bags together to make a tent. The family camped outside. They were afraid their house would fall. People watched rescue workers try to put out the flames with coats and brooms. 3

Soldiers blew up buildings to stop the fire from spreading.

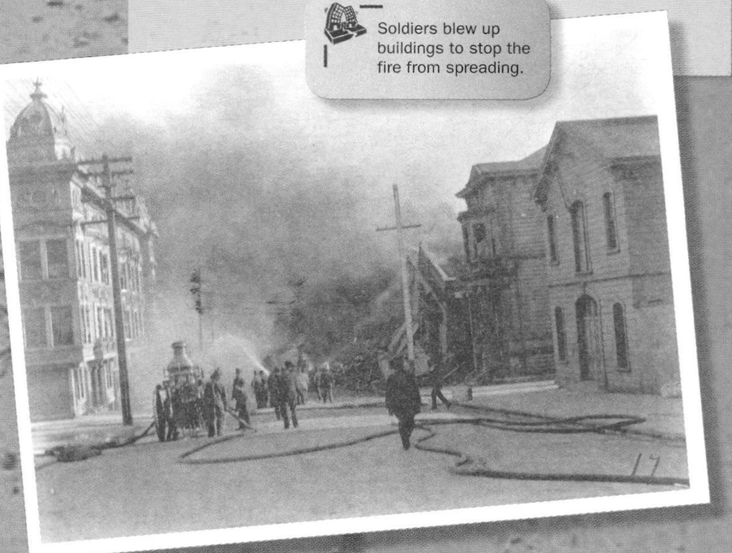

170

A Shattered City

Three days later, the fire was out. The shaking had stopped. The beautiful city of San Francisco was a mess.

The death count was about 700. People who study history, however, say as many as 3,000 people died. About 225,000 people were hurt. The earthquake destroyed 490 city blocks. Over 25,000 buildings had fallen. It would take millions of dollars to rebuild San Francisco.

Without warning, much of San Francisco had been flattened like a sand castle hit by a wave. How did it happen? How does any earthquake happen?

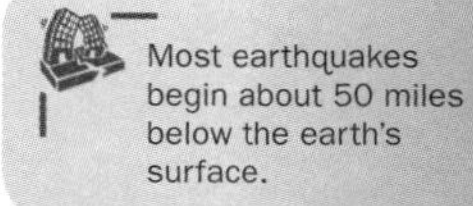

Most earthquakes begin about 50 miles below the earth's surface.

171

2 Making Connections Teacher Prompt: *Who would like to share a connection with this part of the text?* **Possible Student Response** *This part of the text tells us about how Thomas Chase helped people onto the ferryboats. I remember seeing a news report about a man who helped people get out of a fire in a house. They were both very brave men to be helping people during a crisis.*

3 Visualizing Teacher Prompt: *Who would like to share their visualizations with the class?* **Possible Student Response** *I can see the tents made out of bags and the firefighters putting out the flames with coats and brooms.*

Comprehension Check

Why are captions used with the photographs in the text? **Possible Answer** *They help explain the photographs, and they give additional information to the main body of the text.*

Word Structure

Affixes as syllables: flying, sparking, shaking, rebuild, warning

Teacher Tip

THINK ALOUDS Remind students that their own think alouds are always preferred to yours. Continue to encourage the students to model for one another when they use strategies or work out problems as they read. Students may want to record in journals what strategies they have used in a particular selection and why. They can note which strategies were most useful to them.

What Is an Earthquake?

The city had been hit by shock waves. These waves start below the earth's surface, where there are large pieces of rock. These rocks are called tectonic plates. The plates fit against one another like a puzzle. 4

Each plate floats on hot liquid rock. Sometimes plates push against each other. If the plates slip while they're pushing, shock waves occur. These waves travel up and can cause the ground to move.

An earthquake is usually followed by aftershocks. The aftershocks occur as the rocks get into their new positions. The 1906 San Francisco Earthquake had 135 aftershocks.

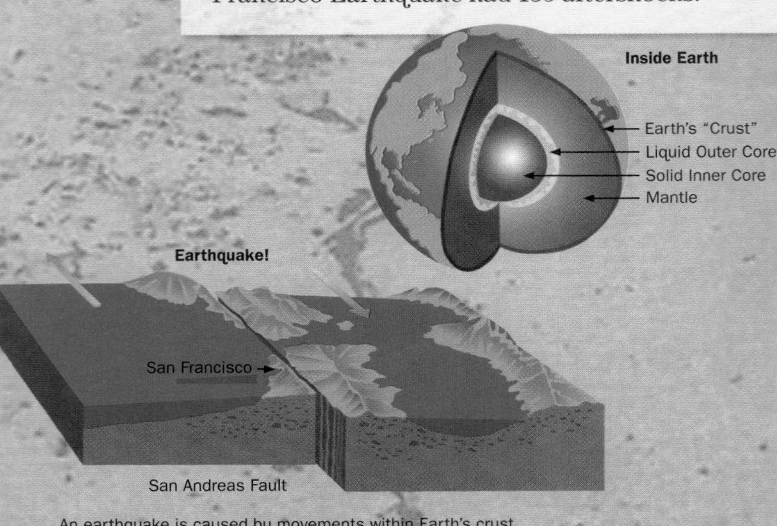

An earthquake is caused by movements within Earth's crust.

172

Whose Fault Is It?

Each year, half a million earthquakes occur around the world. Most are harmless. About a hundred are big enough to cause trouble, mainly those near cities.

Earthquakes usually occur along weak places in the earth's crust called faults. San Francisco sits on the San Andreas Fault. This fault stretches along part of the state. It causes most of California's many earthquakes. 5

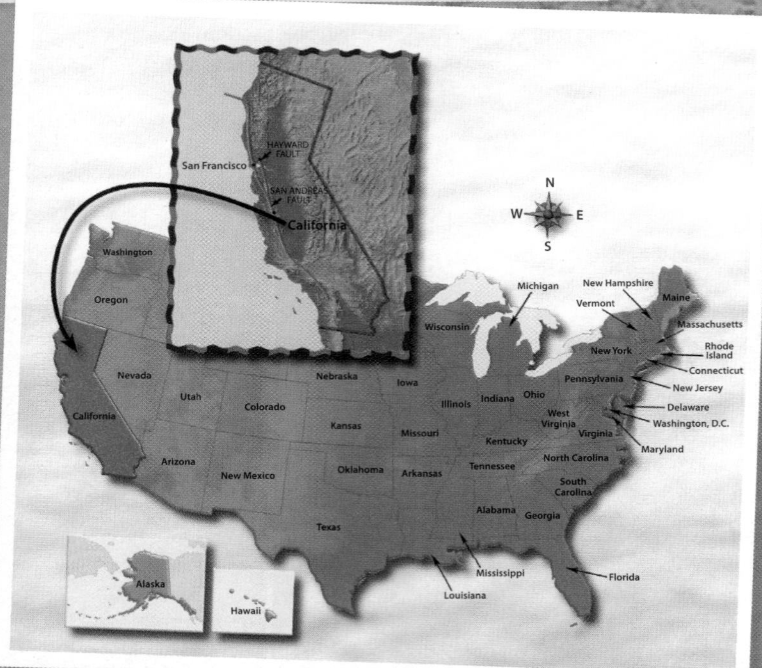

173

Word Structure

Affixes as syllables: below, pushing, harmless, mainly, usually

Differentiating Instruction **English Learner**

IF . . . students need a review of *headings*, **THEN . . .** explain that these are the words at the top of a section that tell what that section will be about. Lead students to understand how the base word head relates to the use of the term.

Comprehension Strategies

4 Visualizing Teacher Prompt: *What can you visualize as you read these words?* **Possible Student Response** *The plates fit against one another like a puzzle. I can see in my mind how the plates would look. If I would push pieces of a jigsaw puzzle together they would slip, too. I can see how huge pieces of rock pushing against each other underground would cause trouble.*

5 Making Connections Teacher Prompt: *Who can make a connection to the text?* **Possible Student Response** *I have heard of the San Andreas Fault before. Now I understand that a fault is a weak place in Earth's crust. I know that weak means "not as strong." Since the San Andreas Fault is a weak spot, it makes sense that more earthquakes would occur there.*

Comprehension Check

What causes aftershocks to occur? They occur when the rocks that have been pushed against each other get into their new positions.

Take a Number

Since 1906, scientists have learned a lot about earthquakes. They have special tools to help them. One is a seismograph. It's used to record the movement of the earth during an earthquake. 6

Scientists give each earthquake a number on the Richter Scale. This scale measures the power of an earthquake. The highest numbers go to the biggest earthquakes.

The scale uses numbers and parts of numbers to measure power exactly. If an earthquake is rated "five point two," that means its number is 5.2. It has more power than an earthquake rated 5.1.

The biggest earthquake in the world measured 9.5 on the Richter Scale. This earthquake occurred in Chile in 1960.

Movements of the earth show up as heavy lines on a seismograph chart.

America's 10 Strongest Earthquakes on Record*			
Rank	Location	Date	Magnitude
1	Prince William Sound, Alaska	March 28, 1964	9.2
2	Andreanof Islands, Alaska	March 9, 1957	9.1
3	Rat Islands, Alaska	February 4, 1965	8.7
4	East of Shumagin Islands, Alaska	November 10, 1938	8.2
5	New Madrid, Missouri	December 16, 1811	8.1
6	Yakutat Bay, Alaska	September 10, 1899	8.0
7	Andreanof Islands, Alaska	May 7, 1986	8.0
8	New Madrid, Missouri	February 7, 1812	8.0
9	(Near) Cape Yakataga, Alaska	September 4, 1899	7.9
10	Fort Tejon, California	January 9, 1857	7.9

* From the United States Geological Survey

The San Francisco Earthquake of 1906 would be number 17 on this list. It hit the Richter Scale at 7.8.

America's Biggest Shake-ups

The 1906 San Francisco Earthquake wasn't the biggest earthquake to ever occur. It was, however, the most harmful earthquake in American history.

It caused so much damage because it hit a big city with lots of buildings and people. Earthquakes that hit places with few people and buildings don't cause as much harm, even if they have more power.

6 Visualizing Teacher Prompt: *Who can visualize this part of the text?* **Possible Student Response** *The text says a seismograph records the movement of the earth during an earthquake. The higher numbers are assigned to the biggest earthquakes. I can just see the rocks pushing against each other under Earth's crust. The harder and faster the rocks push, the higher the number goes on the scale.*

Vocabulary Tip

Point out the word *shattered* in the heading on page 171. Then have students read the paragraph following this term. Ask them how the phrase *The beautiful city of San Francisco was a mess* helps them to remember the meaning of *shattered.* Point out the word *exactly* on page 174. Ask students how knowing that the seismograph can measure the difference between the power of 5.1 and 5.2 helps them remember the meaning of the word *exactly.*

Word Structure

Affixes as syllables: movement, harmful

Teacher Tip

COMPREHENSION Ask students the following questions to make sure they understand what they are reading:

- *Can you summarize what you have read?*
- *Does what you are reading make sense?*

STOP You have read the first half of the story. Continue the story tomorrow on page T210.

Lesson 3 Inquiry Planner

STEP 3: Making Conjectures

Day 1 In groups, students will make conjectures about their investigation questions and post them on the **Concept/Question Board.**

Day 2 Students will read "Earthquake! The 1906 San Francisco Nightmare" for more ideas about the unit theme.

Day 3 As a whole group, students will discuss how ideas in "Earthquake! The 1906 San Francisco Nightmare" relate to students' conjectures.

STEP 4: Identifying Information Needs

Day 4 With their groups, students will discuss things their group needs to know about their investigation topic and make plans for their investigation.

Day 5 Groups will begin collecting sources and carrying out investigation plans.

Teacher Tip

MAKING CONJECTURES Making conjectures might seem difficult for some students. Remind them that a conjecture is a possible answer to their investigation question. Explain that during their investigation, they might find that this answer no longer applies to their question. Or, they might find that they need to change the answer in some way to make it fit better. Students should continue to revise their questions and answers as they investigate.

Inquiry Process

Step 3—Making Conjectures

Whole-Group Time

Whole Group

✦ At this point, student groups have chosen their investigation questions. Now they will begin making conjectures about their questions.

✦ Ask students what a conjecture is. If necessary, remind students that a conjecture is an answer to a question based on what is already known, like an educated guess. After they collect information, students will review their conjectures in light of new information. Remind students that their ideas about their question might change after they do more research.

✦ Return to the investigation question you modeled earlier, *How can our community avoid expanding too much and destroying valuable countryside?* Now model a conjecture about this question, saying something such as this: *I think our community needs to find a way to slow down how fast it's expanding. Both people and wildlife have a right to the land. To protect these rights, my conjecture is,* Some land should be set aside for nature parks and protected wildlife sanctuaries. *People won't be able to live in these places and the wildlife and countryside can be preserved.* Have students contribute their ideas and conjectures about the question you modeled. Remind students that they are free to propose any questions and conjectures about the topics that interest them.

✦ If necessary, model making conjectures using some of the questions raised so far in the unit and in discussions. Example questions: *How has the land affected human beings? How do human beings affect and change the land? What does learning about the past of a community teach us about the present and the future?* Example conjectures might be: *Land can benefit people by providing water and food, but it can harm people through natural occurrences, such as earthquakes, hurricanes, and droughts. Human beings change the land as populations continue to increase and people inhabit more of the natural world. We can learn from past mistakes and also from what was done well in order to improve our communities.*

✦ Review with students what they have learned about the theme from the selections they have read so far in this unit. Remind them to use this information to help make conjectures about their investigation question.

Small-Group Time

Small Group

- In their small groups, students should review their investigation question and any notes they have taken about their topic and the theme in their Writer's Notebooks and ***Skills Practice 2.***
- As you circulate among the groups, continue to model making conjectures with students. Keep in mind, however, that the investigations are student-driven. Groups should develop their questions, conjectures, and presentations based on their own interests.
- Remind students that their conjectures should be based on what they already know about their topic. Have groups discuss what they know about their topic, including what they have learned from the unit selections. Then have them discuss which conjectures are most reasonable, likely, or helpful answers to their question. Students should record their conjectures in their Writer's Notebooks and post them on the **Concept/Question Board.**

Concept/Question Board

Have students continue to write information on the **Concept/Question Board.** Students might

- share interesting findings, quotes, or ideas.
- write and post paragraphs about where their community lives, archaeology, natural disasters, or the environment.
- post photographs or illustrations of our past, present, or future communities.
- list television programs or movies related to the theme.

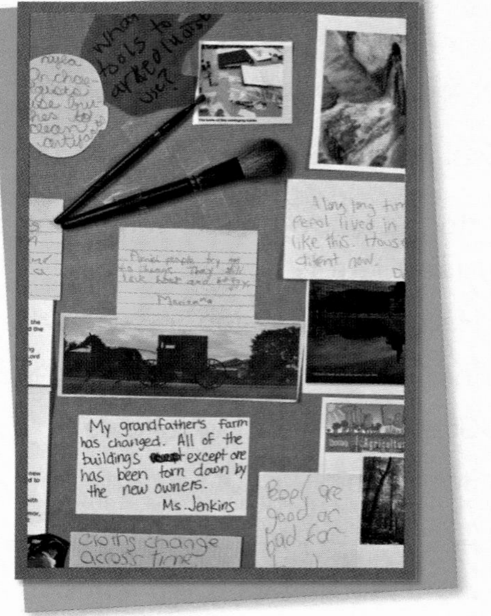

Inquiry Rubric

To assess Making a Conjecture, see the Inquiry Rubrics in the Level Appendix.

Day 1

Language Arts

OBJECTIVES

Students will

- prewrite a business letter.
- take the spelling pretest.
- review cursive *S, G, N, M, P,* and *R.*

MATERIALS

- ***Language Arts Handbook,*** pp. 72–77
- ***Transparencies*** 127, 131, 137, and 142
- ***Skills Practice 2,*** p. 129
- Routine 16

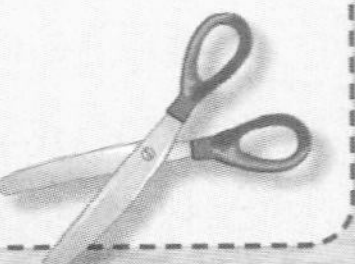

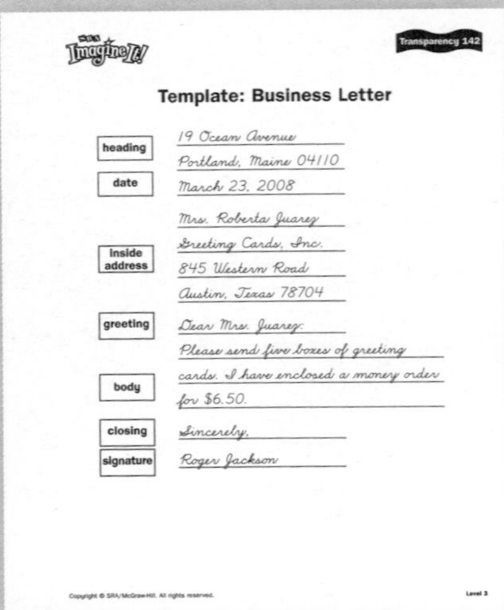

Imagine It! Transparency 142

Template: Business Letter

heading	19 Ocean Avenue Portland, Maine 04110
date	March 23, 2008
inside address	Mrs. Roberta Juarez Greeting Cards, Inc. 845 Western Road Austin, Texas 78704
greeting	Dear Mrs. Juarez:
body	Please send five boxes of greeting cards. I have enclosed a money order for $6.50.
closing	Sincerely,
signature	Roger Jackson

 Level 3

Transparency 142

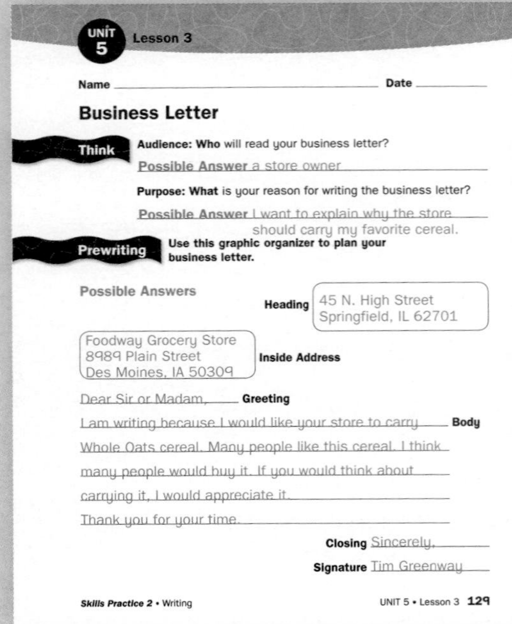

UNIT 5 Lesson 3

Name ______ Date ______

Business Letter

Think **Audience: Who** will read your business letter?

Possible Answer a store owner

Purpose: What is your reason for writing the business letter?

Possible Answer I want to explain why the store should carry my favorite cereal.

Prewriting **Use this graphic organizer to plan your business letter.**

Possible Answers

Heading 45 N. High Street
Springfield, IL 62701

Foodway Grocery Store
8989 Plain Street
Des Moines, IA 50309 **Inside Address**

Dear Sir or Madam, **Greeting**

I am writing because I would like your store to carry Whole Oats cereal. Many people like this cereal. I think many people would buy it. If you would think about carrying it, I would appreciate it. Thank you for your time. **Body**

Closing Sincerely,

Signature Tim Greenway

Skills Practice 2 • Writing UNIT 5 • Lesson 3 129

Skills Practice 2, p. 129

Writing Business Letter

ROUTINE 16

Prewriting

Teach

- Use Routine 16. Ask students what kinds of letters they have written. **Possible Answers** *friendly letters, invitations, persuasive letters* Tell students this time they will write a business letter.
- Explain that people need to communicate with businesses, doctors, employers, and so on. This type of communication is considered formal and is used for a special reason. A business letter, for example, is a formal letter written when people are interested in an issue or worried about an issue. It might also be a letter of request that asks the reader to send information. A business letter could be a letter of complaint that states a problem the writer has with a product or service.
- Display ***Transparency*** 142. Read and discuss the formal business letter.
- Write the following information on the board or chart paper, and explain that business letters have six parts.
    - Heading: writer's address and the date
    - Inside address: the person to whom the letter is addressed
    - Greeting: salutation followed by a colon
    - Body: main part of the letter; paragraphs are not indented
    - Closing: followed by comma
    - Signature: handwritten name
- Tell students they will be completing a graphic organizer in prewriting that will help them remember all the parts of a business letter.
- Refer to the ***Language Arts Handbook*** pp. 72–77 for information about formal business letters.

Writing, continued

Guided Practice

- As a class, brainstorm ideas for business letters. Write ideas on the board. Ideas might include a letter to the principal expressing concern over food in the cafeteria or a letter to a toy manufacturer stating a problem with a toy. Tell students they can use one of these ideas or create one of their own, but it must be for a serious, formal business letter.
- Have students turn to ***Skills Practice 2*** page 129, and read the Think section aloud. Explain to students that before they write their business letters, they must think about the audience and the reason for writing. Remind them that formal business letters require formal language and word choices.
- Create a graphic organizer on the board like the one on page 129 in ***Skills Practice 2***. Select a topic from the ones on the board to model organizing information for your draft. Save this information.

Apply

Composing—Prewriting Have students complete page 129 in ***Skills Practice 2*** as a prewriting activity.

Assessment

You will use the Writing Rubrics found in the Level Appendix to evaluate students' business letters. You may use any of the rubrics for Genre, Writing Process, and Writing Traits. Share with students what you will be looking for when assessing their business letters.

Spelling

Affixes that Change Word Meaning Pretest

Teach

Say the sentences below aloud. Have students write the spelling words on a separate sheet of paper. When they are finished, have them correct any misspelled words.

Pretest Sentences

1. I always bring my **lucky** charm with me.
2. Some say black cats are an **unlucky** sign.
3. The puddle began to **freeze.**
4. We put **antifreeze** in our car's radiator.
5. Because you are tired, you should get some **rest.**
6. The vacation we took was very **restful.**
7. When I am feeling **restless,** I like to go for a walk.
8. The beautiful sunset began to **fade.**
9. Try not to **miswrite** your test answer.
10. How high can you **count?**
11. The furniture store offers a huge **discount.**
12. We decided to **move** closer to the river.
13. We spotted some **movement** in the bushes.
14. I like to hear Grandpa **tell** stories.
15. Would you please **retell** the story?

Challenge Sentences

16. The bracelet was **exactly** what I wanted.
17. You have to **disconnect** the phone.

Diagnose any misspellings by determining whether students misspelled the affixes or some other part of the word. Then have students use the pretest as a take-home list to study the spellings of words with affixes.

Teacher Tip

PENMANSHIP Have students practice legible penmanship as they write their unit investigations.

Differentiating Instruction **English Learner**

IF . . . students have difficulty following your directions for handwriting, **THEN . . .** words such as *undercurve, overcurve, downcurve, slant* and *loop.* Say and demonstrate each word, having students mimic both your words and movements.

Penmanship

Cursive Letters *S, G, N, M, P,* and *R*

Teach

✦ Review capital cursive *S* and *G* as letters with loops. Review capital cursive *N* and *M* as curve forward letters. Review capital cursive *P* and *R* as undercurve slant letters.

✦ For further assistance with this review lesson, refer to Unit 4 Lesson 5, and Unit 5 Lessons 1 and 2; ***Transparencies*** 127, 131, and 137; and the Level Appendix.

✦ Write capital cursive *S, G, N, M, P,* and *R* on the board, you say the strokes aloud as you form the letters.

Guided Practice

Ask for a volunteer to write the letters on the board while you say the strokes aloud. Guide the student as he or she writes.

Apply

Have students practice writing each of the letters four times. Ask them to circle the best formation of each of their letters.

For further practice, have students use classmates' names to practice proper formation of capital *S, G, N, M, P,* and *R.*

Skills Traces

Preparing to Read

Word Structure: Inflectional Ending *-ed*

Introduced in Grade 2, Unit 4, Lesson 5

Grade 3
Reviewed: Unit 3, Lesson 2
Practiced: Unit 5, Lesson 3
Assessed: ***Lesson Assessment Book 2,*** p. 59

Reviewed in Grade 4, Unit 1, Lesson 4

Word Structure: Affixes

Grade 3
Introduced: Unit 5, Lesson 3
Practiced: Unit 5, Lesson 5

Reviewed in Grade 4, Unit 1, Lesson 3

Reading and Responding

Comprehension Skill: Cause and Effect

Reviewed in Grade 2, Unit 2, Lesson 3

Grade 3
Reviewed: Unit 1, Lesson 1
Practiced: Unit 5, Lesson 3
Assessed: ***Lesson Assessment Book 2,*** pp. 60–62

Reviewed in Grade 4, Unit 1, Lesson 3

Comprehension Skill: Drawing Conclusions

Reviewed in Grade 2, Unit 1, Lesson 2

Grade 3
Reviewed: Unit 1, Lesson 4
Practiced: Unit 5, Lesson 3
Assessed: ***Lesson Assessment Book 2,*** pp. 60–62

Reviewed in Grade 4, Unit 1, Lesson 2

Comprehension Skill: Fact and Opinion

Reviewed in Grade 2, Unit 3, Lesson 3

Grade 3
Reviewed: Unit 1, Lesson 1
Practiced: Unit 5, Lesson 3
Assessed: ***Lesson Assessment Book 2,*** pp. 60–62

Reviewed in Grade 4, Unit 2, Lesson 4

Comprehension Strategy: Making Connections

Reviewed in Grade 2, Unit 1, Lesson 1

Grade 3
Reviewed: Unit 1, Lesson 1
Practiced: Unit 5, Lesson 3
Assessed: Unit 5, Lesson 3, p. T195

Reviewed in Grade 4, Unit 1, Lesson 1

Language Arts

Writing: Business Letter

Reviewed in Grade 2, Unit 6, Lesson 3

Grade 3
Reviewed: Unit 5, Lesson 3
Assessed: Unit 5, Lesson 3, p. T248

Grammar, Usage, and Mechanics: Sentence Tense

Reviewed in Grade 2, Unit 5, Lesson 5

Grade 3
Reviewed: Unit 5, Lesson 3
Practiced: Unit 6, Lesson 5
Assessed: ***Lesson Assessment Book 2,*** p. 64

Reviewed in Grade 4, Unit 4, Lesson 5

Day 2

Preparing to Read

OBJECTIVES

Students will
- recognize affixes as syllables.
- build fluency.

MATERIALS

Transparency 140

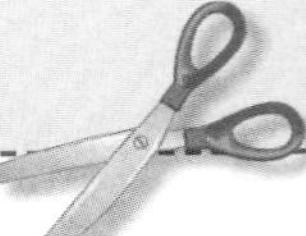

Daily Oral Practice

Daily News Today!

Scientists have extremely important jobs. They do research and study patterns and movements on Earth and in space. They invent machines that help protect people from danger. I want to be a scientist someday.

- Write the daily news on the board or on chart paper. Then have the girls read the daily news in unison to practice fluency.
- As a review of yesterday's word structure lesson, ask a volunteer to identify any words in the message with affixes that add syllables to base words. *extremely, research, movements*

Differentiating Instruction **English Learner**

IF . . . students are native speakers of Vietnamese, Hmong, or Chinese, **THEN . . .** they will need extra help hearing and isolating syllables. In their native languages, all words are monosyllabic. Refer to the ***English Learner Support Guide*** for additional instruction for new English learners.

Word Structure

Affixes as Syllables

✦ Use ***Transparency*** 140 with these word lines from Day 1.

Line 1	harm	harmless	main	mainly
Line 2	bend	bendable	thank	thankful
Line 3	build	rebuild	connect	disconnect
Line 4	treat	mistreat	helpful	unhelpful

✦ Review how affixes are their own syllables in words. If necessary, remind students that prefixes such as *re-* and *un-*, and suffixes, such as *-less* and *-ful*, add new syllables to base words. Remind students that some prefixes and suffixes add more than one syllable to base words, such as *auto-* and *-able*.

Developing Oral Language

Use any or all of the following activities to help students practice reading the words from the word lines.

- Have a volunteer select a base word and use it in a sentence. **Possible Answer** *The city should* build *more parks.* Then have that student select another volunteer to use the other form of the word in another sentence. **Possible Answer** *I had to* rebuild *my sandcastle after the wave came.* Continue until all of the words have been used.
- Ask a student to identify a word in the word lines by naming its location. For example, "Line 2, Word 4." Then ask the student to read it aloud and use it in a sentence. **Possible Answer** *I'm* thankful *that I've never been in an earthquake.* Continue the activity until all the words have been used.
- Have a volunteer choose a line of words from the word lines. Then have the volunteer identify the affixes in the words on that line. **Possible Answer** *Line 2:* -able *in* bendable *and* -ful *in* thankful Ask the student whether the affixes are prefixes or suffixes. *suffixes* Then ask the class to offer other examples of words with these affixes. **Possible Answers** *huggable, squeezable, drinkable; grateful, careful, hopeful* Continue this activity with the other affixes in the words on the word lines.

Differentiating Instruction — English Learner

IF . . . students are native Spanish speakers, **THEN . . .** point out that the English suffix *-able* has the same meaning as the Spanish suffix *-able* and that the word *variable* is identical in the two languages.

Monitor Progress 

to Differentiate Instruction
Formal Assessment

Word Structure During the word structure activity, note how well students understand the words.

APPROACHING LEVEL
IF . . . students do not understand the words on the word lines, **THEN . . .** use pictures, photos, objects, stick drawings, or pantomime to help them visualize the words.

ON LEVEL
IF . . . students need practice with the words on the word lines, **THEN . . .** have them write sentences using the same words on the lines.

ABOVE LEVEL
IF . . . students understand the words on the word lines, **THEN . . .** have them make a list of other words with affixes and use them in sentences.

Looking for Clues

Days later, Thomas Chase was safe at his mother's house in Oakland, California. Lloyd Head's family was still camping outside. Thousands of others were in tents in the city's parks. They hung signs with names like "Camp Thankful." They were glad to be alive. 7

Scientists studied photos and maps of the places hit. Workers hunted through the fallen buildings and homes. They were looking for ideas to help make a safer city. They found that buildings on soft land were damaged more than buildings on solid rock. They learned the fire had caused more problems than the earthquake.

The moon also has "earthquakes." These "earthquakes" don't happen often and they aren't strong.

176

By 1910, many buildings in San Francisco had been rebuilt.

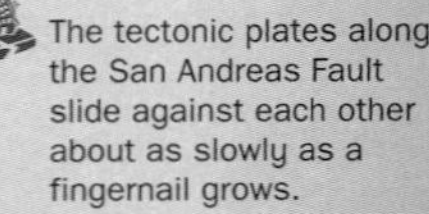

The tectonic plates along the San Andreas Fault slide against each other about as slowly as a fingernail grows.

A New San Francisco

After the earthquake, the city made new building rules. The rules were very tough for buildings on soft ground. Tall buildings were made to move with earthquake shocks instead of falling to pieces. Most new buildings had to have steel frames.

New water pipes that could bend easily were put to use. These pipes would be less likely to burst. New gas lines were made more bendable, too. 8

San Francisco did not put these new rules into effect all at once. The city, however, was ready to welcome visitors to the 1915 World's Fair.

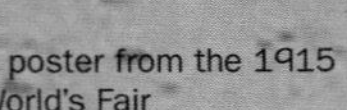

A poster from the 1915 World's Fair

177

OBJECTIVES

Students will

- use the comprehension strategies Making Connections and Visualizing.
- discuss the selection using the handing-off process.
- review vocabulary, genre, and fluency.

MATERIALS

- ***Student Reader,*** Book 2, pp. 176–181
- Routine A
- ***Skills Practice 2,*** pp. 123–124
- ***Transparencies*** 35, 141

Comprehension Strategies

7 Making Connections Teacher Prompt: *Who would like to share a connection they can make with the selection?* **Possible Student Response** *My aunt and uncle lived through a bad hurricane last year. They also had to live in tents for awhile. A lot of people in their community lost their homes and they all camped out together. They helped each other get through the tough times.*

8 Visualizing Teacher Prompt: *Who would like to share their visualizations with the class?* **Possible Student Response** *I've never really seen bendable pipes, but I can picture pipes that could twist and bend. They would be harder to break than stiffer pipes.*

San Francisco Hit Again!

In 1989, another large earthquake shook the city. One place it hit was San Francisco's Candlestick Park. It was before the start of a World Series game. Millions of Americans watched on TV.

This earthquake measured 6.9 on the Richter Scale. This time the city was more prepared. Buildings shook but most did not fall. There was, however, some damage. Parts of the San Francisco-Oakland Bay Bridge fell. A section of the freeway in Oakland fell, too. Forty-two people were killed. Power was knocked out. Fires started around the city. Again, the most damage happened to buildings on soft land.

Damage from the 1989 earthquake cost about 6 billion dollars.

The Future

Scientists think another big earthquake might strike San Francisco in the next 30 years. More than 1,000 earthquake stations are on the lookout for shock waves along California's fault lines. If it seems like an earthquake is about to happen, people can be warned. Families have emergency supplies of food and water. Kids in school practice safety moves such as hiding under a strong table. 9

Earthquake study in America began because of the 1906 San Francisco Earthquake. Now we know much more. We can't stop an earthquake, but we can live through one.

Every year about 500,000 earthquakes occur. Only about 100 cause damage.

9 **Making Connections** Teacher Prompt: *Who can make a connection to the text?* **Possible Student Response** *My family has an emergency supply of food, water, flashlights, and a medical kit in case of emergencies. We also have emergency plans in case of fire or tornadoes. We have fire and tornado drills at school. It scares me a little, sometimes, but I'm glad we'll know what to do if we ever have to.*

Comprehension Check

Why did the San Francisco earthquake of 1989 not cause as much damage as the earthquake of 1906? **Possible Answer** *The city was more prepared because the buildings were built better. Where did most of the damage occur?* **Possible Answer** *Most of the damage occurred to buildings built on soft land. How can people be better prepared for earthquakes?* **Possible Answer** *People can practice safety moves and have emergency supplies ready.*

Vocabulary Tip

Point to the word *frames* on page 177 in the text. Ask students what materials they believe should be used to make *frames* for buildings. If necessary, point to a picture or actual door frames. Point out the word *section* on page 178. Ask students to substitute other words for the word *section* in the sentence such as *part, piece,* or *portion*. Ask them if substituting these words helps them better understand the word *section*.

Word Structure

Affixes as syllables: camping, thankful, hunted, looking, falling, easily, likely, bendable, started, safety

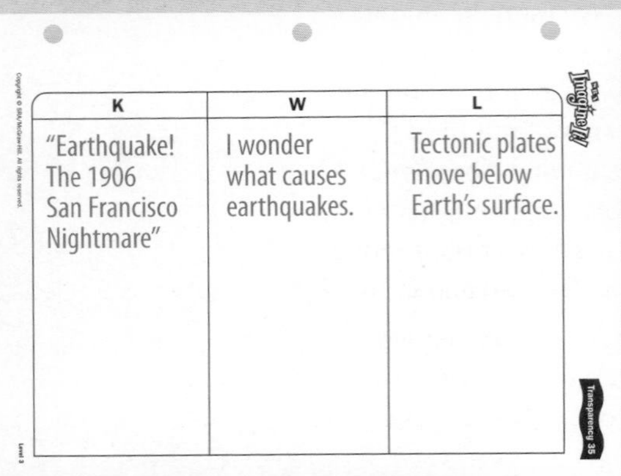

K	W	L
"Earthquake! The 1906 San Francisco Nightmare"	I wonder what causes earthquakes.	Tectonic plates move below Earth's surface.

Transparency 35

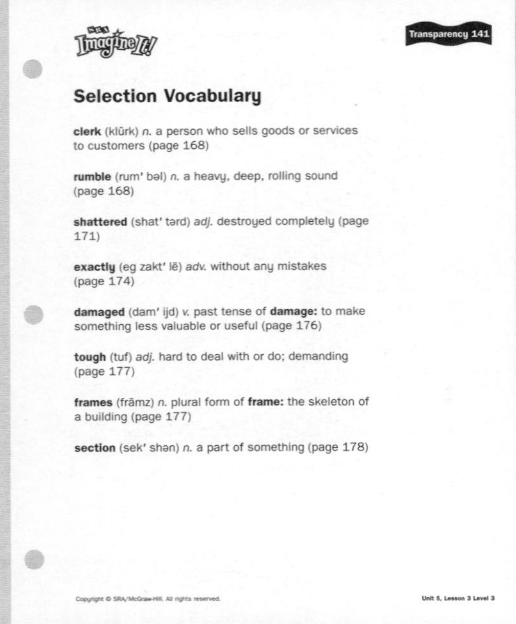

Transparency 141

Selection Vocabulary

clerk (klûrk) *n.* a person who sells goods or services to customers (page 168)

rumble (rum' bəl) *n.* a heavy, deep, rolling sound (page 168)

shattered (shat' tərd) *adj.* destroyed completely (page 171)

exactly (eg zakt' lē) *adv.* without any mistakes (page 174)

damaged (dam' ijd) *v.* past tense of **damage:** to make something less valuable or useful (page 176)

tough (tuf) *adj.* hard to deal with or do; demanding (page 177)

frames (frāmz) *n.* plural form of **frame:** the skeleton of a building (page 177)

section (sek' shən) *n.* a part of something (page 178)

Unit 5, Lesson 3 Level 3

Transparency 141

Differentiating Instruction **English Learner**

IF . . . students need help to participate in the discussion, **THEN . . .** remember to ask questions that can be answered by a nod, a *yes* or *no,* a short phrase, or a simple sentence, depending students' level of proficiency.

IF . . . students would benefit from additional work with the vocabulary of "Earthquake! The 1906 San Francisco Nightmare," **THEN . . .** read the selection to them during Workshop. Encourage them to ask questions about anything they don't understand.

Discussing the Selection

✦ It is important for students to see you as a contributing member of the group. Use Routine A, handing-off, to emphasize that you are part of the group. Actively participate in handing-off by raising your hand to be called on by the last speaker when you have a contribution to make. Point out unusual and interesting insights verbalized by students so that these insights are recognized and discussed.

✦ Engage students in a discussion using handing-off to determine whether they have grasped the following ideas.
- Natural disasters have a tremendous impact on the land.
- People can protect themselves from natural disasters by inventing better instruments to predict events and warn people about them.

✦ Ask students how the selection demonstrates the following key concepts:
- People can be prepared by having emergency plans and supplies ready.
- Cities can be better prepared with tougher building codes, better warning systems, and emergency disaster plans.

✦ Return to the KWL chart on ***Transparency*** 35. Have students discuss whether the selection provided enough information to tell them what they wanted to know. Also have them discuss what they learned by reading the selection. Ask students if the predictions they made while browsing the selection were confirmed or not confirmed.

✦ Have students return to the Focus Questions on page 167. Select a student to read the questions aloud, and have students answer and discuss the questions. Have them return to the text as necessary.

Genre Review

Review the elements of expository text on page T194 with students. Then ask students how they know "Earthquake! The 1906 San Francisco Nightmare" is expository text.

How has my community changed over time?

After reading the selection, read the Big Idea question. Discuss with students how the selection helps answer this question.

Vocabulary Review

Review with students the selection vocabulary words and definitions they wrote in the vocabulary section of the Writer's Notebook. Then refer students to ***Skills Practice 2*** pages 123–124. Help students complete the first two questions, and have students complete the rest on their own. Also, review the concept vocabulary word *community*. Ask students if they can think of other words related to the theme Communities across Time. **Possible Answers** *towns, homes, people, bonds, helpful*

Fluency

- When modeling fluency, practice accuracy. Accuracy, or reading with few errors, is essential to fluency. Reading with accuracy makes the text easier to understand and to remember. Tell students that to read with accuracy, they might need to reread a word, sentence, or passage.
- Read aloud pages 168–169 of "Earthquake! The 1906 San Francisco Nightmare." Model accuracy for students. For example, after reading *The real terror was just starting,* model rereading until you are able to read the sentence accurately. Point out to students that some words, such as *terror,* might be unfamiliar. To read fluently, readers sometimes reread to make sure they understand the text. Tell students that when reading it is important to pay attention to end punctuation and commas. Have students follow along in the ***Student Reader*** and tell them to raise their hands when you pause. Tell students that as they reread, they should practice pausing after commas.

Monitor Progress to Differentiate Instruction

Formal Assessment

Selection Vocabulary Observe students' understanding of the vocabulary words and their definitions.

APPROACHING LEVEL

IF . . .	THEN . . .
IF . . . students need extra help with the selection vocabulary,	**THEN . . .** refer to ***Intervention Guide*** Unit 5 Lesson 3.
IF . . . students need extra help with the selection vocabulary,	**THEN . . .** use ***Reteach*** page 137.

ON LEVEL

IF . . .	THEN . . .
IF . . . students need practice using the selection vocabulary words,	**THEN . . .** have students find words that are related to the selection vocabulary in a dictionary or thesaurus.

ABOVE LEVEL

IF . . .	THEN . . .
IF . . . students understand the selection vocabulary,	**THEN . . .** use ***Challenge Activities*** page 125.

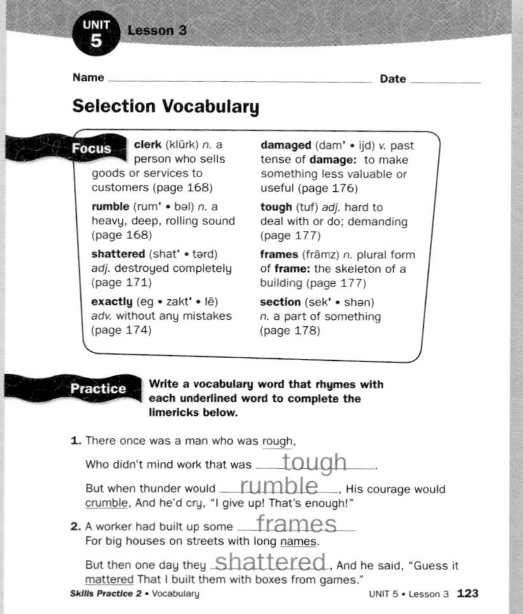

UNIT 5 Lesson 3

Name ____________ Date ______

Selection Vocabulary

Focus

clerk (klûrk) *n.* a person who sells goods or services to customers (page 168)

rumble (rum' • bəl) *n.* a heavy, deep, rolling sound (page 168)

shattered (shat' • tərd) *adj.* destroyed completely (page 171)

exactly (eg • zakt' • lē) *adv.* without any mistakes (page 174)

damaged (dam' • ijd) *v.* past tense of **damage:** to make something less valuable or useful (page 176)

tough (tuf) *adj.* hard to deal with or do; demanding (page 177)

frames (frāmz) *n.* plural form of **frame:** the skeleton of a building (page 177)

section (sek' • shən) *n.* a part of something (page 178)

Practice Write a vocabulary word that rhymes with each underlined word to complete the limericks below.

1. There once was a man who was rough,
   Who didn't mind work that was tough.
   But when thunder would rumble, His courage would crumble, And he'd cry, "I give up! That's enough!"
2. A worker had built up some frames
   For big houses on streets with long names.
   But then one day they shattered, And he said, "Guess it mattered That I built them with boxes from games."

Skills Practice 2 • Vocabulary UNIT 5 • Lesson 3 123

Skills Practice 2, pp. 123–124

Teacher Tip

WORD BANK Review the Word Bank with students. Encourage students to add words to the Word Bank related to the unit theme. You might also want to encourage students to add synonyms and antonyms in the Word Bank as well.

Fluency Tip

FLUENCY By this time in Grade 3, good readers should be reading approximately 137 words per minute with fluency and expression. The only way to gain this fluency is with practice. Have students reread the selection to you and to each other during Workshop to help build fluency. As students read, you may notice that some need work in building fluency. During Workshop, have these students choose a section of the text (a minimum of 160 words) to read aloud several times to build fluency.

Teacher Tips

WORKSHOP During Workshop, have students listen to "Earthquake! The 1906 San Francisco Nightmare" for a model of oral reading. While students listen, have them keep a list in their Writer's Notebooks of any new or unfamiliar words they encounter, and instruct them to check the words using a dictionary or glossary. Also, instruct students to listen for the lesson's vocabulary words and to check that the words make sense within the reading.

WRITE ABOUT IT! In their Writer's Notebooks, have students write about a time when people in their city or town worked together.

BEYOND THE SELECTION Have students summarize what they have learned and tell how they might use this information in future investigations.

Writer's Notebook

- Have students use their Writer's Notebooks to list other nonfiction selections they have read in class or on their own.
- Have students compare the themes in each selection.

Differentiating Instruction **English Learner**

IF . . . students have difficulty understanding the phrase *Bringing the fun of science to children* on page 180, **THEN . . .** rephrase it by saying *Making science fun for children.*

Meet the Author

After students read the information about the author, discuss the following questions with them:

- *Why does Lynn Brunelle write about science?* **Possible Answer** *She wants to bring the fun of science to children.*
- *Why do you think Lynn Brunelle writes about scientific experiments that use items that children can find at home?* **Possible Answer** *She wants all children to be able to experiment and have fun with science. She wants to make it easy for children to experiment.*

Theme Connections

Within the Selection

1. How do you prepare for emergency situations at home and at school? **Possible Answer** *My home has an emergency kit, fire extinguishers, and smoke alarms in case we have an emergency. We have practice drills at school during the year to prepare us in case there is an emergency.*
2. What can people learn from a tragedy like an earthquake? **Possible Answer** *People can use information learned from an earthquake to better prepare for the next time one occurs.*

Across Selections

3. How are scientists who study earthquakes like the scientists in "Days of Digging"? **Possible Answer** *Both groups of scientists carefully record all data they gather in order to understand and learn more about what they are studying.*
4. How are they different? **Possible Answer** *The scientists in "Days of Digging" are studying artifacts left behind by humans to better understand people and their impact on the earth. The scientists in "Earthquake! The 1906 San Francisco Nightmare" are studying the impact of nature on the land.*

Meet the Author

Lynn Brunelle
Bringing the fun of science to children is a goal for Lynn Brunelle. All of her scientific experiments involve items that kids can find at home. In addition to writing her own books, she has written for Bill Nye, the Science Guy, whose TV show appears on PBS. She won an Emmy Award for her writing on this show. Brunelle lives in Seattle, Washington, with her husband and two children.

Theme Connections

Within the Selection

1. How do you prepare for emergency situations at home and at school?
2. What can people learn from a tragedy like an earthquake?

Across Selections

3. How are scientists who study earthquakes like the scientists in "Days of Digging"?
4. How are they different?

Beyond the Selection

5. Why do people continue to live in places where there have been earthquakes?
6. How does a tragedy bring a community closer together?

about It!

Describe a time when people in your city or town worked together.

Remember to find articles on earthquakes to add to the **Concept/Question Board.**

Beyond the Selection

5. Why do people continue to live in places where there have been earthquakes? **Possible Answers** *People might continue to live in areas where there have been earthquakes because their homes, friends, and family are there and they do not want to leave them behind.*

6. How does a tragedy bring a community closer together? **Possible Answer** *By pulling together and helping each other, people can form friendships.*

Concept/Question Board

As students reread "Earthquake! The 1906 San Francisco Nightmare," encourage them to post questions, answers, comments, or other items related to the theme Communities across Time on the **Concept/Question Board.**

OBJECTIVES

Students will
- draft their business letters.
- learn to spell words with affixes that change word meanings.
- learn sentence tense.

MATERIALS

- ***Language Arts Handbook,*** pp. 324–325
- ***Skills Practice 2,*** pp. 133–134

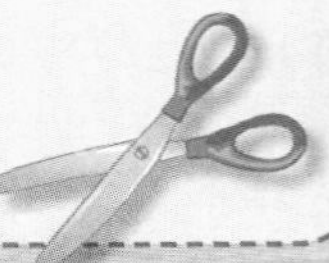

Writing Business Letter

Drafting

Teach—Formality of Language

- At this point, students should have completed the prewriting activity and decided to whom they would like to send a business letter.
- Remind students to use formal language as they begin to draft their letters. Even though they might not be writing complete sentences in their drafts, they should still make note of the formal word choices for their letters.
- Tell students that as they draft their business letters, they should refer to their selection vocabulary words for possible word choices.
- Tell students to draft the body of their letters first so they do not forget the main reasons they are writing their letters. Then they should go back and draft the other parts of the letter.

Guided Practice

- Display the business letter graphic organizer you created to model how to use this graphic organizer as a tool to draft the business letter. Allow students to help you draft. As you draft, circle words you would like to change or find a more formal synonym to use. Tell students you will look up new words during revision.
- Remind students to use the graphic organizer as a reference for all the parts that must be included in their letters, the reasons they are writing their letters, and the formal language they want to include.
- Tell students they can make corrections in spelling, grammar, capitalization, and punctuation during editing/proofreading.

Differentiating Instruction **English Learner**

IF . . . students are beginning English learners, **THEN . . .** they may not know the proper way to write an address. Tell them that an address begins with a person's name and is followed by his or her house number and street where the house is located. Next comes the name of the city, the state, and the postal code. Have students practice by writing their home and school addresses.

IF . . . students have difficulty drafting their letters, **THEN . . .** provide them with additional examples of letters to read and use for reference.

Writing, continued

Apply

Composing—Drafting Have students use their graphic organizers to draft their business letters.

Traits of Good Writing

Voice The writer uses formality of language as a means of distinguishing voice and mood.

Spelling

Affixes that Change Word Meaning

Teach

Use a word sort to teach words that change meaning when an affix is added.

Guided Practice

Write the following headings on the board: *Base Word, Words with Prefixes, Words with Suffixes,* and *Words with a Prefix and a Suffix*. Then write the following word list: *lucky, unlucky, freeze, antifreeze, rest, restful, restless, fade, miswrite, count, discount, move, movement, tell, retell.* Have volunteers write the words under the correct heading. After all the spelling words have been used, ask for students to come to the board and underline the part of each word that reflects the category in which it was placed.

Word Sort Answers

Base Words: *rest, fade, count, move, tell, freeze*

Words with Prefixes: *antifreeze, discount, retell, miswrite*

Words with Suffixes: *lucky, restful, restless, movement*

Word with a Prefix and a Suffix: *unlucky*

Grammar, Usage, and Mechanics

Sentence Tense

Teach

✦ Have students review verb tenses. If necessary, remind them how to form past, present, and future tense verbs.

✦ Ask a student what he or she did yesterday. Write the answer on the board. Ask another student what he or she is doing right now. Write that answer on the board. Finally, ask another student what he or she will do tomorrow. Write that answer on the board. Explain that sentences can happen in the past, the present, or the future. The tense of a sentence is determined by the tense of the verb. Have students indicate the sentence tense of the sentences written on the board.

✦ Use ***Language Arts Handbook*** pages 324–325 for definitions and examples of sentence tenses.

Guided Practice

✦ Have students write three sentences on the board. First, ask a student to write a sentence in the present tense about the theme Communities across Time. Next, have another student rewrite the sentence to make it past tense. Finally, have a third student rewrite the sentence in future tense. As students modify the sentence, have them explain to the rest of the class how they changed the verb to change the tense of the sentence. Tell students to look for the words *yesterday, today,* and *tomorrow*. These words are clues to the tense of a sentence. Have students use *yesterday, today,* and *tomorrow* in the sentences they created.

✦ Have students turn to ***Skills Practice 2*** page 133. Have a student read the directions aloud, and then complete the first two Practice questions as a class.

Verb Tenses

Present, Past, and Future Tenses

The **tense** of a verb tells when an action happens. Verbs in the **present tense** tell what is happening now or what happens all the time.

She **walks** to school.
Josh **is** hungry.

Verbs in the **past tense** tell what has already happened. The past tense of an action verb is often formed by adding *-ed* to the base form of the verb.

She **walked** to school.
Josh **was** hungry.

Verbs in the **future tense** tell what will happen later. The future tense is often formed with the helping verb *will.*

We **will go** to the library on Thursday.

324 Verb Tenses • Usage

Language Arts Handbook, p. 324

Differentiating Instruction **English Learner**

IF . . . students would benefit from additional work with verb tenses, **THEN . . .** have them go through the selection and identify sentences that are in the present tense and past tense sentences.

Apply

Have students complete ***Skills Practice 2*** pages 133–134 to practice using sentence tenses.

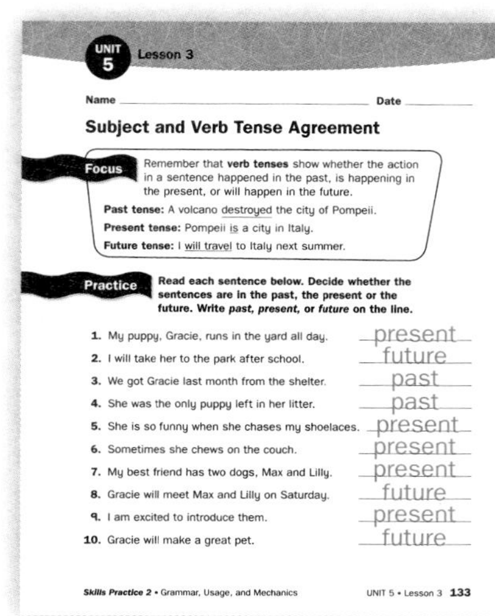

UNIT 5 Lesson 3

Name ______________ Date ______

Subject and Verb Tense Agreement

Focus Remember that **verb tenses** show whether the action in a sentence happened in the past, is happening in the present, or will happen in the future.

Past tense: A volcano destroyed the city of Pompeii.

Present tense: Pompeii is a city in Italy.

Future tense: I will travel to Italy next summer.

Practice **Read each sentence below. Decide whether the sentences are in the past, the present or the future. Write *past, present,* or *future* on the line.**

1. My puppy, Gracie, runs in the yard all day. present
2. I will take her to the park after school. future
3. We got Gracie last month from the shelter. past
4. She was the only puppy left in her litter. past
5. She is so funny when she chases my shoelaces. present
6. Sometimes she chews on the couch. present
7. My best friend has two dogs, Max and Lilly. present
8. Gracie will meet Max and Lilly on Saturday. future
9. I am excited to introduce them. present
10. Gracie will make a great pet. future

Skills Practice 2 • Grammar, Usage, and Mechanics UNIT 5 • Lesson 3 **133**

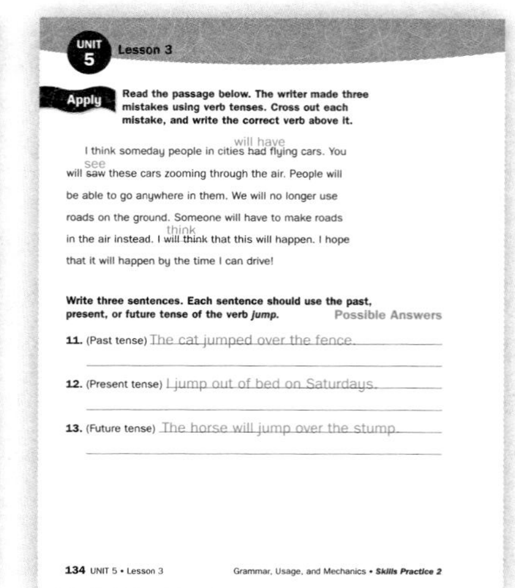

UNIT 5 Lesson 3

Apply **Read the passage below. The writer made three mistakes using verb tenses. Cross out each mistake, and write the correct verb above it.**

I think someday people in cities ~~had~~ will have flying cars. You will ~~saw~~ see these cars zooming through the air. People will be able to go anywhere in them. We will no longer use roads on the ground. Someone will have to make roads in the air instead. I ~~will think~~ think that this will happen. I hope that it will happen by the time I can drive!

Write three sentences. Each sentence should use the past, present, or future tense of the verb *jump*. Possible Answers

11. (Past tense) The cat jumped over the fence.
12. (Present tense) I jump out of bed on Saturdays.
13. (Future tense) The horse will jump over the stump.

134 UNIT 5 • Lesson 3 Grammar, Usage, and Mechanics • ***Skills Practice 2***

Skills Practice 2, pp. 133–134

Monitor Progress to Differentiate Instruction

Formal Assessment

Sentence Tense Note whether students are conjugating verb tenses correctly.

APPROACHING LEVEL

IF . . . students need to practice sentence tense,	**THEN . . .** have them complete ***Reteach*** page 141 during Workshop.
IF . . . students need more practice with sentence tense,	**THEN . . .** refer to Unit 5 Lesson 3 in the ***Intervention Guide.***

ON LEVEL

IF . . . students have an understanding of sentence tense,	**THEN . . .** have them do an activity from the ***Workshop Kit*** during Workshop.

ABOVE LEVEL

IF . . . students need a challenge,	**THEN . . .** have them complete ***Challenge Activities*** page 128 during Workshop.

Differentiating Instruction: English Learners

IF . . . students have difficulty with sentence tenses, **THEN . . .** refer to Unit 5 Lesson 3 in the ***English Learner Support Guide.***

Preparing to Read

OBJECTIVES

Students will
- identify and know affixes used to change word meanings.
- build fluency.

MATERIALS

- ***Transparency*** 143
- Routine 10
- ***Skills Practice 2,*** pp. 121–122

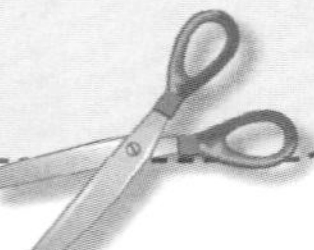

Daily Oral Practice

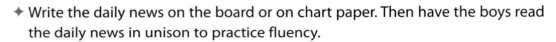

Daily News Today!

My family has an emergency plan in case there were a fire at our house. We regularly practice our drills so we would know what to do, just in case. I hope we never have to use it, but I'm glad we're prepared.

- Write the daily news on the board or on chart paper. Then have the boys read the daily news in unison to practice fluency.
- As a review of yesterday's word structure lesson, ask a volunteer to identify any words in the message with affixes. *regularly, prepared*

Word Structure

ROUTINE 10

Affixes Used to Change Word Meanings

- Write these word lines on the board or use ***Transparency*** 143. The words in boldface are in "Earthquake! The 1906 San Francisco Nightmare."

Line 1	**harm**	**harmless**	**argue**	**argument**
Line 2	**care**	**careful**	**careless**	**carelessness**
Line 3	**wash**	**prewash**	**lock**	**unlock**
Line 4	**take**	**mistake**	**retake**	**unmistakable**

Teacher Tip

SYLLABICATION To help students blend words and build fluency, demonstrate syllabication using the decodable, multisyllabic words in the word lines.

harm • less	ar • gue
ar • gu • ment	care • ful
care • less	care • less • ness
pre • wash	un • lock
mis • take	re • take
un • mis • tak • a • ble	

Line 1 **Suffixes Used to Change Word Meaning**

Use Routine 10 to review how prefixes and suffixes change word meaning. Remind students that suffixes are affixes added to the end of base words. Explain that the meaning of a base word changes when a suffix is added. For example, adding the suffix *-less* to the base word *fear* makes the word *fearless,* which means "without fear."

Point to the words in Line 1, and have students read them in unison. Ask students to identify the suffixes in Line 1. -less *in* harmless *and* -ment *in* argument Have students discuss how the meaning of each base word changes when these suffixes are added. If necessary, remind them that *-less* means "without" or "lacking" and *-ment* means "action" or "process."

Line 2 **Suffixes Used to Change Word Meaning**

Explain that some words can have more than one suffix. Have students read the words in Line 2 in unison. Then ask them to identify the common base word in the line. *care* Have students identify the word with two suffixes. *carelessness* Then have students discuss the meanings of *careful, careless,* and *carelessness*. If necessary, remind them that *-ful* means "full of," and *-ness* means "state of being."

Line 3 **Prefixes Used to Change Word Meaning**

Remind students that prefixes are affixes added to the beginning of base words, and they change their meanings. For example, adding the prefix *un-* to the base word *happy* makes the word *unhappy,* which means "not happy."

Point to the words in Line 3, and have students read them aloud in unison. Ask students to identify the prefixes in Line 3. pre- *in* prewash *and* un- *in* unlock Have students discuss how the meaning of each base word changes when these prefixes are added. If necessary, remind them that *pre-* means "before" and *un-* means "not" or "the opposite of."

Line 4 **Affixes Used to Change Word Meaning**

Explain that some base words can have both prefixes and suffixes added. Have students read the words in Line 4 in unison. Then ask them to identify the common base word in Line 4. *take* Have students identify the two prefixes and the suffix in *unmistakable.* un-, mis-, *and* -able Then have students discuss how the meaning of *take* changes when suffixes are added to make *mistake, retake,* and *unmistakable*. If necessary, remind them that *mis-* means "wrong" and *re-* means "again."

✦ Help students start the word structure activities on ***Skills Practice 2*** pages 121–122. Read the Focus box with them and help them with the first few questions. Then have students complete the pages on their own.

Monitor Progress 

to Differentiate Instruction

Formal Assessment

Word Structure During the word structure activity, note how well students understand how affixes affect word meaning.

APPROACHING LEVEL

IF . . . students need practice with affixes that change word meaning,	**THEN . . .** work with them in small groups on the word structure activities on ***Reteach*** page 136 during Workshop.
IF . . . students need extra practice with affixes that change word meaning,	**THEN . . .** work with them in small groups on the word structure activities for Unit 5 lesson 3 in the ***Intervention Guide*** during Workshop.

ON LEVEL

IF . . . students understand how affixes affect word meaning,	**THEN . . .** have them make lists of base words and practice adding different prefixes and suffixes to them during Workshop.

ABOVE LEVEL

IF . . . students are ready for a challenge with affixes that affect word meaning,	**THEN . . .** have them complete the word structure activities on ***Challenge Activities*** page 124 during Workshop.

Reading and Responding

Shaking at Dawn

On April 18, 1906, the sun had just begun to rise in San Francisco, California. Most people were asleep. Others were getting ready for work.

Thomas Jefferson Chase was a ticket clerk on a ferryboat. As he walked to his job, the streets were empty and quiet. Suddenly, without warning, a loud roar and rumble filled the air. The ground shook so hard that Thomas was thrown flat on his face.

The ground kept shaking. Then it opened up around him. He couldn't stand up.

What was going on? A huge earthquake was happening. It would change San Francisco forever.

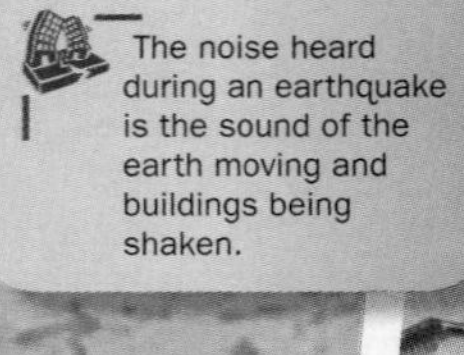

The noise heard during an earthquake is the sound of the earth moving and buildings being shaken.

168

Broken Windows, Broken Lives

Nearby, young Lloyd Head held onto his shaking bed so he wouldn't fall out. The house was rocking back and forth. When the shaking stopped, he ran to his parents' room. The whole family looked outside.

Buildings had fallen down. Windows were broken. There were huge holes in the earth. The sidewalks were cracked and bent. Water flowed from pipes that had burst. Crowds of people were on the streets.

Downtown, Lloyd could see a fire. He didn't know it, but gas was coming out of broken gas lines all over the city. The real terror was just starting.

San Francisco is in northern California. Earthquakes also occur in southern California. About 10,000 small earthquakes occur there each year.

169

OBJECTIVES

Students will

- use the comprehension skills Drawing Conclusions, Fact and Opinion, and Cause and Effect.
- review fluency.
- investigate the theme Communities across Time using the Inquiry process.

MATERIALS

- ***Student Reader,*** Book 2, pp. 168–175
- ***Skills Practice 2,*** 125–126
- ***Transparency*** 23

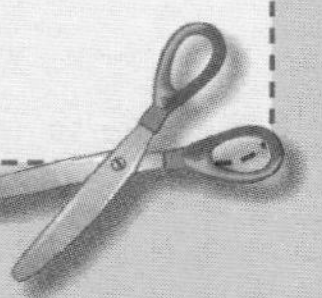

2nd READ

Comprehension Skill

Reread the selection using the comprehension skills Drawing Conclusions, Fact and Opinion, Cause and Effect, and Reading with a Writer's Eye.

Drawing Conclusions

Remind students that writers do not always say the exact information they want to tell. Readers must then "read between the lines" to get the information. This gives the writing more variety and makes reading more interesting. Ask students the following question:

What do you think the writer meant when she wrote, "The real terror was just starting"? **Possible Answer** *Because of the broken gas lines, more trouble was coming for the city.*

Fire!

Thomas Chase had stayed away from flying stones and sparking power lines to get to work. Now he helped people onto ferryboats.

The gas had caught fire and flames covered the city. Horses couldn't get through the broken streets. Firefighters had to get to the fires on foot. When they reached a fire there was no water to put it out. The pipes had burst.

Lloyd Head's mother sewed bags together to make a tent. The family camped outside. They were afraid their house would fall. People watched rescue workers try to put out the flames with coats and brooms.

Soldiers blew up buildings to stop the fire from spreading.

170

A Shattered City

Three days later, the fire was out. The shaking had stopped. The beautiful city of San Francisco was a mess.

The death count was about 700. People who study history, however, say as many as 3,000 people died. About 225,000 people were hurt. The earthquake destroyed 490 city blocks. Over 25,000 buildings had fallen. It would take millions of dollars to rebuild San Francisco.

Without warning, much of San Francisco had been flattened like a sand castle hit by a wave. How did it happen? How does any earthquake happen?

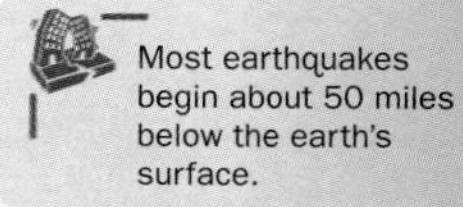

Most earthquakes begin about 50 miles below the earth's surface.

171

Fact and Opinion

Ask students to explain the difference between facts and opinions. If necessary, tell students that facts can be verified, and opinions are judgments or beliefs that cannot be verified. Although expository text generally deals with many facts, sometimes opinions are also expressed. Ask students the following questions:

- *What are some of the facts given on pages 170–171?* **Possible Answers** *Thomas Chase helped people; fire covered the city; most earthquakes start 50 miles below Earth's surface; the earthquake destroyed 490 city blocks; more than 25,000 buildings had fallen.*
- *What are the opinions, if any, given on these pages? Why are they opinions?* **Possible Answers** *The text says that the families thought their houses would fall. This is an opinion because we cannot prove what the families thought.*

Expanding Vocabulary

earthquake (ûrth´ • kwāk) *n.* a shaking or trembling of the ground (page 168)

An *earthquake* can occur on a weak spot in Earth's crust.

burst (bûrst) *v.* to break open suddenly (page 169)

The frozen water pipe *burst*.

gas (gas) *n.* heating or cooking fuel (page 169)

Does *gas* fuel your oven, or is it electric?

power lines (pou´ • ûr līnz) *n.* plural form of **power line:** a wire that carries electricity (page 170)

Power lines were knocked down during the storm.

Day 3

Reading and Responding

What Is an Earthquake?

The city had been hit by shock waves. These waves start below the earth's surface, where there are large pieces of rock. These rocks are called tectonic plates. The plates fit against one another like a puzzle.

Each plate floats on hot liquid rock. Sometimes plates push against each other. If the plates slip while they're pushing, shock waves occur. These waves travel up and can cause the ground to move.

An earthquake is usually followed by aftershocks. The aftershocks occur as the rocks get into their new positions. The 1906 San Francisco Earthquake had 135 aftershocks.

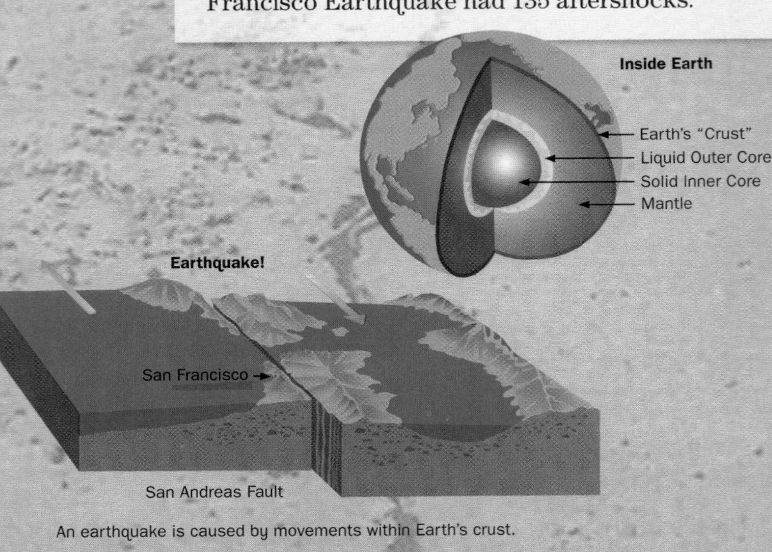

An earthquake is caused by movements within Earth's crust.

Whose Fault Is It?

Each year, half a million earthquakes occur around the world. Most are harmless. About a hundred are big enough to cause trouble, mainly those near cities.

Earthquakes usually occur along weak places in the earth's crust called faults. San Francisco sits on the San Andreas Fault. This fault stretches along part of the state. It causes most of California's many earthquakes.

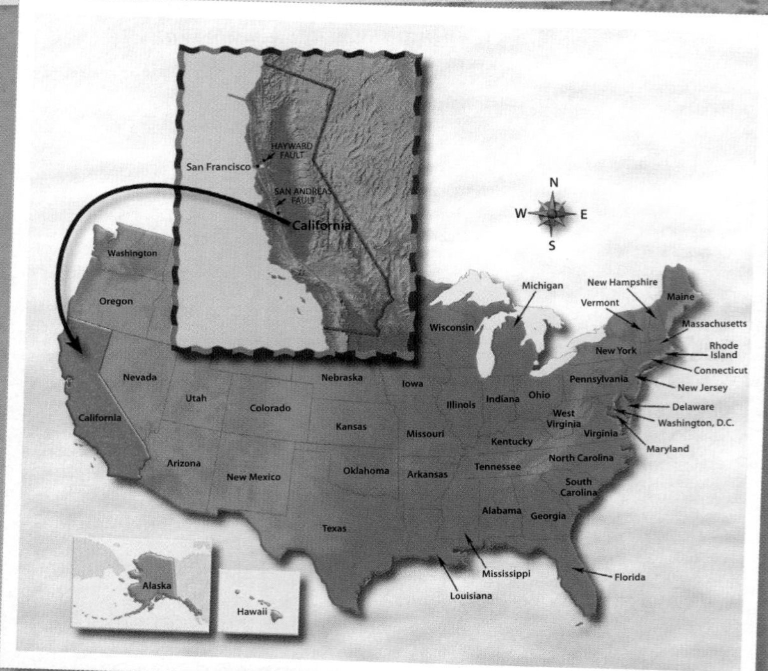

Word Structure

Affixes that change word meaning: movement, harmful, below, pushing, harmless, mainly, usually

Teacher Tip

CAUSE AND EFFECT Observe students as they chart cause-and-effect relationships. In addition to having students write causes and effects, have students orally tell you about the relationships they identify and explain how causes lead to effects, which in turn become the cause for a new effect.

Comprehension Skill

Cause and Effect

Remind students that identifying the cause and effect of events helps readers comprehend what they read. Remind them that the *cause* is "why something happened" and the *effect* is "what happened." Ask students to find examples of cause and effect on ***Student Reader,*** Book 2 pages 172–173. Remind students that cause-and-effect relationships can be recursive. Causes lead to effects which in turn become the cause for another effect and so on.

Cause	Effect
Tectonic plates push against each other.	The plates slip.
The plates slip.	Shock waves occur.

Take a Number

Since 1906, scientists have learned a lot about earthquakes. They have special tools to help them. One is a seismograph. It's used to record the movement of the earth during an earthquake.

Scientists give each earthquake a number on the Richter Scale. This scale measures the power of an earthquake. The highest numbers go to the biggest earthquakes.

The scale uses numbers and parts of numbers to measure power exactly. If an earthquake is rated "five point two," that means its number is 5.2. It has more power than an earthquake rated 5.1.

The biggest earthquake in the world measured 9.5 on the Richter Scale. This earthquake occurred in Chile in 1960.

Movements of the earth show up as heavy lines on a seismograph chart.

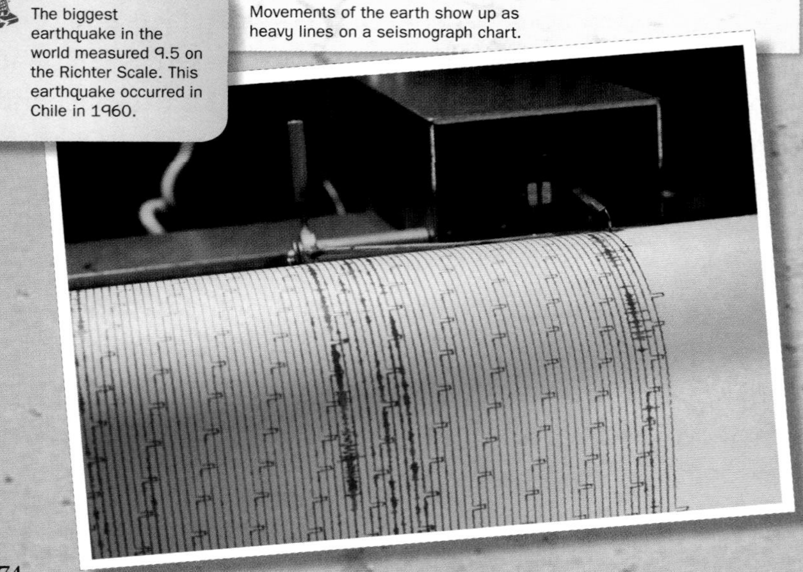

174

America's 10 Strongest Earthquakes on Record*

Rank	Location	Date	Magnitude
1	Prince William Sound, Alaska	March 28, 1964	9.2
2	Andreanof Islands, Alaska	March 9, 1957	9.1
3	Rat Islands, Alaska	February 4, 1965	8.7
4	East of Shumagin Islands, Alaska	November 10, 1938	8.2
5	New Madrid, Missouri	December 16, 1811	8.1
6	Yakutat Bay, Alaska	September 10, 1899	8.0
7	Andreanof Islands, Alaska	May 7, 1986	8.0
8	New Madrid, Missouri	February 7, 1812	8.0
9	(Near) Cape Yakataga, Alaska	September 4, 1899	7.9
10	Fort Tejon, California	January 9, 1857	7.9

* From the United States Geological Survey

The San Francisco Earthquake of 1906 would be number 17 on this list. It hit the Richter Scale at 7.8.

America's Biggest Shake-ups

The 1906 San Francisco Earthquake wasn't the biggest earthquake to ever occur. It was, however, the most harmful earthquake in American history.

It caused so much damage because it hit a big city with lots of buildings and people. Earthquakes that hit places with few people and buildings don't cause as much harm, even if they have more power.

175

Reading with a Writer's Eye

Text Structures—Techniques

Remind students that authors decide on and use certain types of text structure techniques to tell their story. Lynn Brunelle tells the real story of the 1906 San Francisco earthquake. She gives facts, examples, and supporting explanations in her story. Ask students to identify features used by the author to support her facts and examples. *Photographs, charts and captions.* Remind students that they need to present facts and examples in their formal letters. They may even want to support their examples with photographs. Ask students the following question:

How do the photographs and captions on these pages contribute to the information? **Possible Answer** *The photographs of the seismograph show readers what the machine looks like and how it records information.*

Expanding Vocabulary

shock waves (shok′ wāvz) *n.* plural form of **shock wave:** a vibration after a violent collision of tectonic plates (page 172)

The *shock waves* caused the ground to move!

tectonic plates (tek • tôn′ • ik plāts) *n.* plural form of **tectonic plate:** a large piece of rock under the earth's surface (page 172)

When *tectonic plates* shift, an earthquake may result.

aftershocks (af′ • tûr • shoks′) *n.* plural form of **aftershock:** a vibration of rocks or plates shifting into a new position (page 172)

Aftershocks were caused by the earthquake.

STOP

You have reread the first half of the story. Continue the story tomorrow on page T234.

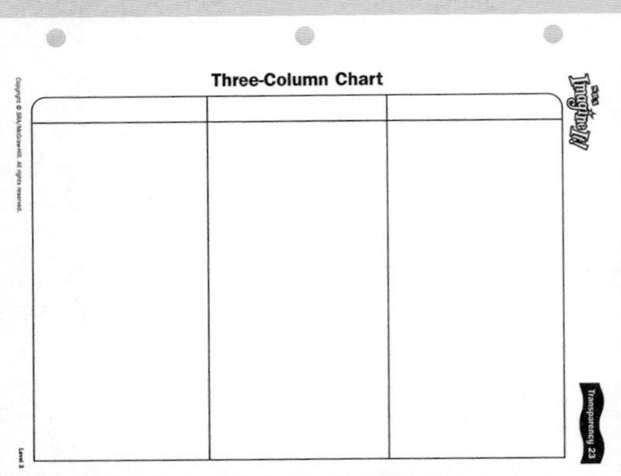

Transparency 23

Monitor Progress

to Differentiate Instruction

Formal Assessment

Comprehension Skill Note the students' understanding of the comprehension skill Fact and Opinion.

APPROACHING LEVEL

IF . . . students need extra help with Fact and Opinion,	THEN . . . use ***Reteach*** page 138.

ON LEVEL

IF . . . students need practice with Fact and Opinion,	THEN . . . have students play a game from the ***Workshop Kit.***

ABOVE LEVEL

IF . . . students understand Fact and Opinion,	THEN . . . use ***Challenge Activities*** page 126.

Supporting the Reading

Comprehension Skill: Fact and Opinion

Teach

Remind students that some forms of writing, such as biographies, reviews, and other types of informative texts, contain both facts and opinions. Expository texts, such as "Earthquake! The 1906 San Francisco Nightmare," give many verifiable facts. However, opinions might also be expressed by the writer or by the people mentioned within the text. As students read more and varied types of texts, they should become better able to distinguish between facts and opinions. Stress to students that sometimes opinions are expressed as facts and readers must be able to make their own judgments about what is truly fact and what is opinion. People should separate facts and opinions when reading or listening to a speaker to form their own judgments.

Guided Practice

Bring in an article from a children's magazine that contains both facts and opinions. Read the article aloud to students. Then select sentences to reread, and ask students to tell whether they are facts or opinions and explain why. Have students determine which statements support the opinions and which statements can be proven facts. Keep track of each sentence and students' explanations on a three-column chart on the board or on ***Transparency*** 23. When you are finished with the activity, count how many facts and how many opinions were in the article. Ask students whether they were or were not surprised at how many opinion statements were in the article. Ask students to share their thoughts with the class. For example:

Factual Statements	Opinion Statements	Explanation
The earthquake registered a 5.0 on the Richter scale.		This is a verifiable fact.
	One person thought the homes were damaged beyond repair.	This was that person's belief. Someone else may believe that the homes could be repaired.

Apply

Have students turn to pages 125–126 in ***Skills Practice 2.*** Have students read aloud the Focus section of the lesson. Work through the Practice section of the lesson with students. Have them look through the selection to find examples of facts and opinions. Have them record examples they can refer to as they work on the Practice and Apply sections of the lesson.

Fluency

"Earthquake! The 1906 San Francisco Nightmare" contains factual information as well as some emotional scenes. Explain to students that even stories that report the facts can reveal human emotions, such as the section of the text that tells about the people living in makeshift tents. Tell students that this can affect the tone of voice used when reading. While a serious voice should be used for this selection, since it is both an expository text and a serious topic, more emotion and a softer tone can be used in the sections that contain human feelings.

- Model fluent reading by reading pages 176–177 from "Earthquake! The 1906 San Francisco Nightmare." Have students follow along in ***Student Reader,*** Book 2. Ask them to raise their hand if they hear an unfamiliar word or passage.
- After you have read through the passage, call on a volunteer to read the passage. Before the student begins, go over any words that the student may need help pronouncing. Review definitions if necessary. Remind students to read the headings.
- After the volunteer has finished, have students read the passage chorally several times until they can read it naturally with good phrasing.

Inquiry

Conjectures

✦ Remind students that they have made conjectures about their research question, but their conjectures might need to be changed based on new things they learn from the unit selections. Have students think about how things they learned from reading "Earthquake! The 1906 San Francisco Nightmare" might relate to their conjectures. Remind students that new information they learn can confirm their conjectures, but it can also challenge or complicate them.

✦ Model how information in the selection relates to your conjecture, saying something like the following: From reading "Earthquake! The 1906 San Francisco Nightmare," I learned that communities need to have a response plan in place before disasters happen. My conjecture was that our community needs to build nature parks before too much countryside becomes developed. Information in this story seems to confirm my conjecture. Ask students to share any ideas about how their conjectures are affected by their understanding of the selection.

✦ Keep a record of any ideas students share, and use them later to help groups confirm or revise their conjectures. Have students take notes in their Writer's Notebooks about how the selection relates to their conjectures.

Leveled Readers

To help students build fluency and strengthen their vocabulary and comprehension skills, have them read the ***Leveled Readers*** for this unit. Use each student's Oral Fluency Assessment score from the previous lesson assessment to diagnose the appropriate ***Leveled Reader.***

Fluency Tip

FLUENCY For additional fluency practice, students can take turns reading different pages of "Earthquake! The 1906 San Francisco Nightmare" to each other during Small-Group Time.

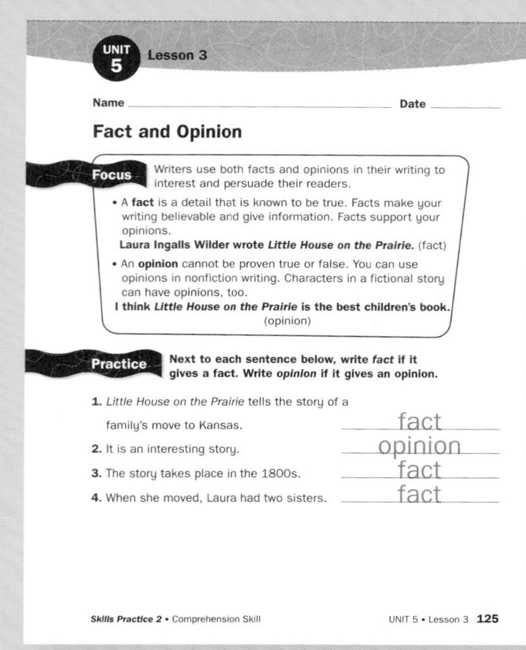

UNIT 5 Lesson 3

Name ______ Date ______

Fact and Opinion

Focus Writers use both facts and opinions in their writing to interest and persuade their readers.

- A **fact** is a detail that is known to be true. Facts make your writing believable and give information. Facts support your opinions.
  Laura Ingalls Wilder wrote *Little House on the Prairie.* (fact)
- An **opinion** cannot be proven true or false. You can use opinions in nonfiction writing. Characters in a fictional story can have opinions, too.
  I think *Little House on the Prairie* is the best children's book. (opinion)

Practice **Next to each sentence below, write *fact* if it gives a fact. Write *opinion* if it gives an opinion.**

1. *Little House on the Prairie* tells the story of a family's move to Kansas. fact
2. It is an interesting story. opinion
3. The story takes place in the 1800s. fact
4. When she moved, Laura had two sisters. fact

Skills Practice 2 • Comprehension Skill UNIT 5 • Lesson 3 **125**

Skills Practice 2, pp. 125–126

Day 3 **Language Arts**

OBJECTIVES

Students will
- ✦ revise their business letters.
- ✦ practice spelling words with affixes that change word meanings.
- ✦ learn different types of maps.
- ✦ practice sentence tenses.

MATERIALS

- ✦ ***Skills Practice 2,*** pp. 130–132 and 135–136
- ✦ ***Transparencies*** 139 and 139A

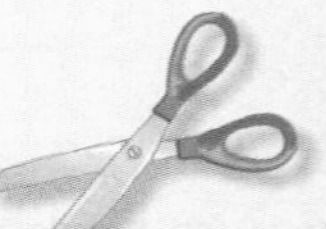

UNIT 5 Lesson 3

Revising **Use this checklist to revise your business letter.**

- ☐ Did you include all of the parts of a letter?
- ☐ Did you stay on topic?
- ☐ Are the sentences in a clear order?
- ☐ Does your business letter sound serious and polite?
- ☐ Does your letter sound like you are talking to an adult whom you respect?

Editing/Proofreading **Use this checklist to correct mistakes.**

- ☐ Did you use correct spellings?
- ☐ Did you capitalize the greeting and the closing?
- ☐ Did you capitalize proper nouns?
- ☐ Did you end each sentence with correct punctuation?

Publishing **Use this checklist to get your business letter ready to send.**

- ☐ Neatly rewrite or type a final copy.
- ☐ Address an envelope.

130 UNIT 5 • Lesson 3 Writing • *Skills Practice 2*

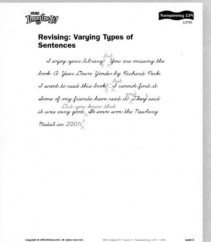

Skills Practice 2, p. 130

Transparency 139 139A

Revising: Varying Types of Sentences

I enjoy your library, but you are missing the book A Year Down Yonder by Richard Peck. I want to read this book, but I cannot find it. Some of my friends have read it, and they said it was very good. Did you know that it even won the Newbery Medal in 2001?

Transparencies 139, 139A

Writing Business Letter

Revising

Teach

✦ Students will use the drafts they have written to revise their business letters.

✦ Use Routine 16, and remind students that as they revise they need to make sure
- all parts of the letter are included.
- they state the reason for writing their letter in the body of the letter.
- they use formal language.
- the letter is polite and stays on topic.

✦ Tell students that as they revise, they need to make sure they use the proper sentence tense throughout the letter and that they are consistent with the tense.

Guided Practice

✦ Display ***Transparency*** 139. Ask a student to read the paragraph aloud. Ask students to look for words they think should be changed to create more formal language. Next, display ***Transparency*** 139A and discuss the new paragraph.

✦ Using the draft you created, have students help you select new words to replace the words you circled during drafting.

✦ Have students turn to ***Skills Practice 2*** page 130 to read and discuss the revising checklist.

Apply

Composing—Revising Have students refer to page 130 in ***Skills Practice 2*** when revising their business letters.

Differentiating Instruction **English Learner**

IF . . . students have difficulty revising their letters, **THEN . . .** go through their letters with them, pointing out some of errors they need to look for. Allow them to find additional errors on their own.

Spelling

Affixes that Change Word Meanings

Teach

- Remind students that affixes are used to change the meaning of a word. A prefix is an affix attached to the beginning of the word, and a suffix is an affix attached to the end of a word.
- Write the word list on the board. Have students volunteer to come to the board and do the following for each word: circle the base word, underline any prefixes one time, and underline any suffixes two times.

Guided Practice

Have students turn to ***Skills Practice 2*** page 131. Read the instructions with them, and complete the first two questions as a class.

Apply

Have students complete ***Skills Practice 2*** pages 131–132 on their own. Remind students that challenge words are not used in ***Skills Practice*** exercises.

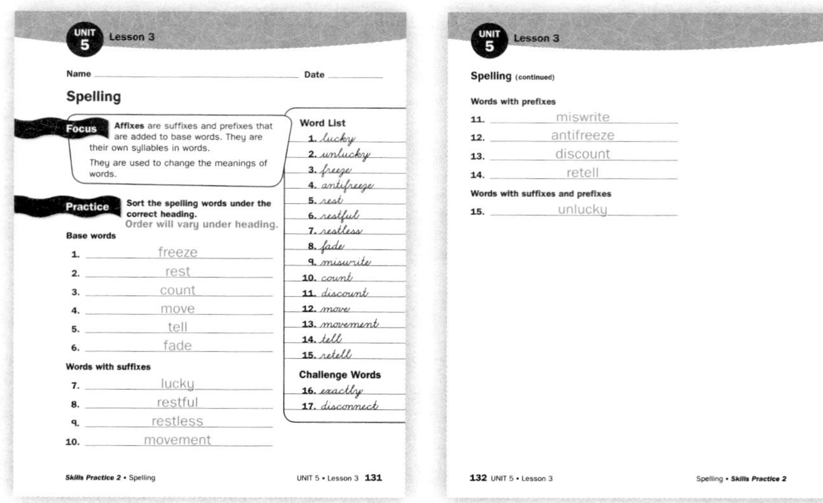

UNIT 5 Lesson 3

Name ____ Date ____

Spelling

Focus Affixes are suffixes and prefixes that are added to base words. They are their own syllables in words.

They are used to change the meanings of words.

Practice Sort the spelling words under the correct heading.

Order will vary under heading.

Base words

1. freeze
2. rest
3. count
4. move
5. tell
6. fade

Words with suffixes

7. lucky
8. restful
9. restless
10. movement

Word List

1. lucky
2. unlucky
3. freeze
4. antifreeze
5. rest
6. restful
7. restless
8. fade
9. miswrite
10. count
11. discount
12. move
13. movement
14. tell
15. retell

Challenge Words

16. exactly
17. disconnect

Skills Practice 2 • Spelling UNIT 5 • Lesson 3 131

UNIT 5 Lesson 3

Spelling (continued)

Words with prefixes

11. miswrite
12. antifreeze
13. discount
14. retell

Words with suffixes and prefixes

15. unlucky

132 UNIT 5 • Lesson 3 Spelling • Skills Practice 2

Skills Practice 2, pp. 131–132

Monitor Progress

to Differentiate Instruction
Formal Assessment

Spelling Note whether students are able to spell the lesson words correctly.

APPROACHING LEVEL

IF . . . students need to practice spelling this week's words, **THEN . . .** have them complete ***Reteach*** page 140.

ON LEVEL

IF . . . students can spell this week's spelling words, **THEN . . .** have them think of other affixes they know. On a separate sheet of paper, have students write a list of those affixes. Ask them to trade papers with a partner, and then write next to each affix whether it is used as a prefix or a suffix.

ABOVE LEVEL

IF . . . students are ready for a challenge, **THEN . . .** have them complete ***Challenge Activities*** page 127.

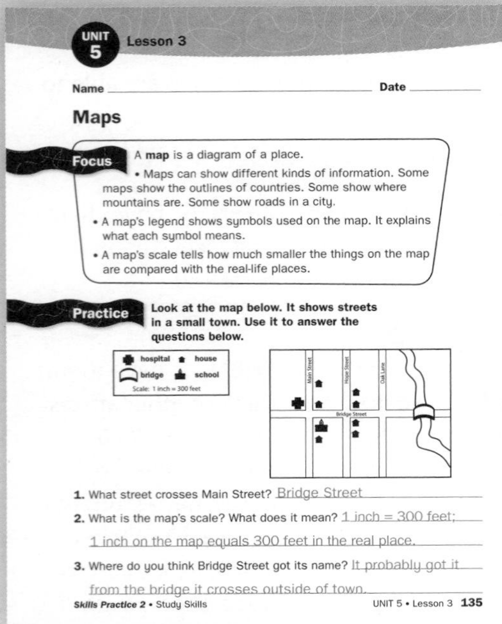
UNIT 5 Lesson 3

Name ______________________ Date ________

Maps

Focus

A **map** is a diagram of a place.

- Maps can show different kinds of information. Some maps show the outlines of countries. Some show where mountains are. Some show roads in a city.
- A map's legend shows symbols used on the map. It explains what each symbol means.
- A map's scale tells how much smaller the things on the map are compared with the real-life places.

Practice **Look at the map below. It shows streets in a small town. Use it to answer the questions below.**

1. What street crosses Main Street? Bridge Street
2. What is the map's scale? What does it mean? 1 inch = 300 feet; 1 inch on the map equals 300 feet in the real place.
3. Where do you think Bridge Street got its name? It probably got it from the bridge it crosses outside of town.

Skills Practice 2 • Study Skills UNIT 5 • Lesson 3 **135**

Skills Practice 2, p. 135

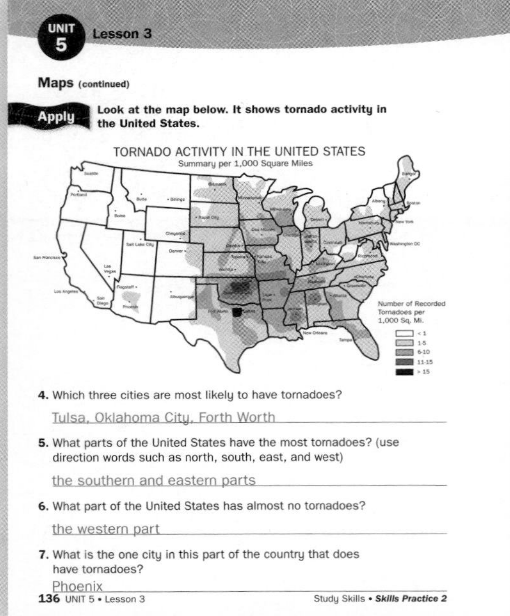
UNIT 5 Lesson 3

Maps (continued)

Apply **Look at the map below. It shows tornado activity in the United States.**

4. Which three cities are most likely to have tornadoes? Tulsa, Oklahoma City, Forth Worth
5. What parts of the United States have the most tornadoes? (use direction words such as north, south, east, and west) the southern and eastern parts
6. What part of the United States has almost no tornadoes? the western part
7. What is the one city in this part of the country that does have tornadoes? Phoenix

136 UNIT 5 • Lesson 3 Study Skills • *Skills Practice 2*

Skills Practice 2, p. 136

Study Skills

Maps

Teach

✦ Invite students to share what they know about maps. Remind students that maps can show a variety of information in addition to their main purpose of showing where places are located. The following is a list of some common maps and the information they provide:

- **Economic map:** shows natural resources of an area
- **Historical map:** shows areas of land from a specific historical time period
- **Physical map:** shows physical features of an area, such as mountains, rivers, lakes, and so on.
- **Political map:** shows state and national boundaries with no physical features
- **Road map:** shows major roads and systems of transportation
- **Topographical map:** shows shape and elevation of areas
- **Weather map:** shows climate and precipitation of areas

Guided Practice

Have students turn to page 135 in ***Skills Practice 2.*** Have a student read the directions aloud. Answer the first Practice question as a class.

Apply

Have students complete ***Skills Practice 2*** pages 135–136 for practice using maps.

Formal Assessment 

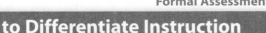

Monitor Progress to Differentiate Instruction

Maps Note whether students are reading and understanding the information on a map.

APPROACHING LEVEL

IF . . . students need to practice reading and understanding the information on a map,	**THEN . . .** have them work with a partner to review maps during Workshop.

ON LEVEL

IF . . . students have an understanding of reading and understanding the information on a maps,	**THEN . . .** have them help another student find information on a map during Workshop.

ABOVE LEVEL

IF . . . students need a challenge,	**THEN . . .** have them create maps for their unit investigations during Workshop.

Grammar, Usage, and Mechanics

Sentence Tenses

Teach

- Have students review the rules for constructing sentences using the appropriate tenses. If necessary, remind students that the verbs in sentences dictate whether a sentence is in the past, the present, or the future tense.
- Write the following sentences on the board and have students identify whether the sentence is in the past tense, the present tense, or the future tense.
  - The horses trot through the open pasture every morning and evening. *present*
  - The horses trotted early yesterday morning. *past*
  - As the sun starts to stay up longer, the horses will trot a little later into the evening. *future*
  - Amanda and Jill will cook dinner tomorrow night. *future*
  - I'll cook dinner tonight. *future*
  - Craig cooked dinner last night. *past*

Guided Practice

Have students rewrite three of the sentences on the board to change the sentence tense.

Apply

Have students write sentences independently on a topic of your choosing. Have students underline the verb and write whether it is past, present, or future tense. Tell students to write one sentence for each verb tense.

Differentiating Instruction English Learner

IF . . . students have difficulty writing sentences independently, **THEN . . .** have them work in pairs or in small groups with proficient English speakers.

Day 4

Preparing to Read

OBJECTIVES

Students will

- ✦ identify and know affixes used to change word meanings.
- ✦ build fluency.

MATERIALS

- ✦ ***Transparency*** 143
- ✦ Routine 10

Differentiating Instruction **English Learner**

IF . . . students are native speakers of Vietnamese, Hmong, or Chinese,
THEN . . . they may need extra practice with the concept of adding affixes to make new words. In their native languages, all words are monosyllabic.

Daily Oral Practice

Daily News

Today!

The land around us is quite changeable. Natural disasters, such as earthquakes, hurricanes, and tornadoes, change what our land looks like. People do have some control over the environment. We can preserve land for the future and rebuild damaged areas.

- ✦ Write the daily news on the board or on chart paper. Then have students read the daily news in unison to practice fluency.
- ✦ As a review of yesterday's word structure lesson, ask a volunteer to identify any words in the message with the affixes *-able, -ment, pre-,* or *re-*. *changeable, environment, preserve, rebuild*

Word Structure 

ROUTINE 10

Affixes Used to Change Word Meanings

✦ Use ***Transparency*** 143 with these word lines from Day 3.

Line 1	harm	harmless	argue	argument
Line 2	care	careful	careless	carelessness
Line 3	wash	prewash	lock	unlock
Line 4	take	mistake	retake	unmistakable

✦ Use Routine 10 to review affixes and how they can change the meaning of base words. If necessary, remind students that many prefixes and suffixes add new meaning to base words. For example, the suffix *-ful* changes the base word from a noun to an adjective, and it means "to be full of" whatever the base word is. *Harmful* means "to be full of harm."

Developing Oral Language

Use any of the following activities to help students practice reading the words.

✦ Have a volunteer choose a base word from the word lines and use it in a sentence. **Possible Answer** *I care a lot about my family.* Then have that student choose another volunteer to read the base word with its affix in another sentence. **Possible Answer** *My dad always tells me to be* careful *with scissors.* Continue until all base words with their affixes have been used.

✦ Have students identify all the different suffixes used on the word lines. *-less, -ment, -ful, -ness, -able* Then have students define each of these suffixes. Ask students to name other words with these suffixes. **Possible Answers** *helpless, coatless, penniless; enjoyment, basement, government; hopeful, bashful, wonderful; happiness, friendliness, hardness; drinkable, adorable, likable*

✦ Have students identify all the different prefixes used on the word lines. *pre-, un-, mis-, re-* Then have students define each of these prefixes. Ask students to name other words with these prefixes. **Possible Answers** *precook, prepare, preplan; unafraid, uncomfortable, unbutton; misplace, misunderstand, misread; rewrite, review, reappear*

✦ Have a student choose one of the word lines. Then ask volunteers to define each word in the line. Have students use a dictionary if necessary. Continue for all the word lines.

Differentiating Instruction — English Learner

IF . . . students would benefit from additional practice identifying affixes, **THEN . . .** choose a page or two from the selection, "Earthquake! The 1906 San Francisco Nightmare," and have students identify words with suffixes and prefixes.

Monitor Progress 

to Differentiate Instruction
Formal Assessment

Word Structure During the word structure activity, note how well students understand the words.

APPROACHING LEVEL

IF . . . students do not understand the words on the word lines, **THEN . . .** use pictures, photos, objects, stick drawings, or pantomime to help them visualize the words.

ON LEVEL

IF . . . students need practice with the words on the word lines, **THEN . . .** have them write sentences using the words on the lines.

ABOVE LEVEL

IF . . . students understand the words on the word lines, **THEN . . .** have them make a list of other affixes and practice adding them to base words.

Reading and Responding

Looking for Clues

Days later, Thomas Chase was safe at his mother's house in Oakland, California. Lloyd Head's family was still camping outside. Thousands of others were in tents in the city's parks. They hung signs with names like "Camp Thankful." They were glad to be alive.

Scientists studied photos and maps of the places hit. Workers hunted through the fallen buildings and homes. They were looking for ideas to help make a safer city. They found that buildings on soft land were damaged more than buildings on solid rock. They learned the fire had caused more problems than the earthquake.

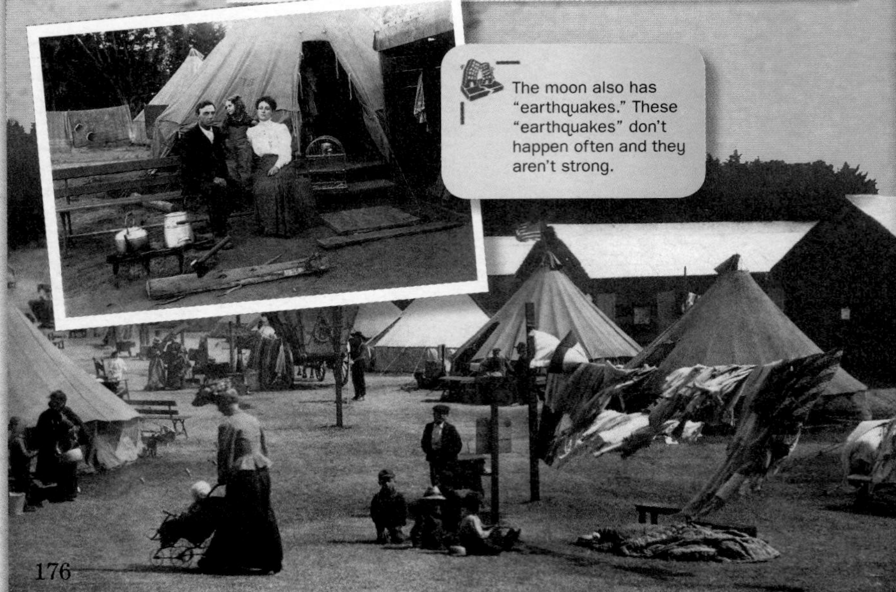

The moon also has "earthquakes." These "earthquakes" don't happen often and they aren't strong.

176

By 1910, many buildings in San Francisco had been rebuilt.

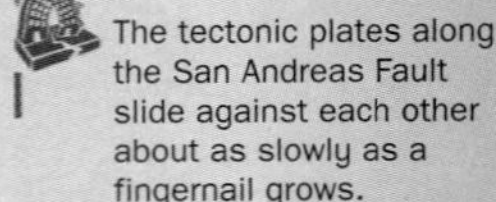

The tectonic plates along the San Andreas Fault slide against each other about as slowly as a fingernail grows.

A New San Francisco

After the earthquake, the city made new building rules. The rules were very tough for buildings on soft ground. Tall buildings were made to move with earthquake shocks instead of falling to pieces. Most new buildings had to have steel frames.

New water pipes that could bend easily were put to use. These pipes would be less likely to burst. New gas lines were made more bendable, too.

San Francisco did not put these new rules into effect all at once. The city, however, was ready to welcome visitors to the 1915 World's Fair.

A poster from the 1915 World's Fair

177

OBJECTIVES

Students will

- use the comprehension skill Fact and Opinion.
- check comprehension.

MATERIALS

- ***Student Reader,*** Book 2, pp. 176–183
- ***Skills Practice 2,*** pp. 127–128

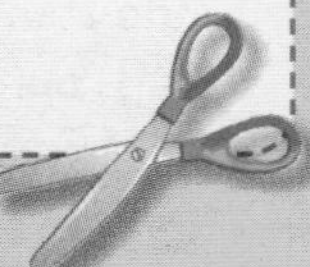

Comprehension Skill

Fact and Opinion

The author of "Earthquake! The 1906 San Francisco Nightmare" continues to provide examples of facts and explanations to her readers. Remind students that facts can be verified by research. Ask students the following questions:

- *What example does the author give for the fact that thousands of people were affected by the earthquake?* **Possible Answer** *Lloyd Head's family and thousands of others were still camping outside days after the earthquake.*
- *What were some of the building rules that would make buildings safer?* **Possible Answer** *Buildings were made to move with earthquake shocks. Buildings had to have steel frames. Bendable pipes were used.*

San Francisco Hit Again!

In 1989, another large earthquake shook the city. One place it hit was San Francisco's Candlestick Park. It was before the start of a World Series game. Millions of Americans watched on TV.

This earthquake measured 6.9 on the Richter Scale. This time the city was more prepared. Buildings shook but most did not fall. There was, however, some damage. Parts of the San Francisco-Oakland Bay Bridge fell. A section of the freeway in Oakland fell, too. Forty-two people were killed. Power was knocked out. Fires started around the city. Again, the most damage happened to buildings on soft land.

Damage from the 1989 earthquake cost about 6 billion dollars.

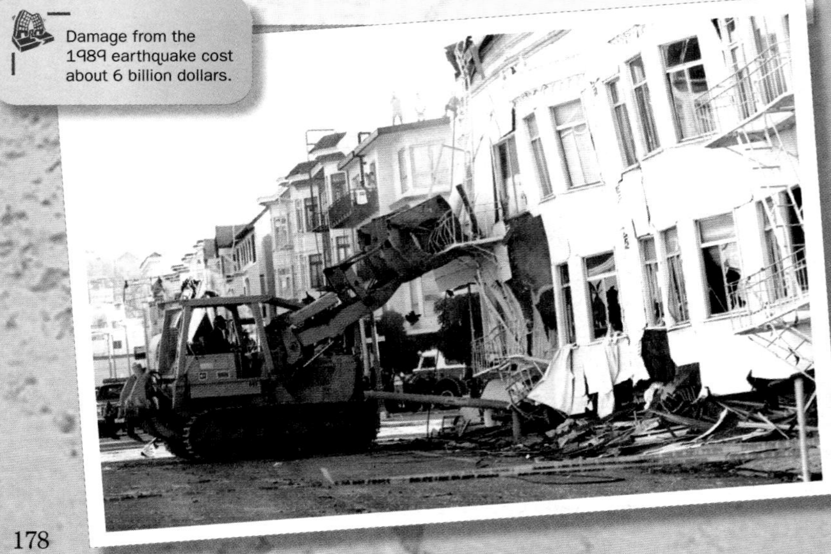

178

The Future

Scientists think another big earthquake might strike San Francisco in the next 30 years. More than 1,000 earthquake stations are on the lookout for shock waves along California's fault lines. If it seems like an earthquake is about to happen, people can be warned. Families have emergency supplies of food and water. Kids in school practice safety moves such as hiding under a strong table.

Earthquake study in America began because of the 1906 San Francisco Earthquake. Now we know much more. We can't stop an earthquake, but we can live through one.

Every year about 500,000 earthquakes occur. Only about 100 cause damage.

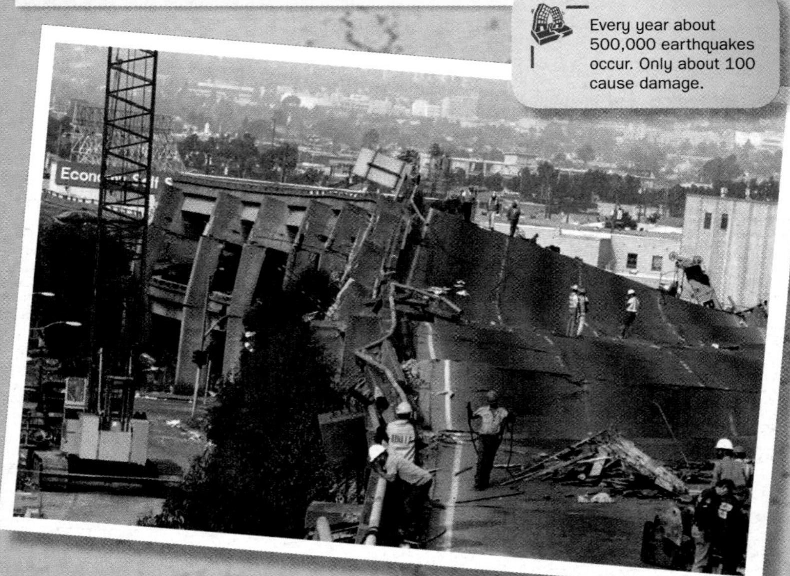

179

Checking Comprehension

Ask students the following questions to check their comprehension of the selection.

- *What happens if the tectonic plates slip while they are pushing against each other?* *Shock waves occur and they travel up through the earth and cause earthquakes.*
- *What did scientists find when they studied the fallen buildings and homes?* **Possible Answer** *They found that buildings on soft land were damaged more than buildings on solid rock.*
- *What did these findings lead to?* **Possible Answer** *Buildings had new, tough rules.*
- *Why was the 1906 San Francisco earthquake so important to us today?* **Possible Answer** *Because of that earthquake, scientists have studied earthquakes and we can now be better prepared.*

Word Structure

Affixes that change word meaning: camping, hunted, looking, started, safety, hiding

Differentiating Instruction: English Learner

IF . . . students have difficulty answering the Checking Comprehension questions, **THEN . . .** ask them questions they can answer by choosing between two options. For example, *What in the selection was compared to a puzzle—Richter scales or tectonic plates?* *tectonic plates*

Reading and Responding

Social Studies Inquiry

Teacher Tips

SILENT READ If some students are having difficulty comprehending the selection as they read silently, read the selection with them in small groups.

SELECTION VOCABULARY Review the meaning of the highlighted selection vocabulary word *tough* in "Shear Joy!"

Differentiating Instruction English Learner

IF . . . students are native speakers of Spanish, Tagalog (Pilipino), Vietnamese, and some other languages, **THEN . . .** they may say /s/ or /ch/ in place of /sh/ in *shear* and *shepherd*. Their native languages lack the /sh/ sound. Demonstrate how to make the /sh/ sound and provide practice saying simple words such as *shop, shape, sheep,* and *shoe.*

IF . . . students are confused by the layout of page 182, **THEN . . .** explain that the *Q:* stands for *question,* meaning that the questions the interviewer asks will follow. The *A:* stands for *answer,* meaning that the answers the interviewee gives will follow.

Genre Interview 

An interview is a series of questions and answers that tells one person's ideas or opinions.

Feature Line Graph

Point to the line graph in "Shear Joy!" Tell students that line graphs can show how something changes over time.

Reading "Shear Joy!"

Have students read "Shear Joy!" silently. Ask students how this interview relates to the theme Communities across Time. Remind students to use word structure, such as the meanings of affixes, to help them decode unfamiliar words. Make sure students read and interpret the line graph. Ask students to point to the line graph and tell what it is showing.

Think Link

1. Why was the Ray family's sheep ranch so successful when it started? **Possible Answer** *The ranch started around the time of the Civil War. Wool was used to make Civil War uniforms, so there was a big demand.*
2. Why is the demand for organic wool growing? **Possible Answer** *More people want natural products, and organic wool is free of chemicals and pesticides.*
3. When was the sheep population in California the highest? *1880*

Social Studies Inquiry

Shear Joy!

Genre

An **interview** is a series of questions and answers that tells one person's ideas or opinions.

Feature

A **line graph** can show how something changes over time.

"Shepherd" is not a job title often heard these days. However, they do still exist. Darryl Ray tells us about his California sheep ranch.

Q: How did you get started as a sheep rancher?

A: The ranch has been in my family for about 150 years. When I was growing up, I wanted to get away and try something else. I lived in the city for a while, but I found that I missed the ranch. So I came back, and I really love the work.

Q: How has the business changed over time?

A: Right after my ancestors settled here, in the late 1850s, there was a big need for wool. It was used to make uniforms for the Civil War. The sheep business was a great success back then. The demand for wool hasn't always been as strong, but there has been enough need to keep the ranch going.

One change in the last ten years or so is the call for organic wool. More and more people want natural products. This is a growing market for us right now.

Q: What makes wool "organic"?

A: There are some tough rules, but it mostly means the wool is free of chemicals. The sheep feed in fields that have not been sprayed with pesticides for at least three years. And the sheep cannot be dipped in pesticides. Also, they have to have plenty of room to graze.

Q: What do you like most about your job?

A: The best part is that I get to spend a lot of time outside. It also makes me proud to keep up the family tradition.

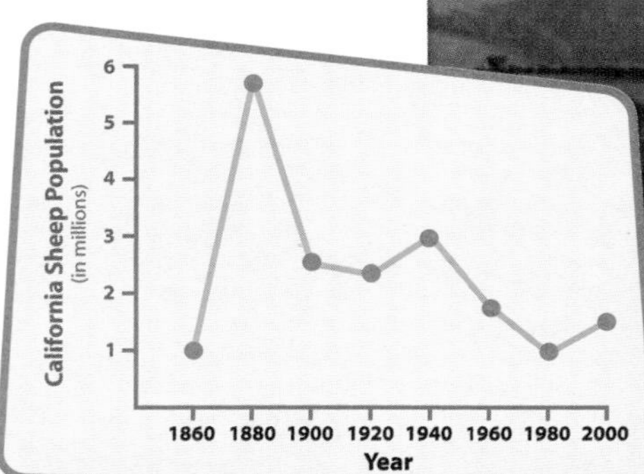

Think Link

1. Why was the Ray family's sheep ranch so successful when it started?
2. Why is the demand for organic wool growing?
3. When was the sheep population in California the highest?

Try It!

As you work on your investigation, think about how you can use a line graph to show your facts.

Inquiry Connection

Have students discuss how line graphs might be helpful in their investigation of communities across time. For example, students might want to use a line graph to show how one aspect of a community has changed over a period of time.

Differentiating Instruction | **English Learner**

IF . . . students are unfamiliar with line graphs, **THEN . . .** explain what each side of the graph represents, and use your finger to show how a line graph is read.

Teacher Tip

COLLECTING INFORMATION Remind students that they can use something they learned from reading "Earthquake! The 1906 San Francisco Nightmare" as an idea for their investigation. Or, they can use other selections they have read.

UNIT 5 Lesson 3

Name ______________ Date ________

Finding Internet Sources

Use this page to help you find Internet sources for your group investigation.

Our group's topic:

The history of our neighborhood, Clintonville.

What things on the Internet could be useful for your investigation?

	Yes	No
Historical Documents/Facts	✓	
Photos/Illustrations		✓
Community Websites		✓
Encyclopedia Information	✓	
Diagrams	✓	
Stories		

Skills Practice 2 • Inquiry UNIT 5 • Lesson 3 127

Skills Practice 2, p. 127

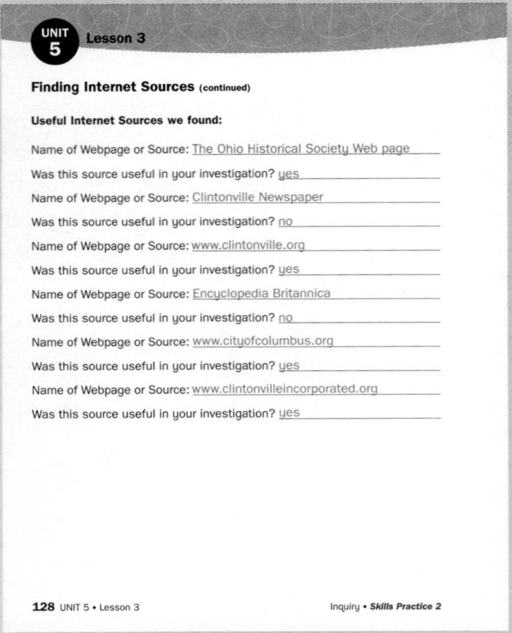

UNIT 5 Lesson 3

Finding Internet Sources (continued)

Useful Internet Sources we found:

Name of Webpage or Source: The Ohio Historical Society Web page

Was this source useful in your investigation? yes

Name of Webpage or Source: Clintonville Newspaper

Was this source useful in your investigation? no

Name of Webpage or Source: www.clintonville.org

Was this source useful in your investigation? yes

Name of Webpage or Source: Encyclopedia Britannica

Was this source useful in your investigation? no

Name of Webpage or Source: www.cityofcolumbus.org

Was this source useful in your investigation? yes

Name of Webpage or Source: www.clintonvilleincorporated.org

Was this source useful in your investigation? yes

128 UNIT 5 • Lesson 3 Inquiry • *Skills Practice 2*

Skills Practice 2, p. 128

Inquiry Process

Step 4—Identifying Information Needs

Whole-Group Time

Whole Group

- Each group has produced a conjecture and discussed it in their investigation groups. Conduct a whole-class discussion of each group's conjectures. Have groups briefly present their conjectures and allow the class to offer suggestions, constructive criticisms, questions, and sources for more information about specific topics. These contributions should help each group as they identify needs and make plans for their investigations.

- Remind students that in their investigations they can use what they learned about the theme from the unit selections. Discuss what students learned from "Earthquake! The 1906 San Francisco Nightmare," especially how the selection relates to their investigations. Have students take notes in their Writer's Notebooks during the discussion.

- Explain that each group needs to construct a plan for their investigation. This plan should include the things they need to find out and where they will get information about their question and conjecture. Have students identify and search for different kinds of reference materials for their investigations, including maps, time lines, charts, photos, and videos.

- To help groups get started with identifying their needs, remind them that they should be asking themselves questions such as: *How can we find out whether our conjectures are right? Where can we find more information about our question? What do we need to understand to improve our conjecture? What community experts might we interview?*

- Students should use these questions to help decide which sources they can use in their investigations. Model identifying research needs and making plans by answering these questions. You might say something such as this: *I need some information about nature parks and wildlife sanctuaries. I could do a library and Internet search for books, articles, and Web sites with this information. I could also interview a park ranger or urban planner.*

Small-Group Time

Small Group

✦ In their groups, students should review their questions and conjectures, as well as any notes they have taken and ideas they have learned from reading the unit selections. These should help them as they identify what they need to know for their investigations and make a plan.

✦ Review with students what they learned about conducting an Internet search. Then students should work in their groups on ***Skills Practice 2*** pages 127–128. Guide each group as they look for Internet sources by helping them choose appropriate keywords to search for Web sites, articles, or multimedia files. During Workshop, help each group find Internet sources that will be genuinely useful for their investigations.

✦ Groups will probably need to find sources in addition to Internet sources. Remind them what they have learned about choosing appropriate sources. Have students record additional plans for their investigations as well as additional sources they could use in their Writer's Notebooks.

Concept/Question Board

✦ Ask students to consult the **Concept/Question Board** for ideas to help them identify needs, find sources, and make plans. Remind them to post articles, book titles, and summaries.

✦ Continue to encourage use of the Board by recognizing and thanking students for their contributions. Incorporate those items into classroom discussions whenever possible. Remember to also model by posting your own items.

Inquiry Rubric

To assess Identifying Information Needs, see the Inquiry Rubrics in the Level Appendix.

Teacher Tip

COLLECTING INFORMATION If students are investigating how the community has changed over time, they might want to consult historical documents in a library or on the Internet that will give information about the town or city's population, economic resources, industries, and so on. Help students navigate through Web pages or library archives to find the right kinds of documents.

OBJECTIVES

Students will
- ✦ edit/proofread their business letters.
- ✦ review spelling words.
- ✦ practice drawing maps.
- ✦ practice effective voice and word choice.

MATERIALS

- ✦ ***Transparencies*** 17, 17A
- ✦ ***Skills Practice 2,*** p. 130

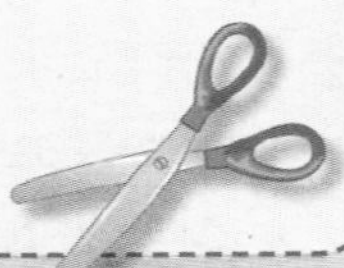

Imagine It! Transparency 17 17A

Proofreading Marks

¶ Indent.	¶ Dad read nursery rhymes to my sister and me when we were young. Each of us had a favorite rhyme. My sister liked "Jack and Jill." Dad must have read it to her 1,000 times!
^ Add something.	I also liked it, but my ^favorite one was "Three Little Kittens."
Take out something.	That rhyme is about the kittens who lost their mittens.
≡ Make a capital letter.	i don't ask dad to read to me anymore.
/ Make a small letter.	Now, I ask if I can read to Him.
Check spelling.	What shood I reed to him first?
⊙ Add a period.	I think he will like this one ⊙

Copyright © SRA/McGraw-Hill. All rights reserved. SRA Imagine It! • Level 3 • Transparency 17 • 17A Level 3

Transparencies 17, 17A

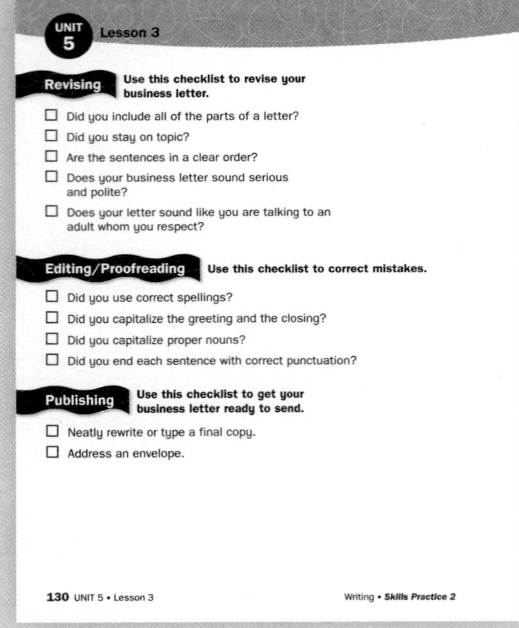

UNIT 5 Lesson 3

Revising Use this checklist to revise your business letter.

- ☐ Did you include all of the parts of a letter?
- ☐ Did you stay on topic?
- ☐ Are the sentences in a clear order?
- ☐ Does your business letter sound serious and polite?
- ☐ Does your letter sound like you are talking to an adult whom you respect?

Editing/Proofreading Use this checklist to correct mistakes.

- ☐ Did you use correct spellings?
- ☐ Did you capitalize the greeting and the closing?
- ☐ Did you capitalize proper nouns?
- ☐ Did you end each sentence with correct punctuation?

Publishing Use this checklist to get your business letter ready to send.

- ☐ Neatly rewrite or type a final copy.
- ☐ Address an envelope.

130 UNIT 5 • Lesson 3 Writing • *Skills Practice 2*

Skills Practice 2, p. 130

Writing Business Letter

Editing/Proofreading

Teach

- ✦ Tell students they will edit/proofread their business letters.
- ✦ Remind students that when they edit, they will be making corrections to spelling, grammar, capitalization, and punctuation.
- ✦ When editing their business letters, remind students to make sure they
  - spelled the person's name and title correctly.
  - put a colon after the greeting.
  - added periods to abbreviations of titles or initials if needed.
  - capitalized the greeting and the closing.
  - signed the letter.

Guided Practice

- ✦ Remind students of the proofreading marks they are to use by displaying ***Transparencies*** 17, 17A.
- ✦ Using the draft you have revised, have students help you edit/proofread for grammar, spelling, and punctuation. Tell them to pay attention to verb tenses and to make sure they do not switch tenses in the middle of a sentence or paragraph. They should also make sure that the verbs agree with the subject or subjects of simple and compound sentences.
- ✦ Have students turn to ***Skills Practice 2*** page 130 to read and discuss the editing/proofreading checklist.

Differentiating Instruction **English Learner**

IF . . . students need help proofreading their letters, **THEN . . .** pair them with a proficient English speaker who can point out any errors in spelling, grammar, or punctuation.

Writing, continued

Apply

Composing—Editing/Proofreading Have students edit and proofread their business letters. Encourage students to complete the checklist on page 130 in ***Skills Practice 2*** after they have edited. Tell them to make any necessary corrections after going through the checklist.

Monitor Progress Formal Assessment
to Differentiate Instruction

Editing/Proofreading Note whether students have an understanding of using grammar principles and practices in their own writing.

APPROACHING LEVEL

IF . . . students need to practice editing/proofreading,	**THEN . . .** have them use ***eSkills*** during Workshop.

ON LEVEL

IF . . . students have an understanding of editing/proofreading,	**THEN . . .** have them continue to edit/proofread during Workshop.

ABOVE LEVEL

IF . . . students need a challenge,	**THEN . . .** have them help a classmate during Workshop.

Spelling

Affixes that Change Word Meanings

Teach

Meaning Strategy Tell students that when they use a word, it is important to make sure it is spelled correctly, and that they are using the correct meaning. Be certain students are able to easily determine whether a word has the proper affix based on the meaning they want to convey, or based on the meaning they think someone is trying to convey to them.

Guided Practice

Write the following sentence on the board: *If you do not understand the story after I ________ it, then I will ________ it.* Ask students which two spelling words would best complete this sentence. *tell; retell* Tell students that thinking how affixes change the meanings of words can help them determine if they are using the correct word.

Study Skills

Maps

Teach

Remind students that many types of maps exist for different purposes. Maps might be helpful as they conduct research for their unit investigations, or they might be helpful to use as a visual aid in presentations.

Guided Practice

Draw a simple map of your state on the board. Ask a volunteer to write the name of your city in its approximate location. Have other students add other features such as a state park or amusement park.

Apply

Have students draw the map from the board on their own paper. Have them fill in the names of other cities or towns, rivers, lakes, and so on, on the map. Encourage students to use sources to fill in more information. If students wish, they can do a different kind of a map, such as a topographical map, weather map, historical map, and so on. Encourage students to create a map they can use in their unit investigations.

Listening/Speaking/Viewing

Effective Voice and Word Choice

Teach

- Tell students that an effective voice is one that uses clear diction, fluent phrasing, rhythm, and changes in volume for emphasis. Explain that using an effective voice while speaking and making presentations can have a powerful impact on an audience.
- Appropriate word choice is also important when writing and making speeches. Students should make careful word choices depending on their audience. Some audiences require more formal word choices, whereas others might accept a more relaxed and informal language. Explain to students that they need to know their audience. Explain various ways speakers can learn about their audience. For example, a political speaker might learn the major concerns of the people who are attending his or her speech.
- Students should also make sure they are choosing words that are powerful and effective. Encourage students to use a thesaurus when writing speeches or presentations so they use variety in word choice.

Guided Practice

Model using effective voice by reciting the poem or speech you selected. Have students discuss the words and why they are so effective, and then allow volunteers to recite some of the speech or poem. Discuss ways to improve presentations.

Apply

- Have students work in small groups. Ask each group to choose a paragraph from one of the selections they have read in this unit. Have each group identify examples of effective word choices. Then have students read their paragraphs for the class, modeling the voice elements mentioned above.
- Ask students listening to the readings to identify effective voice elements and to cite examples of powerful word choices. Have students explain why particular words are effective or powerful.

Teacher Tip

PLAN AHEAD Pick a powerful poem or speech to recite to the class to model effective voice and word choice.

Differentiating Instruction: English Learner

IF . . . students have difficulty reading aloud,
THEN . . . have them echo a proficient English reader, sentence by sentence.

Day 5

Preparing to Read

Review

OBJECTIVES

Students will

- review affixes as syllables and affixes used to change word meaning.
- build fluency.

MATERIALS

Transparencies 140 and 143

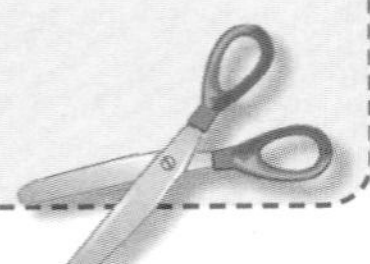

Word Structure

Use ***Transparency*** 140 with the word lines from Days 1 and 2 to review affixes as syllables. Have students read the words on the word lines. Then have students define each word on the lines that have a prefix.

Line 1	harm	harmless	main	mainly
Line 2	bend	bendable	thank	thankful
Line 3	build	rebuild	connect	disconnect
Line 4	treat	mistreat	helpful	unhelpful

Word Structure

Use ***Transparency*** 143 with the word lines from Days 3 and 4 to review affixes used to change word meaning. Have students read the words on the word lines. Then have students use words from the lines in sentences.

Line 1	harm	harmless	argue	argument
Line 2	care	careful	careless	carelessness
Line 3	wash	prewash	lock	unlock
Line 4	take	mistake	retake	unmistakable

OBJECTIVES

Students will

- review selection vocabulary.
- review the comprehension strategies Making Connections and Visualizing.
- review the comprehension skills Cause and Effect, Drawing Conclusions, and Fact and Opinion.
- review fluency.

MATERIALS

- ***Student Reader,*** Book 2, pp. 166–181
- ***Transparency*** 141

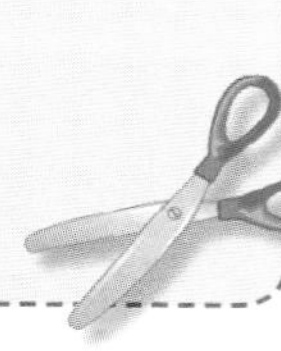

Selection Vocabulary

To review the selection vocabulary with students, organize them into small groups of three or four. Give each group a piece of paper with two or three of the selection vocabulary words. Ask each group to write a definition for each vocabulary word in their own words. When they are finished, have one student from each group read one definition at a time to the class to see whether someone can guess the vocabulary word they have defined.

Selection Vocabulary

clerk (klûrk) *n.* a person who sells goods or services to customers (page 168)

rumble (rum´ • bəl) *n.* a heavy, deep, rolling sound (page 168)

shattered (shat´ • tərd) *adj.* destroyed completely (page 171)

exactly (eg • zakt´ • lē) *adv.* without any mistakes (page 174)

damaged (dam´ • ijd) *v.* past tense of **damage:** to make something less valuable or useful (page 176)

tough (tuf) *adj.* hard to deal with or do; demanding (page 177)

frames (frāmz) *n.* plural form of **frame:** the skeleton of a building (page 177)

section (sek´ • shən) *n.* a part of something (page 178)

Comprehension Strategies  

Review the following comprehension strategies with students:

- **Visualizing** requires readers to mentally picture the events or characters in a story, resulting in a more vivid and imaginative understanding of the story. Ask students to review the selection and find ideas and passages they visualized. Ask students to explain how their visualizations helped them better understand "Earthquake! The 1906 San Francisco Nightmare."
- **Making Connections** helps readers use their own experiences to understand what is happening in a story. Ask students to review "Earthquake! The 1906 San Francisco Nightmare" and find connections they made as they read. Have students share their connections with the class.

Comprehension Skills  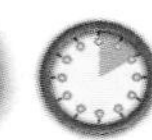 

Review the following comprehension skills with students:

- **Drawing Conclusions** requires readers to find clues within the text to make their own conclusions, judgments, or opinions about events or characters within the story. To review this strategy, ask students to explain how drawing conclusions helped them better understand "Earthquake! The 1906 San Francisco Nightmare."
- **Fact and Opinion** is a skill that helps readers understand the difference between facts, which can be verified or tested, and opinions, which are the writer's own judgments. To review this strategy, ask students to explain how understanding fact and opinion help them understand the selection.
- **Cause and Effect** is a skill that helps readers identify what causes events to happen or what causes characters to behave in certain ways. This helps readers put together logical explanations in the text. To review this strategy, ask students to review "Earthquake! The 1906 San Francisco Nightmare" and find examples of cause-and-effect relationships in the text. Have students explain the relationships they find using words such as *for*, *since*, and *due to*.

Reading with a Writer's Eye 

Review the literary element with students:

Text Structure—Technique is how an author organizes facts and information and uses examples and photographs to explain information. Ask students to review "Earthquake! The 1906 San Francisco Nightmare," and find examples of how Lynn Brunelle uses examples, explanations, and photographs to tell the story of the 1906 San Francisco earthquake. Have students explain how these techniques increased their understanding of the selection.

Fluency

Review

Remind students that accuracy adds to the meaning of text by making it easier to comprehend and enjoy. Read aloud a passage from pages 176–179 from "Earthquake! The 1906 San Francisco Nightmare." Make sure that the passage totals at least 160 words to ensure an appropriate practice length. Model fluency by showing students that words, sentences, and passages often need to be read more than once to gain accuracy. Model rereading for accuracy for students.

Have students read the passage chorally. Encourage students to reread as needed to improve accuracy. Also remind students to pause after commas and end punctuation.

OBJECTIVES

Students will
- ✦ publish formal letters.
- ✦ take the spelling posttest.
- ✦ review cursive *S, G, N, M, P,* and *R.*

MATERIALS

- ✦ ***Skills Practice 2,*** p. 130
- ✦ ***Transparencies*** 127, 131, and 137
- ✦ Routine 17

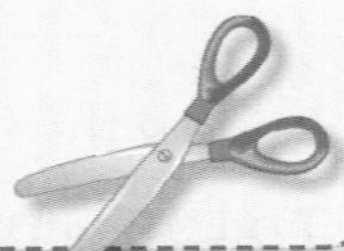

Writing Business Letter

ROUTINE 17

Publishing

Teach

- ✦ Use Routine 17. Tell students they are at the final stage of the writing process publishing.
- ✦ If possible, students should type a neat, clean copy of their business letters.
- ✦ Tell students they will also address an envelope to send their letters. The envelope for a business letter should be typed or written very neatly with black ink and should be free of any errors. If necessary, review addressing an envelope.
- ✦ Some students may want to read their business letters aloud. Encourage those who wish to do so.

Guided Practice

Have students turn to page 130 in ***Skills Practice 2*** to read and discuss the publishing checklist.

Apply

- ✦ **Composing—Publishing** Have students create a finished, error-free copy of their business letters. Have them address an envelope in which to send their letters.

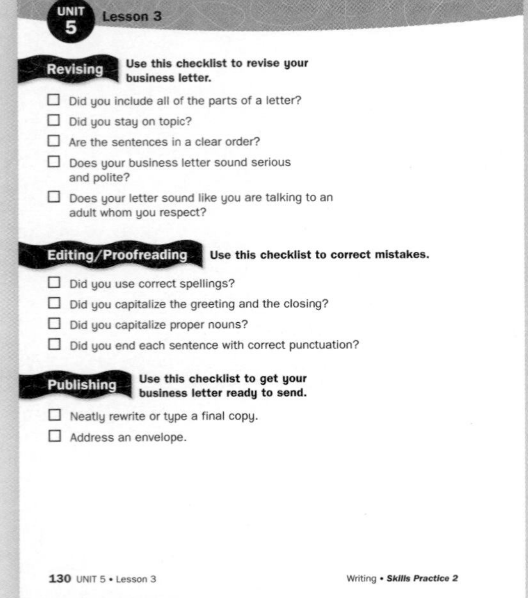

UNIT 5 Lesson 3

Revising Use this checklist to revise your business letter.

- ☐ Did you include all of the parts of a letter?
- ☐ Did you stay on topic?
- ☐ Are the sentences in a clear order?
- ☐ Does your business letter sound serious and polite?
- ☐ Does your letter sound like you are talking to an adult whom you respect?

Editing/Proofreading Use this checklist to correct mistakes.

- ☐ Did you use correct spellings?
- ☐ Did you capitalize the greeting and the closing?
- ☐ Did you capitalize proper nouns?
- ☐ Did you end each sentence with correct punctuation?

Publishing Use this checklist to get your business letter ready to send.

- ☐ Neatly rewrite or type a final copy.
- ☐ Address an envelope.

130 UNIT 5 • Lesson 3 Writing • *Skills Practice 2*

Skills Practice 2, p. 130

Teacher Tip

ASSESSMENT Use the Writing Rubrics found in the Level Appendix to evaluate students' business letters. You may use any of the rubrics for Genre, Writing Process, and Writing Traits.

Spelling

Affixes that Change Word Meanings

Teach

Ask students to write *Spelling* and their names in the top margin of a clean piece of paper. Have them number the first fifteen lines 1–15, then skip a line and number the next two lines 1–2. Read each word, use it in a sentence, and give students time to spell it correctly. Encourage students to try to spell the challenge words, but assure them that misspelling a challenge word will not affect their test scores.

Spelling Words		Challenge Words
lucky	miswrite	exactly
unlucky	count	disconnect
freeze	discount	
antifreeze	move	
rest	movement	
restful	tell	
restless	retell	
fade		

Guided Practice

- Have students proofread for any mistakes they made on the posttest. Tell them to categorize the mistakes as
  - careless errors.
  - errors in spelling the base words.
  - errors in spelling the words with affixes.
- Make certain students are spelling the base words and the words with affixes correctly.

Penmanship

Cursive Letters *S, G, N, M, P* and *R*

Teach

- For further assistance with this review lesson, refer to Unit 4 Lesson 5, and Unit 5 Lessons 1 and 2; ***Transparencies*** 127, 131, and 137; and the Level Appendix.
- To model proper letter formation, write the following sentence on the board: *Norman P. Stanley has lived in Georgia, Montana, and Rhode Island.*

Guided Practice

Ask for a volunteer to write the sentence on the board. Guide the student as needed.

Apply

After reviewing the sentence you wrote on the board, have students practice writing the sentence on a separate piece of paper. Ask students to circle their best sentence based on the correct formation of *S, G, N, M, P,* and *R*.

Teacher Tip

PENMANSHIP If students are not using proper spacing between words, then check to make sure they are positioning their papers correctly, are holding their pencils correctly, and understand how to lift the pencil at the end of the word and reposition it for the next word.

Language Arts

OBJECTIVES

Students will

- review maps.
- review presentation skills.
- review verb tenses.

MATERIALS

Lesson Assessment Book 2, pp. 59–66

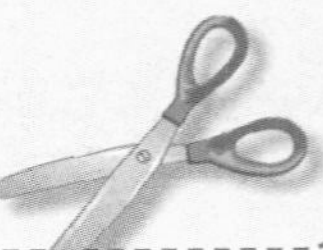

Study Skills

Maps

Remind students of the different types of maps and how they are used.

Ask students to name some of the maps they could use for their unit investigations on the unit theme Communities across Time. *physical map, historical map, topographical map, economic map*

Have students select a map and explain why that map would be a good visual aid to use in their unit investigations.

Listening/Speaking/Viewing

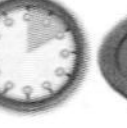

Effective Voice and Word Choice

Remind students of the importance of using an effective voice and making effective word choices when speaking or making presentations.

Ask students to give examples of how someone can speak effectively. Then have them give examples of effective word choices.

Have students review a piece of their own writing for effective word choices.

Grammar, Usage, and Mechanics

Sentence Tense

Write the following sentences on the board. Then have students circle the verbs and indicate whether the sentence is in the past, present, or future tense.

- We will listen to the speaker in class tomorrow. circle: *will listen; future*
- We listened to the speaker in class yesterday. circle: *listened; past*
- We listen to speakers every other week in class. circle: *listen; present*

Have students work in pairs to rewrite a section of "Earthquake! The 1906 San Francisco Nightmare" to make it futuristic. Have students present their modified versions to the class.

Monitor Progress
Formal Assessment

Use pages 59–66 in ***Lesson Assessment Book 2*** to assess students' understanding of the skills taught in this lesson. Intervene with ***Reteach, Challenge Activities, Intervention Guide, eSkills & eGames, Leveled Readers,*** or activities in the ***Workshop Kit*** as needed.

Lesson Planner

	Day 1	Day 2
Preparing to Read MATERIALS ✦ ***Transparencies*** 144, 147 ✦ Routine 10 ✦ ***Skills Practice 2,*** pp. 137–140	**Daily News,** p. T266 ✔ **Word Structure** Word Families, pp. T266–T267	**Daily News,** p. T286 ✔ **Word Structure,** p. T287 **Developing Oral Language,** p. T287
Reading and Responding MATERIALS ✦ ***Student Reader,*** Book 2, pp. 184–205 ✦ ***Transparencies*** 5, 9, 145 ✦ Routines 11, 12, 14, A ✦ ***Skills Practice 2,*** pp. 141–146 ✦ Writer's Notebook ✦ ***Home Connection,*** pp. 57–58 ✦ ***Listening Library CD*** ✦ ***Leveled Reader*** ✦ ***Lesson Assessment Book 2***	**Build Background,** p. T268 **Preview and Prepare,** p. T269 **Selection Vocabulary,** pp. T270–T271 **Reading the Selection,** pp. T272–T275 1st READ 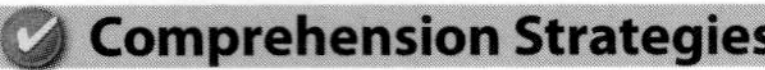 • Clarifying, pp. T272, T276–T279 • Summarizing, pp. T273, T279 ✔ **Comprehension Skill** ☆ Cause and Effect, p. T274 **Inquiry,** pp. T280–T281	✔ **Comprehension Strategies** • Clarifying, pp. T288–T290 • Summarizing, p. T291 **Discussing the Selection,** p. T292 ✔ **Review Selection Vocabulary,** p. T293 **Fluency,** p. T293 **Theme Connections,** p. T294
Language Arts MATERIALS ✦ ***Transparencies,*** 17, 17A, 42, 42A, 146, 148, 148A ✦ ***Skills Practice 2,*** pp. 147–154 ✦ ***Language Arts Handbook,*** pp. 101–103, 308, 324–325 ✦ Routines 16, 17 ✦ ***Lesson Assessment Book 2,*** pp. 67–74	✔ **Writing** Prewriting, pp. T282–283 **Spelling Pretest,** p. T283 ✔ **Penmanship** Cursive Letters *D* and *B,* p. T284	**Writing** Drafting, p. T296 **Spelling,** p. T297 ✔ **Grammar, Usage, and Mechanics** Verb *be* and Irregular Verbs, pp. T298–T299
Monitor Progress ✔ = Formal Assessment	✔ **Word Structure, p. T267** ✔ **Comprehension Strategy, p. T272** ✔ **Comprehension Skill, p. T273** ✔ **Writing, p. T283** ✔ **Spelling Pretest, p. T283**	✔ **Word Structure, p. T287**  **Fluency, p. T293** ✔ **Grammar, Usage, and Mechanics, p. T299**

Literature Overview

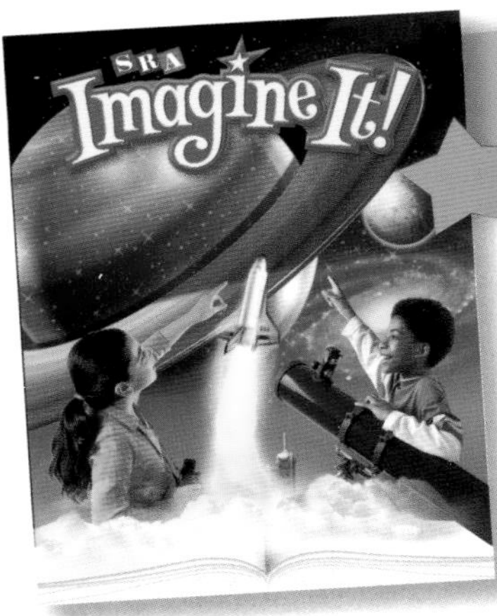

Student Reader

The Disappearing Island

by Corinne Demas

illustrated by Ted Lewin

Social Studies Inquiry

Keeping Track

SRA
Imagine It!

★ Phonics ★ Fluency ★ Vocabulary ★ Comprehension

Day 3

Daily News, p. T300
Word Structure
Multisyllabic Words with Silent Consonants, pp. T300–T301

2nd READ

Comprehension Skills
- Author's Purpose, p. T302
- ☆ Cause and Effect, pp. T303, T304

Reading with a Writer's Eye, p. T305
Supporting the Reading
☆ Comprehension Skill: Cause and Effect, p. T306
Fluency, p. T307
Inquiry, p. T307

Writing
Revising, p. T308
Spelling, p. T309
Study Skills
Calendars, p. T310
Grammar, Usage, and Mechanics, p. T311

Word Structure, p. T301
Fluency, p. T307
Spelling, p. T309
Study Skills, p. T310

Day 4

Daily News, p. T312
Word Structure, p. T313
Developing Oral Language, p. T313

Comprehension Skills
- ☆ Cause and Effect, p. T314
- Author's Purpose, p. T316

Reading with a Writer's Eye, p. T315
Social Studies Inquiry, pp. T318–T319
Inquiry, pp. T320–T321

Writing
Editing/Proofreading, pp. T322–T323
Spelling, p. T323
Study Skills, p. T324
Listening/Speaking/Viewing
Using Multimedia, p. T325

Word Structure, p. T313

Day 5 Review

Word Structure, p. T326

Selection Vocabulary, p. T327
Comprehension Strategies
- Clarifying, p. T328
- Summarizing, p. T328

Comprehension Skills
- Author's Purpose, p. T328
- ☆ Cause and Effect, p. T328

Reading with a Writer's Eye, p. T329
Fluency, p. T329

Writing
Publishing, p. T330
Spelling Posttest, p. T331
Penmanship, p. T331
Study Skills, p. T332
Listening/Speaking/Viewing, p. T332
Grammar, Usage, and Mechanics, p. T333

Spelling Posttest, p. T31
***Lesson Assessment Book 2*, pp. 67–74**

Student Resources

Genre

Realistic Fiction involves stories about people and events that are true to life and that could really happen.

Comprehension Skill

Cause and Effect
As you read, think about what causes certain events to happen.

186

The DISAPPEARING Island

by Corinne Demas
illustrated by Ted Lewin

Focus Questions

What physical or environmental changes could cause a community to disappear? What do communities do to survive major changes in their environments?

187

Student Reader, Book 2, pp. 186–203

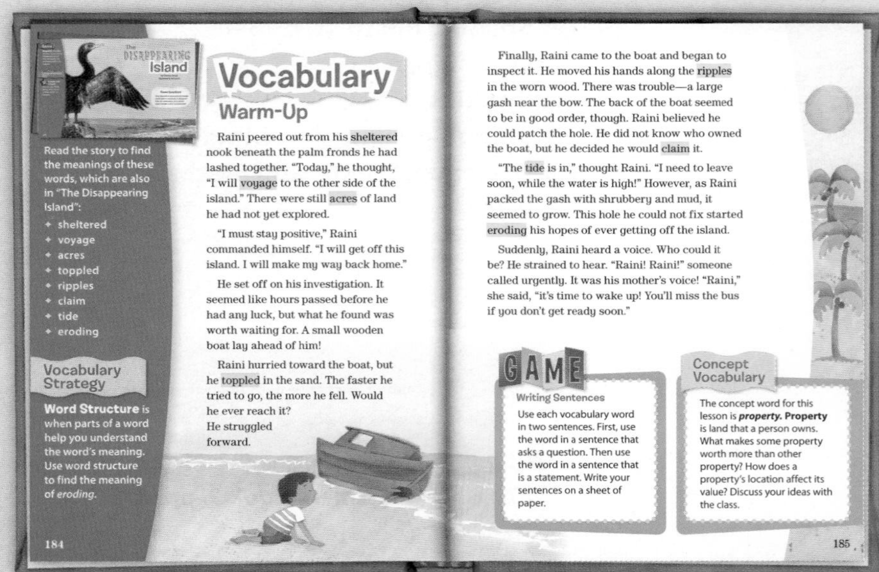

Read the story to find the meanings of these words, which are also in "The Disappearing Island":

- sheltered
- voyage
- acres
- toppled
- ripples
- claim
- tide
- eroding

Vocabulary Strategy

Word Structure is when parts of a word help you understand the word's meaning. Use word structure to find the meaning of *eroding*.

Vocabulary Warm-Up

Raini peered out from his sheltered nook beneath the palm fronds he had lashed together. "Today," he thought, "I will voyage to the other side of the island." There were still acres of land he had not yet explored.

"I must stay positive," Raini commanded himself. "I will get off this island. I will make my way back home."

He set off on his investigation. It seemed like hours passed before he had any luck, but what he found was worth waiting for. A small wooden boat lay ahead of him!

Raini hurried toward the boat, but he toppled in the sand. The faster he tried to go, the more he fell. Would he ever reach it? He struggled forward.

184

Finally, Raini came to the boat and began to inspect it. He moved his hands along the ripples in the worn wood. There was trouble—a large gash near the bow. The back of the boat seemed to be in good order, though. Raini believed he could patch the hole. He did not know who owned the boat, but he decided he would claim it.

"The tide is in," thought Raini. "I need to leave soon, while the water is high!" However, as Raini packed the gash with shrubbery and mud, it seemed to grow. This hole he could not fix started eroding his hopes of ever getting off the island.

Suddenly, Raini heard a voice. Who could it be? He strained to hear. "Raini! Raini!" someone called urgently. It was his mother's voice! "Raini," she said, "it's time to wake up! You'll miss the bus if you don't get ready soon."

GAME

Writing Sentences

Use each vocabulary word in two sentences. First, use the word in a sentence that asks a question. Then use the word in a sentence that is a statement. Write your sentences on a sheet of paper.

Concept Vocabulary

The concept word for this lesson is ***property.* Property** is land that a person owns. What makes some property worth more than other property? How does a property's location affect its value? Discuss your ideas with the class.

185

Student Reader, Book 2, pp. 184–185

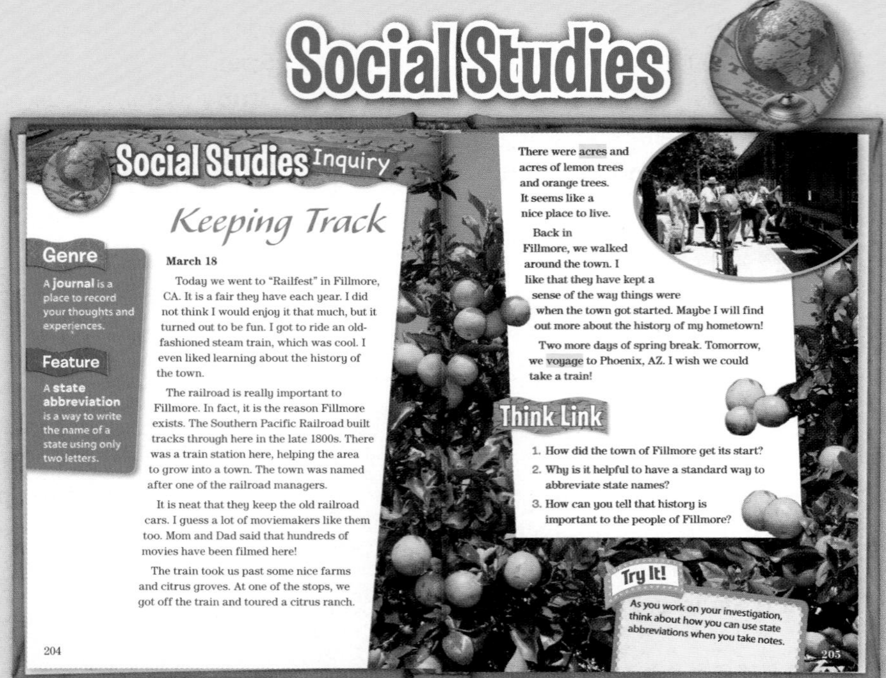

Social Studies

Social Studies Inquiry

Keeping Track

Genre

A **journal** is a place to record your thoughts and experiences.

Feature

A **state abbreviation** is a way to write the name of a state using only two letters.

March 18

Today we went to "Railfest" in Fillmore, CA. It is a fair they have each year. I did not think I would enjoy it that much, but it turned out to be fun. I got to ride an old-fashioned steam train, which was cool. I even liked learning about the history of the town.

The railroad is really important to Fillmore. In fact, it is the reason Fillmore exists. The Southern Pacific Railroad built tracks through here in the late 1800s. There was a train station here, helping the area to grow into a town. The town was named after one of the railroad managers.

It is neat that they keep the old railroad cars. I guess a lot of moviemakers like them too. Mom and Dad said that hundreds of movies have been filmed here!

The train took us past some nice farms and citrus groves. At one of the stops, we got off the train and toured a citrus ranch.

204

There were acres and acres of lemon trees and orange trees. It seems like a nice place to live.

Back in Fillmore, we walked around the town. I like that they have kept a sense of the way things were when the town got started. Maybe I will find out more about the history of my hometown!

Two more days of spring break. Tomorrow, we voyage to Phoenix, AZ. I wish we could take a train!

Think Link

1. How did the town of Fillmore get its start?
2. Why is it helpful to have a standard way to abbreviate state names?
3. How can you tell that history is important to the people of Fillmore?

Try It!

As you work on your investigation, think about how you can use state abbreviations when you take notes.

205

Student Reader, Book 2, pp. 204–205

Cross-Curricular Resources

Curriculum Connections

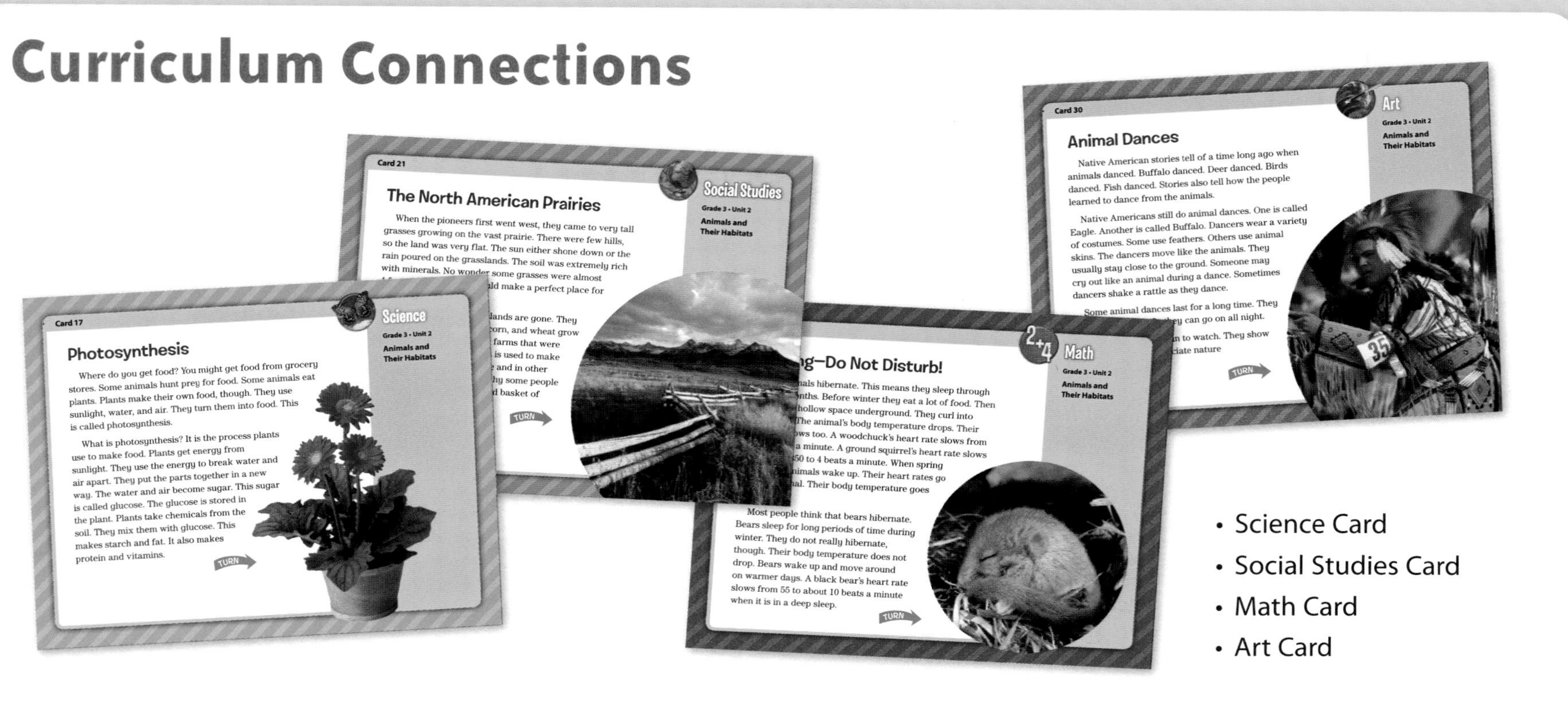

- Science Card
- Social Studies Card
- Math Card
- Art Card

Leveled Social Studies Readers

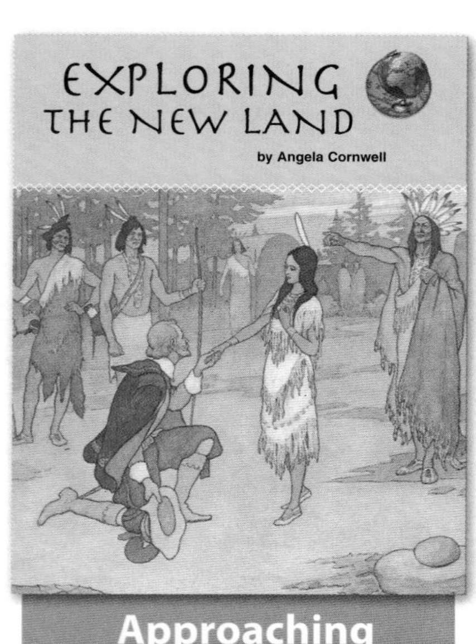

Approaching Level

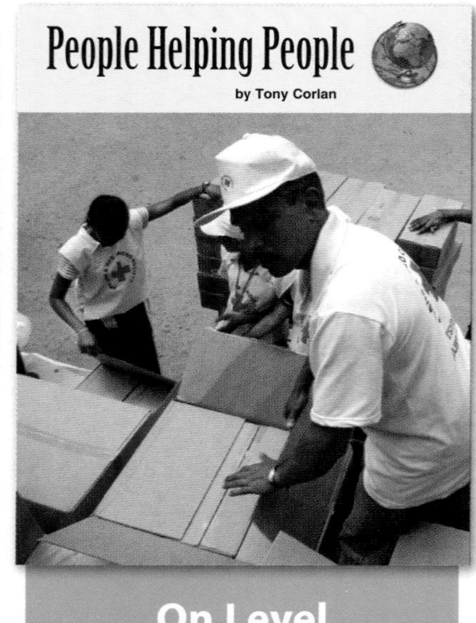

On Level

English Learner

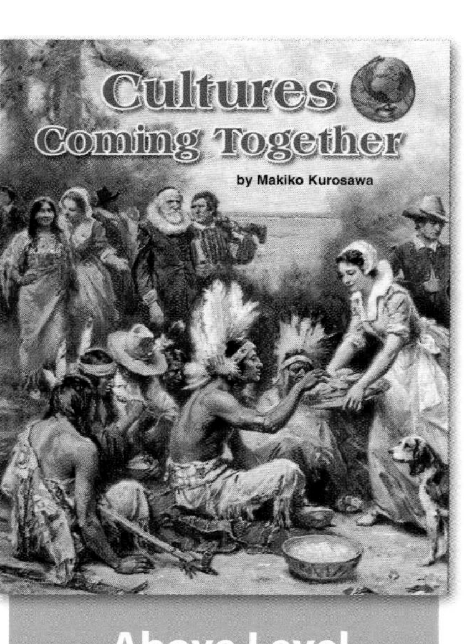

Above Level

Differentiating Instruction
for Workshop

Day 1

	Approaching Level	On Level	English Learner	Above Level
Preparing to Read	**Word Structure:** Review the word lines. Help students in small groups complete ***Reteach*** page 142, or work with them on the word structure activities in the ***Intervention Guide.***	**Word Structure:** Have students make lists of other base words and create new word families with them during Workshop.	**Word Structure:** Use the ***English Learner Support Guide*** for additional word structure instruction.	**Word Structure:** Have students complete ***Challenge Activities*** page 129. Students can make new lists of word families to add to each word family in the word lines.
Reading and Responding	**Vocabulary:** Have students use the selection vocabulary words to write sentences. **Comprehension:** Have students create a list of words and ideas they clarified while reading. Have students share their clarifications and the methods they used to clarify with the class. **Inquiry:** Have students work in groups to find Web sites with information for their investigations.	**Vocabulary:** Have students create illustrations for the selection vocabulary words. **Comprehension:** Have students write a short paragraph summarizing what they have read so far. **Inquiry:** Have students work in groups to find Web sites with information for their investigations.	**Vocabulary:** Use ***English Learner Support Guide,*** Unit 5, Lesson 4. **Comprehension:** Have students write a short paragraph about a scene they can visualize about the story. **Inquiry:** Have students work in groups to find Web sites with information for their investigations.	**Vocabulary:** Have students use the selection vocabulary words in a story. **Comprehension:** Have students create a checklist of clarifications that they have made while reading. **Inquiry:** Have students work in groups to find Web sites with information for their investigations.
Language Arts	**Writing:** Have students work on their graphic organizer with a partner. **Spelling:** Have pairs of students study the spelling words in this lesson.	**Writing:** Have students begin to draft their directions once they have completed the graphic organizer. **Spelling:** Have students proofread their writing activity for spelling errors.	**Writing:** Have students work on their graphic organizers with a more proficient English speaker. **Spelling:** Have students rewrite one paragraph from their selections, spelling the words carefully.	**Writing:** Have students begin drawing a map for their directions. **Spelling:** Have students pick five spelling words and use the letters from those words to correctly spell new words.

Day 2

	Approaching Level	On Level	English Learner	Above Level
Preparing to Read	**Word Structure:** Have students write sentences using words from the word lines. Students can reread "The Disappearing Island" looking for word families.	**Word Structure:** Have students reread "The Disappearing Island" to look for word families.	**Word Structure:** Have students write sentences using words from the word lines. Students can reread "The Disappearing Island" to look for word families.	**Word Structure:** Have students write a paragraph for each word line, making sure to use all the words in the line.
Reading and Responding	**Vocabulary:** Have students use ***Reteach*** page 144. **Comprehension:** Have students create a checklist of clarifications that they have made while reading. **Fluency:** Have students choose a text on their independent level to read silently.	**Vocabulary:** Have students complete a game in the ***Workshop Kit.*** **Comprehension:** Have students summarize the story. **Fluency:** Have students choose a text on their independent level to read silently.	**Vocabulary:** Help students create flash cards for the selection vocabulary words. Have students use them to quiz a partner. **Comprehension:** Have students find a passage they have clarified or need to clarify. Place students in small groups, and let them help each other clarify confusing information. **Fluency:** Have students choose a text on their independent level to read silently.	**Vocabulary:** Have students complete ***Challenge Activities*** page 131. **Comprehension:** Have students write a journal entry about information they learned about Communities across Time after reading the story. **Fluency:** Have students choose a text on their independent level to read silently.
Language Arts	**Writing:** Have students continue to draft their directions. **Spelling:** Have students work in groups to review this week's spelling word list. **Grammar, Usage, and Mechanics:** Have students complete ***Reteach*** page 148.	**Writing:** Have students conference with peers. **Spelling:** Have students write their spelling words on a separate piece of paper. Then have them circle words that are part of the same family as another spelling word, underline multisyllabic words, and draw a box around words with a silent consonant. **Grammar, Usage, and Mechanics:** Have students do an activity from the ***Workshop Kit.***	**Writing:** Have students use a dictionary or thesaurus as they draft. **Spelling:** Have students work in pairs to brainstorm ideas to help them with their spelling. **Grammar, Usage, and Mechanics:** Have students refer to the ***English Learner Support Guide,*** Unit 5, Lesson 4.	**Writing:** Have students share their drafts with other students. **Spelling:** Have students think of and spell new words that contain silent consonants. **Grammar, Usage, and Mechanics:** Have students complete ***Challenge Activities*** page 134.

Differentiating Instruction
for Workshop

Day 3

	Approaching Level	On Level	English Learner	Above Level
Preparing to Read	**Word Structure:** Review the word lines and ***Sound/Spelling Cards*** 11, 14, and 29. Then have students complete ***Reteach*** page 143, or work with them on the word structure activities in the ***Intervention Guide,*** Unit 5, Lesson 4.	**Word Structure:** Have students make lists of multisyllabic words with silent consonants to add to the word lines.	**Word Structure:** Review the word lines. Then use the additional word structure instruction in the ***English Learner Support Guide.***	**Word Structure:** Have students complete ***Challenge Activities*** page 130. Then have students make lists of words to add to the word lines.
Reading and Responding	**Vocabulary:** Have students write functional definitions for three of the selection vocabulary words. **Comprehension:** Have students create a list of comprehension questions. Have students trade their questions with a partner. **Fluency:** Have students use the ***Leveled Readers.***	**Vocabulary:** Have students create a word-search puzzle with the concept vocabulary words and trade them with a partner. **Comprehension:** Have students use graphic organizers to organize cause-and-effect relationships found in the story. **Fluency:** Have students reread a passage from the selection with a partner or individually.	**Vocabulary:** Have students find words related to the selection vocabulary words using online and print reference materials. **Comprehension:** Have students use graphic organizers to organize cause-and-effect relationships in the story. **Fluency:** Have students read into a tape recorder at the beginning and end of the week. Have them listen to themselves at the end of the week so they can hear their progress.	**Vocabulary:** Have students research the Internet for additional words related to erosion and disappearing islands. **Comprehension:** Have students research erosion using reference materials or the Internet to find additional information that might be added to the **Concept/ Question Board.** **Fluency:** Have students use the ***Leveled Readers.***
Language Arts	**Writing:** Have students work with peers to revise their directions. **Spelling:** Have students complete ***Reteach*** page 147. **Grammar, Usage, and Mechanics:** Have students make sure they have conjugated irregular verbs correctly.	**Writing:** Have students continue to revise their directions. **Spelling:** Have students write five sentences using the spelling words. Have them omit the spelling word from the sentence, trade sentences with a partner, and have the partner fill in the blank with the correct spelling word. **Grammar, Usage, and Mechanics:** As students revise their directions, have them look for errors in verb tense.	**Writing:** Have students refer to the checklist as they revise their directions. **Spelling:** Have students write five sentences using the spelling words. Have them omit the spelling word from the sentence, trade sentences with a partner, and have the partner fill in the blank with the correct spelling word. **Grammar, Usage, and Mechanics:** Have students check the conjugation of irregular verbs as they revise their directions.	**Writing:** Have students work with peers. Encourage them to offer suggestions. **Spelling:** Have students complete ***Challenge Activities*** page 133. **Grammar, Usage, and Mechanics:** Have students edit previous writing pieces for irregular verbs.

Day 4

	Approaching Level	On Level	English Learner	Above Level
Preparing to Read	**Word Structure:** Have students write sentences using words from the word lines.	**Word Structure:** Students can scramble words from the word lines and give them to a partner to unscramble.	**Word Structure:** Have students write sentences using words from the word lines. Then have students read other materials looking for multisyllabic words with silent consonants.	**Word Structure:** Students can scramble words from the word lines and give them to a partner to unscramble.
Reading and Responding	**Vocabulary:** Have students create crossword puzzles with the expanding vocabulary words. **Comprehension:** Pair students into small groups in order to discuss what they have learned about Communities across Time by reading the story. Have students post any new information on the **Concept/ Questions Board.** **Inquiry:** Have groups organize their information by using charts, graphs, or time lines.	**Vocabulary:** Have students write sentences using the selection vocabulary words. **Comprehension:** Have students research disappearing islands using reference materials or the Internet to find additional information that might be added to the **Concept/Question Board.** **Inquiry:** Have groups organize their information by using charts, graphs, or time lines.	**Vocabulary:** Have students write sentences using the expanding vocabulary words. **Comprehension:** Divide students into small groups to discuss what they have learned about Communities across Time by reading the story. Have students post any new information on the **Concept/ Question Board.** **Inquiry:** Have groups organize their information by using charts, graphs, or time lines.	**Vocabulary:** Have students write a journal entry about how one of the concept vocabulary words relates to the unit theme. **Comprehension:** Have students write a journal entry explaining nature's effect on the island in "The Disappearing Island." **Inquiry:** Have groups organize their information by using charts, graphs, or time lines.
Language Arts	**Writing:** Have students work with a peer to edit and proofread their directions. **Spelling:** Have students write six spelling words on a piece of paper spelled incorrectly, trade papers with a partner, and correct the words.	**Writing:** Have students begin their final drafts. **Spelling:** Have students write five words that rhyme with spelling words on a piece of paper.	**Writing:** Have students work with a peer to edit and proofread their directions. **Spelling:** Have students circle the spelling words that are part of the same word family as another spelling word.	**Writing:** Have students proceed to publishing once they have edited and proofread their directions. **Spelling:** Have students pick two spelling words and write four words each that rhyme with those words.

Differentiating Instruction for Workshop

Day 5

	Approaching Level	On Level	English Learner	Above Level
Preparing to Read	**Word Structure:** Review the word lines. Then have students write sentences uses words from the lines.	**Word Structure:** Have students write clue sentences for words in the word lines and have a partner guess the word.	**Word Structure:** Review the word lines. Then have students create new lists of word families and write paragraphs using the words from their lists.	**Word Structure:** Have students write clue sentences for words in the word lines and have a partner guess the word.
Reading and Responding	**Vocabulary:** Have students find interesting words and phrases to add to their Writer's Notebooks. **Comprehension:** Have students create review questions for the story and trade questions with a partner. **Fluency:** Have students write answers to comprehension questions from the ***Leveled Readers.***	**Vocabulary:** Have students create a board game that helps players learn the selection vocabulary words. **Comprehension:** Have students write a summary of "The Disappearing Island." **Fluency:** Have students write answers to comprehension questions from the ***Leveled Readers.***	**Vocabulary:** Have students write a poem about their community. **Comprehension:** Have students write a summary of "The Disappearing Island." Encourage students to include illustrations if they have trouble expressing themselves. **Fluency:** Have students use vocabulary from the ***Leveled Readers*** in extended sentences.	**Vocabulary:** Have students write a story using the selection vocabulary words. **Comprehension:** Have students research Billingsgate Island using reference materials and the Internet. Have students share their research with the class. **Fluency:** Have students create a play from the story to use with reader's theater.
Language Arts	**Writing:** Have students share their directions with a small group. **Spelling:** Have students carefully rewrite a paragraph from their selection, while keeping an eye on spelling the words correctly.	**Writing:** Have students publish their directions. **Spelling:** Have students make a list of five spelling words with one letter missing, trade papers with a partner, and fill in the blanks.	**Writing:** Have students share their directions with a peer. **Spelling:** Have students choose five spelling words for a partner to spell on a piece of paper.	**Writing:** Have students share their work with others. **Spelling:** Have students write an imaginary letter to someone using at least six spelling words.

Resources for

Differentiating Instruction 

Leveled Readers

Approaching Level

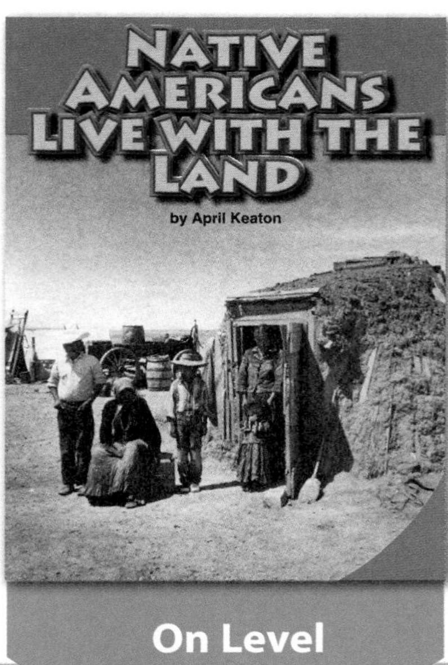

On Level

English Learner

Above Level

Additional Skills Practice

Approaching Level

Reteach

- Word Families, p. 142
- Multisyllabic Words with Silent Consonants, p. 143
- Vocabulary, p. 144
- Cause and Effect, pp. 145–146
- Spelling, p. 147
- Irregular Verb Tenses, p. 148

On Level

Skills Practice 2

- Word Families, pp. 137–138
- Multisyllabic Words, pp. 139–140
- Vocabulary, pp. 141–142
- Cause and Effect, pp. 143–144
- Directions, pp. 147–148
- Spelling, pp. 149–150
- Irregular Verb Tenses, pp. 151–152

English Learner

English Learner Support Activities

Unit 5, Lesson 4

Above Level

Challenge Activities

- Word Families, p. 129
- Multisyllabic Words with Silent Consonants, p. 130
- Vocabulary, p. 131
- Cause and Effect, p. 132
- Spelling, p. 133
- Irregular Verb Tenses, p. 134

Additional Resources for Differentiating Instruction

Workshop Kits

Technology

The following electronic resources are available for students:

- ***eStudent Reader***
- ***eSkills & eGames***
- ***Listening Library CD***

Electronic resources for the teacher include:

- ***ePlanner***
- ***eTeacher's Edition***
- ***eAssess***
- ***ePresentation***

English Learner

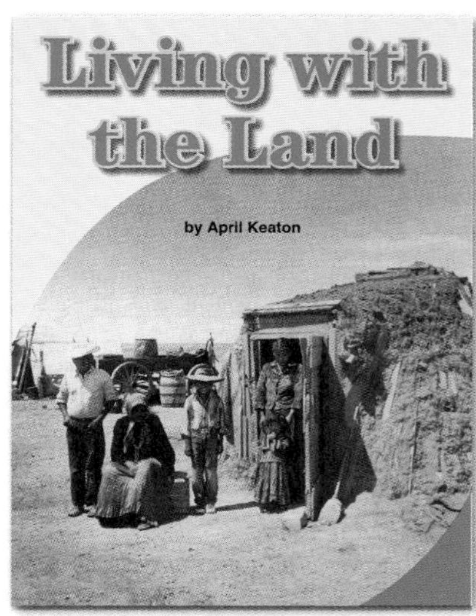

Leveled Reader

English Learner Support Activities, Lesson 4

Listening Library CD, Unit 5

English Learner Support Guide, Lesson 4

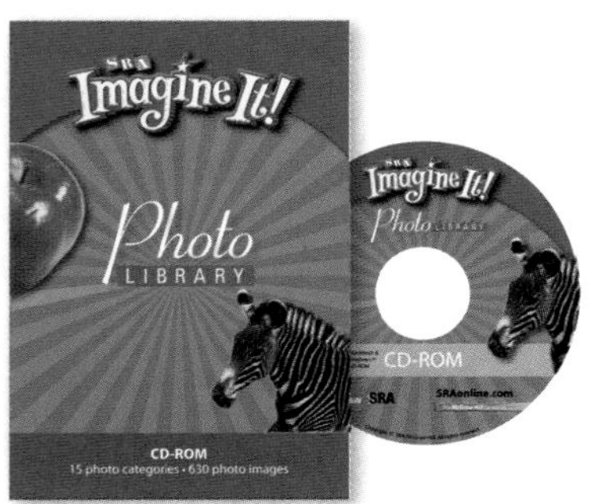

Photo Library CD

Approaching Level

Intervention

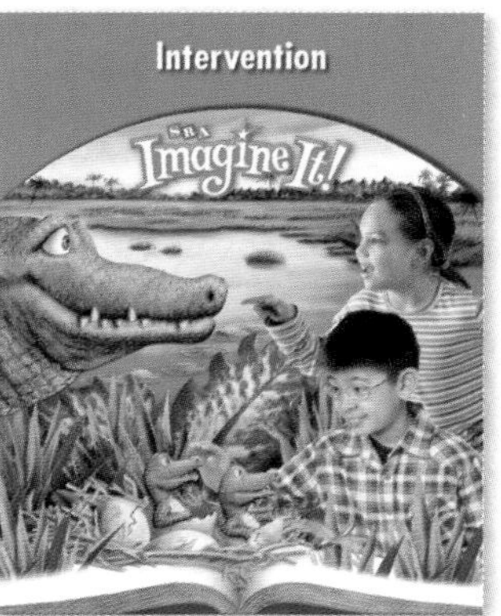

Intervention Workbook

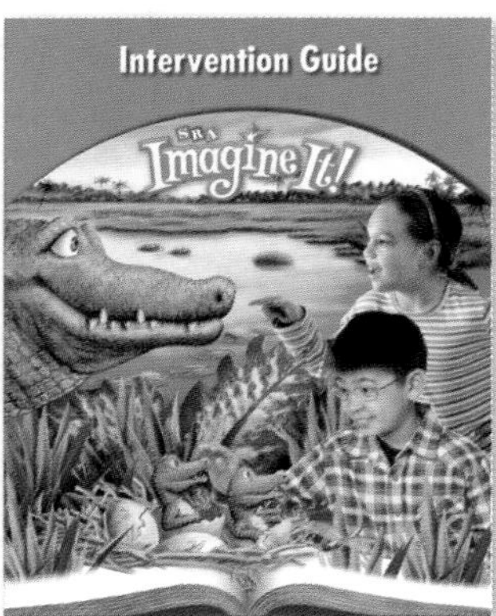

Intervention Guide

Lesson 4 Overview

Lesson Assessment

Monitor Progress to Differentiate Instruction

Comprehension Strategies Rubrics

Use the Comprehension Strategies Rubrics to determine whether a student is using the strategies.

- ✦ Clarifying, p. T272
- ✦ Summarizing, p. T273

Inquiry Rubrics

Use the Inquiry Rubrics to assess a student's performance throughout the stages of the investigation for each unit. In addition, at the end of the unit you can use the rubrics to assess the groups' collaborative work as well as an individual's participation in that group.

- ✦ Collecting Information, p. T321

Writing Rubrics

Use the writing rubrics in the Level Appendix to evaluate each student's directions.

- ✦ Genre
- ✦ Writing Process
- ✦ Writing Traits

Lesson Assessments

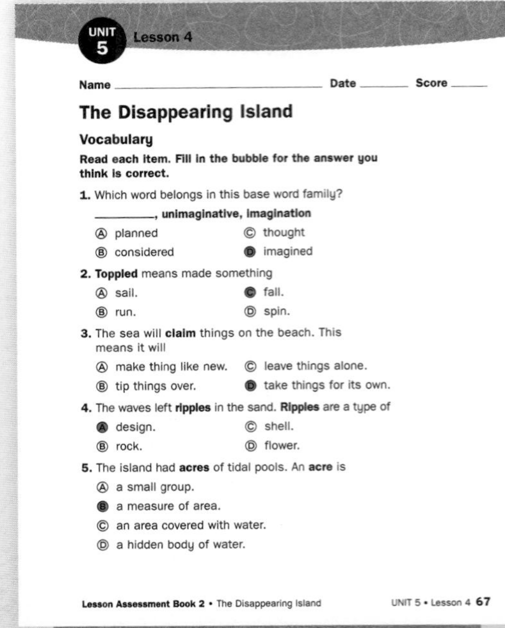

UNIT 5 Lesson 4

Name ______________ Date ______ Score ______

The Disappearing Island

Vocabulary

Read each item. Fill in the bubble for the answer you think is correct.

1. Which word belongs in this base word family?
   ________, **unimaginative, imagination**
   Ⓐ planned Ⓒ thought
   Ⓑ considered ● imagined
2. **Toppled** means made something
   Ⓐ sail. ● fall.
   Ⓑ run. Ⓓ spin.
3. The sea will **claim** things on the beach. This means it will
   Ⓐ make thing like new. Ⓒ leave things alone.
   Ⓑ tip things over. ● take things for its own.
4. The waves left **ripples** in the sand. **Ripples** are a type of
   ● design. Ⓒ shell.
   Ⓑ rock. Ⓓ flower.
5. The island had **acres** of tidal pools. An **acre** is
   Ⓐ a small group.
   ● a measure of area.
   Ⓒ an area covered with water.
   Ⓓ a hidden body of water.

Lesson Assessment Book 2 • The Disappearing Island UNIT 5 • Lesson 4 **67**

Lesson Assessment Book 2, p. 67

UNIT 5 Lesson 4

The Disappearing Island (continued)

Comprehension

Read the following questions carefully. Then completely fill in the bubble of each correct answer. You may look back at the selection to find the answer to each of the questions.

1. Carrie got all of these for her birthday EXCEPT
   Ⓐ a cake.
   Ⓑ a perfect sand dollar.
   ● a new life jacket.
   Ⓓ a trip to a disappearing island.
2. How did Carrie see the island from the boat?
   Ⓐ by looking behind the boat
   ● by looking through binoculars
   Ⓒ by watching a cormorant land
   Ⓓ by wading close to shore

68 UNIT 5 • Lesson 4 The Disappearing Island • **Lesson Assessment Book 2**

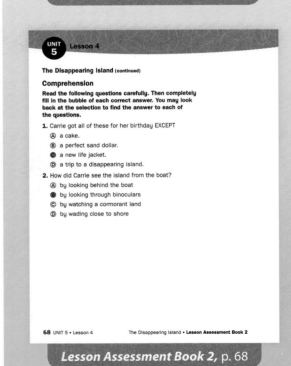

Lesson Assessment Book 2, p. 68

Formal Assessment

Use these summative assessments along with your informal observations to assess student mastery.

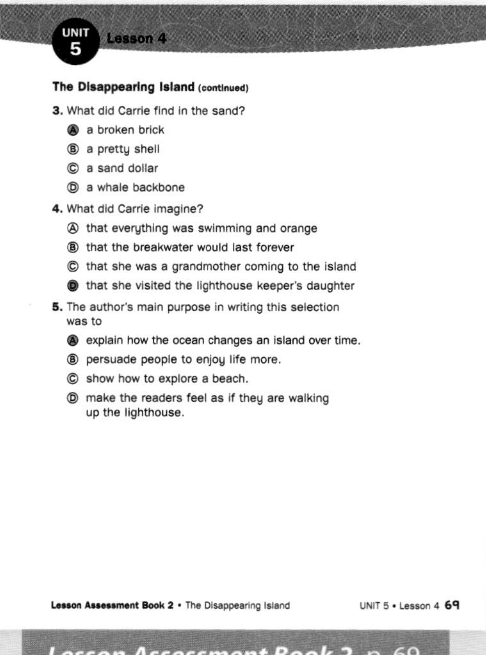

UNIT 5 Lesson 4

The Disappearing Island (continued)

3. What did Carrie find in the sand?
- ● a broken brick
- Ⓑ a pretty shell
- Ⓒ a sand dollar
- Ⓓ a whale backbone

4. What did Carrie imagine?
- Ⓐ that everything was swimming and orange
- Ⓑ that the breakwater would last forever
- Ⓒ that she was a grandmother coming to the island
- ● that she visited the lighthouse keeper's daughter

5. The author's main purpose in writing this selection was to
- ● explain how the ocean changes an island over time.
- Ⓑ persuade people to enjoy life more.
- Ⓒ show how to explore a beach.
- Ⓓ make the readers feel as if they are walking up the lighthouse.

Lesson Assessment Book 2 • The Disappearing Island UNIT 5 • Lesson 4 69

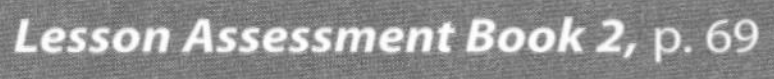

Lesson Assessment Book 2, p. 69

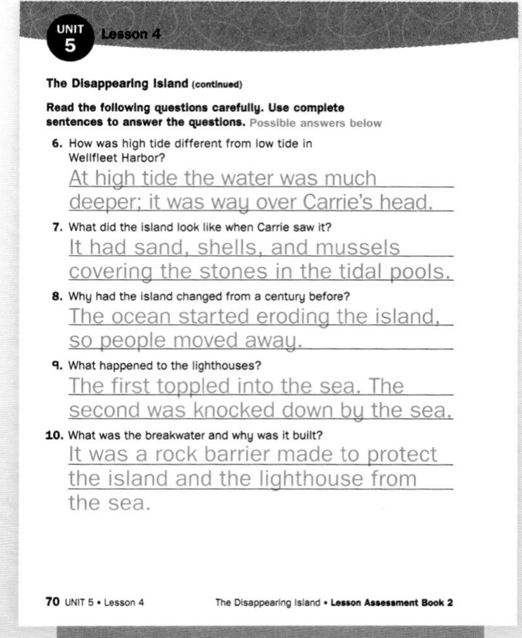

UNIT 5 Lesson 4

The Disappearing Island (continued)

Read the following questions carefully. Use complete sentences to answer the questions. Possible answers below

6. How was high tide different from low tide in Wellfleet Harbor?
At high tide the water was much deeper; it was way over Carrie's head.

7. What did the island look like when Carrie saw it?
It had sand, shells, and mussels covering the stones in the tidal pools.

8. Why had the island changed from a century before?
The ocean started eroding the island, so people moved away.

9. What happened to the lighthouses?
The first toppled into the sea. The second was knocked down by the sea.

10. What was the breakwater and why was it built?
It was a rock barrier made to protect the island and the lighthouse from the sea.

70 UNIT 5 • Lesson 4 The Disappearing Island • Lesson Assessment Book 2

Lesson Assessment Book 2, p. 70

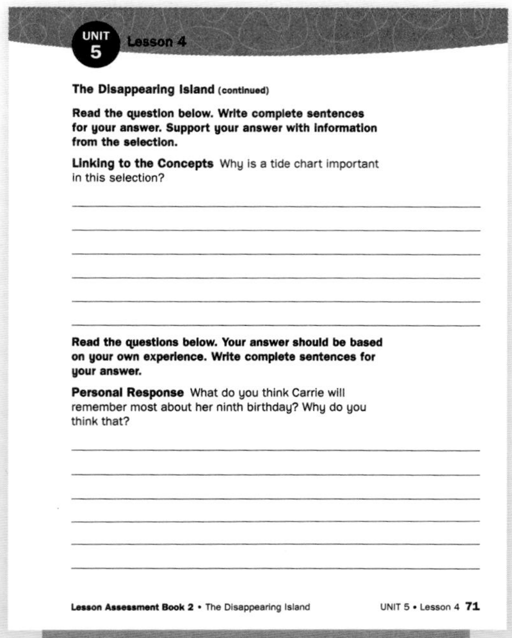

UNIT 5 Lesson 4

The Disappearing Island (continued)

Read the question below. Write complete sentences for your answer. Support your answer with information from the selection.

Linking to the Concepts Why is a tide chart important in this selection?

Read the questions below. Your answer should be based on your own experience. Write complete sentences for your answer.

Personal Response What do you think Carrie will remember most about her ninth birthday? Why do you think that?

Lesson Assessment Book 2 • The Disappearing Island UNIT 5 • Lesson 4 71

Lesson Assessment Book 2, p. 71

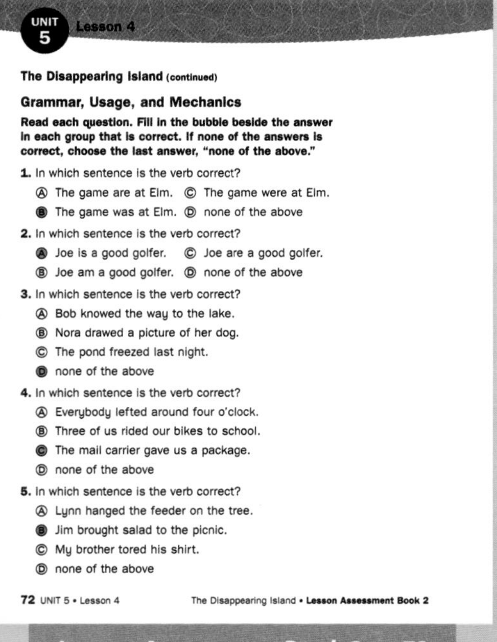

UNIT 5 Lesson 4

The Disappearing Island (continued)

Grammar, Usage, and Mechanics

Read each question. Fill in the bubble beside the answer in each group that is correct. If none of the answers is correct, choose the last answer, "none of the above."

1. In which sentence is the verb correct?
- Ⓐ The game are at Elm.
- ● The game was at Elm.
- Ⓒ The game were at Elm.
- Ⓓ none of the above

2. In which sentence is the verb correct?
- ● Joe is a good golfer.
- Ⓑ Joe am a good golfer.
- Ⓒ Joe are a good golfer.
- Ⓓ none of the above

3. In which sentence is the verb correct?
- Ⓐ Bob knowed the way to the lake.
- Ⓑ Nora drawed a picture of her dog.
- Ⓒ The pond freezed last night.
- ● none of the above

4. In which sentence is the verb correct?
- Ⓐ Everybody lefted around four o'clock.
- Ⓑ Three of us rided our bikes to school.
- ● The mail carrier gave us a package.
- Ⓓ none of the above

5. In which sentence is the verb correct?
- Ⓐ Lynn hanged the feeder on the tree.
- ● Jim brought salad to the picnic.
- Ⓒ My brother tored his shirt.
- Ⓓ none of the above

72 UNIT 5 • Lesson 4 The Disappearing Island • Lesson Assessment Book 2

Lesson Assessment Book 2, p. 72

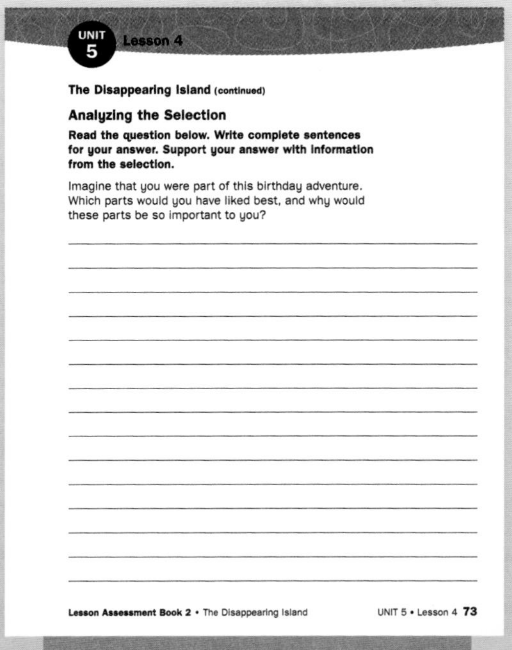

UNIT 5 Lesson 4

The Disappearing Island (continued)

Analyzing the Selection

Read the question below. Write complete sentences for your answer. Support your answer with information from the selection.

Imagine that you were part of this birthday adventure. Which parts would you have liked best, and why would these parts be so important to you?

Lesson Assessment Book 2 • The Disappearing Island UNIT 5 • Lesson 4 73

Lesson Assessment Book 2, p. 73

UNIT 5 Lesson 4

The Disappearing Island (continued)

Oral Fluency Assessment

A New King

All the monkeys in the forest were excited. This was the day 1–12
the new leader of the monkeys would be picked. 13–21
By noon, all of the monkeys had gathered near a sacred tree. 22–33
The old King of the Monkeys was named Butu. He would help 34–45
to choose the new king. 46–50
Many monkeys wanted to be king. They climbed up and 51–60
down the sacred tree quickly. The monkey that did the best 61–71
tricks would be the new king. 72–77
One monkey climbed and jumped better than all the others. 78–87
Butu decided this monkey would be king. When the monkey 88–97
climbed to the top of the tree to receive the crown, everyone 98–109
was surprised. This monkey was a girl! Girls could not be king! 110–121
Butu thought very hard. Chota was the best climber and 122–131
jumper. Yet she was a girl. Then Butu had an idea. He said, 132–144
"Chota is the best climber and jumper, but she can not be king. 145–157
So this year, we will have a queen instead." He gave Chota the 158–170
crown. All the monkeys cheered. 171–175

EVALUATING CODES FOR ORAL FLUENCY

sky (/) words read incorrectly

blue
^ sky (^) inserted word
( ]) after the last word

READING RATE AND ACCURACY

Total Words Read: ____

Number of Errors: ____

Number of Correct Words Read Per Minute (WPM): ____

Accuracy Rate: ____

(Number of Correct Words Read per Minute ÷ Total Words Read)

READING FLUENCY

	Low	Average	High
Decoding ability	○	○	○
Pace	○	○	○
Syntax	○	○	○
Self-correction	○	○	○
Intonation	○	○	○

Record student rates on the Oral Fluency Scores pages.

74 UNIT 5 • Lesson 4 The Disappearing Island • Lesson Assessment Book 2

Lesson Assessment Book 2, p. 74

Day 1

Preparing to Read

OBJECTIVES

Students will
- ✦ identify and know the meaning of word families.
- ✦ build fluency.

MATERIALS

- ✦ ***Transparency*** 144
- ✦ Routine 10
- ✦ ***Skills Practice 2,*** pp. 137–138

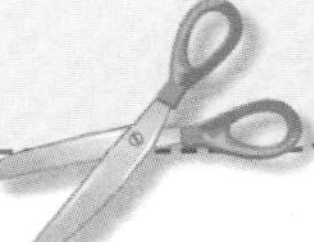

Daily Oral Practice

Daily News

Today!

When I went to the beach, my room overlooked the beautiful ocean. In the morning, I looked out and saw a lot of sand. During the day we built sand castles and swam in the water. When I looked back at the beach in the evening, it looked smaller, and the water looked closer. What happened to the beach?

- ✦ Write the daily news on the board or on chart paper. Then have a volunteer read the daily news aloud to practice fluency.
- ✦ As a word structure review from Lesson 3, ask a volunteer to identify any words in the message with affixes. *beautiful*

Word Structure

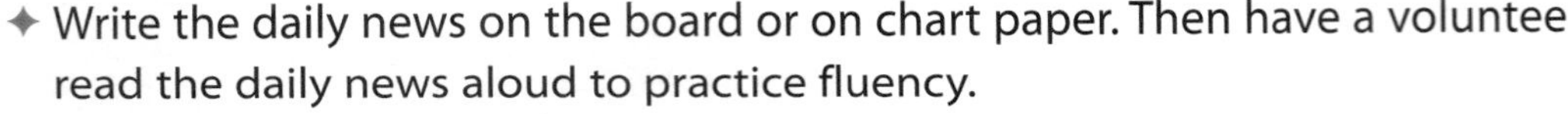

Word Families

- ✦ Write these word lines on the board or use ***Transparency*** 144. The words in boldface are in "The Disappearing Island."

Line 1	safe	safety	safer	unsafe
Line 2	**appear**	**disappear**	**disappeared**	**disappearing**
Line 3	**celebrate**	celebrated	celebrating	celebration
Line 4	imagine	**imagined**	imagining	imagination

Teacher Tip

SYLLABICATION To help students blend words and build fluency, demonstrate syllabication using the decodable, multisyllabic words in the word lines.

safe • ty	saf • er
un • safe	
ap • pear	dis • ap • pear
dis • ap • peared	dis • ap • pear • ing
cel • e • brate	cel • e • bra • ted
cel • e • bra • ting	cel • e • bra • tion
im • ag • ine	im • ag • ined
im • ag • in • ing	im • ag • i • na • tion

Lines 1–4 Word Families

Explain that base words can often have different prefixes, suffixes, or endings added to them. For example, the base word *laugh* can be changed to *laughing, laughingly, laughed, laughable,* or *laughter*. Because all of these words have the same base word, *laugh,* they form a word family. A word family is a group of words that have a common base word.

- Point out that each line of words is a word family because there is a common base word in all the words on the line. Have students identify the common base word in each line. *safe, appear, celebrate, imagine*
- As you point to the words in the lines, have students read them in unison. If students have difficulty pronouncing some words, model the correct pronunciation for them, and have them repeat after you.
- Remind students that the inflectional endings *-ed* and *-ing* are added to base verbs or actions. These endings change the tense of the verb, which means they show when the action takes place. Ask them how *-ed* and *-ing* affect the tense of verbs. *The inflectional ending* -ed *makes the verb or action take place in the past. The inflectional ending* -ing *shows that the action is continuing or ongoing*.
- Use Routine 10 for words with prefixes and suffixes to discuss the meanings of the words on the word lines. Have students discuss how each base word changes meaning, tense, or part of speech with each prefix, suffix, or ending. Remind students, if necessary, that adding *-er* to adjectives, like *safe,* makes them comparative adjectives. In using the word *safer,* you have to compare how safe one thing is to another.
- Help students start the word structure activities on ***Skills Practice 2*** pages 137–138. Read the Focus box with them and help them with the first few questions. Then have students complete the pages on their own.

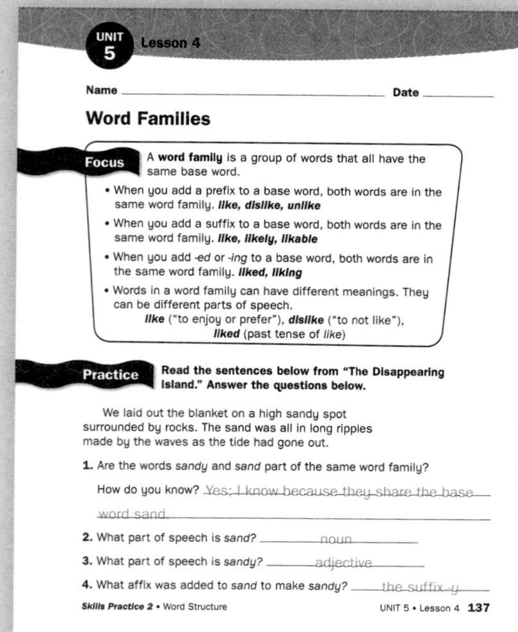

UNIT 5 Lesson 4

Name ______ Date ______

Word Families

Focus A **word family** is a group of words that all have the same base word.

- When you add a prefix to a base word, both words are in the same word family. ***like, dislike, unlike***
- When you add a suffix to a base word, both words are in the same word family. ***like, likely, likable***
- When you add *-ed* or *-ing* to a base word, both words are in the same word family. ***liked, liking***
- Words in a word family can have different meanings. They can be different parts of speech.
  like ("to enjoy or prefer"), ***dislike*** ("to not like"), ***liked*** (past tense of *like*)

Practice **Read the sentences below from "The Disappearing Island." Answer the questions below.**

We laid out the blanket on a high sandy spot surrounded by rocks. The sand was all in long ripples made by the waves as the tide had gone out.

1. Are the words *sandy* and *sand* part of the same word family? How do you know? Yes; I know because they share the base word sand.
2. What part of speech is *sand*? noun
3. What part of speech is *sandy*? adjective
4. What affix was added to *sand* to make *sandy*? the suffix -y

Skills Practice 2 • Word Structure UNIT 5 • Lesson 4 **137**

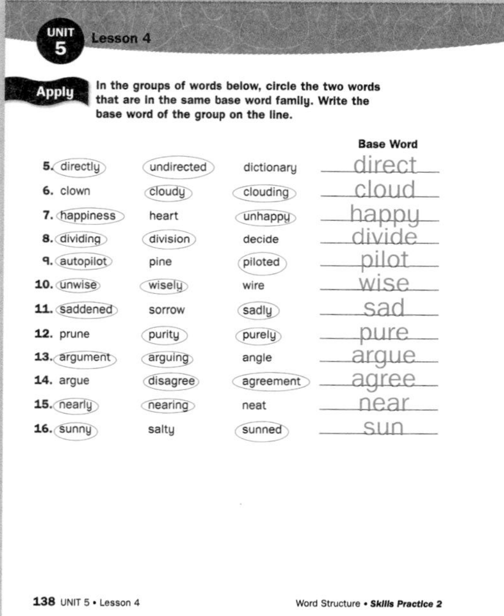

UNIT 5 Lesson 4

Apply **In the groups of words below, circle the two words that are in the same base word family. Write the base word of the group on the line.**

				Base Word
5.	directly	undirected	dictionary	direct
6.	clown	cloudy	clouding	cloud
7.	happiness	heart	unhappy	happy
8.	dividing	division	decide	divide
9.	autopilot	pine	piloted	pilot
10.	unwise	wisely	wire	wise
11.	saddened	sorrow	sadly	sad
12.	prune	purity	purely	pure
13.	argument	arguing	angle	argue
14.	argue	disagree	agreement	agree
15.	nearly	nearing	neat	near
16.	sunny	salty	sunned	sun

138 UNIT 5 • Lesson 4 Word Structure • *Skills Practice 2*

Skills Practice 2, pp. 137–138

Monitor Progress to Differentiate Instruction

Formal Assessment 

Word Structure During the word structure activity, note how well students understand the concept of word families.

	IF . . .	THEN . . .
APPROACHING LEVEL	**IF . . .** students need practice with word families,	**THEN . . .** work with them in small groups on the word structure activities on ***Reteach*** page 142 during Workshop.
	IF . . . students need extra practice with word families,	**THEN . . .** work with them in small groups on the word structure activities for Unit 5 Lesson 4 in the ***Intervention Guide*** during Workshop.
ON LEVEL	**IF . . .** students understand the concept of word families,	**THEN . . .** have them make lists of other base words and then create new word families with them during Workshop.
ABOVE LEVEL	**IF . . .** students are ready for a challenge with word families,	**THEN . . .** have them complete the word structure activities on ***Challenge Activities*** page 129 during Workshop.

Reading and Responding

OBJECTIVES

Students will
- ✦ activate prior knowledge to prepare for reading the story.
- ✦ learn selection vocabulary.
- ✦ learn the elements of realistic fiction.
- ✦ use the comprehension strategies Clarifying and Summarizing.
- ✦ investigate the theme Communities across Time using the Inquiry process.

MATERIALS

- ✦ Routines 11, 12, 14
- ✦ ***Transparency*** 5, 145
- ✦ ***Student Reader,*** Book 2, pp. 184–195
- ✦ ***Home Connection,*** pp. 57–58
- ✦ ***Lesson Assessment Book 2***

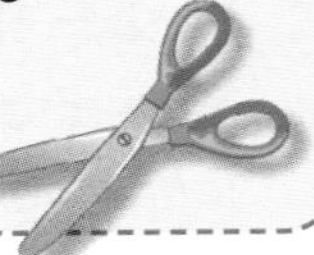

Research in Action

By the time children enter school, most of them have heard hundreds, even thousands, of stories. When they tell us about the events around them, their accounts already bear the mark of this experience. Some children's attempts to put their experience into words are still relatively unsophisticated: little more than fragmented images. Other children's narratives are more sophisticated and reflect their exposure to well-structured literary productions. Regardless of their level of sophistication, however, all children have learned a great deal about stories by the time they reach their school years, and all children have their own story to tell.

(Anne McKeough and Robbie Case)

Differentiating Instruction **English Learner**

IF . . . students are not familiar with the geography of the United States, **THEN . . .** use a classroom map to show them where Cape Cod, Massachusetts, is located.

Build Background

Activate Prior Knowledge

- ✦ Ask students if they have ever been to an island. Remind students that islands are pieces of land surrounded by water.
- ✦ Ask students what they know about tides. Explain that the tide is the rising and falling of the surface of the ocean. Tides are controlled by the ocean's attraction to the moon and the sun. High tide and low tide occur twice each day along the shores of large bodies of water.
- ✦ Tell students that erosion occurs as tides come and go.
- ✦ Ask students if they have read other books about islands, tides, or water erosion. Have students share what they have learned from these stories.
- ✦ Ask students how a story about land erosion might relate to other stories they have read in this unit so far.

Background Information

The following information may help students understand the story they are about to read:

- Tell students that Billingsgate Island is a real place located off the coast of Cape Cod, Massachusetts. In the 1800s, Billingsgate Island was a summer vacation spot and a popular fishing village. Many lighthouses were built on the island, but they were destroyed by tides and storms over the years. The island continues to erode, and geologists predict that it will completely disappear one day.
- The legendary island of Atlantis, written about by Plato, is another famous disappearing island. No one knows for sure whether Atlantis existed. Some believe it to be a myth, some believe it to be real, and others believe it was part of an island that was destroyed by a volcano. Nevertheless, over the centuries many people have searched for Atlantis and the treasures that are said to have disappeared with it.

Preview and Prepare 

ROUTINE 12

Browse

Use Routine 12, the clues, problems, and wonderings routine, to help students identify what they know before reading, what problems they may encounter while reading, and their purposes for reading. Students will chart these on a transparency.

Have students read the title and the names of the author and illustrator, and then give them a few minutes to browse the first few pages of the story. Have students use features such as the story's title and illustrations to predict what this story might have to do with communities across time.

Tell students to look for interesting words or ideas they might come across. They may point out the name of the real island, Billingsgate Island, the name Wellfleet Harbor, or the name of the boat *Aphrodite*.

Use ***Transparency*** 5 to model browsing for students. For example, a Clue might be that Billingsgate Island may be the name of the disappearing island. Under Problems, point out *mooring* as an unfamiliar word. Write *How can an island disappear?* under Wonderings. Record students' observations on the transparency as they browse the story.

Set Purposes

Encourage students to set their own purposes for reading the story. Remind students to set purposes by picking up clues from the title, illustrations, and genre of the text they are going to read. If students are having trouble, suggest that as they read, they learn about the effects the ocean's tides can have on land.

How has my community changed over time?

Before reading the story, read the Big Idea question. Tell students to keep this question in mind as they read the story.

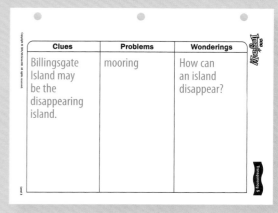

Clues	Problems	Wonderings
Billingsgate Island may be the disappearing island.	mooring	How can an island disappear?

Transparency 5

Give each student a copy of ***Home Connection*** page 57. Encourage students to discuss "The Disappearing Island" with their families and complete the activity provided. The same information is also available in Spanish on ***Home Connection*** page 58.

Differentiating Instruction: English Learner

IF . . . students have limited proficiency,
THEN . . . pair them with proficient English speakers and have the pair browse the story together.

Selection Vocabulary

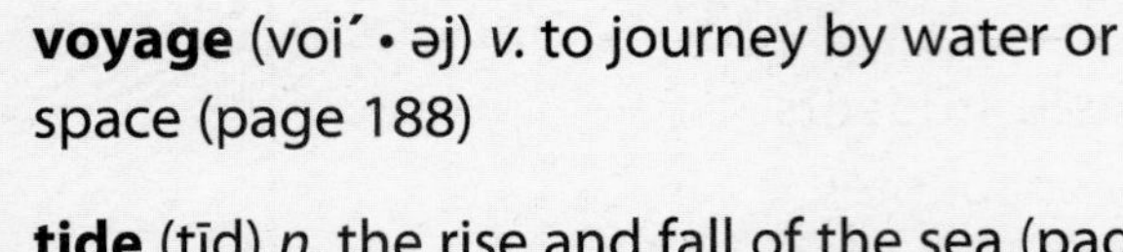

voyage (voi′ • əj) *v.* to journey by water or through space (page 188)

tide (tīd) *n.* the rise and fall of the sea (page 190)

sheltered (shel′ • tərd) *adj.* protected from danger (page 190)

ripples (rip′ • pəlz) *n.* plural form of **ripple:** a design created by waves (page 192)

eroding (ə • rōd′ • ing) *v.* wearing or washing away slowly (page 193)

acres (ā′ • kûrz) *n.* plural form of **acre:** a measurement equal to 43,560 square feet (page 194)

claim (klām) *v.* to take as one's own (page 194)

toppled (top′ • pəld) *v.* past tense of **topple:** to fall or make fall forward (page 195)

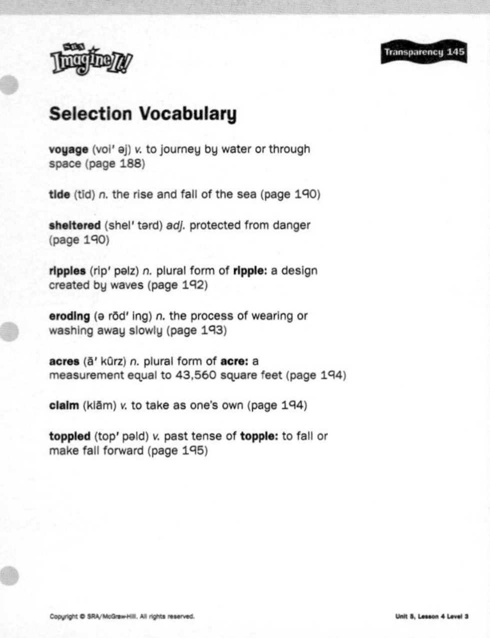

Imagine It! Transparency 145

Selection Vocabulary

voyage (voi′ əj) *v.* to journey by water or through space (page 188)

tide (tīd) *n.* the rise and fall of the sea (page 190)

sheltered (shel′ tərd) *adj.* protected from danger (page 190)

ripples (rip′ pəlz) *n.* plural form of **ripple:** a design created by waves (page 192)

eroding (ə rōd′ ing) *n.* the process of wearing or washing away slowly (page 193)

acres (ā′ kûrz) *n.* plural form of **acre:** a measurement equal to 43,560 square feet (page 194)

claim (klām) *v.* to take as one's own (page 194)

toppled (top′ pəld) *v.* past tense of **topple:** to fall or make fall forward (page 195)

Copyright © SRA/McGraw-Hill. All rights reserved. Unit 5, Lesson 4 Level 3

Transparency 145

Differentiating Instruction English Learner

IF . . . students have difficulty pronouncing the plural endings in the selection vocabulary words *ripples* and *acres,* **THEN . . .** remember to explain that in some words the plural *-s* has the /z/ sound.

Building Vocabulary

ROUTINE 11

Using Routine 11, the selection vocabulary process, have students read aloud the Vocabulary Warm-Up on ***Student Reader,*** Book 2 pages 184–185.

As students read, have them stop to blend any difficult or unfamiliar words. Provide students with the pronunciation of words that are not decodable or that they cannot read automatically or fluently.

Guided Vocabulary Practice

Ask students to identify the highlighted vocabulary words they figured out using the vocabulary strategy Word Structure. **Possible Answers** *sheltered, toppled, rippled, eroding* Have students explain how they figured out the meaning of the other vocabulary words as they read the Vocabulary Warm-Up.

Display ***Transparency*** 145, and have students read the words and definitions. Return to the Vocabulary Warm-Up, and read the sentences containing the vocabulary words with students. Then, if necessary, provide a brief in-context explanation of the words.

Use the vocabulary words on ***Transparency*** 145 to create fill-in-the-blank sentences. Have students fill in the appropriate vocabulary words. For example, "When it began to rain, we stopped playing and looked for ________ spots so we could stay dry." *sheltered*

Read the story to find the meanings of these words, which are also in "The Disappearing Island":

- sheltered
- voyage
- acres
- toppled
- ripples
- claim
- tide
- eroding

Vocabulary Strategy

Word Structure is when parts of a word help you understand the word's meaning. Use word structure to find the meaning of *eroding*.

184

Vocabulary Warm-Up

Raini peered out from his sheltered nook beneath the palm fronds he had lashed together. "Today," he thought, "I will voyage to the other side of the island." There were still acres of land he had not yet explored.

"I must stay positive," Raini commanded himself. "I will get off this island. I will make my way back home."

He set off on his investigation. It seemed like hours passed before he had any luck, but what he found was worth waiting for. A small wooden boat lay ahead of him!

Raini hurried toward the boat, but he toppled in the sand. The faster he tried to go, the more he fell. Would he ever reach it? He struggled forward.

Finally, Raini came to the boat and began to inspect it. He moved his hands along the ripples in the worn wood. There was trouble—a large gash near the bow. The back of the boat seemed to be in good order, though. Raini believed he could patch the hole. He did not know who owned the boat, but he decided he would claim it.

"The tide is in," thought Raini. "I need to leave soon, while the water is high!" However, as Raini packed the gash with shrubbery and mud, it seemed to grow. This hole he could not fix started eroding his hopes of ever getting off the island.

Suddenly, Raini heard a voice. Who could it be? He strained to hear. "Raini! Raini!" someone called urgently. It was his mother's voice! "Raini," she said, "it's time to wake up! You'll miss the bus if you don't get ready soon."

GAME

Writing Sentences

Use each vocabulary word in two sentences. First, use the word in a sentence that asks a question. Then use the word in a sentence that is a statement. Write your sentences on a sheet of paper.

Concept Vocabulary

The concept word for this lesson is ***property*. Property** is land that a person owns. What makes some property worth more than other property? How does a property's location affect its value? Discuss your ideas with the class.

185

Discuss the concept vocabulary word *property* with students. Ask students how they think the word *property* relates to the theme Communities across Time. As students read the selections in this unit, encourage them to think about other words that relate to the theme. Students can record these words in the vocabulary section of their Writer's Notebooks.

GAME

Have students play the Writing Sentences game during Small-Group Time.

Differentiating Instruction — English Learner

IF . . . students have difficulty playing the Writing Sentences game, **THEN . . .** be sure to place English Learners in groups with at least two proficient English speakers.

Concept/Question Board

As students read "The Disappearing Island," encourage them to post questions, answers, comments, or other items related to communities across time on the **Concept/Question Board.**

Monitor Progress

Formal Assessment

Comprehension Observation Log Observe individual students as they read, and use the Comprehension Observation Log, located in ***Lesson Assessment Book 2,*** to record anecdotal information about each student's strengths and weaknesses.

Differentiating Instruction English Learner

IF . . . students need help contributing to the **Concept/Question Board**, **THEN . . .** remind them to post materials in their native languages.

Reading the Selection 

Genre Realistic Fiction

Have students identify the genre of "The Disappearing Island." *realistic fiction* If necessary, remind students of the following elements of realistic fiction:

- The characters behave as people do in real life.
- The setting of the story is a real place or could be a real place.
- The events in the story could happen in real life.

Comprehension Strategies

1st READ

Prompt the use of the following comprehension strategies during the first reading of "The Disappearing Island":

- Clarifying
- Summarizing

Comprehension Strategies Rubrics

Use the Informal Comprehension Strategies Rubrics to determine whether a student is using any of the strategies listed below. Note the strategies a student is using, instead of the degree to which a student might be using any particular strategy. In addition, encourage the student to tell of any strategies other than the ones being taught that he or she is using.

Clarifying

- ✦ The student recognizes when a word or idea is not making sense.
- ✦ The student uses decoding skills to read unfamiliar words.
- ✦ The student uses structural elements in words to read them.
- ✦ The student uses structural elements, context, and questioning to clarify the meanings of unfamiliar words.

Summarizing

- ✦ The student retells information from the story.
- ✦ The student paraphrases or puts the main ideas and details in his or her own words.
- ✦ The student gives a summary that includes only the important or main ideas.
- ✦ The student recognizes when the same ideas are included more than once in a summary and deletes them.

Monitor Progress to Differentiate Instruction

Formal Assessment 

Comprehension Skill Note students' understanding of the comprehension skill Cause and Effect as they read.

APPROACHING LEVEL

IF . . . students are having difficulty understanding cause and effect as they read,

THEN . . . have them create a two-column chart in their Writer's Notebooks. In the first column, have students list actions they performed this week. In the second column, have students list the effects of those actions.

ON LEVEL

IF . . . students are gaining an understanding of cause and effect as they read,

THEN . . . have them create a two-column chart in their Writer's Notebooks. In the first column, have students list three causes they read about in "The Disappearing Island." Then have students trade their papers with a partner, and have the partners fill in the correct effect for each cause.

ABOVE LEVEL

IF . . . students are demonstrating an understanding of cause and effect as they read,

THEN . . . have students write a short essay about physical changes they would like to make to the land in their communities. For example, you could ask students *What would the effects be if a park were added to my community? What would the effects be if everyone had access to places where they could grow their own vegetables?*

Teacher Tip

DECODING As they read, make sure students are recognizing and using their word structure and basic syllabication rules to help them decode unfamiliar words.

Comprehension Skills

Reread "The Disappearing Island" using the following comprehension skills:

- Author's Purpose
- Cause and Effect

Reading with a Writer's Eye

During the rereading of "The Disappearing Island," explain the following literary elements:

- Language Use
- Theme

Focus Questions

Have students read aloud the Focus Questions on page 187 of the ***Student Reader,*** Book 2. Encourage students to think about the Focus Questions as they read "The Disappearing Island."

Reading Recommendation

ROUTINE 14

Oral Reading

Use Routine 14, the reading the selection routine, as you read the entire story. As you read, stop to ask and answer questions. Point out how the pictures reflect the story. Share the images that pop up in your mind as you read and how points in the reading relate to ideas you already know.

The beautiful and descriptive language of this story and its conversational style make it ideal for oral reading.

Technology

eSTUDENT READER Students can access ***SRA Imagine It! Student Reader*** electronically by using the ***eStudent Reader*** online or on CD-ROM.

Genre
Realistic Fiction
involves stories about people and events that are true to life and that could really happen.
Comprehension Skill
Cause and Effect
As you read, think about what causes certain events to happen.
186
The DISAPPEARING Island
by Corinne Demas
illustrated by Ted Lewin
Focus Questions
What physical or environmental changes could cause a community to disappear? What do communities do to survive major changes in their environments?
187

Students will read the story twice over a four-day period.

Day 1 **ORAL READ** Have students read the first half of the story. Prompt the use of the comprehension strategies.

Day 2 **ORAL READ** Have students finish reading the story. Continue to prompt the comprehension strategies.

Day 3 **SILENT READ** Have students reread the story silently. Have students focus on comprehension skills and Reading with a Writer's Eye.

Day 4 **SILENT READ** Have students finish rereading the story.

Differentiating Instruction **English Learner**

IF . . . students would benefit from hearing "The Disappearing Island" before it is read to the class, **THEN . . .** have them listen to the story on ***Listening Library CDs*** during Workshop.

Reading and Responding

For my ninth birthday my grandma gave me a small box. Inside was a perfect sand dollar and a note. The note said:

To celebrate your birthday we will voyage out to the disappearing island where I found this sand dollar when I was just your age.

"How can an island disappear?" I asked.

Grandma laughed. "When I take you out to Billingsgate Island, Carrie, you'll see," she said.

I'd been all around Wellfleet Harbor in Grandma's boat, but this time we were going to go farther out, into Cape Cod Bay, just the two of us, farther than I'd ever been before. 1

188

Grandma's boat is named *Aphrodite,* after the goddess of love who first rose out of the sea foam. It's painted the blue of the sea on the outside and the blue of the sky on the inside.

The next day we rowed out to *Aphrodite* in a rubber boat so small our legs were in a tangle.

We clambered aboard *Aphrodite,* and Grandma hooked the rubber boat to the mooring. To get the 2 old outboard motor started she had to pull the rope nearly ten times. Her arms are all muscles from clamming and swimming and pulling. We put on our life jackets, and I sat up on the bow and pretended I was a figurehead on one of the old ships that used to come into Wellfleet Harbor. Water sprayed me, but it was a hot day so I didn't mind.

189

Word Structure

Word families: celebrate/celebrated/celebrating, disappearing/disappear/disappeared, clambered/clamber/clambering

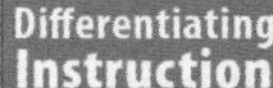

Differentiating Instruction — English Learner

IF . . . students have difficulty understanding the word *clarify*, **THEN . . .** provide a few synonyms, such as *explain*, *help us understand*, and *make more clear*.

1st READ

Comprehension Strategies

This story is broken into two parts. On the first day, read pages 188–195. On the second day, read pages 196–201.

1 Clarifying Teacher Prompt: *Has anyone clarified any words in the text?*
Possible Student Response *I'm not sure what Wellfleet Harbor is, so I'm going to look up the word* harbor *in the dictionary. I see; a harbor is a place where boats can anchor or dock. Wellfleet Harbor must be where Carrie's grandma keeps her boat.*

2 Clarifying Teacher Prompt: *Does anyone have a word they need to clarify?*
Possible Student Response *I don't know what* mooring *means. The text says that Grandma hooked the rubber boat to the mooring, so maybe it's part of the dock. I'll look that word up in the dictionary, too, just to be sure. The word* moor *is a verb that means "to fasten by using ropes, cables, or anchors." Adding the suffix* -ing *to the word makes the word a noun. So a mooring is a place where boats can be fastened.*

When the tide is high in Wellfleet Harbor, the water is way over my head. When the tide is low, it just comes up to my middle. Grandma has a tide chart on her wall. It's like a calendar for the sea. There's low tide and high tide twice a day, and every day it's an hour different. The tide was going out now. A cormorant was drying out its feathers on a rock that hadn't been there an hour before. When we rode out beyond the sheltered part of Wellfleet Harbor, the waves got higher and I went to sit in the back of the boat with Grandma.

"I don't see any island," I said. ❸

She passed me the binoculars. "Keep looking straight ahead," she told me. "At high tide it is completely covered by water. It begins to appear as the tide goes out."

Finally we got close enough so I could see it: a flat stretch of beach out in the middle of the sea. We pulled into a cove, and Grandma anchored *Aphrodite*. We waded to shore, carrying our lunch basket and beach blanket.

190 191

❸ **Clarifying** Teacher Prompt: *Who needs to stop and clarify information on this page?* **Possible Student Response** *What is a cormorant? Oh, I see. The text says that it was drying out its feathers, so it must be a bird. But I'm still not sure why the rock it was sitting on hadn't been there an hour before. I'm going to reread this paragraph to see if I can figure it out. It says that when the tide is high, the water comes over Carrie's head. When it is low, it comes to her middle. The water is rising and falling with the tides. So that must mean that it is now low tide and the bird can sit on the rock because the water is lower. An hour before, it was high tide and the rock was covered by the water.*

Comprehension Check

Why does Grandma have a tide chart on her wall? **Possible Answer** *It is like a calendar so she knows when the tides will be high and when they will be low. Why does the island begin to appear as the tide goes out?* **Possible Answer** *The water is getting lower and the island can be seen again.*

Teacher Tip

CLARIFICATION Encourage students to clarify unfamiliar words or concepts as they read. If students do not ask for clarification and you think there are things that they may not understand, prompt them to ask for clarification.

Word Structure

Word families: sheltered/shelter/sheltering, looking/look/looked, waded/wade/wading

Reading and Responding

We laid out the blanket on a high sandy spot surrounded by rocks—the foundation for the old lighthouse, Grandma said. Then we went off to explore the island.

There were no buildings, no trees, not even a blade of grass. Just sand. The sand was all in long ripples made by the waves as the tide had gone out. I ran as far as I could run without stopping to catch my breath. Grandma ran beside me.

"A century ago, this island was a mile long," Grandma explained. "This was a busy fishing community, and there were thirty-five homes here and a school. There were meadows and gardens. When the sea started eroding the island, people moved off and took their houses with them. When I was a little girl, my dad used to take me out here to go clamming. There was more of the island than there is now, but no one lived here anymore." 4

192

193

Word Structure

Word families: surrounded/surround/surrounding, stopping/stop/stopped, fishing/fish/fished, charred/char/charring, hiked/hike/hiking

Differentiating Instruction **English Learner**

IF . . . students are unclear about what the phrase people *moved off* on page 193 means, **THEN . . .** restate the expression, saying *people moved away*.

Comprehension Strategies

4 Clarifying Teacher Prompt: *Does anyone need to stop and clarify?* **Possible Student Response** *Why did the people who lived on the island leave? I'm going to reread this paragraph. Grandma says that the sea started eroding the island and then people moved off. I think* eroding *is in the same word family as* erosion. Erosion *means "the process of being torn away." So the sea is tearing away the island, and that is why the people had to move.*

Comprehension Check

Why did the people who built the second lighthouse think it would be safe? **Possible Answer** *They built it out of brick and farther inland.* *Why didn't the breakwater work at keeping the lighthouse safe?* **Possible Answer** *The sea just came around it.*

We were the only ones on the island except for the gulls and the terns. There were shells everywhere: jingle shells and quahogs, razor clams and channeled whelks. Mussels, tiny as ants, covered the stones in the acres of tidal pools. They looked like black fur. 5

I found a broken brick, half buried in the sand. One side of it had been charred.

"This was from someone's chimney," Grandma said.

"May I keep it?"

"Sure. The sea would claim it soon enough."

We hiked back to our blanket, and nearby I saw a strange, rusty creature that looked like the backbone of a whale.

"It's the metal spiral staircase from the old lighthouse, lying on its side," Grandma told me. It was too big for us to carry back to safety on the mainland.

"That was the second lighthouse out here. The first one toppled into the sea. They built this one farther inland and they built it out of brick. They thought it would last forever, but the sea kept taking more and more of the island. They built a big breakwater out of rocks, but the sea just came around it."

Grandma pointed to a curve of gray rocks that were covered with barnacles that looked like white lace. 6

194 195

5 Clarifying Teacher Prompt: *Are there any words that you need to clarify?*
Possible Student Response *What are quahogs and whelks? I'm going to have to look those up in a dictionary.* Quahogs *are clams and* whelks *are snails. No wonder Carrie is finding those on the island.*

6 Summarizing Teacher Prompt: *Who can summarize the story for the class?*
Possible Student Response *Grandma is taking Carrie to a disappearing island for her birthday. The island is disappearing because the tides are eroding away the island. Nobody lives on the island anymore, and Carrie and Grandma are exploring it.*

Teacher Tip

COMPREHENSION Ask students the following questions to make sure they understand the story.

- *Can you summarize what you have read?*
- *Does what you are reading make sense?*

Vocabulary Tip

Point out the words *acres* and *toppled* in the text. Ask students what strategies readers can use to figure out the meaning of the word *acres*. Ask students how visualizing what a tall lighthouse would do if it went into the sea helps them remember the meaning of the word *toppled*.

STOP You have read the first half of the story. Continue the story tomorrow on page T288.

Lesson 4 **Inquiry Planner**

STEP 5: Collecting Information

Day 1 With their groups, students will collect resources and information about their investigation questions and topics.

Day 2 Groups will continue collecting information for their investigations. Students will also read "The Disappearing Island" for more information about the unit theme.

Day 3 With the whole group, discuss how ideas in "The Disappearing Island" relate to students' conjectures.

Day 4 Groups will continue collecting information and finalize their presentation ideas.

Day 5 With their groups, students will continue collecting information to use for their group presentation.

Inquiry Process

Step 5—Collecting Information

Whole Group

Whole-Group Time

- ✦ Remind students that their groups should now have a question, a conjecture, some sources for their investigation, and some information from the unit selections and group discussions. Tell them they should continue collecting information to use in some kind of presentation. Encourage students to use the Internet sources they listed on ***Skills Practice 2***, page 128.

- ✦ As groups collect information for their investigations, they need to start thinking about the kind of presentation they want to give at the end of the unit. For each group, suggest possibilities for the kinds of presentations they could give based on the nature of their investigations, but allow them to choose how they want to present the results of their Inquiry. Some presentation possibilities include making posters with photographs, illustrations, charts, graphs, and diagrams; oral presentations with visuals; creating a community timeline, coming up with a community plan of action to deal with a local problem; or written reports that try to answer an investigation question.

- ✦ If possible, arrange to have a speaker or expert visit the class to provide students with more information about their investigation topics. Have students review the skills for listening and responding to presentations. Or you could have students review the interviewing skills they learned and have them interview the guest.

- ✦ Throughout the remaining time in this unit, meet with each group to arrange schedules, discuss problems that students are encountering, hear preliminary presentation ideas, and discuss interesting findings.

Small-Group Time

Small Group

- Meet with each group individually to provide guidance and ensure that they are collecting information, carrying out or revising their plans, and developing final presentation ideas.
- Each group should review any notes in their Writer's Notebooks to see what information they still might need to answer their research questions and evaluate their conjectures.
- Help groups by showing them where to go and how to collect any sources of information they need for their inquiries. You may want to provide time for students to visit the school or community library and, if possible, computer time for Internet research.

Concept/Question Board

Have students write information, ideas, sources of information, quotes, or questions on the **Concept/Question Board.** Students might

- share information they learned from a class speaker or a trip to the library.
- post new ideas learned from whole group or small group discussions.
- post magazine or newspaper articles about important community events or organizations.
- post photographs, illustrations, timelines, or diagrams about things related to the theme.
- list television programs or movies related to the theme. Have students include summaries of the important information about the theme in the program.

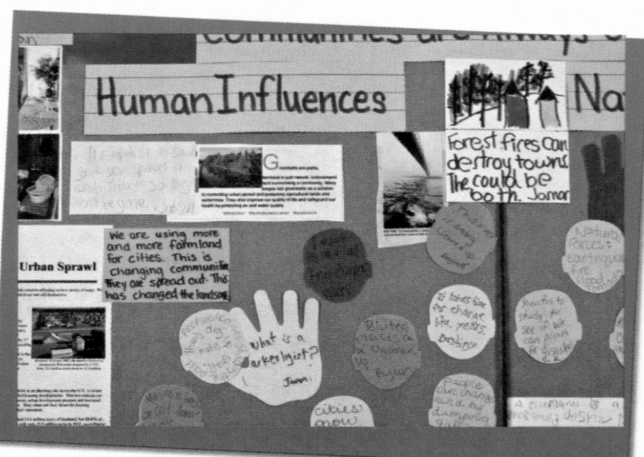

Teacher Tip

COLLECTING INFORMATION As students begin collecting information, review their understanding of different sources and how they are used. For example, tell students that the title of a nonfiction book should give them an idea of the kind of information contained in the book and whether the book will provide the kind of information they need.

Day 1

Language Arts

OBJECTIVES

Students will
- ✦ prewrite ideas for directions.
- ✦ take the spelling pretest.
- ✦ practice cursive *D* and *B.*

MATERIALS

- ✦ ***Language Arts Handbook,*** pp. 101–103
- ✦ ***Transparency*** 146
- ✦ ***Skills Practice 2,*** p. 147
- ✦ Routine 16

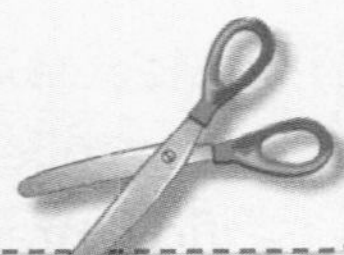

Writing Directions  

ROUTINE 16

Prewriting

Teach

- ✦ Ask students to discuss the directions they wrote in Unit 4. Remind students that when giving directions, you are explaining to someone how to go from one location to another.
- ✦ Ask students to share some of the specific words used when giving directions. *right, left, straight, blocks* or *streets.*
- ✦ Students should also incorporate cardinal directions and landmarks into their directions.
- ✦ Explain to students that visualizing the directions will help them give better directions. Remind students that presenting the directions in the correct order is important when giving directions.
- ✦ For more information on directions, see ***Language Arts Handbook*** pages 101–103.

Guided Practice

- ✦ Brainstorm with students directions they might want to give to someone. Examples might include directions from home to school or from school to home, directions to another school, directions to the park, or directions to a friend's house.
- ✦ Have students turn to ***Skills Practice 2*** page 147, and read the Think section as a class. Have students answer the questions.
- ✦ Select a location that most students are familiar with to use as your model. Use Routine 16, and draw a graphic organizer on the board or chart paper like the one on page 147 in ***Skills Practice 2*** to model inserting information for your directions. Have students help you insert the information.

Giving Directions

When you give someone directions, you tell the person how to get somewhere. You may use words such as *right, left,* and *straight* to clearly explain to your reader. If you are telling someone how to go a long distance, you might also use the word *blocks* or use street names.

To get started, picture a map in your head of the directions you are giving. Imagine you are following the directions yourself. Order is very important. One wrong turn, and your reader is lost!

Nick's mom was coming to help in his classroom. Nick was going to write directions for her. First, he thought about how to get to his room from the front door of the school. This is what he wrote.

turn left
down second hallway
turn right
first hallway

Expository Writing • Giving Directions 101

Language Arts Handbook, p. 101

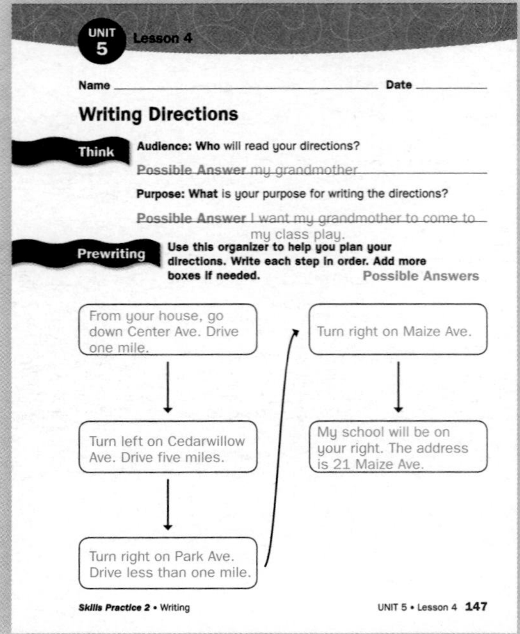

UNIT 5 Lesson 4

Name ______ Date ______

Writing Directions

Think **Audience:** Who will read your directions?

Possible Answer my grandmother

Purpose: What is your purpose for writing the directions?

Possible Answer I want my grandmother to come to my class play.

Prewriting **Use this organizer to help you plan your directions. Write each step in order. Add more boxes if needed.** Possible Answers

From your house, go down Center Ave. Drive one mile.

Turn left on Cedarwillow Ave. Drive five miles.

Turn right on Park Ave. Drive less than one mile.

Turn right on Maize Ave.

My school will be on your right. The address is 21 Maize Ave.

Skills Practice 2 • Writing UNIT 5 • Lesson 4 147

Skills Practice 2, p. 147

Writing, continued

Apply

Have students complete page 147 in ***Skills Practice 2*** as a prewriting activity.

Assessment

You will use the Writing Rubrics found in the Level Appendix to evaluate students' directions. You may use any of the rubrics for Genre, Writing Process, and Writing Traits. Share with students what you will be looking for when assessing their directions.

Monitor Progress to Differentiate Instruction

Formal Assessment 

Brainstorming Note whether students select a destination and audience for their directions.

APPROACHING LEVEL

IF . . . students need to brainstorm ideas,	**THEN . . .** have them create a list of all the places they are familiar with during Workshop.

ON LEVEL

IF . . . students have selected their location,	**THEN . . .** have them work with someone who is less familiar with the surrounding area.

ABOVE LEVEL

IF . . . students need a challenge,	**THEN . . .** have them view different maps of their location during Workshop.

Spelling

Word Families, Multisyllabic Words, and Silent Consonants Pretest

Teach

Say the sentences below aloud. Have students write the spelling words on a separate sheet of paper. When they are finished, have them correct any misspelled words.

Pretest Sentences

1. I **live** only five miles away from school.
2. The clown ended his act with a **lively** dance.
3. It would be fun to **relive** a roller coaster ride.
4. How long have you been **living** in California?
5. She happily received the **honor.**
6. Telling the truth is an **honorable** thing to do.
7. People always appreciate an **honest** leader.
8. **Honesty** is an admirable quality.
9. Are you taking a **direct** flight?
10. The **director** will tell you when to sing.
11. Which **direction** is the beach from here?
12. The ivy plant grows best in **indirect** sunlight.
13. I **doubt** that our team will win this game.
14. I am **doubtful** that it will snow today.
15. The law of gravity is **undoubted.**

Challenge Sentences

16. Do you **know** what time it is?
17. There are many **unknown** planets.
18. Grandma's cooking **knowledge** is great.

Diagnose any misspellings by determining whether students misspelled any words from the word families, any silent consonants or some other part of the word. Then have students use the pretest as a take-home list to study the spellings of words from each word family and words with silent consonants.

Penmanship

Cursive Letters *D* and *B*

Teach

- Remind students that cursive letters are made of four types of strokes (undercurve, overcurve, downcurve, and slant lines). Draw each one of the strokes on the board.
- Introduce capital cursive *D* as a letter with loops and capital *B* as an undercurve slant letter.
- Display ***Transparency*** 146. Using a pointer, trace the letters while saying the formations aloud.
  - **Letter *D*** Starting point, slant down
Loop, curve down and up
Loop and curve right: capital *D*
  - **Letter *B*** Starting point, undercurve
Slant down, retrace up
Curve forward, loop
Curve forward and back
Curve right: capital *B*
- On the board, write capital cursive *D* and *B*, saying the strokes aloud as you form the letters.

Guided Practice

Tell students to hold their index fingers in the air in front of them. Say the strokes aloud as you trace the letters, and have students mimic your movements as if they were writing in the air.

Apply

Have students practice writing each of the letters four times. Ask them to circle the best formation of each of their letters.

Teacher Tips

PENMANSHIP If students are having problems forming cursive *D* or *B*, or their letters are floating between the lines, then review proper paper position, check to make sure students are holding their pencils correctly, or review letter formation.

CONNECTING *D* Show how to connect cursive *D* to other letters.

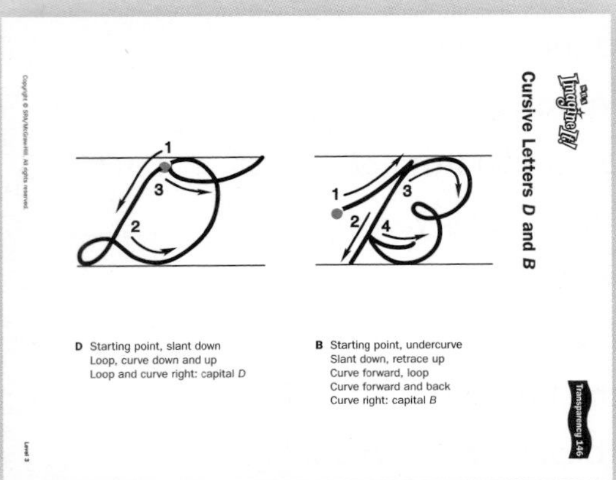

Transparency 146

Differentiating Instruction — English Learner

IF . . . students have difficulty with handwriting, **THEN . . .** keep in mind that some students may be more familiar with other writing systems than they are with the Roman alphabet. Be alert for students who need extra help with handwriting.

Skills Traces

Preparing to Read

Word Structure: Word Families

Introduced in Grade 2, Unit 5, Lesson 5

Grade 3
Reviewed: Unit 5, Lesson 4
Practiced: Unit 5, Lesson 5
Assessed: ***Lesson Assessment Book 2,*** p. 67

Word Structure: Multisyllablic Words

Grade 3
Introduced: Unit 5, Lesson 4
Practiced: Unit 5, Lesson 5

Word Structure: Silent Consonants

Grade 3
Introduced: Unit 1, Lesson 5
Practiced: Unit 5, Lesson 4

Reading and Responding

Comprehension Skill: Author's Purpose

Introduced in Grade 2, Unit 2, Lesson 1

Grade 3
Reviewed: Unit 1, Lesson 2
Practiced: Unit 5, Lesson 4
Assessed: ***Lesson Assessment Book 2,*** pp. 68–70

Reviewed in Grade 4, Unit 1, Lesson 4

Comprehension Skill: Cause and Effect

Reviewed in Grade 2, Unit 2, Lesson 3

Grade 3
Reviewed: Unit 1, Lesson 1
Practiced: Unit 5, Lesson 4
Assessed: ***Lesson Assessment Book 2,*** pp. 68–70

Reviewed in Grade 4, Unit 1, Lesson 3

Comprehension Strategy: Clarifying

Reviewed in Grade 2, Unit 1, Lesson 3

Grade 3
Reviewed: Unit 1, Lesson 5
Practiced: Unit 5, Lesson 4
Assessed: Unit 5, Lesson 4, p. T272

Reviewed in Grade 4, Unit 1, Lesson 4

Comprehension Strategy: Summarizing

Reviewed in Grade 2, Unit 1, Lesson 2

Grade 3
Reviewed: Unit 1, Lesson 2
Practiced: Unit 5, Lesson 4
Assessed: Unit 5, Lesson 4, p. T273

Reviewed in Grade 4, Unit 1, Lesson 2

Language Arts

Writing: Writing Directions

Reviewed in Grade 2, Unit 3, Lesson 3

Grade 3
Reviewed: Unit 4, Lesson 3
Practiced: Unit 5, Lesson 4
Assessed: Unit 5, Lesson 4, p. T330

Grammar, Usage, and Mechanics: Irregular Verb "to be"

Grade 3
Introduced: Unit 5, Lesson 4
Assessed: ***Lesson Assessment Book 2,*** p. 72

Reviewed in Grade 4, Unit 4, Lesson 1

Preparing to Read

OBJECTIVES

Students will
- ✦ identify and know the meaning of word families.
- ✦ build fluency.

MATERIALS

- ✦ ***Transparency*** 144
- ✦ Routine 10

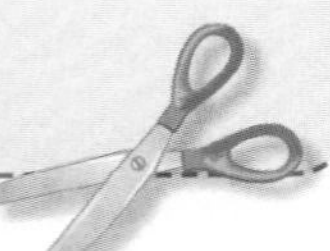

Daily Oral Practice

Daily News

Today!

Carrie is going on an exploration of the island. What do you think she will find? She could find parts of old lighthouses or sea creatures on the beach. Maybe she'll find a buried treasure! What would you look for on a disappearing island?

- ✦ Write the daily news on the board or on chart paper. Then have students read the daily news in unison to practice fluency.
- ✦ As a review of yesterday's word structure lesson, ask a volunteer to identify any words in the message that are part of a word family. *going, exploration, buried, disappearing* Ask students to identify the base word of the family to which these words belong. *go, explore, bury, appear*

Word Structure 

ROUTINE 10

Word Families

✦ Use ***Transparency*** 144 with these word lines from Day 1.

Line 1	safe	safety	safer	unsafe
Line 2	appear	disappear	disappeared	disappearing
Line 3	celebrate	celebrated	celebrating	celebration
Line 4	imagine	imagined	imagining	imagination

✦ Review the meaning of word families. If necessary, remind students that words with the same base word are part of a word family. All the words on Line 1, for example, are in the same word family because they all come from the same base word, *safe*.

✦ Use Routine 10 to review how prefixes and suffixes change word meaning.

Developing Oral Language

Use any or all of the following activities to help students practice reading the words from the word lines.

- Have a volunteer select a word from the lines and use it in a sentence. **Possible Answer** *It's very* unsafe *to ride a bike without a helmet.* Then have that student select a volunteer to use a different form of the word in a new sentence. **Possible Answer** *A bike helmet is for a biker's own* safety. Continue until all of the words have been used.
- Have a volunteer point to a word and use it in a sentence. **Possible Answer** *Sometimes my* imagination *runs wild.* Then select a volunteer to choose a different word from the board and use it in a sentence that extends the story of the first sentence. **Possible Answer** *I once* imagined *that I was a cyclone wind cloud.* Have volunteers use the remaining words in sentences that continue the story.
- Give students other examples of base words, such as *help, cycle, agree, climb, type*, or *desire*. Then ask students to name other words that could be in the same family as these words. **Possible Answers** *cycling, bicycle, cyclist, bicyclist, motorcycle; desirable, desireless, desiring, desired, undesirable* Have students define any examples they give, based on what affixes the words have.

Differentiating Instruction — English Learner

IF . . . students have difficulty blending words, **THEN . . .** keep in mind that syllabication rules vary among languages. Provide English learners with extra practice breaking words into syllables and blending the syllables to decode words. Demonstrate the process, and have students repeat each step after you.

Monitor Progress 

to Differentiate Instruction
Formal Assessment

Word Structure During the word structure activity, note how well students understand the words.

APPROACHING LEVEL

IF . . . students do not understand the words on the word lines, **THEN . . .** use pictures, photos, objects, stick drawings, or pantomime to help them visualize the words.

ON LEVEL

IF . . . students need practice with the words on the word lines, **THEN . . .** have them write sentences using the words on the lines.

ABOVE LEVEL

IF . . . students understand the words on the word lines, **THEN . . .** have them make a list of other words within these word families or other words and their word families.

Reading and Responding

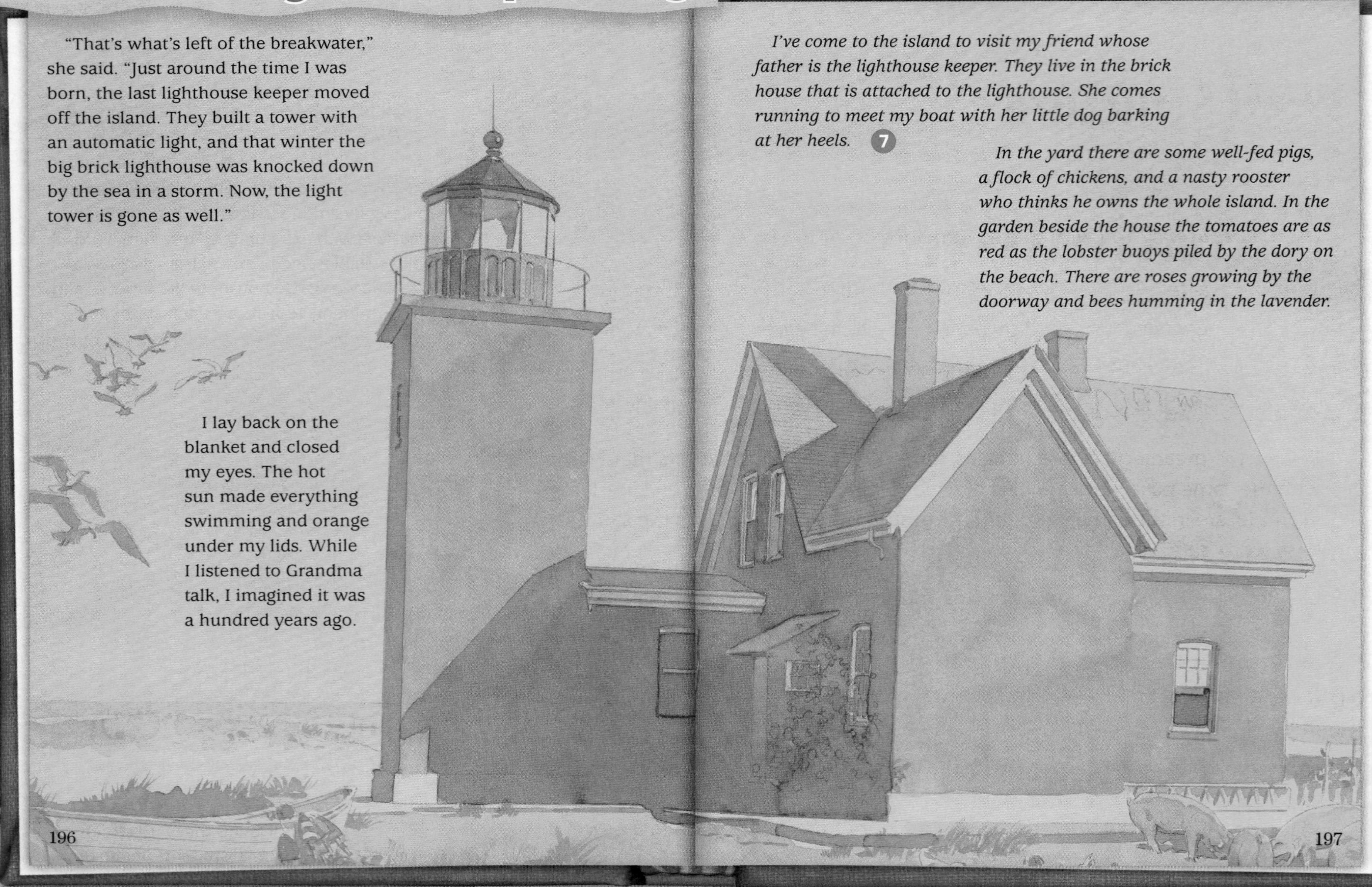

"That's what's left of the breakwater," she said. "Just around the time I was born, the last lighthouse keeper moved off the island. They built a tower with an automatic light, and that winter the big brick lighthouse was knocked down by the sea in a storm. Now, the light tower is gone as well."

I lay back on the blanket and closed my eyes. The hot sun made everything swimming and orange under my lids. While I listened to Grandma talk, I imagined it was a hundred years ago.

I've come to the island to visit my friend whose father is the lighthouse keeper. They live in the brick house that is attached to the lighthouse. She comes running to meet my boat with her little dog barking at her heels. 7

In the yard there are some well-fed pigs, a flock of chickens, and a nasty rooster who thinks he owns the whole island. In the garden beside the house the tomatoes are as red as the lobster buoys piled by the dory on the beach. There are roses growing by the doorway and bees humming in the lavender.

196 197

OBJECTIVES

Students will

- use the comprehension strategies Clarifying and Summarizing.
- discuss the story using the handing-off process.
- review genre, vocabulary, and fluency.

MATERIALS

- ***Student Reader,*** Book 2, pp. 196–203
- Routine A
- ***Skills Practice 2,*** pp. 141–142
- ***Transparencies*** 5, 145

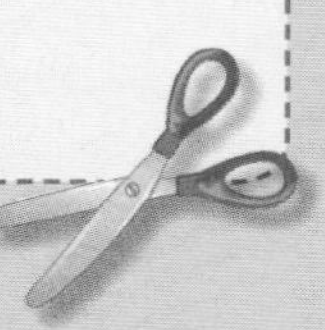

Comprehension Strategies

7 **Clarifying** Teacher Prompt: *I'm not sure why part of the text is written in italics. Can anyone help me clarify why this part is in italics?* **Possible Student Response** *Carrie is lying on her blanket imagining what the island would have been like a hundred years ago. Then the italics part tells about her visiting her friend on the island. I think I understand why this part of the text is written differently. The part that is different is Carrie's daydream. It's like a play in her head.*

Comprehension Check

Why was an automatic light put up on the island? **Possible Answer** *The lighthouse keeper moved away. An automatic light could operate without a person being there.*
What is Carrie daydreaming about? **Possible Answer** *She is daydreaming about what it would have been like visiting the island a hundred years ago.*

Inside the lighthouse it is cool as a cave. It takes a while for my eyes to adjust to the darkness. We climb up the spiral staircase to the top of the lighthouse and step ouside into the glimmering sunshine on the walkway that circles the great lamp. I can see to Provincetown and beyond. I can see as far as anyone has ever seen before. Ships with sails as white as my summer dress are making their way along the horizon. The rooster, who is practicing for sunrise, starts to crow.

A rooster *was* crowing. I opened my eyes. But it wasn't a rooster, it was a herring gull who thought he owned the island. 8

198

In the basket Grandma had packed sandwiches and leftover birthday cake from my party the day before. She lit a candle, and the wind and I blew it out together. Grandma sang "Happy Birthday Plus One."

"Someday," she said, "this island will be completely gone, and you'll tell your granddaughter how you came out here and picnicked on it at low tide."

"I'll show her the brick as proof," I said. 9

Now the tide was coming back in. It moved slowly at first, as if making up its mind, and then it started claiming the edges of the beach.

Grandma stroked the smooth sand beside her.

199

8 Clarifying Teacher Prompt: *Was there a rooster crowing or wasn't there a rooster crowing? How can we clarify this part of the text?* **Possible Student Response** *I'm going to clarify by rereading this part of the text. The rooster was crowing in Carrie's daydream. She thought it was crowing as she opened her eyes, then she realized what she was really hearing was a herring gull.*

9 Clarifying Teacher Prompt: *Is there anything you need to clarify in this part of the story?* **Possible Student Response** *What does Carrie mean when she says, "I'll show her the brick as proof"? Carrie's grandma is telling Carrie how one day she will tell her granddaughter about picnicking on an island that by then will have disappeared. Oh, I see. Carrie will tell her own granddaughter the story of the island and will be able to show her the brick to prove her story.*

Word Structure

Word families: knocked/knock/knocking, glimmering/glimmer/glimmered, practicing/practice/practiced

Reading and Responding

"In this modern world people can do almost anything," she said. "We cut canals and build long bridges and dam rivers. We've tamed almost everything. I'm glad that we haven't completely tamed the ocean, too. What I love about a place like this is that it reminds us that nature still can have its way once in a while." 10

Grandma stood up. "Time to get going," she said.

We each took a corner of the beach blanket and let it flap free of sand in the wind. Then we folded the blanket together, like partners in a square dance. When our hands came together, Grandma kissed my knuckles and my nose.

The tide was coming in faster now, eating up the beach, eating up the island. We waded out to *Aphrodite.* Grandma started the engine in two tries, and we went chugging off. I looked back as Billingsgate Island began to disappear in the distance, and in the sea. The spot where Grandma and I had had our picnic would soon be underwater. Where the chickens once pecked for grain thrown out by the lighthouse keeper's little girl a hundred years ago, fish would peck at plankton.

By the time *Aphrodite* was back at her mooring in Wellfleet Harbor, Billingsgate Island was gone, a secret beneath the waves. 11

200

201

Word Structure

Word families: tamed/tame/taming, folded/fold/folding/refold, kissed/kiss/kissing, chugging/chugged/chug

Teacher Tip

CONCEPT/QUESTION BOARD Remind students to post questions, ideas, or new and interesting things they have learned from reading the story as items on the **Concept/Question Board.**

10 **Clarifying** Teacher Prompt: *How can we clarify what Grandma means when she says that she's glad that we haven't completely tamed the ocean?* **Possible Student Response** *I'm going to reread this paragraph. She is talking about things we can do in the modern world, such as build bridges. Then she says we've tamed almost everything, but not the ocean. I think she means that even though we can build a lot of things, we still can't tell the ocean what to do.*

Comprehension Check

What does Grandma love about Billingsgate Island? **Possible Answer** *It reminds her that nature can still have its way. The ocean is still untamed.*

⑪ **Summarizing** Teacher Prompt: *Since we are at the end of the story, we should summarize the main points. Who would like to summarize the story?* **Possible Student Response** *Grandma took Carrie to a disappearing island. The island was disappearing because the ocean was slowly eroding it away. Grandma told Carrie what it was like when she lived on the island, and then Carrie imagined what it would have been like living on the island a hundred years ago. As the tide started to come back in, Grandma and Carrie gathered their things and left.*

Teacher Tip

SUMMARIZING As students offer suggestions for the summary, note whether their additions are main points in the story. You may have to remind students to state only the main points of the story when summarizing.

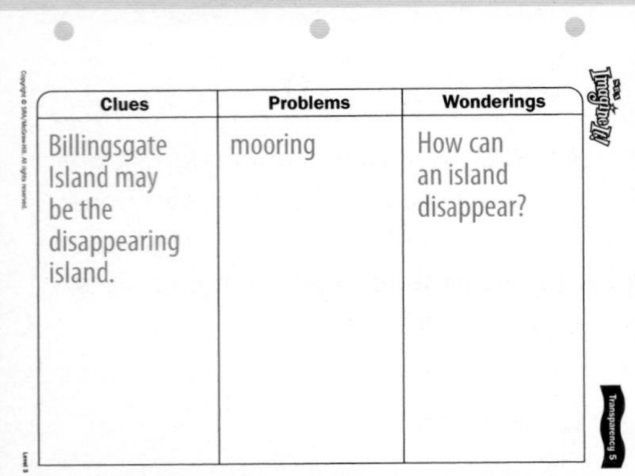

Clues	Problems	Wonderings
Billingsgate Island may be the disappearing island.	mooring	How can an island disappear?

Transparency 5

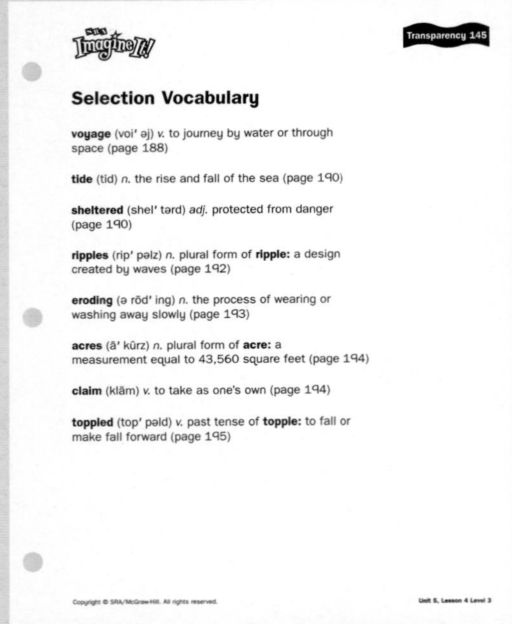

Transparency 145

Selection Vocabulary

voyage (voi' əj) *v.* to journey by water or through space (page 188)

tide (tīd) *n.* the rise and fall of the sea (page 190)

sheltered (shel' tərd) *adj.* protected from danger (page 190)

ripples (rip' pəlz) *n.* plural form of **ripple:** a design created by waves (page 192)

eroding (ə rōd' ing) *n.* the process of wearing or washing away slowly (page 193)

acres (ā' kûrz) *n.* plural form of **acre:** a measurement equal to 43,560 square feet (page 194)

claim (klām) *v.* to take as one's own (page 194)

toppled (top' pəld) *v.* past tense of **topple:** to fall or make fall forward (page 195)

Transparency 145

Discussing the Selection

- ✦ It is important for students to see you as a contributing member of the group. Use Routine A, handing-off, to emphasize that you are part of the group. Actively participate in handing-off by raising your hand to be called on by the last speaker when you have a contribution to make. Point out unusual and interesting insights verbalized by students so that these insights are recognized and discussed.
- ✦ Engage students in a discussion using handing-off to determine whether they have grasped the following ideas:
  - Grandma wants to show Carrie an island that will someday disappear.
  - The ocean has claimed the land and everything on it. No matter how many lighthouses were built, the ocean kept taking them away.
- ✦ Ask students how the story demonstrates the following key concepts.
  - As the tides come and go on Billingsgate Island, the ocean waters are eroding the land. One day, the island will completely erode and will disappear.
  - Despite all that human beings have invented and controlled, nature can still have ultimate control.
- ✦ Return to the Clues, Problems, and Wonderings chart on ***Transparency*** 5. Have students discuss which clues were useful, how they resolved their problems, and how they answered their questions. Also ask students if the predictions they made while browsing the story were confirmed or not confirmed.
- ✦ Have students return to the Focus Questions on ***Student Reader,*** Book 2 page 187. Select a student to read the questions aloud, and have students answer and discuss the questions. Have them return to the text as necessary.

Genre Review

Review the elements of realistic fiction on page T272 fiction with students. Then ask students how they know "The Disappearing Island" is realistic fiction.

How has my community changed over time?

After reading the story, read the Big Idea question. Discuss with students how the story helps answer this question.

Vocabulary Review

Review with students the selection vocabulary words and definitions they wrote in the vocabulary section of their Writer's Notebook. Then refer students to ***Skills Practice 2*** pages 141–142. Help students complete the first two questions. Then have students complete the rest on their own. Also, review the concept vocabulary word *property*. Ask students if they can think of other words related to the theme Communities across Time. **Possible Answers** *land, nature, environment, owner, generations*

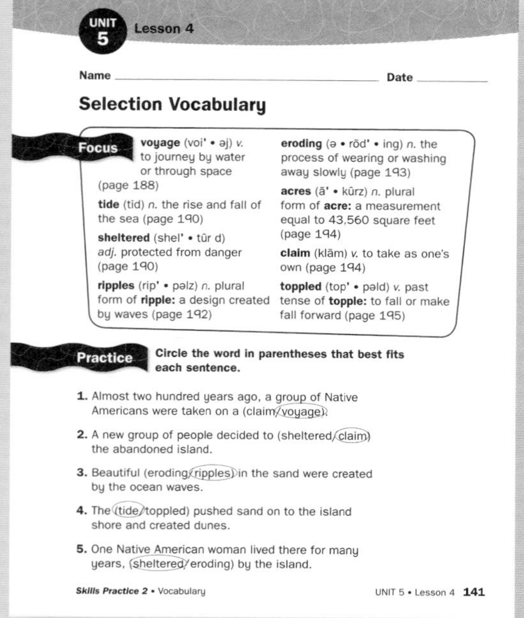
UNIT 5 Lesson 4

Name ______ Date ______

Selection Vocabulary

Focus

voyage (voi' • əj) *v.* to journey by water or through space (page 188)

tide (tīd) *n.* the rise and fall of the sea (page 190)

sheltered (shel' • tûr d) *adj.* protected from danger (page 190)

ripples (rip' • pəlz) *n.* plural form of **ripple:** a design created by waves (page 192)

eroding (ə • rōd' • ing) *n.* the process of wearing or washing away slowly (page 193)

acres (ā' • kûrz) *n.* plural form of **acre:** a measurement equal to 43,560 square feet (page 194)

claim (klām) *v.* to take as one's own (page 194)

toppled (top' • pəld) *v.* past tense of **topple:** to fall or make fall forward (page 195)

Practice **Circle the word in parentheses that best fits each sentence.**

1. Almost two hundred years ago, a group of Native Americans were taken on a (claim/voyage).
2. A new group of people decided to (sheltered/claim) the abandoned island.
3. Beautiful (eroding/ripples) in the sand were created by the ocean waves.
4. The (tide/toppled) pushed sand on to the island shore and created dunes.
5. One Native American woman lived there for many years, (sheltered/eroding) by the island.

Skills Practice 2 • Vocabulary UNIT 5 • Lesson 4 141

Skills Practice 2, pp. 141–142

Fluency

✦ When modeling fluency, practice intonation. Intonation, or pitch of voice, is essential to fluency. Reading with intonation helps readers understand and enjoy the text that is being read. Remind students to note the content of the text and end punctuation while reading to determine the pitch of voice to use while reading. For example, a period tells the reader to stop, a question mark indicates a raised tone at the end of the sentence, and a comma tells the reader to pause slightly.

✦ Read aloud pages 200–201 of "The Disappearing Island." Model intonation for students. For example, after reading *By the time Aphrodite was back at her mooring in Wellfleet Harbor, Billingsgate Island was gone, a secret beneath the waves*, point out how your voice paused at the commas. Have students follow along in the ***Student Reader,*** Book 2, and tell them to raise their hands when you pause.

Monitor Progress to Differentiate Instruction

Formal Assessment

Selection Vocabulary Observe students' understanding of the vocabulary words and their definitions.

APPROACHING LEVEL

IF . . . students need extra help with the selection vocabulary,

THEN . . .
- refer to ***Intervention Guide*** Unit 5, Lesson 4.
- use ***Reteach*** page 144.

ON LEVEL

IF . . . students need practice using the selection vocabulary words,

THEN . . . have students complete ***eSkills & eGames*** vocabulary activites.

ABOVE LEVEL

IF . . . students understand the selection vocabulary,

THEN . . . use ***Challenge Activities*** page 131.

Fluency Tip

FLUENCY By this time in Grade 3, good readers should be reading approximately 137 words per minute with fluency and expression. The only way to gain this fluency is with practice. Have students reread the story to you and to each other during Workshop to help build fluency. As students read, you may notice that some need work in building fluency. During Workshop, have these students choose a section of the text (a minimum of 160 words) to read aloud several times to build fluency.

Teacher Tip

WORD BANK Review the Word Bank with students. Encourage students to add words to the Word Bank related to the unit theme Communities across Time. You might also want to encourage students to add synonyms and antonyms in the Word Bank as well.

Meet the Author and Illustrator 

After students read the information about the author and illustrator, discuss the following questions with them:

- *How might visiting Cape Cod every summer influence Corinne Demas' writing?* **Possible Answer** *After visiting Cape Cod, she can use details about the land, ocean, and people to make her stories that take place there seem more realistic.*
- *Ted Lewin enjoys traveling. How do you think his experiences have helped his illustrating?* **Possible Answer** *Lewin often uses what he sees while traveling in his illustrations.*

Theme Connections 

Within the Selection

1. How would you feel if everyone in your community had to leave? **Possible Answer** *I would feel sad and a little afraid. It would feel strange to leave my home and settle somewhere else.*
2. What do you think you will remember about your community when you are older? **Possible Answer** *I will remember playing basketball in the park with my friends. I'll also remember going to the parade every summer.*

Across Selections

3. How are changes to the land in "The Disappearing Island" like those in "Earthquake!"? **Possible Answer** *In both stories, the changes to the land are similar because they are both caused by nature.*
4. How are the changes different? **Possible Answer** *In "The Disappearing Island," the changes caused by nature cannot be controlled. There is nothing the citizens of the island can do to keep their island from eroding. In "Earthquake! The 1906 San Francisco Nightmare," people learn from the tragedy and are able to prepare for the next time an earthquake occurs; they do not have to leave their homes.*

Beyond the Selection

5. What can people do to make sure places that have disappeared are not forgotten? **Possible Answer** *People can tell their children and grandchildren stories about places that have disappeared so they will be remembered from generation to generation, just like in "The Disappearing Island."*
6. What museums have you visited or would you like to visit? **Possible Answer** *I visited my town's historical museum during a school field trip and learned more about my community there.*

Teacher Tips

WORKSHOP During Workshop, have students listen to "The Disappearing Island" for a model of oral reading. While students listen, have them keep a list in their Writer's Notebooks of any new or unfamiliar words they encounter, and instruct them to check the words using a dictionary or glossary. Also, instruct students to listen for the lesson's vocabulary words and to check that the words make sense within the reading.

BEYOND THE SELECTION Have students summarize what they have learned and tell how they might use this information in further investigations.

WRITE ABOUT IT! Have students describe a souvenir that they or their families have from somewhere special in their Writer's Notebooks.

Research in Action

Comprehension comes as a result of the blending of several things—ability to decode words, knowledge of word meaning, efficient use of context clues, prior knowledge, of the subject or parts of the subject, and the ability to connect what is being read to other materials one has read. The students' ability to participate in class discussion of the reading material is effective proof that all of these aspects of the reading process have indeed come together and resulted in thorough comprehension.

(Michael Pressley)

Meet the Author

Corinne Demas
Corinne Demas is an author, a college English professor, and an editor. She has written two novels, a number of short stories, a memoir, and several books for children. Demas spends her summers near the ocean in Cape Cod, Massachusetts, which is where many of her books take place.

Meet the Illustrator

Ted Lewin
When he was young, Ted Lewin knew he wanted to be an illustrator. He began his career by illustrating for adventure magazines and has since become a fulltime children's book illustrator. Lewin grew up with his parents, a brother, a sister, a lion, an iguana, and a chimpanzee. To pay for college, he worked as a wrestler during the summers. Lewin's book illustrations are often inspired by what he sees in his travels.

Communities across Time

Theme Connections

Within the Selection

1. How would you feel if everyone in your community had to leave?
2. What do you think you will remember about your community when you are older?

Across Selections

3. How are changes to the land in "The Disappearing Island" like those in "Earthquake!"?
4. How are the changes different?

Beyond the Selection

5. What can people do to make sure places that have disappeared are not forgotten?
6. What museums have you visited or would you like to visit?

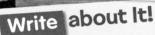

Write about It!

Describe a souvenir you have from a place that is special to you or your family.

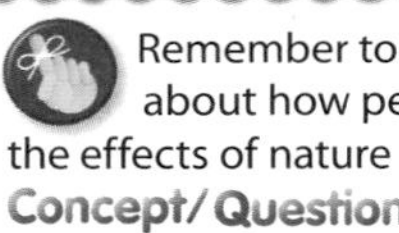

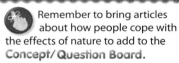

Remember to bring articles about how people cope with the effects of nature to add to the **Concept/Question Board.**

Concept/Question Board

As students discuss "The Disappearing Island" encourage them to post questions, answers, comments, or other items related to communities across time on the **Concept/Question Board.**

Language Arts

OBJECTIVES

Students will

- draw a map and draft directions to a location.
- learn to spell word families, multisyllabic words, and words with silent consonants.
- learn the past tense of *to be* and irregular verbs.

MATERIALS

- ***Skills Practice 2,*** pp. 147, 151–152
- ***Language Arts Handbook,*** pp. 308, 324–325

Writing Directions

Drafting

Teach

- Students should have decided on the location for their directions and completed the graphic organizer on page 147 in ***Skills Practice 2.***
- Tell students they will create a map and draft their directions.
- Tell students they should use cardinal directions, street names, and geographic markers such as landmarks, as they create their maps.

Guided Practice

- After students have drawn their maps, model using the chain of events graphic organizer and a map as tools for drafting. Show students how you transfer information that you have written in the boxes to paper. Allow students to assist you in drafting. If they direct you to write something out of order, you can point out this error during revision.
- Remind students they can make corrections in spelling, punctuation, and grammar during editing/proofreading. For now, they should make sure all the directions are included.
- Tell students to pay attention to word choice as they draft.

Apply

Composing—Drafting Have students use their graphic organizers to write a draft of their directions.

Differentiating Instruction English Learner

IF . . . students have difficulty drafting their directions, **THEN . . .** provide them with additional examples of directions to read and use for reference.

Teacher Tip

VERB TENSE As students draft their directions, have them pay careful attention to the verb tenses they use.

Spelling

Word Families, Multisyllabic Words, and Silent Consonants

Teach

Use a word sort to teach word families, multisyllabic words, and words with silent consonants.

Guided Practice

- On the board, write *Base Words*. Next to that head, write the following headings: *live, honor, direct,* and *doubt*. Then, write the following word list: *honest, director, relive, lively, honorable, indirect, undoubted, doubtful, living, honesty,* and *direction*. Have volunteers write the words under the correct heading. After all the spelling words have been used, ask for students to come to the board and underline the part of each word that reflects the category in which it was placed.
- Ask for volunteers to come to the board and circle the silent consonants in the spelling words that contain them.

Word Sort Answers

Words from the Base Word *Live: lively, relive, living*

Words from the Base Word *Honor: honorable, honest, honesty*

Words from the Base Word *Direct: director, direction, indirect*

Words from the Base Word *Doubt: doubtful, undoubted*

Words with Silent Consonants Underlined: *honor, honorable, honest, honesty, doubt, doubtful, undoubted.*

Verbs

There are different types of verbs. An **action verb** tells about an action of something or someone in a sentence. Actions can be seen or unseen.

Seen action: The dog **ran** all the way home.

Unseen action: Alex **forgot** his library book.

A **state-of-being verb** does not tell about an action. It tells about a condition or a state of being.

Our friends **were** here for a visit.

When a state-of-being verb connects the subject of a sentence with a word in the predicate, the verb is a **linking verb.**

I **am** a student.	My aunt **is** a teacher.
You **are** a good cook.	Josh **was** helpful with the baby.

A **verb phrase** is one or more **helping verbs** followed by the **main verb.** Helping verbs help the main verb express an action or state of being.

She **has won** the race. (helping verb+main verb)

She **could have won** the race. (two helping verbs+main verb)

308 Verbs • Grammar

Language Arts Handbook, p. 308

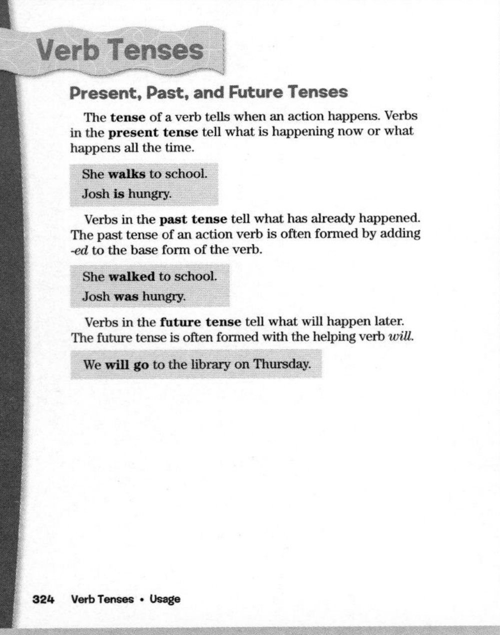

Verb Tenses

Present, Past, and Future Tenses

The **tense** of a verb tells when an action happens. Verbs in the **present tense** tell what is happening now or what happens all the time.

She **walks** to school.
Josh **is** hungry.

Verbs in the **past tense** tell what has already happened. The past tense of an action verb is often formed by adding *-ed* to the base form of the verb.

She **walked** to school.
Josh **was** hungry.

Verbs in the **future tense** tell what will happen later. The future tense is often formed with the helping verb *will.*

We **will go** to the library on Thursday.

324 Verb Tenses • Usage

Language Arts Handbook, p. 324

Grammar, Usage, and Mechanics 

Verb *be* and Irregular Verbs

Teach

✦ Write the following examples on the board while explaining *be* and other irregular verbs.

✦ The forms of the verb *be* include the following:

- *am, are, is, was, were, being,* and *been*

✦ Ask students for examples of each form of *be* used in a sentence. **Possible Answers** I am *happy. They* were *my friends.*

✦ Ask students to remind you of what a helping verb does. *Helping verbs help the main verb express an action.* Forms of *be* can also be helping verbs. Write the following examples on the board:

- I am running on Saturday.
- They were playing golf today.

✦ Remind students that verbs show the action in a sentence. However, the verb *be* does not show action; it is a state-of-being verb. It tells what someone or something *is* or *is like.*

✦ Remind students that a regular verb is one that adds *-ed* to the base verb. However, an irregular verb does not use the same past-tense rule. Instead, the spelling changes when forming the past tense.

✦ Common irregular verbs include:

- *am/was, are/were, begin/began, come/came, do/did, eat/ate, give/gave, has/had, run/ran, go/went,* and *take/took.*

✦ Use ***Language Arts Handbook*** pages 308 and 324–325 for rules and examples of the verb *be* and other irregular verbs.

Guided Practice

Have students turn to ***Skills Practice 2*** page 151. Ask a student to read the directions aloud. Work with students to complete the first two questions in the Practice section. Remind students that verbs, whether regular or irregular, need to agree in number and tense with the subject or subjects of the sentence.

Apply

Have students complete ***Skills Practice 2*** pages 151–152 to practice identifying and using the verb *be* and irregular verbs.

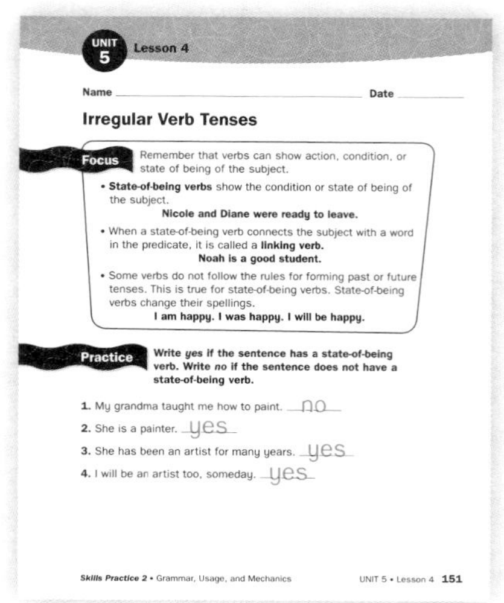

UNIT 5 Lesson 4

Name ______ Date ______

Irregular Verb Tenses

Focus Remember that verbs can show action, condition, or state of being of the subject.

- **State-of-being verbs** show the condition or state of being of the subject.
  Nicole and Diane were ready to leave.
- When a state-of-being verb connects the subject with a word in the predicate, it is called a **linking verb.**
  Noah is a good student.
- Some verbs do not follow the rules for forming past or future tenses. This is true for state-of-being verbs. State-of-being verbs change their spellings.
  I am happy. I was happy. I will be happy.

Practice **Write *yes* if the sentence has a state-of-being verb. Write *no* if the sentence does not have a state-of-being verb.**

1. My grandma taught me how to paint. no
2. She is a painter. yes
3. She has been an artist for many years. yes
4. I will be an artist too, someday. yes

Skills Practice 2 • Grammar, Usage, and Mechanics UNIT 5 • Lesson 4 **151**

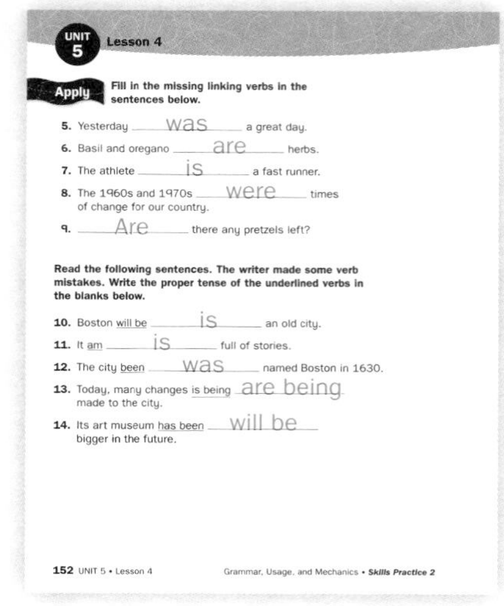

UNIT 5 Lesson 4

Apply **Fill in the missing linking verbs in the sentences below.**

5. Yesterday was a great day.
6. Basil and oregano are herbs.
7. The athlete is a fast runner.
8. The 1960s and 1970s were times of change for our country.
9. Are there any pretzels left?

Read the following sentences. The writer made some verb mistakes. Write the proper tense of the underlined verbs in the blanks below.

10. Boston will be is an old city.
11. It am is full of stories.
12. The city been was named Boston in 1630.
13. Today, many changes is being are being made to the city.
14. Its art museum has been will be bigger in the future.

152 UNIT 5 • Lesson 4 Grammar, Usage, and Mechanics • *Skills Practice 2*

Skills Practice 2, pp. 151–152

Monitor Progress to Differentiate Instruction

Formal Assessment

Irregular *to be* Verb Note whether students conjugate the verb *be* correctly.

APPROACHING LEVEL

IF . . . students need to practice irregular verbs, **THEN . . .** have them complete ***Reteach*** page 148 during Workshop.

IF . . . students need more practice with irregular verbs, **THEN . . .** refer to Unit 5 Lesson 4 in the ***Intervention Guide.***

ON LEVEL

IF . . . students have an understanding of irregular verbs, **THEN . . .** have them do an activity from the ***Workshop Kit*** during Workshop.

ABOVE LEVEL

IF . . . students need a challenge, **THEN . . .** have them complete ***Challenge Activities*** page 134 during Workshop.

Differentiating Instruction: English Learner

IF . . . students have difficulty completing the ***Skills Practice*** page independently, **THEN . . .** have them work in pairs or in small groups with proficient English speakers.

Day 3

Preparing to Read

OBJECTIVES

Students will
- ✦ identify silent consonants in multisyllabic words.
- ✦ build fluency.

MATERIALS

- ✦ ***Transparency*** 147
- ✦ ***Skills Practice 2,*** pp. 139–140

Daily Oral Practice

Daily News — Today!

The school I used to go to has disappeared. A bad storm came through town two years ago. I can still hear the wind howling and the hail knocking at the window. Luckily, nobody was hurt. I miss the school, but the people are what matter most to me.

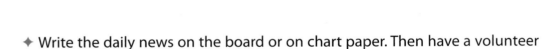

- ✦ Write the daily news on the board or on chart paper. Then have a volunteer read the daily news aloud to practice fluency.
- ✦ As a review of yesterday's word structure lesson, ask a volunteer to identify words in the message that are a part of a word family. *used, disappeared, howling, knocking, luckily* Ask students to identify the base word of the family to which these words belong. *use, appear, howl, knock, luck*

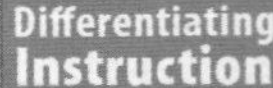

Differentiating Instruction — English Learner

IF . . . students are native Spanish speakers, **THEN . . .** they may have difficulty pronouncing *howling, hail,* and *hurt* in the daily news. In Spanish, *h* is always silent. Provide native Spanish speakers with extra practice pronouncing words with /h/.

Word Structure

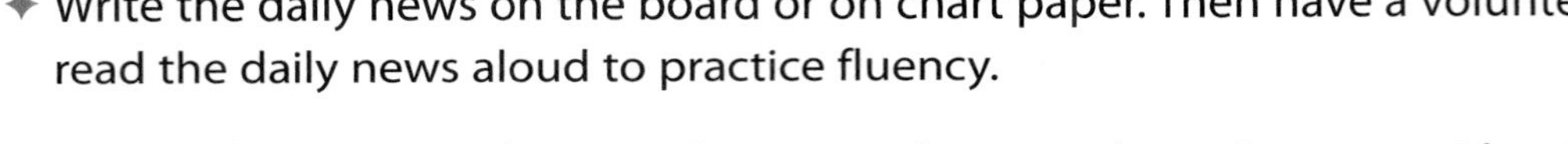

Multisyllabic Words with Silent Consonants

- ✦ Write these word lines on the board or use ***Transparency*** 147. The words in boldface are in "The Disappearing Island."

Line 1	**jackets**	**chickens**	**backbone**	rocket
Line 2	science	scientist	scenery	**muscles**
Line 3	**knuckles**	knitted	knowing	knotted
Line 4	mighty	**higher**	**lighthouse**	rightly

Teacher Tip

SYLLABICATION To help students blend words and build fluency, demonstrate syllabication using the decodable, multisyllabic words in the word lines.

jack • ets	chick • ens
back • bone	rock • et
sci • ence	sci • en • tist
sce • ner • y	mus • cles
knuck • les	knit • ted
know • ing	knot • ted
migh • ty	high • er
light • house	right • ly

Lines 1–4 Multisyllabic Words with Silent Consonants

Explain that some words have consonants that do not add sounds to a word, which makes them silent consonants. For example, write the word *thumb* on the board. Have students read the word aloud to hear that there is no *b* sound in *thumb*, so *b* is a silent consonant in *thumb*. Tell students that the words in Lines 1–4 are multisyllabic words that have silent consonants. Remind students that every syllable in a word has one vowel sound.

Lines 1–2 The Silent Consonant *c*

Tell students that the words in Lines 1–2 have a silent *c*. Point to each word in Lines 1–2 and have students read the words together. Ask them what sound *ck* makes. ck *makes /k/*. Ask them what sound *sc* makes. sc *makes /s/.*

Line 3 The Silent Consonant *k*

Explain that the words on Line 3 are multisyllabic words with a silent *k* consonant. Point to each word in Line 3 and have students read the words aloud in unison. Ask them what sound *kn* makes. kn *makes /n/.*

Line 4 The Silent Consonants *gh*

Explain that the words on Line 4 are multisyllabic words in which the letters *gh* are silent. As you point to each word in Line 4, have students read the words aloud. Ask students what sound *igh* makes in these words. *The letters* igh *make /ī/.*

✦ Help students start the word structure activities on ***Skills Practice 2*** pages 139–140. Read the Focus box with them and help with the first few questions. Then have students complete the pages on their own.

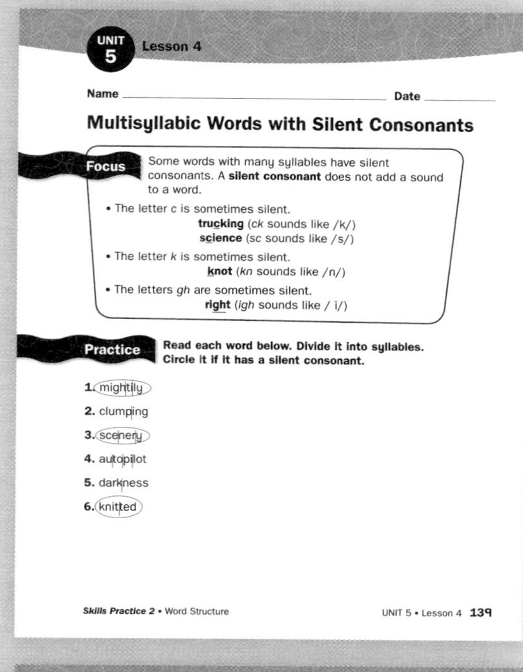

UNIT 5 Lesson 4

Name ____________ Date ________

Multisyllabic Words with Silent Consonants

Focus Some words with many syllables have silent consonants. A **silent consonant** does not add a sound to a word.

- The letter *c* is sometimes silent.
  trucking (*ck* sounds like /k/)
  science (*sc* sounds like /s/)
- The letter *k* is sometimes silent.
  knot (*kn* sounds like /n/)
- The letters *gh* are sometimes silent.
  right (*igh* sounds like /ī/)

Practice **Read each word below. Divide it into syllables. Circle it if it has a silent consonant.**

1. might|i|ly
2. clump|ing
3. scen|er|y
4. au|to|pi|lot
5. dark|ness
6. knit|ted

Skills Practice 2 • Word Structure UNIT 5 • Lesson 4 139

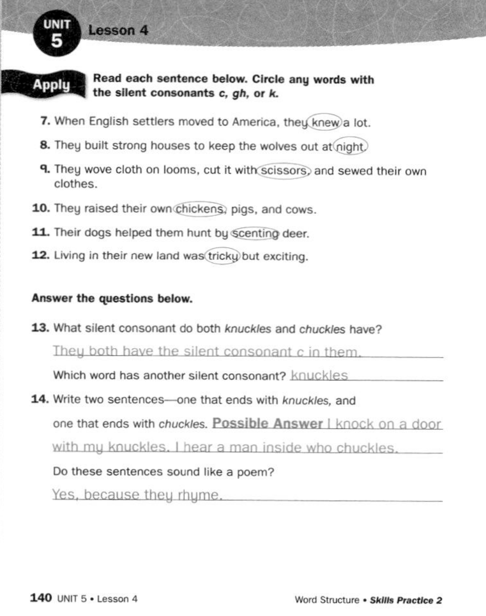

UNIT 5 Lesson 4

Apply **Read each sentence below. Circle any words with the silent consonants *c, gh,* or *k*.**

7. When English settlers moved to America, they knew a lot.
8. They built strong houses to keep the wolves out at night.
9. They wove cloth on looms, cut it with scissors, and sewed their own clothes.
10. They raised their own chickens, pigs, and cows.
11. Their dogs helped them hunt by scenting deer.
12. Living in their new land was tricky but exciting.

Answer the questions below.

13. What silent consonant do both *knuckles* and *chuckles* have?
They both have the silent consonant c in them.
Which word has another silent consonant? knuckles
14. Write two sentences—one that ends with *knuckles*, and one that ends with *chuckles*. **Possible Answer** I knock on a door with my knuckles. I hear a man inside who chuckles.
Do these sentences sound like a poem?
Yes, because they rhyme.

140 UNIT 5 • Lesson 4 Word Structure • *Skills Practice 2*

Skills Practice 2, pp. 139–140

Monitor Progress to Differentiate Instruction

Formal Assessment 

Word Structure During the word structure activity, note how well students recognize silent consonants in multisyllabic words.

APPROACHING LEVEL	**IF . . .** students need practice recognizing silent consonants in multisyllabic words,	**THEN . . .** work with them in small groups on the word structure activities on ***Reteach*** page 143 during Workshop.
	IF . . . students need extra practice recognizing silent consonants in multisyllabic words,	**THEN . . .** work with them in small groups on the word structure activities for Unit 5 Lesson 4 in the ***Intervention Guide*** during Workshop.
ON LEVEL	**IF . . .** students adequately recognize silent consonants in multisyllabic words,	**THEN . . .** have them make lists of other words to add to the word lines during Workshop.
ABOVE LEVEL	**IF . . .** students are ready for a challenge with silent consonants in multisyllabic words,	**THEN . . .** have them complete the word structure activities on ***Challenge Activities*** page 130 during Workshop.

For my ninth birthday my grandma gave me a small box. Inside was a perfect sand dollar and a note. The note said:

To celebrate your birthday we will voyage out to the disappearing island where I found this sand dollar when I was just your age.

"How can an island disappear?" I asked.

Grandma laughed. "When I take you out to Billingsgate Island, Carrie, you'll see," she said.

I'd been all around Wellfleet Harbor in Grandma's boat, but this time we were going to go farther out, into Cape Cod Bay, just the two of us, farther than I'd ever been before.

Grandma's boat is named *Aphrodite,* after the goddess of love who first rose out of the sea foam. It's painted the blue of the sea on the outside and the blue of the sky on the inside.

The next day we rowed out to *Aphrodite* in a rubber boat so small our legs were in a tangle.

We clambered aboard *Aphrodite,* and Grandma hooked the rubber boat to the mooring. To get the old outboard motor started she had to pull the rope nearly ten times. Her arms are all muscles from clamming and swimming and pulling. We put on our life jackets, and I sat up on the bow and pretended I was a figurehead on one of the old ships that used to come into Wellfleet Harbor. Water sprayed me, but it was a hot day so I didn't mind.

OBJECTIVES

Students will

- use the comprehension skills Author's Purpose and Cause and Effect.
- review fluency.
- investigate the theme Communities across Time using the Inquiry process.

MATERIALS

- ***Student Reader,*** Book 2, pp. 188–195
- ***Skills Practice 2,*** pp. 143–144

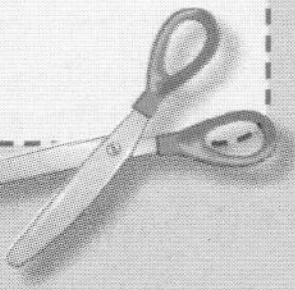

2nd READ

Comprehension Skill

Reread the story using the comprehension skills Author's Purpose and Cause and Effect and Reading with a Writer's Eye.

Author's Purpose

Ask students to explain what possible purposes author's might have for writing. *to entertain, to inform, to persuade, or to explain*

While rereading the story, tell students to look for clues to the author's purposes for writing "The Disappearing Island." Ask students the following questions:

- *What do you think the author's main purpose was for writing "The Disappearing Island"?* **Possible Answer** *to entertain*
- *The author might have had other reasons for writing this story. What could some of those reasons be?* **Possible Answer** *She could have wanted to give information about Billingsgate Island because it is a true story. She also could have wanted to explain how tides work and how nature has control of humans.*

When the tide is high in Wellfleet Harbor, the water is way over my head. When the tide is low, it just comes up to my middle. Grandma has a tide chart on her wall. It's like a calendar for the sea. There's low tide and high tide twice a day, and every day it's an hour different. The tide was going out now. A cormorant was drying out its feathers on a rock that hadn't been there an hour before. When we rode out beyond the sheltered part of Wellfleet Harbor, the waves got higher and I went to sit in the back of the boat with Grandma.

"I don't see any island," I said.

She passed me the binoculars. "Keep looking straight ahead," she told me. "At high tide it is completely covered by water. It begins to appear as the tide goes out."

Finally we got close enough so I could see it: a flat stretch of beach out in the middle of the sea. We pulled into a cove, and Grandma anchored *Aphrodite*. We waded to shore, carrying our lunch basket and beach blanket.

190

191

Cause and Effect

Ask students to explain cause and effect. If necesarry, tell them that the *cause* is *why* something happened and the *effect* is *what* happened. Ask students to give examples of cause and effect on pages 190–191. Remind students that cause-and-effect relationships can be recursive. Causes lead to effects, which in turn can become causes, and so on.

Cause	Effect
The tide is high in Wellfleet Harbor.	The water is over Carrie's head.
The tide is low in Wellfleet Harbor.	The water comes to Carrie's middle.
The tide is high.	The island is completely covered by water.

Expanding Vocabulary

foam (fōm) *n.* a mass of bubbles (page 189)
The waves created *foam* as they came onto the shore.

bow (bou) *n.* the front part of boat (page 189)
The captain was at the ship's *bow*.

waded (wād´• əd) *v.* past tense of **wade:** to walk through water (page 191)
The swimmers *waded* into the ocean.

Word Structure

Another focus in this lesson is multisyllabic words with silent consonants.

Multisyllabic word with silent consonants: jackets

Reading and Responding

We laid out the blanket on a high sandy spot surrounded by rocks—the foundation for the old lighthouse, Grandma said. Then we went off to explore the island.

There were no buildings, no trees, not even a blade of grass. Just sand. The sand was all in long ripples made by the waves as the tide had gone out. I ran as far as I could run without stopping to catch my breath. Grandma ran beside me.

"A century ago, this island was a mile long," Grandma explained. "This was a busy fishing community, and there were thirty-five homes here and a school. There were meadows and gardens. When the sea started eroding the island, people moved off and took their houses with them. When I was a little girl, my dad used to take me out here to go clamming. There was more of the island than there is now, but no one lived here anymore."

192

193

Expanding Vocabulary

foundation (foun • dā´ • shən) *n.* the base upon which a structure is built (page 192)

The crew laid the *foundation* for the house.

century (sen´ • chə • rē) *n.* a period of one hundred years (page 193)

School was different a *century* ago.

Word Structure

Multisyllabic word with silent consonants: backbone

Comprehension Skill

Cause and Effect

Ask students to identify the text structure used by the author to explain why people began to move off the island. *cause and effect* Encourage students to continue to chart examples of cause-and-effect relationships as they read the story. Ask students to find examples on pages 192–193:

Cause	Effect
The sea started eroding the island.	People moved off the island.

We were the only ones on the island except for the gulls and the terns. There were shells everywhere: jingle shells and quahogs, razor clams and channeled whelks. Mussels, tiny as ants, covered the stones in the acres of tidal pools. They looked like black fur.

I found a broken brick, half buried in the sand. One side of it had been charred.

"This was from someone's chimney," Grandma said.

"May I keep it?"

"Sure. The sea would claim it soon enough."

194

We hiked back to our blanket, and nearby I saw a strange, rusty creature that looked like the backbone of a whale.

"It's the metal spiral staircase from the old lighthouse, lying on its side," Grandma told me. It was too big for us to carry back to safety on the mainland.

"That was the second lighthouse out here. The first one toppled into the sea. They built this one farther inland and they built it out of brick. They thought it would last forever, but the sea kept taking more and more of the island. They built a big breakwater out of rocks, but the sea just came around it."

Grandma pointed to a curve of gray rocks that were covered with barnacles that looked like white lace.

195

Reading with a Writer's Eye

Theme

Ask students to explain what a theme is. *what a story is mostly about* The theme of Communities across Time is a broad topic. Corrine Demas, the author of "The Disappearing Island," wants to address a certain aspect of the theme. Ask students the following questions:

- *What aspect of the theme Communities across Time do you think Corrine Demas addresses?* **Possible Answer** *She tells her readers about how nature has changed a community over the years.* How do you know? **Possible Answer** *Readers are given specific details about the changes to the island.*
- *How is this story similar to "Earthquake! The 1906 San Francisco Nightmare"?* **Possible Answer** *In both selections, nature changed the land.*
- *How does the theme of this story differ from the theme in "The House on Maple Street"?* **Possible Answer** *In "The House on Maple Street," people changed the land more than nature did.*

You have reread the first half of the story. Continue the story tomorrow on page T314.

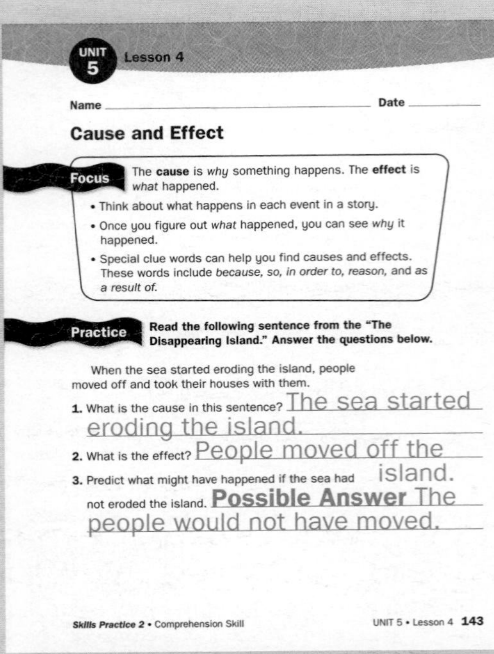
UNIT 5 Lesson 4

Name ______ Date ______

Cause and Effect

Focus The **cause** is *why* something happens. The **effect** is *what* happened.

- Think about what happens in each event in a story.
- Once you figure out *what* happened, you can see *why* it happened.
- Special clue words can help you find causes and effects. These words include *because, so, in order to, reason,* and *as a result of.*

Practice **Read the following sentence from the "The Disappearing Island." Answer the questions below.**

When the sea started eroding the island, people moved off and took their houses with them.

1. What is the cause in this sentence? The sea started eroding the island.
2. What is the effect? People moved off the island.
3. Predict what might have happened if the sea had not eroded the island. **Possible Answer** The people would not have moved.

Skills Practice 2 • Comprehension Skill UNIT 5 • Lesson 4 **143**

Skills Practice 2, p. 143

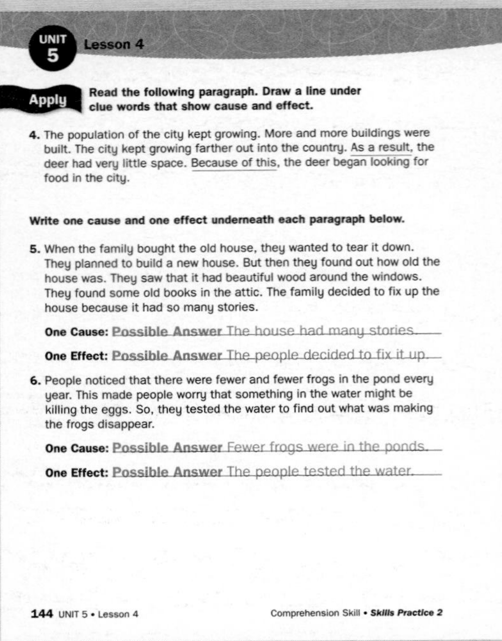
UNIT 5 Lesson 4

Apply **Read the following paragraph. Draw a line under clue words that show cause and effect.**

4. The population of the city kept growing. More and more buildings were built. The city kept growing farther out into the country. As a result, the deer had very little space. Because of this, the deer began looking for food in the city.

Write one cause and one effect underneath each paragraph below.

5. When the family bought the old house, they wanted to tear it down. They planned to build a new house. But then they found out how old the house was. They saw that it had beautiful wood around the windows. They found some old books in the attic. The family decided to fix up the house because it had so many stories.

One Cause: **Possible Answer** The house had many stories.

One Effect: **Possible Answer** The people decided to fix it up.

6. People noticed that there were fewer and fewer frogs in the pond every year. This made people worry that something in the water might be killing the eggs. So, they tested the water to find out what was making the frogs disappear.

One Cause: **Possible Answer** Fewer frogs were in the ponds.

One Effect: **Possible Answer** The people tested the water.

144 UNIT 5 • Lesson 4 Comprehension Skill • ***Skills Practice 2***

Skills Practice 2, p. 144

Supporting the Reading

Comprehension Skill: Cause and Effect

Teach

Identifying cause and effect (or the *what* and the *why*) in stories helps students become involved with the action and improves their comprehension. Words called *causal indicators* sometimes directly alert readers to these relationships. These words include *because, for, since, therefore, so, reason for, so that, due to,* and *as a result.*

Guided Practice

Ask students why cause-and-effect relationships are important in "The Disappearing Island." Have them explain why and how they would use this skill in their own writing.

- Bring in either a nonfiction or fiction article relating to the theme to read to the class. On the board, write a two-column chart with the headings Cause and Effect.
- Ask students to raise their hands as they hear you read cause-and-effect relationships. Write them on the board.
- Point out how cause-and-effect relationships can be recursive. A cause can lead to an effect, which in turn can become another cause and so on. Point these relationships out to students, or have them point them out to you, as you work through this activity.

Apply

Have students turn to pages 143–144 in ***Skills Practice 2.*** Have students read aloud the Focus section of the lesson. Work through the Practice section of the lesson with students. Have them look in the story "The Disappearing Island" to find examples of cause and effect. Have them record examples they can refer to as they work on the Apply section of the lesson.

Monitor Progress to Differentiate Instruction

Formal Assessment

Comprehension Skill Note students' understanding of the comprehension skill Cause and Effect.

APPROACHING LEVEL

IF . . . students need extra help with cause and effect, **THEN . . .** use ***Reteach*** pages 145–146.

ON LEVEL

IF . . . students need practice with cause and effect, **THEN . . .** have students play a game in the Workshop Kit.

ABOVE LEVEL

IF . . . students understand cause and effect, **THEN . . .** use ***Challenge Activities*** page 132.

Fluency

Students should not have trouble reading "The Disappearing Island" with its conversational tone and descriptive language. For some passages, you may want to review pronunciations of select words or vocabulary words prior to the fluency practice.

- Model fluent reading by reading pages 197–198 from "The Disappearing Island." Have students follow along in ***Student Reader,*** Book 2. Ask them to raise their hands if they hear an unfamiliar word or passage.
- After you have read through the passage, call on a volunteer to read the first paragraph. Before the student begins, remind him or her that the italics portion of the story is Carrie's daydream. In her daydream she imagines herself to be living a hundred years ago.
- After the volunteer has finished, have all students read the passage chorally several times until they can read it naturally with good phrasing.

Inquiry

Conjecture

- Remind students that they have made conjectures about their research questions, but their conjectures may change based on new things they learn from the unit selections. Remind students that revising conjectures is a good thing, it now means that they learned something new.

- Have students think about how ideas in "The Disappearing Island" might relate to their conjectures. For example, a group may have conjectured that the perfect place to set up a community would be on an island. After reading "The Disappearing Island," they should realize that an island can disappear into the ocean and the community would be forced to move. This might make a group realize that living on an island presents a community with particular problems that living elsewhere doesn't. Explore with students their ideas about how the selection relates to their conjectures.

LEVELED READERS To help students build fluency and strengthen their vocabulary and comprehension skills, have them read the ***Leveled Readers*** for this unit. Use each student's Oral Fluency Assessment score from the previous ***Lesson Assessment*** to diagnose the appropriate ***Leveled Reader.***

Fluency Tip

FLUENCY For additional fluency practice, have students read this passage and others in the story aloud with a partner.

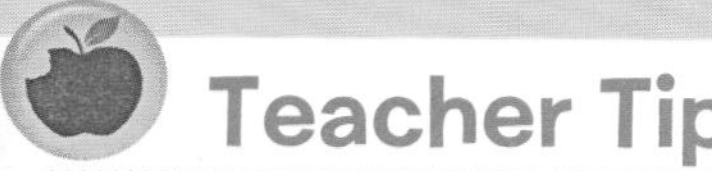

Teacher Tip

THEME The theme of each story in this unit is different. However, some share characteristics and have similarities. You may want students to keep track of the theme of each selection and determine how they relate to each other and to the overall themes of the unit.

Day 3

Language Arts

OBJECTIVES

Students will

- ✦ revise persuasive paragraphs.
- ✦ practice spelling words in word families, multisyllabic words, and silent consonants.
- ✦ work with calendars.
- ✦ practice recognizing forms of *be* and other irregular verbs.

MATERIALS

- ✦ ***Skills Practice 2,*** pp. 148–150 and 153–154
- ✦ ***Transparencies*** 148 and 148A
- ✦ Routine 16

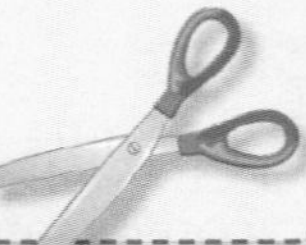

Writing Directions

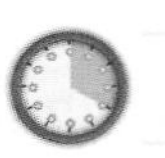

ROUTINE 

Revising

Teach—Sequence

- ✦ Students will use the drafts they have written to revise their directions.
- ✦ Use Routine 16, and tell students that as they revise to make sure their word choice is precise, clear, and specific, so the readers know exactly which direction to take. For example, students should use words such as: *left, right, north, south, two blocks, three lights,* and so on, depending on the type of directions they are giving.
- ✦ Remind students that in addition to precise word choice, it is also important to remember to include every step in the directions and make sure they are in the correct order.
- ✦ Have students work on maintaining a consistent verb tense with regular and irregular verbs as they revise their directions.

Guided Practice

- ✦ Model revising directions by displaying ***Transparency*** 148. Have a student read the transparency aloud. Ask students to list things they think are out of order. Then display ***Transparency*** 148A to discuss the revisions to sequence. Review the importance of placing steps in the correct order and using precise words for directions.
- ✦ Have students turn to ***Skills Practice 2*** page 148 to read and discuss the revising checklist.

Apply

Composing—Revising Have students revise their directions. Remind them to refer to the revising checklist on page 148 in ***Skills Practice 2.***

Differentiating Instruction — English Learner

IF . . . students have limited vocabulary, **THEN . . .** allow them to use words from their native languages for any English words they do not know. After they are finished revising their drafts, they can use a bilingual dictionary to find those unknown English words.

Imagine It! Transparency 148 148A

Revising for Sequence

Aunt Susan mixed up the draft of the directions for Katy to find her birthday present.

1. *Walk to the big rock.*
2. *Go to the fish pond.*
3. *Turn right.*
4. *Your present is hidden there.*
5. *Walk out the back door.*
6. *Turn left.*
7. *Look behind the rock.*

big rock

fishing pond

Transparencies 148, 148A

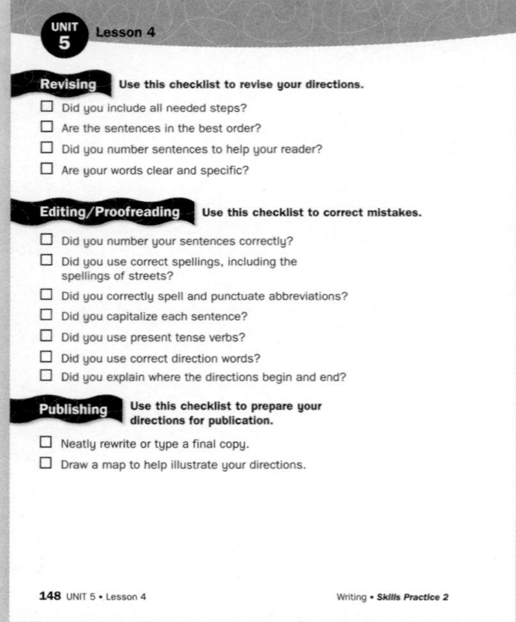

UNIT 5 Lesson 4

Revising Use this checklist to revise your directions.

- ☐ Did you include all needed steps?
- ☐ Are the sentences in the best order?
- ☐ Did you number sentences to help your reader?
- ☐ Are your words clear and specific?

Editing/Proofreading Use this checklist to correct mistakes.

- ☐ Did you number your sentences correctly?
- ☐ Did you use correct spellings, including the spellings of streets?
- ☐ Did you correctly spell and punctuate abbreviations?
- ☐ Did you capitalize each sentence?
- ☐ Did you use present tense verbs?
- ☐ Did you use correct direction words?
- ☐ Did you explain where the directions begin and end?

Publishing Use this checklist to prepare your directions for publication.

- ☐ Neatly rewrite or type a final copy.
- ☐ Draw a map to help illustrate your directions.

148 UNIT 5 • Lesson 4 Writing • *Skills Practice 2*

Skills Practice 2, p. 148

Traits of Good Writing

Organization The writer revises to create the correct sequence.

Spelling

Word Families, Multisyllabic Words, and Silent Consonants

Teach

- Tell students that word families are groups of related words that all derived using the same base word.
- Tell students that multisyllabic words are words that have two or more syllables, and that in this lesson, the individual syllables may have a specific meaning that can be added to or deleted from the word (affixes).
- Tell students that silent consonants are consonants that are part of a word's spelling but are not heard when the word is pronounced.
- Write the word list on the board. Have students do the following for each word: circle the base word, underline prefixes and suffixes one time, and underline silent consonants two times. For words with affixes that change the spelling of the base word, have students tell the class which spelling rule was used to create the word's new spelling.

Guided Practice

Have students turn to ***Skills Practice 2*** page 149. Read the instructions with them, and complete the first two questions as a class.

Apply

Have students complete ***Skills Practice 2*** pages 149–150 on their own. Remind students that challenge words are not used in ***Skills Practice*** exercises.

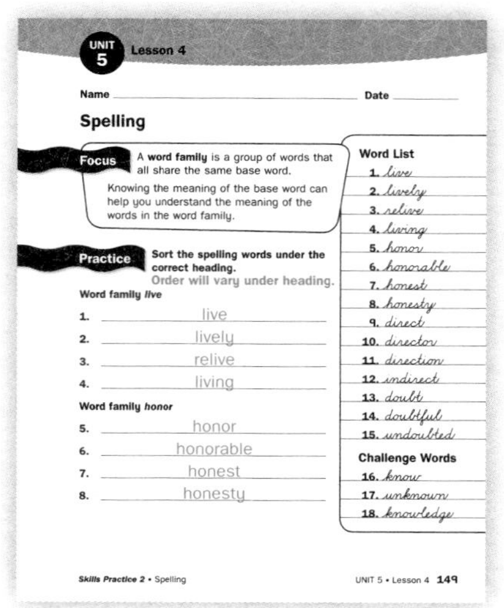
UNIT 5 Lesson 4

Name ______ Date ______

Spelling

Focus A **word family** is a group of words that all share the same base word.

Knowing the meaning of the base word can help you understand the meaning of the words in the word family.

Practice **Sort the spelling words under the correct heading.**
Order will vary under heading.

Word family *live*
1. live
2. lively
3. relive
4. living

Word family *honor*
5. honor
6. honorable
7. honest
8. honesty

Word List
1. live
2. lively
3. relive
4. living
5. honor
6. honorable
7. honest
8. honesty
9. direct
10. director
11. direction
12. indirect
13. doubt
14. doubtful
15. undoubted

Challenge Words
16. know
17. unknown
18. knowledge

Skills Practice 2 • Spelling UNIT 5 • Lesson 4 149

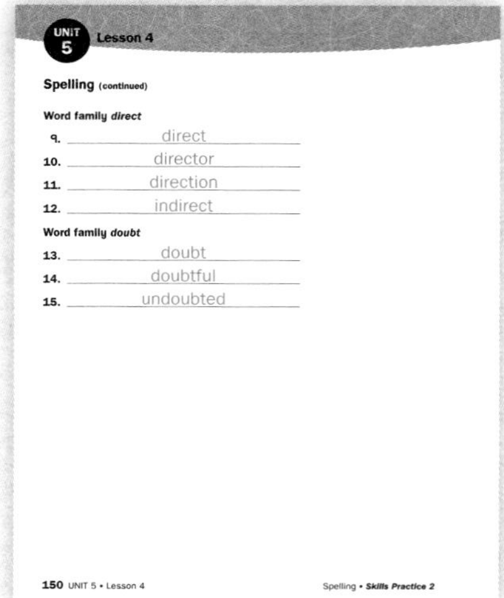
UNIT 5 Lesson 4

Spelling (continued)

Word family *direct*
9. direct
10. director
11. direction
12. indirect

Word family *doubt*
13. doubt
14. doubtful
15. undoubted

150 UNIT 5 • Lesson 4 Spelling • *Skills Practice 2*

Skills Practice 2, pp. 149–150

Monitor Progress

to Differentiate Instruction
Formal Assessment

Spelling Note whether students are able to spell the lesson words correctly.

APPROACHING LEVEL

IF . . . students need to practice spelling this week's words, **THEN . . .** have them complete ***Reteach*** page 147.

ON LEVEL

IF . . . students can spell this week's spelling words, **THEN . . .** have them use five spelling words to write five sentences. Have them spell the spelling word incorrectly, and then trade sentences with a partner and have each student correct the other's sentences.

ABOVE LEVEL

IF . . . students are ready for a challenge, **THEN . . .** have them complete ***Challenge Activities*** page 133.

Monitor Progress 

to Differentiate Instruction
Formal Assessment

Calendars Note whether students are utilizing calendars.

APPROACHING LEVEL

IF . . . students need to familiarize themselves with calendars,	**THEN . . .** have them create their own activity planner calendar during Workshop.

ON LEVEL

IF . . . students have an understanding of calendars,	**THEN . . .** have them keep track of their activities in a calendar.

ABOVE LEVEL

IF . . . students need a challenge,	**THEN . . .** have them create a calendar for their unit investigation during Workshop.

Study Skills

Calendars

Teach

- Ask students to discuss what they know about calendars.
- Explain that there are many reasons for using calendars in addition to keeping track of activities and appointments.
- Remind students of the tidal calendar that Grandma used in "The Disappearing Island." The calendar helped her remember when the tides would be high and when they would be low.
- Some calendars plot seasonal changes. These calendars help farmers and gardeners know when to plant seeds. Other calendars chart planets and constellations in the sky. These types of calendars also help with planting and tides. Some calendars record natural events, such as the ones the scientists in "Earthquake! The 1906 San Francisco Nightmare" may have used.
- Tell students that calendars can be a useful source in some investigations, or they can be used as visual aids in presentations.

Guided Practice

- Ask students how looking at calendars of the past may be beneficial in predicting the future. **Possible Answer** *Following a calendar from the past may help predict patterns in the future.*
- Have students turn to ***Skills Practice 2*** page 153. Have a student read the directions aloud. Do the Practice activity as a class.

Apply

Have students complete ***Skills Practice 2*** pages 153–154.

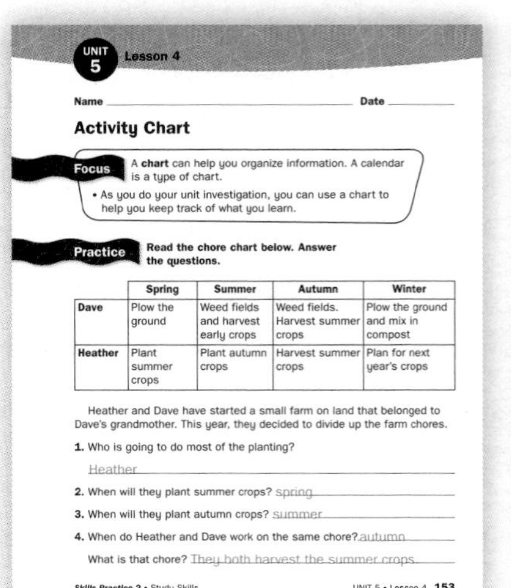

UNIT 5 Lesson 4

Name ______ Date ______

Activity Chart

Focus A **chart** can help you organize information. A calendar is a type of chart.

- As you do your unit investigation, you can use a chart to help you keep track of what you learn.

Practice **Read the chore chart below. Answer the questions.**

	Spring	Summer	Autumn	Winter
Dave	Plow the ground	Weed fields and harvest early crops	Weed fields. Harvest summer crops	Plow the ground and mix in compost
Heather	Plant summer crops	Plant autumn crops	Harvest summer crops	Plan for next year's crops

Heather and Dave have started a small farm on land that belonged to Dave's grandmother. This year, they decided to divide up the farm chores.

1. Who is going to do most of the planting? Heather
2. When will they plant summer crops? spring
3. When will they plant autumn crops? summer
4. When do Heather and Dave work on the same chore? autumn
   What is that chore? They both harvest the summer crops.

Skills Practice 2 • Study Skills UNIT 5 • Lesson 4 **153**

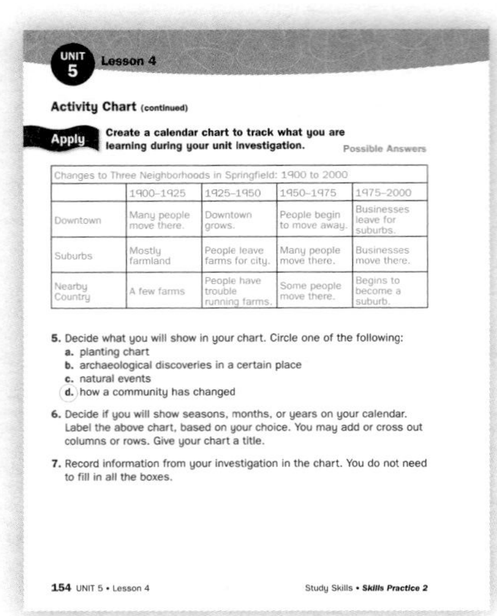

UNIT 5 Lesson 4

Activity Chart (continued)

Apply **Create a calendar chart to track what you are learning during your unit investigation.** Possible Answers

Changes to Three Neighborhoods in Springfield: 1900 to 2000				
	1900–1925	1925–1950	1950–1975	1975–2000
Downtown	Many people move there.	Downtown grows.	People begin to move away.	Businesses leave for suburbs.
Suburbs	Mostly farmland	People leave farms for city.	Many people move there.	Businesses move there.
Nearby Country	A few farms	People have trouble running farms.	Some people move there.	Begins to become a suburb.

5. Decide what you will show in your chart. Circle one of the following:
   a. planting chart
   b. archaeological discoveries in a certain place
   c. natural events
   (d.) how a community has changed
6. Decide if you will show seasons, months, or years on your calendar. Label the above chart, based on your choice. You may add or cross out columns or rows. Give your chart a title.
7. Record information from your investigation in the chart. You do not need to fill in all the boxes.

154 UNIT 5 • Lesson 4 Study Skills • *Skills Practice 2*

Skills Practice 2, pp. 153–154

Grammar, Usage, and Mechanics

Verb *be* and Irregular Verbs

Teach

- ✦ Have students review the rules and usage of the verb *be.* Remind students that this verb can be used as a main verb or as a helping verb.
- ✦ Have students review some of the common irregular verbs and their forms by writing a list on the board or by volunteering sentences with irregular verbs.

Guided Practice

Ask students for examples of the following types of sentences for you to write on the board:

- A sentence using a present singular form of the verb *be*
- A sentence using a past plural form of the verb *be*
- A sentence using a past form of the verb *take*
- A sentence using a past form of the verb *eat*

Apply

Have students write five sentences using the verb *be* or other irregular verbs such as *become, take, fall, draw,* and *eat.*

Differentiating Instruction **English Learners**

IF . . . students are having difficulty with forms of the verb *be* and irregular verbs, **THEN . . .** refer to Unit 5 Lesson 4 in the ***English Learner Support Guide.***

Preparing to Read

OBJECTIVES

Students will
- identify silent consonants in multisyllabic words.
- build fluency.

MATERIALS

Transparency 147

Daily Oral Practice

Daily News

Today!

Is it sad when a place disappears? Some places, like the disappearing island, were once home to many people. Now nature is taking the island away. We may not be able to fully control nature, but we can keep the memories and wonderful stories of such places and their people alive.

- Write the daily news on the board or on chart paper. Then have students read the daily news in unison to practice fluency.
- As a review of yesterday's word structure lesson, ask a volunteer to identify any words in the message with a silent consonant. *island*

Teacher Tip

DAILY NEWS Students may not recognize the silent *s* in *island.* Point this out, and ask them if they can think of other words with a silent *s*. Possibilities include *isle* and *aisle*. Point out that *island, aisle,* and *isle* are related words; they all relate to being completely surrounded by something.

Word Structure

Multisyllabic Words with Silent Consonants

✦ Use ***Transparency*** 147 with these word lines from Day 3.

Line 1	jackets	chickens	backbone	rocket
Line 2	science	scientist	scenery	muscles
Line 3	knuckles	knitted	knowing	knotted
Line 4	mighty	higher	lighthouse	rightly

✦ Review multisyllabic words with silent consonants. Review the silent consonants in /k/ spelled *ck,* /n/ spelled *kn,* /s/ spelled *sc,* and /ī/ spelled *_igh.*

Developing Oral Language

Use any of the following activities to help students practice reading the words.

- Have a student choose a word, calling out only the line and its position in the line, for example, "Line 2, Word 3." Have the student select a classmate to read the word, saying "Line 2, Word 3 is *scenery.*" Then ask the student to use the word in a sentence. **Possible Answer** *The* scenery *in Yellowstone National Park is beautiful.* Continue for all the words.
- Give a clue for one of the words in the word lines. Examples: What pecks around the yard and says "cluck"? *chickens* What is a subject you study in school? *science* Continue with all of the words. After modeling a few examples, ask volunteers to create clues.
- Remind students of these sound/spellings: /r/ spelled *wr* and /m/ spelled *_mb.* Ask them to identify which consonant is silent in these spellings. *w and* b Then have volunteers try to name multisyllabic words using these sound/spellings.

Differentiating Instruction
English Learner

IF . . . students have difficulty decoding the words on Line 4, **THEN . . .** remind them that the spelling *_igh* makes /ī/. Show them other words that have the same sound/spelling. Use the ***English Learner Support Guide*** for additional instruction for new English learners.

Monitor Progress

to Differentiate Instruction
Formal Assessment

Word Structure During the word structure activity, note how well students understand the words.

APPROACHING LEVEL

IF . . . students do not understand the words on the word lines, **THEN . . .** use pictures, photos, objects, stick drawings, or pantomime to help them visualize the words.

ON LEVEL

IF . . . students need practice with the words on the word lines, **THEN . . .** have them write sentences using the same words on the lines.

ABOVE LEVEL

IF . . . students understand the words on the word lines, **THEN . . .** have them make a list of other multisyllabic words with silent consonants and write a poem using as many of them as they can.

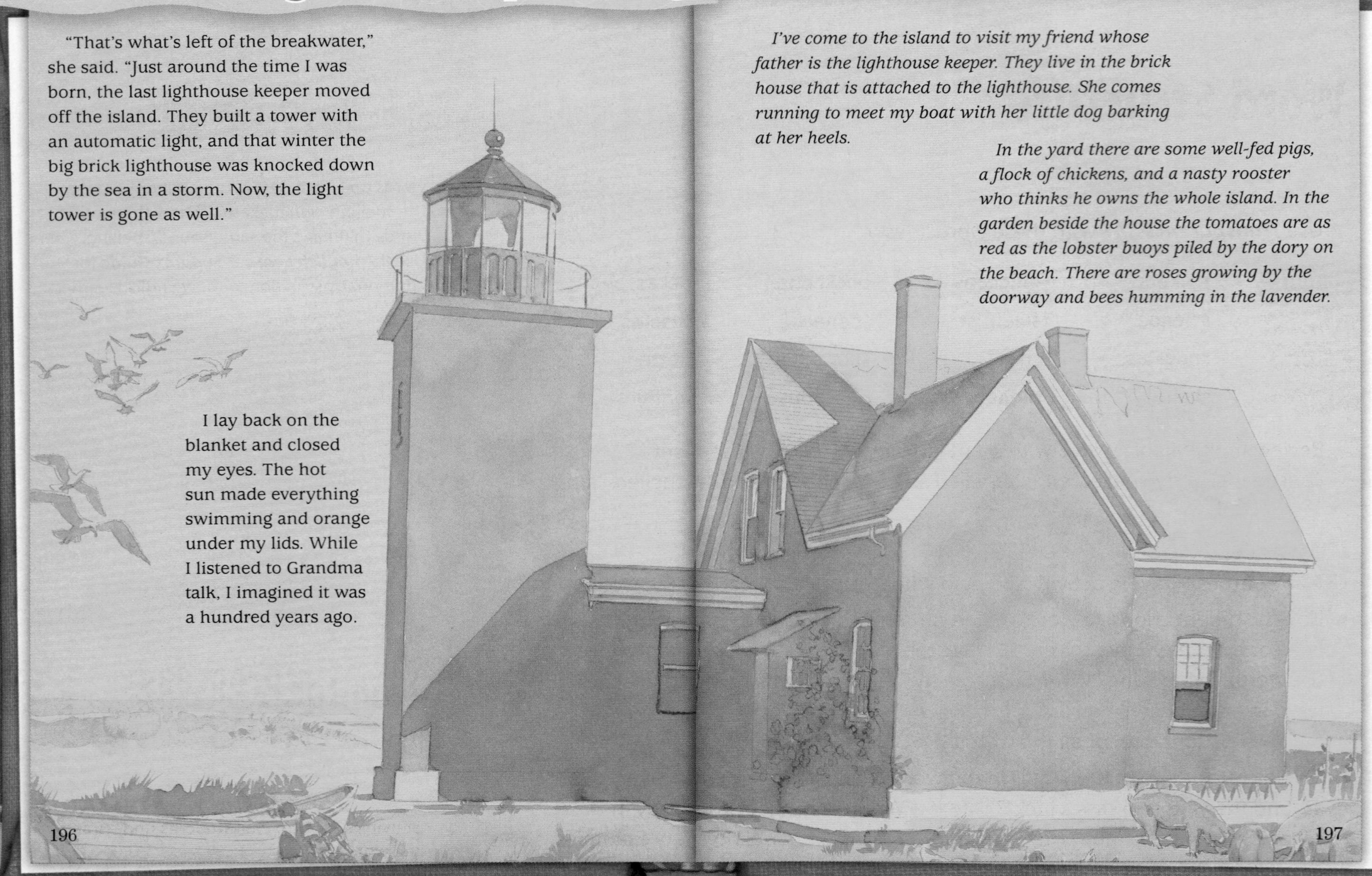

"That's what's left of the breakwater," she said. "Just around the time I was born, the last lighthouse keeper moved off the island. They built a tower with an automatic light, and that winter the big brick lighthouse was knocked down by the sea in a storm. Now, the light tower is gone as well."

I lay back on the blanket and closed my eyes. The hot sun made everything swimming and orange under my lids. While I listened to Grandma talk, I imagined it was a hundred years ago.

196

I've come to the island to visit my friend whose father is the lighthouse keeper. They live in the brick house that is attached to the lighthouse. She comes running to meet my boat with her little dog barking at her heels.

In the yard there are some well-fed pigs, a flock of chickens, and a nasty rooster who thinks he owns the whole island. In the garden beside the house the tomatoes are as red as the lobster buoys piled by the dory on the beach. There are roses growing by the doorway and bees humming in the lavender.

197

OBJECTIVES

Students will

- use the comprehension skills Cause and Effect and Author's Purpose.
- check comprehension.

MATERIALS

- ***Student Reader,*** Book 2, pp. 196–205
- ***Transparency*** 9
- ***Skills Practice 2,*** pp. 145–146

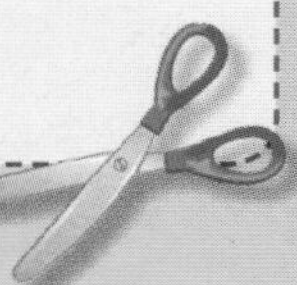

Comprehension Skill

Cause and Effect

Ask students to continue to identify cause-and-effect relationships in the text.

Cause	Effect
The sea destroyed the breakwater.	The lighthouse keeper moved off the island.
The lighthouse keeper moved off the island.	They built a tower with an automatic light.

Inside the lighthouse it is cool as a cave. It takes a while for my eyes to adjust to the darkness. We climb up the spiral staircase to the top of the lighthouse and step ouside into the glimmering sunshine on the walkway that circles the great lamp. I can see to Provincetown and beyond. I can see as far as anyone has ever seen before. Ships with sails as white as my summer dress are making their way along the horizon. The rooster, who is practicing for sunrise, starts to crow.
A rooster *was* crowing. I opened my eyes. But it wasn't a rooster, it was a herring gull who thought he owned the island.
In the basket Grandma had packed sandwiches and leftover birthday cake from my party the day before. She lit a candle, and the wind and I blew it out together. Grandma sang "Happy Birthday Plus One."
"Someday," she said, "this island will be completely gone, and you'll tell your granddaughter how you came out here and picnicked on it at low tide."
"I'll show her the brick as proof," I said.
Now the tide was coming back in. It moved slowly at first, as if making up its mind, and then it started claiming the edges of the beach.
Grandma stroked the smooth sand beside her.
198
199

Reading with a Writer's Eye

Language Use

Remind students that writers can use many different language styles when writing stories. The style writers adopt sets a tone for a particular story or piece of writing. Corinne Demas chose to write about the disappearing lighthouse using vivid imagery, vivid adjectives, similes (comparing two different things using the words *like* or *as*), and personification. Explain to students that personification is giving human qualities to animals or objects. For example, *The breeze sang a beautiful song.* Ask students the following questions:

- *What are examples of similes on page 198?* **Possible Answer** *The lighthouse is cool as a cave. The ships have sails as white as a summer dress.*
- *What is an example of personification on page 199?* **Possible Answer** *The tide moved slowly as if making up its mind.*

Expanding Vocabulary

adjust (əd • just′) *v.* to change for the purpose of correcting something (page 198)

The runner had to *adjust* her speed to keep up with her competitor.

horizon (hə • rī′ • zən) *n.* the line where the sky and the land or sea seem to meet (page 198)

The bluish-green sea blended into the steely blue sky at the *horizon*.

stroked (strōkd) *v.* past tense of **stroke:** to rub gently (page 199)

As Leigh *stroked* her cat Bungee, the cat purred affectionately.

"In this modern world people can do almost anything," she said. "We cut canals and build long bridges and dam rivers. We've tamed almost everything. I'm glad that we haven't completely tamed the ocean, too. What I love about a place like this is that it reminds us that nature still can have its way once in a while."

Grandma stood up. "Time to get going," she said.

We each took a corner of the beach blanket and let it flap free of sand in the wind. Then we folded the blanket together, like partners in a square dance. When our hands came together, Grandma kissed my knuckles and my nose.

The tide was coming in faster now, eating up the beach, eating up the island. We waded out to *Aphrodite*. Grandma started the engine in two tries, and we went chugging off. I looked back as Billingsgate Island began to disappear in the distance, and in the sea. The spot where Grandma and I had had our picnic would soon be underwater. Where the chickens once pecked for grain thrown out by the lighthouse keeper's little girl a hundred years ago, fish would peck at plankton.

By the time *Aphrodite* was back at her mooring in Wellfleet Harbor, Billingsgate Island was gone, a secret beneath the waves.

200

201

Teacher Tip

AUTHOR'S PURPOSE Remind students to keep in mind their own purpose for writing as they complete their writing assignments and any writing they do for their unit investigations. Remind them that keeping their purpose in mind will keep them on track in all of their writing.

Comprehension Skill

Author's Purpose

In addition to writing an entertaining story, Corinne Demas accomplished another purpose for writing "The Disappearing Island." She gives her readers information about the real disappearing lighthouse, and she teaches a lesson about the forces of nature. Ask students the following question:

What is Corinne Demas teaching readers about on page 200? **Possible Answer** *She reminds readers that even though people can invent many things, we cannot always control what nature is going to do.*

Checking Comprehension

Ask students the following questions to check their comprehension of the story:

- *Where did Grandma take Carrie for her ninth birthday?* *Billingsgate Island*
- *Why is the island disappearing?* **Possible Answer** *The ocean is eroding away the land over time.*
- *What was the island like in Grandma's day?* **Possible Answer** *It was a busy fishing community with houses and a school.*
- *What is Grandma glad about toward the end of the story?* **Possible Answer** *She is glad that people have not tamed the ocean.*
- *What is the secret?* **Possible Answer** *To those who never saw it or never would see it, the disappearing island would be a secret.*

Word Structure

Multisyllabic word with silent consonants: chickens

Day 4 **Reading and Responding**

Social Studies Inquiry

Genre Journal 

A journal is a place to record your thoughts and experiences.

Feature State Abbreviations

Point out the state abbreviation in "Keeping Track." Tell students that *CA* is the state abbreviation for California. Other state abbreviations include *FL* for Florida, *OH* for Ohio, and *MI* for Michigan. State abbreviations are used most often in mailing addresses. Tell students that they can find state abbreviations listed with the name of the state in the dictionary and also in phone books.

Reading "Keeping Track"

Have students read "Keeping Track" silently. Ask them to think about how this journal entry relates to the theme Communities across Time. *The journal tells readers about how and why a town developed in the late 1800s and what that town is like today.* Make sure students look at the state abbreviations and understand what they represent. Ask students to point to and read the other state abbreviation they see in "Keeping Track." Ask them the state they think this abbreviation represents. *Arizona*

Think Link

1. How did the town of Fillmore get its start? **Possible Answer** *The Southern Pacific Railroad built tracks and a train station there in the late 1800s. The town developed from that.*
2. Why is it helpful to have a standard way to abbreviate state names? **Possible Answer** *It's good to have a standard way so everyone uses the same abbreviations and everyone understands what they mean.*
3. How can you tell that history is important to the people of Fillmore? **Possible Answer** *The town still has the old railroad cars and it celebrates its history at a fair every year.*

Teacher Tips

SELECTION VOCABULARY Review the meaning of the highlighted selection vocabulary words *acres* and *voyage* in "Keeping Track."

CONCEPT/QUESTION BOARD After students read "Keeping Track," encourage them to post questions, answers, comments, news articles photographs, drawing, or other related items on the **Concept/Question Board.**

SILENT READ If some students are having difficulty comprehending the selection as they read silently, read the selection with them in small groups.

Social Studies Inquiry

Keeping Track

Genre

A **journal** is a place to record your thoughts and experiences.

Feature

A **state abbreviation** is a way to write the name of a state using only two letters.

March 18

Today we went to "Railfest" in Fillmore, CA. It is a fair they have each year. I did not think I would enjoy it that much, but it turned out to be fun. I got to ride an old-fashioned steam train, which was cool. I even liked learning about the history of the town.

The railroad is really important to Fillmore. In fact, it is the reason Fillmore exists. The Southern Pacific Railroad built tracks through here in the late 1800s. There was a train station here, helping the area to grow into a town. The town was named after one of the railroad managers.

It is neat that they keep the old railroad cars. I guess a lot of moviemakers like them too. Mom and Dad said that hundreds of movies have been filmed here!

The train took us past some nice farms and citrus groves. At one of the stops, we got off the train and toured a citrus ranch.

There were acres and acres of lemon trees and orange trees. It seems like a nice place to live.

Back in Fillmore, we walked around the town. I like that they have kept a sense of the way things were when the town got started. Maybe I will find out more about the history of my hometown!

Two more days of spring break. Tomorrow, we voyage to Phoenix, AZ. I wish we could take a train!

Think Link

1. How did the town of Fillmore get its start?
2. Why is it helpful to have a standard way to abbreviate state names?
3. How can you tell that history is important to the people of Fillmore?

Try It!

As you work on your investigation, think about how you can use state abbreviations when you take notes.

Inquiry Connections

Have students discuss how journals might be helpful in their Inquiries about communities across time. For example, if students study the history of their community, a journal would help them keep track of what they learn and their thoughts about their community.

Differentiating Instruction — **English Learner**

IF . . . students would benefit from additional practice with state abbreviations, **THEN . . .** point out that every state has an abbreviation. Write the abbreviation of your state and a few others on the board and see if students can identify each state from its abbreviation.

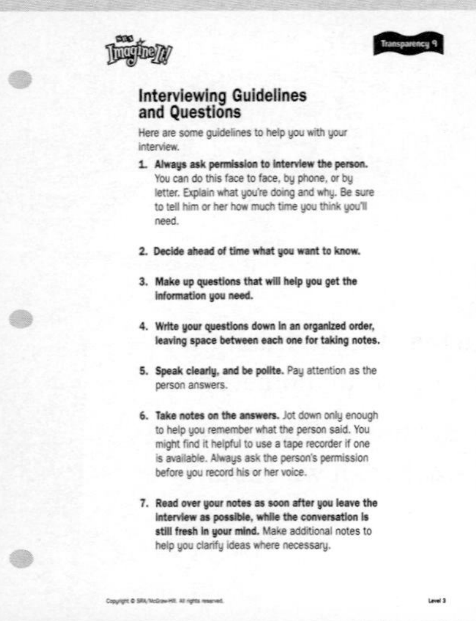
Transparency 9

Interviewing Guidelines and Questions

Here are some guidelines to help you with your interview.

1. **Always ask permission to interview the person.** You can do this face to face, by phone, or by letter. Explain what you're doing and why. Be sure to tell him or her how much time you think you'll need.
2. **Decide ahead of time what you want to know.**
3. **Make up questions that will help you get the information you need.**
4. **Write your questions down in an organized order, leaving space between each one for taking notes.**
5. **Speak clearly, and be polite.** Pay attention as the person answers.
6. **Take notes on the answers.** Jot down only enough to help you remember what the person said. You might find it helpful to use a tape recorder if one is available. Always ask the person's permission before you record his or her voice.
7. **Read over your notes as soon after you leave the interview as possible, while the conversation is still fresh in your mind.** Make additional notes to help you clarify ideas where necessary.

 Level 3

Transparency 9

Inquiry Process

Step 5—Collecting Information

Whole-Group Time

Whole Group

✦ Students should practice the study skills they have learned as they collect information. Encourage students to find useful Internet sources, interview people, use maps, and incorporate calendars in their investigations.

✦ If you were able to arrange for any speakers to come to class, use this as an opportunity for students to practice interviewing as a research skill. Review ***Transparency*** 9 with students before they interview any class guests or other people they have selected. Have students use ***Skills Practice 2*** pages 145–146 for an interview about their investigations.

✦ Discuss new questions or ideas related to the theme that students may have about the selection, "The Disappearing Island." As they read each selection, remind students to ask themselves questions such as: *Does the selection tell me something about the unit theme that I didn't know before? Does the selection make me wonder about something? Has anything I've learned in the selection changed my ideas about the theme or my investigation topic?* Model taking notes by writing students' responses on the board.

✦ As students come closer to their final presentations, hold a discussion with the whole class about the questions and ideas they had at the beginning of the unit. Discuss how students' ideas have changed and what they've learned. Ask if any of their initial questions have been answered and what they know now that they didn't know before about particular communities or about the theme in general.

Small-Group Time

Small Group

- Students should break into their small groups. If an interview would be relevant to their investigations, have students prepare questions for an interview on ***Skills Practice 2*** pages 145–146.
- Students should continue to collect the information and materials they need to re-evaluate their conjectures, answer their investigation question, and work toward their final presentations.
- Give each group time to finalize how they want to present the results of their Inquiry. They should also start planning how each group member will contribute to the group's presentation. Remind students to practice teamwork and to give each group member an equal share of the work and responsibility.

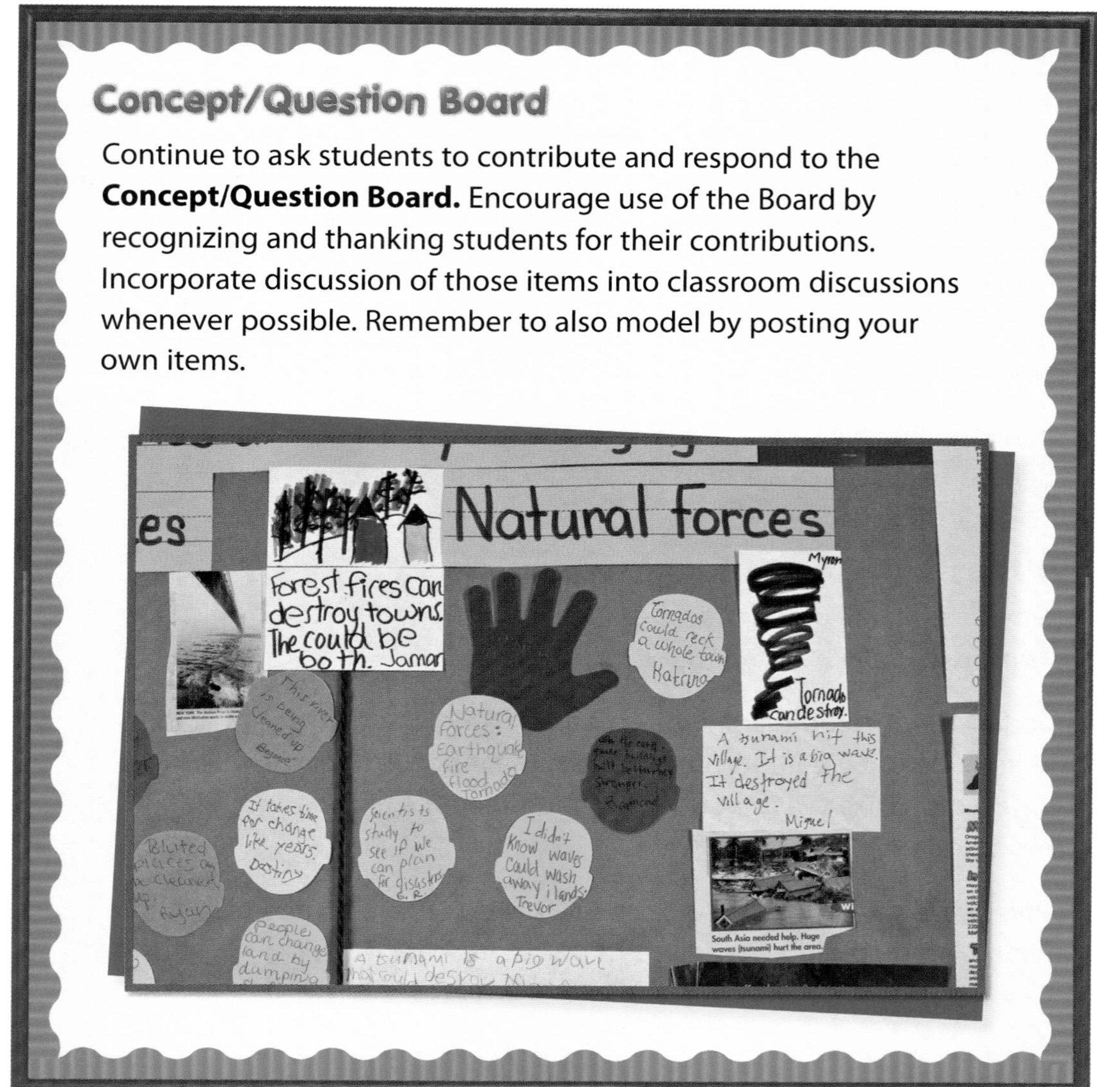

Concept/Question Board

Continue to ask students to contribute and respond to the **Concept/Question Board.** Encourage use of the Board by recognizing and thanking students for their contributions. Incorporate discussion of those items into classroom discussions whenever possible. Remember to also model by posting your own items.

Inquiry Rubric

To assess Collecting Information, see the Inquiry Rubrics in the Level Appendix.

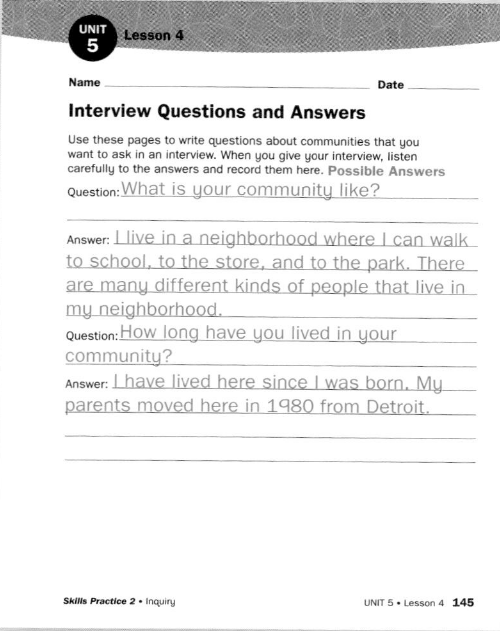

UNIT 5 Lesson 4

Name ____________ Date ______

Interview Questions and Answers

Use these pages to write questions about communities that you want to ask in an interview. When you give your interview, listen carefully to the answers and record them here. **Possible Answers**

Question: What is your community like?

Answer: I live in a neighborhood where I can walk to school, to the store, and to the park. There are many different kinds of people that live in my neighborhood.

Question: How long have you lived in your community?

Answer: I have lived here since I was born. My parents moved here in 1980 from Detroit.

Skills Practice 2 • Inquiry — UNIT 5 • Lesson 4 **145**

Skills Practice 2, p. 145

UNIT 5 Lesson 4

Interview Questions and Answers (continued)

Question: What is the best part of your neighborhood?

Answer: I love to walk my dog to the park and play with him. My neighbor has a dog too. Sometimes we walk our dogs together.

Question: What is bad about your community?

Answer: There is not much parking on our streets. Sometimes it is difficult to find a place to park the car.

Question: What is there to do in your community on Saturdays?

Answer: On Saturdays we play basketball when the weather is nice. Other people from the neighborhood have cookouts in the park. In the winters, we ice skate in the park.

146 UNIT 5 • Lesson 4 — Inquiry • *Skills Practice 2*

Skills Practice 2, p. 146

OBJECTIVES

Students will
- edit/proofread directions.
- review spelling words.
- construct a class calendar.
- learn uses for a computer.

MATERIALS
- ***Transparencies*** 17, 42 and 42A
- ***Skills Practice 2,*** p. 148
- Routine 16

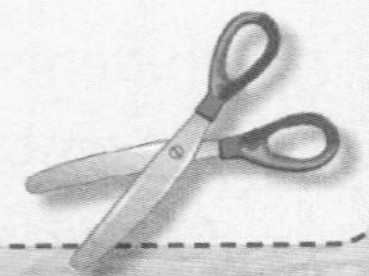

Transparency 17
17A

Proofreading Marks

Indent.	Dad read nursery rhymes to my sister and me when we were young. Each of us had a favorite rhyme. My sister liked "Jack and Jill." Dad must have read it to her 1,000 times!
Add something.	I also liked it, but my one was "Three Little Kittens." (favorite)
Take out something.	That rhyme is about the kittens who lost their mittens.
Make a capital letter.	i don't ask dad to read to me anymore.
Make a small letter.	Now, I ask if I can read to Him.
Check spelling.	What shood I reed to him first?
Add a period.	I think he will like this one

 SRA Imagine It! • Level 3 • Transparency 17 • 17A Level 3

Transparency 17

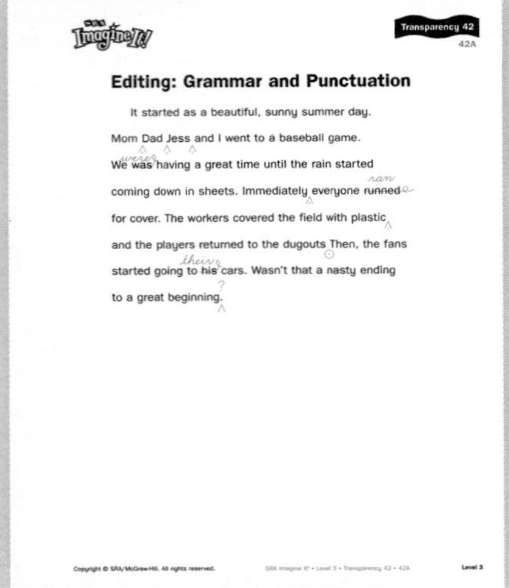

Transparency 42
42A

Editing: Grammar and Punctuation

It started as a beautiful, sunny summer day. Mom Dad Jess and I went to a baseball game. We was having a great time until the rain started coming down in sheets. Immediately everyone runned for cover. The workers covered the field with plastic and the players returned to the dugouts Then, the fans started going to his cars. Wasn't that a nasty ending to a great beginning.

Transparencies 42, 42A

Differentiating Instruction

English Learner

IF . . . students have difficulty understanding print conventions such as the use of spaces, capitalization, and punctuation, **THEN . . .** bear in mind that these conventions vary greatly among languages. English learners may need more time and practice to master English print conventions than their English-speaking peers.

Writing Directions

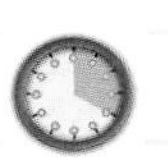

Editing/Proofreading

Teach

- Use Routine 16. Tell students they will now edit/proofread the revised copy of their directions.
- Remind students to look for errors in spelling, grammar, capitalization, and punctuation. Errors such as these can change the directions and cause problems for anyone following the directions. Tell students that if they cannot use spelling patterns to spell a word correctly, then they should look in a dictionary or thesaurus.
- Explain to students that details are important when writing or giving directions and they should edit and proofread the directions carefully.
- After students have completed the editing/proofreading process, encourage them to begin the publishing process by writing their final draft.

Guided Practice

- Remind students of the proofreading marks they are to use by displaying ***Transparency*** 17.
- Model editing/proofreading directions by reviewing ***Transparencies*** 42 and 42A or by editing/proofreading the model students helped you write. Emphasize the importance of proofreading spelling to avoid giving misinformation.
- Have students turn to ***Skills Practice 2*** page 148 to read and discuss the editing/proofreading checklist as a class.

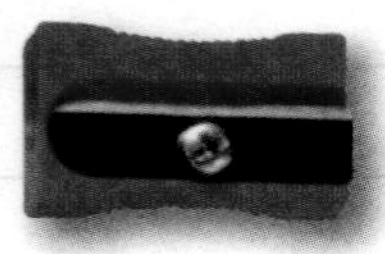

Writing, continued

Apply

Composing—Editing/Proofreading Have students edit/proofread their directions. Encourage students to refer to the checklist on page 148 in ***Skills Practice 2*** as they edit their directions.

UNIT 5 Lesson 4

Revising Use this checklist to revise your directions.

- ☐ Did you include all needed steps?
- ☐ Are the sentences in the best order?
- ☐ Did you number sentences to help your reader?
- ☐ Are your words clear and specific?

Editing/Proofreading Use this checklist to correct mistakes.

- ☐ Did you number your sentences correctly?
- ☐ Did you use correct spellings, including the spellings of streets?
- ☐ Did you correctly spell and punctuate abbreviations?
- ☐ Did you capitalize each sentence?
- ☐ Did you use present tense verbs?
- ☐ Did you use correct direction words?
- ☐ Did you explain where the directions begin and end?

Publishing Use this checklist to prepare your directions for publication.

- ☐ Neatly rewrite or type a final copy.
- ☐ Draw a map to help illustrate your directions.

148 UNIT 5 • Lesson 4 Writing • *Skills Practice 2*

Skills Practice 2, p. 148

Spelling

Word Families, Multisyllabic Words, and Silent Consonants

Apply

Family Strategy Tell students that if they know the family to which a new word belongs, they can use their knowledge about that family's spelling to determine how the new word is spelled.

Guided Practice

Write the word *undoubted* on the board. Ask a volunteer to come to the board and do the following: circle the base word, underline the prefix one time, and underline the suffix two times. Ask the class which words from this lesson are part of the same family as *undoubted. doubt; doubtful* Then ask students which of those words are multisyllabic words. *undoubted, doubtful*

Study Skills

Calendars

Teach

Remind students that calendars are important in many aspects of life, including organizing one's own daily activities. Calendars can be used as a source of information and also used as a tool to explain information as in a presentation.

Guided Practice

- Ask students to discuss the type of information they put on a calendar at school or at home. **Possible Answers** *holidays, sporting events, school events, doctor appointments*
- Ask students the types of events that might be listed on a school calendar. **Possible Answers** *sporting events, music events, plays, academic tournaments*

Apply

Construct a large monthly class calendar. Place students in small groups. Assign each group a different type of school activity. Then have each group research the events occurring at school that are associated with their activity. One member of each group can record those events on the class calendar. Encourage students to add events as they hear of them.

Differentiating Instruction **English Learner**

IF . . . students have intermediate or advanced English proficiency, **THEN . . .** allow them to share information about any other kinds of calendars that may be used in their native countries.

Listening/Speaking/Viewing

Using Multimedia

Teach

- Remind students that using technology and multimedia is a way to make presentations more effective. Assess students' comfort level in this area by leading a general discussion about what technology students have actually used.
- Point out to students some of the multimedia used in presentations, such as computers, televisions, DVD players, CD players, and so on.
- Explain to students that the computer can be used as a tool for creating presentations or as a visual aid for presentations. Students can use computers to create clean, professional, book-like materials. Computers can be used to create different fonts, type sizes, clip art, and to scan photographs. Computers can also be used to create color charts, diagrams, and so on.
- Students might want to use computers to give presentations and display graphics, video clips, audio clips, and so on. Such a display may add to and enhance oral presentations.

Guided Practice

If a computer or computer lab is available to students, allow time for hands-on experience with writing and creating presentations.

Apply

Have students incorporate a multimedia presentation into their unit investigation.

Differentiating Instruction **English Learner**

IF . . . students have limited vocabulary,
THEN . . . be sure to introduce or review multimedia vocabulary with them.

Day 5 **Preparing to Read** Review

OBJECTIVES

Students will

- review word families and multisyllabic words with silent consonants.
- build fluency.

MATERIALS

Transparencies 144 and 147

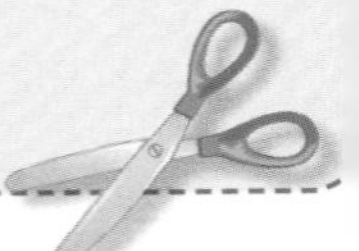

Word Structure

Use ***Transparency*** 144 with the word lines from Days 1 and 2 to review word families. Have students read the words on the word lines. Then have volunteers choose a line of words and use each word on the line in a sentence.

Line 1	safe	safety	safer	unsafe
Line 2	appear	disappear	disappeared	disappearing
Line 3	celebrate	celebrated	celebrating	celebration
Line 4	imagine	imagined	imagining	imagination

Word Structure

Use ***Transparency*** 147 with the word lines from Days 3 and 4 to review multisyllabic words with silent consonants. Have students read the words on the word lines. Then have students identify the silent consonants in each word and use it in a sentence.

Line 1	jackets	chickens	backbone	rocket
Line 2	science	scientist	scenery	muscles
Line 3	knuckles	knitted	knowing	knotted
Line 4	mighty	higher	lighthouse	rightly

Reading and Responding

Review

OBJECTIVES

Students will

- review selection vocabulary.
- review comprehension strategies Clarifying and Summarizing.
- review comprehension skills Author's Purpose and Cause and Effect.
- review fluency.

MATERIALS

- ***Student Reader,*** Book 2, pp. 184–205
- ***Transparencies*** 145

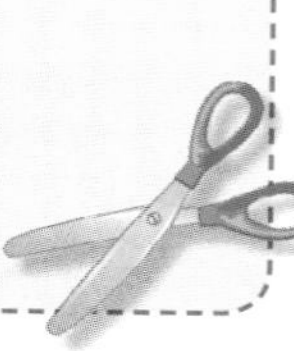

Selection Vocabulary

To review the selection vocabulary with students organize them into three or four teams depending on the size of the class. Give the class one vocabulary word at a time. Tell students that the first team to read aloud the sentence from the selection containing the vocabulary word and use that word correctly in an original sentence will score a point for their team. Repeat this exercise until all of the vocabulary words have been reviewed.

Selection Vocabulary

voyage (voi´ • əj) *v.* to journey by water or through space (page 188)

tide (tīd) *n.* the rise and fall of the sea (page 190)

sheltered (shel´ • tərd) *adj.* protected from danger (page 190)

ripples (rip´ • pəlz) *n.* plural form of **ripple:** a design created by waves (page 192)

eroding (ə • rōd´ • ing) *n.* the process of wearing or washing away slowly (page 193)

acres (ā´ • kûrz) *n.* plural form of **acre:** A measurement equal to 43,560 square feet (page 194)

claim (klām) *v.* to take as one's own (page 194)

toppled (top´ • pəld) *v.* past tense of **topple:** To fall or make fall forward (page 195)

Comprehension Strategies  

Review the following comprehension strategies with students:

- **Clarifying** is used by readers to figure out the meanings of words and difficult ideas. Ask students to go back to "The Disappearing Island" and find a difficult word they clarified as they read or a word that still needs clarification. If students figured out the word as they read, have them explain to the class how they figured it out. Have the class work together to clarify any final words that still need to be clarified. Suggest that students check the words in a dictionary, and remind them to use context clues to figure out the word.
- **Summarizing** prompts readers to keep track of what they are reading and to focus their minds on important information. To review this strategy, ask students to summarize "The Disappearing Island."

Comprehension Skills   

Review the following comprehension skills with students:

- **Author's Purpose** is a skill that helps readers determine the purpose the author had for writing the text. Knowing the author's purpose gives readers an idea of what they can expect to find in a text. To review this strategy, review what the author's purpose, or purposes, were for writing "The Disappearing Island." Ask students why they think Corrine Demas, who spends much of her time near the ocean, would want to tell the story of Billingsgate Island.
-  **Cause and Effect** helps readers identify what causes events to happen or what causes characters to behave in certain ways. This helps readers put together logical explanations in the text. Ask students to return to "The Disappearing Island" and share the cause-and-effect relationships they found with the class.

Reading with a Writer's Eye  

Review the following narrative elements with students:

- **Language Use** is how an author uses words in a story. To review this strategy, have students turn back to "The Disappearing Island" and find examples of figurative language such as similes and personification. Have students write a journal entry describing a place they would like to visit for their birthdays using similes and personification. Have students share their writing with the class.
- **Theme** is the main idea of a story, or a collection of stories. For example, the theme of Unit 5 is Communities across Time. Ask students what they think the theme is of "The Disappearing Island." Have students find specific examples in the story that support their ideas for the story's theme.

Fluency 

Review fluency by modeling intonation for students. Remind students that intonation, or reading with appropriate pitch and tone, makes text easier to comprehend and enjoy. Read a passage from pages 188–191 from "The Disappearing Island." Make sure that the passage totals at least 160 words to ensure an appropriate practice length.

Have students read the passage chorally. Encourage students to use intonation. Remind students to also pause after commas and end punctuation.

Day 5 **Language Arts**

OBJECTIVES

Students will
- ✦ publish their directions.
- ✦ take the spelling posttest.
- ✦ review cursive *D* and *B.*

MATERIALS

- ✦ ***Transparency*** 146
- ✦ ***Skills Practice 2,*** p. 148
- ✦ Routines 16 and 17

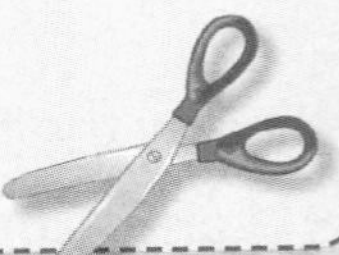

Writing Directions

ROUTINE 16 ROUTINE 17

Publishing

Teach

- ✦ Use Routines 16 and 17 as you instruct students on publishing their directions.
- ✦ Tell students that they are at the final stage of the writing process: publishing. Students should complete their directions and add the map or graphic they created to the published work.
- ✦ Because directions are often given aloud to others, have students trade and read a partner's directions, and then present their directions orally. Encourage students to give constructive feedback about their classmates' directions.

Guided Practice

Have students turn to page 148 in ***Skills Practice 2*** to read and discuss the publishing checklist.

Apply

- ✦ **Composing — Publishing** Have students refer to page 148 in ***Skills Practice 2*** as they publish their directions.
- ✦ Have students reflect upon the writing process and their direction for a journal entry in their Writer's Notebooks. Tell students they should write about
  - what they liked best about their written directions.
  - which stage of the writing process was most helpful, confusing, or fun.
  - feedback from students with whom they shared their directions.
  - whether their writing achieved its purpose.

Teacher Tips

CONSTRUCTIVE FEEDBACK When students read other students' work, encourage them to give positive and constructive feedback.

PORTFOLIOS Students should continue to select writing activities to add to their portfolios.

ASSESSMENT Use the Writing Rubrics found in the Level Appendix to evaluate students' directions. You may use any of the rubrics for Genre, Writing Process, and Writing Traits.

Spelling

Word Families, Multisyllabic Words, and Silent Consonants

Teach

Ask students to write *Spelling* and their names in the top margin of a clean piece of paper. Have them number the first fifteen lines 1–15, then skip a line and number the next three lines 1–3. Read each word, use it in a sentence, and give students time to spell it correctly. Encourage students to try to spell the challenge words, but assure them that misspelling a challenge word will not affect their test scores.

Spelling Words		Challenge Words
live	direct	know
lively	director	unknown
relive	direction	knowledge
living	indirect	
honor	doubt	
honorable	doubtful	
honest	undoubted	
honesty		

Guided Practice

✦ Have students proofread for any mistakes they made on the posttest. Tell them to categorize the mistakes as

- careless errors.
- errors in spelling base words.
- errors in spelling those base words with affixes added (multisyllabic words from the same word family).
- errors in spelling words with silent consonants.

✦ Make certain students are spelling word families, multisyllabic words, and words with silent consonants correctly.

Penmanship

Cursive Letters *D* and *B*

Teach

✦ Review uppercase cursive *D* and *B* with students. Refer to ***Transparency*** 146 for strokes and letter formations.

- **Letter *D*** Starting point, slant down
  Loop, curve down and up
  Loop and curve right: capital *D*
- **Letter *B*** Starting point, undercurve
  Slant down, retrace back up
  Curve forward, loop
  Curve forward and back
  Curve right: capital *B*

✦ To model proper letter formation, write the following sentence on the board: *Dr. Booth buys flowers from A Basket of Daisies.*

Guided Practice

✦ Ask for a volunteer to write the letters on the board. Guide the student as he or she writes.

Apply

After reviewing the sentence that you wrote on the board, have students practice writing the sentence on a separate piece of paper. Ask students to circle their best sentence based on the correct formation of *D* and *B*.

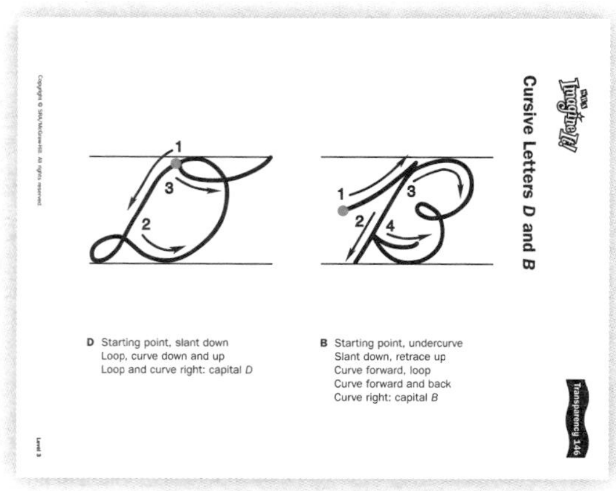

Transparency 146

Language Arts

OBJECTIVES

Students will

- ✦ review calendars.
- ✦ review the use of technology in reports and presentations.
- ✦ review *to be* and other irregular verbs.

MATERIALS

Lesson Assessment Book 2, pp. 67–74

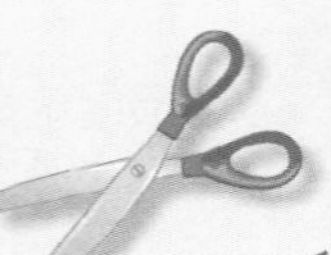

Study Skills 

Calendars

- ✦ Remind students that calendars are useful tools to display information and to organize information.
- ✦ Ask students how they might use calendars. **Possible Answers** *keep track of information about homework assignments, sporting events, music events, chores, and so on*
- ✦ Using a yearly calendar, ask students to look for the day or date and month of the following events:
  - Martin Luther King Jr. Day
  - Presidents' Day
  - First day of spring
  - Memorial Day
  - Labor Day

Listening/Speaking/Viewing 

Using Multimedia

Remind students that using multimedia and technology can help them prepare assignments and projects.

Multimedia and technology can also be used as a visual aid when making presentations.

- Ask students to discuss what types of technology or multimedia they would like to use to prepare assignments or presentations.
- Ask students to discuss what technology or multimedia they would like to use as a part of or as an aid to their presentations.

Grammar, Usage, and Mechanics

Verb *be* and Irregular Verbs

✦ Write the following verbs on the board and have students create sentences for each.

- are
- were
- met
- brought
- gave

Monitor Progress
Formal Assessment

Use pages 67–74 in ***Lesson Assessment Book 2*** to assess students' understanding of the skills taught in this lesson. Intervene with ***Reteach, Challenge Activities, Intervention Guide, eSkills & eGames, Leveled Readers,*** or activities in the ***Workshop Kit*** as needed.

Lesson Planner

	Day 1	Day 2
Preparing to Read MATERIALS ✦ ***Transparencies*** 149, 153 ✦ Routine 10 ✦ ***Skills Practice 2,*** pp. 155–158	**Daily News,** p. T348 ✅ **Word Structure** Review, pp. T348–T349	**Daily News,** p. T370 ✅ **Word Structure,** pp. T371 **Developing Oral Language,** p. T371
Reading and Responding MATERIALS ✦ ***Student Reader,*** Book 2, pp. 206–231 ✦ ***Transparencies*** 5, 150 ✦ Routines 11, 12, 14, A ✦ ***Skills Practice 2,*** pp. 159–162 ✦ Writer's Notebook ✦ ***Home Connection,*** pp. 59–60 ✦ ***Listening Library CD*** ✦ ***Leveled Reader*** ✦ ***Lesson Assessment Book 2***	**Build Background,** p. T350 **Preview and Prepare,** p. T351 **Selection Vocabulary,** pp. T352–T353 **Reading the Selection,** pp. T354–T357 1st READ ✅ **Comprehension Strategies** • Asking Questions, pp. T354, T358, T359, T362 • Making Connections, pp. T355, T360, T363 • Predicting, pp. T355, T362, T363 ✅ **Comprehension Skill** ☆ Main Idea and Details, p. T355 **Inquiry,** pp. T364–T365	✅ **Comprehension Strategies** • Asking Questions, pp. T372, T374, T375 • Making Connections, p. T373 • Predicting, p. T373 **Discussing the Selection,** p. T376 ✅ **Review Selection Vocabulary,** p. T377 **Fluency,** p. T377 **Theme Connections,** pp. T378–T379
Language Arts MATERIALS ✦ ***Transparencies*** 17, 17A, 24, 33, 33A, 82, 82A, 151, 152, 156 ✦ ***Skills Practice 2,*** pp. 163–170 ✦ ***Language Arts Handbook,*** pp. 156–161 ✦ Routine 16, B ✦ ***Lesson Assessment Book 2,*** pp. 75–82	**Writing** Prewriting, pp. T366–T367 ✅ **Spelling Pretest,** p. T367 **Penmanship,** Cursive Letters *Q* and *F*, p. T368	✅ **Writing** Prewriting, pp. T380–T381 **Spelling,** p. T381 ✅ **Grammar, Usage, and Mechanics** Complex Sentences, pp. T382–T383
Monitor Progress ✅ = Formal Assessment	✅ **Word Structure, p. T349** ✅ **Comprehension Strategy, p. T354** ✅ **Comprehension Skill, p. T355** ✅ **Spelling Pretest, p. T367**	✅ **Word Structure, p. T371** ✅ **Selection Vocabulary, p. T377** **Fluency, p. T377** ✅ **Writing, p. T381** ✅ **Grammar, Usage, and Mechanics, p. T383**

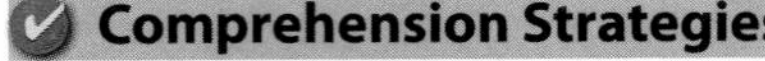

Literature Overview

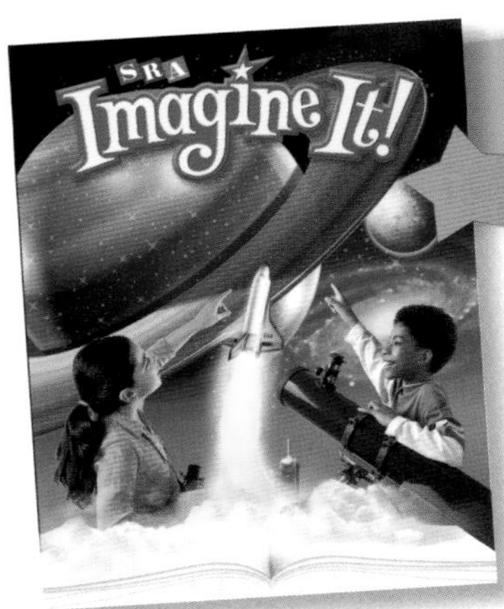

Student Reader

What Ever Happened to the Baxter Place?

by Pat Ross

illustrated by Roger Duvoisin

Notable Children's Trade Book (Social Studies)

Social Studies Inquiry

Hoover Dam

Early Explorers

poem by Marilyn Singer

illustrated by Susan Lawson

Caring for the World

poem by Jane Whittle

illustrated by Se Hee Jung

SRA
Imagine It!

Day 3

Daily News, p. T384
Word Structure
Review, pp. T384–T385

Comprehension Skills
- Main Idea and Details, pp. T386, T388, T390, T391
- Author's Point of View, p. T387

2nd READ

Reading with a Writer's Eye, p. T389
Supporting the Reading
- Comprehension Skill: Main Idea and Details, p. T392

Fluency, p. T393
Inquiry, p. T393

Writing
Prewriting, p. T394
Spelling, p. T395
Study Skills
Story Maps and Character Webs, p. T396
Grammar, Usage, and Mechanics, p. T397

Word Structure, p. T385
Comprehension Skill, p. T392
Fluency, p. T393
Spelling, p. T395
Study Skills, p. T396

Day 4

Daily News, p. T398
Word Structure, p. T399
Developing Oral Language, p. T399

Comprehension Skill
- Main Idea and Details, pp. T400, T402

Reading with a Writer's Eye, p. T401
Inquiry, pp. T404–T405

Writing
Drafting, pp. T406–T407
Spelling, p. T407
Study Skills, p. T408
Listening/Speaking/Viewing
Descriptive Presentations, p. T409

Word Structure, p. T399

Day 5 Review

Word Structure, p. T410

Selection Vocabulary, p. T411
Comprehension Strategies
- Asking Questions, p. T412
- Making Connections, p. T412
- Predicting, p. T412

Comprehension Skills
- Main Idea and Details, p. T412
- Author's Point of View, p. T412

Reading with a Writer's Eye, p. T413
Fluency, p. T413

Writing
Drafting, p. T414
Spelling Posttest, p. T415
Penmanship, p. T415
Study Skills, p. T416
Listening/Speaking/Viewing, p. T416
Grammar, Usage, and Mechanics, p. T417

Spelling Posttest, p. T415
***Lesson Assessment Book 2,* pp. 75–82**

Student Resources

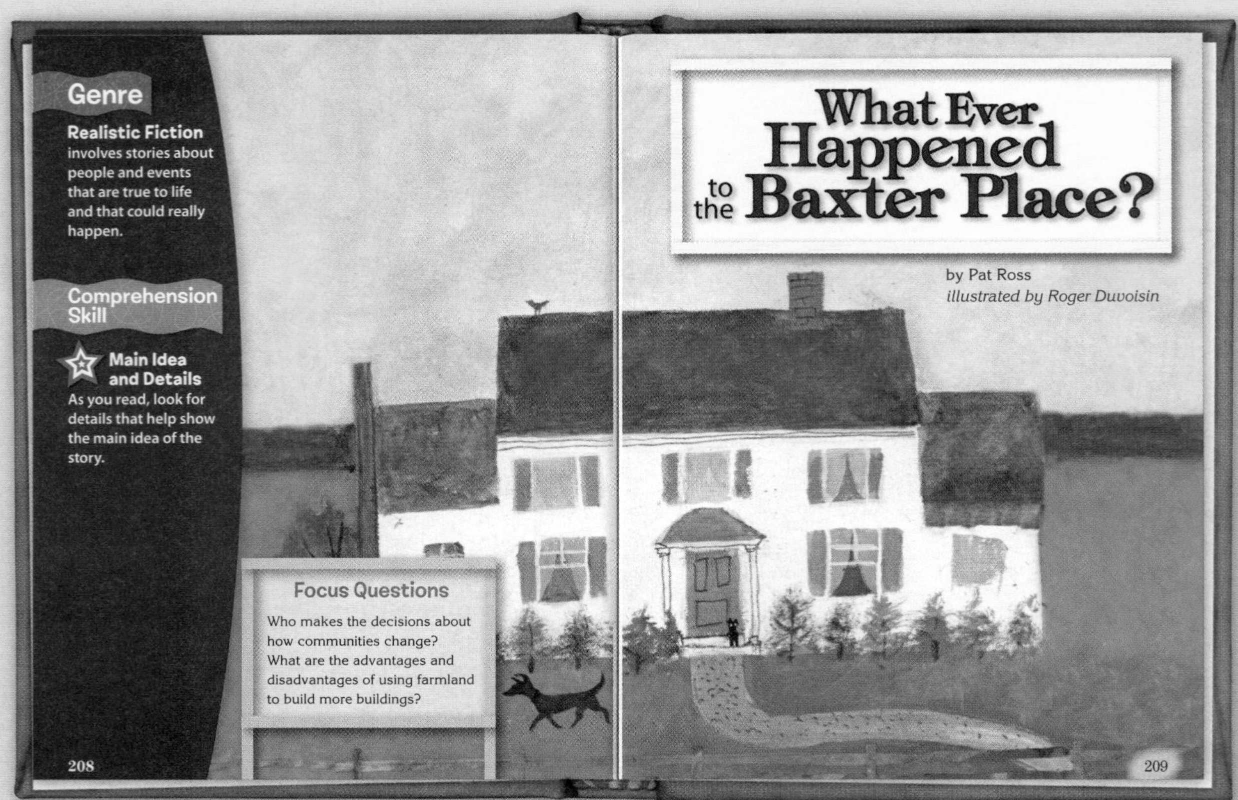

Genre

Realistic Fiction involves stories about people and events that are true to life and that could really happen.

Comprehension Skill

Main Idea and Details
As you read, look for details that help show the main idea of the story.

Focus Questions

Who makes the decisions about how communities change? What are the advantages and disadvantages of using farmland to build more buildings?

208

What Ever Happened to the Baxter Place?

by Pat Ross
illustrated by Roger Duvoisin

209

Student Reader, Book 2, pp. 208–231

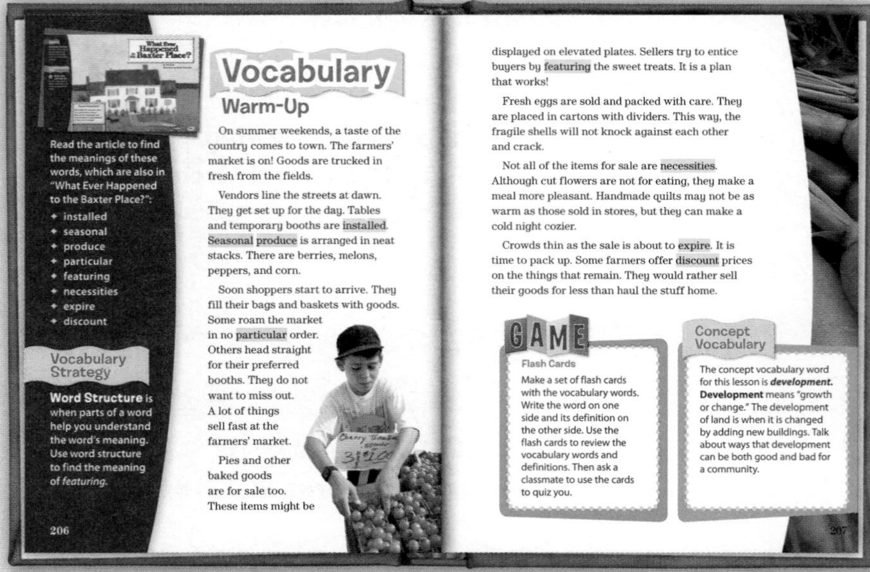

Read the article to find the meanings of these words, which are also in "What Ever Happened to the Baxter Place?":

- installed
- seasonal
- produce
- particular
- featuring
- necessities
- expire
- discount

Vocabulary Strategy

Word Structure is when parts of a word help you understand the word's meaning. Use word structure to find the meaning of *featuring.*

Vocabulary Warm-Up

On summer weekends, a taste of the country comes to town. The farmers' market is on! Goods are trucked in fresh from the fields.

Vendors line the streets at dawn. They get set up for the day. Tables and temporary booths are installed. Seasonal produce is arranged in neat stacks. There are berries, melons, peppers, and corn.

Soon shoppers start to arrive. They fill their bags and baskets with goods. Some roam the market in no particular order. Others head straight for their preferred booths. They do not want to miss out. A lot of things sell fast at the farmers' market.

Pies and other baked goods are for sale too. These items might be displayed on elevated plates. Sellers try to entice buyers by featuring the sweet treats. It is a plan that works!

Fresh eggs are sold and packed with care. They are placed in cartons with dividers. This way, the fragile shells will not knock against each other and crack.

Not all of the items for sale are necessities. Although cut flowers are not for eating, they make a meal more pleasant. Handmade quilts may not be as warm as those sold in stores, but they can make a cold night cozier.

Crowds thin as the sale is about to expire. It is time to pack up. Some farmers offer discount prices on the things that remain. They would rather sell their goods for less than haul the stuff home.

206

GAME

Flash Cards

Make a set of flash cards with the vocabulary words. Write the word on one side and its definition on the other side. Use the flash cards to review the vocabulary words and definitions. Then ask a classmate to use the cards to quiz you.

Concept Vocabulary

The concept vocabulary word for this lesson is ***development.*** **Development** means "growth or change." The development of land is when it is changed by adding new buildings. Talk about ways that development can be both good and bad for a community.

207

Student Reader, Book 2, pp. 206–207

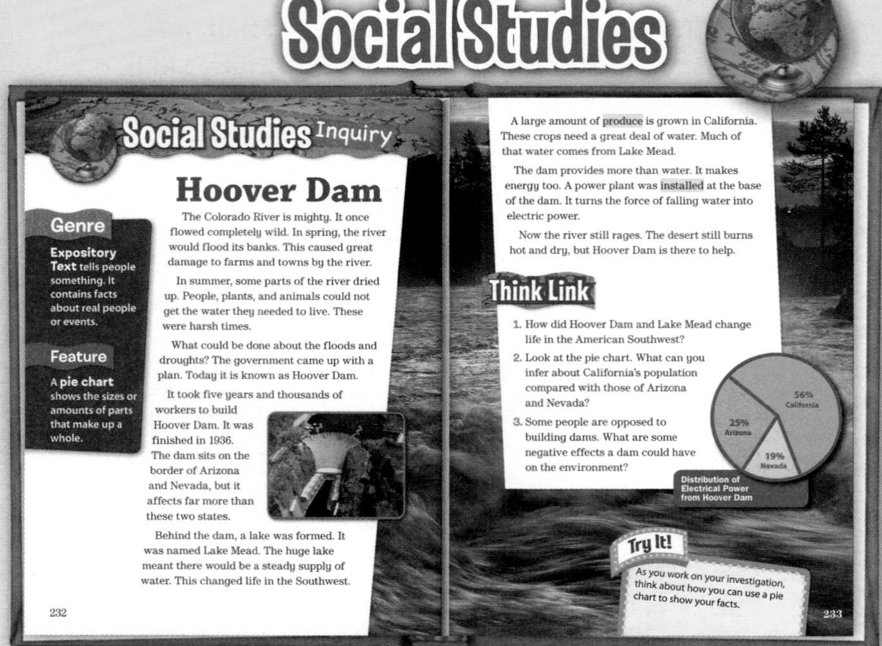

Social Studies

Social Studies Inquiry

Hoover Dam

Genre

Expository Text tells people something. It contains facts about real people or events.

Feature

A **pie chart** shows the sizes or amounts of parts that make up a whole.

The Colorado River is mighty. It once flowed completely wild. In spring, the river would flood its banks. This caused great damage to farms and towns by the river.

In summer, some parts of the river dried up. People, plants, and animals could not get the water they needed to live. These were harsh times.

What could be done about the floods and droughts? The government came up with a plan. Today it is known as Hoover Dam.

It took five years and thousands of workers to build Hoover Dam. It was finished in 1936. The dam sits on the border of Arizona and Nevada, but it affects far more than these two states.

Behind the dam, a lake was formed. It was named Lake Mead. The huge lake meant there would be a steady supply of water. This changed life in the Southwest.

232

A large amount of produce is grown in California. These crops need a great deal of water. Much of that water comes from Lake Mead.

The dam provides more than water. It makes energy too. A power plant was installed at the base of the dam. It turns the force of falling water into electric power.

Now the river still rages. The desert still burns hot and dry, but Hoover Dam is there to help.

Think Link

1. How did Hoover Dam and Lake Mead change life in the American Southwest?
2. Look at the pie chart. What can you infer about California's population compared with those of Arizona and Nevada?
3. Some people are opposed to building dams. What are some negative effects a dam could have on the environment?

56% California
25% Arizona
19% Nevada

Distribution of Electrical Power from Hoover Dam

Try It!

As you work on your investigation, think about how you can use a pie chart to show your facts.

233

Student Reader, Book 2, pp. 232–233

Cross-Curricular Resources

Curriculum Connections

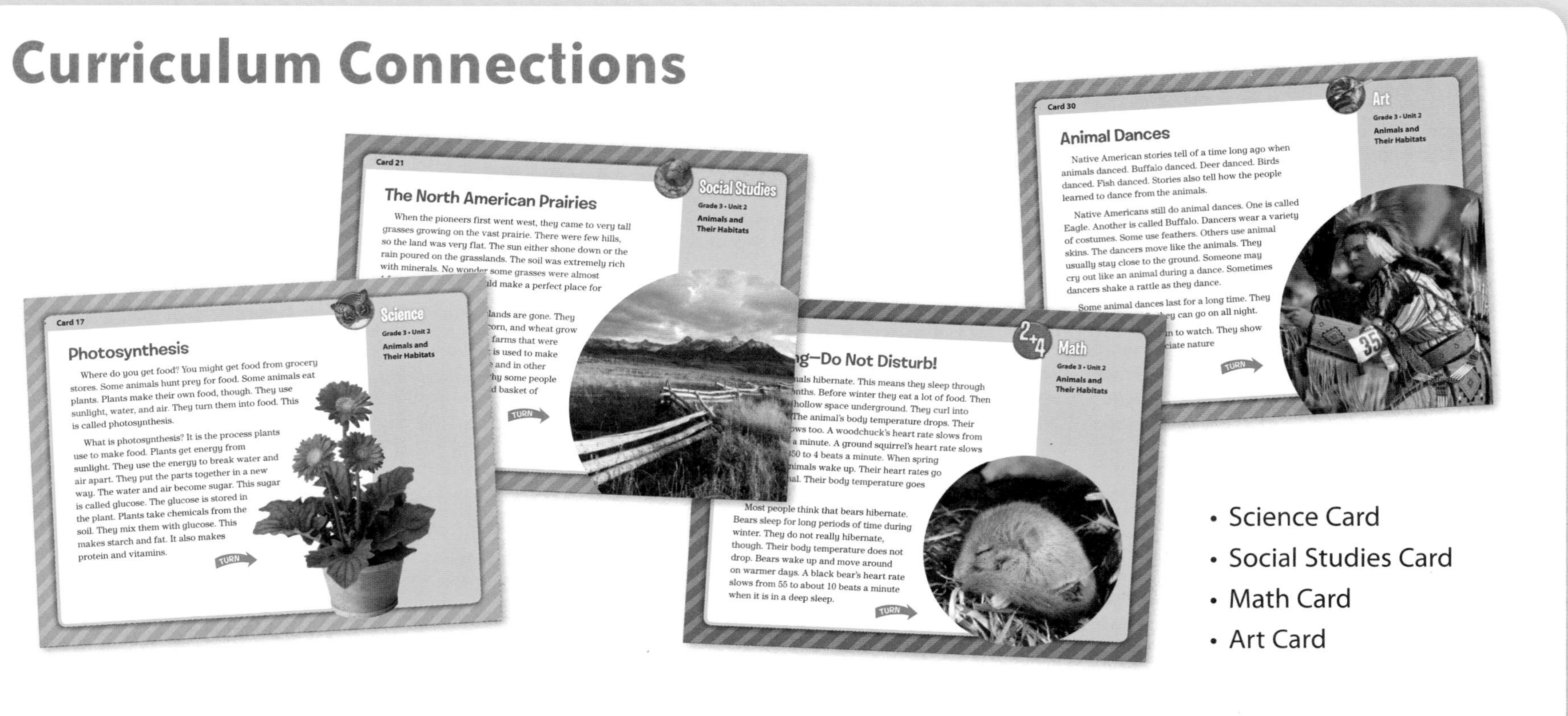

Card 21
The North American Prairies
Social Studies
Grade 3 • Unit 2
Animals and Their Habitats
Card 17
Photosynthesis
Science
Grade 3 • Unit 2
Animals and Their Habitats
Where do you get food? You might get food from grocery stores. Some animals hunt prey for food. Some animals eat plants. Plants make their own food, though. They use sunlight, water, and air. They turn them into food. This is called photosynthesis.
What is photosynthesis? It is the process plants use to make food. Plants get energy from sunlight. They use the energy to break water and air apart. They put the parts together in a new way. The water and air become sugar. This sugar is called glucose. The glucose is stored in the plant. Plants take chemicals from the soil. They mix them with glucose. This makes starch and fat. It also makes protein and vitamins.
TURN
Math
Grade 3 • Unit 2
Animals and Their Habitats
Card 30
Animal Dances
Art
Grade 3 • Unit 2
Animals and Their Habitats
Native American stories tell of a time long ago when animals danced. Buffalo danced. Deer danced. Birds danced. Fish danced. Stories also tell how the people learned to dance from the animals.
TURN

- Science Card
- Social Studies Card
- Math Card
- Art Card

Leveled Readers for Social Studies

The Roman Empire
by Mark Fara

Approaching Level

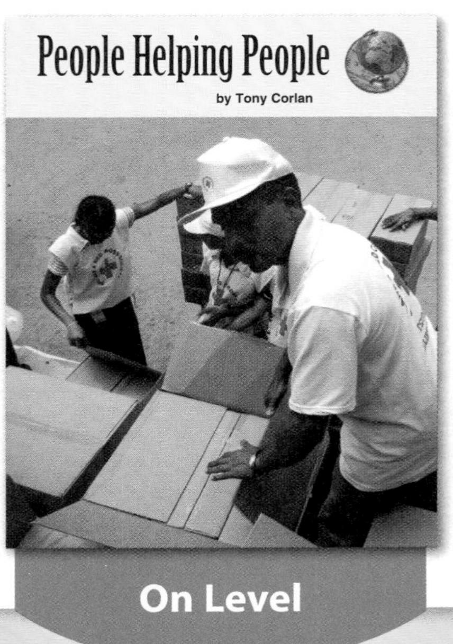

People Helping People
by Tony Corlan

On Level

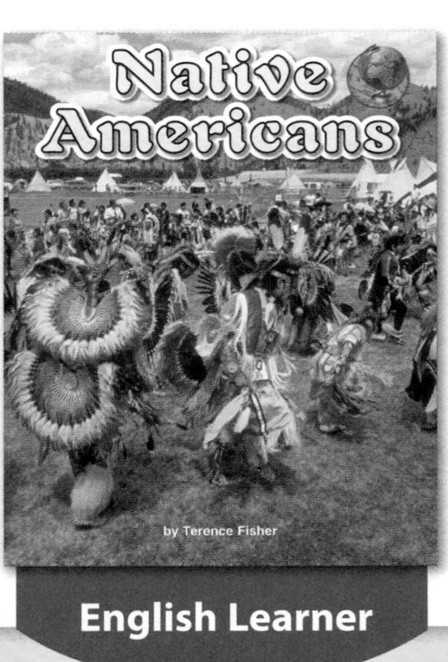

Native Americans
by Terence Fisher

English Learner

Cultures Coming Together
by Makiko Kurosawa

Above Level

Lesson 5 Overview

Differentiating Instruction for Workshop

Day 1

Approaching Level	On Level	English Learner	Above Level
Preparing to Read			
Word Structure: Review the word lines. In small groups, help students complete ***Reteach*** page 149, or work with them on the word structure activities in the ***Intervention Guide,*** Unit 5, Lesson 5.	**Word Structure:** Have students make lists of base words and practice adding different prefixes and suffixes to them.	**Word Structure:** Review the prefix instruction in the ***English Learner Support Guide.***	**Word Structure:** Have students complete ***Challenge Activities*** page 135. In pairs, students can scramble words from the word lines and give them to a partner to unscramble.
Reading and Responding			
Vocabulary: Have students create illustrations for the selection vocabulary words. **Comprehension:** Have students write a journal entry about a connection they can make to the story. **Inquiry:** Have students confirm and revise their conjectures based on new information they collected.	**Vocabulary:** Have students use the selection vocabulary words to write sentences. **Comprehension:** Have students write a journal entry about a prediction they would like to make about the story. Have students explain the reasons behind the predictions they make. **Inquiry:** Have students confirm and revise their conjectures based on new information they collected.	**Vocabulary:** Use ***English Learner Support Guide,*** Unit 5, Lesson 5. **Comprehension:** Have students write a journal entry about a connection they can make to the story. **Inquiry:** Have students confirm and revise their conjectures based on new information they collected.	**Vocabulary:** Have students use the selection vocabulary words in a story. **Comprehension:** Have students write a journal entry about a prediction they have for the story. Have students include reasons for their predictions in their journal entries. **Inquiry:** Have students confirm and revise their conjectures based on new information they collected.
Language Arts			
Writing: Have students continue to brainstorm ideas for plays. **Spelling:** Have students write the spelling words for this week and circle the prefix in each word.	**Writing:** Encourage students to share their play ideas with others. **Spelling:** Have students proofread their plays for spelling errors.	**Writing:** Have students brainstorm ideas for their play with a small group of peers. **Spelling:** Have students work in groups to decide four rules that will help them remember how to spell this lesson's words.	**Writing:** Have students begin working on their graphic organizers after they know have an idea for their plays. **Spelling:** Have students create a list of seven spelling words spelled incorrectly, trade papers with a partner, and correct the lists.

Day 2

	Approaching Level	On Level	English Learner	Above Level
Preparing to Read	**Word Structure:** Have students review their prefix flash cards with a partner. Students can use ***eSkills & eGames*** or an activity in the ***Workshop Kit*** for practice with prefixes.	**Word Structure:** Students can use ***eSkills & eGames*** or an activity in the ***Workshop Kit*** for practice with prefixes.	**Word Structure:** Have students review their prefix flash cards with a partner. Students can use ***eSkills & eGames*** or an activity in the ***Workshop Kit*** for practice with prefixes.	**Word Structure:** Students can use ***eSkills & eGames*** or an activity in the ***Workshop Kit*** for practice with prefixes.
Reading and Responding	**Vocabulary:** Have students use ***Reteach*** page 151. **Comprehension:** Have students apply questions asked about the story to the ***Concept/ Question Board.*** **Fluency:** Have students reread a passage from the story with a partner or individually.	**Vocabulary:** Have students complete a game in the ***Workshop Kit.*** **Comprehension:** Have students review the **Concept/ Question Board.** Have students discuss whether the story has answered any questions that they have about Communities across Time. **Fluency:** Have students read into a tape recorder at the beginning and end of the week. Have them listen to themselves at the end of the week so they can hear their progress.	**Vocabulary:** Help students create flash cards for the selection vocabulary words. Have students use them to quiz a partner. **Comprehension:** Have students help each other clarify confusing or difficult ideas, words, or passages. **Fluency:** Have students engage in echo reading with passages from the story.	**Vocabulary:** Have students complete ***Challenge Activities*** page 137. **Comprehension:** Have students create a checklist of questions they have about the story. Have students check the questions off whenever an answer is given for a question. **Fluency:** Have students choose a text on their independent level to read silently.
Language Arts	**Writing:** Have students continue to work on their graphic organizers. **Spelling:** Have students work in groups to review this week's spelling word list. **Grammar, Usage, and Mechanics:** Have students complete ***Reteach*** activities on page 155.	**Writing:** Have students share their ideas and graphic organizers with peers. **Spelling:** Working in pairs, have students think of and write a list of as many other words with prefixes as they can. **Grammar, Usage, and Mechanics:** Have students create five complex sentences or edit a piece of their writing to correct fragmentation.	**Writing:** Have students work with a peer to fill in graphic organizers. **Spelling:** Have students work in pairs to write a list of as many words with prefixes as they can think of. **Grammar, Usage, and Mechanics:** Refer to the ***English Learner Support Guide,*** Unit 5, Lesson 5.	**Writing:** Encourage students to share their graphic organizers with classmates. **Spelling:** Have students rewrite a paragraph from their selection. Remind them to pay attention to the way the words are spelled. **Grammar, Usage, and Mechanics:** Have students complete ***Challenge Activities*** page 140.

Lesson 5 Overview

Differentiating Instruction for Workshop

Day 3

	Approaching Level	On Level	English Learner	Above Level
Preparing to Read	**Word Structure:** Review the word lines. Then have students complete ***Reteach*** page 150, or work with them on the word structure activities in the ***Intervention Guide,*** Unit 5, Lesson 5.	**Word Structure:** Have students write sentences using words from the word lines.	**Word Structure:** Review the word lines. Then use the ***English Learner Support Guide*** for additional word structure instruction.	**Word Structure:** Have students complete ***Challenge Activities*** page 136. Then have students write paragraphs using words from the word lines.
Reading and Responding	**Vocabulary:** Have students rewrite the definitions of three of the selection vocabulary words. **Comprehension:** Have students create an outline that tracks the main ideas and details given in the story. **Fluency:** Have students use ***Leveled Readers.***	**Vocabulary:** Have students find words in the story that are unfamiliar, find the meaning in a dictionary or the glossary, and use the words in sentences. **Comprehension:** Have students find five sentences that use the third-person point of view and rewrite them in the first person point of view. **Fluency:** Have students read a passage from their favorite story aloud to a partner.	**Vocabulary:** Have students rewrite the definitions for three of the selection vocabulary words. **Comprehension:** Have students create a list of comprehension questions. Have students trade their questions with a partner. **Fluency:** Have students use ***Leveled Readers.***	**Vocabulary:** Have students write functional definitions of three of the selection vocabulary words.. **Comprehension:** Have students draw maps illustrating the Baxter farm and the changes it went through. **Fluency:** Have students use ***Leveled Readers.***
Language Arts	**Writing:** Have students work with a partner to fill in graphic organizers. **Spelling:** Have students complete ***Reteach*** page 154. **Grammar, Usage, and Mechanics:** Have students look for fragments in their writing and revise them to create complex sentences.	**Writing:** Have students work on plot or character development. **Spelling:** Have students think of another word family, write it on a separate sheet of paper, and circle affixes in the words. **Grammar, Usage, and Mechanics:** Have students look for fragments in a piece of their writing and revise them to create complex sentences.	**Writing:** Have students work with a partner to complete the graphic organizer and web. **Spelling:** Have students think of another word family, write it on a separate sheet of paper, and circle affixes in the words. **Grammar, Usage, and Mechanics:** Have students look for fragments in a piece of their writing and revise them to create complex sentences.	**Writing:** Have students work on adding depth to one of their characters. **Spelling:** Have students complete ***Challenge Activities*** page 139. **Grammar, Usage, and Mechanics:** Have students create complex sentences to add depth in their dialogue.

Day 4

	Approaching Level	On Level	English Learner	Above Level
Preparing to Read	**Word Structure:** Have students write sentences using words from the word lines. Have students make lists of new word families from base words.	**Word Structure:** Students can write paragraphs using words from the word lines.	**Word Structure:** Have students make lists of new word families from base words. Then have students write sentences using words from their new word families.	**Word Structure:** Students can read additional materials looking for word families and words with silent consonants.
Reading and Responding	**Vocabulary:** Have students write riddles using the selection vocabulary words. **Comprehension:** Have students create review questions for the story and trade questions with a partner. **Inquiry:** Have groups of students compare and revise their conjectures.	**Vocabulary:** Have students use the selection vocabulary words in extended sentences. **Comprehension:** Have students compare and contrast "What Ever Happened to the Baxter Place?" to "The Disappearing Island." **Inquiry:** Have groups of students compare and revise their conjectures.	**Vocabulary:** Have students write sentences using expanding vocabulary words. **Comprehension:** Have students create review questions for the story and trade them with a partner. **Inquiry:** Have groups of students compare and revise their conjectures.	**Vocabulary:** Have students write a story using the selection vocabulary words. **Comprehension:** Have students use a Venn diagram to show how two selections from Unit 5 are alike and different. **Inquiry:** Have groups of students compare and revise their conjectures.
Language Arts	**Writing:** Have students continue to draft their plays. **Spelling:** Have students work in pairs to review the spelling words.	**Writing:** Have students continue to draft their plays. **Spelling:** Have students write a list of the five words that they hear most often that have affixes.	**Writing:** Have students conference with peers while drafting their plays. **Spelling:** Have students write a list of the five words that they hear most often that have suffixes.	**Writing:** Encourage students to share their ideas with peers. **Spelling:** Have students spell and misspell the spelling words on a piece of paper, trade papers with a partner, and circle the correct words.

Differentiating Instruction for Workshop

Day 5

Section	Approaching Level	On Level	English Learner	Above Level
Preparing to Read	**Word Structure:** Review the word lines. Then have students review their prefix flash cards. Students can also use ***eSkills & eGames*** for practice with prefixes.	**Word Structure:** Have small groups of students make lists of base words. Then have students practice adding appropriate prefixes to the words on their lists. Students also can use ***eSkills & eGames*** for practice with prefixes.	**Word Structure:** Have students review their prefix flash cards. Then have students reread "What Ever Happened to the Baxter Place?" while looking for words with affixes. Students also can use ***eSkills & eGames*** for practice with prefixes.	**Word Structure:** Have small groups of students write clue sentences for words on the word lines.
Reading and Responding	**Vocabulary:** Have students write a poem about their community using words from the Word Bank. **Comprehension:** Have students write a short summary for "What Ever Happened to the Baxter Place?" **Fluency:** Have students write answers to comprehension questions from the ***Leveled Readers.***	**Vocabulary:** Have students use a thesaurus to find antonyms and synonyms for the selection vocabulary words. **Comprehension:** Have students write a summary of "What Ever Happened to the Baxter Place?" **Fluency:** Have students select a book to read on their independent level.	**Vocabulary:** Have students create crossword puzzles using the selection vocabulary words. **Comprehension:** Have students write a summary of "What Ever Happened to the Baxter Place?" Encourage students to include illustrations if they have trouble expressing themselves. **Fluency:** Have students use vocabulary from the ***Leveled Readers*** in extended sentences.	**Vocabulary:** Have students write a story using the selection vocabulary words. **Comprehension:** Have students research issues such as nature and technology that affect farmers' lives. Have students write an essay explaining what they learn from their research. **Fluency:** Have students reread passages from the story.
Language Arts	**Writing:** Have students read their drafts to make sure there is a definite beginning, middle, and end. **Spelling:** Have students work in groups to read each other words aloud and attempt to spell those words on a piece of paper.	**Writing:** Have students conference with peers. **Spelling:** Have students make a list of five spelling words with one letter missing, trade papers with a partner, and fill in the blanks.	**Writing:** Have students use a thesaurus as they draft their plays. **Spelling:** Have students choose five spelling words for a partner to spell on a piece of paper.	**Writing:** Have students review their drafts to make notes of areas that need to be revised. **Spelling:** Have students misspell this lesson's words on a piece of paper, trade with a partner, and write the skill that was misspelled next to each word.

Resources for

Differentiating Instruction 

Leveled Readers

Approaching Level

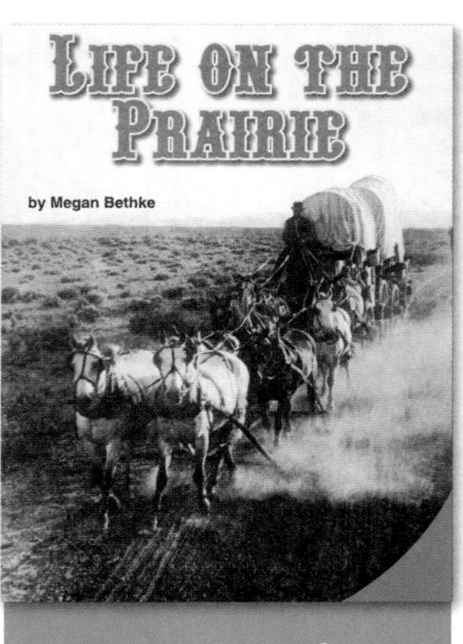

On Level

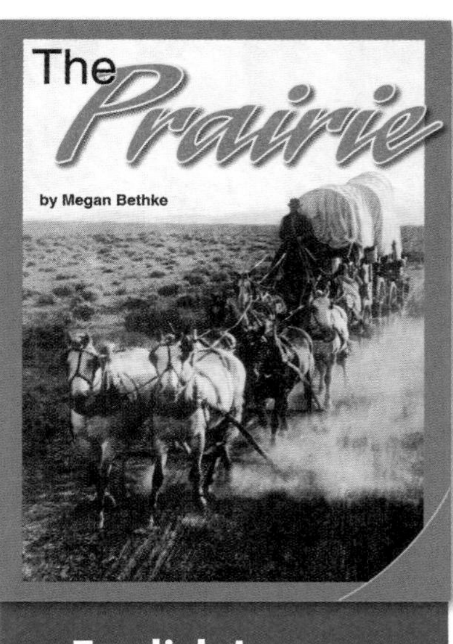

English Learner

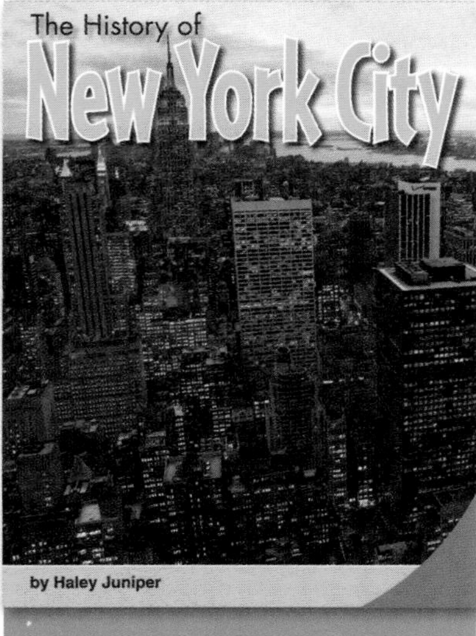

Above Level

Additional Skills Practice

Approaching Level

Reteach

- Review, p. 149
- Words with Silent Consonants, p. 150
- Selection Vocabulary, p. 151
- Main Idea and Details, pp. 152–153
- Spelling, p. 154
- Complex Sentences, p. 155

On Level

Skills Practice 2

- Review, pp. 155–156
- Words with Silent Consonants, pp. 157–158
- Selection Vocabulary, pp. 159–160
- Main Idea and Details, pp. 161–162
- Writing a Play, pp. 163–164
- Spelling, pp. 165–166
- Complex Sentences, pp. 167–168

English Learner

English Learner Support Activities

English Learner Support Activities, Unit 5, Lesson 5

Above Level

Challenge Activities

- Review, p. 135
- Words with Silent Consonants, p. 136
- Selection Vocabulary, p. 137
- Main Idea and Details, p. 138
- Spelling, p. 139
- Complex Sentences, p. 140

Additional Resources for Differentiating Instruction

Workshop Kits

Technology

The following electronic resources are available for students:

- ***eStudent Reader***
- ***eSkills & eGames***
- ***Listening Library CDs***

Electronic resources for the teacher include:

- ***ePlanner***
- ***eTeacher's Edition***
- ***eAssess***
- ***ePresentation***

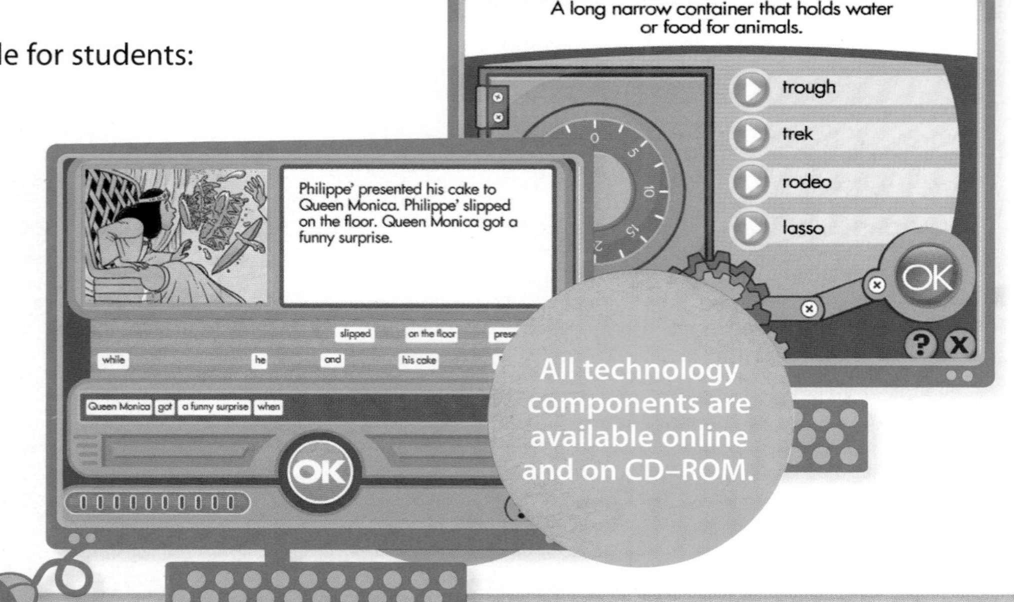

All technology components are available online and on CD–ROM.

English Learner

Leveled Reader

English Learner Support Activities, Lesson 5

Listening Library Unit 5

English Learner Support Guide, Lesson 5

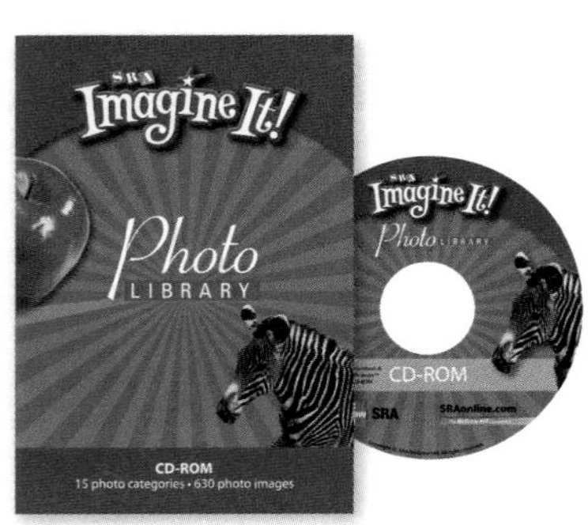

Photo Library

Approaching Level

Intervention

Intervention Workbook

Intervention Teacher's Guide

Lesson 5 Overview

Lesson Assessment

Monitor Progress to Differentiate Instruction

Comprehension Strategies Rubrics

Use the Comprehension Strategies Rubrics to determine whether a student is using the strategies.

- Asking Questions, p. T354
- Making Connections, p. T355
- Predicting, p. T355

Inquiry Rubrics

Use the Inquiry Rubrics to assess a student's performance throughout the stages of the investigation for each unit. In addition, at the end of the unit you can use the rubrics to assess the groups' collaborative work as well as an individual's participation in that group.

- Confirming and Revising Conjectures, p. T405
- Presenting Inquiry Findings, p. T423
- Overall Research, p. T431
- Participation in Collaborative Inquiry, p. T431

Writing Rubrics

Use the writing rubrics in the Level Appendix to evaluate a student's play.

- Genre
- Writing Process
- Writing Traits

Lesson Assessments

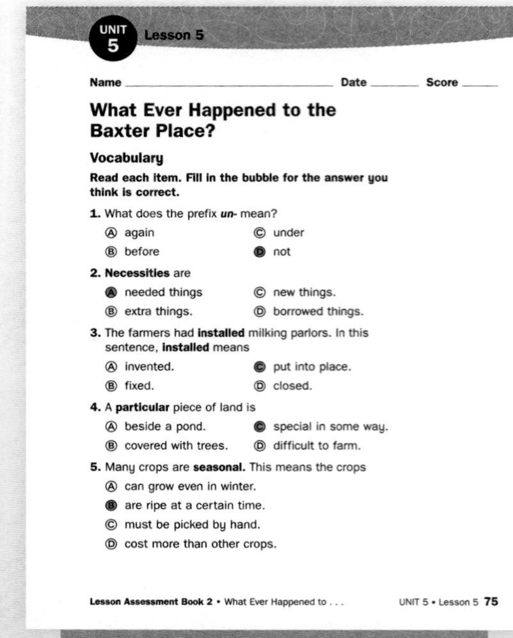

UNIT 5 Lesson 5

Name ______ Date ______ Score ______

What Ever Happened to the Baxter Place?

Vocabulary

Read each item. Fill in the bubble for the answer you think is correct.

1. What does the prefix *un-* mean?
   - Ⓐ again
   - Ⓑ before
   - Ⓒ under
   - ● not
2. **Necessities** are
   - ● needed things
   - Ⓑ extra things.
   - Ⓒ new things.
   - Ⓓ borrowed things.
3. The farmers had **installed** milking parlors. In this sentence, **installed** means
   - Ⓐ invented.
   - Ⓑ fixed.
   - ● put into place.
   - Ⓓ closed.
4. A **particular** piece of land is
   - Ⓐ beside a pond.
   - Ⓑ covered with trees.
   - ● special in some way.
   - Ⓓ difficult to farm.
5. Many crops are **seasonal.** This means the crops
   - Ⓐ can grow even in winter.
   - ● are ripe at a certain time.
   - Ⓒ must be picked by hand.
   - Ⓓ cost more than other crops.

Lesson Assessment Book 2 • What Ever Happened to . . . UNIT 5 • Lesson 5 75

Lesson Assessment Book 2, p. 75

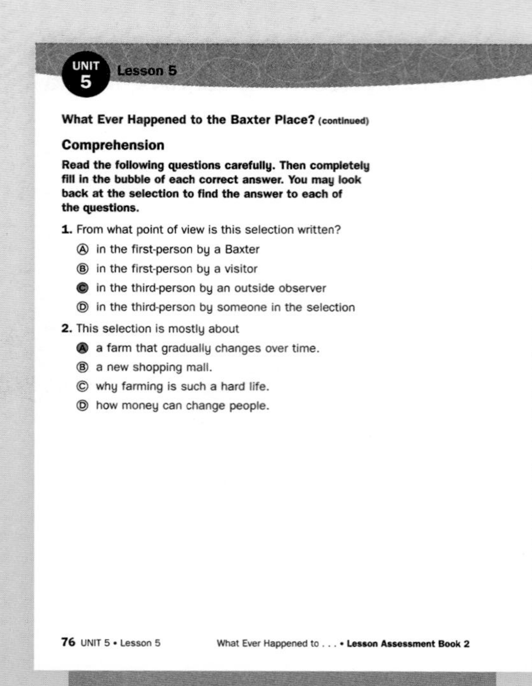

UNIT 5 Lesson 5

What Ever Happened to the Baxter Place? (continued)

Comprehension

Read the following questions carefully. Then completely fill in the bubble of each correct answer. You may look back at the selection to find the answer to each of the questions.

1. From what point of view is this selection written?
   - Ⓐ in the first-person by a Baxter
   - Ⓑ in the first-person by a visitor
   - ● in the third-person by an outside observer
   - Ⓓ in the third-person by someone in the selection
2. This selection is mostly about
   - ● a farm that gradually changes over time.
   - Ⓑ a new shopping mall.
   - Ⓒ why farming is such a hard life.
   - Ⓓ how money can change people.

76 UNIT 5 • Lesson 5 What Ever Happened to . . . • Lesson Assessment Book 2

Lesson Assessment Book 2, p. 76

Use these summative assessments along with your informal observations to assess student mastery.

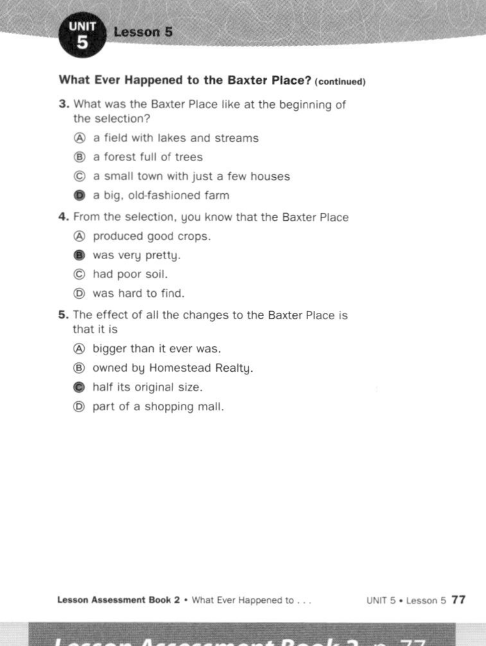

UNIT 5 Lesson 5

What Ever Happened to the Baxter Place? (continued)

3. What was the Baxter Place like at the beginning of the selection?
   - Ⓐ a field with lakes and streams
   - Ⓑ a forest full of trees
   - Ⓒ a small town with just a few houses
   - ● a big, old-fashioned farm
4. From the selection, you know that the Baxter Place
   - Ⓐ produced good crops.
   - ● was very pretty.
   - Ⓒ had poor soil.
   - Ⓓ was hard to find.
5. The effect of all the changes to the Baxter Place is that it is
   - Ⓐ bigger than it ever was.
   - Ⓑ owned by Homestead Realty.
   - ● half its original size.
   - Ⓓ part of a shopping mall.

Lesson Assessment Book 2 • What Ever Happened to . . . UNIT 5 • Lesson 5 77

Lesson Assessment Book 2, p. 77

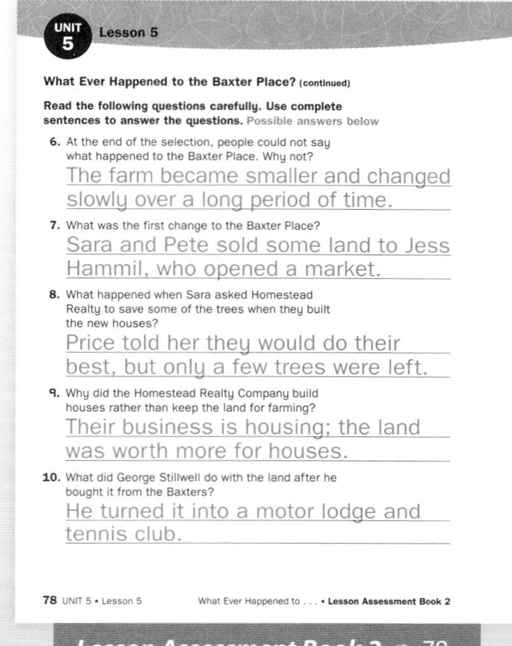

UNIT 5 Lesson 5

What Ever Happened to the Baxter Place? (continued)

Read the following questions carefully. Use complete sentences to answer the questions. Possible answers below

6. At the end of the selection, people could not say what happened to the Baxter Place. Why not?
   The farm became smaller and changed slowly over a long period of time.
7. What was the first change to the Baxter Place?
   Sara and Pete sold some land to Jess Hammil, who opened a market.
8. What happened when Sara asked Homestead Realty to save some of the trees when they built the new houses?
   Price told her they would do their best, but only a few trees were left.
9. Why did the Homestead Realty Company build houses rather than keep the land for farming?
   Their business is housing; the land was worth more for houses.
10. What did George Stillwell do with the land after he bought it from the Baxters?
    He turned it into a motor lodge and tennis club.

78 UNIT 5 • Lesson 5 What Ever Happened to . . . • Lesson Assessment Book 2

Lesson Assessment Book 2, p. 78

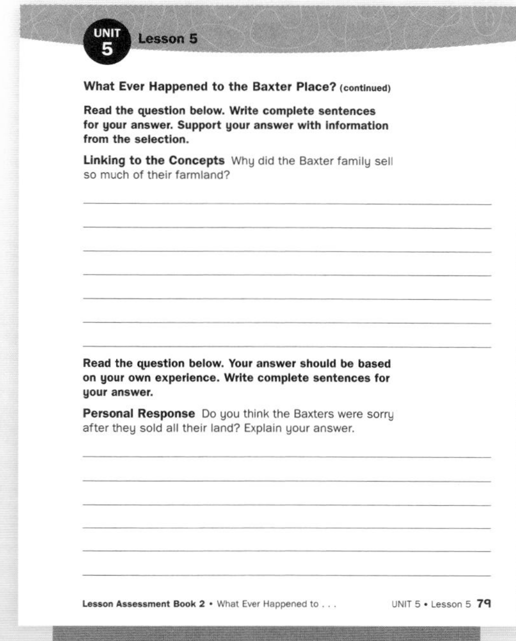

UNIT 5 Lesson 5

What Ever Happened to the Baxter Place? (continued)

Read the question below. Write complete sentences for your answer. Support your answer with information from the selection.

Linking to the Concepts Why did the Baxter family sell so much of their farmland?

Read the question below. Your answer should be based on your own experience. Write complete sentences for your answer.

Personal Response Do you think the Baxters were sorry after they sold all their land? Explain your answer.

Lesson Assessment Book 2 • What Ever Happened to . . . UNIT 5 • Lesson 5 79

Lesson Assessment Book 2, p. 79

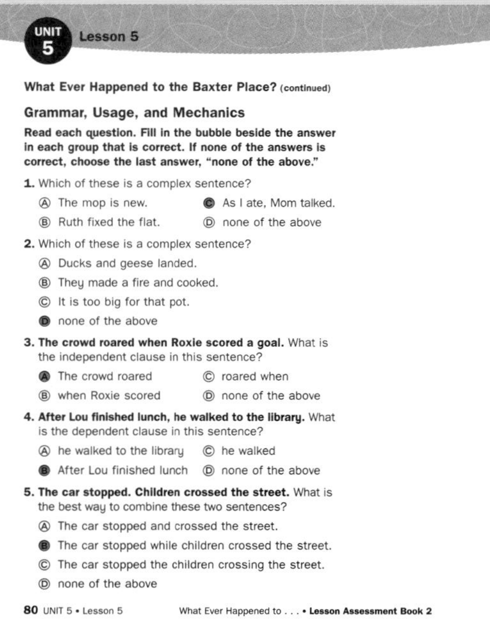

UNIT 5 Lesson 5

What Ever Happened to the Baxter Place? (continued)

Grammar, Usage, and Mechanics

Read each question. Fill in the bubble beside the answer in each group that is correct. If none of the answers is correct, choose the last answer, "none of the above."

1. Which of these is a complex sentence?
   - Ⓐ The mop is new.
   - ● As I ate, Mom talked.
   - Ⓑ Ruth fixed the flat.
   - Ⓓ none of the above
2. Which of these is a complex sentence?
   - Ⓐ Ducks and geese landed.
   - Ⓑ They made a fire and cooked.
   - Ⓒ It is too big for that pot.
   - ● none of the above
3. **The crowd roared when Roxie scored a goal.** What is the independent clause in this sentence?
   - ● The crowd roared
   - Ⓒ roared when
   - Ⓑ when Roxie scored
   - Ⓓ none of the above
4. **After Lou finished lunch, he walked to the library.** What is the dependent clause in this sentence?
   - Ⓐ he walked to the library
   - Ⓒ he walked
   - ● After Lou finished lunch
   - Ⓓ none of the above
5. **The car stopped. Children crossed the street.** What is the best way to combine these two sentences?
   - Ⓐ The car stopped and crossed the street.
   - ● The car stopped while children crossed the street.
   - Ⓒ The car stopped the children crossing the street.
   - Ⓓ none of the above

80 UNIT 5 • Lesson 5 What Ever Happened to . . . • Lesson Assessment Book 2

Lesson Assessment Book 2, p. 80

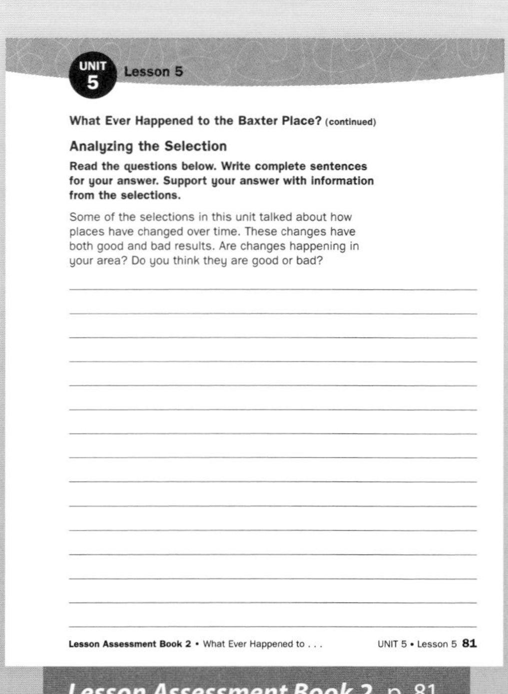

UNIT 5 Lesson 5

What Ever Happened to the Baxter Place? (continued)

Analyzing the Selection

Read the questions below. Write complete sentences for your answer. Support your answer with information from the selections.

Some of the selections in this unit talked about how places have changed over time. These changes have both good and bad results. Are changes happening in your area? Do you think they are good or bad?

Lesson Assessment Book 2 • What Ever Happened to . . . UNIT 5 • Lesson 5 81

Lesson Assessment Book 2, p. 81

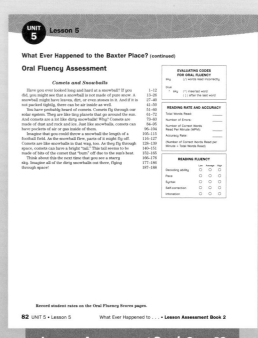

UNIT 5 Lesson 5

What Ever Happened to the Baxter Place? (continued)

Oral Fluency Assessment

Comets and Snowballs

Have you ever looked long and hard at a snowball? If you 1–12
did, you might see that a snowball is not made of pure snow. A 13–26
snowball might have leaves, dirt, or even stones in it. And if it is 27–40
not packed tightly, there can be air inside as well. 41–50
You have probably heard of comets. Comets fly through our 51–60
solar system. They are like tiny planets that go around the sun. 61–72
And comets are a lot like dirty snowballs! Why? Comets are 73–83
made of dust and rock and ice. Just like snowballs, comets can 84–95
have pockets of air or gas inside of them. 96–104
Imagine that you could throw a snowball the length of a 105–115
football field. As the snowball flew, parts of it might fly off. 116–127
Comets are like snowballs in that way, too. As they fly through 128–139
space, comets can have a bright "tail." This tail seems to be 140–151
made of bits of the comet that "burn" off due to the sun's heat. 152–165
Think about this the next time that you see a starry 166–176
sky. Imagine all of the dirty snowballs out there, flying 177–186
through space! 187–188

EVALUATING CODES FOR ORAL FLUENCY

sky (/) words read incorrectly

blue
^ sky (^) inserted word
( ]) after the last word

READING RATE AND ACCURACY

Total Words Read: ____

Number of Errors: ____

Number of Correct Words Read Per Minute (WPM): ____

Accuracy Rate: ____

(Number of Correct Words Read per Minute ÷ Total Words Read)

READING FLUENCY

	Low	Average	High
Decoding ability	○	○	○
Pace	○	○	○
Syntax	○	○	○
Self-correction	○	○	○
Intonation	○	○	○

Record student rates on the Oral Fluency Scores pages.

82 UNIT 5 • Lesson 5 What Ever Happened to . . . • Lesson Assessment Book 2

Lesson Assessment Book 2, p. 82

Preparing to Read

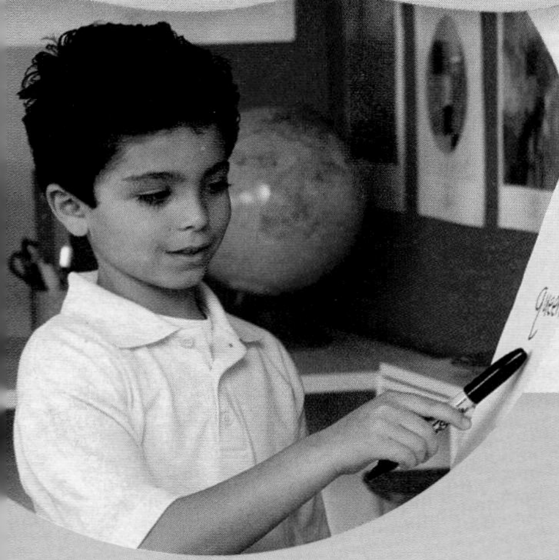

OBJECTIVES

Students will

- review the meanings of the prefixes *re-*, *un-*, *pre-*, *mis-*, *bi-*, *mid-*, *dis-*, and *auto-* and affixes as syllables.
- build fluency.

MATERIALS

- ***Transparency*** 149
- Routine 10
- ***Skills Practice 2,*** pp. 155–156

Daily Oral Practice

Daily News

Today!

When I was little, deer grazed under tall trees in a pretty field across the street. When I was a little older, a family put up a little store beside the field. A few years later, a bigger store took up almost the whole field. I miss the scenic, peaceful field.

Differentiating Instruction — English Learner

IF . . . students need some help understanding the daily news, **THEN . . .** replace the occurrences of *little* in the selection with the following words, respectively: *young, a few years, small*.

- Write the daily news on the board or on chart paper. Then have students read the daily news in unison to practice fluency.
- As a word structure review from Lesson 4, ask a volunteer to identify any words in the message with silent consonants. *scenic*

Word Structure

ROUTINE 10

Review: The Prefixes *re-*, *un-*, *pre-*, *mis-*, *bi-*, *mid-*, *dis-*, and *auto-*; Affixes as Syllables

- Write these word lines on the board or use ***Transparency*** 149. The words in boldface are in "What Ever Happened to the Baxter Place?"

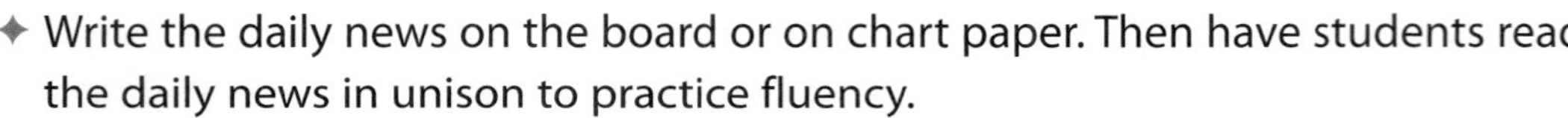

Line 1	**renewed**	**resurface**	**unpaid**	**untold**
Line 2	**preserved**	predawn	misinform	mislead
Line 3	bifocals	bilingual	midfield	midsized
Line 4	**discount**	disinfect	autographed	**automatic**

Teacher Tip

SYLLABICATION To help students blend words and build fluency, demonstrate syllabication using the decodable, multisyllabic words in the word lines.

re • newed	re • sur • face
un • paid	un • told
pre • served	pre • dawn
mis • in • form	mis • lead
bi • fo • cals	bi • lin • gual
mid • field	mid • sized
dis • count	dis • in • fect
au • to • graphed	au • to • mat • ic

Lines 1–4 Affixes as Syllables

As you point to each word, have students say the word and clap for each syllable. Ask students how adding affixes affects the number of syllables in a word. *Affixes add syllables to a word.*

Line 1 The Prefixes *re-* and *un-*

Use Routine 10 for words with prefixes and suffixes to review today's prefixes. Ask students what prefixes are found on this line and what they mean. *the prefixes* re- *and* un-; re- *means "again" and* un- *means "not"* Have students define each word, using a dictionary if necessary.

Line 2 The Prefixes *pre-* and *mis-*

Ask students what prefixes are found on this line and what they mean. *the prefixes* pre- *and* mis-; pre- *means "before," and* mis- *means "wrong" or "bad"* Have students define each word, using a dictionary if necessary.

Line 3 The Prefixes *bi-* and *mid-*

Ask students what prefixes are found on this line and what they mean. *the prefixes* bi- *and* mid-; bi- *means "two," and* mid- *means "middle"* Have students define each word, using a dictionary if necessary.

Line 4 The Prefixes *dis-* and *auto-*

Ask students what prefixes are found on this line and what they mean. *the prefixes* dis- *and* auto-; dis- *means "opposite," and* auto- *means "self"* Ask students to define each of these words.

✦ Help students start the word structure activities on ***Skills Practice 2*** pages 155–156. Read the Focus box with them and help them with the first few questions. Then have students complete the pages on their own.

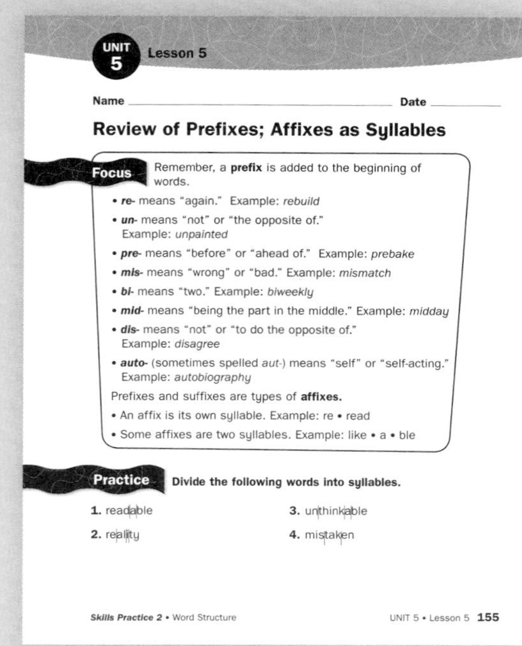

UNIT 5 Lesson 5

Name ______ Date ______

Review of Prefixes; Affixes as Syllables

Focus Remember, a **prefix** is added to the beginning of words.

- ***re-*** means "again." Example: *rebuild*
- ***un-*** means "not" or "the opposite of." Example: *unpainted*
- ***pre-*** means "before" or "ahead of." Example: *prebake*
- ***mis-*** means "wrong" or "bad." Example: *mismatch*
- ***bi-*** means "two." Example: *biweekly*
- ***mid-*** means "being the part in the middle." Example: *midday*
- ***dis-*** means "not" or "to do the opposite of." Example: *disagree*
- ***auto-*** (sometimes spelled *aut-*) means "self" or "self-acting." Example: *autobiography*

Prefixes and suffixes are types of **affixes.**

- An affix is its own syllable. Example: re • read
- Some affixes are two syllables. Example: like • a • ble

Practice Divide the following words into syllables.

1. readable
2. reality
3. unthinkable
4. mistaken

Skills Practice 2 • Word Structure UNIT 5 • Lesson 5 **155**

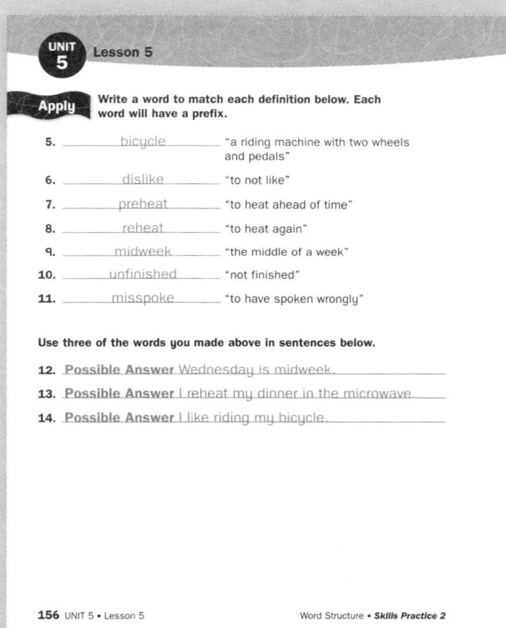

UNIT 5 Lesson 5

Apply Write a word to match each definition below. Each word will have a prefix.

5. bicycle "a riding machine with two wheels and pedals"
6. dislike "to not like"
7. preheat "to heat ahead of time"
8. reheat "to heat again"
9. midweek "the middle of a week"
10. unfinished "not finished"
11. misspoke "to have spoken wrongly"

Use three of the words you made above in sentences below.

12. Possible Answer Wednesday is midweek.
13. Possible Answer I reheat my dinner in the microwave.
14. Possible Answer I like riding my bicycle.

156 UNIT 5 • Lesson 5 Word Structure • *Skills Practice 2*

Skills Practice 2, pp. 155–156

Monitor Progress to Differentiate Instruction

Formal Assessment 

Word Structure During the word structure activity, note how well students recognize prefixes and affixes as syllables.

	IF . . .	THEN . . .
APPROACHING LEVEL	**IF . . .** students need practice recognizing prefixes and affixes as syllables,	**THEN . . .** work with them in small groups on the word structure activities on ***Reteach*** page 149 during Workshop.
	IF . . . students need extra practice recognizing prefixes and affixes as syllables,	**THEN . . .** work with them in small groups on the word structure activities for Unit 5 Lesson 5 in the ***Intervention Guide*** during Workshop.
ON LEVEL	**IF . . .** students adequately recognize prefixes and affixes as syllables,	**THEN . . .** make lists of base words and practice adding different prefixes and suffixes to them during Workshop.
ABOVE LEVEL	**IF . . .** students are ready for a challenge with prefixes and affixes as syllables,	**THEN . . .** have them complete the word structure activities on ***Challenge Activities*** page 135 during Workshop.

Reading and Responding

OBJECTIVES

Students will

- ✦ activate prior knowledge to prepare for reading the selection.
- ✦ learn selection vocabulary.
- ✦ review the elements of realistic fiction.
- ✦ use the comprehension strategies Asking Questions, Making Connections, and Predicting.
- ✦ investigate communities across time using the Inquiry process.

MATERIALS

- ✦ Routines 11, 12, 14
- ✦ ***Transparencies*** 5, 150
- ✦ ***Student Reader,*** Book 2, pp. 206–221
- ✦ ***Home Connection,*** pp. 59–60
- ✦ ***Lesson Assessment Book 2***

Research in Action

A good reader knows when and where to use familiar strategies. Students can become autonomous in their use of strategies only by being given lots of encouragement in choosing appropriate strategies. Thus, you should not tell students when to predict or when to summarize. Rather, you should prompt students who are not using strategies to choose a strategy that helps them make sense of what they are reading.

(Michael Pressley)

Differentiating Instruction **English Learner**

IF . . . students are not familiar with the geography of the United States, **THEN . . .** use a classroom map to show them where the state of Maryland is located.

Build Background

Activate Prior Knowledge

- ✦ Discuss with students how open land, such as fields, meadows, and farms, is often developed for housing or for commercial use such as shopping malls. Ask students if they have noticed new houses or shops on lots that used to be empty.
- ✦ Ask students how they feel about new buildings taking over fields and farms.
- ✦ Discuss what students know about farms or what it would be like to work and live on a farm.
- ✦ Ask students to discuss what other selections from this unit told about land and how it has changed over the years due to increasing population and development.
- ✦ Encourage students to discuss how the land changed in all of the other selections in this unit.

Background Information

The following information might help students understand the story they are about to read:

- This story takes place in the state of Maryland, which is in the eastern part of the United States.
- Farmers earn their livings by planting and selling crops. When crops fail, farmers need to find a way to continue to make money, or they need to live on their savings. If they do not have enough savings, they may have to sell part of their land to earn money.
- People who buy land from farmers may want to continue to farm it. However, often developers, or people who want to build houses and businesses, buy the land to build on and make a profit.

Preview and Prepare

ROUTINE 12

Browse

Use Routine 12, the clues, problems, and wonderings routine, to help students identify what they know before reading, what problems they may encounter while reading, and their purposes for reading. Students will chart these on a transparency.

Have students read the title and the names of the author and illustrator, and then take a few minutes to browse the first few pages of the story. Have students use features such as the story's title and illustrations to predict what this story might have to do with communities across time.

Tell students to look for interesting words or ideas when reading. They may notice the color and black-and-white illustrations.

Use ***Transparency*** 5 to model browsing for students. For example, the illustrations of a farm could be a Clue that the story is about life on a farm. Under Problems, point out *barley* as an unfamiliar word. Write *What happens to the farm?* under Wonderings. Record students' observations on the transparency as they browse the story.

Set Purposes

Encourage students to set their own purposes for reading the story. Remind students to set purposes by picking up clues from the title, illustrations, and genre of the text they are going to read. If students are having trouble determining purpose, suggest that as they read, they think about how the land and the people around it change when more houses and businesses come into a town.

How has my community changed over time?

Before reading the story, read the Big Idea question. Tell students to keep this question in mind when reading.

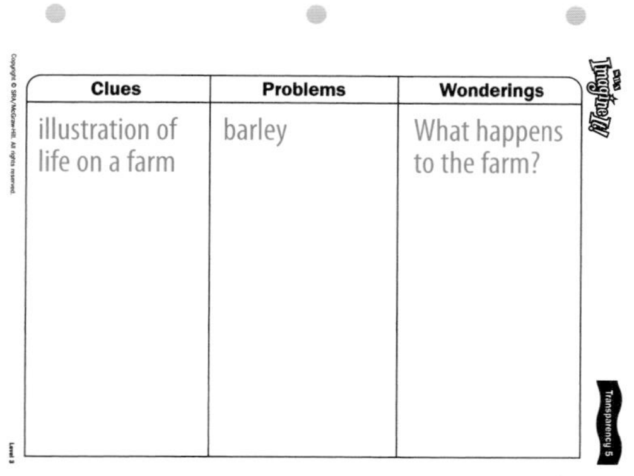

Clues	Problems	Wonderings
illustration of life on a farm	barley	What happens to the farm?

Transparency 5

Give each student a copy of ***Home Connection*** page 59. Encourage students to discuss "What Ever Happened to the Baxter Place?" with their families and complete the activity provided. This same information is also available in Spanish on ***Home Connection*** page 60.

Differentiating Instruction **English Learner**

IF . . . students have limited proficiency,
THEN . . . pair them with proficient English speakers and have the pair browse the story together.

Selection Vocabulary

seasonal (sē´ • zən • əl) *adj.* ripe at a certain time (page 217)

produce (prō´ • dōōs) *n.* farm products, such as fresh fruits and vegetables (page 216)

particular (pär´ • tik´ • ū • lûr) *adj.* special (page 217)

necessities (nəs • es´ • sət • ēz´) *n.* plural form of **necessity:** something that is needed (page 220)

installed (in • stôld) *v.* a form of the verb **install:** to put in place for use or service (page 223)

featuring (fē´ • chûr • ing) *adj.* having as the main attraction (page 227)

discount (dis´ • kount) *adj.* with lowered prices (page 227)

expire (eks • pīr´) *v.* to come to an end (page 228)

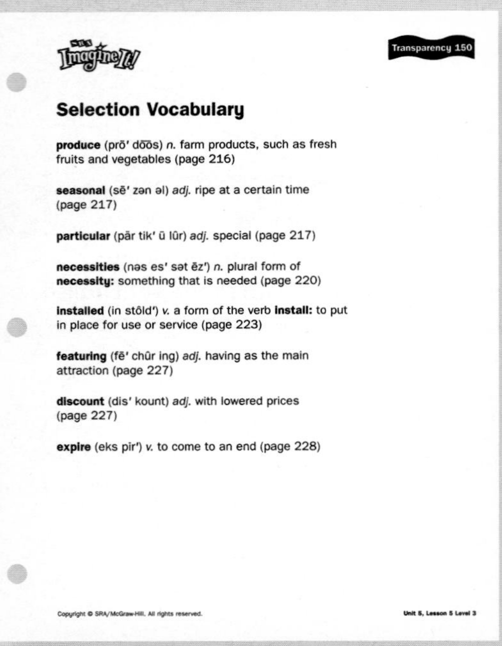
Imagine It! Transparency 150

Selection Vocabulary

produce (prō' dōōs) *n.* farm products, such as fresh fruits and vegetables (page 216)

seasonal (sē' zən əl) *adj.* ripe at a certain time (page 217)

particular (pär tik' ū lûr) *adj.* special (page 217)

necessities (nəs es' sət ēz') *n.* plural form of **necessity:** something that is needed (page 220)

installed (in stôld') *v.* a form of the verb **install:** to put in place for use or service (page 223)

featuring (fē' chûr ing) *adj.* having as the main attraction (page 227)

discount (dis' kount) *adj.* with lowered prices (page 227)

expire (eks pīr') *v.* to come to an end (page 228)

 Unit 5, Lesson 5 Level 3

Transparency 150

Writer's Notebook

Have students copy the vocabulary words and definitions into the vocabulary section of their Writer's Notebooks.

Building Vocabulary

Using Routine 11, the selection vocabulary process, have students read aloud the Vocabulary Warm-Up on ***Student Reader,*** Book 2 pages 206–207.

As students read, have them stop to blend any difficult or unfamiliar words. Provide students with the pronunciation of words that are not decodable or that they cannot read automatically or fluently.

Guided Vocabulary Practice

Ask students to identify the highlighted vocabulary words they figured out using the vocabulary strategy word structure. **Possible Answers** *installed, seasonal, featuring, necessities* Have students explain how they figured out the meaning of the other vocabulary words as they read the Vocabulary Warm-Up.

Display ***Transparency*** 150, and have students read the words and definitions. Return to the Vocabulary Warm-Up, and read the sentences containing the vocabulary words with students. Then, if necessary, provide a brief in-context explanation of the words.

Read the article to find the meanings of these words, which are also in "What Ever Happened to the Baxter Place?":

- installed
- seasonal
- produce
- particular
- featuring
- necessities
- expire
- discount

Vocabulary Strategy

Word Structure is when parts of a word help you understand the word's meaning. Use word structure to find the meaning of *featuring*.

Vocabulary Warm-Up

On summer weekends, a taste of the country comes to town. The farmers' market is on! Goods are trucked in fresh from the fields.

Vendors line the streets at dawn. They get set up for the day. Tables and temporary booths are installed. Seasonal produce is arranged in neat stacks. There are berries, melons, peppers, and corn.

Soon shoppers start to arrive. They fill their bags and baskets with goods. Some roam the market in no particular order. Others head straight for their preferred booths. They do not want to miss out. A lot of things sell fast at the farmers' market.

Pies and other baked goods are for sale too. These items might be displayed on elevated plates. Sellers try to entice buyers by featuring the sweet treats. It is a plan that works!

Fresh eggs are sold and packed with care. They are placed in cartons with dividers. This way, the fragile shells will not knock against each other and crack.

Not all of the items for sale are necessities. Although cut flowers are not for eating, they make a meal more pleasant. Handmade quilts may not be as warm as those sold in stores, but they can make a cold night cozier.

Crowds thin as the sale is about to expire. It is time to pack up. Some farmers offer discount prices on the things that remain. They would rather sell their goods for less than haul the stuff home.

GAME

Flash Cards

Make a set of flash cards with the vocabulary words. Write the word on one side and its definition on the other side. Use the flash cards to review the vocabulary words and definitions. Then ask a classmate to use the cards to quiz you.

Concept Vocabulary

The concept vocabulary word for this lesson is ***development.*** **Development** means "growth or change." The development of land is when it is changed by adding new buildings. Talk about ways that development can be both good and bad for a community.

Use the vocabulary words on ***Transparency*** 150 to create fill-in-the-blank sentences. Have students fill in the appropriate vocabulary words. For example, "Our school __________ a new basketball court on the playground." *installed*

Discuss the concept vocabulary word *development* with students. Ask students how they think the word *development* relates to the theme Communities across Time. As students read the selections in this unit, encourage them to think about other words that relate to the theme. Students can record these words in the vocabulary section of their Writer's Notebooks.

GAME

Have students play the Flash Cards game during Small-Group Time.

Differentiating Instruction: English Learner

IF . . . students have difficulty playing the Flash Cards game, **THEN . . .** be sure to place them in groups with at least two proficient English speakers.

Concept/Question Board

As students read "What Ever Happened to the Baxter Place?" encourage them to post questions, answers, comments, or other items related to communities across time on the **Concept/Question Board.**

Formal Assessment

Comprehension Observation Log Observe individual students as they read, and use the Comprehension Observation Log, located in ***Lesson Assessment Book 2,*** to record anecdotal information about each student's strengths and weaknesses.

Differentiating Instruction **English Learner**

IF . . . students would benefit from hearing "What Ever Happened to the Baxter Place?" before it is read to the class, **THEN . . .** have them listen to the story on ***Listening Library CD*** during Workshop.

Reading the Selection

Genre Realistic Fiction

Have students identify the genre of "What Ever Happened to the Baxter Place?" *realistic fiction* If necessary, remind students of the following elements of realistic fiction:

- The characters behave as people do in real life.
- The setting of the story is a real place or could be a real place.
- The events in the story could happen in real life.

Comprehension Strategies

Prompt the use of the following comprehension strategies during the first reading of "What Ever Happened to the Baxter Place?":

- Asking Questions
- Making Connections
- Predicting

Comprehension Strategies Rubrics

Use the Informal Comprehension Strategies Rubrics to determine whether a student is using any of the strategies listed below. Note the strategies a student is using, instead of the degree to which a student might be using any particular strategy. In addition, encourage the student to tell of any strategies other than the ones being taught that he or she is using.

Asking Questions

✦ The student stops to ask questions—any question.

✦ The student asks questions directly related to the text.

✦ The student asks *who*, *what*, *why*, *when*, *where*, or *how* questions as opposed to *yes* or *no* questions.

✦ The student asks questions that help clarify information in the text.

Making Connections

- ✦ The student makes connections between prior knowledge and information in the text.
- ✦ The student makes connections between or relates personal experiences to what is read in the text (text-to-self connections).
- ✦ The student makes connections across or relates information from different selections (text-to-text connections).
- ✦ The student makes connections or relates information between what is happening in the text to what is happening in the world today (text-to-world connections).

Predicting

- ✦ The student stops to make a prediction about the text.
- ✦ The student identifies the clues in the text used to make a prediction.
- ✦ The student uses clues in the text and prior knowledge to make a prediction.
- ✦ The student recognizes when a prediction is or is not confirmed by the text.

Monitor Progress to Differentiate Instruction

Formal Assessment

Comprehension Skills Note students' use of the comprehension skill Main Idea and Details.

APPROACHING LEVEL

IF . . . students are having difficulty understanding main idea and details as they read,

THEN . . . point out specific paragraphs in "What Ever Happened to the Baxter Place?" and model the skill for students. Continue to model the skill until students are able to find main ideas and details on their own.

ON LEVEL

IF . . . students are gaining an understanding of main idea and details as they read,

THEN . . . have students identify the main idea and some of the supporting details on every page of the story.

ABOVE LEVEL

IF . . . students are demonstrating an understanding of main idea and details as they read,

THEN . . . give students articles and essays that reflect the theme Communities across Time. Have students identify the main ideas and details in the articles. Have students post new information learned on the **Concept/Question Board.**

Technology

eSTUDENT READER Students can access ***SRA Imagine It! Student Reader*** electronically by using the ***eStudent Reader*** online or on CD-ROM.

Reading and Responding

Comprehension Skills

Reread "What Ever Happened to the Baxter Place?" using the following comprehension skills:

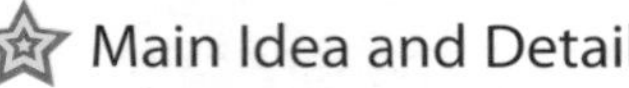

- Main Idea and Details
- Author's Point of View

Reading with a Writer's Eye

During the rereading of "What Ever Happened to the Baxter Place?" explain the following literary element:

Genre Knowledge

Focus Questions

Have students read aloud the Focus Questions on page 208 of ***Student Reader,*** Book 2. Encourage students to think about the Focus Questions as they read "What Ever Happened to the Baxter Place?"

Reading Recommendation

Oral Reading

Use Routine 14, the reading the selection routine, as you read the entire story. As you read, stop to ask and answer questions. Point out how the pictures reflect the story. Share the images that pop up in your mind as you read and how points in the reading relate to ideas you already know.

Because of the unfamiliar ideas and concepts that students may need to discuss (farming methods, leasing property, debt, and so on), this story is well suited for oral reading.

Genre

Realistic Fiction involves stories about people and events that are true to life and that could really happen.

Comprehension Skill

Main Idea and Details

As you read, look for details that help show the main idea of the story.

Focus Questions

Who makes the decisions about how communities change? What are the advantages and disadvantages of using farmland to build more buildings?

208

What Ever Happened to the Baxter Place?

by Pat Ross

illustrated by Roger Duvoisin

209

Students will read the story twice over a four-day period.

Day 1 **ORAL READ** Have students read the first half of the story. Prompt the use of the comprehension strategies.

Day 2 **ORAL READ** Have students finish reading the story. Continue to prompt the comprehension strategies.

Day 3 **SILENT READ** Have students reread the story silently. Have students focus on comprehension skills and Reading with a Writer's Eye.

Day 4 **SILENT READ** Have students finish rereading the story.

Technology

Have students listen to "What Ever Happened to the Baxter Place?" on the ***Listening Library CD***. After students have listened, have them discuss what other things, such as poetry, songs, or nonfiction, they prefer to listen to on the radio or on CDs.

Reading and Responding

Some years ago you could turn off the main road outside a small town in Maryland onto a dirt road which stretched three miles. The old dirt road was called Flatland Road, and it led you straight to the Baxter Place.

It was really a farm belonging to the Baxter family—acres and acres of fields and meadows and woodland—but everybody around just called it the Baxter Place. ❶

A herd of cows grazed in the east meadow. Wild ducks and geese swam in the pond nearby.

Stretching up to a big white farmhouse was a field of soybeans, making a pretty blanket of green in the spring and summer months.

210

The Baxter Place spread out over nearly three hundred acres. The south field—the biggest and flattest—was planted in rotation with corn one year and barley the next. The rolling east field was well-suited for alfalfa, giving three cuttings ❷ each year. The west field, the smallest stretch, was reserved for crops the Baxters might want for their own, with surplus going for sale.

The fields were divided by woods, like nature's markers.

211

Word Structure

This lesson reviews the prefixes *re-*, *un-*, *pre-*, *mis-*, *bi-*, *be-*, *dis-*, and *auto-*.

Prefix *re-*: reserved

Prefix *be-*: belonging

Teacher Tip

GENRE Remind students that this story is realistic fiction. While the events and characters are fictional, the setting and events could be real.

Comprehension Strategies

This story is broken into two parts. On the first day, read pages 210–221. On the second day, read pages 222–229.

❶ **Asking Questions** Teacher Prompt: *Asking questions as you read will help you stay focused on the story. Does anyone have a question about the story so far?* **Possible Student Response** *I have a question already. The Baxter Place is a farm. What do the Baxters grow on their farm? I'll keep reading to find the answer.*

❷ **Answering Questions** Teacher Prompt: *Has anyone found an answer to their question?* **Possible Student Response** *I've already found the answer to my question. The Baxters grow soybeans, corn, barley, and alfalfa.*

There were four in the family. Sara Baxter was a big, strong woman with a friendly way, and Pete Baxter was a tall and wiry man with skin toughened and tanned from being outdoors all year round. Sue Ann, the older child, seemed to take after her mother's side of the family. Last there was young Pete, named after his dad, but everybody called him Pee Wee. It's said he was so tiny when he was born that he fit in a shoe box, so Pee Wee they called him, and the name stuck.

212

The Baxter Place was a business—a farm business. It was also a way of life. ③

Nothing kept Pete Baxter from the work in the fields or in the big dairy barn that had milking stalls for twenty cows at a time. Pete knew every crop, every one of their hundred cows by name, and everything that happened on the farm. For him, farming was more than any regular full-time job, and he liked being outdoors every day all year round. ④

Sara Baxter raised chickens in a chicken house. During the laying season, she collected about a hundred eggs every day, then drove them to town to Hammil's Country Market to be sold. She also grew vegetables, and those that didn't get eaten right away got canned and

213

③ **Asking Questions** Teacher Prompt: *Does anyone have any questions about the story so far?* **Possible Student Response** *Why does the author say that the Baxter Place was a farm business and a way of life? I'll read further and try to find an answer through clues in the text and maybe by looking at the illustrations.*

④ **Answering Questions** Teacher Prompt: *Now that we have read a little further in the text, have any of your questions been answered?* **Possible Student Response** *Farming's more than a regular job for Pete Baxter because he really likes it. I can tell that both Pete and Sara feel that the farm is an important part of their life.*

Comprehension Check

Why do you think the illustrator chose to draw some pictures in color and some in black and white? **Possible Answer** *The black-and-white picture looks like it could be a real photograph of the family, and at that time it could have been a black and white photograph.*

Differentiating Instruction **English Learner**

IF . . . students would benefit from additional practice with adjectives, **THEN . . .** ask them to identify and define as many adjectives as they can on page 212 of the selection.

Reading and Responding

preserved for the long winter or taken to the market along with the eggs. Sara kept careful records of everything that was bought or sold for the farm. She was not only the farm's bookkeeper but also the business-minded one in the family.

Jim and Wally were the hired hands—farmers who work at farming other people's land. Jim was a crackerjack repairman when the tractor and equipment broke down—which was more often than he liked. And Wally knew the planting seasons like the back of his hand. Folks said he could smell a late spring frost in the air. Both Jim and Wally came every morning at six sharp and often stayed till late in the evening. They had worked with Pete for fifteen years.

214

Sue Ann did her chores every morning before the school bus came up Flatland Road. She cleaned the calves' stalls, fed the chickens, helped with the milking, and set the table for breakfast—which came *after* chores.

Pee Wee, being younger, got away with a little less in the way of work. He was in charge of feeding the three big watchdogs and an untold number of cats, cleaning the chicken house, and helping Sara set out breakfast for everyone. 5

215

Word Structure

Prefix *pre-*: preserved
Prefix *re-*: repairman, renewed
Prefix *un-*: untold

Teacher Tip

RESPONSES TO READING Remind students that different readers may picture the same scene quite differently, and this is fine. Every reader responds to a story in his or her own way.

Comprehension Strategies

5 Making Connections Teacher Prompt: *Who would like to share a connection they have with the story?* **Possible Student Response** *I have to do chores too. My chores are different from Sue Ann's and Pee Wee's. I would rather feed animals than wash dishes and take out the garbage. My younger brother and I are like Sue Ann and Pee Wee in one way, though. My brother always gets away with doing less work.*

Comprehension Check

Why do Jim and Wally work for the Baxters instead of farming their own land?
Possible Answer *They probably don't have land of their own, but they still like working on a farm and they're good at it.*

All the folks around those parts said the Baxter Place was the prettiest, neatest farm they'd ever seen, and the Baxters were some of the nicest folks they knew. Luckiest, too. And they were right—until the day the man from the market stopped by. 6

Jess Hammil owned the farmers' market where Sara took her eggs and produce to be sold. Sara, Pete, and Jess had all been in grade school together, so they went way back. Jess came to see the Baxters the day he learned the lease on his small vegetable market in town wasn't going to be renewed. A fancy new building was going up in its place, and he sure couldn't afford those rents.

Now, he figured if he could buy his own land—and not rent—something like this wasn't likely to happen again. He had saved the cash, so maybe the Baxters would be willing to part with that small west field. With those twenty-five acres, Jess could not only have his market, he could also grow much of his own seasonal produce instead of always depending on other farmers. The field was right off the main road from town, so people would be likely to stop and buy.

It was true that particular piece of land was what you might call extra. Sara and Pete had always thought they would save it for Sue Ann and Pee Wee. But Sue Ann was headed for forestry college in a year and planned to move later on to the mountains where her work would be. And Pee Wee, young as he was, had his

6 **Predicting** Teacher Prompt: *Making predictions about what will happen in a story helps readers understand the story. Who would like to make a prediction?*
Possible Student Response *I think something is going to happen to the Baxters. The story says, "the Baxters were some of the nicest folks they knew. Luckiest, too." But then it says, ". . . until the day the man from the market stopped by." I think that the man from the market will do something that will end up costing the Baxters something. I'll keep reading to see what happens.*

Differentiating Instruction

English Learner

IF . . . students have trouble with irregular plurals, **THEN . . .** explain that several words for animals have irregular plurals and that some of these words do not change at all to make the plural. Write *buffalo, buffalo*; *deer, deer*; *elk, elk*; *fish, fish*; *sheep, sheep*; *calf, calves* and *wolf, wolves* on the board. Use pictures to show what each word means.

heart set on being a mathematician, and claimed he was allergic to field work—which certainly seemed to be true!

Jess's being an old friend and all helped the Baxters decide to sell. Also, Sara thought it would be kind of nice to have a market for her sales so close by. They shook hands and made a deal. 7

Within a year, Jess opened a brand-new market. He planted his land with seasonal produce crops. When word got around that the state was planning to widen and resurface Main Road, Jess knew this meant even more business for him.

218

Pete and Sara figured they'd not only made some money to pay the bills more easily, but they'd also done a favor for a friend.

Every year for the past five, Emma Price from Homestead Realty Company had made her call on the Baxters. Every year it was the same: Emma's real estate company was interested in purchasing and developing their meadow and woodland area around the pond. Would they consider selling? The offer would be handsome. 8 9

219

Word Structure

Prefix *re-*: resurface
Prefix *un-*: unpaid

Teacher Tip

ASKING QUESTIONS Help students understand the concept of developing the land. Then encourage them to ask questions about anything they don't understand so far in the story. Help students answer their questions by looking for clues in the text and in the illustrations.

Comprehension Strategies

7 Confirming Predictions Teacher Prompt: *Does this part of the story confirm anyone's predictions?* **Possible Student Response** *My prediction has been confirmed. The Baxters sell part of their land to Jess Hammil, so it does cost them something. I'm glad that even though they're giving up part of their land, they feel that it is a good deal.*

8 Asking Questions Teacher Prompt: *I have more questions. Who else has a question?* **Possible Student Response** *Why does the lady from the realty company want the Baxters' land so much? I'll keep reading and look for clues to answer my questions. I read further and found out that the company wants to develop the meadow and area around the pond. They probably want to put up houses or businesses on this land.*

9 Predicting Teacher Prompt: *I have another prediction to make. Does anyone else have a prediction?* **Possible Student Response** *I don't think the Baxters will sell any more land. It is too special to them.*

Every year they greeted Emma Price politely, but their answer had always been a firm no. They needed the meadow for the cows. And how could they part with the woods and pond? Besides, they didn't need the money. So each year they bade Emma good-by with the same answer.

But one year, things were a little different. The corn harvest that fall had been a total loss. There had been too much rain during planting time and a dry spell just when they needed rain. Corn was their livelihood, and without the crop's sale the bills would go unpaid. Sara figured they could barely pay for the farm's necessities that year. They also owed the bank a mortgage on the house and the land plus money they had borrowed for seed and a new tractor.

They insisted they would not part with the meadow, pond, and woods. Still, they didn't like getting into debt any more if they could help it. Would the Homestead Realty Company consider the rolling east field? they asked. Emma Price was pleasantly surprised and said yes right away. 10

It was the toughest decision they'd ever had to make together. 11

220

Would the company please save some of the trees when they made room for houses? Sue Ann asked. Emma Price assured her they'd make every effort to do just that. Would the Baxters get the best price, even though the east field was the company's second choice? Sara and Pete asked. Emma quoted them a price. Would the new people have children his age? Pee Wee asked. Everyone laughed nervously. Pete quickly figured out loud that they could use the front soybean field for alfalfa, too. There would just be less of a soybean crop, and they would have to sell off some of the older cows in the herd, but the fifty milk-producing cows would not go hungry. 12

221

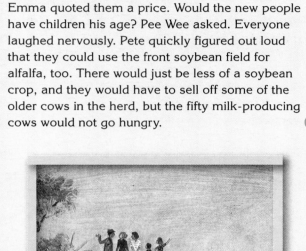

10 Confirming Predictions Teacher Prompt: *Have anyone's predictions been confirmed or not confirmed?* **Possible Student Response** *My prediction was partially confirmed. That land is special to the Baxters, and they also need it for the cows. The Baxters don't sell the land to the realty company. However, I didn't think that they would sell another part of their land.*

11 Making Connections Teacher Prompt: *Who can make a connection here?* **Possible Student Response** *My aunt and uncle had to sell their house and move into a smaller one. They didn't want to, but they could only afford a smaller house. After they moved they liked their new house, so it worked out after all.*

12 Predicting Teacher Prompt: *Who would like to make a prediction?* **Possible Student Response** *I have a feeling the realty company won't save the trees when they build the new houses, even though they say they will try.*

Comprehension Check

Why do the Baxters sell part of the east field? **Possible Answer** *They had a bad year and they need the money.*

Vocabulary Tip

Point out the words *seasonal* and *particular* on page 217 in the text. Ask students what the word *season* means and encourage them to use word structure to help them figure out the meaning of the word *seasonal*. Point out that the Baxters and Jess are discussing only one piece of land. Encourage them to use context clues to help figure out the meaning of *particular*.

STOP

You have read the first half of the story. Continue the story tomorrow on page T372.

Lesson 5 Inquiry Planner

STEP 6: Confirming and Revising Conjectures

Day 1 With their groups, students will start gathering information to evaluate their conjectures.

Day 2 Students will continue thinking about how the information they collected relates to their conjectures.

Day 3 Have a whole-group discussion about how any information in "What Ever Happened to the Baxter Place?" relates to students' conjectures.

Day 4 Discuss new information about the theme in "What Ever Happened to the Baxter Place?". Then students will revise their conjectures and start producing their presentations.

STEP 7: Presenting Inquiry Findings

Day 5 With their groups, students will complete their presentations and rehearse them.

Day 6 Each group will give some kind of presentation about their investigation. Students will also discuss the presentations afterward.

STEP 8: Asking New Questions

Day 7 Students will ask new questions about their specific topics and the unit theme.

Teacher Tip

REVISING CONJECTURES Remind students that revising conjectures is an important part of the investigation process. They have been collecting information along the way that has probably changed their initial conjecture. Now is the time to revise their conjectures before continuing on to their presentations.

Inquiry Process

Step 6—Confirming and Revising Conjectures

Whole-Group Time

Whole Group

- Remind students that they chose an investigation question, made conjectures about that question, and gathered information about their topic. Now they will see how the information they have collected affects their conjectures and their understanding of their topic.

- Have students review any notes, questions, ideas, and conjectures they recorded in their Writer's Notebooks and ***Skills Practice 2.*** As they think about these initial questions and conjectures, they should ask themselves questions such as the following to help confirm or revise them: *What have I learned about my topic that I didn't know before? How has that changed how I think about my topic? How does the information our group has collected relate to my conjecture? What information confirms my conjecture? What information challenges my conjecture? How can I make my conjecture better with what I know now?*

- Have students reflect on their conjectures so that they can revise them. Model this process for students, saying something such as the following: *When I began, my conjecture was that creating nature parks and wildlife sanctuaries would be a way for our community to keep from destroying valuable countryside. I did some research and found some really good places for these parks. The only problem is that someone already owns all the land. Nature parks and wildlife sanctuaries are a good idea, but it might be really hard to get the land for them. I will have to think more about this and revise my conjecture a little.*

Small-Group Time

Small Group

- Students should break into their investigation groups and continue to gather information to evaluate their conjectures.
- Each group should review all of its information up to this point. Remind them of the information they recorded about the selections in their Writer's Notebooks and from any of their other sources such as Web pages, interviews, or historical documents. Encourage students to make use of items on the **Concept/Question Board** as well as any maps, timelines, and calendars.
- Circulate among the groups, and help students think about how their information relates to their conjectures. If the information is leading them in a different direction than their original conjecture, they should consider revising it. Continue to model this process as needed.

Concept/Question Board

Continue to ask students to contribute and respond to the **Concept/Question Board.** Encourage the use of the Board by recognizing and thanking students for their contributions. Incorporate those items into classroom discussions whenever possible. Remember to model by posting your own contributions.

Research in Action

With Inquiry, then, even young children can come to understand knowing as open-ended, changeable, and improvable. They can come to view learning as multiple-sourced and community-based. They can come to view ideas and theories as things that can be evaluated, infinite, and within their grasp.

(McKeough, 2006)

Language Arts

OBJECTIVES

Students will

- ✦ brainstorm ideas for a play.
- ✦ take the spelling pretest.
- ✦ practice writing cursive letters *Q* and *F*.

MATERIALS

- ✦ ***Language Arts Handbook,*** pp. 156–161
- ✦ ***Transparencies*** 151, 152
- ✦ ***Skills Practice 2,*** p. 163

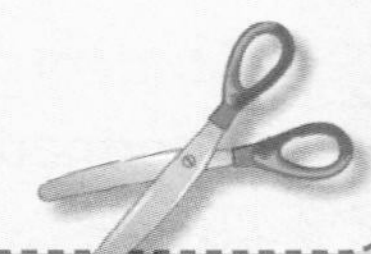

Play

A **play** is a story that is written to be performed in front of an audience. The writer of the play tells the story by writing what the characters do and say.

Like a story, a play has characters, a setting, and events in the plot. The characters are the actors in the play. They may be people or animals. The setting in a play is also called the scene. It is where the action takes place and when it takes place. When you tell where and when the story takes place, you are setting the scene.

A play is different from a story or report. Stories and reports are written to be read. A play is written to be performed. A play has stage directions, lines, and props. Stories and reports don't have them.

Try It! Imagine you are writing a play about your classroom. Name three characters. Set the scene.

156 Play • Narrative Writing

Language Arts Handbook, p. 156

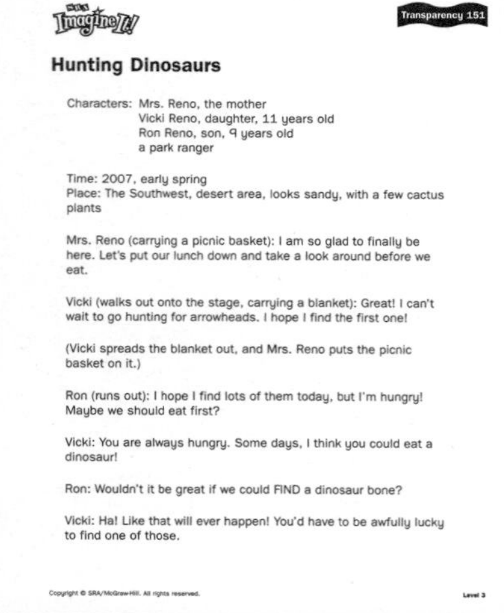

Imagine It! Transparency 151

Hunting Dinosaurs

Characters: Mrs. Reno, the mother
Vicki Reno, daughter, 11 years old
Ron Reno, son, 9 years old
a park ranger

Time: 2007, early spring
Place: The Southwest, desert area, looks sandy, with a few cactus plants

Mrs. Reno (carrying a picnic basket): I am so glad to finally be here. Let's put our lunch down and take a look around before we eat.

Vicki (walks out onto the stage, carrying a blanket): Great! I can't wait to go hunting for arrowheads. I hope I find the first one!

(Vicki spreads the blanket out, and Mrs. Reno puts the picnic basket on it.)

Ron (runs out): I hope I find lots of them today, but I'm hungry! Maybe we should eat first?

Vicki: You are always hungry. Some days, I think you could eat a dinosaur!

Ron: Wouldn't it be great if we could FIND a dinosaur bone?

Vicki: Ha! Like that will ever happen! You'd have to be awfully lucky to find one of those.

 Level 3

Transparency 151

Writing Play

Prewriting

Teach

- ✦ Ask students if they have ever seen a play, and ask those who have to describe the experience.
- ✦ Explain to students that a play is a story that is written to be performed by actors in front of an audience. Remind students that "The Legend of Damon and Pythias" is a play that was written to be performed.
- ✦ Tell students a play has events, called the *plot,* and a setting, called the *scene,* in addition to characters. Tell students that over the next two weeks they will write a play that includes all of these elements.
- ✦ Explain to students that when writing a play, writers must include the following information:
  - Stage directions (given in parentheses): tell the characters where to move or how to speak or feel
  - Lines (speaker's name at the beginning of the first line, all in capital letters, followed by a colon): the words spoken by the characters
  - Props (part of the stage directions): objects that will be used by the actors and sounds made off stage
- ✦ Display ***Transparency*** 151. Have a student or students read the excerpt from the play aloud, and then have students locate the various elements you discussed with them (setting, props, and lines). Tell students they can refer to this transparency as they write their plays.
- ✦ Explain to students that when a play is written, much attention is paid to the planning and the details. Writers of plays have to decide what characters will say and how they will move.
- ✦ If necessary, review the steps of writing a play with students by reading ***Language Arts Handbook*** pages 156–161 as a class.

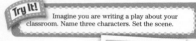

Writing, continued

Guided Practice

- Brainstorm ideas with students. Offer suggestions such as retelling a favorite story; writing a play about someone they know, one of their heroes, or someone they have learned about in school; writing a play about their favorite pet or animal; or writing about their favorite sport or sports hero. Tell students when choosing something to write about, it must be something they know enough about to give good dialogue to the characters, describe a setting with stage directions, and develop a plot with a goal that is achieved or a problem that is solved.

Apply

Have students discuss and then complete the Think section on page 163 in ***Skills Practice 2*** as a prewriting activity. Have students write some of their brainstorming ideas.

Assessment

You will use the Writing Rubrics found in the Level Appendix to evaluate students' plays. You may use any of the rubrics for Genre, Writing Process, and Writing Traits. Share with students what you will be looking for when assessing their plays.

UNIT 5 Lesson 5

Name ______ Date ______

Writing a Play

Think

Audience: Who will read your play?

Possible Answer classmates who will perform it

Purpose: What is your purpose for writing the play?

Possible Answer I want to tell the story of my great-grandmother's move to America.

Prewriting **Use this organizer to help you plan your play.**

Possible Answers

Characters
Kirsten (my great-grandmother); her mom; Pauline

Props
book (to be an English reader)

Setting
a farmhouse in Minnesota, 1900

Plot
Beginning: Kirsten and her mom arrive at the new farmhouse.
Middle: Kirsten misses Sweden, but makes friends with Pauline, who helps her read and spell English.
End: Kirsten does well at the spelling bee.

Skills Practice 2 • Writing UNIT 5 • Lesson 5 163

Skills Practice 2, p. 163

Spelling

Review of Prefixes, Affixes, and Word Families Pretest

Teach

- Students will review words with prefixes, words with affixes that change the word's meaning, and word families.
- Say the sentences below aloud. Have students write the spelling words on a separate sheet of paper. When they are finished, have them correct any misspelled words.

Pretest Sentences

1. The battery that I bought is a **mismatch.**
2. I saw a **preview** for that movie last week.
3. Regular **movement** is important to health.
4. A new **bicycle** would be outstanding.
5. Her mother was **doubtful** about her story.
6. All the excitement made my night **restless.**
7. A **restful** weekend was good for him.
8. Who will **direct** the play?
9. You may go any **direction** that you wish.
10. The new choir **director** is a nice person.
11. The **indirect** flight took a lot of time.
12. Using **autopilot** saves much time and energy.
13. He will **distrust** you if you sound insincere.
14. The outcome seemed **unfair.**
15. A **midsummer** festival sounds wonderful!

Challenge Pretest Sentences

16. Try not to **misspell** the words on this test.
17. Use the **knowledge** that you have gained.

Diagnose any misspellings by determining whether students misspelled words with prefixes, words with affixes that change the word's meaning, or words from the same word family. Then have students use the pretest as a take-home list to study these review concepts.

Penmanship

Cursive Letters *Q* and *F*

Teach

✦ Introduce capital cursive *Q* as an overcurve letter and capital *F* as a doublecurve letter.

✦ Display ***Transparency*** 152. Using a pointer, trace the letters while saying the formations aloud.

- **Letter *Q*** Starting point, downcurve
  Left into undercurve
  Loop and curve right
  Starting point, slant down right: capital *Q*
- **Letter *F*** Starting point, slant down
  Curve up and right to end point
  Starting point
  Slant down, curve up and right
  Starting point, across: capital *F*

✦ On the board, write capital cursive *Q* and *F*, saying the strokes aloud as you form the letters.

Guided Practice

Ask a volunteer to write the letters on the board. Guide the student as he or she writes.

Apply

Have students practice writing each of the letters four times. Ask students to circle the best formation of each of their letters.

Teacher Tips

CONNECTING *Q* Show how to connect cursive *Q* to other letters.

PENMANSHIP If students are having problems forming cursive *Q* and *F*, or their letters are floating between the lines, then review proper paper position, check to make sure students are holding their pencils correctly, or review letter formation.

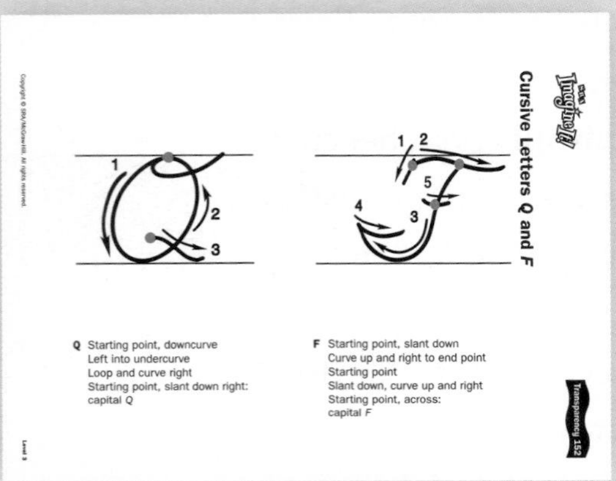

Cursive Letters Q and F

Q Starting point, downcurve
Left into undercurve
Loop and curve right
Starting point, slant down right:
capital Q

F Starting point, slant down
Curve up and right to end point
Starting point
Slant down, curve up and right
Starting point, across:
capital F

Transparency 152

Differentiating Instruction: English Learner

IF . . . students have difficulty with handwriting, **THEN . . .** bear in mind that some languages are written and read vertically or from right to left. Make sure English Learners write and proofread from left to right.

Skills Traces

Preparing to Read

Word Structure: Prefix *un-*

Introduced in Grade 2, Unit 4, Lesson 3

Reviewed: Unit 5, Lesson 1
Practiced: Unit 5, Lesson 5
Assessed: ***Lesson Assessment Book 2,*** p. 75

Reviewed in Grade 4, Unit 1, Lesson 2

Reading and Responding

Comprehension Skill: Author's Point of View

Introduced in Grade 2, Unit 2, Lesson 4

Grade 3
Reviewed: Unit 1, Lesson 3
Practiced: Unit 5, Lesson 5
Assessed: ***Lesson Assessment Book 2,*** pp. 76–78

Reviewed in Grade 4, Unit 1, Lesson 1

Comprehension Skill: Main Idea and Details

Reviewed in Grade 2, Unit 1, Lesson 1

Grade 3
Reviewed: Unit 1, Lesson 5
Practiced: Unit 5, Lesson 5
Assessed: ***Lesson Assessment Book 2,*** pp. 76–78

Reviewed in Grade 4, Unit 2, Lesson 2

Comprehension Strategy: Asking Questions

Reviewed in Grade 2, Unit 1, Lesson 1

Grade 3
Reviewed: Unit 1, Lesson 1
Practiced: Unit 5, Lesson 5
Assessed: Unit 5, Lesson 5, p. T354

Reviewed in Grade 4, Unit 1, Lesson 2

Comprehension Strategy: Predicting

Reviewed in Grade 2, Unit 1, Lesson 3

Grade 3
Reviewed: Unit 1, Lesson 1
Practiced: Unit 5, Lesson 5
Assessed: Unit 5, Lesson 5, p. T355

Reviewed in Grade 4, Unit 1, Lesson 1

Language Arts

Writing: Play

Introduced in Grade 2, Unit 5, Lesson 5

Grade 3
Reviewed: Unit 5, Lesson 5
Assessed: Unit 5, Lesson 5, p. T425

Reviewed in Grade 4, Unit 1, Lesson 4

Grammar, Usage, and Mechanics: Complex Sentences

Grade 3 Introduced in Grade 2, Unit 4, Lesson 3

Introduced: Unit 5, Lesson 5
Assessed: ***Lesson Assessment Book 2,*** p. 80

Reviewed in Grade 4, Unit 2, Lesson 5

Day 2

Preparing to Read

OBJECTIVES

Students will

- review the meanings of the prefixes *re-*, *un-*, *pre-*, *mis-*, *bi-*, *mid-*, *dis-*, and *auto-* and affixes as syllables.
- build fluency.

MATERIALS

- ***Transparency*** 149
- Routine 10

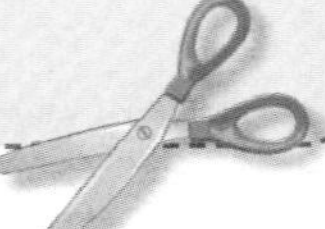

Daily Oral Practice

Daily News

Today!

I visited a farm once. I liked taking care of the animals, planting seeds in the fields, and being outside all day. I could ride my bicycle for miles and miles on one country road. The country is unbelievable. I hope I can return many times and maybe even live there one day.

- Write the daily news on the board or on chart paper. Then have a volunteer read the daily news aloud to practice fluency.
- As a review of yesterday's word structure lesson, ask a volunteer to identify any words in the message with prefixes. *bicycle, unbelievable, return*

Differentiating Instruction **English Learner**

IF . . . students are native Spanish speakers, **THEN . . .** remind them that the personal pronoun *I* is always capitalized. In Spanish, the personal pronoun *yo* is capitalized only when it begins a sentence. For additional instruction for new English learners, refer often to the ***English Learner Support Guide.***

Word Structure 

ROUTINE 10 

Review: The Prefixes *re-, un-, pre-, mis-, bi-, mid-, dis-,* and *auto-;* Affixes as Syllables

✦ Use ***Transparency*** 149 with these word lines from Day 1.

Line 1	renewed	resurface	unpaid	untold
Line 2	preserved	predawn	misinform	mislead
Line 3	bifocals	bilingual	midfield	midsized
Line 4	discount	disinfect	autographed	automatic

✦ Use Routine 10 to review the meaning of the prefixes *re-, un-, pre-, mis-, bi-, mid-, dis-,* and *auto-*. If necessary, remind students that different prefixes change the meaning of base words and add syllables to them. Point out that some affixes, such as the prefix *auto-,* are two syllables.

Developing Oral Language

Use any or all of the following activities to help students practice reading the words from the word lines.

- Ask a volunteer to choose a word from the word lines and use it in a sentence. **Possible Answer** *When they have to* resurface *the highway, it is very expensive.* Then have that student choose another volunteer to use that word's base word in a sentence. **Possible Answer** *The* surface *of the water looked as smooth as silk.* Continue until all words have been used.
- Have individual students point to a word, read it, and then use it in a sentence. Have other students extend the sentence by asking questions about *who, what, when, where, why* and *how*. **Possible Answer** *I want to be* bilingual, *but I have to study another language first.*
- Have one student choose a line of words from the word lines and point to a word in that line. Then have the student choose a classmate to read the word. Have the student read the word a second time, this time clapping for each syllable. Then have that student point to a different word, and choose a classmate to read it and clap the syllables. Repeat the procedure until all of the words on the board have been read.

Teacher Tip

PREFIXES Point out that the word *prefix* has a prefix. Challenge students to define *prefix* by breaking the word down into its parts.

Monitor Progress 

to Differentiate Instruction

Formal Assessment

Word Structure During the word structure activity, note how well students understand the words.

APPROACHING LEVEL

IF . . . students do not understand the words on the word lines,	**THEN . . .** use pictures, photos, objects, stick drawings, or pantomime to help them visualize the words.

ON LEVEL

IF . . . students need practice with the words on the word lines,	**THEN . . .** have them write sentences using the words on the lines.

ABOVE LEVEL

IF . . . students understand the words on the word lines,	**THEN . . .** have them make a list of other words with these prefixes and use them in sentences.

Hurting with the pain of parting with their good land, but having to, the Baxters signed the east field over to Emma Price's company. Homestead Realty paid them without delay. In turn, the Baxters paid for their bad year and looked forward to better ones.

Soon bulldozers were clearing the land, leaving pitifully few of the trees, going against (13) what Emma Price had promised. But it was not all bad, the Baxters told themselves and each other. When the noises and smells of building began to die down, the new houses looked pretty and comfortable, and the people who moved into them seemed friendly enough. It was just strange to see the old alfalfa field planted with so many houses.

Several years of good crops did follow and things seemed to be almost back to normal, even though more and more houses were being built all around. Sue Ann won a partial scholarship to forestry college. Everybody was proud of her, but missed her a lot.

Pee Wee had just started high school when the milking problem came up. Each morning

he'd pitch in to take Sue Ann's place. Jim and Wally still arrived at the crack of dawn, but Jim was getting on in years, and it seemed to take him longer to get the cows milked than it (14) used to. Besides, a lot of the local farmers were putting in new automatic equipment—milking parlors, they called them, with an elevated stall for each cow and tubes leading right to the main tank. The Baxters still relied on the old methods. Not that they wouldn't have changed over. But the cost of the new setup was more than they could swing. So, for a while at least, Pee Wee did his best to help out. Wally never missed a day, but he was no longer up to heavy work, so Sara pitched in more often.

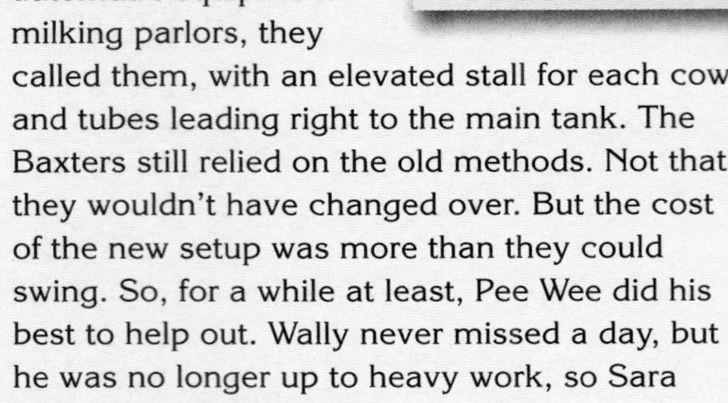

Still, it got harder and harder to compete with the milk production of neighboring farmers who had installed milking parlors to handle larger herds in less time than it took the Baxters. Milk sales were barely bringing in enough to cover costs, so it wasn't long before the Baxters began to sell off the rest of their herd.

OBJECTIVES

Students will

- use the comprehension strategies Predicting, Asking Questions, and Making Connections.
- discuss the story using the handing-off process.
- review vocabulary, genre, and fluency.

MATERIALS

- ***Student Reader,*** Book 2, pp. 222–231
- Routine A
- ***Skills Practice 2,*** pp. 159–160
- ***Transparency*** 5, 150

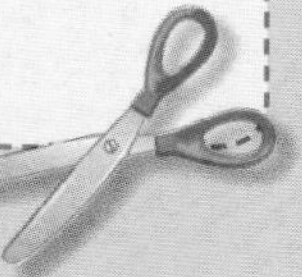

Comprehension Strategies

(13) **Confirming Predictions** Teacher Prompt: *Have any of your predictions been confirmed?* **Possible Student Response** *I predicted that the realty company would not save the trees on the Baxter's land, and I was right. The text says, "... leaving pitifully few trees, going against what Emma Price had promised."*

(14) **Asking Questions** Teacher Prompt: *I have a question on this page. Who else has a question?* **Possible Student Response** *The text says that a lot of the farmers were putting in new milking equipment. How does that affect the Baxters? I'll keep reading to see if I can find the answer. It says that it got harder and harder to compete with those farmers because they could handle larger herds in less time. Unfortunately, the Baxters couldn't keep up and they had to sell their herd.*

Comprehension Check

What does the realty company do with the old alfalfa field? **Possible Answer** *It builds houses on them.*

Finally, only five cows grazed in the meadow. The milking barn was practically empty. And even though the Baxters didn't have their herd, they took comfort in knowing that the milk and butter on their kitchen table was not store-bought, but still their own. 15

The following spring George Stillwell came to see Pete and Sara Baxter about using the pond and meadow area for sports land. He didn't want to *buy* the land—which pleased the Baxters, as they'd made up their minds they'd never part with the pond. George Stillwell proposed leasing the area for eight years. 16

224

He would put up what he called a "rustic cabin" and, in turn, rent it out to hunters during the fall and winter gunning seasons.

Pete figured that was a good enough deal. The pond was a safe distance from the housing development. Besides, the whole area filled up with hunters during the duck and goose seasons anyway. The Baxters had always let some hunters on their land, so a few more couldn't do much harm, except for the noise. And without actually giving up the land, they would be paid for it. This would fill the hole in their pockets left by the loss of milk money, and would help to fill Pee Wee's college savings account. So Sara, too, reluctantly agreed.

225

15 **Making Connections** Teacher Prompt: *Are there any connections we can make to this part of the story?* **Possible Student Response** *The text says that the Baxters still feel good that the milk and butter on their table was their own and not from the store. That reminds me of my grandmother. She always says the same thing about her eggs. She lives in the country and has a yard for her own chickens. She never buys eggs from a store.*

16 **Predicting** Teacher Prompt: *I would like to make another prediction here. How about you?* **Possible Student Response** *George Stillwell says he wants the pond and the meadow area for eight years. The way things are changing for the Baxters, I predict that something will go wrong and they won't get their land back. I hope I'm wrong this time.*

Teacher Tip

PREDICTING Remind students that predictions that are not confirmed are not "wrong answers." Rather, the author simply chose to take the story in another direction. Encourage students whose predictions were refuted to brainstorm how the story might have been different if their predictions had been confirmed.

Reading and Responding

In the next year, the cabin, only a little bigger than the Baxters had expected, went up. They could live with a few hunters for eight years.

Pee Wee, now Petie to everyone except his family, went off to engineering school a whole year ahead of his graduating class. This came as no great surprise to the Baxters, and his ambitions made them proud.

Jim retired officially, but still came around to tinker with the machinery and complain how the new tractor wasn't up to the old model.

226

Again, things returned almost to normal. Pete and Sara had a smaller place, but it was plenty for them and Wally to handle. They still had the big south field for corn and barley, and the front field for other crops. Sara had her chickens and her garden. Life on the farm was different, what with the changes and Sue Ann and Pee Wee away most of the year. Perhaps now things would stay put for a while. And they did in fact—for some time.

But things once set out of order never quite stay put for long. 17

One day something happened that the Baxters found hard to understand. Jess Hammil sold out to a developer, a big developer.

Jess's country market and his land were bulldozed to make Main Shopping Mall, featuring a giant supermarket, a discount drugstore, a dress boutique, a chain department store, and countless other small shops.

227

Word Structure

Prefix *re-*: retire, returned

Vocabulary Tip

Point out the words *featuring* and *discount* in the text. Ask students to name the base word of *featuring*. Ask them how using word structure can help them figure out the meaning of the word. If students do not know the meaning of the word *discount*, have them look up the word in a dictionary.

Comprehension Strategies

17 **Asking Questions** Teacher Prompt: *Who has questions about what we are reading now?* **Possible Student Response** *What does the author mean when she says, "But things once set out of order never quite stay put for long"? Does that mean that because changes had been made more changes were coming? Jess Hammil sold his property to a developer to make a shopping mall. How is that going to affect the Baxters?*

Comprehension Check

Why would Jess Hammil sell his land to a developer? **Possible Answer** *They probably offered him a lot of money for the land.* *Why do the Baxters find his decision to sell hard to understand?* **Possible Answer** *They probably thought he liked his life on the farm the way it was and wasn't interested in changing it.*

Not long after this, Homestead Realty Company made the Baxters an offer on the big south field. This time they didn't *have* to sell, but Wally was about to retire and Pete and Sara were no longer up to heavy work. They could look for new hired hands, but it just didn't seem the same. The offer was tempting, so they finally accepted.

One thing led to another. The man who'd rented the pond made an offer to buy now that the lease was about to expire. Since the pond and meadow would never be the same again, what with a shopping center bordering it, the Baxters could see little reason to hold onto it. It had lost almost all its meaning for them. 18

After the sale to George Stillwell—the most profitable and the most heartbreaking for the Baxters—the cabin was turned into Rustic Manor Motor Lodge and Tennis Club almost overnight.

The Baxter Place was not even half of what it had been not too many years before. But the trees—those that were left—still acted as dividers, trying hard to keep the Baxter Place separate.

Sara and Pete still had the front field leading up to the old farmhouse. In the early years, they had had to struggle hard just to make the place pay for itself. Now they had some money in the bank. That was something.

Folks couldn't still say the Baxter Place was the prettiest, neatest place around—not the way it had gotten so divided up and changed. But folks could still say the Baxters were some of the nicest folks they'd ever known. And they were. That had not changed. But so many things *had*.

"What ever happened to the old Baxter Place?" somebody asked. And nobody could quite say. Not even the Baxters. 19

18 **Confirming Predictions** Teacher Prompt: *Now that we're close to the end of our story, have anyone's predictions been confirmed?* **Possible Student Response** *I was right about the meadow and pond. The Baxters didn't need the money, but the land wasn't the same anymore and they decided to sell. They didn't lose the land like I thought they would; it was their decision to give it up.*

19 **Asking Questions** Teacher Prompt: *I have a question on this page. Who else has a question?* **Possible Student Response** *The text says that the Baxters couldn't say what happened to the Baxter place. I wonder why they don't know. I do know that they kept selling their land over many years; the farm kept getting smaller. The farm became a different place than how it started. I see. It must be hard for the Baxters to look back and understand how it changed over time.*

Differentiating Instruction **English Learner**

IF . . . students are native speakers of Spanish, **THEN . . .** remind them that in English the question mark is placed only at the end of a sentence, never at the beginning. Tell students to quickly skim to the end of a sentence before they read it aloud in order to determine the appropriate expression or inflection to use.

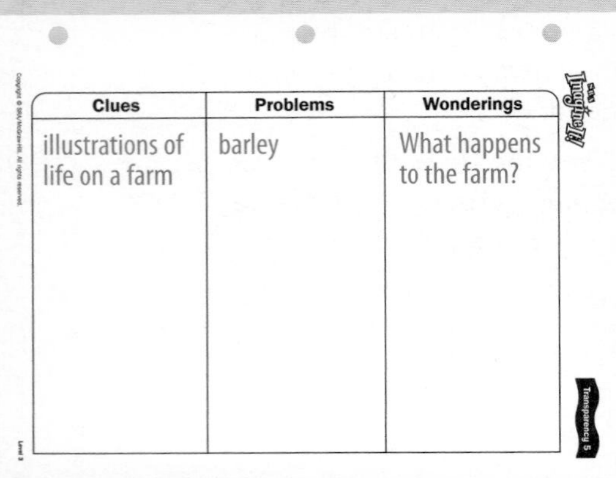

Clues
Problems
Wonderings
illustrations of life on a farm
barley
What happens to the farm?

Transparency 5

Discussing the Selection

✦ It is important for students to see you as a contributing member of the group. Use Routine A, handing-off, to emphasize that you are part of the group. Actively participate in handing-off by raising your hand to be called on by the last speaker when you have a contribution to make. Point out unusual and interesting insights verbalized by students so these insights are recognized and discussed.

✦ Engage students in a discussion using handing-off to determine whether they have grasped the following ideas:

- The Baxter family had a good life on a big farm.
- Life on the farm changed over a period of time. Weather, competition with larger farms, and aging affected the Baxter Place.

✦ Ask students how the story demonstrates the following key concepts:

- The farm was bought by land developers who used the land for businesses and houses and cleared the land of its trees and fields.
- Some people want to keep the land the way it is and farm it in its natural state. Others want to develop the land and build businesses and houses on it.

✦ Return to the Clues, Problems, and Wonderings chart on ***Transparency*** 5. Have students discuss which clues were useful, how they resolved their problems, and how they answered their questions. Also ask students if the predictions they made while browsing the story were confirmed or not confirmed.

✦ Have students return to the Focus Questions on ***Student Reader***, Book 2 page 208. Select a student to read the questions aloud, and have students answer and discuss the questions. Have them return to the text as necessary

Genre Review

Review the elements of realistic fiction with students. Then ask students how they know "What Ever Happened to the Baxter Place?" is realistic fiction.

How has my community changed over time?

After reading the story, read the Big Idea question. Discuss with students how the story helps answer this question.

Vocabulary Review

Review with students the selection vocabulary words and definitions they wrote in the vocabulary section of their Writer's Notebooks. Then refer students to ***Skills Practice 2*** pages 159–160. Help students complete the first two questions. Then have students complete the rest on their own. Also, review the concept vocabulary word *development*. Ask students if they can think of other words related to the theme Communities across Time. **Possible Answers** *land, change, growth, cooperation, nature, ownership, environment*

Fluency

- When modeling fluency, pay careful attention to expression. Expression, or reading words with feeling and emotion, is essential to fluency. Point out to students that stories such as "What Ever Happened to the Baxter Place?" should be read with expression because of the story's content. The Baxters go through a series of hardships and changes. By reading with expression, readers can better understand the story and the characters' feelings.
- Read aloud pages 222–223 of "What Ever Happened to the Baxter Place?" Model expression for students. For example, after reading *Hurting with the pain of parting with their good land, but having to, the Baxters signed the east field over to Emma Price's company*, point out to students that because of the sadness and disappointment felt by the Baxters, the text should be read in a serious way.

Monitor Progress to Differentiate Instruction

Formal Assessment

Selection Vocabulary Observe students' understanding of the vocabulary words and their definitions.

APPROACHING LEVEL

IF . . . students need extra help with the selection vocabulary,	**THEN . . .** refer to ***Intervention Guide*** Unit 5, Lesson 5.
IF . . . students need extra help with the selection vocabulary,	**THEN . . .** use ***Reteach*** page 151.

ON LEVEL

IF . . . students need practice using the selection vocabulary words,	**THEN . . .** have students complete ***eSkills & eGames*** vocabulary activities.

ABOVE LEVEL

IF . . . students understand the selection vocabulary,	**THEN . . .** use ***Challenge Activities*** page 137.

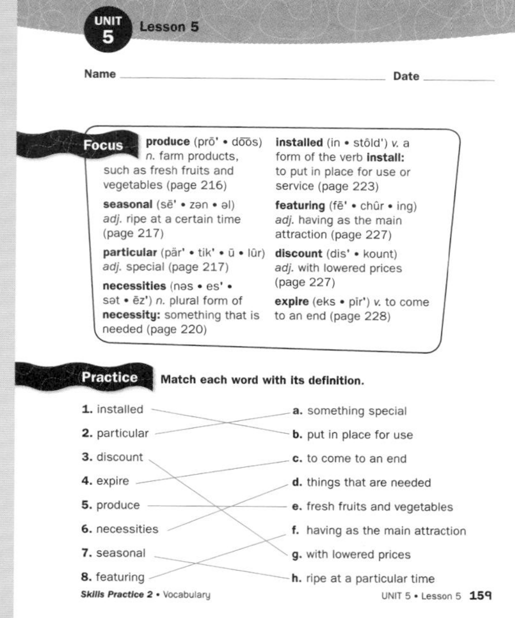

UNIT 5 Lesson 5

Name ______________ Date ________

Focus

produce (prō' • dōōs) *n.* farm products, such as fresh fruits and vegetables (page 216)

seasonal (sē' • zən • əl) *adj.* ripe at a certain time (page 217)

particular (pär' • tik' • ū • lûr) *adj.* special (page 217)

necessities (nəs • es' • sət • ēz') *n.* plural form of **necessity:** something that is needed (page 220)

installed (in • stôld') *v.* a form of the verb **install:** to put in place for use or service (page 223)

featuring (fē' • chûr • ing) *adj.* having as the main attraction (page 227)

discount (dis' • kount) *adj.* with lowered prices (page 227)

expire (eks • pīr') *v.* to come to an end (page 228)

Practice **Match each word with its definition.**

1. installed
2. particular
3. discount
4. expire
5. produce
6. necessities
7. seasonal
8. featuring

a. something special
b. put in place for use
c. to come to an end
d. things that are needed
e. fresh fruits and vegetables
f. having as the main attraction
g. with lowered prices
h. ripe at a particular time

Skills Practice 2 • Vocabulary   UNIT 5 • Lesson 5 **159**

Skills Practice 2, pp. 159–160

Teacher Tips

FLUENCY By this time in Grade 3, good readers should be reading approximately 137 words per minute with fluency and expression. The only way to gain this fluency is with practice. Have students reread the story to you and to each other during Workshop to help build fluency. As students read, you may notice that some need work in building fluency. During Workshop, have these students choose a section of the text (a minimum of 160 words) to read aloud several times to build fluency.

WORD BANK Review the Word Bank with students. Encourage students to add words to the Word Bank that are related to the unit theme Communities across Time. You might also want to encourage students to add synonyms and antonyms in the Word Bank as well.

Meet the Author and Illustrator

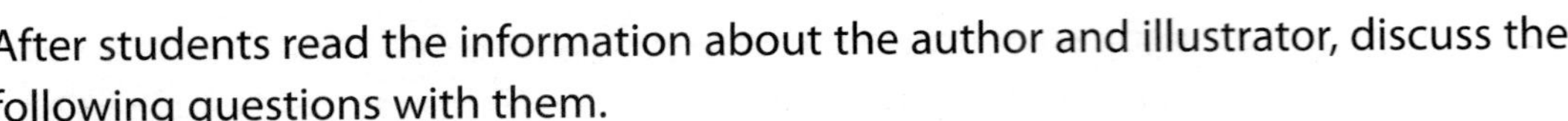

After students read the information about the author and illustrator, discuss the following questions with them.

- *Pat Ross discovered her own voice for writing by editing children's books. Why do you think editing would help her to do this?* **Possible Answer** *She probably read many books as an editor. She may have developed new ideas for stories and wanted to see them made into books too.*
- *Roger Duvoisin is also a successful scenery and textile designer. How would this have helped him illustrate this story?* **Possible Answer** *Scenery is an important part of this story. He had to show how the Baxter place kept changing through the scenery.*

Theme Connections

Within the Selection

1. How would you feel if you were one of the Baxter children? **Possible Answer** *I would be proud of my parents for believing in their farm and their way of life, no matter how difficult it was for them sometimes.*
2. How has land in your area been changed to meet the community's needs? **Possible Answer** *My community now has a hospital where a farm used to be. People were sorry to see the farm go, but having a hospital close by was very important to our town.*

Across Selections

3. How are the Baxters like Grandma in "The Disappearing Island"? **Possible Answer** *The Baxters, like Grandma, love and respect nature. They are disappointed when the land is changed by developers who are building homes and stores.*
4. How are they different? **Possible Answer** *Grandma's island has been changed by nature. There is nothing people can do to keep the island occupied. The Baxter's farm, however, has been changed by people. If the land hadn't been sold, it might not have changed.*

Concept/Question Board

As students reread "What Ever Happened to the Baxter Place?" encourage them to post questions, answers, comments, or other items related to communities across time on the **Concept/Question Board.**

Teacher Tips

BEYOND THE SELECTION Have students summarize what they have learned and tell how they might use this information in further investigations.

WRITE ABOUT IT! Have students describe a farm they have visited or read about in their Writer's Notebooks.

WORKSHOP During Workshop, have students listen to "What Ever Happened to the Baxter Place?" for a model of oral reading. While students listen, have them keep a list in the Writer's Notebook of any new or unfamiliar words they encounter, and instruct them to check the words using a dictionary or glossary. Also, instruct students to listen for the lesson's vocabulary words and to check that the words make sense within the reading.

Writer's Notebook

- Have students use their Writer's Notebooks to list other fiction selections they have read in class or on their own.
- Have students compare the elements found in each selection.

Meet the Author

Pat Ross

Pat Ross began writing and drawing as hobbies. After finishing school, she discovered that she had a gift for writing children's stories. Many of Ross's books focus on the spirit and challenges of young girls. The books in her M & M book series have won many awards.

Meet the Illustrator

Roger Duvoisin

Roger Duvoisin was born in Switzerland and became a citizen of the United States in 1938. Throughout his career, he wrote over 40 children's books and illustrated more than 140 books altogether. Duvoisin loved drawing animals, which seemed to come to life through both his words and drawings. His *Happy Lion* books were very popular. For these, Duvoisin was the illustrator and his wife, Louise Fatio, was the author.

230

Communities across Time

Theme Connections

Within the Selection

1. How would you feel if you were one of the Baxter children?
2. How has land in your area been changed to meet the community's needs?

Across Selections

3. How are the Baxters like Grandma in "The Disappearing Island"?
4. How are they different?

Beyond the Selection

5. Why do some communities protest plans to build strip malls and superstores in their areas?
6. Why do some people want these kinds of stores nearby?

Write about It!

Describe a farm that you have visited or read about.

Remember to bring questions about how farming in America has changed over time to add to the **Concept/Question Board.**

231

Beyond the Selection

5. Why do some communities protest plans to build strip malls and superstores in their areas? **Possible Answer** *Some people are afraid of the land being changed, just like it was in "What Ever Happened to the Baxter Place?" An area that was once peaceful might become busy and crowded.*

6. Why do some people want these kinds of stores nearby? **Possible Answer** *These kinds of stores can bring jobs to a community. Also, it can be convenient for the neighborhood to have these types of stores nearby.*

Language Arts

OBJECTIVES

Students will
- create a play graphic organizer.
- review Unit 5 spelling words and patterns.
- learn complex sentences.

MATERIALS

- ***Skills Practice 2,*** pp. 163, 167–168
- Routine 16

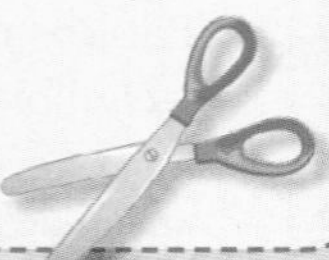

Writing Play

ROUTINE 16

Prewriting

Teach

- Review the three parts of a play with students.
- Use Routine 16. Tell students they will work on a graphic organizer that will help them remember to include all of the characters, props, the setting, and the events of the plot.
- Discuss with students the beginning, middle, and ending of "What Ever Happened to the Baxter Place?" Tell students the characters attempted to solve problems throughout the story, even though they were not always pleased by the outcomes.
- Remind students that they should think about how they want to develop the setting, the personalities of their characters, and the types of props used by the characters.

Guided Practice

- Have students turn to ***Skills Practice 2*** page 163. Draw a graphic organizer on the board like the one on page 163. Using a topic you select to use during modeling, model using the play graphic organizer to record ideas for the plot, characters, setting, and props.
- As you model, remind students to keep the audience in mind when deciding on characters and their dialogue, plot, and setting.
- As you model, explain to students why you use certain props for certain characters, and then ask students to suggest other props that would add dimension to the plot or characters.

Teacher Tip

PLAN AHEAD Plan time for students to type their plays before they present them.

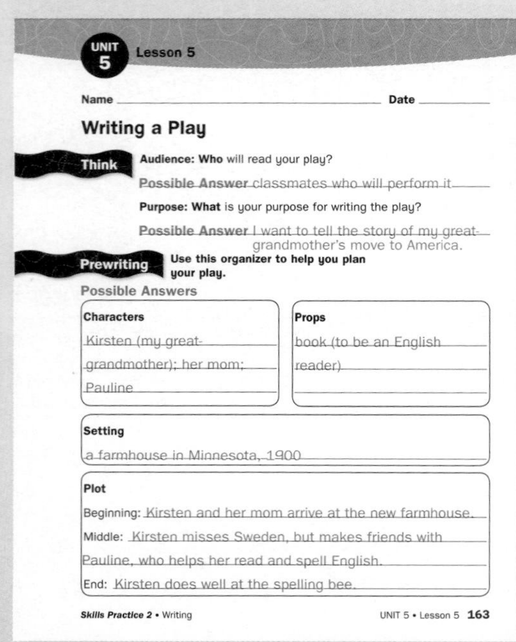

UNIT 5 Lesson 5

Name ______ Date ______

Writing a Play

Think

Audience: Who will read your play?

Possible Answer classmates who will perform it

Purpose: What is your purpose for writing the play?

Possible Answer I want to tell the story of my great-grandmother's move to America.

Prewriting Use this organizer to help you plan your play.

Possible Answers

Characters	Props
Kirsten (my great-grandmother); her mom; Pauline	book (to be an English reader)

Setting: a farmhouse in Minnesota, 1900

Plot
Beginning: Kirsten and her mom arrive at the new farmhouse.
Middle: Kirsten misses Sweden, but makes friends with Pauline, who helps her read and spell English.
End: Kirsten does well at the spelling bee.

Skills Practice 2 • Writing UNIT 5 • Lesson 5 163

Skills Practice 2, p. 163

Writing, continued

Apply

Composing—Prewriting Have students work on inserting information into the play graphic organizer in ***Skills Practice 2*** page 163.

Monitor Progress to Differentiate Instruction

Formal Assessment

Graphic Organizer Note whether students are putting information in appropriate areas of their graphic organizers.

APPROACHING LEVEL

IF . . . students need help with their graphic organizers,	**THEN . . .** pair them with another student during Workshop.

ON LEVEL

IF . . . students understand how to fill in the graphic organizers,	**THEN . . .** have them begin working on characterization during Workshop.

ABOVE LEVEL

IF . . . students need a challenge,	**THEN . . .** have them create a more complex graphic organizer to complete during Workshop.

Spelling

Review of Prefixes, Affixes, and Word Families

Teach

Use a word sort to review words with prefixes, words with affixes that change the word's meaning, and word families.

Guided Practice

Write the following headings on the board: *words with a prefix, words with an affix,* and *words from the same word family.* Then write the following words on the board: *mismatch, preview, movement, bicycle, doubtful, restless, restful, direct, direction, director, indirect, autopilot, distrust, unfair,* and *midsummer.* Have volunteers write the words under the correct heading. After all the spelling words have been used, ask for students to come to the board and underline the part of each word that reflects the category in which it was placed. If a word fits in more than one category, ask students to put the word under the heading that they prefer. Because this is a review lesson, tell students that there will be many words that belong in more than one category.

Word Sort Answers

Words with a Prefix: *mismatch, preview, bicycle, autopilot, distrust, unfair, midsummer, indirect*

Words with an Affix: *mismatch, preview, movement, bicycle, doubtful, restless, restful, direction, director, indirect, autopilot, distrust, unfair, midsummer*

Words From the Same Word Family: *direct/direction/director/indirect, restless/restful*

Grammar, Usage, and Mechanics 

Complex Sentences

Teach

✦ Write a complex sentence on the board. Ask students who and what the sentence is about. Then write a fragment on the board, and ask students who and what it is about. If necessary, explain to students that a fragment is part of a sentence but is missing either the *who* or the *what.*

✦ Ask students if they have ever been told by you or another teacher that they have written a fragment of a sentence, but not a complete sentence. **Possible Answer** *yes* Then explain to students that you are going to show them a way to get rid of these incomplete sentences in their writing.

✦ Write the following examples on the board:

- My friend likes his new school. *independent clause*
- Although I miss him *dependent clause*
- My friend likes his new school, although I miss him. *complex sentence*

✦ Have students identify the subject and predicate in the first sentence. Have students identify the second sentence as a fragment, and explain that it lacks a subject. Then have students identify the third sentences as a complex sentence.

✦ Write the following examples of an independent clause and a dependent clause on the board, and then model combining them to create the complex sentence.

- We'll have a picnic. *independent clause*
- After the storm passes *dependent clause*
- After the storm passes, we'll have a picnic. *complex sentence*

✦ Explain to students that complex sentences can be created by combining an independent clause with a dependent clause using a subordinating conjunction. Common subordinate conjunctions include *after, although, as, because, before, if, since, when, where, while, until,* and *unless*.

✦ Independent and dependent clauses can also be joined with the relative pronouns *who, whose, which, that*.

✦ Using the examples on the board, point out that a comma is used to join the dependent and independent clauses when the sentence begins with a dependent clause.

Guided Practice

Have students turn to ***Skills Practice 2*** page 167. Have a student read the directions aloud. Complete the first two Practice questions as a class.

Apply

Have students complete ***Skills Practice 2*** pages 167–168 to practice creating complex sentences.

Monitor Progress to Differentiate Instruction

Formal Assessment 

Complex Sentences Note whether students understand how to combine dependent and independent clauses.

APPROACHING LEVEL

IF . . . students need to practice complex sentences,	**THEN . . .** have them complete ***Reteach*** page 155 during Workshop.
IF . . . students need more practice with complex sentences,	**THEN . . .** refer to Unit 5 Lesson 5 in the ***Intervention Guide.***

ON LEVEL

IF . . . students have an understanding of complex sentences,	**THEN . . .** edit a piece of their writing to correct fragments during Workshop.

ABOVE LEVEL

IF . . . students need a challenge,	**THEN . . .** have them complete ***Challenge Activities*** page 140 during Workshop.

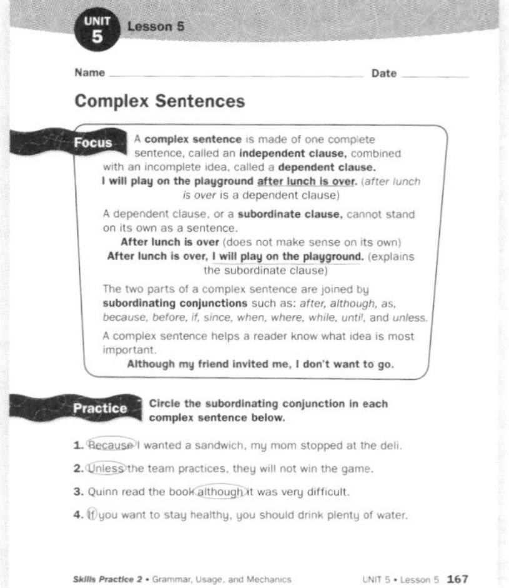

UNIT 5 Lesson 5

Name ____________ Date ______

Complex Sentences

Focus A **complex sentence** is made of one complete sentence, called an **independent clause,** combined with an incomplete idea, called a **dependent clause.**

I will play on the playground after lunch is over. (*after lunch is over* is a dependent clause)

A dependent clause, or a **subordinate clause,** cannot stand on its own as a sentence.

After lunch is over (does not make sense on its own)

After lunch is over, I will play on the playground. (explains the subordinate clause)

The two parts of a complex sentence are joined by **subordinating conjunctions** such as: *after, although, as, because, before, if, since, when, where, while, until,* and *unless.*

A complex sentence helps a reader know what idea is most important.

Although my friend invited me, I don't want to go.

Practice **Circle the subordinating conjunction in each complex sentence below.**

1. Because I wanted a sandwich, my mom stopped at the deli.
2. Unless the team practices, they will not win the game.
3. Quinn read the book although it was very difficult.
4. If you want to stay healthy, you should drink plenty of water.

Skills Practice 2 • Grammar, Usage, and Mechanics UNIT 5 • Lesson 5 167

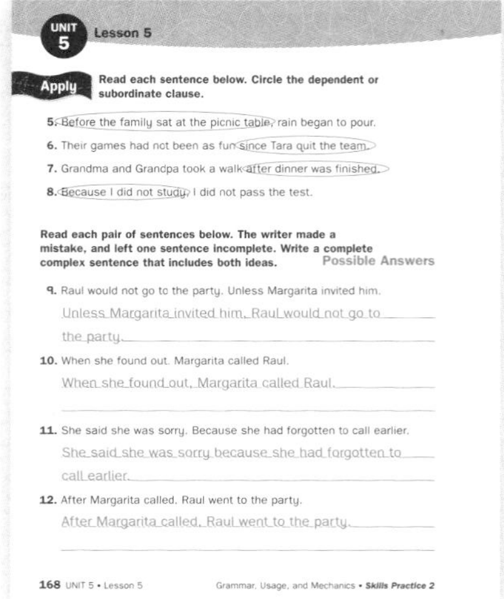

UNIT 5 Lesson 5

Apply **Read each sentence below. Circle the dependent or subordinate clause.**

5. Before the family sat at the picnic table, rain began to pour.
6. Their games had not been as fun since Tara quit the team.
7. Grandma and Grandpa took a walk after dinner was finished.
8. Because I did not study, I did not pass the test.

Read each pair of sentences below. The writer made a mistake, and left one sentence incomplete. Write a complete complex sentence that includes both ideas. Possible Answers

9. Raul would not go to the party. Unless Margarita invited him.
Unless Margarita invited him, Raul would not go to the party.
10. When she found out. Margarita called Raul.
When she found out, Margarita called Raul.
11. She said she was sorry. Because she had forgotten to call earlier.
She said she was sorry because she had forgotten to call earlier.
12. After Margarita called. Raul went to the party.
After Margarita called, Raul went to the party.

168 UNIT 5 • Lesson 5 Grammar, Usage, and Mechanics • *Skills Practice 2*

Skills Practice 2, pp. 167–168

Differentiating Instruction **English Learner**

IF . . . students have difficulty distinguishing between dependent and independent clauses, **THEN . . .** review the meanings of *dependent* and *independent.* You may also wish to introduce words that commonly introduce a dependent clause, such as *who, when,* and *because.*

IF . . . students have difficulty completing the ***Skills Practice*** page independently, **THEN . . .** have them work in pairs or in small groups with proficient English speakers.

Day 3

Preparing to Read

OBJECTIVES

Students will

- review word families and multisyllabic words with silent consonants.
- build fluency.

MATERIALS

- ***Transparency*** 153
- ***Skills Practice 2,*** pp. 157–158

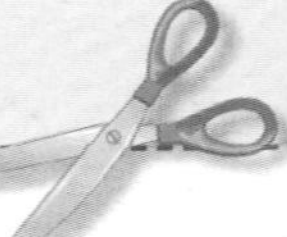

Differentiating Instruction **English Learner**

IF . . . students would benefit from a review of plurals and possessives, **THEN . . .** write the following words on the board: *Baxters, Baxter's and Baxters'*. Point to the word *Baxters'* in the daily news and explain that because this word is both plural and possessive, the last *s* is left off.

Daily Oral Practice

Daily News

Today!

Change can be good, and change can be bad. The land development changed the Baxters' lives. They loved farming, and they saved their farm for as long as they could. In the end, they had only one small piece of their farm to call their own.

- Write the daily news on the board or on chart paper. Then have students read the daily news in unison to practice fluency.
- As a review of yesterday's word structure lesson, ask volunteers to identify any words in the message that have affixes as syllables. *development*

Word Structure

Review: Word Families and Multisyllabic Words with Silent Consonants

- Write these word lines on the board or use ***Transparency*** 153. The words in boldface are in "What Ever Happened to the Baxter Place?"

Line 1	stretch	**stretched**	**stretching**	restretch
Line 2	develop	**developer**	**developing**	**development**
Line 3	**luckiest**	**pockets**	scenic	scissors
Line 4	**kneeling**	knapsack	**overnight**	**highlight**

Teacher Tip

SYLLABICATION To help students blend words and build fluency, demonstrate syllabication using the decodable, multisyllabic words in the word lines.

stretch • ing	re • stretch
de • vel • op	de • vel • op • er
de • vel • op • ing	de • vel • op • ment
luck • i • est	pock • ets
sce • nic	scis • sors
kneel • ing	knap • sack
o • ver • night	high • light

Lines 1–2 Word Families

As you point to each word, have students say the word and clap for each syllable. Point out that the first word on Lines 1–2 is the base word of a word family. Ask students how the words following the base words are different. *Affixes or inflectional endings have been added.* Have students identify any prefixes or suffixes in these words and define them, using a dictionary if necessary.

Line 3 Multisyllabic Words with the Silent Consonant *c*

Point to the words in Line 3 and ask students to read the words together. Explain that the words on Line 3 are multisyllabic words with a silent consonant. Ask students what letter in these words is silent. *The letter* c *is silent.* Ask them what sound *ck* makes. ck *makes /k/.* Ask students what sound *sc* makes. sc *makes /s/.*

Line 4 Multisyllabic Words with the Silent Consonants *k* and *gh*

Point to the words in Line 4 and ask students to read the words together. Explain that the words on Line 4 are multisyllabic words with a silent consonant. Ask students to identify the silent consonants in each word. k *in* kneeling *and* knapsack*;* c *in* knapsack*;* gh *in* overnight *and twice in* highlight

✦ Help students start the word structure activities on ***Skills Practice 2*** pages 157–158. Read the Focus box with them and help them with the first few questions. Then have students complete the pages on their own.

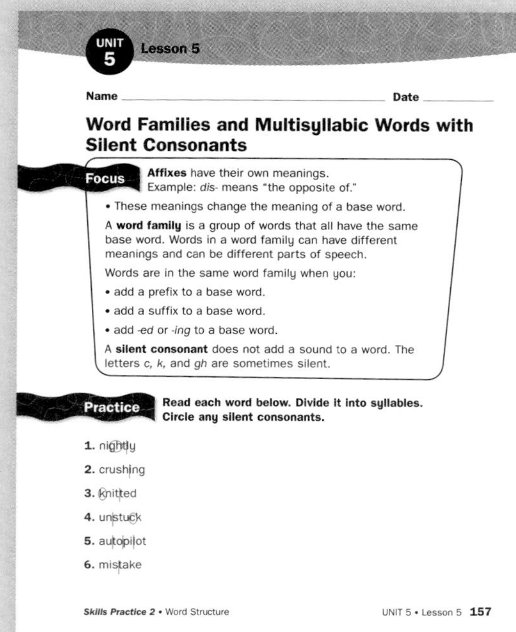
UNIT 5 Lesson 5

Name ______ Date ______

Word Families and Multisyllabic Words with Silent Consonants

Focus **Affixes** have their own meanings.
Example: *dis-* means "the opposite of."

- These meanings change the meaning of a base word.

A **word family** is a group of words that all have the same base word. Words in a word family can have different meanings and can be different parts of speech.

Words are in the same word family when you:

- add a prefix to a base word.
- add a suffix to a base word.
- add *-ed* or *-ing* to a base word.

A **silent consonant** does not add a sound to a word. The letters *c*, *k*, and *gh* are sometimes silent.

Practice **Read each word below. Divide it into syllables. Circle any silent consonants.**

1. nightly
2. crushing
3. knitted
4. unstuck
5. autopilot
6. mistake

Skills Practice 2 • Word Structure UNIT 5 • Lesson 5 **157**

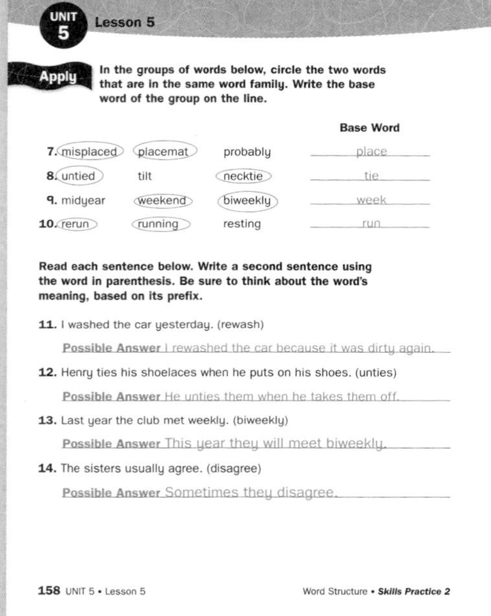
UNIT 5 Lesson 5

Apply **In the groups of words below, circle the two words that are in the same word family. Write the base word of the group on the line.**

			Base Word
7. misplaced	placemat	probably	place
8. untied	tilt	necktie	tie
9. midyear	weekend	biweekly	week
10. rerun	running	resting	run

Read each sentence below. Write a second sentence using the word in parenthesis. Be sure to think about the word's meaning, based on its prefix.

11. I washed the car yesterday. (rewash)
Possible Answer I rewashed the car because it was dirty again.
12. Henry ties his shoelaces when he puts on his shoes. (unties)
Possible Answer He unties them when he takes them off.
13. Last year the club met weekly. (biweekly)
Possible Answer This year they will meet biweekly.
14. The sisters usually agree. (disagree)
Possible Answer Sometimes they disagree.

158 UNIT 5 • Lesson 5 Word Structure • *Skills Practice 2*

Skills Practice 2, pp. 157–158

Monitor Progress to Differentiate Instruction

Formal Assessment 

Word Structure During the word structure activity, note how well students recognize word families and silent consonants.

	IF . . .	THEN . . .
APPROACHING LEVEL	**IF . . .** students need practice with word families or silent consonants,	**THEN . . .** work with them in small groups on the word structure activities on ***Reteach*** page 150 during Workshop.
	IF . . . students need extra practice with word families or silent consonants,	**THEN . . .** work with them in small groups on the word structure activities for Unit 5 Lesson 5 in the ***Intervention Guide*** during Workshop.
ON LEVEL	**IF . . .** students understand word families and silent consonants,	**THEN . . .** have them use words from the word lines in sentences during Workshop.
ABOVE LEVEL	**IF . . .** students are ready for a challenge with word families and silent consonants,	**THEN . . .** have them complete the word structure activities on ***Challenge Activities*** page 136 during Workshop.

Some years ago you could turn off the main road outside a small town in Maryland onto a dirt road which stretched three miles. The old dirt road was called Flatland Road, and it led you straight to the Baxter Place.

It was really a farm belonging to the Baxter family—acres and acres of fields and meadows and woodland—but everybody around just called it the Baxter Place.

A herd of cows grazed in the east meadow. Wild ducks and geese swam in the pond nearby.

Stretching up to a big white farmhouse was a field of soybeans, making a pretty blanket of green in the spring and summer months.

210

The Baxter Place spread out over nearly three hundred acres. The south field—the biggest and flattest—was planted in rotation with corn one year and barley the next. The rolling east field was well-suited for alfalfa, giving three cuttings each year. The west field, the smallest stretch, was reserved for crops the Baxters might want for their own, with surplus going for sale.

The fields were divided by woods, like nature's markers.

211

OBJECTIVES

Students will

- use the comprehension skills Main Idea and Details and Author's Point of View.
- review fluency.

MATERIALS

- ***Student Reader,*** Book 2, pp. 210–221
- ***Skills Practice 2,*** pp. 161–162

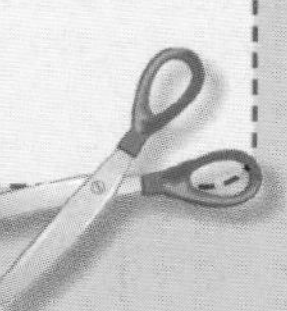

2nd READ

Comprehension Skill

Reread the story using the comprehension skills Main Idea and Details and Author's Point of View and Reading with a Writer's Eye.

Main Idea and Details

Remind students that a main idea is what a paragraph or story is mostly about. Often, a writer provides a clear topic sentence that states the main idea. Sometimes the topic sentence is at the beginning of a paragraph, but it can appear later, as well. Supporting details include facts, reasons, or ideas that add to or clarify the main idea. Ask students the following questions:

- *What is the topic sentence in the first paragraph on page 211? The Baxter Place spread out over nearly three hundred acres.*
- *What are some details that provide more information about the topic sentence?* **Possible Answers** *Information about the south and west fields and what is planted there are details about the three hundred acres.*

There were four in the family. Sara Baxter was a big, strong woman with a friendly way, and Pete Baxter was a tall and wiry man with skin toughened and tanned from being outdoors all year round. Sue Ann, the older child, seemed to take after her mother's side of the family. Last there was young Pete, named after his dad, but everybody called him Pee Wee. It's said he was so tiny when he was born that he fit in a shoe box, so Pee Wee they called him, and the name stuck.

212

The Baxter Place was a business—a farm business. It was also a way of life.

Nothing kept Pete Baxter from the work in the fields or in the big dairy barn that had milking stalls for twenty cows at a time. Pete knew every crop, every one of their hundred cows by name, and everything that happened on the farm. For him, farming was more than any regular full-time job, and he liked being outdoors every day all year round.

Sara Baxter raised chickens in a chicken house. During the laying season, she collected about a hundred eggs every day, then drove them to town to Hammil's Country Market to be sold. She also grew vegetables, and those that didn't get eaten right away got canned and

213

Author's Point of View

Remind students that author's point of view refers to the kind of narrator or speaker that the writer uses to tell the story. In a first-person narrative, the writer tells the story as if the storyteller was a character in the story. Clue words used in first-person narrative include *I, me, we, our,* and *ours*. In a third-person narrative, the writer tells the story as if the narrator is someone outside the story. Clues used in the third-person narrative are *he, him, she, her, they,* and *theirs*. Ask students the following questions:

- *What is the author's point of view in this story?* third person
- *What clue words on pages 212–213 reveal the author's point of view?* her, him, he, she
- *Why do you think Ross wrote the story from this point of view?* **Possible Answer** *It seems like the author is observing the family and describing them from a more objective point of view.*

Word Structure

Word families: tanned/tan/tanning, farming/farm/farmed, canned/can/canning

Expanding Vocabulary

crops (krops) *n.* plural form of **crop:** plants grown to be used as food or sold for profit (page 211)

The weather cooperated and it was a good season for growing *crops.*

surplus (sûr′ • plus) *n.* an amount greater than what is needed. (page 211)

We had *surplus* crops this year and we were able to share with our neighbors.

preserved for the long winter or taken to the market along with the eggs. Sara kept careful records of everything that was bought or sold for the farm. She was not only the farm's bookkeeper but also the business-minded one in the family.

Jim and Wally were the hired hands—farmers who work at farming other people's land. Jim was a crackerjack repairman when the tractor and equipment broke down—which was more often than he liked. And Wally knew the planting seasons like the back of his hand. Folks said he could smell a late spring frost in the air. Both Jim and Wally came every morning at six sharp and often stayed till late in the evening. They had worked with Pete for fifteen years.

214

Sue Ann did her chores every morning before the school bus came up Flatland Road. She cleaned the calves' stalls, fed the chickens, helped with the milking, and set the table for breakfast—which came *after* chores.

Pee Wee, being younger, got away with a little less in the way of work. He was in charge of feeding the three big watchdogs and an untold number of cats, cleaning the chicken house, and helping Sara set out breakfast for everyone.

215

Word Structure

Word families: preserved/preserve/preserving, stayed/stay/staying, helped/help/helping

Multisyllabic words with silent consonants: crackerjack, chickens, chicken

Teacher Tip

MAIN IDEA You may want to keep track of main ideas and supporting details throughout the story on the board or on an overhead transparency.

Comprehension Skill

Main Idea and Details

Encourage students to continue to identify main ideas and supporting details in the text. Identifying main ideas and supporting details keeps readers focused on the text and helps them keep track of what is most important. Ask students the following questions:

- *What is the main idea of page 214? Jim and Wally were the hired hands—farmers who work at farming other people's land. What are the supporting details?* **Possible Answers** *Jim was a crackerjack repairman. Wally knew the planting season like the back of his hand.*
- *What is one of the main ideas on page 215?* **Possible Answer** *Sue Ann did her chores every morning. What are the supporting details?* **Possible Answers** *She cleaned the calves' stalls, fed the chickens, helped with the milking, and set the table for breakfast.*

All the folks around those parts said the Baxter Place was the prettiest, neatest farm they'd ever seen, and the Baxters were some of the nicest folks they knew. Luckiest, too. And they were right—until the day the man from the market stopped by.

Jess Hammil owned the farmers' market where Sara took her eggs and produce to be sold. Sara, Pete, and Jess had all been in grade school together, so they went way back. Jess came to see the Baxters the day he learned the lease on his small vegetable market in town wasn't going to be renewed. A fancy new building was going up in its place, and he sure couldn't afford those rents.

216

Now, he figured if he could buy his own land—and not rent—something like this wasn't likely to happen again. He had saved the cash, so maybe the Baxters would be willing to part with that small west field. With those twenty-five acres, Jess could not only have his market, he could also grow much of his own seasonal produce instead of always depending on other farmers. The field was right off the main road from town, so people would be likely to stop and buy.

It was true that particular piece of land was what you might call extra. Sara and Pete had always thought they would save it for Sue Ann and Pee Wee. But Sue Ann was headed for forestry college in a year and planned to move later on to the mountains where her work would be. And Pee Wee, young as he was, had his

217

Reading with a Writer's Eye

Genre Knowledge

Remind students that genre is the type of literature a story is. The genre could be historical fiction, fantasy, expository, and so on. Remind students that "What Ever Happened to the Baxter Place?" is realistic fiction. In realistic fiction, the characters behave as people do in real life, the setting could be a real place, and the events could really happen. Ask students the following questions:

- *What are some elements of realistic fiction found on page 216–217?* **Possible Answer** *The descriptions of the characters seem real. They behave like real people do.*
- *Why do you think Pat Ross chose to write her story as realistic fiction?* **Possible Answer** *She probably wanted her readers to know that characters like these exist and the events that happen in their lives really could happen.*

Word Structure

Word families: forest/forestry, headed/head/heading, planned/plan/planning

Multisyllabic words with silent consonants: luckiest

Reading and Responding

heart set on being a mathematician, and claimed he was allergic to field work—which certainly seemed to be true!

Jess's being an old friend and all helped the Baxters decide to sell. Also, Sara thought it would be kind of nice to have a market for her sales so close by. They shook hands and made a deal.

Within a year, Jess opened a brand-new market. He planted his land with seasonal produce crops. When word got around that the state was planning to widen and resurface Main Road, Jess knew this meant even more business for him.

218

Pete and Sara figured they'd not only made some money to pay the bills more easily, but they'd also done a favor for a friend.

Every year for the past five, Emma Price from Homestead Realty Company had made her call on the Baxters. Every year it was the same: Emma's real estate company was interested in purchasing and developing their meadow and woodland area around the pond. Would they consider selling? The offer would be handsome.

219

Word Structure

Word families: certainly/certain, opened/open/opening/reopen, seasonal/season/seasoned

Teacher Tip

SETTING This story provides students a chance to talk about setting. Encourage students to discuss why the setting is so important in this story. Remind students that the setting influences how characters behave and events occur. This will be important as they continue to write their plays.

Comprehension Skill

☆ Main Idea and Details

Ask students to continue to identify topic sentences, main ideas, and supporting details. Ask students the following questions:

- *What is the main idea of the second paragraph on page 219? Every year for the past five, Emma Price from Homestead Realty Company had made a call on the Baxters.*
- *What are the supporting details of this paragraph?* **Possible Answers** *Every year it was the same: Emma's real estate company was interested in purchasing and developing their meadow and woodland area around the pond. The offer would be handsome.*

Every year they greeted Emma Price politely, but their answer had always been a firm no. They needed the meadow for the cows. And how could they part with the woods and pond? Besides, they didn't need the money. So each year they bade Emma good-by with the same answer.

But one year, things were a little different. The corn harvest that fall had been a total loss. There had been too much rain during planting time and a dry spell just when they needed rain. Corn was their livelihood, and without the crop's sale the bills would go unpaid. Sara figured they could barely pay for the farm's necessities that year. They also owed the bank a mortgage on the house and the land plus money they had borrowed for seed and a new tractor.

They insisted they would not part with the meadow, pond, and woods. Still, they didn't like getting into debt any more if they could help it. Would the Homestead Realty Company consider the rolling east field? they asked. Emma Price was pleasantly surprised and said yes right away.

It was the toughest decision they'd ever had to make together.

220

Would the company please save some of the trees when they made room for houses? Sue Ann asked. Emma Price assured her they'd make every effort to do just that. Would the Baxters get the best price, even though the east field was the company's second choice? Sara and Pete asked. Emma quoted them a price. Would the new people have children his age? Pee Wee asked. Everyone laughed nervously. Pete quickly figured out loud that they could use the front soybean field for alfalfa, too. There would just be less of a soybean crop, and they would have to sell off some of the older cows in the herd, but the fifty milk-producing cows would not go hungry.

221

Comprehension Skill

Main Idea and Details

Ask the students to continue to identify topic sentences, main ideas, and supporting details. Ask students the following questions:

- *What is the topic sentence of the first paragraph on page 220? Every year they greeted Emma Price politely, but their answer had always been a firm no. What are the supporting details of this paragraph?* **Possible Answers** *The Baxters needed the land for the cows. They didn't want to part with the woods and the pond. They didn't need the money.*
- *What is the main idea of the rest of the page? One year their corn crop was bad and they needed the money. What are the supporting details?* **Possible Answers** *The weather was bad for the crops. They needed money to support the farm, pay the bank, and pay for their equipment.*

Word Structure

Word families: greeted/greet/greeting, politely/polite, needed/need/needing

STOP

You have reread the first half of the story. Continue the story tomorrow on page T400.

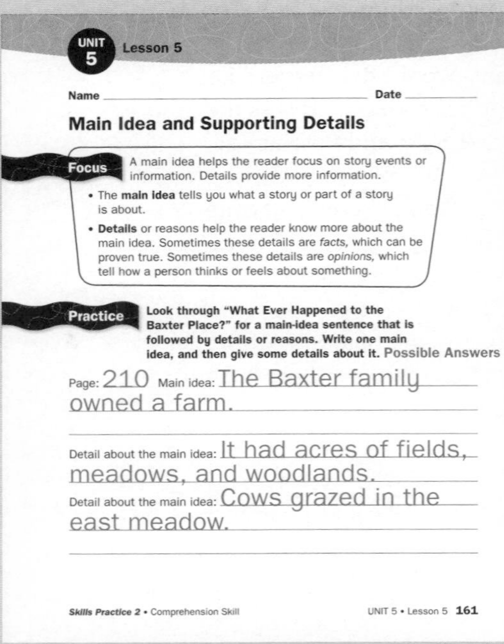

UNIT 5 Lesson 5

Name ______________________ Date __________

Main Idea and Supporting Details

Focus A main idea helps the reader focus on story events or information. Details provide more information.

- The **main idea** tells you what a story or part of a story is about.
- **Details** or reasons help the reader know more about the main idea. Sometimes these details are *facts*, which can be proven true. Sometimes these details are *opinions*, which tell how a person thinks or feels about something.

Practice **Look through "What Ever Happened to the Baxter Place?" for a main-idea sentence that is followed by details or reasons. Write one main idea, and then give some details about it.** Possible Answers

Page: 210 Main idea: The Baxter family owned a farm.

Detail about the main idea: It had acres of fields, meadows, and woodlands.

Detail about the main idea: Cows grazed in the east meadow.

Skills Practice 2 • Comprehension Skill UNIT 5 • Lesson 5 **161**

Skills Practice 2, p. 161

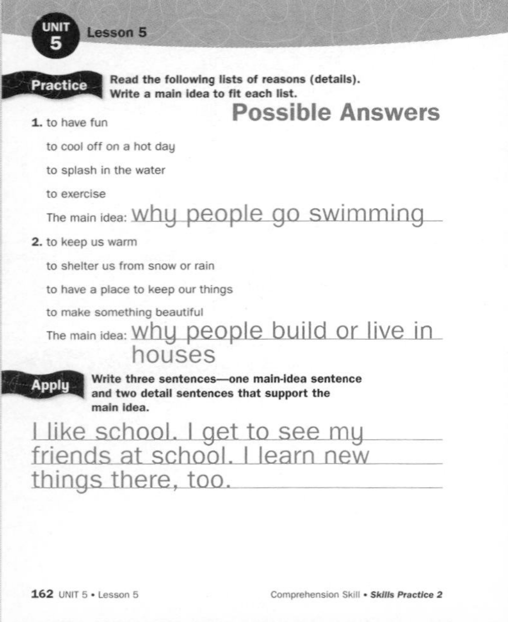

UNIT 5 Lesson 5

Practice **Read the following lists of reasons (details). Write a main idea to fit each list.**

Possible Answers

1. to have fun
   to cool off on a hot day
   to splash in the water
   to exercise
   The main idea: why people go swimming
2. to keep us warm
   to shelter us from snow or rain
   to have a place to keep our things
   to make something beautiful
   The main idea: why people build or live in houses

Apply **Write three sentences—one main-idea sentence and two detail sentences that support the main idea.**

I like school. I get to see my friends at school. I learn new things there, too.

162 UNIT 5 • Lesson 5 Comprehension Skill • *Skills Practice 2*

Skills Practice 2, p. 162

Teacher Tip

HOMEWORK To reinforce this skill, assign students to find an article from the newspaper or a magazine as homework. They should follow the procedure just as they practiced in the Guided Practice portion of this lesson. In class, they can present the main ideas and details of the article. You may wish to post their articles around the room for students to read on their own later.

Supporting the Reading

Comprehension Skill: Main Idea and Details

Teach

Ask students to tell you what they know about main ideas and supporting details. If necessary, remind students that authors of both fiction and nonfiction writing include details that support an overall main idea. In addition, they often organize paragraphs by stating the main idea of that particular paragraph or section and then adding those supporting details. To identify important information in texts, a reader must be able to identify the main ideas in the texts.

Guided Practice

Bring an age-appropriate nonfiction article to class. Share the article with the class. Lead a class discussion by asking students to identify the main idea of each paragraph and then to identify the overall main idea of the article. Remind students that sometimes main ideas are implied and not directly stated. They should tell what they believe is the most important idea or ideas. List the main ideas on the board or on a blank overhead transparency. Reread the article for the class, or have a volunteer read it. During this reading have students share what they believe are the details that support the main ideas that are listed.

Apply

Have students turn to pages 161–162 in ***Skills Practice 2.***

- Have students read aloud the Focus section of the lesson.
- Work through the Practice section of the lesson with students. Have them look back through "What Ever Happened to the Baxter Place?" to find examples of main ideas and supporting details. Have them record examples they can refer to as they work on the Practice and Apply sections of the lesson.

Monitor Progress to Differentiate Instruction

Formal Assessment

Comprehension Skill Note students' understanding of the Comprehension Skill Main Idea and Details.

APPROACHING LEVEL

IF . . . students need extra help with main idea and details, THEN . . . use ***Reteach*** pages 152–153.

ON LEVEL

IF . . . students need practice with main idea and details, THEN . . . have students play a game in the **Workshop Kit.**

ABOVE LEVEL

IF . . . students understand main idea and details, THEN . . . use ***Challenge Activities*** page 138.

Fluency

Students should enjoy reading "What Ever Happened to the Baxter Place?" because of the descriptive characters and the engaging plot. However, some of the concepts and ideas may be challenging. You may want to review vocabulary words, names, or some of the concepts that may be more difficult for students before beginning the fluency practice.

- Model fluent reading by reading pages 262–263 from "What Ever Happened to the Baxter Place?" Have students follow along in ***Student Reader,*** Book 2. Ask them to raise their hands if they hear an unfamiliar word or passage.
- After you have read through the passage, call on a volunteer to read the first page. Before the student begins, make sure he or she knows that the story is being told in the third person by what seems like an observer. The reading should be done as if a narrator were reading it.
- After the volunteer has finished, have students read the passage chorally several times until they can read it naturally with good phrasing.

Inquiry

- ✦ Remind the groups that they are still collecting information about their investigation topics as they are evaluating their conjectures. Explain that they should try to understand how each new piece of information relates to their conjectures.
- ✦ Discuss how any information in "What Ever Happened to the Baxter Place?" may relate to any of the groups' investigations. If any group discovers that information from the selection is relevant, have the class discuss how that information affects their conjectures.
- ✦ As students discuss how the information they collect relates to their conjectures, have them compare and contrast the different topics in each of the unit selections. Explain that by comparing and contrasting the ideas and topics in different selections, students will learn more about how different topics and ideas are related, which will help them confirm or revise their conjectures.

LEVELED READERS To help students build fluency and strengthen their vocabulary and comprehension skills, have them read the ***Leveled Readers*** for this unit. Use each student's Oral Fluency Assessment score from the previous lesson assessment to diagnose the appropriate ***Leveled Reader.***

Fluency Tip

FLUENCY For additional fluency practice, students can read this passage or other pages of the story to you independently.

OBJECTIVES

Students will
- ✦ create a story map graphic organizer.
- ✦ practice Unit 5 spelling words and patterns.
- ✦ learn to use time lines.
- ✦ practice complex sentences.

MATERIALS
- ✦ ***Skills Practice 2,*** pp. 163, 165–166, and 169–170
- ✦ ***Transparency*** 24
- ✦ Routine 16

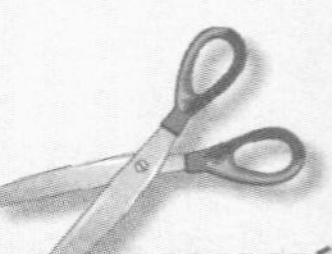

Teacher Tip

SKILLS PRACTICE 2 Have students use the Study Skills pages 169–170 in ***Skills Practice 2*** to expand their plot ideas or to create character webs.

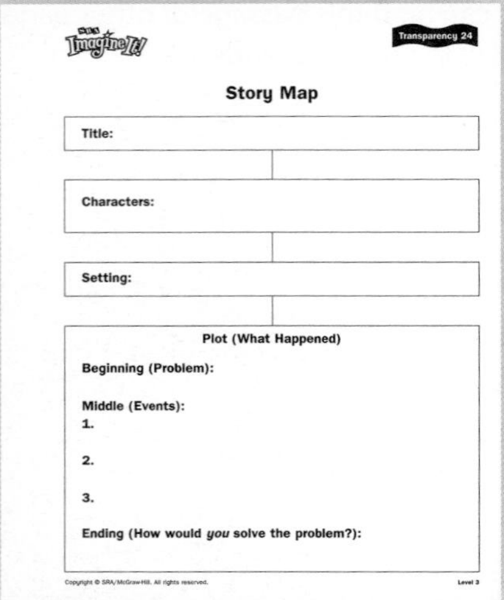

Transparency 24

Story Map

Title:

Characters:

Setting:

Plot (What Happened)

Beginning (Problem):

Middle (Events):
1.
2.
3.

Ending (How would *you* solve the problem?):

Transparency 24

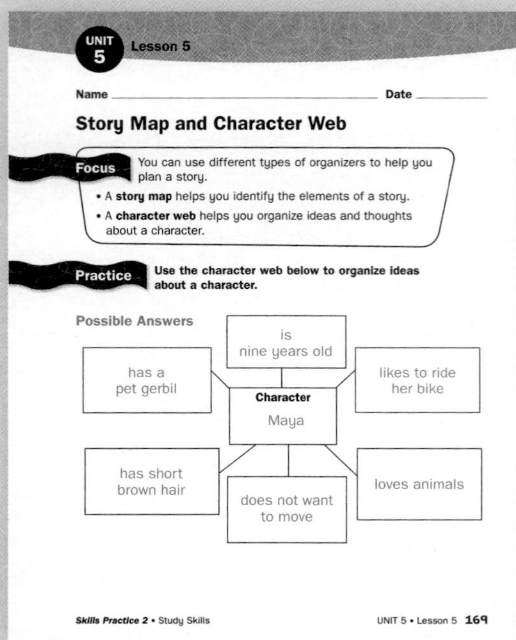

UNIT 5 Lesson 5

Name ____________ Date ______

Story Map and Character Web

Focus You can use different types of organizers to help you plan a story.
- A **story map** helps you identify the elements of a story.
- A **character web** helps you organize ideas and thoughts about a character.

Practice Use the character web below to organize ideas about a character.

Possible Answers

Character: Maya
- is nine years old
- has a pet gerbil
- likes to ride her bike
- has short brown hair
- does not want to move
- loves animals

Skills Practice 2 • Study Skills UNIT 5 • Lesson 5 169

Skills Practice 2, p. 169

Writing Play

Prewriting

Teach

- ✦ Tell students they will continue prewriting their plays by using a story map graphic organizer. Use Routine 16, and explain that this graphic organizer will help them with plot details.

Guided Practice

- ✦ Have students review the information they put in their play graphic organizers on page 163 in ***Skills Practice 2.*** Tell students they are going to use that information to complete a story map graphic organizer.
- ✦ Display ***Transparency*** 24, and have students copy the story map on a separate piece of paper. You may also choose to have students complete the story map and character web on pages 169–170 in ***Skills Practice 2*** as an extension of this lesson.
- ✦ Model using the story map graphic organizer to expand the plot of the story you are developing on your play graphic organizer. Allow students to help with this process. As you model, explain to students that their plots must have a beginning, a middle, and an ending; and the story must include a goal that is achieved or a problem that is solved.

Apply

Composing—Prewriting Have students complete a story map for their plays in ***Skills Practice 2*** page 169 or on a separate piece of paper.

Spelling

Review of Prefixes, Affixes, and Word Families

Teach

- Students will review words with prefixes, words with affixes that change the word's meaning, and word families.
- For further assistance with this review, refer to:
  - Unit 5, Lesson 1 for the prefixes *re-*, *un-*, *pre-* and *mis-*.
  - Unit 5, Lesson 2 for the prefixes *bi-*, *mid-*, *dis-*, and *auto-*.
  - Unit 5, Lesson 3 for affixes.
  - Unit 5, Lesson 4 for word families, multisyllabic words, and silent consonants.
- Write the following word pairs on the board: *preveuw/preview, doubtfull/doubtful, restles/restless, restfull/restful, direct/durect, direcshin/direction, director/derector, indirect/indurect, ottopilot/autopilot,* and *unfair/unfaire.* Ask for a volunteer to come to the board and pick out the correctly spelled word from one of the pairs. Then ask the student to say the word aloud, and use it in a sentence.

Guided Practice

Have students turn to ***Skills Practice 2*** page 165. Read the instructions with them, and complete the first two questions as a class.

Apply

Have students complete ***Skills Practice 2*** pages 165–166 on their own. Remind students that challenge words are not used in ***Skills Practice*** exercises.

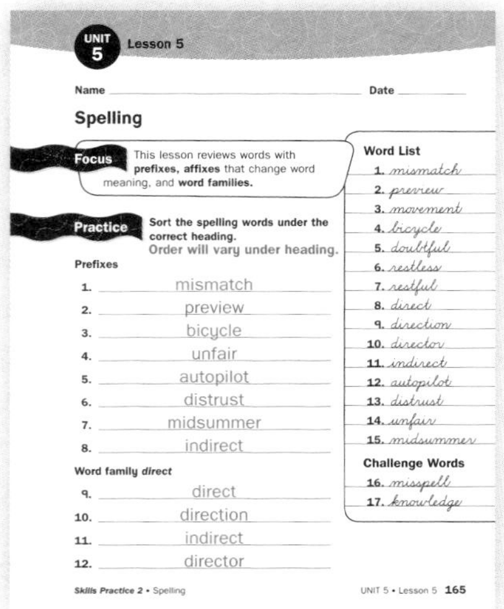

UNIT 5 Lesson 5

Name ______ Date ______

Spelling

Focus This lesson reviews words with **prefixes, affixes** that change word meaning, and **word families.**

Practice **Sort the spelling words under the correct heading.**
Order will vary under heading.

Prefixes

1. mismatch
2. preview
3. bicycle
4. unfair
5. autopilot
6. distrust
7. midsummer
8. indirect

Word family *direct*

9. direct
10. direction
11. indirect
12. director

Word List

1. mismatch
2. preview
3. movement
4. bicycle
5. doubtful
6. restless
7. restful
8. direct
9. direction
10. director
11. indirect
12. autopilot
13. distrust
14. unfair
15. midsummer

Challenge Words

16. misspell
17. knowledge

Skills Practice 2 • Spelling   UNIT 5 • Lesson 5 **165**

UNIT 5 Lesson 5

Spelling (continued)

Affixes that change word meaning

13. movement — mismatch
14. doubtful — preview
15. restful — bicycle
16. restless — unfair
17. autopilot — distrust
18. midsummer — direction
19. indirect — director

166 UNIT 5 • Lesson 5   Spelling • ***Skills Practice 2***

Skills Practice 2, pp. 165–166

Monitor Progress 

to Differentiate Instruction
Formal Assessment

Spelling Note whether students are able to spell the lesson words correctly.

APPROACHING LEVEL

IF . . . students need to practice spelling this week's words,	**THEN . . .** have them complete ***Reteach*** page 154.

ON LEVEL

IF . . . students can spell this week's spelling words,	**THEN . . .** have them think of another word family. Have students write the family on a separate sheet of paper, and then circle any affixes that the words from the word family contain.

ABOVE LEVEL

IF . . . students are ready for a challenge,	**THEN . . .** have them complete ***Challenge Activities*** page 139.

Monitor Progress to Differentiate Instruction

Formal Assessment

Graphic Organizers Note whether students are utilizing graphic organizers for their writing activities and unit investigations.

APPROACHING LEVEL

IF . . . students need practice with graphic organizers, **THEN . . .** have them work with a partner to fill out a graphic organizer during Workshop.

ON LEVEL

IF . . . students have an understanding of graphic organizers, **THEN . . .** have them work on organizing information for their unit investigations or their plays during Workshop.

ABOVE LEVEL

IF . . . students need a challenge, **THEN . . .** have them work with another student who does not understand how to place information in graphic organizers during Workshop.

Differentiating Instruction: English Learner

IF . . . students have limited vocabulary, **THEN . . .** allow them to use descriptive words from their native languages for any English word they do not know. Help them use a bilingual dictionary to find those unknown English words.

Teacher Tip

CONNECTING CONTENT Have students use the story maps and character webs from the Study Skills lesson for further ideas about the plot and characters they are creating in their plays.

Study Skills

Story Maps and Character Webs

Teach

- Ask students to discuss how prewriting using graphic organizers has helped them develop their ideas and build their writing skills.
- Tell students two graphic organizers in particular are especially beneficial when writing narratives, realistic fiction stories, or plays. Story maps and character webs help writers collect and organize story ideas and characters personality traits before they start to write.

Guided Practice

Have students turn to ***Skills Practice 2*** page 169. Read the directions and discuss the character web graphic organizer and the story map graphic organizer.

Ask students to explain what information would go on the character web. **Possible Answer** *A description of each character could go on the web, for example, a physical description, a personality description, how they are important to the story, and so on.*

Apply

Have students complete the two graphic organizers on ***Skills Practice 2*** pages 169–170 with information for their plays or for another activity.

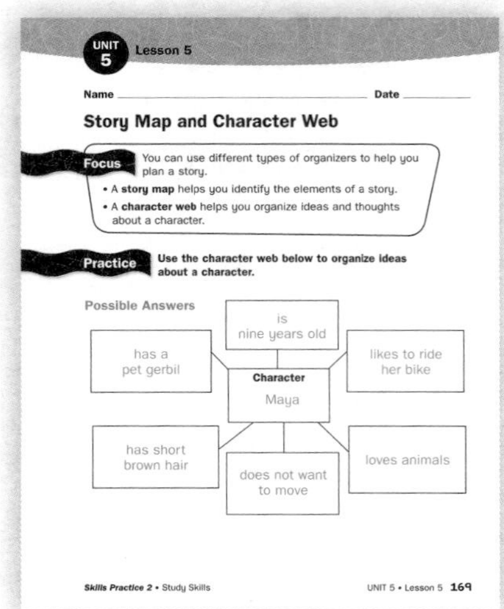

UNIT 5 Lesson 5

Name ______ Date ______

Story Map and Character Web

Focus You can use different types of organizers to help you plan a story.

- A **story map** helps you identify the elements of a story.
- A **character web** helps you organize ideas and thoughts about a character.

Practice **Use the character web below to organize ideas about a character.**

Possible Answers

Character: Maya

- is nine years old
- has a pet gerbil
- likes to ride her bike
- has short brown hair
- does not want to move
- loves animals

Skills Practice 2 • Study Skills — UNIT 5 • Lesson 5 169

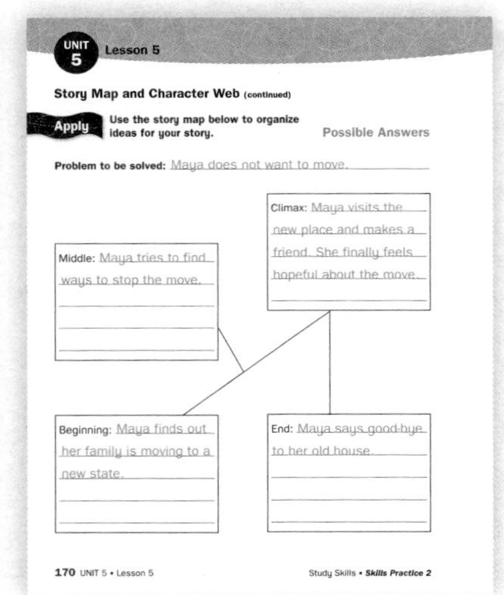

UNIT 5 Lesson 5

Story Map and Character Web (continued)

Apply **Use the story map below to organize ideas for your story.**

Possible Answers

Problem to be solved: Maya does not want to move.

Beginning: Maya finds out her family is moving to a new state.

Middle: Maya tries to find ways to stop the move.

Climax: Maya visits the new place and makes a friend. She finally feels hopeful about the move.

End: Maya says good-bye to her old house.

170 UNIT 5 • Lesson 5 — Study Skills • *Skills Practice 2*

Skills Practice 2, pp. 169–170

Grammar, Usage, and Mechanics

Complex Sentences

Teach

- Ask students how and why complex sentences are made. *Complex sentences include an independent clause (a sentence that could stand alone) and a dependent clause (an idea that could not stand alone as a sentence). Complex sentences add variety to writing, and prevent fragments.*
- Remind students that conjunctions join dependent and independent clauses.

Guided Practice

Practice with students combining complete simple sentences with thoughts or fragments to create complex sentences. You may want to begin by having students list things they know or have learned about storytelling, and then combine their ideas on the board.

Apply

Using the examples written on the board, have students create 3–5 complex sentences on their own or with a partner.

Differentiating Instruction **English Learners**

IF . . . students are having difficulty with complex sentences, **THEN . . .** refer to Unit 5 Lesson 5 in the ***English Learner Support Guide*** for support activities.

Preparing to Read

OBJECTIVES

Students will

- ✦ review word families and multisyllabic words with silent consonants.
- ✦ build fluency.

MATERIALS

Transparency 153

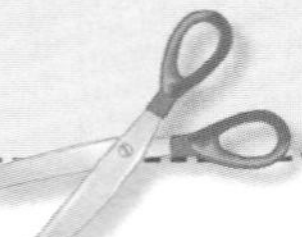

Daily Oral Practice

Daily News

Today!

Do you live in a big city, or a small town? Do you shop in big stores, or small ones? There is a place for both big stores and small local shops, housing developments and country fields. It's important to respect both, and preserve the natural world, where we all must live.

- ✦ Write the daily news on the board or on chart paper. Then have a volunteer read the daily news aloud to practice fluency.
- ✦ As a word structure review from Day 3, ask volunteers to identify any words in the message that belong to a word family. *housing, developments, preserve* Then have students identify the base words in these words. *house, develop, serve*

Differentiating Instruction **English Learner**

IF . . . students are native speakers of Vietnamese, Hmong, or Chinese, **THEN . . .** they may need extra practice blending multisyllabic words. In these languages, all words are monosyllabic.

Word Structure

Review: Word Families and Multisyllabic Words with Silent Consonants

✦ Use ***Transparency*** 153 with these word lines from Day 3.

Line 1	stretch	**stretched**	**stretching**	restretch
Line 2	develop	**developer**	**developing**	**development**
Line 3	**luckiest**	**pockets**	scenic	scissors
Line 4	kneeling	knapsack	**overnight**	highlight

✦ Review the meaning of word families. If necessary, remind students that words with the same base word are part of a word family. All the words on Line 2, for example, are a word family because they all come from the base word *develop.*

✦ Review multisyllabic words with silent consonants. If necessary, remind students of the silent consonants in these sound/spellings: /k/ spelled *ck,* /s/ spelled *sc,* /n/ spelled *kn,* and /ī/ spelled *_igh.*

Developing Oral Language

Use any of these activities to help students practice reading the words.

- Ask a volunteer to use the first word from Lines 1 or 2 in a sentence. **Possible Answer** *I need to* develop *my pictures from vacation last summer.* Then have that student choose a volunteer to use one of the other forms of that word in a sentence. **Possible Answer** *A person that develops pictures is called a* developer. Continue until all forms on the lines have been used.
- Have one student choose a line of words and point to a word in that line. Then have the student choose a classmate to read the word. Have the student read the word a second time, this time clapping for each syllable. Then have that student point to a different word and choose a classmate to read it and clap the syllables. Repeat the procedure until all of the words on the word lines have been read.
- Have a volunteer choose a word and use it in a sentence to begin a story. **Possible Answer** *Only the* luckiest *people find four-leaf clovers.* Have another volunteer continue the story by supplying a sentence that uses another word from the line. **Possible Answer** *One guy was so lucky that he filled his whole* knapsack *with four-leaf clovers.* Continue until all the words are used.

Monitor Progress

to Differentiate Instruction
Formal Assessment

Word Structure During the word structure activity, note how well students understand the words.

APPROACHING LEVEL

IF . . . students do not understand the words on the word lines,	**THEN . . .** use pictures, photos, objects, stick drawings, or pantomime to help them visualize the words.

ON LEVEL

IF . . . students need practice with the words on the word lines,	**THEN . . .** have them write sentences using the words on the lines.

ABOVE LEVEL

IF . . . students understand the words on the word lines,	**THEN . . .** challenge them to think of word families that have multisyllabic words with silent consonants.

Hurting with the pain of parting with their good land, but having to, the Baxters signed the east field over to Emma Price's company. Homestead Realty paid them without delay. In turn, the Baxters paid for their bad year and looked forward to better ones.

Soon bulldozers were clearing the land, leaving pitifully few of the trees, going against what Emma Price had promised. But it was not all bad, the Baxters told themselves and each other. When the noises and smells of building began to die down, the new houses looked pretty and comfortable, and the people who moved into them seemed friendly enough. It was just strange to see the old alfalfa field planted with so many houses.

Several years of good crops did follow and things seemed to be almost back to normal, even though more and more houses were being built all around. Sue Ann won a partial scholarship to forestry college. Everybody was proud of her, but missed her a lot.

Pee Wee had just started high school when the milking problem came up. Each morning

222

he'd pitch in to take Sue Ann's place. Jim and Wally still arrived at the crack of dawn, but Jim was getting on in years, and it seemed to take him longer to get the cows milked than it used to. Besides, a lot of the local farmers were putting in new automatic equipment—milking parlors, they called them, with an elevated stall for each cow and tubes leading right to the main tank. The Baxters still relied on the old methods. Not that they wouldn't have changed over. But the cost of the new setup was more than they could swing. So, for a while at least, Pee Wee did his best to help out. Wally never missed a day, but he was no longer up to heavy work, so Sara pitched in more often.

Still, it got harder and harder to compete with the milk production of neighboring farmers who had installed milking parlors to handle larger herds in less time than it took the Baxters. Milk sales were barely bringing in enough to cover costs, so it wasn't long before the Baxters began to sell off the rest of their herd.

223

OBJECTIVES

Students will

- use the comprehension skill Main Idea and Details.
- check comprehension.

MATERIALS

- ***Student Reader,*** Book 2, pp. 222–229

Comprehension Skill

Main Idea and Details

Ask students the following questions:

- *What is the topic sentence for page 222?* **Possible Answer** *Hurting with the pain of parting with their good land, but having to, the Baxters signed the east field over to Emma Price's company.*
- *What details support this main idea?* **Possible Answer** *The Baxters were able to pay for their bad year with the extra money. Bulldozers soon cleared the land.*

Finally, only five cows grazed in the meadow. The milking barn was practically empty. And even though the Baxters didn't have their herd, they took comfort in knowing that the milk and butter on their kitchen table was not store-bought, but still their own.

The following spring George Stillwell came to see Pete and Sara Baxter about using the pond and meadow area for sports land. He didn't want to *buy* the land—which pleased the Baxters, as they'd made up their minds they'd never part with the pond. George Stillwell proposed leasing the area for eight years.

224

He would put up what he called a "rustic cabin" and, in turn, rent it out to hunters during the fall and winter gunning seasons.

Pete figured that was a good enough deal. The pond was a safe distance from the housing development. Besides, the whole area filled up with hunters during the duck and goose seasons anyway. The Baxters had always let some hunters on their land, so a few more couldn't do much harm, except for the noise. And without actually giving up the land, they would be paid for it. This would fill the hole in their pockets left by the loss of milk money, and would help to fill Pee Wee's college savings account. So Sara, too, reluctantly agreed.

225

Reading with a Writer's Eye

Genre Knowledge

Writers tell a story with words, and illustrators tell a story with their pictures. In nonfiction, actual photographs are often used. In realistic stories, usually an illustrator draws pictures of the events, characters, and setting of a story. Roger Duvoisin's illustrations are very revealing. Ask students the following questions:

- *What do we learn about the story from Roger Duvoisin's illustrations?* **Possible Answer** *We learn that the Baxter farm is changing. The farm and fields are starting to look empty.*
- *What does the picture on page 225 tell us?* **Possible Answer** *This picture tells readers that the land has changed. The Baxters have leased the land to George Stillwell to rent out to hunters during hunting season.*

Expanding Vocabulary

partial (pär′ shəl) *adj.* part of; incomplete (page 222)

The student wrote only a *partial* summary; he would have to go back and finish it after the break.

elevated (el′ • əv • āt • əd) *v.* raised above the ground (page 223)

The room had an *elevated* window to allow in even more light.

practically (prak′ • tik • əl • lē) *adv.* almost (page 224)

The glass of milk was *practically* full when he knocked it over.

reluctantly (rə • luk′ • tənt • lē′) *adv.* unwillingly (page 225)

The team *reluctantly* left the court after the buzzer sounded and they lost by one point.

Day 4 Reading and Responding

In the next year, the cabin, only a little bigger than the Baxters had expected, went up. They could live with a few hunters for eight years.

Pee Wee, now Petie to everyone except his family, went off to engineering school a whole year ahead of his graduating class. This came as no great surprise to the Baxters, and his ambitions made them proud.

Jim retired officially, but still came around to tinker with the machinery and complain how the new tractor wasn't up to the old model.

226

Again, things returned almost to normal. Pete and Sara had a smaller place, but it was plenty for them and Wally to handle. They still had the big south field for corn and barley, and the front field for other crops. Sara had her chickens and her garden. Life on the farm was different, what with the changes and Sue Ann and Pee Wee away most of the year. Perhaps now things would stay put for a while. And they did in fact—for some time.

But things once set out of order never quite stay put for long.

One day something happened that the Baxters found hard to understand. Jess Hammil sold out to a developer, a big developer.

Jess's country market and his land were bulldozed to make Main Shopping Mall, featuring a giant supermarket, a discount drugstore, a dress boutique, a chain department store, and countless other small shops.

227

Expanding Vocabulary

ambitions (am • bish´ • ənz) *n.* plural form of **ambition:** a strong desire to do or succeed at something (page 226)

The students have *ambitions* of becoming scientists.

Teacher Tip

INQUIRY Remind students that they can use information or ideas they learn from this story in their unit investigation.

Comprehension Skill

Main Idea and Details

Ask students the following questions:

- *Page 226 has two main ideas. What are they?* **Possible Answers** *Pee Wee went to engineering school. Jim retired.*
- *What details support these ideas?* **Possible Answers** *Pee Wee graduated early and his parents were proud. Jim still came around to tinker with the machinery.*
- *Page 227 also has two main ideas. They are contrasting ideas. What are the two main ideas on this page?* **Possible Answers** *Things on the farm were normal for Pete and Sara for a while. Jess Hammil sold his land to a developer.*
- *What details support these ideas?* **Possible Answers** *Pete and Sara still had land for crops and a garden. Jess sold his land to a developer who was building a shopping mall.*

Not long after this, Homestead Realty Company made the Baxters an offer on the big south field. This time they didn't *have* to sell, but Wally was about to retire and Pete and Sara were no longer up to heavy work. They could look for new hired hands, but it just didn't seem the same. The offer was tempting, so they finally accepted.

One thing led to another. The man who'd rented the pond made an offer to buy now that the lease was about to expire. Since the pond and meadow would never be the same again, what with a shopping center bordering it, the Baxters could see little reason to hold onto it. It had lost almost all its meaning for them.

After the sale to George Stillwell—the most profitable and the most heartbreaking for the Baxters—the cabin was turned into Rustic Manor Motor Lodge and Tennis Club almost overnight.

The Baxter Place was not even half of what it had been not too many years before. But the trees—those that were left—still acted as dividers, trying hard to keep the Baxter Place separate.

228

Sara and Pete still had the front field leading up to the old farmhouse. In the early years, they had had to struggle hard just to make the place pay for itself. Now they had some money in the bank. That was something.

Folks couldn't still say the Baxter Place was the prettiest, neatest place around—not the way it had gotten so divided up and changed. But folks could still say the Baxters were some of the nicest folks they'd ever known. And they were. That had not changed. But so many things *had*.

"What ever happened to the old Baxter Place?" somebody asked. And nobody could quite say. Not even the Baxters.

229

Checking Comprehension

Ask students the following questions to check their comprehension of the story:

- *Why was the farm business considered a way of life for the Baxters?* **Possible Answer** *It wasn't a job where they went to work and then came home at the end of the day. The work involved the whole family. It took most of their time, and they liked it that way.*
- *How much control do you think the Baxters had over their land? Do you think they made good or bad decisions? Why?* **Possible Answer** *The Baxters had control over their land, but when things started going wrong for them, they were forced to give up their control to survive. I think they made the right decisions because they did what they thought was best.*
- *Why is the story called "What Ever Happened to the Baxter Place?"* **Possible Answer** *The title sums up the main idea. The Baxter farm gets smaller and smaller over a period of time because the owners have to sell some of their land to pay their bills. But the owners don't realize the long-term effects some of their decisions have as developers change the land.*

Expanding Vocabulary

profitable (prof′ • it • ə • bəl) *adj.* moneymaking; rewarding (page 228)

The bake sale was *profitable* and raised a lot of money for the children's charity.

Word Structure

Word families: engineering/engineer/engine, rented/rent/renting, shopping/shop/shopped, bordering/border/bordered

Multisyllabic word with silent consonants: chickens

To help students support their ideas or conjectures, have them read the ***Leveled Social Studies Readers.*** If students are working in a group, encourage them to share their information with their group members. Use each student's Oral Fluency Assessment score from the previous unit to diagnose the appropriate ***Leveled Social Studies Reader.***

Inquiry Process

Step 6—Confirming or Revising Conjectures

Whole-Group Time

Whole Group

- Students have been collecting information about their investigation topics and conjectures. Now they should be getting ready to confirm or revise their conjectures based on what they've learned.
- Remind students that they might find that their conjectures are not confirmed or only partially confirmed as they find new information.
- Model revising your own conjecture, saying something such as this: *My original conjecture was that some land should be set aside for nature parks and protected wildlife sanctuaries. I still think this is a good idea, but it will be hard to create these parks because the best land is already privately owned. So something else needs to be done to keep our community from expanding too much and destroying the countryside. I need to revise my original conjecture. This is my new conjecture:* Our community has to either find a way to buy the right land for nature parks, or it has to convince people to stop developing all of the countryside. Now I wonder how other national and state parks were established.
- Remind students that conjectures can be partially correct like the one you just modeled. The purpose of making conjectures is to do further research to find out how to improve it. To make partially correct conjectures better, they need to be revised.
- As much as time permits, each group should continue to collect information, which might help them improve their conjectures. Lead a group discussion about new things students learned about the theme from reading "What Ever Happened to the Baxter Place?" Have students take notes in their Writer's Notebooks.

Small-Group Time

Small Group

- Remind each group of all the information they have recorded and collected so far about their topic. Groups need to gather all this information and review it before revising their conjectures.
- As necessary, continue to model revising conjectures for individual groups. If groups are having trouble seeing how their conjectures could be revised, point out places where more information could make their conjectures better.
- Have students revise their conjectures and record them in their Writer's Notebooks. Then have them post their revised conjectures on the **Concept/ Question Board.**
- Make sure groups have finalized how they will publish or present the results of their investigations. Review what students learned about using multimedia, and, if possible, encourage them to incorporate multimedia in their presentations. Have groups work on their presentations. Encourage them to incorporate visual aids, graphs, diagrams, or timelines into their presentations where appropriate. Allow groups enough time during Workshop to prepare and rehearse their presentations.

Concept/Question Board

Continue to encourage use of the **Concept/Question Board** by recognizing and thanking students for their contributions. Incorporate those items into classroom discussions whenever possible. Remember to also model by posting your own questions and ideas.

Inquiry Rubric

To assess Confirming and Revising Conjectures, see the Inquiry Rubrics in the Level Appendix.

Teacher Tips

FLEXIBILITY Remind students of the importance of sticking to their project plans while still being flexible to change. Try to encourage the students' changes of interest while keeping them on task.

CONCEPT/QUESTION BOARD All items on the **Concept/Question Board** should be labeled clearly. Revised questions and conjectures can be written on paper of a different color so that students have a record of how their understanding has changed over the course of the unit. Remind students to initial their contributions to the Board.

OBJECTIVES

Students will
- begin drafting their plays.
- review Unit 5 spelling words and patterns.
- practice using time lines.
- learn to create descriptive presentations.

MATERIALS

- ***Skills Practice 2,*** p. 163
- Routine B

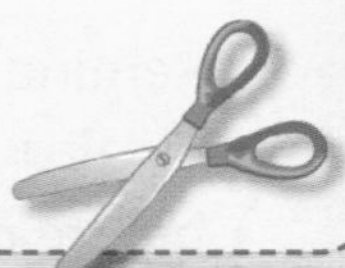

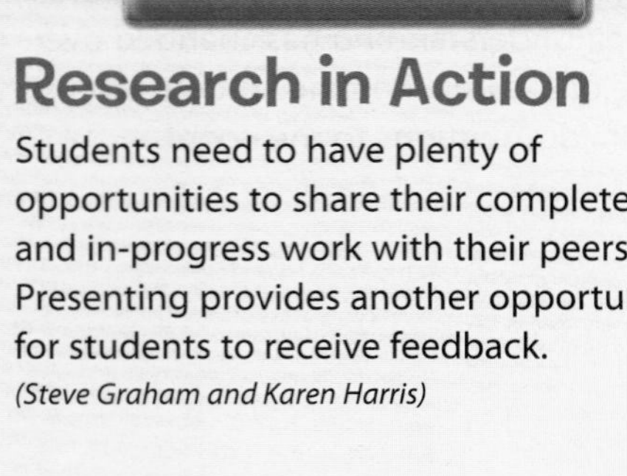

Research in Action

Students need to have plenty of opportunities to share their completed and in-progress work with their peers. Presenting provides another opportunity for students to receive feedback.
(Steve Graham and Karen Harris)

Writing Play

ROUTINE B

Drafting

Teach

- Tell students that it is time for them to begin writing the drafts of their plays.
- Remind students that when writing drafts, it is most important to write ideas, words, passages, and so on. They can go back and fix spelling, grammar, and punctuation later.
- Tell students to use their story map graphic organizers and their play graphic organizers to assist them as they draft their plays.
- Tell students they will begin by drafting their plot. In later writing sessions they will be drafting character dialogue, stage directions, and props.
- Have students review their story maps and play maps before they begin drafting. Model how to use these graphic organizers as a guide to drafting the plot of a play. Tell students they can add more detail to their drafts than what is in their graphic organizers.
- Tell students they will begin by writing a couple of paragraphs that summarize the plot of their plays. Tell them to concentrate on creating a beginning, a middle with rising action, and an ending in which the problem is solved or the situation is resolved. Tell students that once they have the basic plot written, it will be easier to write it in play form.

Writing, continued

Guided Practice

Using the maps you have modeled, ask students for suggestions on drafting your play. Tell them to focus on giving you suggestions for developing the plot.

Apply

- **Composing — Drafting** Students will use their story map graphic organizers and play graphic organizers to write the plot of their plays.
- Use Routine B to conduct individual conferences with students.

Spelling

Review of Prefixes, Affixes, and Word Families

Teach

- Students will review words with prefixes, words with affixes that change the word's meaning, and word families.
- **Visualizing Strategy** Tell students that sometimes the correct spelling of a word can be determined by looking at a word to see if it "looks right." Students can use spelling patterns from words they already know to decide whether a new word has used an incorrect pattern even if they have not seen the word before.

Guided Practice

Write this sentence on the board: *After dinnur, I ate my desert so fast that I started to hikup.* Have students circle the misspelled words and rewrite them correctly. *After dinner, I ate my dessert so fast that I started to hiccup.*

Study Skills

Story Maps and Character Webs

Teach

Remind students that story maps and character webs are graphic organizers that are helpful when writing stories.

Guided Practice

- Ask students to tell you why a story map is useful when writing a story. *It helps the writer organize the beginning, middle, and ending of a story. It helps the writer know who the characters are going to be and what the problem and solution of the story will be.*
- Ask students how a character web is useful when writing a story. *By writing about characters on the web, writers work out the details of what traits the character has before starting to write about them in the draft.*

Apply

Have students review the story maps and character webs they created earlier. Have them check to make sure the map includes a beginning, a middle, and an ending for their stories. Have students check the character web. Ask them if they could think of a believable description of the character based on the information on the web. Have students continue to complete information in the graphic organizers.

Differentiating Instruction — English Learner

IF . . . students have difficulty completing their graphic organizers independently, **THEN . . .** have them work in pairs or in small groups with proficient English speakers.

Listening/Speaking/Viewing

Descriptive Presentations

Teach

- Explain to students that some presentations are enhanced by using specific sensory details to explain and describe people, places, things, and experiences. These sensory details can be words or objects speakers use in presentations.
- Point out that using such descriptive details brings presentations to life for audiences by making them more identifiable. People can identify with the sights, sounds, smells, and so on, of the descriptive words or objects.
- Choosing descriptive words or interesting objects will help audiences connect with the information in your presentations and more fully understand the information being presented.
- Remind students that when presenting information to an audience, the presenter must use an effective volume and tone of voice, must make eye contact with the audience, and must use appropriate nonverbal gestures to enhance the presentation.

Guided Practice

- Model giving a presentation about why people should buy fruit and vegetables from a small, local market. Talk about how the produce is fresh and in-season. Tell your audience how consumers of the small, local market will be supporting their community in addition to getting fresher and better-tasting produce.
- Leave out many of the descriptive words you might use in such a presentation. Then ask students what kinds of words you might use to engage your audience's senses. Ask them about the kinds of props that might be useful in such a presentation. Have them help you revise your presentation.

Apply

Have students work with a partner to create a one-minute presentation on the Reading with a Writer's Eye lesson from Unit 5 Lesson 5 regarding the genre knowledge realistic fiction.

Teacher Tip

DESCRIPTIVE LANGUAGE Tell students to use descriptive language in the written and oral portions of their presentations. Remind students that while they are listening to speakers or presentations they should face the speaker and maintain eye contact.

Day 5

Preparing to Read

Review

OBJECTIVES

Students will
- ✦ review the prefixes *re-*, *un-*, *pre-*, *mis-*, *bi-*, *mid-*, *dis-*, and *auto-* and review affixes as syllables.
- ✦ review word families and multisyllabic words with silent consonants.
- ✦ build fluency.

MATERIALS

Transparencies 149 and 153

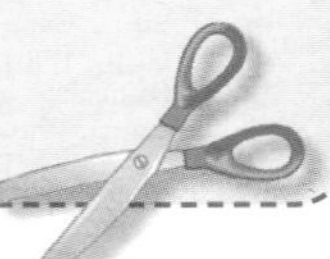

Word Structure

Use ***Transparency*** 149 with the word lines from Days 1 and 2 to review the prefixes *re-*, *un-*, *pre-*, *mis-*, *bi-*, *mid-*, *dis-*, and *auto-* and affixes as syllables. Have students read the words on the word lines. Then have students define each of the prefixes used in the words.

Line 1	**renewed**	**resurface**	**unpaid**	**untold**
Line 2	**preserved**	predawn	misinform	mislead
Line 3	bifocals	bilingual	midfield	midsized
Line 4	**discount**	disinfect	autographed	**automatic**

Word Structure

Use ***Transparency*** 153 with the word lines from Days 3 and 4 to review word families and multisyllabic words with silent consonants. Have students read the words on the word lines. Then have students use words on the lines in sentences.

Line 1	stretch	**stretched**	**stretching**	restretch
Line 2	develop	**developer**	**developing**	**development**
Line 3	**luckiest**	**pockets**	scenic	scissors
Line 4	kneeling	knapsack	**overnight**	highlight

OBJECTIVES

Students will
- review selection vocabulary.
- review comprehension strategies Asking Questions, Making Connections, and Predicting.
- review comprehension skills Main Idea and Details and Author's Point of View.
- review fluency.

MATERIALS

- ***Student Reader,*** Book 2, pp. 206–233
- ***Tranparency*** 150

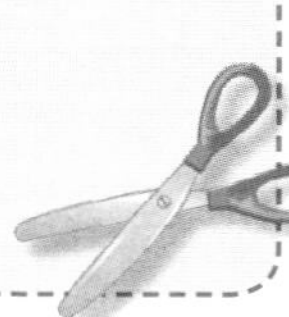

Selection Vocabulary

To review the selection vocabulary with students, organize them into small groups of three or four. Give each group 2 or 3 words. Ask each group to write a definition for each vocabulary word in their own words. When they are finished, have a volunteer from each group share their definitions with the class.

Selection Vocabulary

seasonal (sē´ • zən • əl) *adj.* ripe at a certain time (page 217)

produce (prō´ • dōōs) *n.* farm products, such as fresh fruits and vegetables (page 216)

particular (pär´ • tik´ • ū • lûr) *adj.* special (page 217)

necessities (nəs • es´ • sət • ēz´) *n.* plural form of **necessity:** something that is needed (page 220)

installed (in • stôld´) *v.* a form of the verb **install:** to put in place for use or service (page 223)

featuring (fē´ • chûr • ing) *adj.* having as the main attraction (page 227)

discount (dis´ • kount) *adj.* with lowered prices (page 227)

expire (eks • pīr´) *v.* to come to an end (page 228)

Comprehension Strategies  

Review the following comprehension strategies with students:

- **Asking Questions** helps readers focus attention on what they are reading by asking, and then finding the answers to, questions they have about the text. Have students review questions about the theme on the **Concept/Question Board.** Have students return to "What Ever Happened to the Baxter Place?" and find possible answers or ideas they can add about the theme Communities across Time to the Board.
- **Making Connections** requires readers to activate prior knowledge and connect what they know or have experienced to what they are reading. Ask students to find examples in the story of people, settings, or ideas they can make a personal connection with in "What Ever Happened to the Baxter Place?" Have students share their connections with the class.
- **Predicting** requires readers to analyze information given about story events and characters and to make logical connections to the story's conclusion. Ask students how making predictions as they read helped them better enjoy reading the story. Have students review "What Ever Happened to the Baxter Place?" and find examples of predictions they made while reading the story. Have students share with the class their predictions and the information they used to make predictions.

Comprehension Skills   

Review the following comprehension skills with students:

- **Main Idea and Details** helps readers identify important information in a text, including the details that support the main ideas. Ask students to identify the main ideas on page 229. Have students find specific details in the story that support their main ideas.
- **Author's Point of View** tells readers who is telling the story. Review the point of view of "What Ever Happened to the Baxter Place?" *third-person* Have students point out clue words in the story that helped them figure out the point of view of the story. Ask students how the story would have been different if it had been written from a first-person point of view. Have students share their answers with the class.

Reading with a Writer's Eye 

Review the following literary element with students:

Genre Knowledge is a category or type of literature, such as realistic fiction, nonfiction, fairy tales, and so on. Review the genre of "What Ever Happened to the Baxter Place?" with students. *realistic fiction* Have students find specific examples from the story which show the elements that compose this genre.

Fluency 

Review fluency by modeling expression for students. Remind students that expression, or reading with feeling and emotion, adds to the meaning of text by making it easier to comprehend and enjoy. Read a passage from pages 226–229 from "What Ever Happened to the Baxter Place?" Make sure that the passage totals at least 160 words to ensure an appropriate practice length.

Have students read the passage chorally. Encourage students to use expression. Also remind students to pause after commas and end punctuation.

OBJECTIVES

Students will

- ✦ draft plays.
- ✦ take the spelling posttest.
- ✦ review cursive *Q* and *F*.

MATERIALS

- ✦ ***Transparencies*** 151 and 152

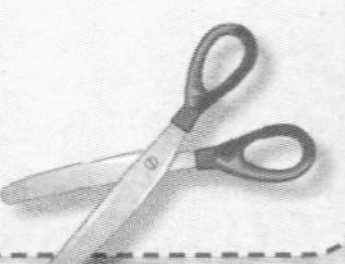

Writing Play

Drafting

Teach

- ✦ Students will draft their plays, using the summary of the plot they wrote during the previous lesson. They will focus on characters and dialogue.
- ✦ Remind students that the plot of their plays will be revealed through their characters' dialogue and actions. Students should use plots they have drafted as well as the play graphic organizer as they write the dialogue for their characters.
- ✦ For examples of character and narrator dialogue, students may silently reread sections of "The Legend of Damon and Pythias" in Unit 1 Lesson 2.
- ✦ If students are handwriting their plays, tell them to write on every other line so that they can make changes more easily and make additions to their drafts later.

Guided Practice

- ✦ Display ***Transparency*** 151 to remind students of how to write character dialogue. Remind students to write the speaker's name at the beginning of the line in all capital letters followed by a colon.
- ✦ Model how to use a plot summary to write the characters' dialogue. For example, if the plot says, "John and Chuck are running late for school," then the dialogue might read:
    - MOM: Hurry up, John and Chuck! You're going to miss the bus.
    - JOHN: I can't find my bag. I think I left it in the kitchen.
    - CHUCK: Oh, John, you're always losing everything.

Apply

Composing—Drafting Students will use their plot summaries to write a draft of their plays. Remind them to focus on writing the characters' dialogue.

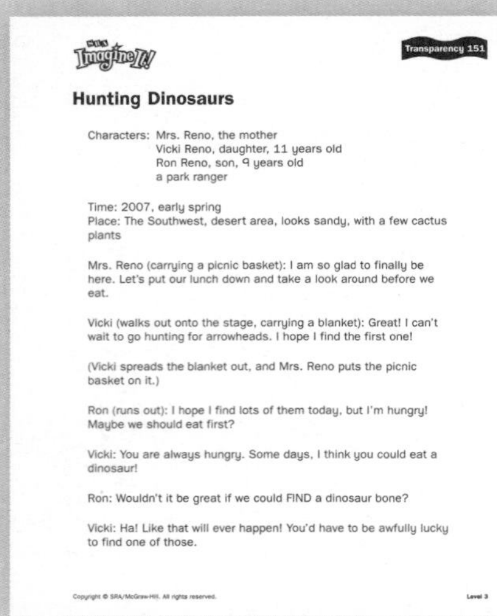

Imagine It! Transparency 151

Hunting Dinosaurs

Characters: Mrs. Reno, the mother
Vicki Reno, daughter, 11 years old
Ron Reno, son, 9 years old
a park ranger

Time: 2007, early spring
Place: The Southwest, desert area, looks sandy, with a few cactus plants

Mrs. Reno (carrying a picnic basket): I am so glad to finally be here. Let's put our lunch down and take a look around before we eat.

Vicki (walks out onto the stage, carrying a blanket): Great! I can't wait to go hunting for arrowheads. I hope I find the first one!

(Vicki spreads the blanket out, and Mrs. Reno puts the picnic basket on it.)

Ron (runs out): I hope I find lots of them today, but I'm hungry! Maybe we should eat first?

Vicki: You are always hungry. Some days, I think you could eat a dinosaur!

Ron: Wouldn't it be great if we could FIND a dinosaur bone?

Vicki: Ha! Like that will ever happen! You'd have to be awfully lucky to find one of those.

 Level 3

Transparency 151

Teacher Tip

ASSESSMENT Use the Writing Rubrics found in the Level Appendix to evaluate students' plays. You may use any of the rubrics for Genre, Writing Process, and Writing Traits.

Spelling

Review of Prefixes, Affixes, and Word Families

Teach

✦ Ask students to write *Spelling* and their names in the top margin of a clean piece of paper. Have them number the first fifteen lines 1–15, then skip a line and number the next two lines 1–2. Read each word, use it in a sentence, and give students time to spell it correctly. Encourage students to try to spell the challenge words, but assure them that misspelling a challenge word will not affect their test scores.

Spelling Words		Challenge Words
mismatch	direction	misspell
preview	director	knowledge
movement	indirect	
bicycle	autopilot	
doubtful	distrust	
restless	unfair	
restful	midsummer	
direct		

Guided Practice

✦ Have students proofread for any mistakes they made on the posttest. Tell them to categorize the mistakes as

- careless errors.
- errors in spelling words with prefixes.
- errors in spelling words whose is changed by adding an affix.
- errors in spelling words from the same word family.

✦ Make certain students are correctly spelling words with prefixes, words that change meaning when an affix is added, and words from the same word family.

Penmanship

Cursive Letters *Q* and *F*

Teach

✦ Review cursive *Q* and cursive *F* with students, using ***Transparency*** 152 if necessary.

- **Letter *Q*** Starting point, downcurve
  Left into undercurve
  Loop and curve right
  Starting point, slant down right: capital *Q*
- **Letter *F*** Starting point, slant down
  Curve up and right to end point
  Starting point
  Slant down, curve up and right
  Starting point, across: capital *E*

✦ To model proper letter formation, write the following sentence on the board: *We shop at Fred's Quality Farm.*

Guided Practice

Ask a volunteer to write the sentence on the board. Guide the student as needed.

Apply

After reviewing the sentence that you wrote on the board, have students practice writing the sentence on a separate piece of paper. Ask students to circle their best sentence based on the correct formation of *Q* and *F*.

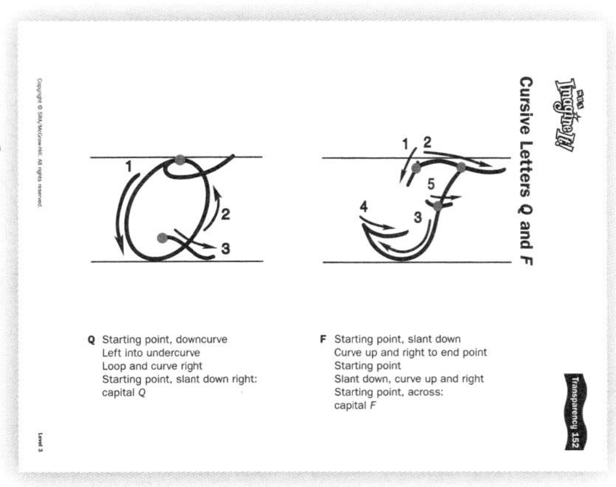

Transparency 152

Teacher Tip

IF . . . students are not using proper spacing between words, **THEN . . .** check to make sure they are positioning their papers correctly, are holding their pencils correctly, and understand how to lift the pencil at the end of the word and reposition it for the next word.

Day 5 **Language Arts**

OBJECTIVES

Students will
- review story maps and character webs.
- review the use of descriptive words in presentations.
- review complex sentences.

MATERIALS

Lesson Assessment Book 2, pp. 75–82

Study Skills

Story Maps and Character Webs

- Ask student to discuss why story maps and character webs are helpful graphic organizers.
- Ask students how they might use these graphic organizers in the future. **Possible Answer** *to write fiction and nonfiction stories*

Listening/Speaking/Viewing

Descriptive Presentations

Remind students that presentations can be enhanced with descriptive sensory details. Speakers can use descriptive words and descriptive objects.

- Ask students how the author of "What Ever Happened to the Baxter Place?" used descriptive words to enhance her characters and scenes. **Possible Answers** *She used sensory details to give her characters physical descriptions. She used sensory details to describe the setting.*
- Ask students how they plan to use descriptive details in their own writing. **Possible Answer** *I want to use sensory words to make my readers be able to picture what I writing about.*

Grammar, Usage, and Mechanics

Complex Sentences

✦ Write the following sentences on the board. Have students combine the sentences using a subordinate conjunction or a relative pronoun. Have students review where subordinating conjunctions and relative pronouns can be placed in a sentence. *beginning or middle*

✦ Subordinate conjunctions: *after, although, as, because, before, if, since, when, where, while, until, unless*

✦ Relative pronouns: *who, whose, which, that*

- Scarlet and Jill took a long walk. It was a beautiful day. *Scarlet and Jill took a long walk because it was a beautiful day.*
- He is hungry now. He'll wait until later to eat. *Although he is hungry now, he'll wait until later to eat.*
- We need to exercise. Let's go to the gym before dinner. *Because we need to exercise, let's go to the gym before dinner.*
- Marina, John, and Lisa plan to play ball after dinner. They have too much homework. *Marina, John, and Lisa plan to play ball after dinner unless they have too much homework.*
- We buy our produce from Frank's Market. It is the best in town. *We buy our produce from Frank's Market, which is the best in town.*

✦ Have students review a piece of writing from their writing portfolios. Tell them to look for fragments and then revise the writing to create complex sentences.

Monitor Progress

Formal Assessment

Use pages 75–82 in ***Lesson Assessment Book 2*** to assess students' understanding of the skills taught in this lesson. Intervene with ***Reteach, Challenge Activities, Intervention Guide, eSkills, Leveled Readers,*** or activities in the ***Workshop Kit*** as needed.

Lesson Planner

MATERIALS

- ***Student Reader,*** Book 2, pp. 232–241
- ***Transparencies*** 17, 17A, 33, 33A, 82, 82A, 151, 155, 156
- ***Skills Practice 2,*** p. 164
- Routines 15, 16
- ***Lesson Assessment Book 2,*** pp. 43–84

Day 6

Reading and Responding

Social Studies Inquiry, pp. T420–T421
Inquiry, pp. T422–T423

Language Arts

Writing
Drafting, pp. T424–T425
Penmanship, p. T425

Workshop

Inquiry: Have students practice and rehearse their Inquiry presentations. Have the group provide feedback.

Writing: Have students begin revising their plays after they complete their drafts.

Day 7

Reading and Responding

Poetry, pp. T426–T429
Inquiry, pp. T430–T431

Language Arts

Writing
Revising, p. T432
Editing and Proofreading, p. T433

Workshop

Inquiry: Have students work in a group to identify and list new questions about communities and post them on the Concept/Question Board.

Writing: Have students edit, proofread, and publish their plays.

Monitor Progress

✔ = **Formal Assessment**
Ⓑ = **Benchmark Assessment**

Day 8

Reading and Responding

Test Prep, pp. T434–T435

Language Arts

Writing
Publishing, pp. T436–T437
Penmanship, p. T437

Writing: Have students present their plays to the class.

Expository Writing Prompt, ***Lesson Assessment Book 2,*** pp. 83–84

Day 9 Review

Preparing to Read

Word Structure, Review, p. T438

Reading and Responding

Selection Vocabulary, Review, p. T439
Comprehension Strategies and Skills
Review, p. T440
Reading with a Writer's Eye
Review, p. T441
Fluency, Review, p. T441

Language Arts

Spelling, Review, p. T442
Study Skills, Review, p. T442
Listening/Speaking/Viewing
Review, p. T443
Grammar, Usage, and Mechanics
Review, p. T443

Day 10

Unit Celebration, pp. T446–T447

Lesson Assessment Book 2, pp. 43–84
B ***Benchmark Assessment,*** Benchmark 6

Social Studies Inquiry

OBJECTIVES

Students will

- read the Social Studies Inquiry Link.
- investigate the unit theme Communities across Time by using the Inquiry process.

MATERIALS

- ***Student Reader,*** Book 2, pp. 232–233

Teacher Tips

SELECTION VOCABULARY Review the meaning of the highlighted selection vocabulary words *produce* and *installed* in "Hoover Dam."

SILENT READ If some students are having difficulty comprehending the selection as they read silently, read the selection with them in small groups.

Genre **Expository Text** 

Expository text tells people facts about real people or events.

Feature **Pie Chart**

Point to the pie chart in "Hoover Dam." Tell students that pie charts show the sizes or amounts of parts that make up a whole.

Ask students to point to and read the information in the pie chart. Then ask students what they think the article might be about.

Reading "Hoover Dam"

Have students read "Hoover Dam" silently. Ask students how this article relates to other selections they have read in this unit. Make sure students read the information in the pie chart and understand how the chart adds to the information in the article.

Think Link

1. How did Hoover Dam and Lake Mead change life in the American Southwest? **Possible Answer** *The dam provides a steady supply of water to the states in the Southwest. People and crops have water and the dam also provides energy for the power plant.*
2. Look at the pie chart. What can you infer about California's population compared with those of Arizona and Nevada? **Possible Answer** *California uses more energy and resources so maybe there are more people there.*
3. Some people are opposed to building dams. What are some negative effects a dam could have on the environment? **Possible Answer** *Because a dam changes the natural flow of a river or lake, some people argue that it has adverse affects on plants and animals near the dam.*

Social Studies Inquiry

Hoover Dam

Genre

Expository Text tells people something. It contains facts about real people or events.

Feature

A **pie chart** shows the sizes or amounts of parts that make up a whole.

The Colorado River is mighty. It once flowed completely wild. In spring, the river would flood its banks. This caused great damage to farms and towns by the river.

In summer, some parts of the river dried up. People, plants, and animals could not get the water they needed to live. These were harsh times.

What could be done about the floods and droughts? The government came up with a plan. Today it is known as Hoover Dam.

It took five years and thousands of workers to build Hoover Dam. It was finished in 1936. The dam sits on the border of Arizona and Nevada, but it affects far more than these two states.

Behind the dam, a lake was formed. It was named Lake Mead. The huge lake meant there would be a steady supply of water. This changed life in the Southwest.

A large amount of produce is grown in California. These crops need a great deal of water. Much of that water comes from Lake Mead.

The dam provides more than water. It makes energy too. A power plant was installed at the base of the dam. It turns the force of falling water into electric power.

Now the river still rages. The desert still burns hot and dry, but Hoover Dam is there to help.

Think Link

1. How did Hoover Dam and Lake Mead change life in the American Southwest?
2. Look at the pie chart. What can you infer about California's population compared with those of Arizona and Nevada?
3. Some people are opposed to building dams. What are some negative effects a dam could have on the environment?

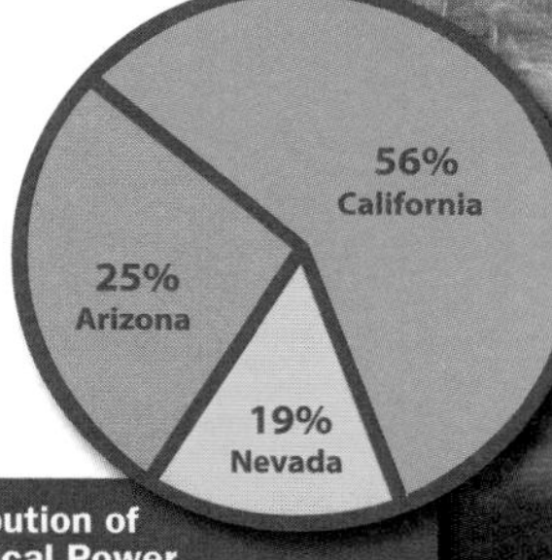

Distribution of Electrical Power from Hoover Dam

Try It!

As you work on your investigation, think about how you can use a pie chart to show your facts.

Inquiry Connection

Have students discuss how pie charts might be helpful in their Inquiries about communities across time. For instance, they may use pie charts to show their city's consumption of a product or resource twenty years ago as compared to today.

Differentiating Instruction: English Learner

IF . . . students need help understanding how to read a pie chart, **THEN . . .** write the percentage numbers on the board and show how all the numbers add up to 100 percent.

Inquiry Process

Step 7—Presenting Inquiry Findings

Whole-Group Time

Whole Group

- Throughout the unit, groups have been researching their own questions and conjectures within the unit theme Communities across Time. Now they will share the results of their investigations. Remind students that sharing knowledge is one main goal of Inquiry because it benefits the whole class.
- Consider letting groups choose the order of the presentations by volunteering. Remind students to be considerate while other groups are making their presentations. Tell them not to interrupt the presentation while it is in progress; there will be time for discussion after each presentation.
- Review the Listening/Speaking/Viewing skills students have learned so they can use them during the presentations. Encourage them to be good listeners, speak clearly, and use effective word choices.
- Remind students that the purpose of Inquiry is not to learn the correct answers to their questions, but rather to discover things they didn't know before.
- Allow time after each presentation for students to ask the group appropriate questions about their presentations and investigations. To encourage students to ask questions, model doing this after each presentation. Asking the groups what they liked most about the investigation is a simple, positive question to ask. You could also ask any group what they found that was most interesting or surprising about their topic.

Small-Group Time

- Have students meet in their small groups to finalize their investigations and discuss how their presentation went. Also have them discuss things they would have done differently if they could do their investigations again.
- Have students discuss questions or ideas they might have about their own and other group's investigations.
- As you circulate among the groups, ask them how the other groups' presentations affected their understanding of the theme Communities across Time.
- Allow each group time to discuss other questions they have about the Inquiry process or the theme Communities across Time.

Concept/Question Board

Continue to encourage use of the **Concept/Question Board** by recognizing and thanking students for their contributions. Incorporate discussion of those items into classroom discussions whenever possible. Remember to also model by posting your own questions and ideas.

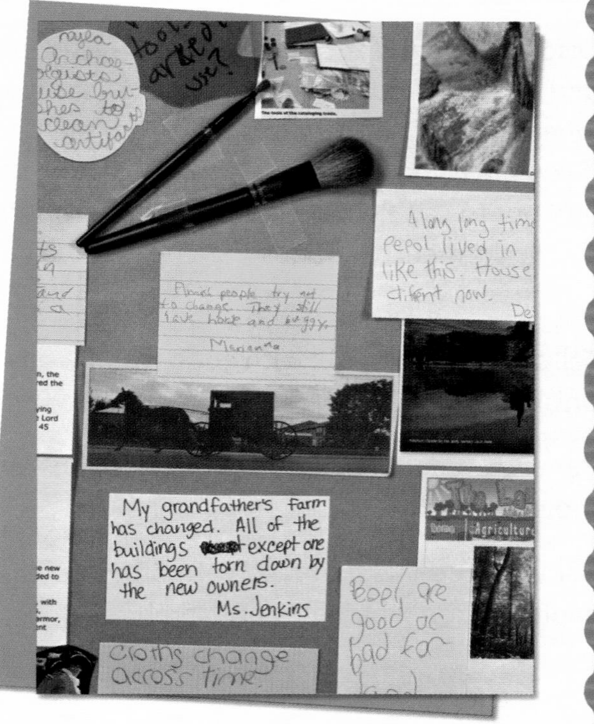

Inquiry Rubric

To assess Presenting Inquiry Findings, see the Inquiry Rubrics in the Level Appendix.

Teacher Tip

SHARING PRESENTATIONS Remind students of the flexible nature of the investigation process. Questions and answers change over the course of the process. Their presentations represent what they have learned about their conjecture up to this point in time.

OBJECTIVES

Students will

- ✦ use visualization techniques to draft stage directions.
- ✦ practice cursive letters *H* and *K*.

MATERIALS

- ✦ ***Transparencies*** 151, 156
- ✦ Routine 15

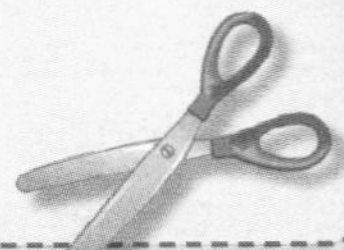

Transparency 151

Hunting Dinosaurs

Characters: Mrs. Reno, the mother
Vicki Reno, daughter, 11 years old
Ron Reno, son, 9 years old
a park ranger

Time: 2007, early spring
Place: The Southwest, desert area, looks sandy, with a few cactus plants

Mrs. Reno (carrying a picnic basket): I am so glad to finally be here. Let's put our lunch down and take a look around before we eat.

Vicki (walks out onto the stage, carrying a blanket): Great! I can't wait to go hunting for arrowheads. I hope I find the first one!

(Vicki spreads the blanket out, and Mrs. Reno puts the picnic basket on it.)

Ron (runs out): I hope I find lots of them today, but I'm hungry! Maybe we should eat first?

Vicki: You are always hungry. Some days, I think you could eat a dinosaur!

Ron: Wouldn't it be great if we could FIND a dinosaur bone?

Vicki: Ha! Like that will ever happen! You'd have to be awfully lucky to find one of those.

 Level 3

Transparency 151

Traits of Good Writing

Vocabulary The writer uses a variety of words and descriptions to make characters and their personalities unique.

Differentiating Instruction **English Learner**

IF . . . students are still having difficulty writing the drafts of their plays, **THEN . . .** allow them to use words from their native languages for any English words they do not know. After they are finished revising their drafts, they can use a bilingual dictionary to find those unknown English words.

Writing Play

ROUTINE 15

Drafting

Teach—Using Visualization

- ✦ Use Routine 15 and tell students a technique they can use to help them when writing stage directions is visualization. Have them visualize what it might look like if their characters were actors performing on a stage.
- ✦ Have students refer to the selection "The Legend of Damon and Pythias" in Unit 1 to see an example of stage directions, or bring in other examples of plays for students to browse.
- ✦ Display ***Transparency*** 151 to remind students of how to write stage directions and include props. Remind students that stage directions tell the characters where to move or how to speak. They are given in parentheses, or in italics if you are using a computer, so the performers know it is something to do and not to say. Remind students that props are objects that will be used by the performers or sounds that are made offstage. They are part of the stage directions.
- ✦ Tell students to begin with adding stage directions and props before they finish drafting their play.
- ✦ Remind students that the stage directions are based on characters' movements.
- ✦ Remind students that they will correct spelling, punctuation, grammar, and capitalization when they edit/proofread.

Writing, continued

Guided Practice

- Block off an area of the classroom to be used as a stage. Show students the basic directions of a stage (up left, down right, and so on), and then model visualizing your characters moving around on the stage. Have students act as your characters, and show them how you would move them. Write this into your play.
- Show students how to use visualization to make a scene more interesting. For example, if the character is late for the school bus and he is trying to catch it, the stage directions might say:

  JOHN: *(waving at the bus as he runs toward it)* Wait! Wait! I'm here! *(John has a book bag slung over his shoulder. The sound of a bus as it starts to move and the sound of a door slamming shut in the background.)*
- Tell students that visualizing this scene will help them write stage directions that are interesting and believable.

Apply

Composing—Drafting Students will add stage directions and props to their play drafts. Encourage them to visualize moving the characters around the stage. Students may want to work together to act as characters for each other and take turns setting stage directions.

Assessment

Use the Writing Rubrics found in the Level Appendix to evaluate students' plays. You may use any of the rubrics for Genre, Writing Process, and Writing Traits.

Penmanship

Cursive Letters *H* and *K*

Teach

- Review capital cursive *H* and *K* as curve forward letters.
- Display ***Transparency*** 156. Using a pointer, trace the letters while saying the formations aloud.
  - **Letter *H*** Starting point, undercurve
    Slant down to end point
    Starting point
    Curve back and slant down
    Retrace up slant, loop left and
    curve right: capital *H*
  - **Letter *K*** Starting point, undercurve
    Slant down to end point
    Starting point
    Doublecurve back to slant
    Curve forward
    Undercurve up: capital *K*
- On the board, write capital cursive *H* and *K*, saying the strokes aloud as you form the letters.

Guided Practice

Tell students to hold their index fingers in the air in front of them. Say the strokes aloud as you trace the letters, and have students mimic your movements as if they were writing in the air.

Apply

Have students practice writing each of the letters four times. Ask them to circle the best formation of each of their letters.

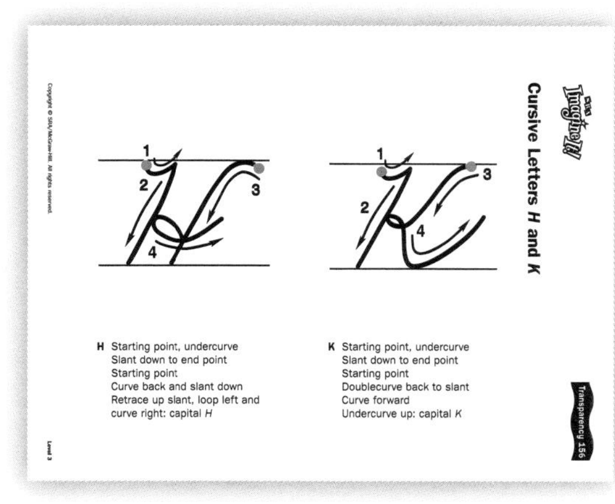

Transparency 156

Day 7 # Reading and Responding

OBJECTIVES

Students will
- discuss tone and rhythm.
- build fluency.
- understand pace, rate, and volume.
- share theme connections.

MATERIALS

- ***Student Reader,*** Book 2, pp. 234–237

Poetry

Activating Prior Knowledge

- Ask students if they have thought about very remote places in the world, where very few people have been. Ask them if people have not visited such remote places, what else might have?
- Have students read the title of the poem and look at the illustration. What do they think the poem might be about?

Reading the Poem

Tone

- Have students close their eyes and listen as you read "Early Explorers." Read the poem with a sense of wonder and awe. Then ask students which phrases in the poem made them feel a certain way. **Possible Answers** *"No place on earth is ever undiscovered" made me feel curious. "Whole mountains hidden under ice," "hottest desert the deepest jungle,"* and *"wings whirring," made me feel excited and curious.*
- Tell students that a poem's tone reflects the poet's or speaker's attitude toward the subject of the poem. The tone can reflect a mood that is happy, serious, sad, or any other emotion. The words poets use and the rhythm and rhyme of the poem can all contribute to the poem's tone. Ask students to identify the poem's tone. **Possible Answers** *curious, amazed, full of the wonder of nature*

Fluency

Before students read the poem aloud, tell them that some lines are meant to flow together and some lines have a pause at the end. Suggest that students read through the poem a couple of times silently, thinking about which lines to flow together and where they should pause. Then have students read the poem aloud. Model fluent reading when needed. Encourage students to read the poem in a tone of wonder, amazement, and curiosity.

Differentiating Instruction **English Learner**

IF... students would benefit from work with the poem's vocabulary, **THEN...** read the selection to them during Workshop. Encourage them to ask questions about any of the words they don't understand. Be sure to keep a picture dictionary handy to help illustrate the words.

Teacher Tip

POETRY Ask students whether they enjoyed listening to the poem. Do they usually like listening to poetry? What other kinds of literature or material (such as nonfiction or songs) do they like to listen to?

Focus Questions

Have students read aloud the Focus Questions on page 234 of the ***Student Reader,*** Book 2. Encourage students to think about the Focus Questions as they read the poem "Early Explorers."

Focus Questions What does it mean to discover a new place? What animals do you suppose lived in your neighborhood before people settled it?

EARLY EXPLORERS

by Marilyn Singer
illustrated by Susan Lawson

No place on earth
is ever undiscovered

Even in Antarctica
where whole mountains are hidden
under ice
penguins already laid shambling tracks
in the snow
before we traveled there

234

The hottest desert
the deepest jungle
where none of us have ever been
all have been crossed
and crossed again
by wings whirring or silent
feet furred or scaled
hoofed or bare

By adventurers we will never know
explorers who will never tell us
what wonders they have seen

235

Listening/Speaking/Viewing

Pace

- Tell students that *pace* is the speed at which a poem is read or spoken. When reading poetry aloud, the speaker must pay attention to the poem's meaning to determine what the pace should be. Determining the tone of the poem helps in determining its pace.
- Have students practice reading the poem aloud in pairs or in small groups. They should focus on a slow and careful reading, slower than their normal rate of speaking.

Theme Connection

- Have students return to the Focus Questions. Ask a student to read the questions aloud, and have students answer and discuss the questions.
- In the Response section of their Writer's Notebooks, have students tell how this poem tells something about communities across time.

Reading and Responding

Teacher Tip

POETRY Ask students whether they enjoyed listening to the poem. Do they usually like listening to poetry? What other kinds of literature or material (such as nonfiction or songs) do they like to listen to?

Activating Prior Knowledge

✦ Ask students what it is like, or would be like, to be completely surrounded by nature. Ask students *what would it be like to know that you always had a place to be free in nature?*

✦ Have students read the title of the poem and look at the illustration. What do they think the poem might be about?

Reading the Poem

Rhythm

✦ Have students close their eyes and listen as you read, "Caring for the World." Explain to students that poets express the mood of a poem through rhythm or the movement or flow of a poem. Ask students to identify the words which create a pattern in this poem. **Possible Answers** *rhyming words: flowing/growing, seas/trees, skies/butterflies, day/play, sand/land, sea/be*

✦ Explain that the rhyming helps establish the rhythm and emphasizes the meaning of the poem. Reread the poem. Ask students what the poet is trying to express through her rhythm and words. **Possible Answer** *The words express feelings of playfulness and freedom in nature.*

Fluency

As students read the poem aloud, remind them to pause at punctuation. Point out that they should pause slightly longer at semicolons than they do for commas, and even a little longer at periods. Remind them to change the tone of their voices when reading the interrogative sentence. Encourage students to read the poem with the same sense of hopefulness and playfulness that the poet suggests.

Focus Questions

Have students read aloud the Focus Questions on page 236 of the ***Student Reader,*** Book 2. Encourage students to think about the Focus Questions as they read the poem "Caring for the World."

Focus Questions What are your favorite places to play outside? How can you help care for your community?

Caring for the World

by Jane Whittle
illustrated by Se Hee Jung

Save me a clean stream, flowing
to unpolluted seas;

lend me the bare earth, growing
untamed flowers and trees.

May I share safe skies
when I wake, every day,

with birds and butterflies?
Grant me a space where I can play

with water, rocks, trees, and sand;
lend me forests, rivers, hills, and sea.

Keep me a place in this old land,
somewhere to grow, somewhere to be.

236

237

Listening/Speaking/Viewing

Rate and Volume

✦ Point out that the rate and volume used when reading a poem is the speed and how loudly or softly it is read.

✦ Read the poem aloud again for students. Read the poem slowly and softly. Ask students why they think you read the poem with this rate and volume. **Possible Answer** *The poem is about someone who enjoys nature and hopes that there will always be safe and clean places to play and grow. It is almost dreamlike.*

Theme Connection

✦ Have students return to the Focus Questions. Ask a student to read the questions aloud, and have students answer and discuss the questions.

✦ In the Response section of their Writer's Notebooks, have students discuss how this poem tells something about communities across time. Encourage them to share their responses with a partner.

Inquiry Process

Step 8—Asking New Questions

Whole-Group Time

- Remind students that even though they have given their presentations, there are still a lot of interesting, unanswered questions about communities. Explain that Inquiry is an on-going process. Each answer raises new questions, and students should be continually asking questions and proposing new conjectures.
- Have students discuss what they learned and identify anything else they want or need to learn about related to the theme. Model asking new questions by saying something such as the following: *After investigating how our community should avoid expanding into too much of the countryside, there is a lot more that I would like to know. Now I have these new questions:* How can our community acquire countryside land to prevent it from being developed?, How long can our city keep expanding? Why do so many people want to live on newly developed land? Have students raise other questions they have related to yours.
- Ask students to share how any of their ideas or opinions about communities—either past, present, or future—have changed over the course of the unit investigation.
- Allow students a chance to share anything else they would still like to know about the unit's theme, especially given all that they have learned in their investigations.

Small-Group Time

Small Group

- Allow time for students to informally discuss their Inquiries and any new questions they have. Encourage them to talk about what they liked about their project as well as what they learned about the theme Communities across Time.
- Ask students to think about and discuss what went well in their group and how well they worked as a group.
- Give each group time to think about what they found most challenging about their project, and remind them to keep this in mind for the next unit investigation.

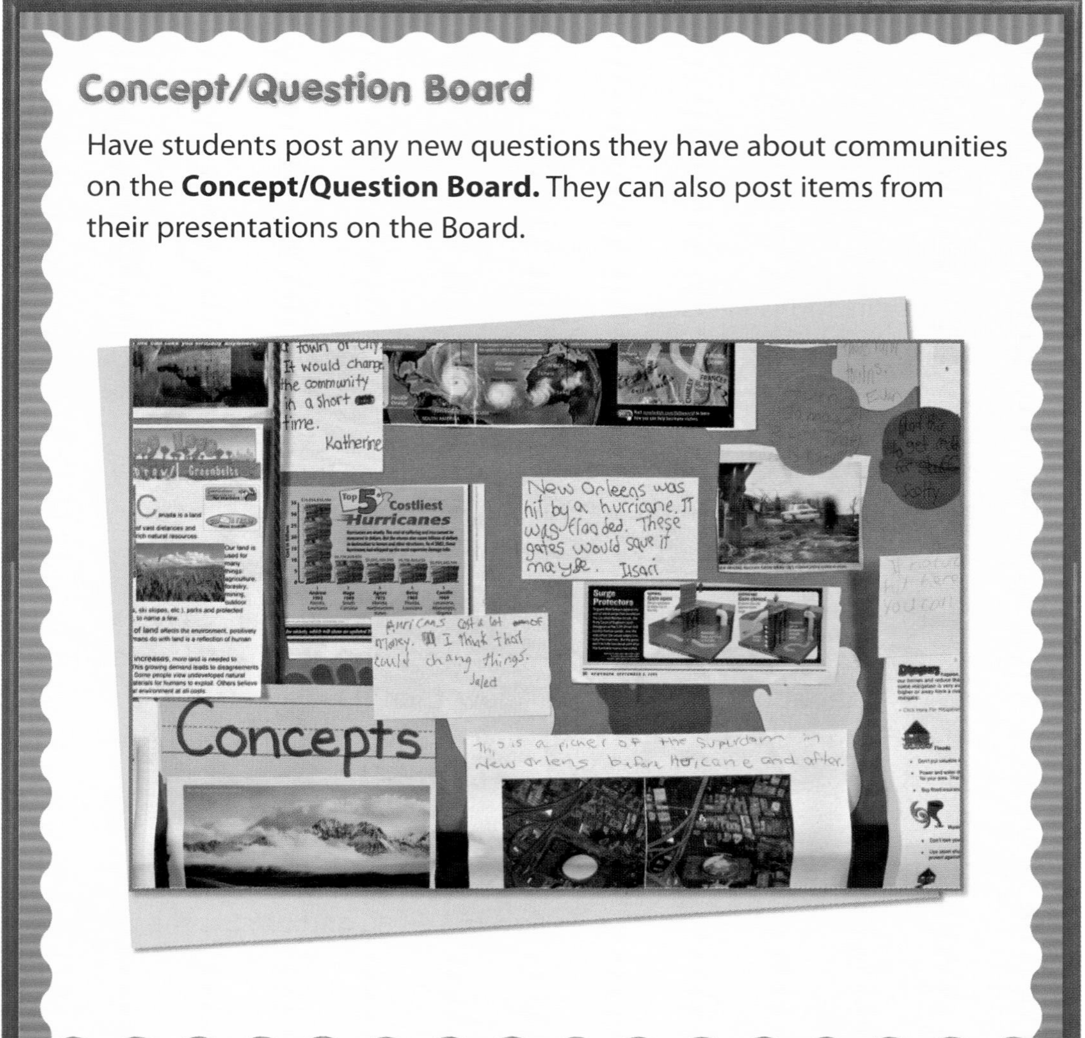

Concept/Question Board

Have students post any new questions they have about communities on the **Concept/Question Board.** They can also post items from their presentations on the Board.

Inquiry Rubric

To assess Overall Research and Participation in Collaborative Inquiry, see the Inquiry Rubrics in the Level Appendix.

Teacher Tip

CONTINUING INQUIRY Students who wish to continue an investigation of these topics and issues on their own might find the following organizations helpful:

- **Roots and Shoots** Founded by Jane Goodall, the Roots and Shoots program encourages young people to become involved in their communities through programs that promote care for the environment, animals, and the human community.
- **National Wildlife Federation** The National Wildlife Federation and its members have been working to protect the environment and wildlife since 1936. The NWF sponsors youth programs and provides youth publications.
- **Defenders of Wildlife** Defenders of Wildlife is dedicated to the protection of native wild animals and plants and the natural community.
- **Sierra Club** Founded by John Muir, the Sierra Club's more than 750,000 members work together to protect our community and our planet.

Language Arts

OBJECTIVES

Students will
- revise and edit/proofread their plays.

MATERIALS

- ***Transparencies*** 17, 33, 33A, 82, and 82A
- ***Skills Practice 2,*** p. 164
- Routine 16

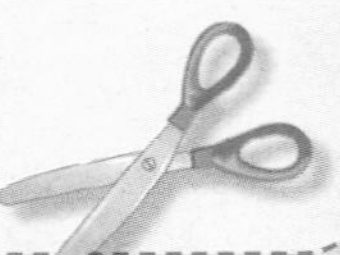

Traits of Good Writing

VOICE The writer maintains a set purpose.

Research in Action

An environment in which writing is central provides a multifaceted context for the development of higher-order thinking. Students learn to plan, which allows them to work out ideas in their heads; to set goals, which promotes interest and the ability to monitor progress; to edit, which enables the creation of text that conforms to conventional standards and heightens its acceptability; and to revise content, which engages students in the reworking and rethinking activities that elevate writing from a craft to a tool of discovery. *(Marsha Roit)*

Writing Play

ROUTINE 16

Revising

Teach—Evaluating Purpose

- Students will revise the drafts of their plays.
- Use Routine 16. Remind students that when revising they should make sure that
  - the most important events of the story are included and told in the right order.
  - the characters' lines tell the story.
  - the stage directions are clear and go with the action taking place.
  - there is a clear beginning, middle, and ending to the story.
  - the play has a title.
- As they did with stage directions, explain to students that visualizing a scene may lead writers to create more interesting and vivid scenes. Tell students that they should reread their plays while visualizing the scenes.
- Model how to evaluate whether one's writing is meeting its intended purpose. For example, if you had stated in a prewriting assignment that the purpose of your play is to tell about someone you know, then the play should be mostly about that person. Tell students that if they strayed from their purpose, now is the time to revise their plays to obtain better focus.

Guided Practice

Have students turn to ***Skills Practice 2*** page 164. Read and discuss the revising checklist with students.

Apply

- **Composing—Revising** Have students revise the drafts of their plays. Also, have them review the revising checklist in ***Skills Practice 2*** page 164 to make sure they are making all necessary revisions.

Play

Editing/Proofreading

Teach

- Remind students that it is important to look closely at the details as they edit/proofread their plays. They should look for errors in spelling, grammar, capitalization, and punctuation.
- When proofreading plays, tell students to make sure that
  - the characters' names are at the beginning of their lines.
  - parentheses are around the stage directions and props.
- Tell students as they edit, they should make sure their characters are talking in complete sentences. If necessary, they can still revise to combine sentences for clarity. Remind students to check for subject and verb agreement and noun and pronoun agreement as subjects and objects.
- Once students have finished the editing/proofreading process, encourage them to type the final copy of their plays.

Guided Practice

- Remind students of the proofreading marks to use by displaying ***Transparency*** 17.
- For further guidance with editing/proofreading, display and discuss ***Transparencies*** 33 and 33A, or ***Transparencies*** 82 and 82A, or model editing/proofreading using the sample you have been modeling.

Apply

Composing—Editing/Proofreading Have students edit and proofread their plays. Encourage them to refer to page 164 in ***Skills Practice 2*** as a checklist after they have edited their plays. Have students type the final draft.

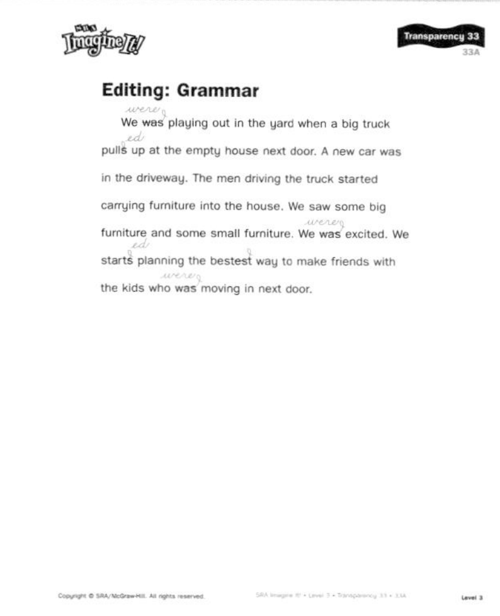
SRA Imagine It! Transparency 33 33A

Editing: Grammar

We was playing out in the yard when a big truck pulls up at the empty house next door. A new car was in the driveway. The men driving the truck started carrying furniture into the house. We saw some big furniture and some small furniture. We was excited. We starts planning the bestest way to make friends with the kids who was moving in next door.

Transparencies 33, 33A

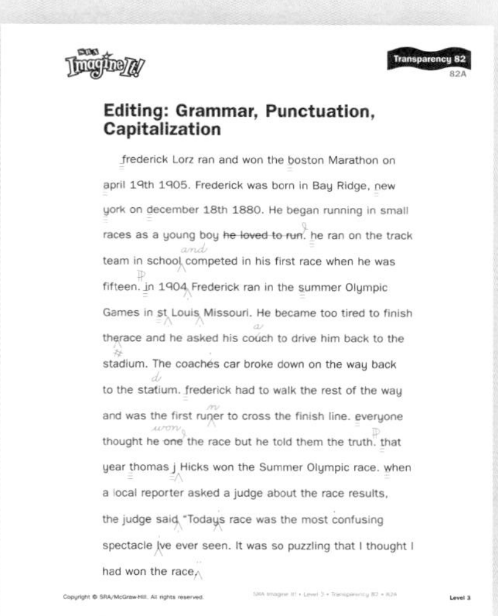
SRA Imagine It! Transparency 82 82A

Editing: Grammar, Punctuation, Capitalization

frederick Lorz ran and won the boston Marathon on april 19th 1905. Frederick was born in Bay Ridge, new york on december 18th 1880. He began running in small races as a young boy he loved to run. he ran on the track team in school competed in his first race when he was fifteen. in 1904 Frederick ran in the summer Olympic Games in st Louis Missouri. He became too tired to finish therace and he asked his couch to drive him back to the stadium. The coaches car broke down on the way back to the statium. frederick had to walk the rest of the way and was the first runer to cross the finish line. everyone thought he one the race but he told them the truth. that year thomas j Hicks won the Summer Olympic race. when a local reporter asked a judge about the race results, the judge said "Todays race was the most confusing spectacle Ive ever seen. It was so puzzling that I thought I had won the race

 Level 3

Transparencies 82, 82A

Differentiating Instruction: English Learner

IF . . . students have difficulty editing their plays, **THEN . . .** go through it with them, pointing out some of the errors they need to look for. Allow them to find additional errors on their own.

IF . . . students have difficulty editing and proofreading their plays, **THEN . . .** be sure to pair them with proficient English speakers for this activity.

OBJECTIVES

Students will

- understand that the answers can usually be found in the reading passage.
- learn the importance of referring to the story to answer questions.
- apply what they have learned about referring to a story to answer questions.

MATERIALS

- ***Student Reader,*** Book 2, pp. 238–241

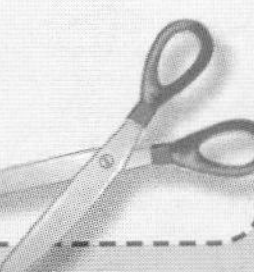

Teacher Tip

REFERRING TO A STORY Tell students that they may not have time to reread the entire story to answer the questions. Remind them to read the story carefully. This will help them better remember where the information they need is located when they refer to the story to answer questions.

Differentiating Instruction English Learner

IF . . . students need additional support reading, "Losing Our Beaches," **THEN . . .** read the story with them during Workshop.

Teaching Test-Taking Strategies

Teach

- Discuss with students how the answers to questions on standardized tests can be found directly in the text or can be inferred from information in the passage. Sometimes students will need to refer to the story to answer a question.
- Have students turn to ***Student Reader,*** Book 2 page 238. As a class, read the text on the far left side of the page as well as the first paragraph at the top of the page. Tell students they should not reread the entire story to answer each question. They usually will not have enough time to do this.

Guided Practice

- Have students read the sample directions, story, question, and answer choices in the box on page 238. Ask a volunteer to answer the question and share why he or she chose that answer. Read and discuss the rest of the page with students.
- Before students begin reading "Losing Our Beaches," point to the words "Go On" as well as the arrows at the bottom of pages 239 and 240. Tell them that when they see these words with the arrow on a test, they should go to the next page.
- Point to the stop sign at the bottom of page 241. Tell students that when they come to a stop sign on a test, they should go back and check their answers until they are told to stop.

Apply

- Have students silently read "Losing Our Beaches" on pages 239–240. Then on a separate piece of paper, have them answer the questions about the story on page 241.
- Remind students to refer to the story to answer questions. Encourage students to use the other test-taking strategies they have learned.
- When students are finished, discuss how referring to the story to answer questions helped them choose the correct answers.

Unit 5

Test Prep

Test-Taking Strategy: Referring to a Story to Answer Questions

To answer some questions on a test, you may have to read a story. You must use the information in the story to answer the question.

Referring to a Story to Answer Questions

Sometimes you will read a story on a test. Do not memorize the story. Just read it, and try to understand what you read. Look back at the story to answer the questions about it.

Read this story. Use the story to choose the correct answer.

The steep climb to the top of the mountain is not easy. It gets colder as you go higher. The air at the top is also thinner. It is harder to breathe. Some people feel faint or dizzy when they get to the top.

All of these make the climb to the top of the mountain hard EXCEPT

- Ⓐ The climb is steep.
- Ⓑ There are many steps.
- Ⓒ It gets colder as you go higher.
- Ⓓ The air is thinner.

Compare each answer to the story. Which answer is NOT mentioned in the story? It mentions all of the answers except the second one. The story says nothing about steps.

Remember to always use the story to answer questions.

Test-Taking Practice

Read "Losing Our Beaches." Then answer numbers 1 through 4.

Ocean states like Florida, New Jersey, Texas, and California are known for their beaches. People come from all over to enjoy them. Beaches also protect us from ocean waves. These beaches, however, are changing. Some are wearing out.

When a beach wears out, it is called *erosion.* This is often caused by natural events, such as a storm. Big waves can push sand from one beach to another or to the bottom of the ocean.

Wind can cause beaches to wear out. A strong wind can blow sand away from a beach. Wind erosion happens more slowly than water erosion.

When an earthquake happens in the ocean, a huge wave can form. This dangerous wave is called a *tsunami.* It can be over 30 feet tall. A wave this big can wash away an entire beach.

Beaches can also wear out if we do not take care of them. In the past, sand was taken from beaches and used for building.

Another way people can cause beach erosion is by hurting sand dunes. A dune is a sandy hill. Sand dunes are sometimes made flat to build houses. Grass and bushes growing on sand dunes might be taken away. This changes the beach so that wind and water can damage it more quickly.

Many people build their homes by the beach. Over time, the land around the homes may wear away. The houses fall apart and people are forced to move. These people can often build new houses farther back. Sometimes, however, they must move away. There is not enough beach left to build a house.

There are things people can do to prevent beach erosion. One is to keep or make more sand dunes. Another is to build walls or put big stones in the water. These will change the way that waves hit the beach. The sand will stay on the beach, and people will be able to enjoy it for a long time. It may not always work, but sometimes it does.

GO ON

Use what you learned from "Losing Our Beaches" to answer Numbers 1 through 4. Write your answers on a piece of paper.

Test Tips

- Read the directions carefully.
- Look back at the story to find the answer.
- Read each question carefully.

1. The last paragraph of this story mainly tells
   - Ⓐ how sand dunes are created by wind.
   - Ⓑ what a tsunami can do.
   - Ⓒ what causes beach erosion.
   - Ⓓ how to prevent beach erosion.
2. What is the author's main purpose for writing "Losing Our Beaches"?
   - Ⓐ To compare new and old beaches
   - Ⓑ To teach about beaches wearing out
   - Ⓒ To explain why beaches are important
   - Ⓓ To warn beach visitors about tsunamis
3. How are storm erosion and tsunami erosion DIFFERENT?
   - Ⓐ Tsunamis are more natural than storms.
   - Ⓑ Tsunamis are more powerful than storms.
   - Ⓒ Tsunamis happen more often than storms.
   - Ⓓ Tsunamis happen in more places than storms.
4. When erosion takes sand away from a beach, where does it go?
   - Ⓐ To other beaches or the bottom of the ocean
   - Ⓑ To rivers that empty into the ocean
   - Ⓒ To deserts far from the ocean
   - Ⓓ To dunes beside the ocean

OBJECTIVES

Students will
- ✦ publish their plays.
- ✦ practice cursive letters *H* and *K*.

MATERIALS

- ✦ ***Skills Practice 2,*** p. 164
- ✦ ***Transparency*** 156

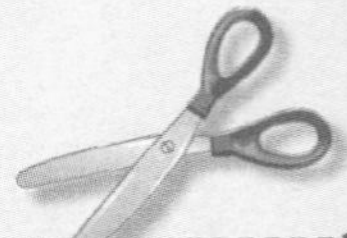

Writing Play

Publishing

Teach—Using Multimedia to Publish

- ✦ Tell students they are at the final stage of the writing process: publishing.
- ✦ Students should have a typed copy of their plays and should make covers for the titles using publishing software if possible. You might want to encourage students to assemble all of their plays into a play book for the classroom library.
- ✦ Invite students to perform their plays. Ask for volunteers who would like to be actors and prop managers. The writer of each play can be the director and will be responsible for casting the play and gathering props.
- ✦ Form small groups for each play. Allow time for rehearsals.
- ✦ Students could either perform their plays live, or ask volunteers to be camera operators and have their plays videotaped.

Guided Practice

- ✦ Using the model you began earlier in the lesson, have students discuss title options and then select a title for your play.
- ✦ Have students turn to ***Skills Practice 2*** page 164 to read and discuss the publishing checklist.

UNIT 5 Lesson 5

Revising **Use this checklist to revise your play.**

- ☐ Does your play have well-developed characters and dialogue?
- ☐ Does it have a specific setting?
- ☐ Does the plot have a problem that is solved?
- ☐ Are your stage directions clear?
- ☐ Do the stage directions support what the characters are saying?
- ☐ Does your story happen in an order that makes sense?
- ☐ Could actors on a stage perform your play?

Editing/Proofreading **Use this checklist to correct mistakes.**

- ☐ Are the characters' names at the beginning of their lines?
- ☐ Did you use correct spellings?
- ☐ Did you put the stage directions in parentheses?
- ☐ Did you use correct punctuation?

Publishing **Use this checklist to prepare your play for an audience.**

- ☐ Give your play a title.
- ☐ Neatly rewrite or type a final copy.
- ☐ Make a sketch of how you will set up your stage.
- ☐ If possible, perform your play with classmates.

164 UNIT 5 • Lesson 5 Writing • *Skills Practice 2*

Skills Practice 2, p. 164

Teacher Tip

PORTFOLIOS Encourage students to add their plays to their writing portfolios.

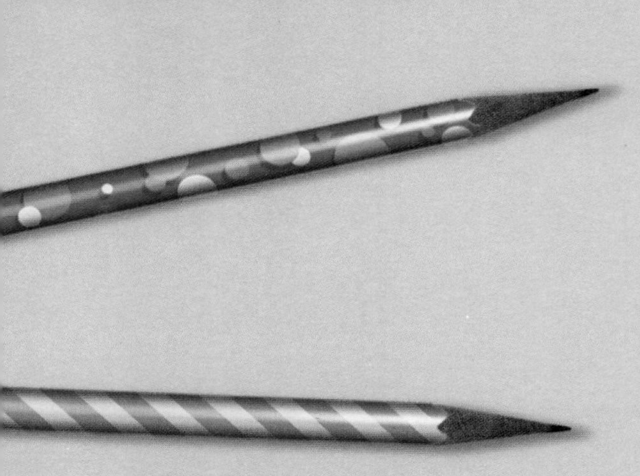

Writing, continued

Apply

✦ **Composing—Publishing** Have students complete page 164 in ***Skills Practice 2*** as a guide to publishing their plays. Have groups performing their plays.

✦ After students have completed their final drafts and performed their plays, encourage them to take their plays home to share with their families, and then to return them to school to add to their writing portfolios.

Traits of Good Writing

Presentation The writer uses multimedia to present and publish written work.

Differentiating Instruction English Learner

IF . . . students have limited vocabulary, **THEN . . .** be sure to review multimedia vocabulary with them.

Penmanship

Cursive Letters *H* and *K*

Teach

✦ Review cursive *H* and *K* with students, using ***Transparency*** 156 if necessary.

✦ Review cursive *H* and *K* as curve forward letters.

- **Letter *H*** Starting point, undercurve
  Slant down to end point
  Starting point
  Curve back and slant down
  Retrace up slant, loop left and
  curve right: capital *H*
- **Letter *K*** Starting point, undercurve
  Slant down to end point
  Starting point
  Doublecurve back to slant
  Curve forward
  Undercurve up: capital *K*

✦ To model proper letter formation, write the following words on the board: *Hawaii, Kansas, The Hobbit,* and *King Kong.*

Guided Practice

Ask for a volunteer to write the words on the board. Guide the student as he or she makes his or her formations.

Apply

✦ Have students practice writing each of the letters two times.

✦ After reviewing the words you wrote on the board, have students practice writing the words on a separate piece of paper. Ask students to circle the best of each word based on the correct formation of *H* and *K*.

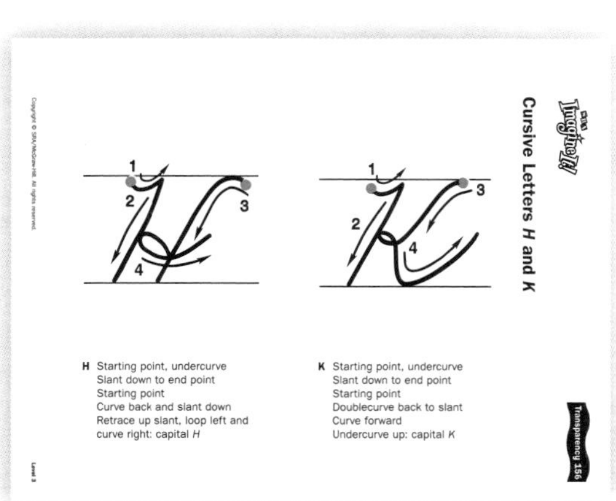

Transparency 156

Unit 5

Unit Review

Use the following activities to review the skills taught in Unit 5.

Word Structure 

Write these word lines on the board or use **Transparency 155** to review Lessons 1–5. Have students read the words on the word lines and give definitions for them. Then have volunteers choose words from the lines and use them in sentences.

Lesson 1	prefixes *re-*, *un-*, *pre-*, and *mis-*	replay	unwrap	preview	misplace
Lesson 2	prefixes *bi-*, *mid-*, *dis-*, and *auto-*	bicycle	midnight	discover	autobiography
Lesson 3	affixes as syllables and affixes used to change word meaning	thankful	rebuild	believable	colorless
Lesson 4	word families and silent consonants	celebrate	celebrating	jackets	knuckles
Lesson 5	Review of Lesson 1	resurface	unaware	preplan	misunderstood
	Review of Lesson 2	biweekly	midway	discontinue	automatic
	Review of Lesson 3	harm	harmful	harmless	harmlessness
	Review of Lesson 4	know	knowing	knew	knowledge

Selection Vocabulary

To review some of the selection vocabulary words from Lessons 1–5, organize students into five teams. Have each team write definitions for their set of words. When they are finished, have the teams take turns sharing their definitions with the class. Their classmates should try to guess each definition's word.

Lesson 1 **Vocabulary**

burrows (bûr′ • rowz) *n.* plural form of **burrow:** a hole in the ground where some animals live (page 135)

settlers (set′ • tlûrz) *n.* plural form of **settler:** a person who makes a new home in a new land or country (page 135)

treasures (trezh′ • ûrz) *n.* plural form of **treasure:** something special; a keepsake (page 143)

Lesson 2 **Vocabulary**

charted (chärt′ • əd) *v.* a form of the verb **chart:** to map; to show information as a picture (page 153)

challenge (chal′ • lənj) *v.* to give the best of (page 156)

developed (də • vel′ • əpd) *v.* past tense of **develop:** to grow; to change (page 157)

Lesson 3 **Vocabulary**

clerk (klûrk) *n.* a person who sells goods or services to customers (page 168)

exactly (eg • zakt′ • lē) *adv.* without any mistakes (page 174)

section (sek′ • shən) *n.* a part of something (page 178)

Lesson 4 **Vocabulary**

acres (ā′ • kûrz) *n.* plural form of **acre:** a measurement equal to 43,560 square feet (page 194)

eroding (ə • rōd′ • ing) *n.* the process of wearing or washing away slowly (page 193)

sheltered (shel′ • tərd) *adj.* protected from danger (page 190)

Lesson 5 **Vocabulary**

necessities (nəs • es′ • sət • ēz′) *n.* plural of **necessity:** something that is needed (page 220)

produce (prō′ • dōōs) *n.* farm products, such as fresh fruits and vegetables (page 216)

seasonal (sē′ • zən • əl) *adj.* ripe at a certain time (page 217)

Unit 5

Unit Review

Comprehension Strategies and Skills

Divide students into five teams. Have each team review one of the comprehension strategies or skills. Then have the teams share their strategy or skill and examples with the class.

Author's Purpose is a skill that allows readers to determine the purpose the author had for writing the text. Readers can then sort out what is important in a text from what is less important. Knowing the author's purpose also gives readers an idea of what they can expect to find in the text. Ask students to review the selections in Unit 5 and discuss the purpose for each selection. Have students find details in each story that support the purposes they choose.

Asking Questions helps readers focus attention on what they are reading by asking and finding the answers to questions they have about the text. Have students review the questions on the **Concept/Question Board,** and discuss whether each of the selections in Unit 5 answered the questions presented. If so, have students write the answers and share their information with the class.

Fact and Opinion is a skill that helps readers understand the difference between facts, which can be verified or tested, and opinions, which are the writer's own judgments which cannot be tested and which might vary between sources. Ask students to find examples of facts and opinions in the selections of this unit.

Cause and Effect is a skill that helps readers identify what causes events to happen or what causes characters to behave in certain ways. This helps readers put together logical explanations in the text. Ask students to review Unit 5 and name cause-and-effect relationships they identified in the selections in this unit.

Main Idea and Details is a skill that helps readers identify important information in a text, including the details that support the main ideas. Ask students what the main idea was for each of the selections in this unit.

Reading with a Writer's Eye

Small Group

In their teams, have students review one of the following literary elements. When they are finished, ask each team to share their narrative element and examples with the class.

Setting is the time and place or places where the story takes place. Ask students to discuss the settings of the selections in this unit. Have students find examples of descriptive sentences and details provided by the author that describe the settings in the selections.

Genre Knowledge is a category or type of literature, such as realistic fiction, expository text, myths, biography, and so on. Ask students to identify the genres of the selections in this unit.

Text Structure—Technique is how an author organizes facts and information and uses examples and photographs to explain information. Ask students how the writers of the units' selections used this technique. Have students discuss how the techniques used added to the meanings of the selections.

Theme is the main idea of something. For example, the main idea of Unit 5 is Communities across Time. Ask students to discuss the themes of each selection in Unit 5.

Characterization is how authors describe and portray their characters. Ask students to describe some of the characters in the selections in this unit.

Fluency

Whole Group

Write the sentences on the board and model reading them aloud. Point out how you paused after the commas. Choose a few students to read the sentences aloud, pausing after the commas. Continue this process until students are reading the sentences fluently.

- What is more important than the land, the sea, and the sky?
- They protect us, entertain us, and give us places in which to dream and explore.
- Now it is our turn to protect them, keep them safe, and ensure that they will be here for generations to come.

Unit 5 Unit Review

Spelling  

Whole Group

Review spelling words from Lessons 1–5 with students. Say each word, and have students spell it on a sheet of paper. When you are finished, have students exchange papers with a partner. Write each word on the board, and have students check their partner's spelling.

Lesson 1

reread unzip preview

Lesson 2

disprove midtown within

Lesson 3

lucky unlucky movement

Lesson 4

honor honorable honesty

Lesson 5

mismatch restful indirect

Study Skills 

Whole Group

Review the following skills with students:

- **Conducting an Internet Search** Invite students to share how they used the Internet to conduct research for their unit investigations or writing activities.
- **Interviews** Ask students to discuss the benefits of conducting interviews for research. Invite students to share their experiences. Whom did they interview? Why did they interview that person? What did they learn from the interview?
- **Maps** Ask students to discuss what types of maps they use in everyday life. Ask them to discuss whether they used maps in their unit investigations. If so, what type of map was used and how was it useful?
- **Calendars** Invite students to display any calendars they use or calendars they have used for school projects. Ask students why calendars are important and how they can be used to organize information.
- **Story Maps and Character Webs** Invite students to share the story maps and character webs they have created, and ask how they helped with their writing assignments.

Listening/Speaking/Viewing

Whole Group

Review the following Listening/Speaking/Viewing skills with students.

- **Group Discussions** Remind students that we interact to share information, to acquire information, to share or learn ideas or feelings, and to enjoy the company of others. Group discussions involve skills in both listening and speaking. Invite students to break into small groups and hold conversations about what they learned about communities across time.
- **Following Directions** Remind students that many times throughout our lives we will be asked to follow directions. Review following directions by playing Simon Says.
- **Effective Voice and Word Choice** Remind students that using an effective voice while speaking and making appropriate word choices can have a powerful impact on audiences. Ask students to give examples of an effective voice and word choices.
- **Using Multimedia** Remind students that using technology and multimedia are ways to make presentations more effective. Ask students to give examples of different technology and media that can be used while making speeches or giving presentations. Ask them to discuss technology and media they have used in the unit investigations.
- **Descriptive Presentations** Ask students to give examples of descriptive words and objects that can be used for unit investigations.

Grammar, Usage, and Mechanics

Whole Group

To review the unit, write the following invitation on the board. Ask students to underline irregular verbs and circle prepositional phrases.

Dear Diary,

Today my class went (on a nature hike). We saw many different kinds (of trees and flowers). We also saw deer, rabbits, frogs, and lots (of birds). Our teacher said that a new shopping center may be built (near the trails). I hope it does not disturb any (of the woods). They can have their spot, just as long as nature can have its place, too. I want to bring my children here someday, to see the trees, flowers, and all (of the animals) (in this amazing forest).

Until next time,
Jane

Unit 5

Benchmark Assessment

Day 9

Monitor Progress

Formal Assessment Options

You will need the following materials, along with your informal observations and ***Lesson Assessment*** results, to monitor student progress throughout the year.

Monitor student progress using ***SRA Imagine It!*** assessment tools.

Technology

- ***eAssess***
- ***eAssess CD-ROM***

Benchmark Assessment for Unit 5 addresses the following skills:

- **Phonics**
- **Vocabulary**
- **Comprehension**
- **Grammar, Usage, and Mechanics**
- **Spelling**

Results on ***Benchmark Assessment*** will serve as a performance indicator that shows how well students are prepared to take an end-of-the-year standardized test. ***Benchmark Assessment*** results also will allow you to intervene with students who are at risk for failure.

Diagnose
students'
strengths and
weaknesses.

Monitor Progress with Benchmark Assessment

Below are two sets of ***Benchmark Assessment*** cutoffs that can be used for predicting student performance — one for Benchmark Skills Assessments and the other for Oral Fluency Assessments. Each cutoff begins with a baseline score under Benchmark 1, which is given at the beginning of the year and ends with Benchmark 7, which is given at the end of the year. The cutoffs are determined by finding the amount of growth a student must make over the course of the year to ensure he or she will not be at risk for reading failure.

Benchmark Skills Assessment

The Benchmark Skills Assessment is a 100-point test, consisting of questions covering phonics; vocabulary; comprehension, grammar, usage, and mechanics; and spelling. The table below shows how many points out of 100 third-grade students should score on a particular Benchmark Skills Assessment over the course of the year. The highlighted score indicates where your students should be at this time.

Benchmark 1	Benchmark 2	Benchmark 3	Benchmark 4	Benchmark 5	Benchmark 6	Benchmark 7
20	30	42	54	66	78	90

Oral Fluency Assessment

The Oral Fluency Assessment is an individually administered assessment, consisting of a passage that students read aloud to the teacher to assess how many words per minute students can read fluently. The table below shows how many words per minute third-grade students should read on a particular Oral Fluency Assessment over the course of the year. The highlighted score indicates where your students should be at this time.

Benchmark 1	Benchmark 2	Benchmark 3	Benchmark 4	Benchmark 5	Benchmark 6	Benchmark 7
44	60	75	91	106	122	137

Independent Tools to Monitor Progress

DIBELS and TPRI

Based on your DIBELS or TPRI scores, use the appropriate ***Leveled Reader*** or the fluency passages from the ***Workshop Resource Book.***

Unit Celebration

Day 10

BIG Idea

How has my community changed over time?

Write the Big Idea question on the board. Ask students what they learned about communities across time. Which selections added something new to their understanding of communities across time? Encourage students to share their thoughts about the unit overall.

Theme Wrap-Up and Review

Small Group

Have students look in ***Student Reader,*** Book 2 at the five selections from the unit. Have students choose which selection they liked best. Organize students into small groups based on the selections they chose. Within their small groups, have students

- retell the selection.
- discuss why they liked the selection.
- identify ways in which the selection related to the theme.
- share their ideas with rest of the class.

Ask students to discuss their thoughts and feelings about the unit. To begin a discussion, ask the following questions:

- *What is the most interesting thing you learned about communities and how they change?*
- *Why is it important to know the history of communities?*
- *What kinds of things would you still like to learn about your community or other past and present communities?*
- *How can you use what you learned about communities to help others?*

Unit Review

Discuss with students how sharing knowledge helps us and others learn. Ask them how they would like to share what they have learned about communities and how they change. For example, students may choose to

- perform a short play about an important historical event in their community.
- write and illustrate a story about a real or fictional community's history.
- create a list of things that could improve the way people live in their community.

Concept/Question Board

- Have students review items on the **Concept/Question Board.**
- Ask students to suggest other ideas related to communities across time that they could still learn more about.
- Discuss how their ideas about communities have changed over the course of the unit.

Pronunciation Key

a as in at	**ô** as in bought and raw	**ə** as in about, chicken, pencil, cannon, circus
ā as in late	**oi** as in coin	**ch** as in chair
â as in care	**o͝o** as in book	**hw** as in which
ä as in father	**o͞o** as in too	**ng** as in ring
e as in set	**or** as in form	**sh** as in shop
ē as in me	**ou** as in out	**th** as in thin
i as in it	**u** as in up	**t̸h** as in there
ī as in kite	**ū** as in use	**zh** as in treasure
o as in ox	**ûr** as in turn, germ, learn, firm, work	
ō as in rose		

The mark (ˊ) is placed after a syllable with a heavy accent, as in **chicken** (**chik**ˊ ən).

The mark (ˊ) after a syllable shows a lighter accent, as in **disappear** (**dis**ˊ əp pērˊ).

Glossary

A

acres (āˊ kûrz) *n.* Plural form of **acre:** A measurement equal to 43,560 square feet.

adjust (əd justˊ) *v.* To change for the purpose of correcting something.

admire (əd mīrˊ) *v.* To look at with pleasure.

affectionately (əf fekˊ shən ət lēˊ) *adv.* With love.

aftershocks (afˊ tûr shoksˊ) *n.* Plural form of **aftershock:** A vibration of rocks or plates shifting into a new position.

alarm (əl ärmˊ) *n.* A sudden fear of danger.

ambitions (am bishˊ ənz) *n.* Plural form of **ambition:** A strong desire to do or succeed at something.

ancestors (anˊ ses tûrzˊ) *n.* Plural form of **ancestor:** An older family member from long ago.

arrowhead (ârˊ rō hed) *n.* The tip of an arrow.

artifacts (ärˊ ti faktsˊ) *n.* Plural form of **artifact:** An old tool, a weapon, or other thing made by people in the past.

astronaut (asˊ tro notˊ) *n.* A person who is trained to pilot or be a part of the crew of a spacecraft.

Astronomers (as tronˊ əm ûrzˊ) *n.* Plural form of **astronomer:** Someone who studies stars.

astronomy (as tronˊ əm ēˊ) *n.* The study of objects in space.

atmosphere (atˊ məs fērˊ) *n.* Area of gas surrounding a planet.

aurora (ə rorˊ ə) *n.* The appearance of light in the night sky.

axis (akˊ sis) *n.* A real or an imaginary straight line through the center of an object, around which the object turns.

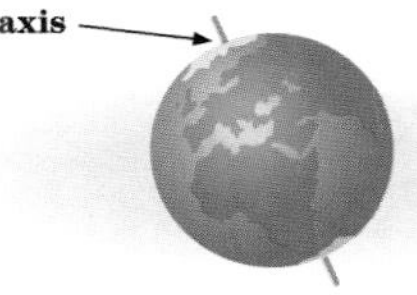

Pronunciation Key: **a**t; l**ā**te; c**â**re; f**ä**ther; s**e**t; m**ē**; **i**t; k**ī**te; **o**x; r**ō**se; **ô** in b**ou**ght; c**oi**n; b**o͝o**k; t**o͞o**; f**or**m; **ou**t; **u**p; **ū**se; t**û**rn; **ə** sound in **a**bout, chick**e**n, penc**i**l, cann**o**n, circ**u**s; **ch**air; **hw** in **wh**ich; ri**ng**; **sh**op; **th**in; **th**ere; **zh** in trea**s**ure.

B

bald (bôld) *adj.* Without hair on the head.

battered (bat´ tûrd) *v.* Past tense of **batter:** To hit over and over again with heavy blows.

beats (bēts) *v.* A form of the verb **beat:** To come down strong and continuously.

boasted (bōst´ əd) *v.* Past tense of **boast:** To brag.

boiled (boil d) *v.* Past tense of **boil:** To heat until steaming.

bolt (bōlt) *n.* A lightning streak.

borrow (bor´ rōw) *v.* To take something from another person with the understanding that it must be given back.

bough (bou) *n.* A tree branch.

bow (bou) *n.* The front part of a boat.

brandishing (bran´ dish ing) *v.* Form of **brandish:** to shake threateningly.

brave (brāv) *adj.* Not afraid; showing courage.

broil (broil) *v.* To make very hot.

burrows (bûr´ rowz) *n.* Plural form of **burrow:** A hole in the ground where some animals live.

burst (bûrst) *v.* To break open suddenly.

bursts (bûrsts) *n.* Plural form of **burst:** An explosion.

bushy (bo͝osh´ ē) *adj.* Shaggy and thick.

C

calculate (kal´ kū lāt´) *n.* To figure out.

carpenters (kär´ pən dûrz´) *n.* Plural form of **carpenter:** A person who builds and repairs houses and other things made of wood.

century (sen´ chə rē) *n.* A period of one hundred years.

certain (sûr´ tən) *adj.* Sure.

challenge (chal´ lənj) *v.* To give the best of.

chant (chant) *v.* To sing words over and over.

charted (chärt´ əd) *v.* A form of the verb **chart:** To map; to show information as a picture.

chronicle (kron´ ik əl) *n.* A written record of events.

clay (klā) *n.* Soft sticky mud.

claim (klām) *v.* 1) To take as one's own. 2) To say that something is true.

clap (klap) *n.* A loud sound.

cleared (klērd) *v.* Past tense of **clear:** To remove things from.

clerk (klûrk) *n.* A person who sells goods or services to customers.

commander (kəm mand´ ûr) *n.* The captain leading a ship or voyage.

common (kom´ mən) *adj.* Happening often; familiar.

community (kəm mū´ ni tē) *n.* A group of people who live in the same area or have a shared interest.

concentrate (kon´ sən trāt) *v.* To give careful attention.

constellation (kon´stəl lā´ shən) *n.* A related group of stars.

contain (kən tān´) *v.* To hold.

cot (kot) *n.* A type of bed.

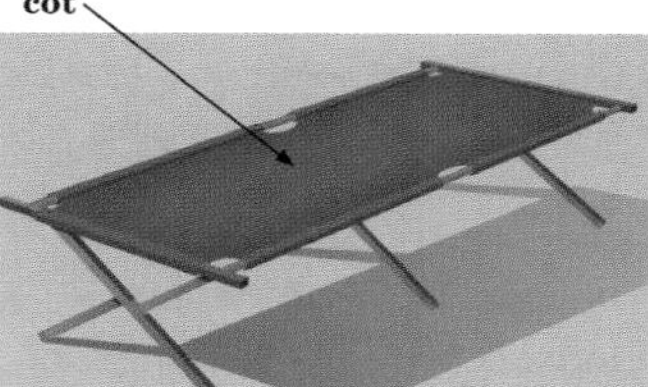

crackled (krak´ əl d) *v.* Past tense of **crackle:** To make a snapping noise.

creative (krē āt´ əv´) *adj.* Able to make or invent new things.

crescent moon (kres´ ənt mo͞on´) *n.* The curved shape of the waxing or waning moon.

crops (krops) *n.* Plural form of **crop:** Plants grown to be used as food or sold for profit.

crumbling (krum´ bəl ing) *v.* A form of the verb **crumble:** To fall to pieces.

Student Reader Glossary

Pronunciation Key: **at**; **lāte**; **câre**; **fäther**; **set**; **mē**; **it**; **kīte**; **ox**; **rōse**; **ô** in bought; **coin**; **bo͝ok**; **to͞o**; **form**; **out**; **up**; **ūse**; **tûrn**; **ə** sound in **a**bout, chick**e**n, penc**i**l, cann**o**n, circ**u**s; **chair**; **hw** in **wh**ich; **ring**; **shop**; **thin**; **th**ere; **zh** in trea**s**ure.

cultures (kəl´ chûrz) *n.* Plural form of **culture:** The arts, beliefs, and customs that make up a way of life for a group of people at a certain time.

curve (kûrv) *n.* A bending line.

customs (kus´ təmz) *n.* Plural form of **custom:** A practice that has become accepted by many people; a tradition.

cycle (sī´ kəl) *n.* A series of events that happens regularly.

cylinder (sil´ in dûr) *n.* A solid or hollow object shaped like a drum or a soup can.

D

damaged (dam´ ijd) *v.* Past tense of **damage:** To make something less valuable or useful.

den (den) *n.* A place where wild animals rest or sleep.

deny (də nī´) *v.* To say that something is not true.

desolation (des´ ə lā´ shən) *n.* Emptiness.

developed (də vel´ əpd) *v.* Past tense of **develop:** To grow; to change.

development (də vel´ əp mənt´) *n.* Growth or change.

devices (də vīs´ əz) *n.* Plural form of **device:** A machine.

directions (də rek´ shənz) *n.* Plural form of **direction:** The way to get somewhere.

discount (dis´ kount) *adj.* With lowered prices.

downtown (doun´ toun) *adv.* The main part or business district of a town.

draft (draft) *n.* A current of air in a room.

drenched (drenchd) *v.* Past tense of **drench:** To soak completely.

drenched

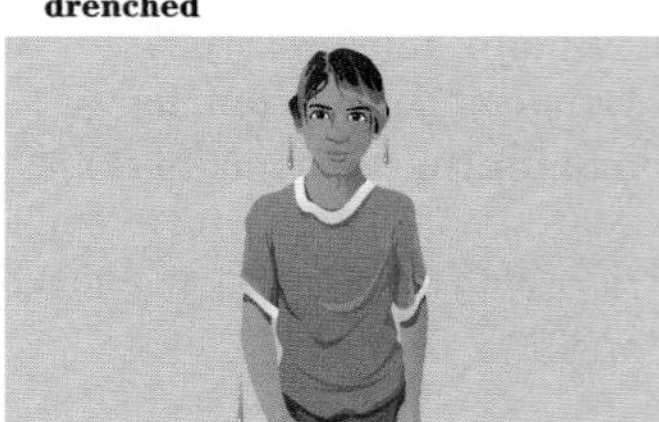

dump (dump) *n.* A place where garbage and trash are thrown.

E

eager (ē´ gûr) *adj.* Wanting very much to do something.

earthquake (ûrth´ kwāk) *n.* A shaking or trembling of the ground.

elevated (el´ əv āt´ əd) *adj.* Raised above the ground.

engineers (en´ jən ērz´) *n.* Plural form of **engineer:** A person trained to plan and design things such as bridges, roads, or airplanes.

eroding (ə rōd´ ing) *n.* The process of wearing or washing away slowly.

errand (er´ rənd) *n.* A short trip to do something.

exactly (eg zakt´ lē) *adv.* Without any mistakes.

exaggerated (egz aj´ jûr āt´ əd) *v.* Past tense of **exaggerate:** To go beyond the truth.

excavation (eks´ kav ā´ shən) *n.* A site created by digging. The process of creating the site.

exhausted (egz ôst´ əd) *adj.* Very weak or tired.

experiences (eks pē´ rē əns´ əz) *n.* Plural form of **experience:** The event that a person has seen, done, or participated in.

expire (eks pīr´) *v.* To come to an end.

F

faucet (fô´ sət) *n.* A water tap.

featuring (fē´ chûr ing) *adj.* Having as the main attraction.

fierce (fērs) *adj.* Strong and wild; raging.

filters (fil´ tûrz) *n.* Plural form of **filter:** A device or material used to block certain light rays.

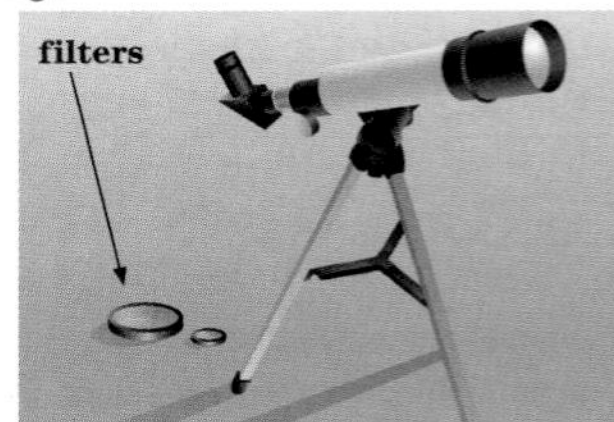

finally (fī´ nəl lē) *adv.* At last.

flickers (flik´ ûrz) *n.* Plural form of **flicker:** A short burst of light.

Pronunciation Key: at; lāte; câre; fäther; set; mē; it; kīte; ox; rōse; ô in bought; coin; bo͝ok; to͞o; form; out; up; ūse; tûrn; ə sound in about, chicken, pencil, cannon, circus; chair; hw in which; ring; shop; thin; there; zh in treasure.

foam (fōm) *n.* A mass of bubbles.

foundation (foun dā´ shən) *n.* The base upon which a structure is built.

frames (frāmz) *n.* Plural form of **frame:** The skeleton of a building.

full moon (fəl mo͞on) *n.* Seeing the whole circle of the moon.

funnel (fun´ nəl) *n.* A utensil with a wide cone at one end and a thin tube at the other, used to pour something into a container with a small opening without spilling.

gas (gas) *n.* Heating or cooking fuel.

gases (gas´ əz) *n.* Plural form of **gas:** A form of matter that is not solid or liquid.

gathered (gath´ ûrd) *v.* Past tense of **gather:** To collect.

gazed (gāzd) *v.* Past tense of **gaze:** To stare.

generations (jen´ ûr ā´ shənz) *n.* Plural form of **generation:** A period of about thirty years.

gigantic (jī gan´ tik) *adj.* Very big.

gravity (gra´ və tē´) *n.* The force pulling things toward the center of a body in space, such as Earth or the moon.

grieved (grēvd) *v.* Past tense of **grieve:** To mourn; to feel sad.

gulps (gulps) *n.* Plural form of **gulp:** A large amount swallowed at one time.

gust (gust) *n.* A sudden, strong rush of wind or air.

half (haf) *adj.* One of two equal parts.

haste (hāst) *n.* Quickness in moving or in acting; speed.

hibernate (hī´ bûr nāt) *v.* To sleep through the winter months.

history (his´ tûr ē) *n.* Events that happened in the past as well as stories about the events.

horizon (hə rī´ zən) *n.* The line where the sky and the land or sea seem to meet.

howling (houl´ ing) *v.* A form of the verb **howl:** To make a loud, wailing cry.

huddled (hud´ dəld) *v.* Past tense of **huddle:** To crowd together.

humor (hū´ mûr) *n.* A quality that makes something funny.

imagination (i maj´ ə nā´ shən) *n.* The ability to form mental images, or pictures.

inspired (in spīrd) *v.* Past tense of **inspire:** To fill with a strong, encouraging feeling.

installed (in stôld) *v.* A form of the verb **install:** To put in place for use or service.

invaded (in vād´ əd) *v.* Past tense of **invade:** To attack in order to conquer the land or people.

iron (ī´ ûrn) *n.* A gray-white metal used to make steel.

jumped (jumpd) *v.* Past tense of **jump:** To move or get up suddenly.

Pronunciation Key: **a**t; l**ā**te; c**â**re; f**ä**ther; s**e**t; m**ē**; **i**t; k**ī**te; **o**x; r**ō**se; **ô** in b**ou**ght; c**oi**n; b**o͝o**k; t**o͞o**; f**or**m; **ou**t; **u**p; **ū**se; t**û**rn; **ə** sound in **a**bout, chick**e**n, penc**i**l, cann**o**n, circ**u**s; **ch**air; **hw** in **wh**ich; ri**ng**; **sh**op; **th**in; **th**ere; **zh** in trea**s**ure.

kiln (kiln) *n.* A type of oven used for making bricks, pottery, and charcoal.

kiln

kneads (nēdz) *v.* A form of the verb **knead:** To mix and press together with the hands.

laboratory (la´ brə tor´ ē) *n.* A room for science experiments and tests.

lap (lap) *v.* To drink a liquid by lifting it up with the tongue.

layer (lā´ ûr) *n.* A single thickness of something.

lighted (līt´ əd) *adj.* That which is showing light.

magnetic field (mag ned´ ik fēld´) *n.* The space around a magnet in which the magnet has the power to attract other metals.

mantel (man´ təl) *n.* A shelf above a fireplace.

mantel

mesa (mā´ sə) *n.* A hill or mountain with a flat top and steep sides.

missions (mish´ ənz) *n.* Plural form of **mission:** A special job or task given to a person or group.

modeling (mod´ əl ing) *n.* The making or designing of something.

modern (mod´ ûrn) *adj.* From the present or recent time.

mounted (mount´ əd) *v.* A form of the verb **mount:** To place or fix on to something.

natural (nach´ ûr əl) *adj.* Found in nature; not made by people.

necessities (nəs es´ sət ēz´) *n.* Plural form of **necessity:** Something that is needed.

new moon (no͞o mo͞on´) *n.* The moon when it cannot be seen or when it appears as a thin crescent.

occur (ək kûr´) *v.* To happen.

orbit (or´ bit) *n.* The path in space that an object follows as it moves in a circle around a planet, moon, or star. *v.* To circle around a heavenly body, such as Earth or the moon.

origins (or´ ə gənz) *n.* Plural form of **origin:** The cause or source of something; what something begins as or comes from.

oval (ov´ əl) *adj.* Egg-shaped.

overcome (o vûr cum´) *v.* To beat or conquer.

package (pak´ əj) *n.* A thing or group of things packed, wrapped up, or tied together; a bundle.

partial (pär´ shəl) *adj.* Part of; incomplete.

particular (pär´ tik´ ū lûr) *adj.* Special.

patches (pach´ əz) *n.* Plural form of **patch:** An area different than what is around it.

path (path) *n.* The route along which something travels.

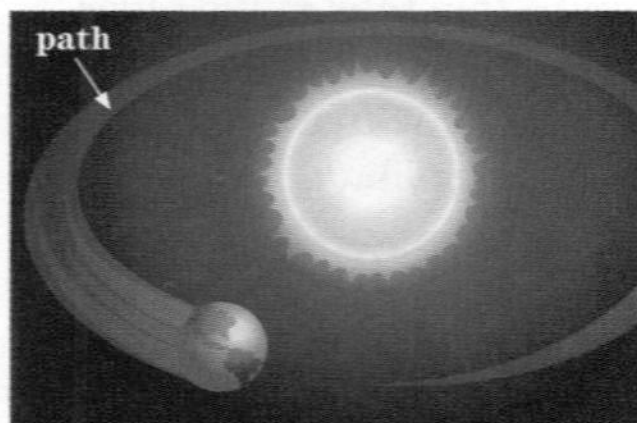
path

penetrate (pen´ ət rāt) *v.* To go into or pass through.

Pronunciation Key: at; **lāte**; **câre**; **fäther**; **set**; **mē**; **it**; **kīte**; **ox**; **rōse**; **ô** in **bought**; **coin**; **bo͝ok**; **to͞o**; **form**; **out**; **up**; **ūse**; **tûrn**; **ə** sound in **about**, **chicken**, **pencil**, **cannon**, **circus**; **chair**; **hw** in **which**; **ring**; **shop**; **thin**; **th͟ere**; **zh** in **treasure**.

phases (fāz´ əz) *n.* Plural form of **phase:** The appearance and shape of the moon or a planet as it is seen at a particular time.

pile (pīl) *n.* A number of things lying one on top of the other; a heap.

pluck (pluk) *v.* To pull off; to pick.

power lines (pou´ ûr līnz) *n.* Plural form of **power line:** A wire that carries electricity.

practically (prak´ tik əl lē) *adv.* Almost.

precious (presh´ əs) *adj.* Of great value.

pressure (presh´ ûr) *n.* Weight of one thing pushing against another.

produce (prō´ do͞os) *n.* Farm products, such as fresh fruits and vegetables.

profitable (prof´ it ə bəl) *adj.* Moneymaking; rewarding.

property (prop´ ûr dē) *n.* Land that a person owns.

pueblo (po͞o e´ blō) *n.* A Native American village consisting of adobe and stone houses joined together.

pure (pūr) *adj.* Not mixed with anything else.

quarantine (quor´ən tēn´) *n.* The keeping of a person, an animal, or a thing away from others to stop the spread of disease.

quarter moon (kwor´ tər mo͞on´) *n.* Phase of the moon in which it looks like a half circle.

raged (rāj d) *v.* Past tense of **rage:** To storm violently.

rays (rāz) *n.* Plural form of **ray:** A beam of light or energy.

recalled (rē käld´) *v.* Past tense of **recall:** To remember.

recollections (rek əl lek´ shənz) *n.* Plural form of **recollection:** A memory.

relic (rel´ ik) *n.* Something that survives from an earlier time or place.

reluctantly (rə luk´ tənt lē´) *adv.* Not wanting to do something.

remained (rə mānd´) *v.* Past tense of **remain:** To stay.

research (rē sûrch´) *n.* A careful study to find and learn facts.

revolution (rev´ ə lo͞o´ shən) *n.* One time around a planet or star.

ringed (ringd) *adj.* Marked with a circular pattern.

ripples (rip´ pəlz) *n.* Plural form of **ripple:** A design created by waves.

ripples

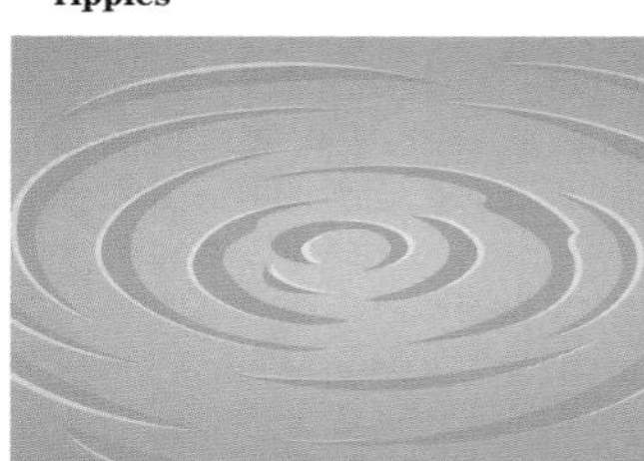

rotation (rō tā´ shən) *n.* Motion about a center point, or an axis.

ruin (ro͞o´ in) *n.* Destruction, damage, or collapse.

rumble (rum´ bəl) *n.* A heavy, deep, rolling sound.

rusty (rust´ ē) *adj.* Covered with rust; the reddish brown or orange coating that forms on iron exposed to moisture or air.

scale (skāl) *n.* The size of a map, picture, or model compared with what it represents.

scarcely (skârs´ lē) *adv.* Barely.

scowling (skoul´ ing) *adj.* Frowning.

scraped (skrāpd) *v.* Past tense of **scrape:** To push or pull an object over another.

seasonal (sē´ zən əl) *adj.* Ripe at a certain time.

section (sek´ shən) *n.* A part of something.

Pronunciation Key: at; **lāte**; **câre**; **fäther**; **set**; **mē**; **it**; **kīte**; **ox**; **rōse**; **ô** in **bought**; **coin**; **bo͝ok**; **to͞o**; **form**; **out**; **up**; **ūse**; **tûrn**; **ə** sound in **about**, **chicken**, **pencil**, **cannon**, **circus**; **chair**; **hw** in **which**; **ring**; **shop**; **thin**; **t͟here**; **zh** in **treasure**.

setting (set´ ting) *v.* A form of the verb **set:** To go down below the horizon.

settlers (set´ tlûrz) *n.* Plural form of **settler:** A person who makes a new home in a new land or country.

shared (shârd) *v.* Past tense of **share:** To use with another or others.

shattered (shat´ tûrd) *adj.* Destroyed completely.

sheltered (shel´ tûrd) *adj.* Protected from danger.

shingle (shin´ gəl) *v.* To cover with shingles.

shock waves (shok´ wāvz) *n.* Plural form of **shock wave:** A vibration after a violent collision of tectonic plates.

sigh (sī) *n.* A long, deep breathing sound caused by sadness, tiredness, or relief.

signs (sīnz) *n.* Plural form of **sign:** A trace.

siren (sī´ rən) *n.* A device that makes a loud, shrill sound.

site (sīt) *n.* A location.

slightly (slīt´ lē) *adv.* Just a little.

sliver (sliv´ ûr) *n.* A thin, narrow piece.

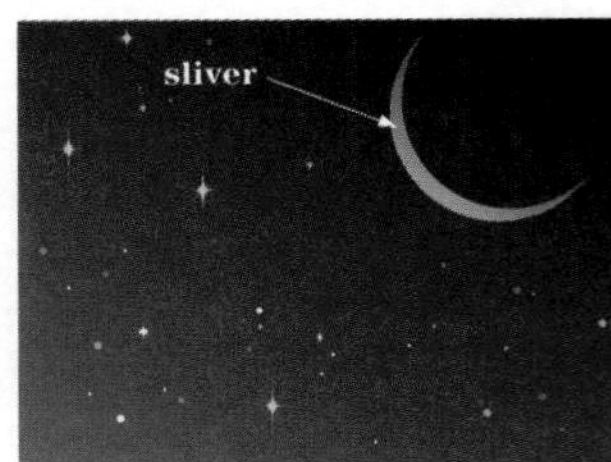

sneak (snēk) *v.* To go quietly without being seen.

soaked (sōkd) *v.* A form of the verb **soak:** To take in; to absorb.

soared (sord) *v.* Past tense of **soar:** To fly.

solar system (sō´ lûr sis´ təm) *n.* The sun and all the planets, satellites, asteroids, and comets that revolve around it.

squinty (skwint´ ē) *adj.* Eyes partly closed.

stark (stärk) *adj.* Lonely empty.

stored (stord´) *v.* Past tense of **store:** To put away for future use.

stormed (stormd´) *v.* Past tense of **storm:** To rush in with boldness and force.

streaming (strēm´ ing) *adj.* Running; flowing.

stroked (strōkd) *v.* Past tense of **stroke:** To rub gently.

struggled (strug´ gəld) *v.* Past tense of **struggle:** To make a great effort.

stump (stump) *n.* Part of tree left over after cutting away at the trunk.

stump

sturdy (stûr´ dē) *adj.* Strong; hardy.

surplus (sûr´ plus) *n.* An amount greater than what is needed.

survived (sûr vīvd´) *v.* Past tense of **survive:** To stay alive.

T

tectonic plates (tek tôn´ ik plāts) *n.* Plural form of **tectonic plate:** A large piece of rock under the earth's surface.

telescopes (tel´ ə scōps) *n.* Plural form of **telescope:** An instrument that makes distant objects seem larger and nearer.

tepees (tē´ pēz) *n.* Plural form of **tepee:** A portable house used by Native Americans.

thrilling (thril´ ing) *adj.* Exciting.

tide (tīd) *n.* The rise and fall of the sea.

tight (tīt) *adj.* Fitting very closely together.

tilted (tilt´ əd) *adj.* On a slant.

timid (tim´ id) *adj.* Easily frightened; lacking boldness.

Pronunciation Key: **a**t; l**ā**te; c**â**re; f**ä**ther; s**e**t; m**ē**; **i**t; k**ī**te; **o**x; r**ō**se; **ô** in b**ou**ght; c**oi**n; b**o͝o**k; t**o͞o**; f**or**m; **ou**t; **u**p; **ū**se; t**û**rn; **ə** sound in **a**bout, chick**e**n, penc**i**l, cann**o**n, circ**u**s; **ch**air; **hw** in **wh**ich; ri**ng**; **sh**op; **th**in; **th**ere; **zh** in trea**s**ure.

top (top) *n.* A spinning toy.

top

toppled (top´ pəld) *v.* Past tense of **topple:** To fall or make fall forward.

tough (tuf) *adj.* Hard to deal with or do; demanding.

traditions (trəd ish´ ənz) *n.* Plural form of **tradition:** The practice of passing down customs, beliefs, or other knowledge from parents to their children.

transform (trans form´) *v.* To change the form or condition of something.

treasured (trezh´ ûrd) *adj.* Valued highly.

treasures (trezh´ ûrz) *n.* Plural form of **treasure:** Something special; a keepsake.

trembled (trem´ bəld) *v.* Past tense of **tremble:** To shake.

trickle (trik´ əl) *n.* A small amount.

universe (ū´ ni vûrs) *n.* Everything that exists in our solar system and all of space.

vegetation (vej´ ə tā´ shən) *n.* Plant life.

voyage (voi´ əj) *v.* To journey by water or through space.

voyage

waded (wād´ əd) *v.* Past tense of **wade:** To walk through water.

waning (wān´ ing) *adj.* Becoming smaller.

waxing (waks´ ing) *adj.* Becoming bigger.

works (wûrks) *v.* A form of the verb **work:** To shape, as by pressing or rolling.

Appendices

Unit 5 • NAT-L3-U5-6-A

SRA
Imagine It!

SRA Imagine It!

The Program Appendix includes a step-by-step explanation of procedures for research-based, effective practices in reading instruction that are repeatedly used throughout ***SRA Imagine It!*** These practices may also be used in other instructional materials.

Table of Contents

Phonological and Phonemic Awareness

The key to learning to read is the ability to identify different sounds and to connect those sounds to the letters of the alphabet. The basic purpose of providing structured practice in phonemic awareness is to help students hear and understand the sounds from which words are made. Before students can be expected to understand the sound/symbol correspondence that forms the base of written English, they need to have a strong working knowledge of the sound relationships that make up the spoken language. This understanding of spoken language lays the foundation for the transition to written language.

Phonological awareness is an umbrella term. It incorporates a range of oral language skills that involve the ability to notice, think about, and manipulate individual sounds in words. Phonological awareness involves working with sentences, words, rhyme, syllables, and sounds. The objective is for students to be able to manipulate words, word parts, and sounds without regard to meaning.

Phonological and phonemic awareness activities initially provide students with the opportunity to think about sentences and to break them into words and then to play with words and to break them into parts. It involves easy and fun activities that engage students in playing with and exploring the parts and sounds of language. The goal of these gamelike activities is to help students understand that speech is made of distinct, identifiable sounds. The playful nature of the activities makes them appealing and engaging, while giving students practice and support for learning about language. When students begin reading and writing, this experience with manipulating sounds will help them use what they know about sounds and letters to sound out and spell unfamiliar words when they read and write.

Developing phonological awareness engages students in activities that move from working with words and syllables — the larger units of language — to individual sounds (phonemes). Students progress by

- Identifying sentences
- Identifying words
- Working with rhymes
- Exploring compound words
- Listening for syllables
- Blending syllables
- Oral blending
- Deleting and substituting sounds
- Segmenting phonemes

As students progress through various phonemic awareness activities, they will become proficient at listening for and reproducing the sounds they hear. It is essential for their progression to phonics and reading that they are able to hear the sounds and the patterns used to make up recognizable words. The phonemic awareness activities support the phonics instruction. Initially students are not expected to read the words they are exploring and manipulating, so any consonant and vowel sounds may be used, even if students have not been formally taught the sounds and their spellings.

As students progress through various phonemic awareness activities, they will become proficient at listening for and reproducing the sounds they hear.

After students have an awareness of phonemes, they can begin to connect sounds to letters and to engage in a variety of activities in which sounds and letters are substituted to make new words. Students begin to understand that if a sound changes, a letter must change, and a new word is created. As students move into phonics, research suggests that connecting sounds to spellings actually heightens their awareness of language. Phonological and phonemic awareness is both a prerequisite for and a consequence of learning to read.

Research suggests that the majority of instructional time should be focused on two critical phonemic awareness formats: phoneme or oral blending and phoneme segmentation. These are supported by discrimination and elision activities (deleting and substituting sounds) and general wordplay. Oral blending encourages students to combine sounds to make words and lays the foundation for decoding and reading. Segmentation, conversely, requires students to break words into discrete sounds and lays the foundation for spelling. Other activities support discrimination, or recognition, of particular sounds. Sometimes simple songs, rhymes, or games engage students in wordplay. In these, students manipulate words in a variety of ways. From these playful activities, students develop serious knowledge about their language.

Oral Blending

Purpose

In oral blending, students are led through a progression of activities designed to help them hear how sounds are put together to make words.

Until students develop an awareness of the component parts of words, they have no tools with which to decode words or to put letters together to form words. Oral blending helps students understand these component parts of words, from syllables down to single sounds, or phonemes. Oral blending is not to be confused with the formal blending of specific sounds whose spellings students will be taught through phonics instruction. Oral blending does not depend on the recognition of written words; it focuses instead on hearing the sounds.

Oral blending focuses on hearing sounds through a sequence that introduces the most easily distinguished word parts and then systematically moves to oral blending of individual sounds that contains all the challenges of phonic decoding (except letter recognition). This sequence provides support for the least-prepared student—one who comes to school with no concept of words or sounds within words. At the same time, the lively pace and playful nature of oral blending activities hold the interest of students who already have some familiarity with words and letters.

Oral blending prepares students for phonics instruction by developing an awareness of the separate sounds that make up speech. Oral blending activities then continue in concert with phonics instruction to reinforce and extend new learning. And because these activities involve simply listening to and reproducing sounds, oral blending need not be restricted to the sounds students have been or will be taught in phonics.

The tone of the activities should be playful and informal and should move quickly. Although these activities will provide information about student progress, they are not diagnostic tools. Do not expect mastery. Those students who have not caught on will be helped more by varied experiences than by more drilling on the same activity.

Procedure

The following is a description of the progression of oral blending activities.

Word-Part Blending

Syllables are easier to distinguish than individual sounds (phonemes), so students can quickly experience success in forming meaningful words. Tell students that you are going to say some words in two parts. Tell them to listen carefully so they can discover what the words are. Read each word, pronouncing each part distinctly with a definite pause between syllables. The lists of words that follow are arranged in sequence from easy to harder. They cover different types of cues. Whenever they fit into the sequence, include multisyllabic names of students in the class.

Model

Teacher: dino . . . saur. What's the word?
Students: dinosaur

Example Words

- First part of the word cues the whole word:
  vita . . . min
  vaca . . . tion
  hippopot . . . amus
  ambu . . . lance
- Two distinct words easily combined:
  butter. . . fly
  straw. . . berry
  surf . . . board
  basket . . . ball
- Two distinct words, but first word could cue the wrong ending:
  tooth . . . ache
  tooth . . . paste
  water . . . fall
  water . . . melon
- First part, consonant + vowel, not enough to guess whole word:
  re . . . member
  re . . . frigerator
  bi . . . cycle
  bi . . . ology
- Identifying cues in second part:
  light . . . ning
  sub . . . ject
  in . . . sect
- Last part, consonant + vowel sound, carries essential information:
  yester . . . day
  rain . . . bow
  noi . . . sy
  pota . . . to
- Changing the final part changes the word:
  start . . . ing
  start . . . er
  start. . . ed

Initial Consonant Sounds

Initial consonant blending prepares students for consonant replacement activities that will come later. Tell students that you will ask them to put some sounds together to make words. Pronounce each word part distinctly, and make a definite pause at the breaks indicated. When a letter is surrounded by slash marks, pronounce the letter's sound, not its name. When you see /s/, for example, you will say "ssss," not "ess." The words that follow are arranged from easy to harder. Whenever they fit into the sequence, include names of students in the class.

Model

Teacher: /t/ . . . iger. What's the word?
Students: tiger

Example Words

- Separated consonant blend, with rest of word giving strong cue to word identity:
  /b/ . . . roccoli   */k/ . . . racker*
  /f/ . . . lashlight   */k/ . . . reature*
- Held consonant that is easy for students to hear, with rest of word giving strong cue:
  /s/ . . . innamon   */l/ . . . adybug*
  /s/ . . . eventeen   */n/ . . . ewspaper*
- Stop consonant that is harder for students to hear preceding vowel, with rest of word giving strong cue:
  /t/. . . adpole   */p/ . . . iggybank*
  /d/ . . . ragonfly   */b/ . . . arbecue*
- Single-syllable words and words in which the second part gives a weaker cue:
  /s/ . . . ing   */l/ . . . augh*   */v/ . . . ase*

Final Consonant Sounds

In this phase of oral blending, the last sound in the word is separated.

Model

Teacher: cabba . . . /j/. What's the word?
Students: cabbage

Example Words

- Words that are easily recognized even before the final consonant is pronounced:
  bubblegu . . . /m/   *Columbu . . . /s/*
  crocodi . . . /l/   *submari . . . /n/*
- Multisyllabic words that need the final consonant for recognition:
  colle . . . /j/ (college)   *come . . . /t/ (comet)*
- Single-syllable words:
  sa . . . /d/   *gra . . . /s/ (grass)*   *snai . . . /l/*

Initial Consonant Sound Replacement

This level of oral blending further develops awareness of initial consonant sounds. The activity begins with a common word then quickly changes its initial consonant sound. Most of the words produced are nonsense words, which helps keep the focus on the sounds in the word. Note that the words are written on the board, but students are not expected to read them. The writing is to help students see that when the sounds change, the letters change, and vice versa.

Model

Teacher: [Writes word on board.] This word is *magazine*. What is it?
Students: magazine
Teacher: Now I'm going to change it. [Erases initial consonant.] Now it doesn't start with /m/; it's going to start with /b/. What's the new word?
Students: bagazine
Teacher: That's right . . . [Writes *b* where *m* had been.] It's *bagazine*. Now I'm going to change it again. . . .

Repeat with different consonant sounds. Then do the same with other words such as *remember, Saturday, tomorrow, lotion,* and *million*. Continue with single-syllable words such as *take, big, boot, cot, seat, look, tap, ride,* and *late*. There are two stages in using written letters:

- The replacement letter is not written until ***after*** the new "word" has been identified.

- Later, the replacement letter is written at ***the same time*** the change in the initial phoneme is announced. For example, erase *d* and write *m* while you say, "Now it doesn't start with /d/; it starts with /m/."

When the consonants used have already been introduced in phonics, you may wish to alter the procedure by writing the replacement letter and having students sound out the new word. Feel free to switch between the two procedures within a single exercise. If students are not responding orally to written spellings that have been introduced in phonics, do not force it. Proceed by saying the word before writing the letter, and wait until another time to move on to writing before pronouncing.

One-Syllable Words

Students now begin blending individual phonemes to form words. This important step can be continued well into the year. Continued repetitions of this activity will help students realize how they can use the sound/spellings they are learning to read and write real words.

At first, the blended words are presented in a story context that helps students identify the words. They soon recognize that they are actually decoding meaningful words. However, the context must not be so strong that students can guess the word without listening to the phonemic cues. Any vowel sounds and irregularly spelled words may be used because there is no writing involved.

Model

Teacher: When I looked out the window, I saw a /l/ /ī/ /t/. What did I see?
Students: A light.
Teacher: Yes, I saw a light. At first I thought it was the /m/ /o͞o/ /n/. What did I think it was?
Students: The moon.
Teacher: But it didn't really look like the moon. Suddenly I thought, maybe it's a space /sh/ /i/ /p/. What did I think it might be?
Students: A spaceship!

When students are familiar with this phase of oral blending, they can move to blending one-syllable words without the story context.

Example Words

- CVC (consonant/vowel/consonant) words beginning with easily blended consonant sounds (/sh/, /h/, /r/, /v/, /s/, /n/, /z/, /f/, /l/, /m/):
  nip nap
- CVC words beginning with any consonant:
  ten bug lip
- Add CCVC words:
  flap step
- Add CVCC words:
  most band went
- Add CCVCC words:
  stamp grand scuffs

Final Consonant Sound Replacement

Final consonant sounds are typically more difficult for students to use than initial consonants.

- Begin with multisyllabic words, and move to one-syllable words.
- As with initial consonants, first write the changed consonant after students have pronounced the new word.
- Then write the consonant as they pronounce it.
- For sound/spellings introduced in phonics instruction, write the new consonant spelling, and have students identify and pronounce it.

Model

Teacher: [Writes word on board.] This word is *teapot.* What is it?
Students: teapot
Teacher: Now I'm going to change it. [Erases final consonant.] Now it doesn't end with /t/; it ends with /p/. What's the word now?
Students: teapop
Teacher: That's right . . . [Writes *p* where *t* had been.] It's *teapop.* Now I'm going to change it again. . . .

Example Words

- Words that are easily recognized even before the final consonant is pronounced:
  picnic picnit picnis picnil picnid
  airplane airplate airplabe airplafe
- Multisyllabic words that need the final consonant for recognition:
  muffin muffil muffim muffip muffit
  amaze amate amake amale amade
- Single-syllable words:
  neat nean neap neam neaj nead neaf
  broom broot brood broof broop broon

Initial Vowel Replacement

Up to now, oral blending has concentrated on consonant sounds because they are easier to hear than vowels. As you move to vowel play, remember that the focus is still on the sounds, not the spellings. Use any vowel sounds.

Model

Teacher: [Writes word on board.] This word is *elephant.* What is it?
Students: elephant
Teacher: Now I'm going to change it. [Erases initial vowel.] Now it doesn't start with /e/; it starts with /a/. What's the word now?
Students: alephant
Teacher: That's right . . . [Writes *a* where *e* had been.] It's *alephant.* Now I'm going to change it again. . . .

Example Words

- Multisyllabic words:
  angry ingry oongry ungry engry
  ivy avy oovy evy ovy oivy
- One-syllable words:
  ink ank oonk unk onk oink
  add odd idd oudd edd udd

Segmentation

Purpose

Segmentation and oral blending complement each other: Oral blending puts sounds together to make words, while segmentation separates words into sounds. Oral blending will provide valuable support for decoding when students begin reading independently.

Procedure

Syllables

The earliest segmentation activities focus on syllables, which are easier to distinguish than individual sounds, or phonemes. Start with students' names, and then use other words. As with the oral blending activities, remember to move quickly through these activities. Do not hold the class back waiting for all students to catch on. Individual progress will vary, but drilling on one activity is less helpful than going on to others. Return to the same activity often. Frequent repetition is very beneficial and allows students additional opportunities to catch on.

- Say, for example, "Let's clap out Amanda's name. A-man-da."
- Have students clap and say the syllables along with you. Count the claps.
- Tell students that these word parts are called syllables. Don't try to explain; the idea will develop with practice. After you have provided the term, simply say, "How many syllables?" after students clap and count.
- Mix one-syllable and multisyllabic words: *fantastic* *tambourine* *good* *imaginary* *stand* *afraid*

Oral blending will provide valuable support for decoding when students begin reading independently.

Comparative Lengths of Words

Unlike most phonemic awareness activities, this one involves writing on the board or on an overhead transparency. Remember, though, that students are not expected to read what is written. They are merely noticing that words that take longer to say generally look longer when written.

- Start with students' names. Choose two names, one short and one long, with the same first letter (for example, *Joe* and *Jonathan*).
- Write the two names on the board, one above the other, so that the difference is obvious.
- Tell students that one name is *Jonathan* and that one is *Joe*. Have them pronounce and clap each name. Then have them tell which written word they think says *Joe*.
- Move your finger under each name as students clap and say it syllable by syllable.
- Repeat with other pairs of names and words such as *tea/telephone, cat/caterpillar, and butterfly/bug*. Be sure not to give false clues. For example, sometimes write the longer word on top, sometimes the shorter one; sometimes ask for the shorter word, sometimes the longer; sometimes ask for the top word, sometimes the bottom; and sometimes point to a word and ask students to name it, and sometimes name the word and ask students to point to it.

Listen for Individual Sounds

Activities using a puppet help students listen for individual sounds in words. Use any puppet you have on hand. When you introduce the puppet, tell students that it likes to play word games. Each new activity begins with the teacher speaking to and for the puppet until students determine the pattern. Next, students either speak for the puppet or correct the puppet. To make sure all students are participating, alternate randomly between having the whole group or individuals respond. The activities focus on particular parts of words, according to the following sequence:

1. Repeating last part of word. Use words beginning with easy-to-hear consonants such as *f, l, m, n, r, s,* and *z*. The puppet repeats only the rime, the part of the syllable after the initial consonant.

Model

Teacher: farm
Puppet: arm
After the pattern is established, students respond for the puppet.
Teacher: rope
Students: ope

Example Words

Use words such as the following:
mine . . . ine *soup . . . oup* *feet . . . eet*

2. Restoring initial phonemes. Now students correct the puppet. Be sure to acknowledge the correction.

Model

Teacher: lake
Puppet: ake
Teacher: No, lllllake. You forgot the /l/.
Teacher: real
Puppet: eal
Teacher: What did the puppet leave off?
Students: /r/. It's supposed to be *real.*
Teacher: That's right. The word is *real.*

Example Words

Use words such as the following:
look . . . ook *mouse . . . ouse*
sand . . . and

3. Segmenting initial consonants. The puppet pronounces only the initial consonant.

Model

Teacher: pay
Puppet: /p/

Example Words

Use words such as the following:
moon . . . /m/ *nose . . . /n/* *bell . . . /b/*

4. Restoring final consonants. Students correct the puppet. Prompt if necessary: "What's the word? What did the puppet leave off?"

Model

Teacher: run
Puppet: ru
Students: It's run! You left off the /n/.
Teacher: That's right. The word is *run.*

Example Words

Use words such as the following:
meet. . . mee *cool . . . coo* *boot. . . boo*

5. Isolating final consonants. The puppet pronounces only the final consonant.

Model

Teacher: green
Puppet: /n/

Example Words

Use words such as the following:
glass . . . /s/ *boom . . . /m/* *mice . . . /s/*

6. Segmenting initial consonant blends. The sounds in blends are emphasized.

Model

Teacher: clap
Puppet: lap
Next have students correct the puppet.
Teacher: stain
Puppet: tain
Students: It's stain! You left off the /s/.
Teacher: That's right. The word is *stain.*

Example Words

Use words such as the following:
blaze . . . laze *draw. . . raw*
proud . . . roud

Discrimination

Purpose

Discrimination activities help students focus on particular sounds in words.

Listening for long-vowel sounds is the earliest discrimination activity. Vowel sounds are necessary for decoding, but young students do not hear them easily. This is evident in students' invented spellings, where vowels are often omitted. Early in the year, students listen for long-vowel sounds, which are more easily distinguished than short-vowel sounds:

- Explain to students that vowels are special because sometimes they say their names in words.
- Tell students which vowel sound to listen for.
- Have them repeat the sound when they hear it in a word. For example, if the target-vowel sound is long *e,* students will say long *e* when you say *leaf,* but they should not respond when you say *loaf.*
- Initially students should listen for one long vowel sound at a time. Later they can listen for two vowel sounds. All Example Words, however, should contain one of the target vowels.

Procedure

Listening for short-vowel sounds

These discrimination activities should be done after the short vowels /a/ and /i/ have been introduced. Short vowels are very useful in reading. They are generally more regular in spelling than long vowels, and they appear in many short, simple words. However, their sounds are less easily distinguished than those of long vowels. Thus, the activities focus only on /a/ and /i/. All the words provided have one or the other of these sounds. Either have students repeat the sound of a specified vowel, or vary the activity as follows: Write an *a* on one side of the board and an *i* on the other. Ask students to point to the *a* when they hear a word with the /a/ sound and to point to the *i* when they hear a word with the /i/ sound. Use words such as the following:

bat mat sat sit spit
pit pat pan pin spin

Consonant sounds in multisyllabic words

Discriminating these sounds helps students attend to consonant sounds in the middle of words.

- Say the word *rib,* and have students repeat it. Ask where they hear the /b/ in *rib.*
- Then say *ribbon,* and ask students where they hear the /b/ in *ribbon.*
- Tell students that you will say some words and that they will repeat each word.
- After they repeat each word, ask what consonant sound they hear in the middle of that word. Use words such as the following:
  famous message picky
  jogger flavor zipper

Phonemic Play

Purpose

Wordplay activities help students focus on and manipulate sounds, thus supporting the idea that words are made of specific sounds that can be taken apart, put together, or changed to make new words. Through wordplay, students gain important knowledge about language.

Procedure

Producing rhymes

Many phonemic play activities focus on producing rhymes. A familiar or easily learned rhyme or song is introduced, and students are encouraged to substitute words or sounds. An example is "Willaby Wallaby Woo," in which students change the rhyming words in the couplet "Willaby Wallaby Woo/ An elephant sat on you" so that the second line ends with a student's name and that the first line ends with a rhyme beginning with *W;* for example, "Willaby Wallaby Wissy/An elephant sat on Missy."

Generate alliterative words

Students can also say as many words as they can think of that begin with a given consonant sound. This is a valuable complement to discrimination activities in which the teacher produces the words and students identify them.

The Alphabetic Principle: How the Alphabet Works

The Alphabetic Principle

Purpose

A major emphasis in the kindergarten program is on letter recognition and attending to sounds. Students need to learn the alphabetic principle: that letters work together in a systematic way to connect spoken language to written words. This understanding is the foundation for reading. Students are not expected to master letter/sound correspondence at the beginning of kindergarten, nor are they expected to blend sounds into words themselves. They are expected to become an "expert" only on their Special Letters as they learn how the alphabet works. Through this introduction to the alphabetic principle, students will have the basic understanding required to work through the alphabet letter by letter, attaching sounds to each.

Key concepts of the alphabetic principle include the following:

- A limited number of letters combine in different ways to make many different words.
- Words are composed of sounds, and letters represent those sounds.
- Anything that can be pronounced can be spelled.
- Letters and sounds can be used to identify words.
- Meaning can be obtained by using letters and sounds to determine words.

Procedures for Kindergarten

The following steps can be used for introducing letters and sounds in kindergarten. These steps may be adapted for students at other grades if they do not understand the alphabetic principle. The tone of these activities should be informal, fun, and fast-paced. The purpose of these activities is to familiarize students with how the alphabet works by having them participate in group play with letters and sounds.

I Can Spell Anything

- Reinforce the idea that anything that can be pronounced can be spelled with the letters of the alphabet.
- Tell students that you can spell any word. Have them give you words to spell.
- Write the words on the board, naming each letter as you write it. This shows students that the words contain the letters displayed on the ***Alphabet Sound Wall Cards.***
- Have students help you spell the words again by pointing to letters as you say them.
- Encourage students to spell each word letter by letter.

The alphabetic principle is the understanding that speech sounds can be mapped onto print.

Letter Expert Groups

- Have ***Alphabet Letter Cards*** (Levels K and 1) available for the following set of letters: *b, d, f, h, l, m, n, p, s, t*. You will need two or three cards for each letter. (You will not need the ***Alphabet Sound Cards*** until later.)
- You will be the letter expert for the vowels.
- Organize the class into groups of two or three, and assign each group a letter. Give each student the appropriate ***Alphabet Letter Card.***
- Tell students that they are now in their Letter Expert groups and that they are going to become experts on their Special Letter's name, shape, and sound.

Making Words

- Begin each lesson with a rehearsal of each group's letter name.
- Demonstrate how letters work by writing a word in large letters on the board.
- Tell students the experts for each letter in the word should hold up their ***Alphabet Letter Cards*** and name the letter. One member of the group should stand in front of their letter on the board.
- Continue until all letters in the word are accounted for. Remember that you are responsible for the vowels.
- Demonstrate that you can make different words by changing a letter or by changing the letter order.

Identifying Sounds in Words

- Use the ***Alphabet Sound Cards*** to demonstrate that every letter has at least one sound.
- Give each student the ***Alphabet Sound Card*** for his or her Special Letter.
- Point out the pictures on the cards. Explain that each card has a picture of something that makes the letter's sound. The picture will help them remember the sound.
- Tell each group the sound for its letter. (Remember, you are the expert for the vowels.)
- Quickly have each group rehearse its letter's name and sound.
- Write a word on the board in large letters. First say the word sound by sound, and then blend the word.
- For each letter/sound in the word, have one student from each Letter Expert group come forward, stand in front of the appropriate letter, and hold his or her card. Although only one member of the group may come forward with the ***Alphabet Letter Card*** or ***Alphabet Sound Card,*** all students in a Special Letter group should say the name or sound of their letter when it occurs in words.
- Say the word again, pointing to the ***Alphabet Sound Cards.***
- Ask students who are not already standing to help you hold the vowel cards.
- Vary the activity by changing one letter sound and having an expert for that letter come forward.

- End the activity for each word by saying the sounds in the words one by one and then saying the entire word. Encourage students to participate.

Tips

- Remind students to use the picture on the ***Alphabet Sound Card*** for their Special Letter to help them remember the letter's sound. Students are expected to "master" only their own Special Letter and to share the information with their classmates. At this point in the year, they are not expected to blend and read the words by themselves. These are group activities in which you work with students to help them gain insight into the alphabet.
- Be sure to connect what students learn about the letters and words to the words they work with in ***Big Book*** selections.
- Occasionally, have students find their special letters in a ***Big Book*** selection. Play some of the letter replacement and rearrangement games with words encountered in the ***Big Books.***

Developing the Alphabetic Principle

Purpose

The alphabetic principle is the understanding that speech sounds can be mapped onto print. It is the association of sounds with letters and the understanding that speech can be turned into print and that print can be turned into speech sounds. Activities associated with the alphabetic principle help kindergarten students develop a more thorough understanding of how sounds "work" in words. In this group of activities, students are introduced to specific letter/sound correspondences, consonants, and short vowels. While students have previously been introduced to vowels and their special characteristics, students' understanding is extended by introducing students to the convention that a vowel has a short sound in addition to its long sound. With this information and a carefully structured set of activities, students can begin to explore and understand the alphabetic principle in a straightforward and thorough manner. Students not only listen for sounds in specified positions in words, they also link sounds to their corresponding letters. The activities in this group of lessons lay the groundwork for students to work their way through the entire alphabet as they learn letter-sound associations and to understand the purpose and the value of this learning.

Move students quickly through these activities. Do not wait for all students to master each letter/sound correspondence before going on. They will have more opportunities to achieve mastery. The goal of these activities is for students to obtain a basic understanding of the alphabetic principle.

Students need to learn the alphabetic principle: that letters work together in a systematic way to connect spoken language to written words. This understanding is the foundation for reading.

Procedures

Introducing Consonant Letters and Sounds

- Point to the ***Alphabet Sound Wall Card*** and ask students what they know about the card (the letter name, the capital and lowercase letter, and so on).
- Turn the card, and point to the picture. Name the picture, and point to and name the letter. Tell students the sound of the letter and how the picture helps them remember the sound. Repeat the sound several times.
- Tell students you will read them the short story or an alliterative sentence to help them remember the sound of the letter. Read the story several times, emphasizing the words with the target sound. Have students join in and say the sound.
- After introducing and reviewing a letter/sound correspondence, summarize the information on the ***Alphabet Sound Wall Card:*** the name of the card, the sound, and the letter.

Generating Words with the Target Sound

Brainstorm to create a list of words that begin with the target sound. Write the words on the board or on a chart. Include any of the students' names that begin with the target sound.

Listening for Initial Sounds

- Give each student an ***Alphabet Letter Card*** for the target sound.
- Point to the picture on the ***Alphabet Sound Wall Card,*** and have students give the sound.
- Tell students to listen for the first sound in each word you say. If it is the target sound, they should hold up their cards. Establish a signal so that students know when to respond.
- Read the list of words, some beginning with the target sound and some beginning with other sounds.

Listening for Final Sounds

The procedure for listening for the final sound of a word is the same as that for listening for the initial sound. Students may need to be reminded throughout the activity to pay attention to the final sound.

Read a list of words, some ending with the target sound and some ending with other sounds. Avoid words that begin with the target sound.

Linking the Sound to the Letter

- **Word Pairs (initial sounds).** Write pairs of words on the board. One of each pair should begin with the target sound. Say the word beginning with the target sound, and ask students to identify it. Remind them to listen for the target sound at the beginning of the word, to think about which letter makes that sound, and to find the word that begins with that letter. For example,
  Target sound: /s/
  Word pair: *fit sit*
  Which word is *sit?*
- **Word Pairs (final sounds).** Follow the same procedure used for initial sounds, and direct students to think about the sound that they hear at the end of the word. Because it is often more difficult

for students to attend to the ending sound, you may need to lead them through several pairs of words. Remind students to listen for the target sound and to think about which letter makes that sound.

- **Writing Letters.** Using either of the handwriting systems outlined in this Program Appendix or the system in use at your school, have students practice writing uppercase and lowercase letters. Remind students about the letter sound, and have them repeat it.

Other activities that support the development of the alphabetic principle include the following:

Comparing Initial Consonant Sounds

This activity is exactly like Listening for Initial Sounds except that students must discriminate between two sounds. They are given ***Alphabet Letter Cards*** for both sounds and must hold up the appropriate card when they hear the sound.

Comparing Final Consonant Sounds

This activity is exactly like Listening for Final Sounds except that students must discriminate between two sounds. They are given ***Alphabet Letter Cards*** for both sounds and must hold up the appropriate card when they hear the sound.

Linking the Consonant Sound to the Letter

In these activities students will link beginning and ending sounds and letters.

- **I'm Thinking of Something That Starts (Ends) with ___ Game.** Begin with the target sound, and add clues until students guess the word. If students give a word that does not begin with the target sound, emphasize the beginning sound, and ask if the word begins with the target sound.
- **Silly Sentences.** Make silly sentences with students that include many words with the target sound. Encourage students to participate by extending the sentences: Mary mopes. Mary mopes on Monday. Mary and Michael mope on Monday in Miami. For older students, have them make silly sentences using the sound at the beginning of their first name. Have them use the dictionary to find more words beginning or ending with the target sound.

Introducing Short-Vowel Sounds

- Tell students that the vowels are printed in red to remind them that they are special letters. (They are not special because they are printed in red.) They are special because they have more than one sound, and every word in English must have a vowel sound.
- Point to the long *Aa* ***Alphabet Sound Wall Card,*** and remind students that this letter is called a vowel. Tell them vowels sometimes say their names in words (for example, *say, day, tray)*. When the vowel says its name, the sound is long. Tell them this vowel sound is called long *a*.
- Have students repeat the sound.
- Tell students sometimes vowels say different sounds. Point to the picture of the lamb on the short *Aa* card, and tell students that *a* also makes the sound heard in the middle of *lamb*. This is the short *a*. Read the short vowel story to help students remember the short *a*.
- Have all students join in saying/a/ /a/ /a/.

Listening for Short-Vowel Sounds Versus Long-Vowel Sounds

- Tell students that you will read words with long *a* and short *a*. Review the two sounds.
- Give students a signal to indicate when they hear the vowel sound. You may want one signal for short *a,* such as scrunching down, and another for long *a,* such as stretching up tall.
- Continue with lists of words such as *add, back, aid, tan, bake,* and *tame.*

Linking the Vowel Sound to the Letter

- **Writing Letters.** Have students practice writing the letter and review the sound of the letter.
- In this activity to help students link sounds and letters, students will make words either by adding initial consonants to selected word parts or by adding a different final consonant to a consonant-vowel-consonant combination. Change the beginning of the word or the word ending, but retain the vowel sound to make new words:

at	hat	mat	pat
ap	map	tap	sap
am	Sam	Pam	ham

Comparing Short-Vowel Sounds

This activity requires students to discriminate between short-vowel sounds in the middle of words. Review the short-vowel sounds.

- Say a word, and have students repeat it. Establish a signal to indicate whether they hear short *a* or short *o* in the middle of the word. For example, they can hold up the appropriate ***Alphabet Letter Card*** when they hear a sound. Sample words: *cap, cot, rat, rot, rack,* and *rock.*

Linking the Sound to the Letter

- In this activity, write a word on the board, and help students say it.
- Change the word by changing the vowel. Help students say the new word, for example, *map, mop; hot, hat; pot, pat.*
- For a variation of this activity, write the pairs of words, and simply have students say which word is the target word. For example, students see *tap* and *top*. Ask which word *top* is, directing students' attention to the vowel.

Introducing Long-Vowel Sounds

The introduction of short vowels and consonants helps students internalize the alphabetic principle—a sound can be mapped onto a letter. In English, however, some sounds are represented by more than one letter, for example, the /ē/ can be represented by the letter *e* as in *me* but also represented by e_e as in *Pete*. Toward the end of kindergarten, students will be introduced to long vowels and two common representations of those sounds. These include the single vowel such as *a* or *e* and the vowel consonant silent *e* (VCe). The introduction of the VCe pattern or unit gives students a wide range of common words to read by the end of kindergarten and sets a solid foundation for first grade.

- If necessary, remind students that vowels are written in red. Point to the long *Aa* card, and tell students that the sound of long *a* is /ā/.

- Have students say the sound with you.
- Tell students that long *a* can be written in more than one way; it can be written as *a* just like short *a* but it can also be written as *a_e*. When we see the blank, it is a clue that another sound and letter needs to be put on the blank or line to make a word.
- Write a_e, and have students give the sound: /ā/. Then write a *t* on the blank, say the sound, and blend the word: *ate*.
- The goal is to have students see the *a_e* or any of the other VCe patterns as a unit.
- While students have been blending and reading short-vowel words, long vowels create a shift in thinking: Combinations of letters can be used to represent a sound. Here are some easy tips when you are first working with the VCe patterns:
  - The VCe patterns are not written on the ***Alphabet Sound Cards.*** You may want to write the *a_e, e_e, i_e, o_e,* and *u_e* units on the respective long-vowel cards as a reminder for students. Do this as you introduce each long vowel unit. Use an erasable marker so you can reintroduce these special patterns each year.
  - Provide maximum support when first using the long-vowel units in blending.
  - Write the letter for the first sound, for example, /m/, and have students give the sound.
  - Write the unit for /ā/: *a_e*. Tell students this says /ā/. Be sure to write the whole unit.
  - Write the final letter ON the blank, for example, *k*. Give the sound for the *k*, and then blend the word.
  - Let students hear your voice during the blending, but gradually reduce it so they are doing more of the thinking.
  - Help students blend long vowel words as they are reading their ***Decodables.***

Tips

- Model and support the activities as necessary until students begin to catch on and can participate with confidence.
- To keep students focused on the various activities, have them tell you the task for each activity. For example, after telling students to listen for final sounds, ask students what they will be listening for.
- Actively involve students by giving them opportunities to tell what they know rather than supplying the information for them. *What is the letter name? What is the sound? What words begin with the sound?*
- Keeping students focused on the idea that they are learning about sounds and letters so they can read books themselves makes the lessons more relevant for students.

Introducing Sounds and Letters

Purpose

In ***SRA Imagine It!*** students learn to relate sounds to letters in kindergarten through the use of thirty-one ***Alphabet Sound Wall Cards.*** In the upper grade levels, ***Sound/Spelling Wall Cards*** (Levels 1–3) are used to relate sounds and spellings. The purpose of the ***Alphabet Sound Wall Cards*** is to remind students of the sounds of the English language and their letter correspondences. These cards are a resource for students to use to remember sound-letter associations for both reading and writing.

Each card contains the capital and small letter and a picture that shows the sound being produced. For instance, the Sausage card introduces the /s/ sound and shows sausages sizzling in a pan. The sound the sausages make sizzling in the pan is /s/ /s/ /s/. The name of the picture on each card contains the target sound at the beginning of the word for the consonants and in the middle for the vowels. Vowel letters are printed in red, and consonants are printed in black. In addition, the picture associates a sound with an action. This action-sound association is introduced through a short, interactive story found in the ***Teacher's Edition,*** in which the pictured object or character "makes" the sound of the letter. Long vowels are represented by a tall—or "long"—picture of the letters themselves rather than by a picture for action-sound association. Short vowels have a green background, and long vowels have a yellow background.

Procedures

- Display Cards 1–26 with the picture sides to the wall. Initially post the first twenty-six cards in alphabetical order so that only the alphabet letters on the back show. The short-vowel cards may be posted as they are introduced later. As you introduce the sound of each letter, you will turn the card to show the picture and the letter on the other side. Because students will be referring to these cards for reading and writing, post them where all students can easily see them.
- Before turning a card, point to the letter. Ask students to tell what they know about the letter. For example, they are likely to know its name if the letter is one with which they have already worked. They might also note that there is an upper- and lowercase for the letter or that the letter is a consonant or a vowel.
- Turn the card, and point to the picture. Tell students the name of the picture (card), and explain that it will help them remember the sound the letter makes.
- Tell students the name and the sound of the letter.
- Read the story that goes with the card. Read it expressively, emphasizing the words with the target sound and the isolated sound when it occurs. Have students join in to produce the sound.

> *The purpose of the **Alphabet Sound Wall Cards** is to remind students of the sounds of the English language and their letter correspondences.*

- Repeat the story a few times, encouraging all students to say the sound along with you.
- Repeat the name of the letter and the sound.
- Follow the story with the cards for the target sound. (These are listed within the lessons.)
- Name each picture, and have students listen for the target sound at the beginning of the word. Ask students to repeat the words and the sound.
- Listening for the sound in different positions in words provides additional work with phonemic awareness. Give each student the letter card for the introduced sound and letter. Read the words from Listening for the Sound, and have students raise their letter card if they hear the target sound at the beginning of the word. For many letters, students will also listen for the sound at the end of words as well.
- To link the sound and the letter, demonstrate how to form the uppercase and lowercase letters by writing on the board or on an overhead transparency. Have students practice forming the letter and saying the sound as they write.

Alphabet Sound Cards

The pictures and letters on the ***Alphabet Sound Wall Cards*** also appear on the small sets of individual ***Alphabet Sound Cards.*** The ***Teacher's Edition*** specifically suggests that you use the individual ***Alphabet Sound Cards*** for Workshop and small-group activities for review, reteaching, and practice sessions. Place sets of the cards in the appropriate Workshop area for students to use alone or with partners. Add each small card to the Activity Center after you have taught the lesson in which the corresponding individual ***Alphabet Sound Card*** is introduced. Here are some suggestions for activities using the individual ***Alphabet Sound Cards:***

1. **Saying sounds from pictures.** The leader flashes pictures as the others say the sound each picture represents.
2. **Saying sounds.** The leader flashes the letters on the cards as the others say the sound that the letters represent.
3. **Naming words from pictures.** The leader flashes pictures. The others say the sound and then say a word beginning with that sound.
4. **Writing letters from the pictures.** Working alone, a student looks at a picture and then writes the letter for the sound that picture represents.
5. **Making words using the pictures.** A student uses the pictures (Sausages, Pig, Timer for *sit*) or the letters to make words.

Tips

- Throughout the beginning lessons, help students remember that vowels are special by reminding them that vowels sometimes say their names in words. For example, tell them the picture of the *a* on the long *a* ***Alphabet Sound Wall Card*** is long because the long *a* says its name. The short *a* ***Alphabet Sound Wall Card*** pictures the lamb because the lamb makes the short *a* sound, and you can hear the sound in the word *lamb.*
- From the very beginning, encourage students to use the ***Alphabet Sound Wall Cards*** as a resource to help them with their work.
- Mastery of letter recognition is the goal students should reach so that they will be prepared to link each letter with its associated sound. If students have not yet mastered the names of the letters, it is important to work with them individually in Workshop, or at other times during the day.
- Both the *Cc* and the *Kk* cards have the same picture—a camera. A camera makes the /k/ sound when it clicks, and the word *camera* begins with the /k/ sound. However, the word *camera* is not spelled with a *k*. Remember, the first sound of the word helps students remember the sound of the letter.
- The picture on the *Qq* card depicts quacking ducks. Make sure that students consistently call them quacking ducks, not ducks, and that they focus on the /kw/ sound.

Explicit, Systematic Phonics

The purpose of phonics instruction is to teach students the association between the sounds of the language and the written symbols—spellings—that have been chosen to represent those sounds.

As with all alphabetic languages, English has a limited number of symbols—twenty-six—that are combined and recombined to make the written language. These written symbols are a visual representation of the speech sounds we use to communicate. This is simply a code. The faster students learn the code and how it works, the faster the whole world of reading opens up to them.

Beginning at the kindergarten level, students are introduced to sounds and letters. Students learn that sounds can be mapped onto letters and that those sounds and letters can be blended to read words.

In Grade 1, students make the shift from mapping sounds onto letters to mapping sounds onto spellings. The introduction of both sounds and letters in kindergarten and the sounds and spellings in Grade 1 is done in a very systematic, sequential manner. This allows students to continually build on what they learned the day before. As each sound/symbol relationship is introduced, students learn about and practice with words containing the target sound and letter in kindergarten and sound/spelling in Grade1. This new knowledge is then reinforced through the use of engaging text specifically written for this purpose.

It can be very difficult for students to hear the individual sounds, or phonemes, that make up words. When phonics instruction is explicit—students are told the sounds associated with the different written symbols—there is no guesswork involved. They know that the sound /b/ is spelled *b*. Therefore, students in an ***SRA Imagine It!*** classroom spend time learning to discriminate individual speech sounds, and then they learn the spellings of those sounds. This systematic, explicit approach affords students the very best chance for early and continuing success.

Sound/Spelling Wall Cards

(Grade 1 on) See The Alphabetic Principle for information on the introduction of sounds and letters in pre-kindergarten and kindergarten.

Purpose

The purpose of the ***Sound/Spelling Wall Cards*** (Levels 1–3) is to remind students of the sounds in English and their spellings. The name of the picture on each card contains the target sound at the beginning of the name for consonants and in the middle for the short vowels. Long vowels are represented by elongated pictures of the vowel. The variant vowels such as /aw/ and /oi/ contain the vowel sound in the name as well. In addition, the picture associates a sound with an action. This association is introduced through an interactive story in which the pictured object or character "makes" the sound. This "action" cue is particularly helpful for students whose primary language is not English. In some cases, the name of the card and the initial sound may be similar to words in other languages. For example, the word for *lion* in Spanish is *león,* which begins with the same sound as the English word. This is not true for other languages. In Russian the word for *lion* is *лев* and in Japanese it is *raion*. The word for *zipper* in Spanish is *cremallera,* in Russian it is *застежка-молния* and in Japanese it is *jippa*. But all students can remember the actions and sounds and use them as a resource for both reading and writing.

The faster students learn the code and how it works, the faster the whole world of reading opens up to them.

Procedure

Posting the Cards

In Grade 1, initially post the first twenty-six cards with the picture to the wall so that only the alphabet letters on the backs show. As you introduce each card, you will turn it to show the picture and the spellings on the front of the card. Some Grade 1 teachers who have students who are familiar with the cards from kindergarten choose to place the first twenty-six cards (the alphabet) with the pictures facing the class. Because students are familiar with the cards and how to use them, this provides support for writing. Even these first-grade teachers, however, cover the spellings not introduced in kindergarten. In second- or third-grade classrooms in which students are reviewing what they learned the year before, place all the cards with the pictures and the spellings facing forward so students can use these as a resource from the beginning of the school year. Make sure that the cards are positioned so that you can touch them with your hand or with a pointer when you refer to them and so that all students can see them easily. The cards should be placed where students can readily see and reference them throughout the day.

Special Devices

- Vowel spellings are printed in red to draw attention to them. It is the vowels and their different spellings that challenge us all. Consonants are printed in black. The blank line in a spelling indicates that a letter will take the place of the blank in a word. For example, the replacement of the blank with *t* in the spelling *a_e* makes the word *ate*. The blank lines may also indicate the position of a spelling in a word or a syllable. The blank in *h_*, for example, means that the sound /h/ spelled *h_* occurs at the beginning of a word or a syllable.
- The blanks in *_ie_* indicate that the *ie* spelling will not come at the beginning or the end of a word or a syllable as in *babies,* while the blank in *_oy* shows that the *oy* spelling comes at the end of a word or a syllable as in *toy*. Uses of blanks in specific spellings are discussed in the lessons. Please note now, however, that when you write a spelling of a sound on

the board or an overhead transparency, you should include the blanks.

- The color of the background behind the spellings also has a meaning. Consonants have a white background. The colors behind vowel spellings are pronunciation clues. Short-vowel spellings have a green background, which corresponds to the green box that appears before some consonant spellings. Thus, before *ck, tch,* or *x,* you will see a green box, which indicates that a short vowel always precedes that spelling. Long-vowel spellings have a yellow background; other vowel spellings such as *r*-controlled vowels, diphthongs, and variant vowels have a blue background. The color code reinforces the idea that vowels are special and have different pronunciations.

Introducing the Sound/Spelling Wall Cards

In first grade, each sound and spelling is introduced by using a see/hear/say/write sequence. In Grades 2 and 3 the same sequence is used in the review of the cards.

1. *See:* Students see the spelling or spellings on the ***Sound/Spelling Wall Card*** and the board or an overhead transparency.
2. *Hear:* Students hear the sound used in words and in isolation in the story. The sound is, of course, related to the picture (and the action) shown on the ***Sound/Spelling Wall Card.***
3. *Say:* Students say the sound.
4. *Write:* Students write the spelling(s) for the sound.

There are a number of important points to remember about this routine.

- Take down the ***Sound/Spelling Wall Card,*** tell the class the name of the card, the sound, and the spelling.
- Read the alliterative story so students hear the sound used in words as well as in isolation, and say the sound.
- After you present the sound and spelling, have several students go to the board to write the spelling. Have them say the sound as they write the spelling. After they have written the spelling of the sound, give them an opportunity to proofread their own work. Then give the other students the opportunity to help with proofreading by noting what is good about the spelling and then suggesting how to make it better.
- Difficulty in blending may be the result of not knowing the sounds or not being able to pronounce the sounds. Teach the sounds thoroughly during the introduction of the ***Sound/Spelling Wall Card*** and during initial sounding and blending. To help ensure success for all students, make certain that every student is able to see the board or screen.

Introducing the Sound /s/ spelled *s*

- Point to the back of ***Sound/Spelling Wall Card*** 19—Sausages, and have students tell you what they know about the card: it is a consonant and there is an upper and lowercase *s* on the card. Turn the card, and tell the class the name of the card: Sausages. Point to the sausages in the picture, and say the word *sausages,* emphasizing the initial consonant sound—*ssssssausages.* Note: teachers usually place a sticky note over the other spellings of /s/—the *ce, ci_,* and *cy*—in order to help students focus on the single spelling being introduced in the lesson.
- Point to the spelling *s.* Tell students that /s/ is spelled *s.*
- Read the alliterative story. In Grades 2 and 3, the stories for the card are printed in the Level Appendix of the ***Teacher's Edition.*** If your students in Grades 2 and 3 are familiar with the cards, have them tell you the name of the card, the sound, and the spelling and tell the story.
- If students had ***SRA Imagine It!*** before, you can ask them if they learned an action to help them remember the sound. If your students do not already have an action they associate with the sound, make some up with your students. They will have fun, and it will be another way for them to remember the sound/spelling relationships.
- Write *s* on the board or on an overhead transparency, and say the sound. Write the spelling again and ask students to say the sound with you as they write the spelling on slates, on paper, or with their index fingers in the air or in the palm of their hands. Repeat this activity several times.
- Have several students come to the board and write the upper- and lowercase spelling while the others continue to write them on slates or with their fingers. Be sure to encourage students to say the sound as they make the spelling. For students writing at the board, take time to have them proofread their work.
- Have students listen for words beginning with /s/, indicating by some signal, such as thumbs-up or thumbs-down, whether they hear the /s/ sound and saying /s/ when they hear it in a word. Repeat with the sound in various positions in words. Encourage students to tell you and the class words with /s/ at the beginning, as well as at the ends of words.
- Check students' learning by pointing to the card. Have students identify the sound, name the spelling, and discuss how the card can help them remember the sound.

Remember that saying the sound, listening to the alliterative story, and listening for the sound (discriminating it from other sounds) in different positions in words are all phonemic awareness activities that have been integrated into phonics.

Individual Sound/Spelling Cards

Use the individual ***Sound/Spelling Cards*** for review and for small-group reteaching and practice sessions. Students can use them alone or with partners. Here are some suggestions for activities using the individual ***Sound/Spelling Cards:***

1. **Saying sounds from pictures.** The leader flashes pictures as the others say the sound each picture represents.
2. **Saying sounds.** The leader flashes the spellings on the cards as the others say the sound that the spellings represent.
3. **Naming spellings from pictures.** The leader flashes pictures. The others name the card, say the sound, and then name as many spellings as they can.
4. **Writing spellings from the pictures.** Working alone, a student looks at a picture and then writes as many spellings for that ***Sound/Spelling Card*** as he or she can remember.
5. **Saying words from pictures.** The leader presents a series of individual cards, for example, Sausages, Lamb, Timer. The others tell the word by blending the sounds represented—*sat.*

Blending

Purpose

The purpose of blending is to teach students a strategy for figuring out unfamiliar words. Initially students will be blending sound by sound as they learn how to blend. After they understand the process, they will move to whole-word blending and develop the strategy they will use to read unfamiliar words. Ultimately students will sound and blend only those words that they cannot read. Eventually the blending process will become quick and comfortable for them.

Procedure

Learning the sounds and their spellings is only the first step in learning to read and write. The second step is learning to blend the sounds into words.

Blending Techniques

Blending lines are written on the board or an overhead transparency as students watch and participate. The lines and sentences should not be written out before class begins. It is through the sound-by-sound blending of the words and the sentences that students learn the blending process.

Sound-by-Sound Blending

- Write the spelling of the first sound in the word. Point to the spelling, and say the sound. For example, the word students will be blending is *sat.*
- Have students say the sound with you as you say the sound again. Write the spelling of the next sound. Point to the spelling, and say the sound. Have students say the sound with you as you say the sound again. After you have written the vowel spelling, blend through the vowel (unless the vowel is the first letter of the word), making the blending motion—a smooth sweeping of the hand beneath the sounds, linking them from left to right, for example, *sa.* As you make the blending motion, make sure that your hand is under the letter that corresponds to the sound you are saying at the moment.
- Write the spelling of the next sound—*t.* Point to the spelling, and have students, say the sound with you as you touch the spelling. If this is the last sound and spelling in the word, then have students blend and read the word—*sat.* If this is not the final sound and spelling, continue pointing to the spelling and asking for the sound. For example, in the word *sand,* you would blend through the vowel then ask for the sounds for the spellings *n* and *d* before blending the word. After pronouncing the final sound in the word, make the blending motion from left to right under the word as you blend the sounds. Then have students blend the word. Let them be the first to pronounce the word normally.
- Ask a student to read the word again naturally, as he or she would say or speak it. Then have a student use it in a sentence. Ask another student to extend the sentence, that is, make it more interesting by giving more information. Help the student by asking an appropriate question about the sentence, using, for example, *How? When? Where?* or *Why?* Continue blending the rest of the words in the blending line. At the end of each line, have students reread the words naturally.

> *Blending is the heart of phonics instruction and the key strategy students must learn to open the world of written language.*

Whole-Word Blending

When students are comfortable with sound-by-sound blending, they are ready for whole-word blending.

- Write the whole word to be blended on the board or display the overhead transparency.
- Ask students to blend the sounds as you point to each spelling.
- Then have students say the whole word.
- Ask students to use the word in a sentence and then to extend the sentence.
- After blending each line, have students read the words naturally, as they would say them.
- When all of the words have been blended, point to words randomly, and ask individuals to read them.

Blending Syllables

In reading the ***Student Readers,*** students will often encounter multisyllabic words. Some students are intimidated by long words, yet many multisyllabic words are easily read by reading and blending the syllables rather than the individual sounds. Beginning in first grade, students will learn about different syllable generalizations, open and closed syllables, consonant *-le*, and the like. Following a set of rules for syllables is difficult because so many of the rules have exceptions. Students need to remember that each syllable in a word contains one vowel sound. Early in the process, you will need to provide support.

- Have students identify the vowel sounds and spellings in the word.
- Have students blend the first syllable sound by sound if necessary or read the first syllable.
- Handle the remaining syllables the same way.
- Have students blend the syllables together to read the word.

Blending Sentences

Blending sentences is the logical extension of blending words. Blending sentences helps students develop fluency, which is critical to comprehension. Encourage students to reread sentences with phrasing and natural intonation.

Write the sentence on the board, underlining any high-frequency sight words—words that students cannot decode either because they are irregular or because they contain sounds or spellings that students have not yet learned or reviewed—or display the transparency. High-frequency sight words are taught before blending. Write the word or words on the board or the overhead transparency, and introduce them before writing the sentence. Read the word, and have students repeat the word then spell the word. Use each word in a sentence. Point to the word or words, and have students read them again. These words should not be blended but read as whole words.

Tips

- The goal of blending in first grade is not to have students blend words sound by sound for the whole year. Sound-by-sound instruction should begin with maximum instructional support—with teachers and students blending together. As students understand the sound-by-sound blending routine, drop the verbal cues (sound, sound, blend, sound, blend), and simply point to the spellings after they are written, and have the class give the sounds.

- How do you know when to move from sound-by-sound to whole-word blending? When you are writing the final spelling and students are reading the word, it is time to move on to whole-word blending. This often occurs around Unit 3 in first grade.
- Keep in mind, however, that when you introduce more complex long-vowel and variant vowel spellings, you can always drop back to sound-by-sound blending for the first couple of blending lines in the lesson.
- Even though the entire class may be doing whole-word blending, sound-by-sound blending is an excellent preteaching tool for students needing extra help. After all the sounds and spellings have been introduced, students may be ready to move just to reading the words in the blending line. Have them read the words, stopping to blend only words they cannot read fluently and automatically.
- In Grades 2 and 3, teachers often begin the phonics review in the Getting Started lessons with sound-by-sound blending and then quickly move into whole-word blending. Again, the goal is to have students reading the words as quickly and automatically as possible. If the majority of the class can do this, then use whole-word blending. Use sound-by-sound blending to preteach the blending lines with students who need more support.

Building for Success

A primary cause of students' blending failure is their failure to understand how to use the ***Sound/Spelling Cards.*** Students need to practice sounds and spellings when the ***Sound/Spelling Cards*** are introduced and during initial blending. They also need to understand that if they are not sure of how to pronounce a spelling, they can check the cards. You may need to lead the group almost constantly. Soon, however, leaders in the group will take over. Watch to see whether any students are having trouble during the blending. Include them in small-group instruction sessions. At that time you may want to use the vowel-first procedure to reteach blending lines.

Extra Help

In working with small groups during Workshop, you may want to use some of the following suggestions to support students who need help with blending.

Vowel-First Blending

Vowel-first blending is an alternative to sound-by-sound and whole-word blending for students who need special help. Used in small-group sessions, this technique helps students who have difficulty with the other two types of blending focus on the most important part of each word—the vowels—and do only one thing at a time. These students are not expected to say a sound and blend it with another at virtually the same time. The steps to use in vowel-first blending follow:

1. Across the board or on an overhead transparency, write the vowel spelling in each of the words in the line. For a short vowel, the line may look like this:
   a a a
   For a long vowel, the line may look like this: *ee ea ea*
2. Point to the spelling as students say the sound for the spelling.
3. Begin blending around the vowels. In front of the first vowel spelling, add the spelling for the beginning sound of the word. Make the blending motion, and have students blend through the vowel, adding a blank to indicate that the word is still incomplete. Repeat this procedure for each partial word in the line until the line looks like this:
   ma__ sa__ pa__
   see__ mea__ tea__
4. Have students blend the partial word again as you make the blending motion, and then add the spelling for the ending sound.
5. Make the blending motion, and have students blend the completed word—for example, *mat* or *seed.*
6. Ask a student to repeat the word and to use it in a sentence. Then have another student extend the sentence.
7. Repeat steps 4, 5, and 6 for each word in the line, which might look like this:
   mat sad pan
   or
   seed meat team

Tips

- In the early lessons, blend with as much direction and dialogue as is necessary for success. Reduce your directions to a minimum as soon as possible. You have made good progress when you no longer have to say, "Sound—Sound—Blend," because students automatically sound and blend as you write.
- Blending is more than just reading words; it is an opportunity to build vocabulary and to develop oral language.

Always ask students to use less familiar words in sentences and then to extend the sentences. This sentence extension is a technique that can be applied to writing as well. Students will naturally extend sentences by adding phrases to the ends of the sentences. Encourage them to add phrases at the beginning or in the middle of the sentence as well.

- Use the vowel-first procedure in small-group preteaching or reteaching sessions with students who are having a lot of trouble with blending. Remember that you must adapt the blending lines in the lessons to the vowel-first method.
- The sight words in the sentences cannot be blended. Students must approach them as sight words to be memorized. If students are having problems reading sight words, tell them the words.
- Cue marks written over the vowels may help students.
  - Straight line cue for long vowels EXAMPLES: āpe, mē, fīne, sō, ūse
  - Curved line cue for short vowels EXAMPLES: căt, pĕt, wĭn, hŏt, tŭg
  - Tent cue for variations of *a* and *o* EXAMPLES: âll, ôff
  - Dot cue for schwa sound with multisyllabic words EXAMPLES: salȧd, planėt, pencil, wagȯn

Dictation and Spelling

Purpose

The purpose of dictation is to teach students to segment words into individual sounds and to spell words by connecting sounds to spellings. In addition, learning dictation gives students a new strategy for reflecting on the sounds they hear in words to help them with their own writing.

As students learn about sounds and spellings, they begin to learn the standard spellings that will enable others to read their writing. As students learn to encode, they develop their visual memory for spelling patterns and words (spelling ability) and hence increase their writing fluency. Reinforcing the association between sounds and spellings and words through dictation gives students a spelling strategy that provides support and reassurance for writing independently. Reflecting on the sounds they hear in words will help students develop writing fluency as they apply the strategy to writing unfamiliar words.

A dictation activity is a learning experience; it is not a test. Students should be encouraged to ask for as much help as they need. The proofreading technique is an integral part of dictation. Students' errors lead to self-correction and, if need be, to reteaching. The dictation activities must not become a frustrating ordeal. Students should receive reinforcement and feedback.

There are two kinds of dictation: Sounds-in-Sequence Dictation and Whole-Word Dictation. The two types differ mainly in the amount of help they give students in spelling the words. The instructions vary for each type.

Procedure

Sounds-in-Sequence Dictation

Sounds-in-Sequence Dictation gives students the opportunity to spell words sound by sound, left to right, checking the spelling of each sound as they write. (Many students write words as they think they hear and say the words, not as the words are actually pronounced or written.)

- Pronounce the first word to be spelled. Use the word in a sentence, and say the word again (word/sentence/word). Have students say the word.
- Tell students to think about the sounds they hear in the word. Ask, "What's the first sound in the word?"
- Have students say the sound.
- Point to the ***Sound/Spelling Card,*** and direct students to check the card. Ask what the spelling is. Students should say the spelling and then write it.
- Proceed in this manner until the word is complete.
- **Proofread.** You can write the word on the board as a model, or have a student do it. Check the work by referring to the ***Sound/Spelling Cards.*** If a word is misspelled, have students circle the word and write it correctly, either above the word or next to it.

Whole-Word Dictation

Whole-Word Dictation gives students the opportunity to practice this spelling strategy with less help from the teacher.

- Pronounce the word, use the word in a sentence, and then repeat the word (word/sentence/word). Have students repeat the word. Tell students to think about the word and each sound in the word. Remind students to check the ***Sound/Spelling Cards*** for spellings and to write the word.
- **Proofread.** Write or have a volunteer write the word on the board as a model. Check the word by referring to the ***Sound/Spelling Cards.***

Sentence Dictation

Writing dictated sentences. Help students apply this spelling strategy to writing sentences. Dictation supports the development of fluent and independent writing. Dictation of a sentence will also help students apply conventions of written language, such as capitalization and punctuation.

- Say the complete sentence aloud.
- Dictate one word at a time, following the procedure for Sounds-in-Sequence Dictation.

Continue this procedure for the rest of the words in the sentence. Remind students to put a period at the end. Then proofread the sentence sound by sound or word by word. When sentences contain sight words, the sight words should be dictated as whole words, not sound by sound. Students should be encouraged to check the high-frequency sight words posted in the room if they are unsure how to spell them. As students learn to write more independently, the whole sentence can be dictated word by word.

Proofreading

Whenever students write, whether at the board or on paper, they should proofread their work. Proofreading is an important technique because it allows students to learn by self-correction, and it gives them an immediate second opportunity for success. It is the same skill students will use as they proofread their writing. Students should proofread by circling—not by erasing—each error. After they circle an error, they should write the correction beside the circle. This type of correction allows you and students to see the error as well as the correct form. Students also can see what needs to be changed and how they have made their own work better.

You may want to have students use a colored pencil to circle and write in the correction. This will make it easier for them to see the changes.

Procedure for Proofreading

- Write—or have a student write—the word or sentence on the board or on an overhead transparency.
- Have the other students tell what is good; for example, it is spelled correctly.
- Have students check their words and identify whether anything can be made better, the word needs to be spelled differently, or the handwriting needs to be improved.
- If there is a mistake, have the student circle it and write it correctly—make it better.
- Have the rest of the class proofread their own work.

The Word Building Game (Grades K and 1)

The major reason for developing writing alongside reading is that reading and writing are complementary communicative processes. Decoding requires that students blend the phonemes together into familiar cohesive words. Spelling requires that students segment familiar cohesive words into separate phonemes. Both help students develop an understanding of how the alphabetic principle works.

The Word Building game gives students a chance to exercise their segmentation abilities and to practice using the sounds and spellings they are learning. The game is a fast-paced activity in which students spell related sets of words with the teacher's guidance. (Each successive word in the list differs from the previous one by one sound.)

For the Word Building game, students use their ***Alphabet Letter Cards*** (Levels K and 1) to build the words. (As an alternative they can use pencil and paper.) You will be writing at the board.

Give students the appropriate ***Alphabet Letter Cards.*** For example, if the list for the Word Building game is *am, at,* and *mat,* they will need their *a, m,* and *t* ***Alphabet Letter Cards.***

- Say the first word, such as *am.* (Use it in a sentence if you wish.) Have students repeat the word. Say the word slowly sound by sound. Tell students to look at the ***Alphabet Sound Cards*** to find the letters that spell the sounds. Touch the first sound's card, in this case the Lamb card, and have students say the sound. Continue the process with the second sound. Write the word on the board while students use their ***Alphabet Letter Cards*** to spell it. Have students compare their words with your word, make changes as needed, and then blend and read the word with you.
- Students will then change the first word to make a different word. Say the next word in the list, (at). Segment the sounds of the word, and have students find the ***Alphabet Letter Cards*** that correspond. Write the new word *(at)* under the first word *(am)* on the board, and have students change their cards to spell the new word. Have them compare their words to yours and make changes as needed. Blend and read the word with students. Continue in a like manner through the word list.

Word Structure

Purpose

As students move into the upper grades, there is a shift from Phonics to Word Structure. Phonology is the study of the sounds that make up words. In the early grades, students learn to map sounds with spellings to read words. However, as students move into the upper grades and encounter more complex and longer words, the understanding of morphology and the morphological units that make up words is important for fluent reading, vocabulary development, and comprehension.

Morphology is the study of Word Structure. Word Structure activities support the development of fluency as students learn to identify and read meaningful chunks of words rather than individual spellings. Word Structure also supports the development of vocabulary as students learn how inflectional endings change a word's tense, number, and so on and how affixes can be added to a base word to create or derive a new but related meaning.

Morphemes are the smallest units that have semantic meaning. Morphemes may be free or bound. A free morpheme can stand alone, such as the words *dog, man,* or *woman.* A bound morpheme, on the other hand, is a unit of meaning that must be combined with another morpheme to make a meaningful word. For example, in *rewrite* the prefix *re-* means "to do again", and in *dogs* the *-s* changes the meaning to plural. Both *re-* and *-s* are bound morphemes because they must combine with other words to create new words.

Learning about word structure helps the reader on several levels. Being able to identify key-word parts not only helps with the pronunciation of longer, unfamiliar words but it also helps with meaning. In Word Structure, students learn how to deconstruct words—to identify the root of the word as well as the affixes. When affixes occur at the beginning of a word, they are called prefixes, and when they occur at the end of a word they are called suffixes. The prefix, root word, and suffix are all morphemes.

In the word *restatement,* there are three morphemes: the prefix *re-,* the root *state* and the suffix *-ment.*

prefix	*root*	*suffix*
re-	*state*	*-ment*

Suffixes, in particular, can impact the root word in different ways. Suffixes such as *-s* and *-ed* can change the tense of a verb; suffixes such as *-s* can change the number of a noun to make it a plural. Derviational morphemes, in contrast, can be added to words to create or derive another word, for example the addition of *-ness* to *sad* creates the new word *sadness,* or the addition of *-ly* changes *sad* to an adverb, *sadly.*

Word structure includes the study of the following:

- **Compound words** are made of two words that combine to form a new word. Compounds can be open or closed.
- **Root words** focus on learning about the basic element of words. Root words are the foundations upon which the meaning of a word is formed. A root may be a real word as in *audio,* meaning "sound," but it can also used with a suffix to become *audible,* changing the noun to an adjective. Although *audible* can have other elements, it does not need other elements to be complete. Most roots, however, do need other elements. Roots such as *duct, anthrop,* and *cred* require affixes to form the words *deduct, anthropology,* and *incredible,* respectively. Knowledge of root words and affixes provides students with critical tools for understanding derived words.
- **Prefixes** include any morpheme that is attached to the beginning of a root or word and changes the meaning of that word. Prefixes do not change the form of the word, only the meaning. Common prefixes include: *con-, com-, ad-, de-, di-, dis-, per-, re-, sub-, hyper-, un-,* and so on as well as numbers *(bi-, tri-, uni-, mono-, octo-,* and so on.)
- **Suffixes** include any morpheme that is attached to the end of a word or root and that changes the meaning of that word. Suffixes often change the function of the word and often require a spelling change in the root as well. For example, the addition of *-ial* to *colony* changes a noun to an adjective.

Common Latin Roots

Aud: auditory, auditorium, inaudible, audible, audition
Dict: dictate, predict, contradict, prediction
Ject: reject, inject, project, object, projection, objection
Port: transport, import, export, portable, support, report
Rupt: rupture, erupt, eruption, disrupt, interruption
Scrib/script: scribe, describe, manuscript, inscription, transcript, description, prescription
Spect: spectator, inspect, inspector, respect, spectacle, spectacular
Struct: structure, construct, instruct, destruction, reconstruction
Tract: tractor, traction, attract, subtraction, extract, retract, attractive
Vis: vision, visual, visit, supervisor, invisible, vista, visualize, visionary

Common Greek Roots

Auto: automatic, autograph, autobiography, automobile
Bio: biology, biography
Graph: graphite, geography, graphic, photograph, phonograph
Hydr: hydrogen, hydrant
Meter: speedometer, odometer, thermometer, metronome
Ology: geology, zoology, phonology
Photo: photography, photocopy, photosynthesis, photogenic
Scope: telescope, stethoscope, microscope, microscopic, periscope
Tele: telephone, television, telegraph
Therm: thermos, thermostat

Other examples of suffixes that change the word form include the following:

- Noun suffixes: *-age, -al, -ance, -ant, -ate, -ee, -ence, -ent, -er, -or, -ar, -ese, -ess, -hood, -ice, -isn, -ist, -ment, -ness, -sion, -tain, -tion, -ure*
- Suffixes that form adjectives: *-able, -al, -er, -est, -ette, -let, -ful, -fully, -ible, -ic, -ical, -ish, -ive, -less, -ous, -some, -worthy*
- Suffixes that form adverbs: *-ly, -wards, -ways, -wide, -wise*
- Suffixes that create verb forms: *-ate, -ed, -en, -ing, -ise, -ize, -yze*
- Inflectional endings are a special set of suffixes that change the number (singular to plural), case, or gender when added to nouns and change tense when added to verbs.

Teaching Word Structure

- ✦ *Have students read the words in a line.
- ✦ Tell students that words can be made of several individual parts.
- ✦ Examine the words in each line for meaningful parts, roots, and affixes.
- ✦ Identify the root or base word, and discuss the meaning.
- ✦ Underline and discuss the meaning of the prefix or suffix or both. If there is a prefix and a suffix, begin with the prefix. Tell students a prefix is a group of letters that is attached to the beginning of a base or root word. These letters have a specific meaning. For example, *un-* means "not" or "the opposite of," *non-* means "not," and *re-* means "again." A suffix is a group of letters that comes at the end of the base or root word and changes the meaning of the word. For example, *-er* changes a verb to a noun or the person doing the action as in *sing* and *singer,* or *-al* or *-ial* change nouns to adjectives as in *colony* and *colonial.*
- ✦ Reassemble the word, thinking about the meaning of the word parts.
- ✦ Say the word.
- ✦ Use the word in a sentence.

*Sometimes students are intimidated by longer words. Understanding syllable breaks helps when reading these longer words. The following chart includes information on syllable "generalizations." These may help your students when reading longer words during Word Structure activities and in the reading.

Word	Break into Syllables	Syllable Generalizations
Puppet	Pup-pet	Closed. If a word has two consonants in the middle, divide the word between the two consonants. The first syllable is closed, and the vowel pronunciation is short.
Music	Mu-sic	Open. If a word has a VCV pattern, break the syllables before the consonant, which makes the first syllable an open syllable and the first vowel long.
Closet	Clos-et	Some VCV patterns have the break after the consonant, which makes the first syllable a closed syllable and the vowel pronunciation short.
Hundred	Hun-dred	When there is a VCCCV pattern, the break is usually between the consonants. The first syllable is closed, and the vowel pronunciation is short.
Coward	Cow-ard	When there are two diphthongs, the syllable break comes between them.
Chaos	Cha-os	When there is a VV pattern, the syllable break comes between the vowels, and the first vowel is usually long.
Handle	Han-dle	Consonant plus *-le.* If a word has an *-le* (or *-el*) at the end, it usually forms a separate syllable and is pronounced with the consonant and /ə/ /l/.
Excitement Reform	Ex-cite-ment Re-form	Prefixes and suffixes are separate syllables.
Entertain Hurdle	En-ter-tain Hur-dle	*R*-controlled vowels. In most syllables where the vowel is followed by an *r,* the vowel sound is *r*-controlled.
Complete	Com-plete	Final *e.* When there is a vowel, consonant, and then an *e* at the end, the vowel before the consonant is pronounced long, and the *e* is silent.

Developing Vocabulary

For students to develop a deeper understanding of words, they should have multiple experiences with them. There are any number of activities that students can do to help them use words and internalize their meanings. The following activities can be used with the whole class or in small groups during Workshop.

- ✦ Give a word, and ask the student to find it in the line and to give a definition.
- ✦ Give a word, and ask the student to add a prefix or a suffix and to tell the meaning of the new word and the new part of speech.
- ✦ If the word is a multiple-meaning word, have the student point to the word, and then have the student give one meaning and use it in a sentence. Then have a second student give another meaning and use it in a sentence. (Be sure that the words that are used are truly multiple-meaning words and not words that can be used as different parts of speech, for example, a verb and a noun that have the same basic meaning.)
- ✦ Give two words, and have the student point to them. Ask what is the difference between these two words. For example, *hot* and *cold* are antonyms. The same could be done for synonyms, homonyms,

and homophones. This gets students to use the vocabulary and do the thinking. Point to two words, and have students tell how they are alike and different. For example, *history, historical,* and *historian* all have the same roots. All three words have a common root, but *history* and *historian* are nouns, and *historical* is an adjective.

- Give students a word, and have them point to the word. If it is a singular noun, have them change it to a plural or vice versa. If it is a verb, have students change the tense, or if it is an adjective, change it into an adverb if appropriate. In all cases, be sure that students spell the new word.
- Give students a word, have them point to and read the word, and then give the part of speech.
- Give a student a word, and have him or her use the word in a sentence. Have the class decide if the sentence truly shows the meaning of the word. For example, if the word is *camouflage,* and the student says, "Animals use camouflage," have the class add to the sentence to show the meaning: "Animals use camouflage to protect themselves from predators."
- Give students a word with a base word, and ask them to point to the word and read it and then to tell the root of the word.
- Give students a word with a Greek or Latin root. Have them point to and read the word, and then have them identify the root. Challenge students to think of other words that have the same root.
- Give students a word with a prefix or suffix. Have a student point to and read the word and then identify the prefix or suffix and tell the meaning of the affix. Then, if appropriate, have the student or a different student replace the affix with a different one and tell the meaning of the new word.
- When appropriate, give students a word, and have them give a synonym or antonym. When appropriate, work on gradations of words. For example, if the word is *hot* then the opposite is *cold.* Gradations would be *hot, warm, tepid, cool, cold.* These kinds of activities expand vocabulary.
- Give two words that are connected in some way, for example, *colony* and *colonial.* Have students come to the board, point to the words, and read them. Then have them tell why or how the words are connected.
- Have students find other words that follow comparable patterns to those taught in the lesson. If *colony, colonial, colonist* is a line in Word Structure, many students could find related nouns and use them with affixes, *(history, historical, historian)*. Challenge students to think more about words.

Tips

- Be sure students understand the limits of structural analysis. The *un-* in *unhappy* is a prefix, but the *un* in *under* and *uncle* is not.
- Help students realize that many words are related and that using their knowledge of a word can help them understand related words.
- Encourage students to use their knowledge of word structure during all reading to clarify unfamiliar words.

Fluency

Fluency is the ability to read or access words effortlessly with seemingly little attention to decoding. Fluent readers decode words not only automatically but accurately. In addition, fluent readers group words into meaningful units, utilize punctuation to guide their voices, and use expression appropriately to help them comprehend what they are reading. Fluent readers also adjust their reading rate as necessary.

To become proficient readers who fully understand what they read, the whole process of decoding must become automatic. Readers need to be so familiar with the sound/spellings, with common meaningful units like prefixes and suffixes and with the most common nondecodable sight words that they automatically process the spellings and word chunks. This enables them to read the word effortlessly and expend most of their energy on comprehending the meaning of the text. Automaticity is a key component of fluency.

The concept of fluency is introduced in the early grades, even before students are reading. When reading aloud, teachers are modeling fluency and using expression and intonation to support meaning. In pre-kindergarten and kindergarten, emergent readers learn about concepts of print that support fluency: learning about spaces and ending punctuation, reading from left to right, and automatically recognizing high-frequency sight words. Students apply this knowledge to reading ***Pre-Decodables.*** These skills are then applied to reading ***Decodables.*** While fluency begins in first grade, many students will continue to need practice in building fluency in second and third grades. Initially students can use the ***SRA Imagine It! Decodable Stories*** in Grades 2 and 3, but fluency practice should include using materials from a variety of different sources, including selections from the ***Student Readers, Leveled Readers,*** and the ***Leveled Science*** and ***Social Studies Readers.*** At all grade levels using ***Pre-Decodables, Decodables, Readers,*** or any other materials, students need to appreciate that fluency is about meaning. Take time to ask questions after students have read, talk about new and interesting words, and discuss any problems students encountered.

Building Fluency: Reading Pre-Decodables (K–1)

Purpose

Pre-Decodables play an important role in students' early literacy development by providing them with meaningful "reading" experiences before they are actually reading on their own and by expanding their awareness of the forms and uses of print. By following along as you read aloud a ***Pre-Decodable,*** students learn about the left-to-right and top-to-bottom progression of print on a page, the clues that indicate the beginnings and endings of sentences, the connections between pictures and words, and important book conventions such as front and back covers, authors' and illustrators' names, title pages, and page numbers.

The ***Pre-Decodables*** provide students with opportunities to apply their growing knowledge of letter names, shapes, and sounds and to become familiar with individual words. In addition, students practice reading high-frequency sight words. The automatic recognition of these words, the identification of ending punctuation, and reading with expression support the development of foundational fluency skills.

Through retelling the story in a ***Pre-Decodable,*** predicting or wondering about what will happen, and asking and responding to questions about the book, students not only learn about the relationship between spoken and written language, they learn to think about what they have read.

About the Pre-Decodables

Each ***Pre-Decodable*** contains a story that engages students' interest as it provides them with opportunities to practice what they are learning in their lessons. These "pre-decodable" stories each contain several high-frequency words that most students already have in their spoken vocabularies and that are a basic part of all meaningful stories. Learning to identify high-frequency words quickly, accurately, and effortlessly is a critical part of students' development as fluent, independent readers. The inside back cover of each ***Pre-Decodable*** contains a list of high-frequency words.

How to Use the Pre-Decodables

- Before reading a ***Pre-Decodable,*** take time to familiarize students with any new high-frequency words in the book and to review previously introduced words. To reinforce the idea that it is important to know these words because they are used so often in print, always point out the words in context. For example, focus students' attention on the words in ***Big Book*** selections or on signs and posters around the classroom.
- Give each student a copy of the book. Tell students that you will read the book together. Hold up your book. Read the title. If the title has a rebus picture, point to it, and tell students what it is. Then point to the word beneath it, and explain that the picture represents that word. Point to and read the names of the author and illustrator, reminding students that an author writes a book, and an illustrator draws the pictures. Page through the book, pointing to and naming the rebus pictures. Have students say the name of each rebus. To avoid confusion, always tell them the exact word that a rebus represents. Do not encourage them to guess at its meaning.
- Allow students time to browse through the book on their own, commenting on what they see in the illustrations and making predictions about what they think the book will be about. Encourage them to comment on anything special they notice about the story, the illustrations, or the words in the book.
- Help students find page 3. Read the book aloud without stopping. As you read, move your hand beneath the words to show the progression of print. Pause at each rebus as you say the word it represents, pointing first to the rebus then to the word beneath it.
- Reread the book. This time, ask students to point to and read the high-frequency words.
- Tell students to follow along in their books as you read the story again. Read the title aloud, and then have students read it with you. Reread page 3. Point to each rebus picture, and ask a volunteer

to "read" it. Point to the word beneath the picture, and remind students that the picture shows what the word is. Continue through each page of the book, calling on volunteers to "read" and stopping as necessary to clarify and help students with words.

- ✦ After reading, answer any questions students might have about the book. Encourage them to discuss the illustrations and to explain what is happening in each one.

Building Fluency: Reading Decodables (K–3)

Purpose

The most urgent task of early reading instruction is to make written thoughts intelligible to students. This requires a balanced approach that includes systematic instruction in phonics as well as experiences with authentic literature. Thus, from the very beginning, ***SRA Imagine It!*** includes the reading of literature. At the beginning of first grade, when students are learning phonics and blending as a tool to access words, the teacher reads aloud. During this time students are working on using comprehension strategies and skills and discussing stories. As students learn to code and blend words, recognize critical sight words, and develop some level of fluency, they take more responsibility for the actual reading of the text.

This program has a systematic instruction in phonics that allows students to begin reading independently. This instruction is supported by ***SRA Imagine It! Decodables.***

About the Decodables

The ***SRA Imagine It! Decodables*** are designed to help students apply, review, and reinforce their expanding knowledge of sound/spelling correspondences. Each story supports instruction in new phonic elements and incorporates elements and words that have been learned earlier. There are eight-page and sixteen-page ***Decodables.*** Grade K has eight-page ***Decodables.*** In Grade 1, the eight-page books focus on the new element introduced in the lesson, while the sixteen-page books review and reinforce the elements that have been taught since the last sixteen-page book. They review sounds from several lessons and provide additional reading practice. Grades 2–3 have eight-page ***Decodable Stories*** in Getting Started, and eight- and sixteen-page stories in Units 1–3 in Grade 3 and Units 1–6 in Grade 2. The primary purpose is to provide practice reading the words. It is important that students also attach meaning to what they are reading. Questions are often included in the ***Teacher's Edition*** to check both understanding and attention to words.

How to use Decodables

Preparing to Read

- ✦ Introduce and write on the board or cards any nondecodable high-frequency or story words introduced or reviewed in the story. Tell students how to pronounce any newly introduced high-frequency words. Then point to each new word, and have students spell and say it. Have them read any previously introduced sight words in the Word Bank list. All the ***SRA Imagine It! Decodables*** contain high-frequency words that may not be decodable. For example, the word *said* is a common high-frequency word that is not decodable. Including words such as *said* makes the language of the story flow smoothly and naturally. Students need to be able to recognize and read these words quickly and smoothly.
- ✦ Read the title. At the beginning of the year, you may need to read the title of the book to students, but as the year goes on, you should have a student read it whenever possible. In Grade 1, selected sixteen-page ***SRA Imagine It! Decodables*** contain two related chapters, each using the same sounds and spellings. In such cases, read the title of the ***Decodable,*** and then point out the two individual chapter titles. Have volunteers read the title of the chapter you are about to read.
- ✦ Browse the story. Have students look through the story, commenting on whatever they notice in the text or illustrations and telling what they think the story will tell them.

Reading the Story

After this browsing, students will read the story a page at a time. Again, these stories are designed to support the learning of sounds and spellings. The focus should not be on comprehension. Students should understand what they are reading, and they should feel free to discuss anything in the story that interests them. Any areas of confusion are discussed and clarified as they arise, as described below.

- ✦ Have students read a page to themselves. Then call on one student or groups of students to read the page aloud, or have the entire group read it aloud.
- ✦ If a student has difficulty with a word that can be blended, help her or him blend the word. Remind the student to check the ***Sound/Spelling Cards*** for help. If a word cannot be blended using the sound/spellings learned so far, pronounce the word for the student.
- ✦ If a student has trouble with a word or sentence, have the reader call on a classmate for help and then continue reading after the word or sentence has been clarified. After something on a page has been clarified or discussed, have a different student reread that page before moving on to the next page.
- ✦ Repeat this procedure for each page.
- ✦ Reread the story twice more, calling on various students to read or reading it in unison. These readings should go more quickly, with fewer stops for clarification.

Responding to the Story

After the story has been read aloud a couple of times, have students respond as follows:

- ✦ Ask students which difficult words they found in the story and how they figured them out. They may mention high-frequency words they did not recognize, words they had to blend, and words whose meanings they did not know.
- ✦ Have students tell about the story, retelling it in their own words, describing what they liked about it, or citing what they found interesting or surprising. Specific suggestions to use are listed in the ***Teacher's Edition.***
- ✦ Questions are often provided in the ***Teacher's Edition.*** They are designed to focus students' attention on the words and not just the pictures. Ask students the questions, and have all students point to the answer in the story rather than having one student respond orally. Having students point to the answers is important. First, it ensures that all students are engaged in finding

the answer, not just one. Second, by pointing to the answer, you know that students know the answer from reading and not just from having heard it read. Third, locating information in a text is an important skill. Finally, by pointing to the answer, you can quickly monitor who is understanding the story and who may still need more support during Workshop.

- Have students reread the story with partners. Circulate among the pairs, listening to individual students read. This allows you to monitor students' reading and to identify any students who may need additional help during Workshop.

Building Fluency beyond Decodables (middle of grade 1 on)

For some students, fluency develops naturally, seemingly without instruction. Other students, however, can benefit from more explicit instruction. There are students who can decode and read words but lack the critical phrasing, intonation, and expression that support meaning. Teach the text characteristics that support fluency, model them for students, and then provide students regular opportunities to practice fluency. Instruction can focus on any or all of the following areas:

- Discuss and model ending punctuation and what this means in terms of expression and intonation. This should be modeled and then discussed with students. Begin with ending punctuation, and then move to internal punctuation such as commas and semicolons. During modeling,
  - pause longer at a period or other ending punctuation.
  - raise your voice at a question mark.
  - use expression when you come to an exclamation point.
  - pause at commas or other internal punctuation such as semicolons.
  - when you come to quotation marks, think of the character and how he or she might say his or her words.
  - pause at an ellipsis.
  - pause at dashes.
- Discuss and model words written in a special way—typographical signals such as underlined words, boldfaced words, or those in all caps—need to be read with expression and changed in intonation for emphasis.
- Talk about reading rate. Oral reading should be done at a normal speaking rate. Students should not be reading so fast that someone listening could not hear the individual words and make sense of what is being read.
- Discuss and model intonation. Let students hear how voices change with different ending punctuation, how voices change when reading dialogue, and how intonation changes with cues from the author. In dialogue, think of the difference between "screamed Jennifer" versus "pleaded Jessie."
- Work on phrase cue boundaries. A good way to teach this is by using an overhead of what students are reading. Mark natural phrase boundaries—for example, clauses, prepositional phrases, subject phrases, verb phrases, and so on, with slashes. For example, *In the summertime,/Josh likes to play baseball/ at the park/down the street from his house.* Have students listen to you read the text, noticing how you paused at the markers. Then have students read the sentences naturally, using the markers as guides. Scaffold the instruction. In the beginning, mark the boundaries, and have students practice reading using the already marked passages. As students become comfortable, have them mark what they are reading with boundary markers. Gradually fade out the markers or slashes.

Fluency develops over time, and students should be given repeated opportunities to practice fluency with a variety of different texts. After students have read a text, take time to go back and discuss any new vocabulary or interesting words that students encountered while reading. Fluency is not an isolated activity; it is about supporting comprehension.

There are a number of techniques for practicing fluency: repeated readings, partner reading, tape-assisted reading, and Reader's Theater. All of these techniques can be done with a variety of different reading materials, including selections from the ***Student Readers,*** the ***Leveled Readers,*** and the ***Science*** and ***Social Studies Leveled Readers.***

- Repeated readings increase reading rate, accuracy, and comprehension by providing students with multiple exposures to words and spelling patterns. In addition, it helps students improve their ability to break sentences into meaningful phrases and to use intonation. It is effective with both older and younger students. Repeated readings involve the students reading segments of text between 50 to 200 words, depending upon students' ability. Students should practice repeated readings with a variety of different text types. While repeated readings can be done with materials from ***SRA Imagine It!*** using segments from science and social studies texts helps students in the upper grades apply their reading knowledge across the curriculum. The goal is to have students read the text fluently and automatically at a per-minute rate commensurate with grade-level norms.
- CD-assisted readings help build confidence and are excellent support for second-language learners. Tape-assisted reading allows students to hear good models of reading and to develop their awareness of phrasing and prosody, or expressive reading. Tapes should provide students with experiences from a variety of text types. Tape selections should be read at approximately 80–100 words per minute by fluent readers with natural intonation, phrasing, and expression. Students read along with the text, aloud or subvocalizing. When the student is comfortable with the text, the student should practice reading the text independently and then read a portion of it to the teacher. The CDs in ***SRA Imagine It!*** can help students develop fluency with selections in the ***Student Readers.***
- Reader's Theater legitimizes practicing fluency because it involves reading a script. While students do not memorize the script the way actors do in a play, they must be able to read the script fluently so the audience—the rest of the class—can enjoy the play. Several students can work together on a single play or playlet. They will need to practice reading the script several times before presenting it to the class. Reader's Theater also provides students with a writing opportunity. They can use a selection from their ***Student Readers,***

write a playlet, and then practice it for Reader's Theater.

- Radio Reading, like Reader's Theater, connects reading aloud to real-life situations. Students, with copies of the text, read aloud in front of the class as if they were news broadcasters. Expository text works particularly well for this. Students can practice, and then once a week, several students can be the radio announcers. Students can also write weekly news reports and read them.
- Partner Reading involves students reading with a partner. They can take turns reading pages or the entire selection. While one student reads, the listening-partner should note misread words and then discuss them with the partner after the reading. If the pairs are reading for one-minute-fluency checks, the nonreading partner can be responsible for timing the reading. Selections should be read multiple times with the goal being that students achieve a higher fluency rate on successive readings.

Assessing Fluency

Fluency should be assessed periodically to determine students' growth and to monitor progess. Listening to students read regularly is key. Fluency assessment should include not just reading rate but decoding accuracy, prosody (phrasing and intonation), and expression. In addition, checks should be done using various text types.

Generally accepted procedures for assessment include the following:

- Use a passage of approximately 250 words at student's reading level. In the first half of first grade, use the appropriate ***Decodable*** in the Practice set. Have two copies—one for the student and one for you to mark.
- Have the student read the passage for one minute. Use a timer, if possible, so you do not have to keep watching a stopwatch or the minute hand on a clock. You can also tape-record the reading. The goal is to have students read the text aloud in a natural way, the way they would speak the words. This is not a race! Use the following scoring conventions. Mark any errors made by the reader.
- Draw a line through any misread word, and count it as an error.
- Circle any words the student omits or refuses to read, and count them as errors.
- Indicate with a caret any extra words the student inserts.
- Draw an arrow between words that student reverses, and count as one error.
- Put two check marks above a word that a student repeats, but do not count it as an error.
- Draw a box around the last word student reads in the one-minute time frame.

To calculate the student's accuracy rate, count the total number of words read in one minute. Subtract the number of errors from the total number of words read, and use that number to find the number of correct words read per minute.

For example, to calculate the rate:

Total words read – errors = words correct per minute

75 words read – 10 errors = 65 words per minute

For example, to calculate the accuracy:

Number of words ÷ the total number of words = percent of accuracy

145 (words correct) ÷ 156 (total number of words) = 93%

Descriptive Statistics for Oral Reading Fluency by Season for Grades 1–6 (Medians)

		Fall	Winter	Spring
Grade	Percentile	WCPM[2]	WCPM	WCPM
1	75		46.75	82
	50		23	53
	25		6	15
2	75	79	100	117
	50	51	72	89
	25	25	42	61
3	75	99	120	137
	50	71	92	107
	25	44	62	78
4	75	119	139	152
	50	94	112	123
	25	68	87	98
5	75	139	156	168
	50	110.25	127	139
	25	85	99	109
6	75	153	167	177
	50	127	140	150
	25	98	111	122

[2]WCPM = words correct per minute

SOURCE
From "Curriculum-Based Oral Reading Fluency Norms for Students in Grades 1 Through 6" (2005) by Jan E. Hasbrouck and Gerald Tindal. *Behavioral Research and Teaching.*

In addition, watch for and note the following:

- Expression
- Ability of the reader to read words in natural syntactic clusters

Assessing accuracy, pace or rate, and expression provide information for instruction.

In addition to the qualitative information, some teachers like to use rubrics in their evaluation of fluency.

- **Level 1:** Reads basically word by word with limited phrasing, little expression. Reading is labored with difficulty in reading words automatically and fluently.
- **Level 2:** Reads in limited phrases of two words, but grouping of words is not natural. There is little or no appropriate expression or intonation.
- **Level 3:** Reads in phrases with most having appropriate breaks. Most of the reading has appropriate expression and intonation. There is limited comprehension.
- **Level 4:** Reads with appropriate phrasing, intonation, and expression and demonstrates understanding of the piece.

Interpreting Fluency Data

First compare the student's number of correct words per minute with accepted fluency norms.

Then examine the student's accuracy percentage. Reading accuracy should remain constant or gradually increase within and between grades until it stabilizes at 90 percent or higher. Compare the student's accuracy percentage after each assessment to ensure that his or her accuracy percentage is holding constant or improving.

Next examine the types of errors the student made, and consider what they mean for instruction.

- Inserting extra words suggest that the student understands what is being read but is reading perhaps impulsively or carelessly.
- Refusing to attempt to read words suggests that the student may be uncertain of his or her abilities, unwilling to take risks, or needs additional work with decoding at the sound/spelling or morpheme level. Look at the words the student does not read. Are they one-syllable words or multisyllabic words?
- Misreading routine CVC and CVCe words suggest that the student may need more work with the sounds and spellings. In some cases, a student may be able to read words with common sounds and spellings but needs more work with long vowels, diphthongs, and diagraphs.
- Looking for patterns in errors is key.
- Using or not using intonation, expression, and phrasing but reading quickly and accurately suggests that students need to think about how words combine to make meaning and how our expression can support understanding.

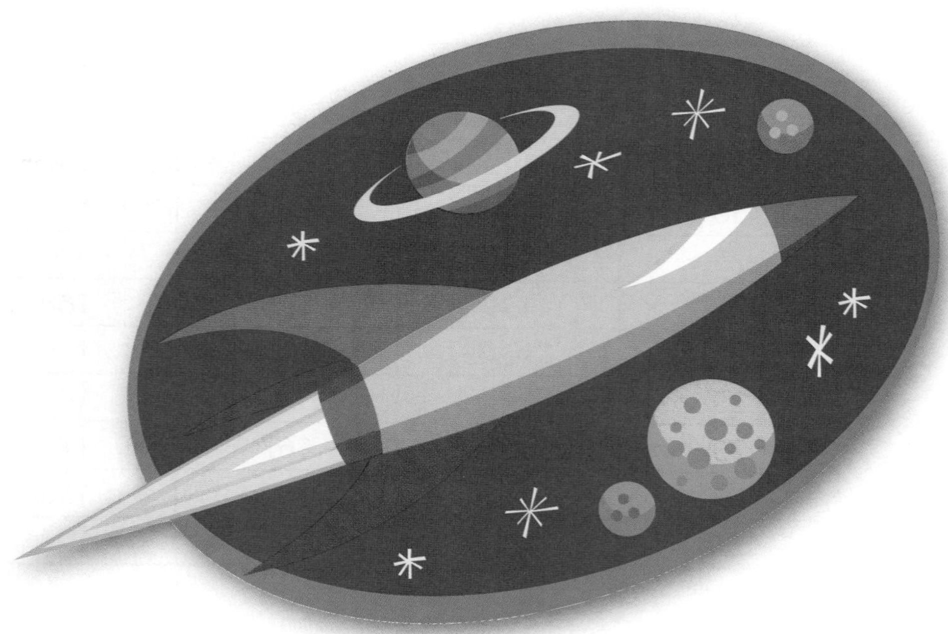

Tips

- Use Workshop time for building fluency. Introduce different ways to practice fluency one at a time.
- Set up a listening area for Workshop that students can use for tape-assisted instruction.
- Make sure ***Pre-Decodables, Decodables,*** and ***Leveled Readers*** are available to students.
- Have simple timers available for students to check their fluency rate.
- Encourage students to chart their fluency growth. If students are doing repeated reading, have them chart the number of words read each day for several days so they can see their fluency improving.
- When students have developed some degree of fluency with a ***Pre-Decodable, Decodable,*** or ***Leveled Reader,*** send the materials home for additional practice.
- Use a range of materials to practice building fluency throughout the day. Remember, fluency practice can be as short as one minute several times a day.

Reading Aloud

Purpose

Adults read aloud a variety of materials to students. In this program there are ***Big Books,*** picture books, novels, and excerpts for reading aloud. Research has shown that students who are read to are more likely to develop the skills they need to read successfully on their own.

In kindergarten and Grade 1, there are ***Big Books.*** In every grade level of ***SRA Imagine It!*** there are opportunities for teachers to read aloud to students. At the beginning of each unit is a Read Aloud selection tied to the unit theme. This Read Aloud selection allows students the opportunity to think about the unit theme before reading selections on their own.

Reading aloud at any age serves multiple purposes. Reading aloud

- provokes students' curiosity about text.
- conveys an awareness that text has meaning.
- demonstrates the various reasons for reading text (to find out about the world, to learn useful new information and new skills, or simply for pleasure).
- exposes students to the "language of literature," which is more complex than the language they ordinarily use and hear.
- provides an opportunity to teach the problem-solving strategies that good readers employ. As students observe you interacting with the text, expressing your own enthusiasm, and modeling your thinking aloud, they perceive these as valid responses and begin to respond to text in similar ways.

Procedures

The following set of general procedures for reading aloud is designed to help you maximize the effectiveness of any Read Aloud session.

- **Read-Aloud sessions.** Set aside time each day to read aloud.
- **Introduce the story.** Tell students that you are going to read a story aloud to them. Tell its title, and briefly comment on the topic. To allow students to anticipate what will happen in the story, be careful not to summarize.
- **Activate prior knowledge.** Ask whether anyone has already heard the story. If so, ask them to see if this version is the same as the one they have heard. If not, activate prior knowledge by saying, "First, let's talk a little about ______." If the story is being read in two (or more) parts, before reading the second part, ask students to recall the first part.
- **Before reading.** Invite students to interrupt your reading if there are any words they do not understand or ideas they find puzzling or to ask questions. Throughout the reading, encourage them to do this.
- **Read the story expressively.** Occasionally react verbally to the story by showing surprise, asking questions, giving an opinion, expressing pleasure, or predicting events. Expressive reading not only supports comprehension but serves as a model for fluency. Think-aloud suggestions are outlined below.
- **Use Comprehension Strategies.** While reading aloud to students, model the use of comprehension strategies in a natural, authentic way. Remember to try to present a variety of ways to respond to text. These include visualizing, asking questions, predicting, making connections, clarifying, and summarizing.
- **Retell.** When you have finished reading the story, call on volunteers to retell it.
- **Discuss.** After reading, discuss with students their own reactions: how the story reminded them of things that have happened to them, what they thought of the story, and what they liked best about the story.
- **Reread.** You may wish to reread the selection on subsequent occasions, focusing the discussion on the unit theme.

Think-Aloud Responses

The following options for modeling thinking aloud will be useful for reading any story aloud. Choose responses that are most appropriate for the selection you are reading.

- React emotionally by showing joy, sadness, amusement, or surprise.
- Ask questions about ideas in the text. This should be done when there are points or ideas that you really do wonder about.
- Identify with characters by comparing them to yourself.
- Show empathy with or sympathy for characters.
- Relate the text to something you already know or something that has happened to you.
- Show interest in the text ideas.
- Question the meaning or clarity of the author's words and ideas.

Questions to Help Students Respond

At reasonable stopping points in reading, ask students general questions to get them to express their own ideas and to focus their attention on the text. These types of generic questions will help students discuss their reactions to the reading and demonstrate their comprehension.

- What do you already know about this?
- What seems really important here? Why do you think so?
- Was there anything that you did not understand? What?
- What did you like best about this?
- What did you not like about this?
- What new ideas did you learn from this?
- What does this make you wonder about?
- What surprised you in the story?

Vocabulary

Purpose

Strong vocabulary skills are correlated to achievement throughout school. The purpose of vocabulary instruction is to introduce students to new words (and ideas) and to teach students a range of strategies for learning, remembering, and incorporating unknown vocabulary words into their existing reading, writing, speaking, and listening vocabularies.

Words chosen for inclusion in ***SRA Imagine It!*** are based upon the vocabulary research of Andrew Biemiller, who has developed a comprehensive database of words students with large vocabularies know by the end of sixth grade. Biemiller's work identifies words that all students need to know and provides evidence that students from various backgrounds acquire these word meanings in roughly the same order. It appears that for students with small vocabularies, improving vocabulary mainly means moving them through the sequence faster. Because vocabulary knowledge is so critical to comprehension, vocabulary instruction is integrated throughout ***SRA Imagine It!***

Vocabulary is taught throughout every part of the lesson.

Part 1: Preparing to Read

- In Grades 2–6, Word Structure develops vocabulary and the understanding that words can be deconstructed and related through known elements to determine meaning. In addition, students are learning about Greek and Latin roots, antonyms, synonyms, and multiple-meaning words. The emphasis on root words and affixes, in particular, serves to expand students' knowledge of words and their vocabulary.
- In Grades K–1, students are using words they blend in sentences to develop vocabulary and oral language. Learning about inflectional endings also helps children see the relationship between root words and various forms of the root. Reviews of blending lines focus on using words based on teacher clues as well as finding synonyms and antonyms.

Part 2: Reading and Responding

- The selection vocabulary instruction in this part of the lesson focuses on teaching specific vocabulary necessary for understanding the literature selection more completely.
- In kindergarten and the first half of Grade 1, the teacher introduces the selection vocabulary orally before reading the selection. Suggestions are made throughout the reading to discuss new and interesting words as the class reads the ***Big Books.*** Work from Biemiller suggests that clarifying words in the context of reading is an effective technique for expanding student vocabulary. Suggestions for which words to stop and clarify are suggested throughout the lessons. Vocabulary review activities are found throughout the lesson.
- From the middle of Grade 1 on, critical word meanings needed to understand the story are pre-taught as students read the Vocabulary Warm-Up in the ***Student Reader.*** This provides an initial exposure to the selection vocabulary. This is followed by guided vocabulary practice in which students discuss the definitions of critical words; learn to apply critical skills such as context, structure and apposition; use the vocabulary words in a variety of activities, and then return to the Vocabulary Warm-Up to reread the sentences containing the vocabulary words and to discuss the words. The clarification of additional vocabulary words is highlighted throughout the reading of each selection. Vocabulary review activities are found throughout the lesson.
- Students write the words and their definitions in their Writer's Notebooks.
- Vocabulary words, along with any other words students find interesting, are posted on charts to remind students to use these words in discussion of their reading as well as in their writing.

Part 3: Language Arts

During writing, students are encouraged to use their new vocabulary.

General Strategies

There is no question that having students read and reading to students are effective vocabulary instructional strategies. Most word learning occurs through exposure to words in listening and reading. Multiple exposures to words, particularly when students hear, see, say, and write words, is also effective. Wordplay, including meaning and dictionary games, helps develop a word consciousness as well.

Vocabulary Strategies for Unknown Words

Different strategies have been shown to be particularly effective for learning completely new words. These strategies are included in the Vocabulary Warm-Up lessons and ***Skills Practice*** activities.

Key Word This strategy involves providing or having students create a mnemonic clue for unknown vocabulary. For example, the word *mole* is defined in chemistry as a "gram molecule." By relating *mole* to *molecule,* students have a key to the meaning of the word.

Definitions Copying a definition from a dictionary is somewhat effective in learning new vocabulary. Combining this with using the word in writing and speaking adds to the effectiveness of this strategy. Requiring students to explain a word or to use it in a novel sentence helps ensure that the meaning is understood. It is not uncommon when students use words in sentences that the meaning of the vocabulary word is not clear. For example, a typical sentence a student might give for the word *camouflage* is "The octopus uses camouflage." The word *camouflage* is correctly used, but there is no real indication that the student knows the meaning of the word. Having students extend the sentence to explain why or how in the sentence helps: "The octopus uses camouflage to protect itself from predators." Or "The camouflage an octopus uses when it is in danger is to change its shape and color."

Context Clues Some words can be inferred from context and can be learned with repeated exposure to words in reading and listening. While using context can be useful, it is not the most effective way to learn new words. Also, as students move into content area reading, context becomes a less effective tool for determining the meaning of unfamiliar words.

- **Syntax** How a word is used in a sentence may provide some clue as to its meaning. This is particularly effective with homographs. "The lead pipe is a hazard to the community." Here lead is an adjective and is pronounced with a short e. In the sentence "He will lead the troops into battle," *lead* has a very different meaning, is a verb, and is pronounced with a long e.
- **Apposition** Sometimes the word is actually defined within the text. In an appositive, the definition of a word is often set off by commas for the reader.

Word Structure Examining the affixes and roots of a word often provides clues to its meaning. Knowing the meaning of at least part of the word can provide a clue as to its meaning. For example, *unenforceable* can be broken down into meaningful word parts. This is a particularly important tool in content area reading.

Developing Vocabulary

Purpose

Vocabulary is closely connected to comprehension. Considerable vocabulary growth occurs incidentally during reading. A clear connection exists between vocabulary development and the amount of reading a person does, and there are strong indications that vocabulary instruction is important and that understanding the meanings of key words helps with comprehension.

In ***SRA Imagine It!*** vocabulary is addressed before, during, and after reading. Before reading, the teacher presents vocabulary words from the selection. Students use skills such as context clues, apposition, and structural analysis to determine the meanings of the words. These selection vocabulary words are not only important to understanding the text but are also high-utility words that can be used in discussing and writing about the unit theme.

During reading, students monitor their understanding of words and text. When they do not understand something, they stop and clarify what they have read. Students will use these same skills—context clues, apposition, structural elements, and so on—to clarify the meanings of additional words encountered while reading. Determining the meanings of words while reading prepares students for the demands of independent reading both in and out of school.

After reading, students review the vocabulary words that they learned before reading the selection. They also review any interesting words that they identified and discussed during reading. Students record in their Writer's Notebooks both the selection vocabulary words and the interesting words they identified during their reading and are encouraged to use both sets of words in discussion and in writing.

Procedure

Before students read the selection, they read the Vocabulary Warm-Up in the ***Student Reader.*** As they read, students use context clues, word structure, or apposition to figure out the highlighted selection vocabulary. If students cannot determine the meaning of a word using one of the skills, they can consult the glossary or dictionary. After reading the Vocabulary Warm-Up, the teacher displays an overhead transparency to review the selection vocabulary.

Below are suggestions for modeling the use of context clues, apposition, or word structure to determine the meaning of a word.

Modeling Using Context Clues

Write the following sentences on the board or on a transparency. Explain to students that they will use context clues, or other words in the sentence, to determine the meaning of the underlined word.

1. Mrs. Frisby must undertake a treacherous journey to take her son some medicine.
2. We took a treacherous walk near a swamp filled with crocodiles.

Have students look for clues in the sentences that might help them understand the meaning of the underlined word. Point out that a good clue in the second sentence is "near a swamp filled with crocodiles." This clue should help them understand that *treacherous* probably has something to do with danger. Guide students until they can give a reasonable definition of *treacherous.* To consolidate understanding of the word, ask another student to use the definition in a sentence.

Modeling Using Apposition

Write the following sentences on the board or on a transparency. Explain to students that they will use apposition to determine the meaning of the underlined word. In apposition, the word is followed by the definition, which is set off by commas.

1. The conductor thought he was an abolitionist, a person who wanted to end slavery.
2. John Brown was a famous abolitionist, a person who wanted to end slavery.

It should be clear to students using apposition that the definition of the word *abolitionist* is "a person who wanted to end slavery."

Modeling Using Word Structure

Write the following sentences on the board or on a transparency. Explain to students that they will use word structure, or parts of the word, to determine the meaning of the underlined word.

1. The strong wind blew Ivan's ship away into uncharted seas.
2. The explorers Lewis and Clark went into uncharted territory.

Have students look at the word *uncharted* and break it into parts: the prefix *un-*, *chart*, and the suffix *-ed*. Students should know that the suffix *un-* means "not" and that the suffix *-ed* usually indicates the past tense of a verb. However, you may need to remind students about the meanings of these affixes. Ask students for the meaning of the word *chart*. Students should know that a chart could be a map or a table. Guide them as they put together the definitions of the word parts: *un-* (not), *charted* (mapped or tabled). They should be able to come up with the definition "not mapped" or "unmapped" or even "unknown." Have them substitute their definition in the sentences to see if the definition makes sense. For instance, the first sentence would read, "The strong wind blew Ivan's ship away into unmapped (or unknown) seas." Confirm with students that the new sentence makes sense, and then repeat the same process for the second sentence.

Everything students learn about phonemic awareness, phonics, word structure and decoding has one primary goal—to help them understand what they are reading. Without comprehension, there is no reading.

Take time to review words and their meanings. Help students connect new words to familiar words. Each unit in ***SRA Imagine It!*** revolves around a theme, and there are key words. In every lesson, there is a concept.

Semantic Mapping Having students create a semantic map of an unknown word after learning its definition helps them learn it. Have students write the new word and then list in a map or web all words they can think of that are related to it.

Semantic Feature Analysis A semantic feature analysis helps students compare and contrast similar types of words within a category to help secure unknown words. Have students chart, for example, the similarities and differences between various types of sports, including new vocabulary such as *lacrosse* and *cricket*.

Reading Comprehension

Purpose

The primary aim of reading is comprehension. Without comprehension, neither intellectual nor emotional responses to reading are possible—other than the response of frustration. Reading is about problem solving. Expert readers bring their critical faculties to bear on everything they read. They generally understand most of what they read, but just as importantly, they recognize when they do not understand, and they have at their command an assortment of strategies for monitoring and furthering their understanding.

The goal of comprehension strategy instruction is to turn responsibility for using strategies over to students as soon as possible. Research has shown that students' comprehension and learning problems are not a matter of mental capacity but rather their inability to use strategies to help them learn. Expert readers use a variety of strategies to help them make sense of the text and to get the most out of what they read. Trained to use a variety of comprehension strategies, students dramatically improve their learning performance. To do this, the teacher models strategy use and gradually incorporates various kinds of prompts and possible student think-alouds as examples of the types of thinking students might do as they read to comprehend what they are reading.

Setting Reading Goals

Even before they begin reading and using comprehension strategies, good readers set reading goals and expectations. Readers who have set their own goals and have definite expectations about the text they are about to read are more engaged in their reading and notice more in what they read. Having determined a purpose for reading, they are better able to evaluate a text and to determine whether it meets their needs. Even when the reading is assigned, the reader's engagement is enhanced when he or she has determined ahead of time what information might be gathered from the selection or how the selection might interest him or her.

Comprehension Strategies

Descriptions of strategies expert readers use to comprehend the text follow.

Good readers continually monitor their speed and ability to understand throughout reading.

Summarizing

Periodically it is important to summarize and check our understanding as we read. Sometimes readers reread to fill in gaps in their understanding. They use the strategy of summarizing to keep track of what they are reading and to focus their minds on important information. The process of putting the information in one's own words not only helps good readers remember what they have read but also prompts them to evaluate how well they understand the information. Sometimes the summary reveals that one's understanding is incomplete, in which case it might be appropriate to reread the previous section to fill in the gaps. The strategy of summarizing is particularly helpful when readers are reading long or complicated text. When to stop and summarize depends on the difficulty of the text as well as the type of text. Often in content area reading, it makes sense to stop and summarize the key ideas after each section. In narratives, the reader often stops to summarize after an episode has been read. Many of us will automatically summarize what has happened if we have put down a book and are about to continue reading it again. Students should think to themselves the following:

- ✦ Does this make sense? What is this selection about?
- ✦ What are the big ideas the writer is trying to get at?
- ✦ What can I delete from my summary? What is not important?
- ✦ Have I said the same thing more than once in my summary?
- ✦ How can I put what I just read into my own words?
- ✦ What is unclear? What is the meaning of the word or sentence? How can I determine this?

Clarifying

Monitoring understanding is key to reading. It allows readers to make sure they understand what they read. They note the characteristics of the text, such as whether it is difficult to read or whether some sections are more challenging or more important than others are. In addition, when readers become aware that they do not understand, they stop and take appropriate action, such as rereading, to understand the text better. As they read, good readers stay alert for problem signs such as loss of concentration, unfamiliar vocabulary, or lack of sufficient background knowledge to comprehend the text. This ability to self-monitor and identify aspects of the text that hinder comprehension is crucial to becoming a proficient reader. Clarifying may occur at the word, the sentence, the paragraph, or at the whole-text level. Students should think to themselves the following:

- ✦ What does not make sense? If it is a word, how can I figure it out? Do I use context, structure, or apposition, or do I need to ask someone or look it up in the dictionary or glossary?
- ✦ What does not make sense? The paragraph is long and full of details. What can I do? I can take some notes, I can reread it more slowly; I can discuss it with someone.
- ✦ These sentences are endless. How can I deal with long, complicated sentences?
- ✦ What is the main idea of what I just read?
- ✦ Can I summarize what I just read?

Asking Questions

Asking questions allows the reader to constantly check his or her understanding and to follow the writer's train of thought. Good readers ask questions that may prepare them for what they will learn. If their questions are not answered in the text, they may try to find answers elsewhere and thus add even more to their store of knowledge. Certain kinds of questions occur naturally to a reader, such as to clear up confusion or to wonder why something in the text is as it is. Intentional readers take this somewhat informal questioning one step further by formulating questions with the specific intent of checking their understanding. They literally test themselves by thinking of questions a teacher might ask and then by determining answers to those questions. Students should think to themselves the following:

- Why is this the way it is? What else is there to know about this?
- What question can I ask to check if I have understood what I just read?
- How does this connect to the unit theme? What new information will I learn?
- What questions do I think the author will answer as I read this selection?
- Do I understand the author? What is not making sense?
- What is interfering with my understanding?

Predicting

Predicting what will happen in the story allows the reader to summarize what has been read so far, to identify clues and events in the text, and to use prior knowledge and personal experience to make inferences about what will happen next. When reading fiction, readers make predictions about what they are reading and then confirm or revise those predictions as they go. Predictions are not wild guesses. They are made based on information provided by the author as well as the reader's background knowledge. Students should think to themselves the following: What do I already know that will help me predict? What are the clues in the text that will help me predict?

- Why was my prediction confirmed?
- Why was my prediction not confirmed?
- What clues did I miss that would have helped me make a better prediction?

The responsibility for using strategies by students should begin as soon as they understand that reading is about problem solving and making sense of text and that these strategies will help them do both.

Making Connections

Making connections between the text and what is known from personal experience or previous reading deepens our understanding of text and expands our understanding. Comprehension is enhanced when we relate what is read to what is known. Students should think to themselves the following:

- What does this remind me of? What else have I read like this?
- What does this remind me of in my own life? In my own experiences?
- How does this connect with other selections I have read?
- How does this connect with what is going on in the world today?

Visualizing

Creating a mental image about the text involves not just the literal interpretation of the author's word but going beyond the literal to incorporating prior knowledge and experiences that deepen understanding. Readers form mental images as they read. They picture the setting, the characters, and the action in a story. Visualizing can also be helpful when reading expository text. Visualizing helps readers understand descriptions of complex activities or processes. When a complex process or an event is being described, the reader can follow the process or the event better by visualizing each step or episode. Sometimes an author or an editor helps the reader by providing illustrations, diagrams, or maps. If no visual aids have been provided, it may help the reader to create one. Creating mental images helps the reader create pictures that can be stored efficiently in his or her long-term memory. Students should think to themselves the following:

- What picture does the words create in my mind? How do the words suggest feelings, actions, and settings?
- Would a drawing help me understand the process?
- How does my mental picture extend beyond the words in the text?
- How did this picture help me understand what I am reading?

Adjusting Reading Speed

Some texts are easy to read; others are more challenging. How difficult a text is to read depends on both author and reader variables. Good readers understand that not all text is equal. Because of this, they continuously monitor what they are reading and adjust their reading speed accordingly. Efficient readers skim parts of the text that are not important or relevant to their reading goals, and they purposely slow down when they encounter difficulty in understanding the text. Students should think to themselves the following:

- When I reread does this make sense?
- This is a long and involved sentence. Rereading may help.

Procedures

Modeling and Thinking Aloud

One of the most effective ways to help students understand and use critical comprehension is to make strategic thinking public. Modeling these behaviors and encouraging students to think aloud as they attempt to address comprehension problems and to understand text can demonstrate for everyone in a class how these behaviors are put into practice. Suggestions for think-alouds are provided throughout the ***Teacher's Edition.***

The most effective models you can offer will be those that come from your own reading experiences. What kinds of questions did you ask yourself? What kinds of things surprised you the first time you read a story? What kinds of new information did you learn? What kinds of things were confusing until you reread or read further? Drawing on these questions and on your students' questions and comments as they read will make the strategic reading process more meaningful to students. Below are suggestions for modeling each of the comprehension strategies.

Before Reading

- **Modeling Setting Reading Goals.** To model setting reading goals, engage students in the following:
  - **Activate prior knowledge.** As you approach a new text, consider aloud what you already know about the subject or what your experiences have been in reading similar material.
  - **Browse the text.** To get an idea of what to expect from a text, look at the title and the illustrations. When students are reading fiction, they will browse the text to look for Clues, Problems and Wonderings. Possible clues will support comprehension—for example, genre, content, author, setting, and so on—potential problems might include things such as difficult words or dense paragraphs as well as unfamiliar concepts; and wonderings are the things students are curious to find out about from their reading— questions about the selection. Wonderings are students' purposes for reading. When students read nonfiction, they will use a KWL chart— this is what I know (K), this is what I want to find out (W), and this is what I have learned (L). Both these activities— Clues, Problems, and Wonderings and KWL—engage students in thinking before reading the selection by having them activate their own background knowledge, identify potential problems, and set purposes for reading. Have students glance quickly at the selection, looking briefly at the illustrations and the print. Have them tell what they think they might be learning about as they read the selection. Early in the year, model the thinking involved with these activities and then begin to turn the responsibility for completing them over to students.

During Reading

Modeling— or thinking aloud— about how to use strategies to solve problems is a powerful tool for teaching comprehension. While think-aloud models are included in all lessons, relate your own thinking and experiences to the lesson and the think-alouds. Early in the process you will need to model thinking about how, when, and why to use the strategies. Encourage students to stop and use them as well; engage them in thinking!

- **Modeling Summarizing.** Just as the strategy of summarizing the plot and then predicting what will happen next can enhance a student's reading of fiction, so too can the same procedure be used to the student's advantage in reading nonfiction. In expository text, it is particularly logical to stop and summarize at the end of a chapter or section before going on to the next. One way to model the valuable exercise of making predictions and at the same time to expand knowledge is to summarize information learned from a piece of expository writing and then to predict what the next step or category will be. Appropriate times to stop and summarize include the following:
  - When a narrative text has covered a long period of time or a number of events
  - When many facts have been presented
  - When an especially critical scene has occurred
  - When a complex process has been described
  - Any time there is the potential for confusion about what has happened or what has been presented in the text
  - When returning to a selection
- **Modeling Clarifying.** A reader may need clarification at any point in the reading. Model this strategy by stopping at points that confuse you or that may confuse your students. Indicate that you are experiencing some confusion and need to stop and make sure you understand what is being read. Difficulty may arise from a challenging or unknown word or phrase. It may also stem from the manner in which the information is presented. Perhaps the author did not supply needed information. As you model this strategy, vary the reasons for stopping to clarify so that students understand that good readers do not simply skip over difficult or confusing material—they stop and determine what they do not understand.
- **Modeling Asking Questions.** Learning to ask productive questions is not an easy task. Students' earliest experiences with this strategy take the form of answering teacher-generated questions. However, students should be able to move fairly quickly to asking questions like those a teacher might ask. Questions that can be answered with a simple *yes* or *no* are not typically very useful for helping them remember and understand what they have read. Many students find it helpful to ask questions beginning with *Who? What? When? Where? How?* and *Why?* As students become more accustomed to asking and answering questions, they will naturally become more adept at phrasing their questions. As their question asking becomes more sophisticated, they progress from simple questions that can be answered with explicit information in the text to questions that require making inferences based on the text.
- **Modeling Predicting.** Predicting can be appropriate at the beginning of a selection—on the basis of the titles and the illustrations—or at any point while reading a selection. At first, your modeling will take the form of speculation about what might happen next, but tell students from the start what clues in the text or illustrations helped you predict to make it clear that predicting is not just guessing. When a student makes a prediction—especially a far-fetched one—ask on what in the selection or in his or her own experience the prediction is based. If the student can back up the prediction, let the prediction stand; otherwise, suggest that the student make another prediction on the basis of what he or she already knows. Often it is appropriate to summarize before making a prediction. This will help students consider what has come before as they make their predictions about what will happen next. When reading aloud, stop whenever a student's prediction has been confirmed or contradicted. Have students tell whether the prediction was correct. If students seem comfortable with the idea of making predictions but rarely do so on their own, encourage them to discuss how to find clues in the text that will help them.

- **Modeling Making Connections.** To model making connections, share with students any thoughts or memories that come to mind as you read the selection. Perhaps a character in a story reminds you of a childhood friend, allowing you to better identify with interactions between characters. Perhaps information in an article on Native American life in the Old West reminds you of an article that you have read on the importance of the bison to Native Americans. Sharing your connections will help students become aware of the dynamic nature of reading and show them another way of being intentional, active learners.
- **Modeling Visualizing.** Model visualizing by describing the mental images that occur to you as you read. A well-described scene is relatively easy to visualize, and if no one does so voluntarily, you may want to prompt students to express their own visualizations. If the author has not provided a description of a scene, but a picture of the scene would make the story more interesting or comprehensible, you might want to model visualizing as follows: "Let's see. The author says that the street was busy, and we know that this story is set during the colonial period. From what I already know about those times, there were no cars, and the roads were different from the roads of today. The street may have been paved with cobblestones. Horses would have been pulling carriages or wagons. I can almost hear the horses' hoofs going clip-clop over the stones." Remind students that different readers may picture the same scene quite differently, which is fine. Every reader responds to a story in her or his own way.
- **Modeling Adjusting Reading Speed.** Just as readers need to monitor for problems, they need to be aware that various texts can be approached in various ways. For example, if reading a story or novel for enjoyment, the reader will typically read at a relaxed speed that is neither so fast as to miss information nor as slow as they might read a textbook. If on the other hand, the reader is reading a textbook, he or she will probably decrease speed to assure understanding and make sure that all important information is read and understood. When modeling this strategy, be sure you indicate why you, as the reader, have chosen to slow down or speed up. Good readers continually monitor their speed and ability to understand throughout reading.

If your students have not previously engaged in the sort of strategic thinking aloud that is promoted throughout ***SRA Imagine It!,*** you will have to do all or most of the modeling at first, but encourage students to participate as soon as possible. Remember, however, the goal is for students to use these strategies independently as they read both in and out of school. In addition to the think-alouds for the teachers, there are also prompts to encourage students to do the thinking. The responsibility for using strategies by students should begin as soon as they understand that reading is about problem solving and making sense of text and that these strategies will help them do both.

Reading Aloud

At the beginning of the year, students should be encouraged to read selections aloud. This practice will help you and them understand some of the challenges posed by the text and how individual students approach these challenges.

Reading aloud helps students build fluency, which in turn will aid their comprehension. Students in Grades K–3 can use ***Decodables*** to build fluency, while students in Grades 4–6 can use the literature from the ***Student Readers. Leveled Readers*** are also available for Grades 1–6. Fluent second graders read between 79 and 117 words per minute with accuracy and understanding, depending on the time of the year (fall/spring). Fluent third graders can be expected to read between 99 and 137 words per minute; fourth (119/152); fifth (139/168); sixth (123/177).

Make sure that you set aside time to hear each student read during the first few days of class—the days devoted to Getting Started are perfect for this—so that you can determine students' abilities and needs. Workshop is also a good time to listen to any students who do not get to read aloud while the class is reading the selection together.

As the year progresses, students should continue reading aloud often, especially with particularly challenging text. Model your own use of strategies, not only to help students better understand how to use strategies but also to help them understand that actively using strategies is something that good, mature readers do constantly.

Most students are unaccustomed to thinking aloud. They will typically stand mute as they try to determine an unfamiliar word or to deal with a confusing passage. When this happens, students should be encouraged to identify specifically with what they are having difficulty. A student might identify a particular word, or he or she may note that the individual words are familiar but that the meaning of the passage is unclear.

Active Response

Not only are good readers active in their reading when they encounter problems, but they respond constantly to whatever they read. In this way they make the text their own. As students read they should be encouraged to

- make as many connections as they can between what they are reading and what they already know.
- visualize passages to help clarify their meanings or simply to picture appealing descriptions.
- ask questions about what they are reading. The questions that go through their minds during reading will help them examine, and thus better understand, the text. Doing so may also interest them in pursuing their own investigations. The questions may also provide a direction for students' research or exploration.
- summarize and make predictions as a check on how well they understand what they are reading.

Tips

- Remember that the goal of all reading is comprehension. If a story or article does not make sense, the reader needs to choose whatever strategies will help make sense of it. If one strategy does not work, the reader should try another.
- Always treat problems encountered in text as interesting learning opportunities rather than something to be avoided or dreaded.
- Encourage students to think aloud about text challenges.
- Encourage students to help each other build meaning from text. Rather than telling each other what a word is or what

a passage means, students should tell each other how they figured out the meanings of challenging words and passages.

- Assure students that these are not the only strategies that can be used while reading. Any strategy that they find helpful in understanding text is a good, useful strategy.
- Encourage students to freely share strategies they have devised on their own. You might want to write these on a large sheet of paper and tape them onto the board.
- An absence of questions does not necessarily indicate that students understand what they are reading. Be especially alert to students who never seem to ask questions. Be sure to spend tutorial time with these students occasionally, and encourage them to discuss specific selections in the context of difficulties they might have encountered and how they solved them as well as their thoughts about unit concepts.
- Observing students' responses to text will enable you to ascertain not only how well they understand a particular selection but also their facility in choosing and applying appropriate strategies. Use the strategy rubrics to evaluate students' understanding of and ability to use the different reading strategies. Take note of the following:
  - Whether the strategies a student uses are effective in the particular situation.
  - Whether the student chooses from a variety of appropriate strategies or uses the same few over and over.
  - Whether the student can explain to classmates which strategies to use in a particular situation and why.
  - Whether the student can identify alternative resources to pursue when the strategies she or he has tried are not effective.
  - Whether students' application of a given strategy is becoming more effective over a period of time.
- Encourage students to use the reading strategies throughout the day in all their reading activities.

Becoming familiar and comfortable with these self-monitoring techniques gives readers the confidence to tackle material that is progressively more difficult. A good, mature reader knows when understanding what he or she is reading is becoming a problem and can take steps to correct the situation. He or she has internalized the strategies, values them, and uses strategies automatically.

Comprehension Skills

Purpose

An important purpose of writing is to communicate thoughts from one person to another. The goal of instruction in reading comprehension skills is to make students aware of the logic behind the structure of a written piece. If the reader can discern the logic of the structure, he or she will be more able to understand the author's logic and to gain knowledge both of the facts and the intent of the selection. By keeping the organization of a piece in mind and considering the author's purpose for writing, the reader can go beyond the actual words on the page and make inferences or draw conclusions based on what was read. Strong, mature readers utilize these "between the lines" skills to get a complete picture of not only what the writer is saying but what the writer is trying to say.

Effective comprehension skills include the following:

Author's Point of View

Point of view involves identifying who is telling the story. If a character in the story is telling the story, that one character describes the action and tells what the other characters are like. This is first-person point of view. In such a story, one character will do the talking and use the pronouns *I, my,* and *me.* All other characters' thoughts, feelings, and emotions will be reported through this one character.

If the story is told in third-person point of view, someone outside the story who is aware of all of the characters' thoughts, feelings, and actions is relating them to the reader. All of the characters are referred to by their names or the pronouns *he/she, him/her,* and *it.*

If students stay aware of who is telling a story, they will know whether they are getting the full picture or the picture of events as seen through the eyes of only one character.

Sequence

The reader cannot make any decisions about relationships or events if he or she has no idea in which order the events take place. The reader needs to pay attention to how the writer is conveying the sequence. Is it simply stated that first this happened and then that happened? Does the writer present the end of the story first and then go back and let the reader know the sequence of events? Knowing what the sequence is and how it is presented helps the reader follow the writer's line of thought.

Fact and Opinion

Learning to distinguish fact from opinion is essential to critical reading and thinking. Students learn what factors need to be present for a statement to be provable. They also learn that an opinion, while not provable itself, should be based on fact. Readers use this knowledge to determine for themselves the validity of the ideas presented in their reading.

Main Idea and Details

An author always has something specific to say to his or her reader. The author may state this main idea in different ways, but the reader should always be able to tell what the writing is about.

To strengthen the main point or main idea of a piece, the author provides details to help the reader understand. For example, the author may use comparison and contrast to make a point, to provide examples, to provide facts, to give opinions, to give descriptions, to give reasons or causes, or to give definitions. The reader needs to know what kinds of details he or she is dealing with before making a judgment about the main idea.

Compare and Contrast

Using comparison and contrast is one of the most common and easiest ways a writer gets his or her reader to understand a subject. Comparing and contrasting unfamiliar thoughts, ideas, or things with familiar thoughts, ideas, and things gives the reader something within his or her own experience base to use in understanding.

Cause and Effect

What made this happen? Why did this character act the way he or she did? Knowing the causes of events helps the reader see the whole story. Using this information to identify the probable outcomes (effects) of events or actions will help the reader anticipate the story or article.

Classify and Categorize

The relationships of actions, events, characters, outcomes, and such in a selection should be clear enough for the reader to see the relationships. Putting like things or ideas together can help the reader understand the relationships set up by the writer.

Author's Purpose

Everything is written for a purpose. That purpose may be to entertain, to persuade, or to inform. Knowing why a piece is written—what purpose the author had for writing the piece—gives the reader an idea of what to expect and perhaps some prior idea of what the author is going to say.

If a writer is writing to entertain, then the reader can generally just relax and let the writer carry him or her away. If, on the other hand, the purpose is to persuade, it will help the reader understand and keep perspective if he or she knows that the purpose is to persuade. The reader can be prepared for whatever argument the writer delivers.

Drawing Conclusions

Often, writers do not directly state everything—they take for granted their audience's ability to "read between the lines." Readers draw conclusions when they take from the text small pieces of information about a character or event and use this information to make a statement about that character or event.

Reality and Fantasy

Students learn to distinguish reality from fantasy as they read different genres, including expository text, realistic fiction, fables, fairy tales, and so on. As students read, they note that a fantasy contains people, animals, and objects that do things that could not happen in the real world. Reality contains people, animals, and objects that can exist and do things in the real world.

Making Inferences

Readers make inferences about characters and events to understand the total picture in a story. When making inferences, readers use information from the text, along with personal experience or knowledge, to gain a deeper understanding of a story event and its implications.

Procedures

Read the Selection

First, have students read the selection using whatever skills they need to help them make sense of the selection. Then discuss the selection to assure that students did, indeed, understand what they read. Talk about any confusion they may have, and make any necessary clarifications.

Reread

Revisiting or rereading a selection allows the reader to note specific techniques that authors use to organize and present information in narratives and expository genres. When students have a basic understanding of the piece, have them reread the selection in whole or in part, concentrating on selected skills. Students learn to appreciate that writers use different structures, for example, cause and effect or compare/contrast, to organize their work and that recognizing these structures can help readers understand what they have read. It is these same structures that students will use in their own writing.

Limit this concentration on specific comprehension/writing skills to one or two that can be clearly identified in the piece. Trying to concentrate on too many things will just confuse students and make it harder for them to identify any of the organizational devices used by the writer. If a piece has many good examples of several different aspects, then go back to the piece several times over a span of days.

Write

Solidify the connection between how an author writes and how readers make sense of a selection by encouraging students to incorporate these organizational devices into their own writing. As they attempt to use these devices, they will get a clearer understanding of how to identify them when they are reading.

Remind students often that the purpose of any skill exercise is to give them tools to use when they are reading and writing. Unless students learn to apply the skills to their own reading—in every area of reading and study—then they are not gaining a full understanding of the purpose of the exercise.

Writing is a complicated process. A writer uses handwriting, spelling, vocabulary, grammar, usage, genre structures, and mechanics skills with ideas to create readable text. In addition, a writer must know how to generate content, or ideas, and understand genre structures to effectively present ideas in writing. Many students never progress beyond producing a written text that duplicates their everyday speech patterns. Mature writers, however, take composition beyond conversation. They understand the importance of audience and purpose for writing. They organize their thoughts, eliminating those that do not advance their main ideas, applying what they have learned in reading, and elaborating on those that do so that their readers can follow a logical progression of ideas in an essay or story. Mature writers also know and can use the conventions of grammar, usage, spelling, and mechanics. They proofread and edit for these conventions, so their readers are not distracted by errors.

Reading Big Books

Purpose

Many students come from homes where they are read to often, but a significant number of other students have not had this valuable experience. ***Big Books*** (Levels K and 1) offer all students crucial opportunities to confirm and expand their knowledge about print and reading, to develop vocabulary, and to enjoy literacy experiences. They are especially useful for shared reading experiences in the early grades.

The benefits of reading ***Big Books*** include engaging even nonreaders in

- unlocking the books' messages.
- developing print awareness.
- participating in good reading behaviors.
- observing what a good reader does: remarking on the illustrations and the title, asking questions about the content and what might happen, making predictions, and clarifying words and ideas.
- promoting the insights about print, for example, that a given word is spelled the same way every time it occurs as high-frequency words are identified.
- reinforcing the correspondence between spoken and written words and spelling patterns.
- enjoying the illustrations and connecting them to the text to help students learn to explore books for enjoyment and information.
- learning about different genre and the language of print.
- developing vocabulary and academic language.
- interpreting and responding to literature and expository text before they can read themselves.

Procedure for Reading Big Books

During the first reading of the ***Big Books,*** you will model reading behaviors and comprehension strategies similar to those that will later apply to their own reading. This focus on strategies encourages students to think about the ideas in the stories, to ask questions, and to learn new vocabulary. During the second reading, you will address print awareness and teach comprehension skills such as classifying and categorizing or sequencing, which help the reader organize information and focus on the specifics in the selection. In addition, you will teach skills such as making inferences and drawing conclusions, which help the reader focus on the deeper meaning of the text. At first, teachers should expect to do all of the reading but should not prevent students from trying to read on their own or from reading words they already know.

- **Activate Prior Knowledge.** Read the title of the selection and the author's and illustrator's names. At the beginning of each ***Big Book,*** read the title of the book and discuss what the whole book is about before going on to reading the first selection. Initiate a brief discussion of any prior knowledge students have that might help them understand the selection.

> **Big Books** *offer all students opportunities to confirm and expand their knowledge about print and reading.*

- **Browse the Selection.** Explain to the class that browsing means to look through the pages of the story to get a general idea of what the story is about, to see what interests them, and to ask questions. Ask students to tell what they think the story might be about just from looking at the illustrations. This conversation should be brief so that students can move on to a prereading discussion of print awareness.
- **Develop Print Awareness.** The focus of browsing the ***Big Books*** is to develop awareness of print. Urge students to tell what words or letters they recognize rather than what they expect the selection to be about.

  To develop print awareness, have students look through the selection page by page and to comment on whatever they notice in the text. Some students may know some of the words, while others may recognize only specific letters or sounds. The key is to get students to look at the print separately from the illustrations even before they have heard the actual text content. This process isolates print awareness so that it is not influenced by content. It also gives you a clearer idea of what your students do or do not know about print.
- **Read Aloud.** Read the selection aloud expressively, using intonation and pauses at punctuation. Not only does this enable students to hear and enjoy the text as it is read through once, it serves as an early model for fluency. Good fluency and expression support comprehension. As you read, you will stop periodically to model behaviors and comprehension strategies that all students will need to develop to become successful readers—for example, asking questions; clarifying unfamiliar words, first by using the pictures and later by using context; or predicting what might happen next.
- **Reread.** Read the selection expressively again. During the second reading of the stories, you will focus on teaching comprehension skills. Also, to develop print awareness, point to each word as it is read, thus demonstrating that text proceeds from left to right and from top to bottom and helping advance the idea that words are individual spoken and written units. Invite students to

identify the rhyming words in a poem or to chime in on repetitive parts of text as you point to the words. Or students can read with you on this second reading, depending on the text. As students' knowledge of words and phonics grows, they can participate in decoding words and reading high-frequency sight words.

- **Discuss Print.** Return to print awareness by encouraging discussion of anything students noticed about the words. Young students should begin to realize that you are reading separate words that are separated by spaces. Later, students will begin to see that each word is made of a group of letters. Students should be encouraged to discuss anything related to the print. For example, you might ask students to point to a word or to count the number of words on a line. Or you might connect the words to the illustrations by pointing to a word and saying it and then asking students to find a picture of that word.
- **Responding.** Responding to a selection is a way of insuring comprehension. Invite students to tell about the story by asking them what they like about the poem or story or calling on a student to explain in his or her own words what the poem or story tells about. Call on others to add to the telling as needed. For nonfiction selections, this discussion might include asking students what they learned about the topic and what they thought was most interesting.

Tips for Using Big Books

- Make sure the entire group is able to see the book clearly while you are reading.
- If some students are able to read words, encourage them to do so during the rereading.
- Encourage students to use their knowledge of print.
- Encourage students' use of academic language as they talk about reading. Students should be comfortable using strategic reading words such as *predict* and *clarify* and book and print words such as *author* and *illustrator.*
- Allow students to look at the ***Big Books*** whenever they wish.
- Provide small versions of the ***Big Books*** for students to browse through and to try to read at their leisure.
- The reader of the ***Big Book*** should try to be part of the collaborative group of learners rather than the leader.

Strategic Reading

Purpose

Reading is a complex process that requires students not only to decode automatically and correctly what they read but also to understand and respond to it. The purpose of this section is to help you identify various reading behaviors used by good readers and to encourage those behaviors in your students.

Reading Behaviors and Comprehension Strategies

There are four basic behaviors that good readers engage in during reading: Setting Reading Goals and Expectations, Responding to Text, Checking Understanding, and Monitoring and Clarifying Unfamiliar Words and Passages. Engaging in these behaviors involves the application of certain comprehension strategies. These strategies are initially modeled while reading the ***Big Books*** (Level K and the first half of Level 1) and ***Student Readers*** (Levels 1–6). The goal of strategy instruction, however, is to ultimately turn over responsibility for using strategies to students so they set their own goals for reading, respond to text, and check their own understanding and solve problems while reading. Students need to take responsibility for doing the thinking and making sense of text.

Setting Reading Goals and Expectations

Good readers set reading goals and expectations before they begin reading. This behavior involves a variety of strategies that will help students prepare to read the text.

- **Activate prior knowledge.** When good readers approach a new text, they consider what they already know about the subject or what their experiences have been in reading similar material.
- **Browse the text.** To get an idea of what to expect from a text, good readers look at the title and the illustrations. They may look for potential problems, such as difficult words. When browsing a unit, have students glance quickly at each selection, looking briefly at the illustrations and the print. Have them tell what they think they might be learning about as they read the unit.
- **Decide what they expect from the text.** When reading for pleasure, good readers anticipate enjoying the story or the language. When reading to learn something, they ask themselves what they expect to find out.

Responding to Text

Good readers are active readers. They interact with text by using the following strategies:

- **Making connections.** Good readers make connections between what they read and what they already know. They pay attention to elements in the text that remind them of their own experiences. Readers make connections to personal experiences, to other stories they have read, and to world knowledge.
- **Visualizing, or picturing.** Good readers visualize what is happening in the text. They not only form mental images as they read but make inferences based on their own experiences. Visualizing goes beyond the words in text. They imagine the setting and the emotions it suggests, they picture the characters and their feelings, and they visualize the action in a story. When reading expository text, good readers picture the objects, processes, or events described. Visualizing helps readers understand descriptions of complex activities or processes.
- **Asking questions.** Good readers ask questions that may prepare them for what they will learn. If their questions are not answered in the text, they may try to find answers elsewhere and thus add even more to their store of knowledge.
- **Predicting.** Good readers predict what will happen next. When reading fiction, they make predictions about what they are reading and then confirm or revise those predictions as they go.
- **Thinking about how the text makes you feel.** Well-written fiction touches readers' emotions; it sparks ideas.

Checking Understanding

One of the most important behaviors good readers exhibit is the refusal to continue reading when something fails to make sense. Good readers continually assess their understanding of the text with strategies such as the following:

- **Interpreting.** As they read, good readers make inferences that help them understand and appreciate what they are reading.
- **Summarizing.** Good readers summarize to check their understanding as they read. Sometimes they reread to fill in gaps in their understanding.
- **Adjusting reading speed.** Good readers monitor their understanding of what they read. They slow down as they come to difficult words and passages. They speed up as they read easier passages.

Monitoring and Clarifying Unfamiliar Words and Passages

Monitoring understanding involves knowing when meaning is breaking down. The reader needs to stop and identify what the problem or source of confusion is. It might be an unfamiliar word, complex and hard-to-understand sentences or unfamiliar concepts that need clarifying. At the word level, the reader might

- apply decoding skills to sound out unknown words.
- apply context clues in text and illustrations to figure out the meanings of words.
- use structural elements to figure out the meaning of the word.
- ask someone the meaning of the word.
- reread the passage to make sure the passage makes sense.
- check a dictionary or the glossary to understand the meanings of words not clarified by clues or rereading.

Complex sentences may require the reader to look for the main idea in the sentence, to pull out clauses that may interfere with the main idea, or to ask for help. When faced with unfamiliar concepts, readers often ask for clarification from someone.

These cognitive activities engage the reader in thinking about text before, during, and after reading. Readers think about text before they read by activating background knowledge, anticipating content, setting purposes, and wondering about the text and what they will learn. During reading, the reader is constantly checking understanding—asking whether what is being read makes sense and constructing conclusions or summary statements. When the text is not making sense, the reader uses strategies to clarify words, ideas, and larger units of text or may reread more slowly for clarification. After reading, the reader reflects on what was read, connecting new information to prior knowledge, evaluating purposes, and connecting the relevance of the new information to the purpose.

Procedures

Modeling and Thinking Aloud

Modeling and encouraging students to think aloud as they attempt to understand text can demonstrate for everyone how reading behaviors are put into practice. Modeling and thinking aloud helps students learn how to process information and learn important content. It is more than asking students questions; it is letting students in on the thinking that helps readers make sense of text, solve problems while reading, and use strategies differentially and intentionally. The most effective models will be those that come from your own reading. As you model the different strategies, let students know what strategy you are using and why you are using it.

Model comprehension strategies in a natural way, and choose questions and comments that fit the text you are reading. Present a variety of ways to respond to text.

- Pose questions that you really do wonder about.
- Identify with characters by comparing them with yourself.
- React emotionally by showing joy, sadness, amusement, or surprise.
- Show empathy with or sympathy for characters.
- Relate the text to something that has happened to you or to something you already know.
- Show interest in the text ideas.
- Question the meaning or clarity of the author's words and ideas.

Encourage Students' Responses and Use of Strategies

Most students will typically remain silent as they try to figure out an unfamiliar word or a confusing passage. Encourage students to identify specifically with what they are having difficulty. When the problem has been identified, ask students to suggest a strategy for dealing with the problem. Remind students to

- treat problems encountered in text as interesting learning opportunities.
- think aloud about text challenges.
- help each other build meaning. Rather than tell what a word is, students should tell how they figured out the meanings of challenging words and passages.
- consider reading a selection again with a partner after reading it once alone. Partner reading provides valuable practice in reading for fluency.
- make as many connections as they can between what they are reading and what they already know.
- visualize to clarify meanings or enjoy descriptions.
- ask questions about what they are reading.
- notice how the text makes them feel.

In addition, using open-ended questions such as the following, as well as your students' questions and comments, will make both the text and the strategic reading process more meaningful to students.

- What kinds of things did you wonder about?
- What kinds of things surprised you?
- What new information did you learn?
- What was confusing until you reread or read further?

Discussion

The more students are able to discuss what they are learning, to voice their confusions, and to compare perceptions of what they are learning, the deeper and more meaningful their learning becomes.

Purpose

Through discussions, students are exposed to points of view different from their own and learn how to express their thoughts and opinions coherently. Through discussion, students add to their own knowledge that of their classmates and learn to explain themselves coherently. They also begin to ask insightful questions that help them better understand what they have read and all that they are learning through their inquiry/research and explorations. The purpose of classroom discussion is to provide a framework for learning.

Procedure

Reflecting on the Selection

After students have finished reading a selection, provide an opportunity for them to engage in discussion about the selection. Students should

- check to see whether the questions they asked before reading as part of Clues, Problems, and Wonderings and KWL (What I Know, What I Want to Know and What I Have Learned) have been answered. Encourage them to discuss whether any unanswered questions should still be answered. If unanswered questions are related to the theme, add those questions to the **Concept/ Question Board.**
- discuss any new questions that have arisen because of the reading. Encourage students to decide which of these questions should go on the **Concept/ Question Board.**
- share what they expected to learn from reading the selection and tell whether expectations were met.
- talk about whatever has come to mind while reading the selection. This discussion should be an informal sharing of impressions of, or opinions about, the selection; it should never take on the aspects of a question-and-answer session about the selection.
- give students ample opportunity to ask questions and to share their thoughts about the selection. Participate as an active member of the group, making your own observations about information in a selection or modeling your own appreciation of a story. Be especially aware of unusual and interesting insights suggested by students so that these insights can be recognized and discussed. To help students learn to keep the discussion student-centered, have each student choose the next speaker instead of handing the discussion back to you.

The purpose of classroom discussion is to provide a framework for learning.

Recording Ideas

As students finish discussions about their reactions to a selection, they should be encouraged to record their thoughts, feelings, reactions, and ideas about the selection or the subject of the selection in their Writer's Notebooks. This will not only help keep the selections fresh in students' minds; it will strengthen their writing abilities and help them learn how to write about their thoughts and feelings.

Students may find that the selection gave them ideas for their own writing, or it could have reminded them of some person or incident in their own lives. Perhaps the selection answered a question that has been on their minds or raised a question they had never thought before. Good, mature writers—especially professional writers—learn the value of recording such thoughts and impressions quickly before they fade. Students should be encouraged to do this also.

Handing Off

Handing off (Levels 1–6) is a method of turning over to students the primary responsibility for controlling discussion. Often, students who are taking responsibility for controlling a discussion tend to have all "turns" go through the teacher. The teacher is the one to whom attention is transferred when a speaker finishes, and the teacher is the one who is expected to call on the next speaker—the result being that the teacher remains the pivotal figure in the discussion.

Having students "hand off" the discussion to other students instead of the teacher encourages them to retain complete control of the discussion and to become more actively involved in the learning process. When a student finishes his or her comments, that student should choose (hand off the discussion to) the next speaker. In this way, students maintain a discussion without relying on the teacher to decide who speaks.

When handing off is in place, the teacher's main roles are to occasionally remind students to hand off, to help students when they get stuck, to encourage them to persevere on a specific point, and to get them back to a discussion, and to monitor the discussion to ensure that everyone gets a chance to contribute. The teacher may say, for example, "Remember, not just boys (or girls)." or "Try to choose someone who has not had a chance to talk yet." It is not unusual early in the process for students to roam from the topic and selection. To bring the discussion back to the topic and selection, be a participant, raise your hand, and ask a question or make a statement that refocuses students' thinking and discussion.

For handing off to work effectively, a seating arrangement that allows students to see one another is essential. It is hard to hold a discussion when students have their backs to each other. A circle or a semicircle is effective. In addition, all students need to have copies of the materials being discussed.

Actively encourage this handing-off process by letting students know that they, not you, are in control of the discussion.

If students want to remember thoughts about, or reactions to, a selection, suggest that they record these in the Response Journal section of their Writer's Notebooks.

Encourage students to record the thoughts, feelings, or reactions that are elicited by any reading they do.

Exploring Concepts within the Selection

To provide an opportunity for collaborative learning and to focus on the concepts, you may want to have students form small groups and spend time discussing what they have learned about the concepts from this selection. Topics may include new information that they have acquired, new ideas that they have had, or new questions that the selection raised.

Students should always base their discussions on postings from the **Concept/ Question Board** as well as on previous discussions of the concept. The small-group discussions should be ongoing throughout the unit; during this time, students should continue to compare and contrast any new information with their previous ideas, opinions, and impressions about the concepts. How does this selection help confirm their ideas? How does it contradict their thinking? How has it changed their outlook?

As students discuss the concepts in small groups, circulate around the room to make sure that each group stays focused upon the selection and the concepts. After students have had some time to discuss the information and the ideas in the selection, encourage each group to formulate some statements about the concept that apply to the selection.

Sharing Ideas about Concepts

Have a representative from each group report and explain the group's ideas to the rest of the class. Then have the class formulate one or more general statements related to the unit concepts and write these statements on the **Concept/Question Board.** As students progress through the unit, they will gain more and more confidence in suggesting additions to the **Concept/Question Board.**

- **Visual Aids** During this part of the discussion, you may find it helpful to use visual aids to help students as they build the connections to the unit concepts. Not all units or concepts will lend themselves to this type of treatment; however, aids such as time lines, charts, graphs, and pictographs may help students see how each new selection adds to their growing knowledge of the concepts.

Encourage students to ask questions about the concepts that the selection may have raised. Have students list on the **Concept/Question Board** those questions that cannot be answered immediately and that they want to explore further.

Through discussions, students are exposed to points of view different from their own and learn how to express their thoughts and opinions coherently.

Exploring Concepts across Selections

As each new selection is read, encourage students to discuss its connection with the other selections and with the unit concepts. Also encourage students to think about selections that they have read from other units and how they relate to the concepts for this unit.

Ultimately, this ability to make connections between past knowledge and new knowledge allows any learner to gain insights into what is being studied. The goal of the work with concepts and the discussions is to help students to start thinking in terms of connections—how is this like what I have learned before? Does this information confirm, contradict, or add a completely different layer to that which I already know about this concept? How can the others in the class have such different ideas than I do when we just read the same selection? Why is so much written about this subject?

Learning to make connections and to delve deeper through self-generated questions and substantive discussions give students the tools they need to become effective, efficient, lifelong learners.

Tips

- Create an environment that facilitates discussion. Have students sit in circles or some other configuration so everyone can see each other.
- When students are discussing the selection, they should have their books with them, and students should feel free to refer to them throughout the discussion.
- Discussions offer a prime opportunity for you to introduce, or seed, new ideas about the concepts. New ideas can come from a variety of sources: Students may draw on their own experiences or on the books or videos they are studying; you may introduce new ideas into the discussion; or you may at times invite experts to speak to the class.
- If students do not mention an important idea that is necessary to the understanding of some larger issue, you may "drop" that idea into the conversation and, indeed, repeat it several times to make sure that it does get picked up. This seeding may be subtle ("I think that might be important here") or quite direct ("This is a big idea, one that we will definitely need to understand and one that we will return to regularly").
- To facilitate this process for each unit, you must be aware of the unit concepts and be able to recognize and reinforce them when they arise spontaneously in discussions. If central unit concepts do not arise naturally, then, and only then, will you seed these ideas by direct modeling. The more you turn over discussions to students, the more

involved they will become, and the more responsibility they will take for their own learning. Make it your goal to become a participant in, rather than the leader of, class discussions.

- Help students see that they are responsible for carrying on the discussion. After a question is asked, always wait instead of jumping in with a comment or an explanation. Although this wait time may be uncomfortable at first, students will come to understand that the discussion is their responsibility and that you will not jump in every time there is a hesitation.
- As the year progresses, students will become more and more adept at conducting and participating in meaningful discussions about what they have read. These discussions will greatly enhance students' understanding of the concepts that they are exploring.

Discussion Starters and Questions

The following examples of discussion starters can be modeled initially, but then the responsibility for using them should be turned over to students. The starters provide the opportunity for open-ended discussions by students.

- I didn't know that . . . .
- Does anyone know . . . .
- I figured out that . . . .
- I liked the part where . . . .
- I'm still confused about . . . .
- This made me think . . . .
- I agree with ______________ because . . . .
- I disagree with ______________ because . . . .
- The reason I think _________ is . . .
- I found _______ interesting because. . . .
- I learned . . .
- What I learned in this selection reminds me of what we read in _________ because . . .
- This author's writing reminds me of . . .
- I had problems understanding _______ because . . .
- I wonder why the author chose to . . .
- I still do not understand . . .
- I was surprised to find out . . .
- I like the way the author developed the character by . . .
- The author made the story really come alive by . . .

In addition to these open-ended discussion starters, students should be encouraged to ask open-ended questions. When students ask questions, other students should respond to the question before moving on to another idea or topic. One student asking a question often helps to clarify something for the whole class and places a value on asking questions as a critical part of learning.

- Why did the author . . .?
- What did the author mean when he or she wrote . . . ?
- Who can help me clarify . . . ?
- Who can help me figure out . . . ?
- How does this piece connect to the unit theme?
- What does this section mean?

Writing

Purpose

The writing program in ***SRA Imagine It!*** teaches students how to write skillfully. This is essential, as writing is a powerful tool that fosters learning, communication, creativity, and self-discovery. ***SRA Imagine It!*** writing teaches students how to use writing effectively for these purposes.

Writing is a complex process. It involves deftly juggling a variety of skills, strategies, and knowledge. Writers must make plans, consider the reader, draw ideas from memory, develop new ideas, organize thoughts, consider the conventions of the genre, translate ideas into words, craft sentences, evaluate decisions, make needed revisions, transcribe words into correctly spelled print, and monitor the writing process, among other things.

SRA Imagine It! writing is designed to ensure that students acquire the skills, knowledge, strategies, and dispositions they need to become skilled writers. This includes the following:

- Knowledge about the qualities of good writing, characteristics of different genres, intended audience, and writing topics. Skilled writers know how to obtain information about their topics, are familiar with basic features of different genres, and possess basic schemas or frameworks for accomplishing common writing tasks.
- The writing strategies involved in basic composing processes such as prewriting, drafting, monitoring, evaluating, revising, editing/proofreading, and publishing. Skilled writers flexibly employ these strategies to create text.
- Command of basic writing skills such as handwriting, spelling, sentence construction, grammar, and usage. Skilled writers execute these basic writing skills with little conscious effort.
- Interest and motivation to write as well as perceptions of competence as a writer. Skilled writers possess an "I can do" attitude.

Procedures

With ***SRA Imagine It!*** writing, evidence-based practices are used to teach students to write skillfully. These evidence-based practices are drawn from research on the effectiveness of specific writing interventions that show that the quality of students' writing can be improved by

- explicitly teaching strategies for prewriting, drafting, revising, editing/proofreading, and publishing.
- modeling effective use of writing strategies.

*Children start school wanting to learn how to write and enjoying writing. The goal of **SRA Imagine It!** writing is for children to become lifelong writers—people who enjoy writing and use writing effectively at work as well as in their personal lives.*

- having students work together to prewrite, draft, revise, edit/proofread, and publish their compositions.
- using prewriting tools such as graphic organizers to gather information.
- involving students in inquiry activities designed to help them further develop their ideas for writing.
- making the goals for writing assignments clear and specific.
- teaching students how to construct more sophisticated sentences.
- providing students with the opportunity to read, evaluate, and emulate models of good writing.
- teaching students how to use word processing as a tool for composing.

The evidence-based practices in ***SRA Imagine It!*** are also based on the study of expert teachers who

- make sure their students are engaged, spending most of their writing time doing something that involves thoughtfulness, such as crafting a story or learning how to construct a complex sentence.
- teach basic writing skills, strategies, and knowledge balanced by ample opportunity to apply what is learned.
- involve students in writing for a variety of different purposes.
- create a writing classroom environment that is supportive, pleasant, and motivating.
- encourage students to accomplish as much as possible on their own (to act in a self-regulated fashion), but who are ready to offer support and instruction as needed.
- use reading to support writing development and vice versa.
- monitor students' growth in writing and encourage students to monitor their own growth.
- provide extra assistance to students who experience difficulty.
- are passionate about writing.

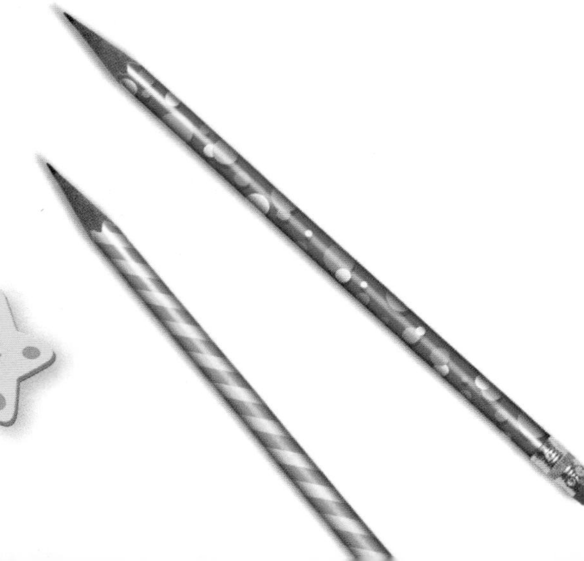

Knowledge about Writing

Purpose

Writing can be used to communicate, entertain, inform, reflect, persuade, and learn. To take full advantage of this flexible tool, students must acquire knowledge about the qualities of good writing and the various purposes and forms of writing. They must also carefully consider their audience and be knowledgeable about the topics they write about.

Procedures

Qualities of Good Writing

One way students learn about the qualities of good writing is by directly teaching them that good writing is characterized by the following seven traits:

- Clearly presented and fully developed ideas
- Writing that is easy to follow and logically organized
- Effective and precise word choice
- Varied use of sentence structure to promote fluency, rhythm, and natural speech patterns
- Writing that captures appropriate tone or mood to make the desired impact on the reader
- Correct spelling, usage, and grammar
- A written product that is legible, attractive, and accessible

For each writing assignment, teachers concentrate on one or more of these traits, teaching students strategies for enhancing the trait(s) in their writing. For example, students are taught to circle words that are vague in their writing and to replace them with more precise ones.

Another way that students learn about the qualities of good writing is through reading. The reading material in ***SRA Imagine It!*** provides concrete models that illustrate the characteristics of good writing, such as how authors

- present, develop, and organize ideas.
- use words to evoke specific images and feelings.
- manipulate sentences to speed up or slow down the flow of text.
- set and change the mood to match the action of the characters.
- use illustrations to reinforce and sharpen readers' understanding.

This knowledge is fostered in ***SRA Imagine It!*** through Reading with a Writer's Eye. Teachers and students discuss what the author of a reading selection did to achieve certain purposes. For example, after reading a mystery, the class discusses how the author planted a false lead to make the story more interesting and complex. Students are then encouraged to use the same technique in a mystery they write.

Different Purposes and Forms of Writing

Students learn the purposes and forms of a wide range of genres they need to master for success both in and out of school. This includes using writing to do the following:

- Communicate with others (personal letters, business letters, notes, cards, and e-mail)
- Create personal narratives (journal writing, autobiography, writing about a personal event, and so on)
- Entertain (stories, plays, poems, and so on)
- Learn (learning logs, reports, journal entries, summarizing, and biographies)
- Inform (writing lists, explaining how to do something, describing objects or places, describing events, news reports, reports, and biographies)
- Respond to literature (book evaluations, book reports, and book reviews)
- Persuade (advertisements, opinions about controversial topics)
- Demonstrate knowledge (for example, traditional classroom tests, high-stakes tests involving writing, high-stakes tests involving multiple-choice answers)

In ***SRA Imagine It!*** writing, students learn to write stories, poetry, plays, journal entries, summaries, book reviews, informative reports, descriptions, explanations, letters, critiques, and e-mail. They also use these various forms of writing to gather, think about, and report what they have learned when doing extended Inquiry projects.

One way they learn about the purposes and forms of these various genres is through the use of models of each type of writing. As students begin working on a new genre, the class analyzes an exemplary model of this type of writing to determine its characteristics and functions. They are encouraged to incorporate these features in their writing. In addition, what they write is frequently tied to what they read, so their reading material provides a model and source of information on the purpose and form of their writing.

Students are also asked to carefully consider the purpose for each of their compositions and include this determination as part of the planning process. As they plan, the form and purpose of their compositions is further emphasized through the use of graphic organizers, in which students typically generate and organize ideas for each of the basic elements included in the type of composition they are composing.

Knowledge of Writing Topics

To write well, students must have something to write about. Good writers typically know a lot about their topics or have strategies for acquiring such information. With ***SRA Imagine It!*** writing, students are taught effective strategies for gathering information to write about. This includes how to

- locate information in written and electronic sources.
- obtain information through interviews or surveys.
- summarize information in notes.
- reference informational sources.

Developing a Sense of Audience

While writing is often viewed as a solitary activity, it is typically meant to be read by others. Children and adults most often use writing to communicate, persuade, or inform others. Because the writer is usually not present when the composition is read, he or she must carefully consider the needs of the readers. ***SRA Imagine It!*** writing helps students develop a sense of audience by asking them to identify their audience when they write collaboratively or independently. Students are also encouraged to share what they write with their peers and others. The following are procedures for presenting and sharing:

- Before presenting, have the writer
  - decide what will be shared.
  - practice what will be shared.
- During presenting,
  - have the writer tell what is to be shared and why.

- have the writer read aloud his or her work or idea.
- remind students to listen carefully.

✦ After presenting,

- have students tell what they like.
- have students offer the writer helpful suggestions.
- take notes of students' comments to share with the writer.

Tips

✦ Have students keep a log of new information they have learned about the attributes of good writing.

✦ Develop wall charts that specify the purpose and attributes of specific writing genres.

✦ Ask students to evaluate their writing and the writing of others based on seven traits of good writing.

✦ Before students begin work on a writing assignment, hold a class discussion on the topic to share information, clarify misperceptions, and identify information students still need to locate.

Mastering the Writing Process

Purpose

To write skillfully, young writers must master the basic processes involved in writing. These processes include the strategic "know-how" involved in writing and include the following:

✦ **Prewriting:** Writers spend time thinking about and planning their topics. They consider their purposes, audience, and the focus of their topics. Writers make plans to guide the composing process, establishing goals for what to do and say. They gather possible ideas for their writing, drawing on memory and external sources such as books, interviews, articles, and the Internet. Writers make decisions about which information to include and how to organize it.

✦ **Drafting:** Writers draft or put their ideas into words, using the initial plans they developed as a guide. These plans are expanded, modified, and even reworked as writers create a first draft of their composition, often in a rough form.

✦ **Revising:** While some revising may occur during prewriting and drafting, writers revisit and revise their first drafts. They reread them to see whether the drafts say what the writers intended. Writers check to be sure the drafts make sense and that the meaning is clear for the audience. They consider whether their writing will have the desired impact on the audience. As they make changes in their text, they discover new things to say and new ways to present their ideas.

Writers need feedback throughout the writing process. Feedback is one of our most powerful tools for helping developing writers.

✦ **Editing/Proofreading:** Writers edit/proofread their work. They recognize that spelling, grammar, and usage errors make it harder for others to understand and enjoy their published work. Writers know that readers are more likely to value their message when they correct these mistakes.

✦ **Publishing:** Writers share their writing by reading their entire work, or part of their work, to others. They publish their work in books, newspapers, magazines, anthologies, and so on.

Skilled writers move back and forth through these processes—from prewriting to drafting to revising and back—to create their final pieces.

Procedures

Much of what happens during writing is not visible. It occurs inside the writer's head. ***SRA Imagine It!*** writing makes the processes involved in writing concrete and visible in the following four ways:

✦ Establishing a predictable writing routine during which students are expected to prewrite, draft, revise, edit/proofread, and publish.

✦ Using graphic organizers and revising, editing/proofreading, and publishing checklists that help developing writers carry out basic writing processes.

✦ Teaching strategies for prewriting, drafting, revising, editing/proofreading, and publishing.

✦ Providing feedback throughout the writing process through writing conferences and students' presentation of their works in progress and completed compositions.

Establishing a Predictable Writing Routine

One way to make the basic writing processes more concrete is to create a predictable classroom writing routine, during which students plan, draft, revise, edit, proofread, and publish their work. This establishes that these processes are important and ensures that time is provided for each process. It also allows students to work with minimum teacher direction and at their own pace.

Tips

✦ Guide students through the steps of the writing routine. Model each step of prewriting, drafting, revising, editing/proofreading, and publishing.

✦ Make sure students learn that the processes of writing do not always occur in the same order but are recursive. For example, revising may occur at any stage of the composing process. You should not only model this by showing how this is done, but the predictable routine should vary at times to reflect this flexibility.

Using Graphic Organizers and Revising, Editing/Proofreading, and Publishing Checklists

Graphic organizers and revising, editing/proofreading, and publishing checklists provide students with assistance in carrying out the thinking activities involved in a writing assignment. They provide structure and information for how to carry out the process. The graphic organizer typically includes a series of prompts that ask the student to think about the purpose for writing a particular piece and the intended audience. It also provides prompts designed to help the student generate and organize possible writing ideas. This frequently involves generating possible content for each part of the target composition. The revising, editing/proofreading, and publishing checklists direct students' attention to specific features or aspects of text that would be useful to consider while writing.

Tips

It is important to be sure that students understand how to use graphic organizers and revising, editing/proofreading, and publishing checklists. Be sure to

- explain the purpose of the graphic organizer or revising, editing/proofreading, and publishing checklist.
- describe how students are to use the graphic organizer or revising, editing/proofreading, and publishing checklist.
- model aloud how to carry out the basic activities on the graphic organizer or revising, editing/proofreading, and publishing checklist.
- make sure students understand each part of the graphic organizer or revising, editing/proofreading, and publishing checklist.

Teaching Strategies for Carrying Out Basic Writing Processes

A strategy involves a series of actions a writer undertakes to achieve a desired goal. In ***SRA Imagine It!*** students are taught strategies to help them carry out each of the basic writing processes—prewriting, drafting, revising, editing/proofreading, and publishing. Each strategy is also designed to enhance one or more of the seven traits of good writing. These include clearly presented and fully developed ideas; writing that is easy to follow and logically organized; effective and precise word choice; varied use of sentences to promote fluency, rhythm, and natural speech patterns; writing that captures appropriate tone or mood to make maximum impact on readers; correct spelling, usage, and grammar; and a written product that is legible, attractive, and accessible.

The goal is for students to be able to use the strategy independently and to make it part of their writing tool kit. The steps for teaching writing strategies are to

- describe the strategy.
- tell why the strategy is important.
- tell students when they should use the strategy.
- model how to use the strategy when writing, making your thoughts visible by saying aloud each thing you are doing and thinking.
- make sure students understand why the strategy is important, when to apply it, and how to use it.
- provide students with assistance in applying the strategy until they can do it on their own.
- remind students to use the strategy when they write.

Tips

- Ask students to evaluate their progress and how the strategy improved their writing.
- Be enthusiastic about learning the strategy.
- Establish the importance of effort in learning and using the strategy.
- Provide opportunities for students to see how the strategy improves their writing.
- Praise and reinforce students' use of the strategy.
- Foster students' ownership of the strategy.

Providing Feedback through Conferencing and Presentation

Writers need feedback throughout the writing process. They need reactions to ideas, drafts, and revisions. Feedback is one of our most powerful tools for helping developing writers. Writers want to know how their works-in-progress sound to someone else, whether their compositions make sense, whether they contain any incorrect or misleading information, and where and how to make changes.

Regular feedback encourages developing writers to solve problems and make meaningful changes throughout the writing process.

One way of providing feedback is through conferences. Teachers may initiate conferences, but students should also be encouraged to call conferences on an as-needed basis. Because conferences can be held at various times throughout the writing process, the focus will vary. Conferences held during the early stages of the writing process help students identify and refine a topic or identify research references. During the revision process, conferences help students learn to elaborate and reorganize their writing. During the final stages, students learn to edit and proofread stories before they are published. Conferences offer an excellent opportunity for the teacher and student to evaluate jointly the student's progress and set goals for future growth.

The basic procedures for writing conferences are as follows:

- Have the student read aloud his or her work.
- Review any feedback the student has received so far.
- Identify positive elements of the work.
- Use one or more of these strategies to help the student improve his or her work.
  - Have the student explain how he or she got his or her ideas.
  - Have the student think aloud about how he or she will address the feedback he or she has received.
  - Ask the student to help you understand any confusion you may have about his or her writing.
  - Have the student add, delete, or rearrange something in the work, and ask how it affects the entire piece.
  - Think aloud while you do a part of what the student was asked to do. Then ask the student to compare what you did to what he or she did.
  - Have the student prescribe as if to a younger student how to revise the work.
- Ask two or three questions to guide the student through revising (see below).
- Conclude the conference by having the student state his or her plan for continuing work on the piece of writing.

Tips

- Set aside a special area of the classroom for you to work with students or for students to work with each other.
- You don't have to meet with every student every day.
- Conferences should be brief; don't overwhelm students with too many comments or suggestions. Several short conferences are often more effective than one long one.
- If appropriate, suggest that students take notes to help them remember where changes are to be made.

- Don't take ownership of the students' work. Encourage students to identify what is good and what needs to be changed, and let the students make the changes.
- Focus on what is good about the students' work; discuss how to solve problems rather than telling students what to do.
- Peer conferencing should be encouraged during Workshop.
- As students engage in peer conferencing, note which students are participating, the types of questions they ask, and the comments they make. Use this information to help students become more effective in peer conferencing.
- You may need to structure peer conferences by asking students to first explain what they liked about the composition, and then teaching them how to give constructive feedback.

Having students present or share their work provides another opportunity for them to receive feedback about their writing. Student presentations can involve

- presenting an initial idea or plan for a writing assignment.
- sharing a first draft of a paper.
- presenting orally part or all of a final piece of writing.

Tips

- Everyone must listen carefully and provide constructive feedback. Focus on what is good about a piece and ways to make it better.
- The student author has ownership and can decide which suggestions to use. The author does not have to incorporate all suggestions from the audience.
- Have a chair designated as the "Author's Chair" from which the student author can read his or her work or share ideas. This lends importance to the activity.
- The student author should be encouraged to give a bit of background, including where he or she is in the process, why he or she chose a particular part, or what problem he or she is having. This helps orient the audience.
- Short pieces of writing can be read in their entirety. As students become more proficient and write longer papers, they should be encouraged to read just a part of their writing; for example, a part they need help with, a part that has been revised, or a part they particularly like.
- Take notes during the presentations, and encourage older students to do the same.
- Be sensitive to the attention span of the class and the feedback being given. Students have a tendency to repeat the same comments to each author.

Word Processing and Other Aspects of Electronic Composing

Using a word processor to compose a piece of writing makes many aspects of the writing process easier. Text can easily be changed, deleted, or moved during drafting or revising. Software such as spell-checkers or word prediction provides assistance with basic writing skills. Information for writing can be obtained on-line or through other electronic sources, such as encyclopedias. Students can use publishing software to develop a more polished and attractive final product by adding pictures to their composition, developing a cover, changing fonts, and so on. ***SRA Imagine It!*** supports the use of these technologies.

Teaching Basic Writing Skills

Purpose

Young writers need to learn many basic writing skills to the point that the skills can be executed with minimal effort so they do not interfere with other writing processes. Correct handwriting, spelling, and grammar should be mastered to the point that they require little attention on the part of the writer. While sentences cannot and should not be constructed without conscious attention and effort, developing writers need to become familiar with different sentence types, and they need to become proficient at building them.

Procedures

Sentence Construction

SRA Imagine It! teaches sentence construction skills through the use of sentence frames, sentence expansion, and sentence combining.

- **Sentence Frames** With sentence frames, students are given part of a sentence and asked to generate the rest of it. For example, students can be taught to write a simple sentence, with a single subject and predicate, by giving them a frame containing the subject (The dog ____________.) and asking them to complete the sentence by telling what happened (The dog ran.).
- **Sentence Expansion** With sentence expansion, students are given a kernel sentence and asked to expand it by adding additional words. For example, students can be taught to make sentences more colorful by adding descriptive words to a kernel sentence: *Rewrite* ***The cat and dog like the toy*** *so the sentence tells more about the cat and dog and the toy — The big dog and gray cat like the fuzzy little toy.*
- **Sentence combining** With sentence combining, students learn how to combine two or more kernel sentences into a more complex single sentence. For example, you can lead students to produce sentences with relative clauses by combining the following two sentences:

  John will win the race.

  John is very fast. (who)

  John, who is very fast, will win the race.

When teaching sentence construction skills, the following three steps should be followed:

- Describe the skill, establish why it is important, and model how to use it.
- Provide students with assistance until they can apply the skill correctly and independently.
- Ask students to apply the skill when they write.

Tips

- Use more than one method to teach a sentence construction skill.
- Ask students to monitor how often they use the sentence construction skill.
- Encourage students to set goals to use sentence construction skills in their writing.

Handwriting

Students need to develop both legible and fluent handwriting. An important aspect of meeting this goal is to teach them an efficient pattern for forming individual letters (both lowercase and uppercase letters). Effective teaching procedures include

- modeling how to form the letter.
- describing how the letter is similar to and different from other letters.
- using visual cues, such as numbered arrows, as a guide to letter formation.
- providing practice tracing, copying, and writing the letter from memory.
- keeping instructional sessions short, with frequent review and practice.
- asking students to identify or circle their best formed letter or letters.
- encouraging students to correct or rewrite poorly formed letters.
- monitoring students' practice to ensure that letters are formed correctly.
- reinforcing students' successful efforts and providing corrective feedback as needed.

In addition to learning how to write the letters of the alphabet correctly, students must be able to produce them quickly. Fluency generally develops as a consequence of writing frequently, but it can also be fostered by having students copy short passages several times, and trying to write them a little faster each time.

Tips

- Make sure that each student develops a comfortable and efficient pencil grip.
- Encourage students to sit in an upright position, leaning slightly forward, as they write.
- Show students how to place or position their papers when writing.
- Implement appropriate procedures for left-handed writers, such as how to properly place or position their papers when writing.
- Monitor students' handwriting, paying special attention to their instructional needs in letter formation, spacing, slant, alignment, size, and line quality.
- Encourage students to make all final drafts of their papers neat and legible.

Spelling

Purpose

To become good spellers, students must learn to spell correctly and easily the words they are most likely to use when writing. They need to be able to generate and check plausible spellings for words whose spellings are uncertain. They also need to learn to use external sources such as spell-checkers to ensure correct spelling during writing. In ***SRA Imagine It!*** students are taught how to spell words they frequently use when writing as well as spelling patterns that help them spell untaught words.

Tips

- Teach students an effective strategy for studying spelling words.
- Reinforce the correct spelling of taught words in students' writing.
- Have students build words from letters or letters and phonograms, for example, c - at.
- Teach strategies for determining and checking the spelling of unknown words.
- Model the use of correct spelling and how to correct spelling errors when you write in front of the class.
- Encourage students to correct misspelled words in all final drafts of their writing.
- Provide instruction and practice in proofreading.
- Encourage students to use spell-checkers, dictionaries, and so on to determine the correct spelling of unknown words.

Grammar and Usage

Traditional methods of teaching grammar and usage skills are not effective. With such instruction, students are initially provided with an abstract definition, such as an adjective is a word that describes a noun or pronoun. This is often followed by asking students to practice applying the skill correctly without actually generating any textual material longer than a word or a phrase. For example, students might be asked to complete the following sentence: The ___________ wagon rolled through the ___________ town. It is not surprising that many students do not understand the rules they are taught or how to use them in their writing, because such instruction is abstract and decontextualized.

To make grammar instruction effective, ***SRA Imagine It!*** applies the following five principles. To make these principles concrete, the program illustrates each as it would apply to the rule for capitalizing the first letter in a person's name.

- Grammar and usage skills need to be defined in a functional and concrete manner. The rule of capitalizing the first letter in a person's name can be introduced by writing a sentence with two or three familiar names on the board. With the students' help, identify each name in the sentence, and ask them what they notice about the first letter in each name—They are capital letters. Repeat this process with a second sentence, and then establish the "capitalization rule" with students' help.
- As soon as the skill is functionally described or defined, establish why it is important—Capitalizing the first letter in a person's name makes the name stand out and shows respect for the person named. This is an important rule for writing.
- Show students how to use the skill when writing. Generate a sentence using the names of students in the class, or have your students help you generate such a sentence. Write it on the board, capitalizing the first letter while simultaneously telling the class what you are doing.

- Provide students with guided practice in applying the skill when writing. Generate with the class another sentence that includes three of your students' names. Tell the class you will write the sentence on the board, but they will need to tell you when to capitalize a word. Next, have students work together in pairs to generate two sentences using names of their friends, capitalizing the first letter in each name. Provide support as needed. Finally, have each student generate one sentence of his or her own containing two names. Monitor to ensure that students capitalize the first letter in each name. Have them share their sentences with a peer.
- Ask students to apply the skill in their compositions. Have students look at one of the papers in their writing portfolio and correct any capitalization mistakes involving people's names. Remind students to capitalize people's names when writing and revising subsequent writing assignments.

Tips

- Ask students to correct other students' papers, focusing on specific grammar and usage rules and mistakes.
- Encourage students to read their papers aloud when revising. This will help them spot grammar and usage mistakes.

Fostering Motivation

Purpose

Children start school wanting to learn how to write and enjoying writing. Too quickly, however, many begin to view writing as a chore or something to be avoided. The goal of ***SRA Imagine It!*** writing is for children to become lifelong writers—people who enjoy writing and use writing effectively at work as well as in their personal lives.

Procedures

One way to foster an interest in writing is to have students write for real purposes and audiences. This includes having students identify why they are writing and what they hope to accomplish. Likewise, students need to share their writing with others. They are more likely to do their best writing when there is an audience. Students can share their plans, an initial draft, a portion of their composition, or the completed paper with you, their peers, or other children or adults.

Students are also likely to give their best effort when the writing environment is supportive and pleasant. This can be accomplished by the following:

- Establishing clear rules for student behavior during the writing period. Keep the rules simple and reasonable in number and consistently reinforce them. Students are not likely to enjoy writing, or learn well, if the classroom environment is chaotic.
- Creating a low-risk environment in which students feel comfortable taking risks with their writing. This means being accepting and encouraging of students' efforts and encouraging them to act in the same manner. For example, make it a rule in your class that when someone shares his or her writing, the first thing that you or other students do is say what you liked most about it.
- Supporting students as they begin to apply the knowledge, skills, or strategies you teach them. This can include reteaching, providing hints and reminders, giving useful feedback, and initially helping students apply what was taught.
- Having students help each other as they plan, draft, revise, edit/proofread, and publish their work. This is most effective when the process of working together is structured. For instance, students are more likely to give good advice for revising if they are asked to focus on specific aspects of the composition, such as identifying places where the writing is unclear or more detail is needed.
- Celebrating student success by displaying their work. This can be done by prominently displaying student work in the classroom or in other places in the school. Students can also be asked to publish their work in a class or school newspaper or to read their compositions aloud to younger children, in other classes, or at a special event.
- Fostering an "I can do" attitude among your students. Consistently emphasize that the key to good writing is effort and the use of what they have learned.
- Setting a positive mood during writing time. Be enthusiastic about writing and what your students write.

Tips

- Allow students to make their own decisions and to accomplish as much on their own as possible.
- Increase students' ownership of a writing topic by allowing them to develop unique interpretations of the topic.
- Encourage students to take ownership of their writing. This includes allowing them to arrange a suitable writing environment, construct a personal plan for accomplishing the writing task, to work at their own pace when possible, and to decide what feedback from you and their peers is most pertinent for revising their writing.
- Look for opportunities to give students positive feedback about their work. Let them know when they have done something well in their writing.
- Encourage students to monitor their progress. For example, have students select their best writing to keep in a writing portfolio, identifying why they selected each piece.
- Show your students that you are a writer too. Share your writing with them. Talk about the various ways you use writing each day.
- Connect writing to students' lives and the world in general. Have them document the types of writing they do outside school. Develop a wall chart on which the class can identify how they use writing away from school.
- Provide incentives for writing at home. For example, have parents document that their child writes for twenty minutes at home a set number of nights for a month. Provide a special party for these children, allowing each one to select a book to keep from an array of books donated by parents or a sponsoring business partner.

Spelling Strategies

Spelling

Many people find English difficult, because English sound/spelling patterns seem to have hundreds of exceptions. The key to becoming a good speller, however, is not just memorization. The key is recognizing and internalizing English spelling patterns. Some people do this naturally as they read and develop large vocabularies. They intuitively recognize spelling patterns and apply them appropriately. Others need explicit and direct teaching of vocabulary and spelling strategies and spelling patterns before they develop spelling consciousness.

Purpose

Spelling is a fundamental skill in written communication. Although a writer may have wonderful ideas, he or she may find it difficult to communicate those ideas without spelling skills. Learning to spell requires much exposure to text and writing. For many it requires a methodical presentation of English spelling patterns.

English Spelling Patterns

A basic understanding of English spelling patterns will help provide efficient and effective spelling instruction. Just as the goal of phonics instruction is to enable students to read fluently, the goal of spelling instruction is to enable students to write fluently so they can concentrate on ideas rather than spelling.

Sound Patterns Many words are spelled the way they sound. Most consonants and short vowels are very regular. When a student learns the sound/spelling relationships, he or she has the key to spelling many words.

Structural Patterns Structural patterns are employed when adding endings to words. Examples of structural patterns include doubling the final consonant, adding *-s* or *-es* to form plurals, and dropping the final *e* before adding *-ing, -ed, -er,* or *-est.* Often these structural patterns are very regular in their application. Many students have little trouble learning these patterns.

Meaning Patterns Many spelling patterns in English are morphological; in other words, the meaning relationship is maintained regardless of how a sound may change. Prefixes, suffixes, and root words that retain their spellings regardless of how they are pronounced are further examples of meaning patterns.

Foreign Language Patterns Many English words are derived from foreign words and retain those language patterns. For example, kindergarten (German), boulevard (French), and ballet (French from Italian) are foreign-language patterns at work in English.

Developmental Stages of Spelling

The most important finding in spelling research in the past thirty years is that students learn to spell in a predictable developmental sequence, much as they learn to read. It appears to take the average student three to six years to progress through the developmental stages and emerge as a fairly competent, mature speller.

Prephonemic The first stage is the prephonemic stage, characterized by random letters arranged either in continuous lines or in wordlike clusters. Only the writer can "read" it, and it may be "read" differently on different days.

Semiphonemic As emergent readers learn that letters stand for sounds, they use particular letters specifically to represent the initial consonant sound and sometimes a few other very salient sounds. This marks the discovery of phonemic awareness that letters represent speech sounds in writing.

Phonemic When students can represent most of the sounds they hear in words, they have entered the phonemic stage of spelling. They spell what they hear, using everything they know about letter sounds, letter names, and familiar words. Many remedial spellers never develop beyond this stage and spell a word the way it sounds whenever they encounter a word they cannot spell.

Transitional or Within-Word Pattern As they are exposed to more difficult words, students discover that not all words are spelled as they sound. They learn that they must include silent letters, spell past tenses with *-ed,* include a vowel even in unstressed syllables, and remember how words look. The transitional stage represents the transition from primarily phonemic strategies to rule-bound spelling.

Derivational The derivational stage occurs as transitional spellers accumulate a large spelling vocabulary and gain control over affixes, contractions, homophones, and other meaning patterns. They discover that related or derived forms of words share spelling features even if they do not sound the same. As spellers gain control over these subtle word features and spell most words correctly, they become conventional spellers.

Procedures

The spelling lessons are organized around different spelling patterns, beginning with phonetic spelling patterns and progressing to other types of spelling patterns in a logical sequence. Word lists including words from the literature selection focus on the particular patterns in each lesson. In general, the sound patterns occur in the first units at each grade, followed by structural patterns, meaning patterns, and foreign-language patterns in the upper grade levels.

- As you begin each new spelling lesson, have students identify the spelling pattern and how it is like and different from other patterns.
- Give the pretest to help students focus on the lesson pattern.
- Have students proofread their own pretests immediately after the test, crossing out any misspellings and writing the correct spelling.
- Have them diagnose whether the errors they made were in the lesson pattern or in another part of the word. Help students determine where they made errors and what type of pattern they should work on to correct them.
- As students work through the spelling pages from ***Skills Practice,*** encourage them to practice the different spelling strategies in the exercises.

Sound Pattern Strategies

Pronunciation Strategy As students encounter an unknown word, have them say the word carefully to hear each sound. Encourage them to check the ***Sound/Spelling Cards.*** Then have them spell each sound. (/s/ + /i/ + /t/: sit). This strategy builds directly on the Dication and Spelling introduced in kindergarten and taught in Levels 1–3.

Consonant Substitution Have students switch consonants. The vowel spelling usually remains the same. (bat, hat, rat, flat, splat) This is a natural extension of Phonemic Awareness activities begun in prekindergarten and kindergarten.

Vowel Substitution Have students switch vowels. The consonant spellings usually remain the same. (CVC: hit, hat, hut, hot; CVCV: mane, mine; CVVC: boat, beat, bait, beet) This is a natural extension of Phonemic Awareness activities begun in prekindergarten and kindergarten.

Rhyming Word Strategy Have students think of rhyming words and the rhymes that spell a particular sound. Often the sound will be spelled the same way in another word. (cub, tub, rub) This is a natural extension of Phonemic Awareness activities begun in prekindergarten and kindergarten.

Structural Pattern Strategies

Conventions Strategy Have students learn the rules and exceptions for adding endings to words (dropping *y,* dropping *e,* doubling the final consonant, and so on).

Proofreading Strategy Many spelling errors occur because of simple mistakes. Have students check their writing carefully and specifically for spelling.

Visualization Strategy Have students think about how a word looks. Sometimes words "look" wrong because a wrong spelling pattern has been written. Have them double-check the spelling of any word that looks wrong.

Meaning Pattern Strategies

Family Strategy When students are not sure of a spelling, have them think of how words from the same base word family are spelled. (critic, criticize, critical; sign, signal, signature; nation, national, nationality)

Meaning Strategy Have students determine a homophone's meaning to make sure they are using the right word. Knowing prefixes, suffixes, and base words will also help.

Compound Word Strategy Tell students to break apart a compound and to spell each word. Compounds may not follow convention rules for adding endings. (homework, nonetheless)

Foreign-Language Strategy Have students think of foreign-language spellings that are different from English spelling patterns. (ballet, boulevard, sauerkraut)

Dictionary Strategy Ask students to look up the word in a dictionary to make sure their spelling is correct. If they do not know how to spell a word, have them try a few different spellings and look them up to see which one is correct. (fotograph, photograph) Have students use the ***Sound/Spelling Cards*** to help them look up words. This develops a spelling consciousness.

Use the post test to determine understanding of the lesson spelling pattern and to identify any other spelling pattern problems. Encourage student understanding of spelling patterns and use of spelling strategies in all their writing to help transfer spelling skills to writing.

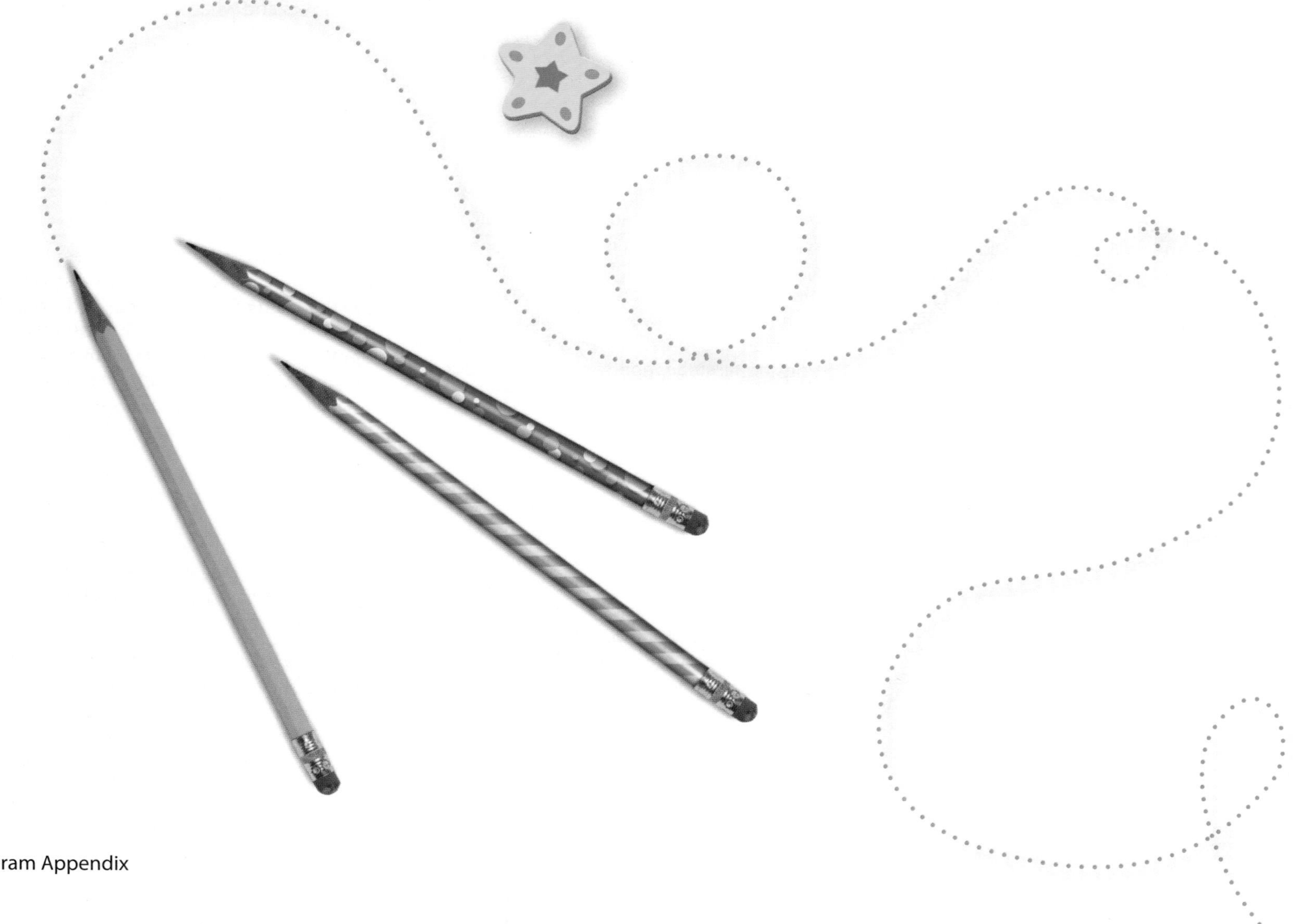

Grammar, Usage, and Mechanics

Purpose

The Study of English Conventions

Over the years the study of grammar, usage, and mechanics has gone in and out of favor. In the past century much research has been done to demonstrate the effectiveness of traditional types of instruction in the conventions of English. Experience and research have shown that learning grammatical terms and completing grammar exercises have little effect on the student's practical application of these skills in the context of speaking or writing. These skills, in and of themselves, do not play a significant role in the way students use language to generate and express their ideas—for example, during the prewriting and drafting phases of the writing process. In fact, emphasis on correct conventions has been shown to have a damaging effect when it is the sole focus of writing instruction. If students are evaluated only on the proper use of spelling, grammar, and punctuation, they tend to write fewer and less complex sentences.

Knowledge of English conventions is, however, vitally important in the editing and proofreading phases of the writing process. A paper riddled with mistakes in grammar, usage, or mechanics is quickly discounted. Many immature writers never revise or edit. They finish the last sentence and turn their papers in to the teacher. Mature writers employ their knowledge of English language conventions in the editing phase to refine and polish their ideas.

The study of grammar, usage, and mechanics is important for two reasons.

1. Educated people need to know and understand the structure of their language, which in large part defines their culture.
2. Knowledge of grammar gives teachers and students a common vocabulary for talking about language and makes discussions of writing tasks more efficient and clearer.

Procedure

The key issue in learning grammar, usage, and mechanics is how to do it. On the one hand, teaching these skills in isolation from writing has been shown to be ineffective and even detrimental if too much emphasis is placed on them. On the other hand, not teaching these skills and having students write without concern for conventions is equally ineffective. The answer is to teach the skills in a context that allows students to directly apply them to a reading or writing activity. Students should be taught proper use of punctuation or subject/verb agreement at the same time they are taught to proofread for those conventions. As they learn to apply their knowledge of conventions during the final stages of the writing process, they will begin to see that correcting errors is an editorial rather than a composition skill.

A paper riddled with mistakes in grammar, usage, or mechanics is quickly discounted.

History of English

A basic understanding of the history and structure of the English language helps students understand the rich but complex resource they have for writing.

Old English

The English language began about A.D. 450 when the Angles, Jutes, and Saxons––three tribes that lived in northern Europe–– invaded the British Isles. Much of their language included words that had to do with farming (*sheep, dirt, tree, earth*). Many of their words are the most frequently used words in the English language today. Because of Latin influences, English became the first of the European languages to be written.

Middle English

In 1066 William the Conqueror invaded England and brought Norman French with him. Slowly Old English and Norman French came together, and Middle English began to appear. Today forty percent of Modern English comes from French. With the introduction of the printing press, English became more widespread.

Modern English

With the Renaissance and its rediscovery of classical Greek and Latin, many new words were created from Greek and Latin word elements. This continued intensively during the Early Modern English period. This rich language was used in the writings of Shakespeare and his contemporaries and profoundly influenced the nature and vocabulary of English. With dictionaries and spelling books, the English language became more standardized, although it continues to be influenced by other languages and new words and trends. These influences continue to make English a living, dynamic language.

Punctuation

Early writing had no punctuation or even spaces between words. English punctuation had its beginning in ancient Greece and Rome. Early punctuation reflected speaking rather than reading. By the end of the eighteenth century, after the invention of printing, most of the rules for punctuation were established, although they were not the same in all languages.

The Structure of English

Grammar is the sound, structure, and meaning system of language. People who speak the same language are able to communicate because they intuitively know the grammar system of that language, the rules to make meaning. All languages have grammar, and yet each language has its own grammar.

Traditional grammar study usually involves two areas:

- **Parts of speech** (nouns, verbs, adjectives, adverbs, pronouns, prepositions, conjunctions) are typically considered the content of grammar. The parts of speech involve the form of English words.
- **Sentence structure** (subjects, predicates, objects, clauses, phrases) is also included in grammar study. Sentence structure involves the function of English.

Mechanics involves the conventions of punctuation and capitalization. Punctuation helps readers understand writers' messages. Proper punctuation involves marking off sentences according to grammatical structure. In speech students can produce sentences as easily and unconsciously as they can walk, but in writing they must think about what is and what is not a sentence.

In English there are about fourteen punctuation marks (period, comma, quotation mark, question mark, exclamation point, colon, semicolon, apostrophe, hyphen, ellipsis, parenthesis, bracket, dash, and underscore). Most immature writers use only three: period, comma, and question mark. The experienced writer or poet with the command of punctuation adds both flexibility and meaning to his or her sentences through his or her use of punctuation.

Usage is the way in which we speak in a given community. Language varies over time, across national and geographical boundaries, by gender, across age groups, and by socioeconomic status. When the variation occurs within a given language, the different versions of the same language are called dialects. Every language has a prestige dialect associated with education and financial success. In the United States, this dialect is known as Standard English and is the language of school and business.

Usage involves the word choices people make when speaking certain dialects. Word choices that are perfectly acceptable in conversation among friends may be unacceptable in writing. Usage is often the most obvious indicator of the difference between conversation and composition. Errors in word usage can make a writer seem ignorant and thus jeopardize his or her credibility, no matter how valid or important his or her overall message might be. Usage depends on a student's cultural and linguistic heritage. If the dialect students have learned is not the formal language of school settings or if it is not English, students must master another dialect or language in order to write Standard English.

The Grammar, Usage, and Mechanics lessons in ***SRA Imagine It!*** are structured to focus on skills presented in a logical sequence. A skill is introduced with appropriate models and then practiced in reading and writing on subsequent days to ensure that skills are not taught in isolation. Encourage students to use the focused English language convention presented in each lesson as they complete each Writing Process Strategies activity. Also encourage them to reread their writing, checking for proper use of the conventions taught. With practice, students should be able to apply their knowledge of conventions to any writing they do.

Tips

- Some of the errors students make in writing are the result simply of not carefully reading their final drafts. Many errors occur because the writer's train of thought was interrupted and a sentence is not complete or a word is skipped. These may look like huge errors that a simple rereading can remedy. Most often the writer can correct these types of errors on his or her own. A major emphasis of any English composition program should be to teach the editing and proofreading phases of the writing process so students can eliminate these types of errors themselves. This involves a shift in perception—from thinking of grammar as a set of discrete skills that involve mastery of individual rules to understanding grammar as it applies to the act of communicating in writing.
- As students learn English language conventions, they should be expected to incorporate them into their written work.
- Sometimes, students write sentences that raise grammatically complex problems that require a deep understanding of English grammar. Use the Sentence Lifting strategies outlined in the Proofreading part of the Appendix to identify and discuss these more sophisticated types of errors that can include the following:
- **Faulty Parallelism.** Parts of a sentence parallel in meaning are not parallel in structure.
- **Nonsequiturs.** A statement does not follow logically from something said previously.
- **Dangling Modifiers.** A phrase or clause does not logically modify the word next to it.
- **Awkwardness.** Sentences are not written simply.
- **Wordiness.** Thoughts are not written in as few words as possible. Precise words are not used.

Listening/Speaking/Viewing

Some people are naturally good listeners, and others have no trouble speaking in front of groups. Many people, however, need explicit instruction on how to tune in for important details and how to organize and make an oral presentation. While some people naturally critique what they read, hear, and see, many others need specific guidance to develop skills for analyzing what they encounter in images and the media. The abilities to listen appropriately and to speak in conversations and in groups, as well as to critically evaluate the information with which they are presented, are fundamental skills that will serve students throughout their lives.

Purpose

In addition to reading and writing, listening, speaking, and viewing complete the language arts picture. Through the development of these language arts skills, students gain flexibility in communicating orally, visually, and in writing. When speaking and listening skills are neglected, many students have difficulty speaking in front of groups, organizing a speech, or distinguishing important information they hear. A top anxiety for many adults is speaking in front of groups. Much of this anxiety would not exist if listening, speaking, and viewing skills were taught from the early years.

The Listening/Speaking/Viewing instruction focuses on the literature selection or the Writing Process Strategies to provide context, to reinforce other elements of the lesson, and to integrate the other language arts. Many of the listening, speaking, and viewing skills are very similar to reading or writing skills. For example, listening for details is the same type of skill as reading for details. Preparing an oral report employs many of the same skills as preparing a written report. Learning to use these skills effectively gives students flexibility in how they approach a task. Furthermore, listening and speaking are naturally integrated into all aspects of learning as students listen and respond to each other during discussions, writing, and Inquiry.

Procedure

Listening, speaking, and viewing skills are presented with increasing sophistication throughout every grade level of ***SRA Imagine It!*** in the Language Arts part of each lesson. Every unit includes at least one lesson on each of the following skills so that students encounter the skills again and again throughout a grade level:

- **Listening.** Listening skills include comprehending what one hears and listening for different purposes, such as to identify sequence or details, to summarize or draw conclusions, or to follow directions.
- **Speaking.** Speaking skills include speaking formally and conversationally, using appropriate volume, giving oral presentations, and using effective grammar. Speaking skills also include using descriptive words, figurative language, and formal and informal language.
- **Viewing.** Viewing skills include comprehending main ideas and messages in images, mass media, and other multimedia.
- **Interaction.** Interaction instruction focuses on a combination of listening and speaking skills. These include asking and responding to questions; nonverbal cues such as eye contact, facial expression, and posture; and contributing to and interacting in group settings.
- **Presenting Information.** The last Listening/Speaking/Viewing lesson in every unit usually focuses on presentation skills. These include sharing ideas, relating experiences or stories, organizing information, and preparing for speeches. These lessons often parallel the Writing Process Strategies instruction so that students can prepare their information in written or oral form. These skills are an integral part of the Inquiry process as students share their ideas, questions, conjectures, and findings.

Tips

- Identify the parallels among the language arts skills: providing written and oral directions, telling or writing a narrative, and so on. Encourage students to see that they have choices for communicating. Discuss the similarities and differences between different forms of communication, and determine whether one is preferable in a given situation.
- Ensure that all students have opportunities to speak in small groups and whole-class situations.
- Provide and teach students to allow appropriate wait time before someone answers a question.
- Encourage students (when they are able) to take notes to help them remember what they heard so they can better respond.
- Remind students to use visuals when appropriate in their presentations to support their presentations and to help keep the listeners' attention.
- Set up simple class rules to show respect for the listener and speaker. These rules should be used during Inquiry or handing off or any time of the day and should foster respect for the speaker and listeners.
  - Students should speak in a voice loud and clear enough for everyone in the class to hear.
  - Students should raise their hands and not interrupt.
  - If someone asks a question, then the person who responds should address the question before going on to another idea or topic.
  - The speaker should look at the audience, and the audience should look at the speaker.

Inquiry

Even in elementary school, students can produce works of genuine research—research that seeks answers to real questions or solutions to real problems.

Inquiry—research, investigation, and exploration—forms the heart of the ***SRA Imagine It!*** program. To encourage students to understand how reading and writing are tools for learning that can enhance their lives and help them become mature, educated adults, they are asked in each unit to use the content they are learning in the unit as the basis for further inquiry, exploration, and research. The unit information is simply the base for their investigations.

There are two types of units in the ***SRA Imagine It!*** program—units based on universal topics of interest such as friendship, heritage, and courage and content units that provide students a very solid base of information upon which they can begin their own inquiry and research. Units delving into science-related areas such as camouflage, energy, and ecology or into social studies units that address American history, geography, or money invite students to become true researchers by exploring personal areas of interest driven by problems or questions raised by students. Based upon common areas of interest, students conduct Inquiry in small collaborative groups and then present their findings to their classmates. In this way, students recognize the importance of sharing knowledge and gain much more knowledge of the unit theme than they would have simply by reading the selections in the unit.

The selections in the units are organized so that each selection will add more information or a different perspective to students' growing bodies of knowledge.

Inquiry through Reflective Activities

Purpose

The units in ***SRA Imagine It!*** that deal with universal topics tend to be explored through reflective activities. These units—such as Courage, Friendship, and Risks and Consequences—are organized to help students expand—perhaps even change—their perspectives of familiar concepts. As they explore and discuss the concepts that emerge from reading selections related to each unit topic, students are involved in activities that extend their experiences and offer opportunities for reflection. Such activities include writing, drama, art, interviews, debates, and panel discussions. Students will choose the activities and presentation format best suited to explore or investigate their research questions. Throughout each unit, students may be involved in a single ongoing investigative activity, or they may participate in a number of different activities. They may choose to produce a final written project or a multimedia presentation. They will share with the rest of the class the new knowledge that they have gained from their investigations. Workshop provides an ideal time for students to work individually or in collaborative groups on their investigation and/or projects.

The Inquiry activities will be those of students' own choosing, thereby allowing them to explore the unit concepts more fully. They are free, of course, to make other choices or to devise activities of their own.

Procedure

Choosing an Area to Investigate

Students may work on activities alone, in pairs, or in small groups. They have the option of writing about or using other methods for presenting their findings to the entire group. Students should decide what concept-related question or problem they wish to explore. Generally, it is better for students to generate wonderings, questions, or problems after they have engaged in some discussion at the beginning of each unit. This should be done, however, before they have had a chance to consult source materials. The goal is to have students ask questions that will drive their inquiry. This approach is more likely to bring forth ideas that students actually wonder about or wish to understand. Students may also look at the questions posted on the **Concept/Question Board** or introduce fresh ideas inspired by material they have just finished reading.

Inquiry pairs or groups are developed based upon common areas of interest or common questions that appear on the **Concept/Question Board.** Students who share a common interest for inquiry should work together to develop a common question to explore. Some of students may need your assistance in deciding upon, or narrowing down, a question or a problem so that it can be explored more easily. A good way to model this process for students is to make webs for a few of your own ideas on the board and to narrow down these ideas to a workable question or problem.

Organizing the Group

After a question or a problem has been chosen, students may choose an activity that will help them investigate that problem or question. For example, if students in Grade 3 are exploring the question "What are the common characteristics that define friendship?" they may want to develop and conduct a survey of classmates, friends, and so on. To develop the survey, group participants may want to do some additional reading about friendship, explore resources on the Internet, and so on to have a sense of the kinds of questions to include in the survey. Students' next responsibility is to decide who is going to investigate which facet of the question or the problem (when they are conducting a literature search, for example) or who is going to perform which activity related to the particular reflective activity (when they are writing and performing an original playlet or puppet show, for example). Lastly, students need to decide how, or if, they want to present their findings. For instance, after conducting a literature search, some students may want to read and discuss passages from a book with a plot or theme that relates to a unit concept. Other students may prefer performing and discussing scenes from the book.

Deciding How to Investigate

The following suggestions may help you and your students choose ways in which to pursue their investigations. For units on universal topics that are more literary in nature, students may want to do one of the following activities to pursue answers to their questions.

- Conduct a literature search to pursue a question or a problem. Discussion or writing may follow.

- Write and produce an original playlet or puppet show based on situations related to the concepts.
- Play a role-playing game to work out a problem related to the concepts.
- Stage a panel discussion with audience participation on a question or problem.
- Hold a debate on an issue related to the concept.
- Write an advice column dealing with problems related to the concepts.
- Write a personal-experience story related to the concepts.
- Invite experts to class. Formulate questions to ask.
- Conduct an interview with someone on a subject related to the concepts.
- Produce and carry out a survey on an issue or a question related to the concept.
- Produce a picture or photo-essay about the concept.

You may want to post this list in the classroom so that groups have access to it as they decide what they want to investigate and how they want to proceed. Encourage students to explore other possibilities as well and to add these ideas to the list.

EXAMPLE: In the Heritage unit in Grade 5 of ***SRA Imagine It!,*** students read "In Two Worlds: A Yup'ik Eskimo Family." This selection is about how three generations of Eskimos living in Alaska near the Arctic strive to adopt the best of modern ways without abandoning their traditional values. During the class discussion, some students may note that Alice and Billy Rivers want their students to learn both the new and the old ways of living. As the discussion continues, many students may conclude from the story that the older generations hope that future generations will continue to value their roots and their cultural traditions. Students then relate this story to their own heritage. Some students may share information about their customs or traditions.

Students choose some reflective activities that will help them learn more about family heritage and that will answer some of their questions about the unit concepts. These questions may relate to the value of maintaining traditional customs and values versus. adopting contemporary ones. Other students may ask exploring questions related to how to maintain traditional values in the face of contemporary changes. Some students may be interested in interviewing family members or close family friends about their cultural traditions and heritages or interviewing students in their class about their cultural heritage and then looking for commonalities and differences. These students review what they know about interviewing. They should proceed by performing the following:

- Researching examples of interviews to see what they might look like and how to build in space to write answers
- Preparing a list of questions to ask
- Preparing a list of subjects to interview, deciding how to record the interview (by audiotape, videotape, or taking notes)
- Contacting in advance the person(s) they want to interview
- Deciding whether to photograph the person and, if so, getting permission to do so in advance—collecting the equipment necessary for conducting the interview
- After they conduct the interviews, students decide how they wish to present the information that they have collected.

EXAMPLE: Another group of students in the same fifth-grade class may be more interested in planning a photo-essay about one family or about a neighborhood with many families belonging to a particular culture. These students may decide to reexamine "In Two Worlds" in terms of how the text and the photographs complement each other and what information is conveyed in each photograph. They may also decide to examine some photo-essays listed in the unit bibliography. These students will need to make some advance preparations as well. They should proceed by performing the following:

- Determining which neighborhood and which family or families to photograph
- Contacting in advance the persons to be interviewed and photographed
- Touring the neighborhood in advance of the photo shoot
- Making a list of questions to ask the family or families about their heritage or about their neighborhood
- Thinking about what information to include in their essay so that they can determine what photographs to take
- Collecting the equipment necessary for conducting interviews and photographing subjects

After students collect the information and take photographs, they may write and organize the photo-essay and present it to the class. The teacher should remind students of the phases of the writing process and encourage them to plan, draft, revise, and edit/proofread their work until they are completely satisfied with it.

Not all questions on the **Concept/Question Board** will be explored in depth. Throughout the unit, students can continue discussing family heritage and raising and posting new questions. The teacher should remind them that as they read further, they may think of additional ways to explore the unit concepts. Students should sign or initial their questions or ideas so that they can identify classmates with similar interests and exchange ideas with them. The teacher should encourage students to feel free to write an answer or a note on someone else's question or to consult the Board for ideas for their own explorations. From time to time, the teacher should post his or her own questions on the **Concept/Question Board.**

Tips

- The ***Leveled Readers*** contain books related to the unit concepts. Remind students that these are good sources of information and that they should consult them regularly—especially when they are investigating concept-related ideas and questions.
- Some students work better within a specified time frame. Whenever they are beginning a new activity, discuss with students a reasonable period of time within which they will be expected to complete their investigations. Post the completion date somewhere in the classroom so that students can refer to it and pace themselves accordingly. At first, you may have to help them determine a suitable deadline, but eventually they should be able to make this judgment on their own.
- Some teachers like to do the Inquiry for the first unit with a common question decided upon by the whole class. Then students break into small groups and work on different ways to explore the question. One group may do a literature search while another might conduct a survey. The end results in students sharing new knowledge that addresses

the common research question.

Inquiry through Research

Purpose

Students come to school with a wealth of fascinating questions. Educators need to capitalize on this excitement for learning and natural curiosity. A classroom in which the teacher is the only person who asks the questions and defines the assignments, only correct answers are accepted, and students are not allowed to make errors and consider alternative possibilities to questions can quickly deaden this natural curiosity and enthusiasm. The purpose of the inquiry and research aspect of this program is to capitalize on students' questions and natural curiosity by using a framework or structure based upon the scientific method. This structure helps students ask questions and preserve the open-ended character of real research, which can lead to unexpected findings and to questions that were not originally considered.

The conventional approach to school research papers can be found, with minor variations, in countless textbooks and instructional resources. This approach consists of a series of steps such as the following: Select a topic or choose a topic from a list suggested by the teacher, narrow the topic to something of interest, collect materials, take notes, outline, and write. By following these steps, a student may produce a presentable paper, but the procedure does not constitute research in a meaningful sense. Indeed, this restrictive approach gives students a distorted notion of what research is about. We see students in universities and even in graduate schools still following this procedure when they do library research papers or literature reviews; we see their dismay when their professors regard such work as mere cutting and pasting and ask them where their original contribution is.

Elementary school students can produce works of genuine research—research that seeks answers to real questions or solutions to real problems—when they are provided the opportunity, taught how to ask good questions and develop conjectures, and work collaboratively to find information or data that will support or refute their conjecture. Being able to collect, analyze, and evaluate information are critical twenty-first century skills. In the adult world, as knowledgeable consumers, productive members of a sophisticated workforce, and lifelong learners, students will be expected to constantly identify problems, raise questions, analyze new information, and make informed decisions on the basis of this information. Preparing students for the analytic demands of adult life and teaching them how to find answers to their questions are goals of education.

Procedure

To make the research productive, the following important principles are embodied in this approach:

1. Research is focused on problems, not topics.
2. Questions and wonderings are the foundation for inquiry and research.
3. Conjectures—opinions based on less than complete evidence or proof—are derived from questions and guide the research; the research does not simply produce conjectures.
4. New information and data are gathered to test and revise conjectures.
5. Discussion, ongoing feedback, and constructive criticism are important in all phases of the research but especially in the revising of problems and conjectures.
6. The cycle of true research is essentially endless, although presentations of findings are made from time to time; new findings give rise to new problems and conjectures and thus to new cycles of research.

Following a Process

While working with the science and social studies units, students are encouraged to use this framework to keep their research activities focused and on track. Within this framework, there is flexibility. Students may begin with a question, develop a conjecture, and begin collecting information only to find that they need to redefine their conjecture. Like the writing process, there is a recursive nature to this framework. Students may go through these steps many times before they come to the end of their research. Certainly for adult researchers, this cycle of question, conjecture, research, and reevaluation can go on for years and, in some cases, lifetimes.

This cycle uses the following process:

1. Decide on a problem or question to research. Students should identify a question or problem that they truly wonder about or wish to understand and then form research groups with other students who have the same interests.
   - My problem or question is _________.
2. Formulate an idea or conjecture about the research problem. Students should think about and discuss with classmates possible answers to their research problems or questions and meet with their research groups to discuss and record their ideas or conjectures.
   - My idea/conjecture/theory about this question or problem is _________.
3. Identify needs and make plans. Students should identify knowledge needs related to their conjectures and meet with their research groups to determine which resources to consult and to make individual job assignments. Students should also meet periodically with the teacher, other classmates, and research groups to present preliminary findings and to make revisions to their problems and conjectures on the basis of these findings.
   - I need to find out _________.
   - To do this, I will need these resources: _________
   - My role in the group is _________.
   - This is what I have learned so far: _________
   - This is what happened when we presented our findings ___________
4. Reevaluate the problem or question based on what we have learned so far and the feedback we have received.
   - My revised problem or question is ___________.
5. Revise the idea or conjecture.
   - My new conjecture about this problem is _________.
6. Identify new needs and make new plans.
   - Based on what I found out, I still need to know _________.
   - To do this, I will need these resources: _________
   - This is what I have learned: _________
   - This is what happened when we presented our new findings: _________

Procedure for Choosing a Problem to Research

1. Discuss with students the nature of the unit. Explain to students that the

unit they are reading is a research unit and that they will produce and publish in some way the results of their explorations. They are free to decide what problems or questions they wish to explore, with whom they want to work, and how they want to present their finished products. They may publish a piece of writing, produce a poster, write and perform a play, or use any other means to present the results of their investigations and research. They may work individually, with partners, or in small groups.

2. Discuss with students the schedule you have planned for their investigations: how long the project is expected to take, how much time will be available for research, when the first presentation will be due. This schedule will partly determine the nature of the problems that students should be encouraged to work on and the depth of the inquiry students will be encouraged to pursue.
3. Have students talk about things they wonder about that are related to the unit subject. For example, in the Grade 3 unit Money, students might wonder where money in the money machine comes from or how prices are determined. Conduct a free-floating discussion of questions about the unit subject.
4. Brainstorm possible questions for students to think about. It is essential that students' own ideas and questions be the starting point of all inquiry. Helpful hint: For the first research unit, you might wish to generate a list of your own ideas, having students add to this list and having them choose from it.
5. Using their wonderings, model for students the difference between a research topic and a research problem or question by providing several examples. For example, have them consider the difference between the topic *California* and the problem *Why do so many people move to California?* Explain to them that if they choose to research the topic *California*, everything they look up under the subject heading or index entry *California* will be related in some way to their topic. Therefore, it will be quite difficult to choose which information to record. This excess of information also creates problems in organizing their research. Clearly, then, this topic is too broad and general. Choosing a specific question or problem, one that particularly interests them, helps them narrow their exploration and advance their understanding. Some possible ideas for questions can be found in the unit introduction. Ideas can also be generated as you and your students create a web of their questions or problems related to the unit concept. For example, questions related to the topic *California* might include the following: Why do so many people move to California? How have the different groups of people living in California affected the state?
6. A good research problem or question not only requires students to consult a variety of sources but is engaging and adds to the groups' knowledge of the concepts. Furthermore, good problems generate more questions. Help students understand that the question *Why do so many people move to California?* is an easy one to research. Many sources will contribute to an answer to the question, and all information located can be easily evaluated in terms of usefulness in answering the question. Helpful hint: Students' initial responses may indeed be topics instead of problems or questions. If so, the following questions might be helpful: What aspect of the topic really interests you? Can you turn that idea into a question?
7. Remember that this initial problem or question serves only as a guide for research. As students begin collecting information and collaborating with classmates, their ideas will change, and they can revise their research problem or question. Frequently, students do not sufficiently revise their problems until after they have had time to consider their conjectures and to collect information.
8. As students begin formulating their research problems, have them elaborate on their reasons for wanting to research their stated problems. They should go beyond simple expressions of interest or liking and indicate what is puzzling, important, or potentially informative, and so forth about the problems they have chosen.
9. At this stage, students' ideas will be of a very vague and limited sort. The important thing is to start them thinking about what really interests them and what value it has to them and the class.
10. Have students present their proposed problems or questions, along with reasons for their choices, and have an open discussion of how promising proposed problems are. As students present their proposed problems, ask them what new things they think they will be learning from their investigations and how that will add to the group's growing knowledge of the concepts. This constant emphasis on group knowledge building will help set a clear purpose for students' research.
11. Form research groups. To make it easier for students to form groups, they may record their problems on the board or on self-sticking notes. Final groups should be constituted in the way you find best for your class—by self-selection, by assignment on the basis of common interests, or by some combination of methods. Students can then meet during Workshop to agree on a precise statement of their research problem, the nature of their expected research contributions, and lists of related questions that may help later in assigning individual roles. They should also record any scheduling information that can be added to the planning calendar.

Using Technology

Students and teachers can access the Web site **www.SRAonline.com** to find information about the themes in their grade level.

What does Inquiry look like in the classroom?

Inquiry is a new concept for many students and is performed over an extended period of time. The following series of vignettes are an example of what Inquiry might look like in a third-grade classroom that is studying the third-grade unit Money.

Lesson 1

Developing questions

For the unit on money, Ms. Hernandes introduced the theme through "A New Coat for Anna" and now is focusing on having her students generate some questions. To maximize the number of resources available to her students to do their inquiry, she talked with the librarian at her local library as well as local high school teachers who are knowledgeable in the area. Both were able to provide resources for the class. Ms. Hernandes began with a discussion of money. She had prepared some basic questions to get the class started.

- Why do you think it is important to have a system of money like ours?
- What is money?
- Why do you think we have both paper money and coins?
- How have you learned about money?
- How would your life change if suddenly there were no money in the world?
- When people are using credit cards to pay for something, are they paying with real money?
- When someone writes a check, are they paying with real money?
- What is the difference between credit cards and checks and cash, or actual money?
- Why do you think people use credit cards and checks instead of cash?

The teacher felt that using open-ended questions like these would help get her students talking about what they know about money as well as give her an opportunity to informally assess students' background knowledge.

Students were able to provide some basic information such as the following:

- Money is used to buy things.
- There was not always money in the world.
- Some people used things such as animals instead of money.
- Sometimes people traded things to get something they wanted.
- Coins are made of metal.
- Some things cost more than other things.
- Sometimes you need to determine ways to get things when you do not have money.

But there were some basic misunderstandings that arose during the conversation, such as the following:

- All countries use dollars and cents.
- Everything costs the same no matter where you live.
- Money is made of paper.
- You can use credit cards whenever you want.

By discussing money in such general terms, students were able to share basic information.

To move students to the next level—asking questions—Ms. Hernandes began by thinking aloud about things related to the unit that interested her.

"I really am curious about how money is made. And another thing I've wondered about is how the government knows how much money to print." Ms. Hernandes encouraged her students to share some of their wonderings or things they are curious about. Some student wonderings included the following:

- What kind of money do people in other countries use?
- Does everyone make the same amount of money?
- What would happen if there were only credit cards and no money?
- How much money do people make?
- Does ripped money get thrown away?
- How come we cannot make our own money?

Lesson 2

Forming groups based on shared interest

Developing good research questions

Ms. Hernandes and her class have been reading about money for the past week. Many students read different trade books during Workshop to learn more about money. Every day at the end of Workshop, they shared some of their new questions. Some students even started bringing in articles from newspapers and magazines and posting them on the **Concept/Question Board.**

By now there are a number of questions on the **Concept/Question Board** and Ms. Hernandes wants to work with the class to generate more questions that will help students connect what they are learning in school to the real world. She began by modeling or thinking aloud and sharing some of her own thoughts: "I know that at the checkout stand in stores, you can buy plastic cards that have a dollar amount printed on them. I wonder how might this change our whole idea about money. Maybe instead of getting cash from the automatic money machines, we'll get a coded card."

The focus is on asking questions. She recognized that students' questions needed to be refined to lead to functional conjectures. The class discussed what makes a good question.

- Questions or wonderings should be things that students are truly curious about.
- Questions should be generated without consulting an encyclopedia or a reference source.
- Good questions cannot be answered with a simple *yes* or *no*.
- Questions should help students deepen their understanding of the unit theme rather than focus on a character or incident in a specific story.
- A good research question often begins with *how*.

Ms. Hernandes and the class talked about their questions and how to refine them. For example, one question the class raised earlier was "Does money change?" The class decided to change the question to "How does money change over time?"

- What possible changes might we see in the future?
- Given the changes in technology today, how might our use of money change over time?

Based on the selections the class has read, students generated the following questions to add to their existing ones on the **Concept/Question Board:**

- I wonder when and how the government decided to change coins and bills.
- I wonder if the government can ever run out of money.
- What happens when people make fake money?
- How do people choose the metals they use to make coins?
- How can money be made so people cannot copy it or make counterfeits?
- What do other countries use for money?
- Where do you save money?

To help move students toward developing some good questions for inquiry, the class reviewed all the questions and grouped them together. They discussed these groups of questions and decided to think of a good representative question. The class worked over the next couple of days to think of a question they were all interested in.

Lesson 3

Forming Conjectures

Identifying Needs and Making Plans

A goal of Inquiry is to have students move from asking questions to forming conjectures. Ms. Hernandes explained to the class that they were now going to take their question and develop a conjecture. Developing a conjecture simply means thinking of what they think the best answer is, given what they know now and have read so far.

Ms. Hernandes modeled this by using one of the questions students raised in the earlier lesson. The question was "How do people choose the metals to make coins?" Ms. Hernandes thought aloud about possible answers to this question: "I think that people choose a strong metal that will last a long time but that is not too heavy for people to carry."

Then Ms. Hernandes wrote the question the class thought of last week. They discussed the question and talked about what possible answers they might find. The question the class decided to focus on was "How is money made so that people cannot copy it?"

The class conjecture was "Special paper and really detailed pictures are used so no one can copy it." However, Ms. Hernandes realized that there could be other conjectures for the same question. She arranged the class into small groups and had them think about other possible conjectures. Some additional conjectures included the following:

- Every dollar has a different number that is recorded in a computer.
- Special ink is used so colors cannot be duplicated.
- When you hold up a bill to the light, you can see a special band in it that maybe only a special government machine can make.

At the end of the lesson, Ms. Hernandes created a chart with the question and all the conjectures students developed.

During the week, Ms. Hernandes continued working with the class on Inquiry. To help the group get started on identifying needs and materials related to their conjecture, Ms. Hernandes asked the following questions:

- What information will we need to help us decide if our conjecture is accurate?
- Where can we find this information?
- Who can help us find information related to our conjecture?
- What people in our school might be able to help us?
- What family members might know something about this?
- What words could we plug in on the Internet to help us get more information?

During the rest of this week, students started collecting different resources and reading various books during Workshop. Students were encouraged to take notes and to share with their groups each day.

Lesson 4

Revising Plans as Necessary

Collecting Data and Information

Now that students have started collecting material, they need to identify individual job assignments so they are not duplicating efforts. At the beginning of this week, Ms. Hernandes took time to have students meet in their groups. During this time she met with the small groups to track their progress, discuss any problems, and help them focus their research efforts.

The group working with the conjecture "Every dollar has a different number that is recorded in a computer" was having trouble finding information to support or refute their conjecture. They had looked in books but did not really find anything. As they talked with the teacher, someone mentioned the term *mint*. As they discussed what happened in the mint, someone suggested that they write the mint with their question to see if they could get some help. This simple activity led students to the Internet to find out the address of the mint. They then spent the rest of that period composing a letter.

At the end of Inquiry that day, Ms. Hernandes made time for each group to present a summary of what it had done. If the group had any unsolved problems, it shared them with the class to get possible suggestions on how to solve the problems. When the group who wrote to the mint shared its problem and solution, several other groups realized that the Internet would be a good resource for them to use as well.

Lesson 5

Continuing Working and Planning Final Presentation

At this point students are beginning to conclude their investigations. Several of the groups realized as they collected information that they really needed to change or revise their conjectures. Ms. Hernandes asked in what ways their ideas have changed—what do they know now that they did not know before? For example, the group that had the conjecture that special ink was used so colors cannot be duplicated revised its conjecture by broadening it. After doing some research, their new conjecture was that there are many different things that the government does in addition to using special ink to protect money from being copied.

As groups presented their conjectures and progress, Ms. Hernandes modeled constructive comments such as the following: "Your points are clearly made." "Your charts and graphs help us understand each of your points." "Each one of you presented different pieces of information that all connect to your conjecture." "How was your conjecture supported?" After the lesson, Ms. Hernandes took time to reflect and realized that it was very hard for her students to give constructive feedback. She knew that this is an area they would need to work on. She would have to continue modeling but also thought about having groups exchange conjectures and provide feedback in writing to each other. This might reduce anxiety as well as give students time to reflect on the questions and conjectures and to develop some thoughtful feedback.

During this week, Ms. Hernandes took time to discuss possible ways that students could present their findings. The class brainstormed other ideas including the following:

- Writing a series of articles on their information for a magazine
- Creating a poster with diagrams of a process
- A panel discussion
- A computer presentation

Students returned to their groups to decide how they wanted to present their findings.

Final Presentation

Students have been busy working on completing their investigations and developing their presentations. While the class decided on a single research question at the beginning of the unit, different groups developed their own conjectures. Because their conjectures guided their research, each group will be presenting different information. Ms. Hernandes has created a simple web with the class's research question in the center and circles around the question. After groups present their work, the class will discuss what information was found to address the research question. As presentations are made, students will also be encouraged to make connections not only to the question but to each other's findings.

Throughout the unit, Ms. Hernandes recognized that students need more work on asking questions of each other and providing constructive feedback. She plans on modeling questions and comments as groups complete their presentations. Some examples include the following:

- How does what you presented support or refute your conjecture?
- Would you clarify . . .
- It would be helpful if . . .
- Have you thought about . . .
- Your visuals really helped me better understand your ideas.
- That was a great idea. Where can we find more information on it so we can learn more about it?
- What other questions did you think of as you were researching your conjecture?

Overall, Ms. Hernandes felt that this first attempt at Inquiry with the entire class focusing on a single question but generating multiple conjectures made Inquiry manageable for students and herself. Ms. Hernandes is now thinking about how to plan the next Inquiry unit so there are multiple questions as well as multiple conjectures. From the final presentations, she has really begun to appreciate how Inquiry incorporates all the reading and writing skills she has been teaching and how it takes students to the next level of learning—delving deeper into ideas that personally interest them, taking time and responsibility to learn about something, working collaboratively, and sharing new ideas and information.

Tips

- ✦ Inquiry takes time to develop. You may want to do the first unit as an entire class.
- ✦ Provide time throughout the unit for students to work on Inquiry. Use Workshop as well as computer and library time to support Inquiry.
- ✦ If students are careful about the problems or questions they choose to research, they should have few problems in following through with the research. If the problem is too broad or too narrow, they will have problems.
- ✦ Have students take sufficient time in assessing their needs—both knowledge needs and physical needs in relation to their research. Careful preplanning can help the research progress smoothly with great results.
- ✦ Encourage students to reevaluate their needs often so they are not wasting time finding things they already have or ignoring needs that they have not noticed.
- ✦ Interim presentations of material are every bit as important, if not more so, than final presentations. It is during interim presentations that students have the opportunity to rethink and reevaluate their work and change direction or to decide to carry on with their planned research.
- ✦ Connect Inquiry to learning in the content areas. Have students apply their Inquiry skills to learning science, social studies, and the arts.

Assessment

Assessment can be your most effective teaching tool if it is used with the purpose of informing instruction and highlighting areas that need special attention.

Purpose

The assessment components of ***SRA Imagine It!*** are designed to help you make informed instructional decisions, make adequate yearly progress, and help ensure you meet the needs of all your students. The variety of assessments is intended to be used continuously and formatively. That is, students should be assessed regularly as a follow-up to instructional activities, and the results of the assessment should be used to inform subsequent instruction.

You can use assessment as a tool to monitor students' progress, to diagnose students' strengths and weaknesses, to prescribe forms of intervention as necessary, and to measure student outcomes. Both formal and informal assessment can be used, though formal assessment will be your main assessment tool. Formal assessment of student learning consists of performance assessment (both reading and writing), objective tests (multiple choice, short answer, and essay), progress assessment (through students' everyday oral and written work), and assessment rubrics (used for writing, inquiry, and comprehension strategies). Informal assessment can be done by observing or listening to students as they work and jotting down notes either in the Comprehension Observation Log or in a notebook.

Procedure

Formal Assessment

Formal assessment is addressed in ***SRA Imagine It!*** in the form of ***Benchmark Assessments*** and ***Lesson Assessments.*** Both will help you use the results to differentiate instruction, especially for students needing some type of intervention to ensure they will not be at risk for reading failure.

Benchmark Assessments

The ***Benchmark Assessments*** are a form of general outcome measurement that offer an overall framework for assessment and serve as a predictor of how well students will perform at the end of the school year. Each ***Benchmark Assessment*** has material that students will learn over the course of the school year, and each ***Benchmark Assessment*** is of equivalent difficulty. Students are not expected to score high on the initial screening benchmark; instead, students are expected to show growth as they move on to each subsequent benchmark. Only at the end of the year are students expected to have mastered the materials on these assessments.

Observing students as they go about their regular classwork can be an effective way to learn your students' strengths and areas of need.

One ***Benchmark Assessment*** will be administered at the beginning of the year for screening. This can serve as a baseline score against which you can measure students' progress throughout the year. Subsequent benchmarks will also be given at regular intervals—at the end of every other unit in grades K–1, for a total of six assessments, and at the end of each unit for students in grades 2–6, for a total of seven assessments. Since the tests are of equivalent difficulty and contain the same types of items, students' higher scores will reflect their increasing mastery of the curriculum over the course of the year. Use the data from the ***Benchmark Assessments*** to identify students who are at risk for reading failure, to identify strengths and weaknesses of students, and to gauge student progress toward high-stakes tests.

Depending upon the grade level, tested benchmark skills include the following:

- letter recognition,
- phonemic/phonological awareness,
- phonics,
- high-frequency word recognition,
- vocabulary,
- spelling,
- grammar, usage, and mechanics,
- comprehension,
- oral fluency, and
- maze fluency.

In addition, a writing assessment is given in the initial screening, at midyear, and also again at the end of the year for students in grades 3–6. This assessment is the type of on-demand writing performance students will encounter in high-stakes tests. Each writing assessment is of equal difficulty, and student outcomes should reflect an increased mastery of writing convention and genre expectations.

Lesson Assessments

The ***Lesson Assessments*** cover the most important skills featured in the lesson of a given unit—skills that are closely related to reading success and are typically in state and national standards. These assessments will help you determine how well students are grasping the skills and concepts as they are taught and will help inform you about any additional instruction they might need.

The ***Lesson Assessments*** are easily administered and scored. They feature the same language used in the instructional components of ***SRA Imagine It!*** and correspond to its sequence of instruction. The format of these weekly assessments range from multiple choice questions to short answer to an extended writing response. Depending upon the grade level, skills assessed include the following:

- letter and number recognition
- phonological and phonemic awareness
- phonics
- print and book awareness
- high frequency words

- selection vocabulary
- spelling
- grammar, usage, and mechanics skills
- comprehension skills
- oral fluency
- writing

The ***Lesson Assessments*** are offered in several formats so that students can demonstrate their knowledge of content in a number of developmentally appropriate ways. Wherever possible, the assessments are designed to be administered to the whole class or small groups of students. In some cases, however, individually administered assessments are included, such as the oral fluency assessments, as well as critical pre-literacy skills such as phoneme blending or segmentation as well as letter and number recognition.

The ***Lesson Assessments*** will allow you to monitor students' progress as they are assessed on the specific skills taught in a given lesson. The results will provide instructionally relevant information that you can use to differentiate instruction for students who may need additional learning opportunities.

Progress Assessment

Written Practice

Students work on several different skills throughout the day. Each of these assignments can provide you with valuable information about your students' progress. One very helpful resource that students will work in daily is the ***Skills Practice Book*** (Levels K–6). The ***Skills Practice Books*** include lessons that act as practice and reinforcement for the skills lessons taught before and during the reading of the lesson as well as in conjunction with the Language Arts lesson. These skills pages give you a clear picture of students' understanding of the skills taught. Use them as a daily assessment of student progress in the particular skills taught through the program.

Also included in the ***Skills Practice Books*** are lessons that help students with their Inquiry activities. Students can record what they know about the concepts and what they learn, they can keep a record of their research, and they can practice study and research skills that will help them in all of their schooling. You will be able to monitor their growing ability to make connections, find resources, and enhance their knowledge base as they find the answers to the research questions they have posed.

Dictation

In grades 1–3, students use dictation to practice the sound/spelling associations they are learning and/or reviewing. Collect the dictation papers and look through them to see how the students are doing with writing and with proofreading their words. Record notes on the papers and keep them in the student portfolios.

Portfolios

Portfolios are more than just a collection bin or gathering place for student projects and records. They add balance to an assessment program by providing unique benefits to teachers, students, and families.

- ✦ Portfolios help build self-confidence and increase self-esteem as students come to appreciate the value of their work. More importantly, portfolios allow students to reflect on what they know and what they need to learn. At the end of the school year, each student will be able to go through their portfolios and write about their progress.
- ✦ Portfolios provide the teacher with an authentic record of what students can do. Just as important, portfolios give students a concrete example of their own progress and development. Thus, portfolios become a valuable source of information for making instructional decisions.
- ✦ Portfolios allow families to judge student performance directly. Portfolios are an ideal starting point for discussions about a student's achievements and future goals during teacher/family conferences.

You will find that there are many opportunities to add to students' portfolios.

Fluency

- ✦ During partner reading, during Workshop, or at other times of the day, invite students, one at a time, to sit with you and read a story from an appropriate ***Decodable*** (grades 1–3), ***Leveled Readers*** (grades 1–6), ***Leveled Readers for Science*** or ***Social Studies*** (grades 1–6), or the ***Student Reader.***
- ✦ As each student reads to you, follow along and make note of any recurring problems the student has while reading. Note students' ability to decode unknown words as well as any attempt—successful or not—to use strategies to clarify or otherwise make sense of what they are reading. From time to time, check students' fluency by timing their reading and noting how well they are able to sustain the oral reading without faltering.
- ✦ If a student has trouble reading a particular ***Decodable*** or ***Leveled Reader,*** encourage the student to read the story a few times on her or his own before reading it aloud to you. If the ***Decodable*** has two stories, use the alternate story to reassess the student a day or two later.
- ✦ If after practicing with a particular Decodable Book or Leveled Reader and reading it on his or her own a few times, a student is still experiencing difficulty, try the following:
    - Drop back two ***Decodables***. (Continue to drop back until the student is able to read a story with no trouble.) If the student can read that book without problems, move up one book. The same is true for ***Leveled Readers.***
    - Continue the process until the student is able to read the current ***Decodable*** or ***Leveled Readers.***

Assessment Rubrics

In addition to the formal assessment opportunities available in ***Benchmark Assessments, Lesson Assessments,*** and progress assessment, ***SRA Imagine It!*** provides rubrics for you to evaluate students' performance in comprehension, Inquiry, and writing. Rubrics provide criteria for different levels of performance. Rubrics established before an assignment is given are extremely helpful in evaluating the assignment. When students know what the rubrics for a particular assignment are, they can focus their energies on the key issues. Rubrics can be found in the Level Appendix.

Informal Assessment

Observation

Informal assessment is a part of the everyday classroom routine. Observing students as they go about their regular classwork can be an effective way to learn your students' strengths and areas of need. The more students become accustomed to you jotting down informal notes about their work, the more it will become just another part of classroom life that they accept and take little note of. This gives you the opportunity to assess their progress constantly without the interference and possible drawback of formal testing situations.

One tool that will help you make

informal assessment of student progress a part of your everyday classroom routine is the Comprehension Observation Log. You can record information quickly on this observation sheet and even extend your observations over several days, until you have had a chance to observe each student's performance in a particular area.

- Enter students' names in the Comprehension Observation Log, found in the ***Lesson Assessment Books.***
- Before each day's lesson begins, decide which students you will observe.
- Keep the Comprehension Observation Log available so that you can easily record your observations.
- Decide what aspect of the students' learning you wish to monitor.
- During each lesson, observe this aspect in the performances of several students.
- When observing students, do not pull them aside; rather, observe students as part of the regular lesson, either with the whole class or in small groups.
- Record your observations.
- It may take four to five days to make sure you have observed and recorded the performance of each student. If you need more information about performance in a particular area for some of your students, you may want to observe them more than once.

Responding to Assessment Results

The point of assessment is to monitor progress in order to inform instruction, diagnose students' strengths and weaknesses, and differentiate instruction for students who need extra practice in certain skills or an extra challenge. ***SRA Imagine It!*** offers you opportunities to diagnose areas that may cause problems for students, differentiate instruction according to their abilities, monitor their progress on an ongoing basis, and measure student outcomes through ***Lesson Assessments*** or ***Benchmark Assessments,*** in addition to high-stakes state assessments. ***SRA Imagine It!*** also provides several ways to differentiate instruction based on the results of the various assessments. These include the following:

- Reteach lessons are available for students who are approaching level and appear to grasp a given concept but need more instruction and practice to solidify their learning. Many skills taught in the ***Skills Practice Books*** are available in a ***Reteach*** format.
- Intervention lessons provide options for you to use with students who need more intensive support and who are struggling to understand the on-level material. In addition to the support for the weekly lesson, controlled vocabulary lessons and specific skills lessons can help bring students up to grade level.
- ***English Learner Support*** lessons are available for students who are having difficulty with the concepts because they lack the necessary English language background. These resources will provide English Learners with the vocabulary, phonics, comprehension, grammar, and writing support they need to access the ***SRA Imagine It!*** lessons.
- ***Challenge Activities*** provide continued stimulation for those students who are doing well and working above grade level. Many skills covered in the ***Skills Practice Books*** are also available in ***Challenge Activities.***
- ***Workshop Resource Book*** activities give students alternative activities to strengthen or extend their skills in areas such as letter recognition, phonics, vocabulary, comprehension, fluency, word structure, and grammar.
- ***Leveled Readers*** provide students at all different levels of instruction—Approaching Level, On Level, Above Level, and English Learners—with additional opportunities to practice fluency, vocabulary, and comprehension skills. Besides the general ***Leveled Readers, Leveled Readers for Science*** and ***Leveled Readers for Social Studies*** provide students cross-curricular opportunities.

These materials, along with formal and informal assessments, help ensure that assessment and instruction work together to meet every student's needs.

Workshop

Every teacher and every student needs time during the day to organize, to take stock of work that is done, to make plans for work that needs doing, and to finish up incomplete projects. In addition, teachers need time for differentiating instruction, for holding conferences with students, and for doing fluency checks.

Purpose

Workshop is the period of time each day in which students work independently or collaboratively to practice and review material taught in the lessons.

A variety of activities may occur during this time. Students may work on a specific daily assignment, complete an ongoing project, work on unit inquiry activities, focus on writing, or choose from a wide range of possibilities. With lots of guidance and encouragement, students gradually learn to make decisions about their use of time and materials and to collaborate with their peers.

A goal of Workshop is to get students to work independently and productively. This is essential because Workshop is also the time during which the teacher can work with individuals or groups of students to reinforce learning, to provide extra help for those having difficulties, to extend learning, or to assess the progress of the class or of individuals.

Procedure

Initially for many students you will need to structure Workshop carefully. Eventually students will automatically go to the appropriate areas, take up ongoing projects, and get the materials they will need. Workshop will evolve slowly from a very structured period to a time when students make choices and move freely from one activity to the next.

Setting up Workshop guidelines is key. By the time students have completed the first few weeks of school, they should feel confident during Workshop. If not, continue to structure the time and limit options. For young students, early periods of Workshop may run no more than five to eight minutes. The time can gradually increase to fifteen minutes or longer as students gain independence. Older students may be able to work longer and independently from the very beginning of the school year.

Introducing Workshop

Introduce Workshop to students by telling them that every day there will be a time when they are expected to work on activities on their own or in small groups. For younger students explain that in the beginning there may be just a couple of activities but that gradually new ones will be introduced and that students can choose what they want to do. With older students and for those who have experienced Workshop in early grades, you may want to introduce the concept of Workshop and discuss the range of Workshop options from working on fluency to completing their writing.

Workshop is the period of time each day in which students work independently or collaboratively to practice and review material taught in the lessons.

Establish and discuss rules for Workshop with students. Keep them simple and straightforward. You may want to write the finalized rules on the board or on a poster. You may want to review these rules each day at the beginning of Workshop for the first few lessons or so. You may also wish to revisit and revise the rules from time to time. Suggested rules include the following:

- Share.
- Use a quiet voice.
- Take only the materials you need.
- Return materials.
- Always be working.
- When the teacher is working with a student or small group, do not interrupt.

Early in the process, review rules routinely, and discuss how Workshop is going. Is the class quiet enough for everyone to work on his or her own? Are there any rules that need changing? What problems are students having with materials?

For young students in the beginning you will assign the Workshop activities to help them learn to work on their own. Point out the shelf or area of the classroom where Workshop materials are stored. Tell students that when they finish working with the materials for one activity, they will choose something else from the Workshop shelf. New activity materials will be added to the shelf from time to time. Make sure students know that they may always look at books during Workshop.

Tell older students that they will have an opportunity each day to work on their unit inquiry activities, their writing, and other projects. Students will be working independently and collaboratively during this time.

Guidelines

- ✦ Make sure each student knows what he or she needs to do during Workshop.
- ✦ Demonstrate for the entire group any activity or game assigned for Workshop, for example, teaching students a new game, introducing new materials or projects, or explaining different areas.
- ✦ For young students, it is essential to introduce and demonstrate different activities and games before students do them on their own. With games, you may want to have several students play while the others watch. Make sure that all students know exactly what is expected of them.
- ✦ In the beginning, plan to circulate among students, providing encouragement and help as necessary.
- ✦ When students are engaged in appropriate activities and can work independently, meet with those students who need your particular attention. This may include individual students or small groups.
- ✦ Let students know that they need to ask questions and to clarify assignments during Workshop introduction so that you are free to work with small groups.
- ✦ Be sure that students know what they are to do when they have finished an activity and where to put their finished work.

Setting Up Your Classroom for Workshop

Carefully setting up your classroom to accommodate various Workshop activities will help assure that the Workshop period progresses smoothly and effectively. While setting up your classroom, keep the primary Workshop activities in mind. During Workshop, students will be doing independent and collaborative activities. In kindergarten and first grade, these activities may include letter recognition and phonemic awareness activities and writing or illustrating stories or projects. In addition, they will be working on individual or small-group projects.

Many classrooms have areas that students visit on a regular or rotating basis. Unlike traditional centers, all students do not rotate through all the areas each day.

The following are suggestions for space and materials for use during Workshop:

1. Reading Area supplied with books and magazines. The materials in the Reading Area should be dynamic—changing with students' abilities and reflecting unit themes they are reading. You may wish to add books to your classroom library.
2. Writing Area stocked with various types and sizes of lined and unlined paper, pencils, erasers, markers, crayons, small slates, and chalk. The area should also have various ***Letter Cards*** and other handwriting models for those students who want to practice letter formation or handwriting. Students should know that this is where they come for writing supplies. In addition to the supplies described above, the Writing Area can also have supplies to encourage students to create and write on their own:
    - Magazines and catalogs to cut up for pictures; stickers, paint, glue, glitter, and so on to decorate books and book covers; precut and stapled blank books for students to write in (Some can be plain and some cut in special shapes.)
    - Cardboard, tag board, construction paper, and so on for making book covers (Provide some samples.)
    - Tape, scissors, yarn, hole punches for binding books
    - Picture dictionaries, dictionaries, thesauruses, word lists, and other materials that may encourage independence
3. Listening Area supplied with tape recorder, CD player, optional headphones, and CDs of stories, poems, and songs for students to listen to and react to. You might also want to provide blank tapes and encourage students to retell and record their favorite stories or to make up and tell stories for their classmates to listen to on tape. You may also want to make available the Listening Library CDs that are available with the program.
4. Phonics Activities supplied with ***Alphabet Flash Cards,*** individual ***Alphabet Sound Card*** sets (Kindergarten), individual ***Sound/Spelling Cards*** and ***High-Frequency Flash Cards*** (Grades K, 1, 2, and 3), and other materials that enhance what students are learning. Other commonly used classroom materials that enhance reading can be included, for example, plastic letters, puzzles, and games.
5. Fluency Area supplied with ***Pre-Decodables and Decodables, Leveled Readers, Leveled Science Readers*** and ***Leveled Social Studies Readers,*** and other resources for practicing fluency. Some teachers have folders for each student with materials to practice during the week. In addition, some Fluency areas have timers and tape recorders as well.

Because students will be working on their inquiry/investigations during Workshop, make sure there are adequate supplies to help them with their research. These might include dictionaries, encyclopedias, magazines, newspapers, and computers—preferably with Internet capability.

Students thrive in an environment that provides structure, repetition, and routine. Within a sound structure, students will gain confidence and independence. This setting allows you to differentiate instruction to provide opportunities for flexibility and individual choice. This will allow students to develop their strengths, abilities, and talents to the fullest.

Suggestions for English Learners

Workshop affords students who are English Learners a wealth of opportunities for gaining proficiency in English. It also encourages them to share their backgrounds with peers. Since you will be working with all students individually and in small groups regardless of their reading ability, students who need special help with language will not feel self-conscious about working with you. In addition, working in small groups made of students with the same interests rather than the same abilities will provide them with the opportunity to learn about language from their peers during the regular course of Workshop activities.

Some suggestions for meeting the special needs of students with diverse backgrounds are as follows:

- Preread a selection with English Learners to help them identify words and ideas they wish to talk about. This will prepare them for discussions with the whole group.
- Preteach vocabulary and develop selection concepts that may be a challenge for students.
- Negotiate the meaning of selections by asking questions, checking for comprehension, and speaking with English Learners as much as possible.
- Draw English Learners into small-group discussions to give them a sense that their ideas are valid and worth attention.
- Pair English Learners with native English speakers to share their experiences and to provide new knowledge to other students.
- Have English Learners draw or dictate to you or another student a description of a new idea they may have during Workshop activities.

Book Review

Sessions can be small or large. Workshop is a good time for students to share the reading they do on their own. They can discuss a book they have all read, or one person can review a book for the others and answer questions from the group.

During Workshop, students can discuss and review a variety of books:

- Full-length versions of ***Student Reader*** selections
- Books that students learn about when discussing authors and illustrators
- Books related to the investigations of unit concepts that can be shared with others who might want to read them
- Interesting articles from magazines, newspapers, and other sources

When a student reviews a book others have not read, he or she can use some of the sentence starters to tell about the book. These may include "This book is about . . . ," "I chose this book because . . . ," "What I really like/don't like about this book is . . . ," and so on.

- When several students read the same book and discuss it during Workshop, they can use discussion starters.

Encouraging Reading

- Read aloud to your students regularly. You can read from your classroom library or full-length versions of ***Student Reader*** selections.
- Provide a time each day for students to read silently. This time can be as short as 10–15 minutes but should be strictly observed. You should stop what you are doing and read. Students should be allowed to choose their own reading materials during this time and record their reactions in the response journal section of their Writer's Notebooks.
- Establish a classroom library and reading center with books from the school or local library, or ask for donations of books from students, parents, and community members.
- Take your students to the school library or to the public library.

Workshop Management Tips

Use the following Workshop management tips to ensure that Workshop runs smoothly.

Note that these suggestions for a weekly unit/lesson may not exactly correspond to a particular unit/lesson in a given grade level but will give you a sense of how Workshop should progress. All of the time suggestions depend upon the needs of the class and their readiness to work independently.

Kindergarten through Grade 1

Unit 1, Week 1 Introduce Workshop as whole-class workshop. Explain Workshop and its rules. Give the class an activity to do, for example, putting letters in alphabetical order (Grade 1) or copying their names (kindergarten). Tell the class that they will be doing Workshop today. As they do their activity, you will walk around, observing students and noting how well Workshop is going. The class is working quietly and independently. Workshop may last only a few minutes in kindergarten and about ten minutes in first grade.

Unit 1, Weeks 2 and 3 Depending upon your class, you can move to whole-group Workshop with two activities. Give half the class one activity and the other half the other. Explain to the class that for the next few Workshop sessions, there will be two different activities but that the class is supposed to work quietly and independently. Switch activities for the next day, and repeat this format for the next few days or so. Introduce the concept of "debriefing." Take a few minutes at the end, have several students share what they did or learned during Workshop. You may want to have students tell what they like about Workshop and if any changes need to be made.

Unit 2, Week 1 Begin introducing Workshop Areas, explaining the materials and how they can be used. Explain to students that the materials in these areas will be changing regularly so students will be able to practice and use their new reading and writing skills. Workshop activities should change routinely and reflect the changing nature of the curriculum. Often, during the early weeks of Workshop, teachers assign students to different activities and, as students become ready, turn over to students the responsibility for choosing activities.

Unit 3 Add new activities for students. Encourage them to do a couple of Workshop activities each day, perhaps working on their writing in progress and fluency practice (reading a Pre-Decodable or Decodable). Other options might include on-line phonemic awareness and phonics activities, phonics activities such as word sorts, using blended words in written sentences, practicing high-frequency sight words, and so on.

Unit 4 By this time, students should be making choices and working independently. Each Workshop session may be fifteen minutes long with the teacher working with small groups. Take time to review Workshop activities to be sure they are being used and that students are learning from the activities. If activities become stale, vary them, or change them altogether.

Grades 2–6

Unit 1, Lesson 1 Introduce Workshop to students. Make sure they know where materials are located. Post the rules on the board or other prominent place in the classroom. Keep Workshop time short (less than thirty minutes) and very directed during the first few weeks until students can work independently.

Unit 1, Lesson 2 Discuss using small groups for pre-/reteaching purposes and how you will indicate who will be in the groups. Start by forming one small group randomly and having other students do something specific such as a writing assignment. When you have finished with the small group, send them to do independent work. Call another small group of students to work with you. Continue this each day until students are accustomed to forming groups and working independently.

Unit 1, Lesson 3 Reading Roundtable is a student-formed and student-run book discussion. Encourage students participating in Reading Roundtable to choose a book that they all will read and discuss. Several different Reading Roundtable groups may form on the basis of the books students choose.

Unit 1, Lesson 4 For the first few weeks of the school year, make sure each student has a plan for using Workshop time.

Unit 1, Lesson 5 (Days 1–5) Allow time for presentation and discussion of research activities. Use an entire Workshop day, and have all groups present their findings, or split the presentations over several days, depending on the small-group needs of your class.

Unit 1, Lesson 5 (Days 6–10) Review how students have used Workshop during this unit. Have they used their time well? Do they have the materials they need? Discuss suggestions for improving their use of this time. Take a few minutes at the beginning of each Workshop to make sure students know what they will be doing.

Unit 2, Lesson 1 Form small extra-practice groups with the more advanced students from time to time, as they also need special attention.

Unit 2, Lesson 2 To keep the entire class informed about the independent research being done, every other day or so invite a research group to explain what it is doing, how the research is going, and any problems they are encountering.

Unit 2, Lesson 3 Discuss the use of Workshop time for doing Inquiry and research projects, and share ***eInquiry*** with different research activities.

Unit 2, Lesson 4 Make sure small extra-practice groups are formed based on your observations of students' work on the different daily lessons. Small groups should be fluid and based on demonstrated need rather than become static and unchanging.

Unit 2, Lesson 5 (Days 1–5) One purpose of Workshop is to help students learn independence and responsibility. Assign students to monitor Workshop materials. They should alert you whenever materials are running low or missing, and they can be responsible for checking on return dates of library books and making sure the books are either returned or renewed.

Unit 2, Lesson 5 (Days 6–10) Students sometimes have difficulty starting discussions in Reading Roundtable. Try some of these discussion starters with students, and print them on a poster for student use.

I didn't know that . . .
I liked the part where . . .
Does anyone know . . .
I'm still confused by . . .
I figured out that . . .
This made me think . . .
I agree/disagree with because . . .

Unit 3, Lesson 1 By this time students should be accustomed to the routines, rules, expectations, and usage of Workshop time and be moving smoothly from small teacher-led groups to independent work. Monitor small groups occasionally to see that they are on task and making progress on their activities.

Unit 3, Lesson 2 Make a practice of reading aloud to students. All students enjoy being read to, no matter their age or grade. Encourage them to discuss the shared reading in groups and to bring books and read them aloud to their classmates.

Unit 3, Lesson 3 Encourage cooperation and collaboration by providing students with opportunities to engage in small groups.

Unit 3, Lesson 4 Spend a few minutes each day circulating around the room and monitoring what students are doing independently or in small groups. Students can then share with you on a timely basis any questions or problems they are having.

Unit 3, Lesson 5 (Days 1–5) Take note of various small groups. Make sure that quieter students are able to participate in the discussions. Often the stronger, more confident students dominate such discussions. Encourage them to give all participants an opportunity to share their ideas.

Unit 3, Lesson 5 (Days 6–10) If students are not productive during Workshop, keep them in the small group you are working with until they can successfully benefit from independent work. Discuss strategies they could use to become more independent.

Unit 4, Lesson 1 Individual students can monitor Workshop materials and alert you when materials or supplies are running low or missing and can check that library books are either returned or renewed.

Unit 4, Lesson 2 From time to time, join a Reading Roundtable group, and take part in their discussion. Make sure students lead the discussion.

Unit 4, Lesson 3 Encourage responsibility and independence by reminding students to show respect for each other and the materials provided.

Unit 4, Lesson 4 Be sure students discuss during Reading Roundtable what they like or dislike about a book, why they wanted to read it, and how the book either lived up to their expectations or disappointed them. Discussions should not be about basic comprehension but should help students think more deeply about the ideas presented in the book.

Unit 4, Lesson 5 (Days 1–5) Make sure students continue to use the activities provided for use with this unit at **SRAonline.com.**

Unit 4, Lesson 5 (Days 6–10) If students are not productive in Workshop, keep them in the small group you are working with until they can successfully benefit from independent work. Discuss strategies they could use to become more independent.

Unit 5, Lesson 1 Students often make great tutors for other students. They are uniquely qualified to understand problems that others might be having. Encourage students to pair up during Workshop to help each other with their daily lessons.

Unit 5, Lesson 2 Form small extra-practice groups with the more advanced students from time to time, as they also need special attention.

Unit 5, Lesson 3 To keep the entire class informed about the independent research being done, every other day or so, invite a research/investigation group to explain what it is doing, how the research is going, and any problems they are encountering.

Unit 5, Lesson 4 Most of the authors of the ***Student Reader*** selections are well known and have written many, many pieces of fine literature. Encourage students who enjoy the selections to find other books by the same author. Encourage them to think about and discuss what about that particular author's work attracts them.

Unit 5, Lesson 5 (Days 1–5) Share your impressions of books from your classroom library or other readings during Reading Roundtable. Note which students initiate sharing and which are reluctant to share.

Unit 5, Lesson 5 (Days 6–10) Review with students the time they have used in Workshop. Have they used their time well? Do they have the materials they need? Discuss suggestions for improving the use of this time.

Unit 6, Lesson 1 Spend a few minutes each day circulating and monitoring what students are doing independently or in small groups. Students can share with you on a timely basis any questions or problems they are having.

Unit 6, Lesson 2 Students should be accustomed to the routines, rules, expectations, and usage of Workshop time and be moving smoothly from small teacher-led groups to independent work. Make sure to monitor small groups occasionally to see that they are on task and making progress with their activities.

Unit 6, Lesson 3 Make sure students continue to use the activities provided for use with this unit at **SRAonline.com.**

Unit 6, Lesson 4 If the reading selection is an excerpt from a longer piece, encourage students to read the book from which the excerpt is taken and to discuss how the excerpt fits into the larger work.

Unit 6, Lesson 5 (Days 1–5) Students often make great tutors for other students. The fact that they, too, are just learning the materials makes them uniquely qualified to understand problems that others might be having. Encourage students to pair up during Workshop to help each other on their daily lessons.

Unit 6, Lesson 5 (Days 6–10) Allot time for presentation and discussion of research activities. You may want to use a whole Workshop day and have all groups present their findings or split the presentations over several days, depending on the urgency of the small-group instruction your class needs.

Scope and Sequence

Reading

	K	1	2	3	4	5	6
Print/Book Awareness (Recognize and understand the conventions of print and books)							
Capitalization	X	X					
Constancy of Words		X					
Differentiate between Letter and Word	X						
Differentiate between Word and Sentence	X						
End Punctuation	X	X					
Follow Left-to-Right, Top-to-Bottom	X	X					
Letter Recognition and Formation	X	X					
Page Numbering	X	X					
Parts of a Book	X	X					
Picture/Text Relationship	X	X					
Punctuation	X	X					
Quotation Marks	X	X					
Relationship Between Spoken and Printed Language	X	X					
Sentence Recognition	X	X					
Spacing Between Sentences	X	X					
Spacing Between Words	X	X					
Table of Contents	X	X					
Text Features		X					
Text Relationships		X					
Word Length	X	X					
Word Boundaries		X					
Write Left-to-Right, Top-to-Bottom	X	X					
Phonemic Awareness (Recognize Discrete Sounds in Words)							
Oral Blending: Words/Word Parts	X	X					
Oral Blending: Onset and Rime	X	X					
Oral Blending: Syllables	X	X					
Oral (Phoneme) Blending: Initial Sounds	X	X					
Oral (Phoneme) Blending: Final Sounds	X	X					
Oral Blending: Initial Vowels		X					
Oral Blending: Vowel Replacement		X					
Rhyming	X	X					
Phoneme Matching: Initial Sounds	X	X					
Phoneme Matching: Final Sounds	X	X					
Phoneme Matching: Medial Sounds	X	X					
Phoneme Manipulation: Initial Sounds	X	X					
Phoneme Manipulation: Final Sounds	X	X					
Phoneme Manipulation: Medial Sounds	X	X					
Segmentation: Final Consonants	X	X					
Segmentation: Initial Consonants/Blends		X					
Segmentation: Words/Word Parts	X	X					
Segmentation: Syllables	X	X					
Segmentation: Identifying the Number and Order of Sounds in Words	X	X					

Reading (continued)

	K	1	2	3	4	5	6
How the Alphabet Works							
Letter Knowledge (Alphabetic Knowledge)	X	X					
Letter Order (Alphabetic Order)	X	X					
Letter Sounds	X	X					
Sounds in Words	X	X					
Phonics (Associate Sounds and Spellings to Read Words)							
Blending Sounds into Words	X	X	X	X			
Consonant Clusters		X	X	X			
Consonant Digraphs		X	X	X			
Phonograms		X	X	X			
Schwa			X	X			
Silent Consonants			X	X			
Syllables		X	X	X			
Vowel Diphthongs		X	X	X			
Vowels: Long Sounds and Spellings	X	X	X	X			
Vowels: r-controlled		X	X	X			
Vowels: Short Sounds and Spellings	X	X	X	X			
Comprehension Strategies							
Adjusting Reading Speed			X	X	X	X	X
Asking Questions/Answering Questions	X	X	X	X	X	X	X
Clarifying	X	X	X	X	X	X	X
Making Connections	X	X	X	X	X	X	X
Predicting/Confirming Predictions	X	X	X	X	X	X	X
Summarizing		X	X	X	X	X	X
Visualizing	X	X	X	X	X	X	X
Comprehension Skills							
Author's Point of View			X	X	X	X	X
Author's Purpose			X	X	X	X	X
Cause and Effect	X	X	X	X	X	X	X
Classify and Categorize	X	X	X	X	X	X	X
Compare and Contrast	X	X	X	X	X	X	X
Drawing Conclusions	X	X	X	X	X	X	X
Fact and Opinion			X	X	X	X	X
Main Idea and Details	X	X	X	X	X	X	X
Making Inferences		X	X	X	X	X	X
Reality and Fantasy	X	X	X	X			
Sequence	X	X	X	X	X	X	X
Vocabulary							
Apposition		X	X	X	X	X	X
Concept Words		X	X	X	X	X	X
Context Clues		X	X	X	X	X	X
Expanding Vocabulary		X	X	X	X	X	X
High-Frequency Words	X	X	X	X			
Idioms				X	X	X	X
Multiple-Meaning Words		X	X	X	X	X	X
Selection Vocabulary	X	X	X	X	X	X	X
Time and Order Words (Creating Sequence)	X	X	X	X	X	X	X
Utility Words (Colors, Classroom Objects, etc.)	X	X					

Reading (continued)

	K	1	2	3	4	5	6
Reading with a Writer's Eye							
Author's Purpose	X		X	X	X	X	
Alliteration			X		X		X
Captions and Headings			X	X		X	X
Characterization	X	X	X	X	X	X	X
Choosing Good Examples				X	X		
Description		X	X	X	X	X	X
Diagrams							X
Dialect						X	
Dialogue		X	X	X	X	X	X
Effective Beginnings					X	X	
Effective Endings					X		
Event Sequence	X	X	X	X		X	
Expository Writing Techniques					X	X	
Fable Characteristics					X		
Figurative Language		X	X	X	X	X	X
Flashback							X
Genre Knowledge	X		X	X	X	X	X
Idiom						X	X
Irony					X		
Language Use	X		X	X	X	X	X
Mood and Tone		X	X	X			X
Onomatopoeia			X	X	X		X
Personification			X	X		X	X
Persuasive Techniques					X	X	
Plot (Problem/Solution)	X	X	X	X	X	X	X
Point of View					X	X	
Punctuation					X	X	
Quoting Sources					X		
Rhyme	X		X			X	X
Sensory Details		X		X		X	
Sentence Variety						X	
Setting	X	X	X	X	X	X	X
Sidebars							X
Similes and Metaphors				X	X		X
Stage Directions					X		
Style							X
Suspense and Surprise				X		X	
Text Structure	X		X	X	X	X	X
Theme	X		X	X	X	X	X
Transitions					X		X
Using Comparisons		X	X	X		X	
Voice					X	X	X
Word Choice				X			X
Word Structure							
Antonyms			X	X	X	X	X
Comparatives/Superlatives			X	X	X	X	
Compound Words	X	X	X	X	X	X	X
Contractions			X	X	X	X	
Connotation and Denotation							X
Content/Concept Words							X

Reading (continued)

	K	1	2	3	4	5	6
Foreign Words and Phrases						X	X
Gerunds							X
Greek and Latin Roots				X	X	X	X
Homographs			X	X	X	X	X
Homonyms/Homophones			X	X	X	X	X
Inflectional Endings			X	X	X	X	X
Irregular Plurals			X	X	X	X	
Multiple-Meaning Words					X	X	X
Multisyllabic Words			X	X	X	X	
Plurals			X	X	X	X	
Position Words	X	X					
Prefixes			X	X	X	X	X
Root or Base Words			X	X	X	X	X
Shades of Meaning/Levels of Specificity						X	X
Suffixes			X	X	X	X	X
Synonyms			X	X	X	X	X
Word Families			X	X	X	X	X
Word Origins					X	X	X

Inquiry and Study Skills

	K	1	2	3	4	5	6
Study Skills							
Comparing Information across Sources		X		X		X	
Charts, Graphs, and Diagrams/Visual Aids	X	X	X	X	X	X	X
Collaborative Inquiry	X	X	X	X	X	X	X
Communicating Research Progress Results		X	X	X	X	X	X
Compile Notes			X		X	X	X
Conducting an Interview		X	X	X	X	X	X
Finding Needed Information	X	X	X	X	X	X	X
Follow Directions	X		X	X	X		X
Formulate Questions for Inquiry and Research	X	X	X	X	X	X	X
Give Reports	X		X	X	X	X	X
Make Outlines			X	X	X	X	X
Making Conjectures	X	X	X	X	X	X	X
Maps	X	X	X	X	X	X	
Note Taking		X	X	X	X	X	X
Parts of a Book	X	X	X	X	X		
Planning Inquiry		X	X	X	X	X	X
Recognizing Information Needs		X	X	X	X	X	X
Revising Questions and Conjectures	X	X	X	X	X	X	X
Summarize and Organize Information		X	X	X	X	X	X
Time Lines			X	X	X	X	
Use Appropriate Resources (Media Sources, Reference Books, Experts, Internet)		X	X	X	X	X	X
Using a Dictionary/Glossary		X	X	X	X		
Using a Media Center/Library		X	X	X	X		
Using a Thesaurus			X	X	X	X	
Using an Encyclopedia		X	X	X	X		
Using Newspapers and Magazines		X	X		X		X
Using Technology	X	X	X	X	X	X	X

Language Arts

Writing/Composition

	K	1	2	3	4	5	6
Approaches							
Collaborative Writing	X	X	X	X	X	X	X
Individual Writing	X	X	X	X	X	X	X
Writing Process							
Brainstorming/Prewriting	X	X	X	X	X	X	X
Drafting	X	X	X	X	X	X	X
Revising	X	X	X	X	X	X	X
Editing	X	X	X	X	X	X	X
Proofreading	X	X	X	X	X	X	X
Publishing	X	X	X	X	X	X	X
Writing Genres							
Action Tale			X				
Autobiography/Biography	X	X	X	X	X	X	X
Book Review		X	X	X	X	X	
Business Letter			X	X		X	X
Describe a Process		X	X	X	X	X	X
Descriptive Writing	X	X	X	X	X	X	X
Expository/Informational Text	X	X	X	X	X	X	X
Fantasy		X	X	X			
Folklore (Folktales, Fairy Tales, Tall Tales, Legends, Myths)		X	X	X	X	X	
Friendly Letter	X	X	X	X	X	X	X
Historical Fiction					X		X
Invitation		X		X		X	
Journal Writing			X	X	X		
Magazine Article						X	X
Making a List	X	X	X	X	X	X	X
Mystery				X			
Narrative	X	X	X	X	X	X	X
News Story		X	X	X	X		
Personal Writing	X	X	X	X	X	X	X
Persuasive Writing	X	X	X	X	X	X	X
Play/Dramatization			X	X	X	X	X
Poetry	X	X	X	X	X	X	X
Realistic Fiction		X	X	X	X	X	X
Summary		X	X	X	X	X	X
Timed Writing		X	X	X	X	X	X
Writing Traits							
Audience		X	X	X	X	X	X
Conventions	X	X	X	X	X	X	X
Elaboration		X	X	X	X	X	X
Focus		X	X	X	X	X	X
Ideas/Content	X	X	X	X	X	X	X
Organization		X	X	X	X	X	X
Presentation	X	X	X	X	X	X	X
Purpose		X	X	X	X	X	X
Sentence Fluency	X	X	X	X	X	X	X
Sentence Variety		X			X	X	X
Vocabulary		X	X	X	X	X	X
Voice	X	X	X	X	X	X	X
Word Choice	X	X	X	X	X	X	X

Language Arts

Writing/Composition (continued)

Writing Strategies	K	1	2	3	4	5	6
Action and Describing Words	X	X	X	X			
Adding Details	X	X	X	X	X	X	X
Addressing Audience Needs		X	X	X	X	X	X
Brainstorming	X	X	X	X	X	X	X
Categorizing Ideas							X
Cause and Effect					X	X	X
Character Sketch					X	X	
Choosing a Topic	X	X	X	X	X	X	X
Compare and Contrast			X			X	X
Conveying a General Mood				X	X	X	
Creating Suspense				X			X
Creating Vivid Images		X		X	X	X	
Dialogue	X	X	X	X	X	X	X
Effective Beginnings					X	X	X
Elements of a Letter		X	X	X	X	X	X
Elements of Persuasion			X	X	X	X	
Eliminating Irrelevant Information		X	X	X	X	X	X
Eliminating Wordiness			X	X	X	X	X
Evaluate Personal Growth as a Writer			X	X	X	X	
Explanatory Paragraphs		X					
Figurative Language			X	X	X	X	X
Formality of Language		X	X	X	X	X	
Format		X			X	X	X
Generate Additional Ideas		X	X	X	X		
Highlight a Memorable Event		X			X		
Identifying Best Feature of Something Written			X	X			
Illustrations and Drawings	X	X	X	X			
Information from Multiple Sources				X	X	X	X
Main Idea and Details					X	X	
Making Connections							X
Organizing a Multi-Paragraph Composition					X	X	X
Planning		X			X	X	X
Plot Structure—Beginning, Middle, Climax, and End		X		X	X	X	X
Point of View						X	X
Presenting Facts and Examples Objectively				X	X	X	X
Proofreading	X	X	X	X	X	X	X
Purpose		X	X	X	X	X	X
Realism					X	X	X
Referencing a Source					X	X	
Revising	X	X	X	X	X	X	X
Rhythm and Rhyme		X	X			X	
Sensory Details				X	X	X	X
Sentence Combining			X	X	X	X	X
Sequence	X	X	X	X		X	
Setting		X	X	X	X	X	X
Story Elements		X	X	X	X	X	
Style							X
Summary			X	X	X	X	X
Taking Notes		X	X	X	X	X	X

Language Arts

Writing/Composition (continued)

	K	1	2	3	4	5	6
Timed Writing		X	X	X	X	X	X
Time Line			X	X		X	
Transition Words/Devices			X	X	X	X	X
Using a Checklist		X	X	X	X	X	
Using a Graphic Organizer		X	X	X	X	X	X
Using a Model as a Guide to Writing			X	X		X	
Using Outlines to Organize Information				X	X	X	X
Using Multimedia Sources			X	X	X	X	X
Vary Sentence Beginnings			X	X	X	X	
Vary Sentence Length		X	X			X	
Vary Sentence Types	X	X	X	X	X	X	
Voice				X		X	
Voicing an Opinion		X				X	X
Word Choice		X	X	X	X	X	X
Working Collaboratively						X	X
Writing Coherent Paragraphs		X	X	X	X	X	X

Language Arts

Grammar

	K	1	2	3	4	5	6
Parts of Speech							
Adjectives (Describing Words)	X	X	X	X	X	X	X
Adverbs			X	X	X	X	X
Conjunctions			X	X	X	X	X
Nouns	X	X	X	X	X	X	X
Prepositions				X	X	X	X
Pronouns	X	X	X	X	X	X	X
Verbs	X	X	X	X	X	X	X
Sentences							
Complete and Incomplete Sentences		X	X	X	X	X	X
Fragments			X	X	X	X	X
Independent and Dependent Clauses							X
Parts (Subjects and Predicates)			X	X	X	X	X
Run-on Sentences					X		X
Sentence Combining			X	X	X	X	X
Structure (Simple, Compound, Complex, Compound-Complex)			X	X	X	X	X
Subject/Verb Agreement		X	X	X	X	X	X
Types (Declarative, Interrogative, Exclamatory, Imperative)	X	X	X	X	X	X	X
Usage							
Adjectives		X	X	X	X	X	X
Adverbs			X	X	X	X	X
Antonyms		X	X				
Articles			X	X		X	X
Contractions			X	X	X		
Nouns		X	X	X	X	X	X
Pronouns		X	X	X	X	X	X
Regular and Irregular Plurals					X	X	X
Synonyms		X	X				
Verb Tenses		X	X	X	X	X	X
Verbs (Action, Helping, Linking, Regular/Irregular)		X	X	X	X	X	X

Language Arts

Grammar (continued)

	K	1	2	3	4	5	6
Mechanics							
Capitalization (Sentence, Proper Nouns, Titles, Direct Address, Pronoun "I")	X	X	X	X	X	X	X
Punctuation (End Punctuation, Comma Use, Quotation Marks, Apostrophe, Colon, Semicolon, Hyphen, Parentheses)	X	X	X	X	X	X	X
Spelling							
Antonyms					X	X	X
Base or Root Words					X	X	
Comparatives/Superlatives				X	X	X	X
Compound Words				X	X	X	
Connotation and Denotation							X
Content/Concept Words							X
Contractions				X	X		X
Foreign Words and Phrases							X
Gerunds							X
Greek and Latin Roots				X	X	X	X
Homographs				X	X	X	X
Homonyms/Homophones				X	X	X	X
Inflectional Endings		X		X	X	X	X
Irregular Plurals		X		X	X	X	
Irregular Verbs						X	
Long Vowel Patterns		X	X	X	X		
Multiple-Meaning Words					X	X	X
Multisyllabic Words		X	X	X	X		X
Phonograms		X					
Prefixes				X	X	X	X
r-Controlled Vowel Spellings		X	X				
Shades of Meaning					X		X
Short Vowel Spellings		X	X	X	X		
Silent Letters			X	X	X		
Sound/Letter Relationships	X	X	X				
Special Spellings Patterns/Rules		X	X	X	X	X	
Special Vowel Spellings		X	X	X			
Suffixes		X		X	X	X	X
Synonyms					X	X	X
Word Families		X		X		X	X

Listening/Speaking/Viewing

Listening/Speaking/Viewing	K	1	2	3	4	5	6
Listening							
Analyze/Evaluate Intent and Content of Speaker's Message		X	X	X		X	X
Ask Questions		X	X	X	X	X	X
Determine Purposes for Listening		X	X	X	X	X	X
Drawing Conclusions and Making Inferences						X	
Follow Directions	X	X		X	X	X	X
Learn about Different Cultures through Discussion				X	X		
Listen for Poetic Language (Rhythm/Rhyme)	X	X			X		X
Listening for Details			X	X	X		
Listening for Information				X	X		
Participate in Group Discussions	X	X	X	X	X	X	X
Recalling What Was Heard				X			
Recognizing Fact and Opinion				X			
Respond to Speaker	X	X	X	X	X	X	X
Use Nonverbal Communication Techniques		X		X	X	X	X
Speaking							
Answer Questions	X	X	X	X	X	X	X
Asking Questions		X		X	X		
Describe Ideas and Feelings	X	X	X				X
Effective Word Choice/Voice			X	X	X	X	
Engaging the Audience					X	X	
Give Directions		X			X	X	X
Learn About Different Cultures through Discussion		X		X			X
Listen and Respond		X		X	X		
Making Announcements and Introductions		X					
Organizing Presentations				X	X	X	X
Paraphrasing			X	X			
Participate in Group Discussion	X	X	X	X	X	X	X
Present Oral Reports		X	X	X	X	X	X
Purposes of Speech			X				
Read Fluently with Expression, Phrasing, and Intonation		X	X	X	X	X	X
Read Orally	X	X	X	X	X	X	X
Share Information		X	X	X	X	X	X
Small Group Discussion			X	X	X	X	X
Speak Clearly at Appropriate Volume		X	X	X	X	X	X
Speaking Strategies				X	X		
Staying on Topic		X					
Summarize/Retell Stories	X	X	X	X	X	X	X
Understand Formal and Informal Language		X		X	X	X	X
Use Appropriate Language for Audience		X		X	X	X	X
Use Nonverbal Communication Techniques		X	X	X	X	X	X

Listening/Speaking/Viewing (continued)

	K	1	2	3	4	5	6
Viewing							
Analyze Purposes and Techniques of the Media			X	X	X	X	X
Appreciate/Interpret Artist's Techniques		X					
Compare Visual and Written Material on the Same Subject		X					X
Culture in Media		X			X	X	
Describe Pictures			X				
Gather Information from Visual Images		X	X	X	X	X	X
Interpreting Media				X	X		
Language Development							X
Literary Devices				X			X
Relating to Content				X	X		
Understanding Gestures				X	X		
Using Multimedia				X	X	X	
View Critically		X		X	X	X	X
Penmanship							
Cursive Letters			X	X			
Manuscript Letters	X	X					
Numbers	X	X					

Unit Themes

	Level K	Level 1	Level 2
Unit 1	Off to School	Back to School	Kindness
Unit 2	Patterns	Where Animals Live	Let's Explore
Unit 3	Finding Friends	I Am Responsible!	Around the Town
Unit 4	By the Sea	Our Neighborhood at Work	Look Again
Unit 5	Stick to It	What's the Weather?	Courage
Unit 6	My Shadow	North, South, East, West	America's People
Unit 7	Teamwork	I Think I Can	
Unit 8	Ready, Set, Grow!	Away We Grow!	
Unit 9	Red, White, and Blue	Home, Sweet Home	
Unit 10	Windy Days	I Am Brave	

Level 3	Level 4	Level 5	Level 6
Friendship	Risks and Consequences	Heritage	Taking a Stand
Animals and Their Habitats	Nature's Delicate Balance	Energy at Work	Ancient Civilizations
Money	A Changing America	Making a New Nation	Ecology
Earth, Moon, and Sun	Science Fair	Our Corner of the Universe	Great Expectations
Communities across Time	America on the Move	Going West	Earth in Action
Storytelling	Dollars and Sense	Call of Duty	Art and Impact

Glossary of Reading Terms

This glossary includes linguistic, grammatical, comprehension, and literary terms that may be helpful in understanding reading instruction.

acronym a word formed from the initial letter of words in a phrase, **scuba (self-contained underwater breathing apparatus)**.

acrostic a kind of puzzle in which lines of a poem are arranged so that words or phrases are formed when certain letters from each line are used in a sequence.

adjective a word or group of words that modifies or describes a noun.

adventure story a narrative that features the unknown or unexpected with elements of excitement, danger, and risk.

adverb a word or group of words that modifies a verb, adjective, or other adverb. An adverb answers questions such as **how, when, where,** and **how much.**

affective domain the psychological field of emotional activities such as interests, attitudes, opinions, appreciations, values, and emotional sets

affix a word part, either a prefix or a suffix, that changes the meaning or function of a word root or stem.

affricate a speech sound that starts as a stop but ends as a fricative, the /ch/ in **catch.**

agreement the correspondence of syntactically related words; subjects and predicates are in agreement when both are singular or plural.

alliteration the repetition of the initial sounds in neighboring words or stressed syllables.

alphabet the complete set of letters representing speech sounds used in writing a language. In English there are twenty-six letters.

alphabet book a book for helping young children learn the alphabet by pairing letters with pictures whose sounds they represent.

alphabetic principle the association between sounds and the letters that represent them in alphabetic writing systems.

alveolar a consonant speech sound made when the tongue and the ridge of the upper and lower jaw stop to constrict the air flow, as /t/.

anagram a word or phrase whose letters form other words or phrases when rearranged, for example, **add** and **dad.**

analogy a likeness or similarity.

analytic phonics also deductive phonics, a whole-to-part approach to phonics in which a student is taught a number of sight words and then phonetic generalizations that can be applied to other words.

antonym a word that is opposite in meaning to another word.

appositive a word that restates or modifies a preceding noun, for example, **my daughter, Charlotte.** Appositives are also definitions of words usually set off by commas.

aspirate an unvoiced speech sound produced by a puff of air, as /h/ in **heart.**

aspirated stop a stop consonant sound released with a puff of air, as /k/, /p/, and /t/.

auditory discrimination the ability to hear phonetic likenesses and differences in phonemes and words.

author's purpose the motive or reason for which an author writes; includes to entertain, inform, persuade, and explain how.

automaticity fluent processing of information, requiring little effort or attention.

auxiliary verb a verb that precedes another verb to express time, mood, or voice; includes verbs such as **has, is,** and **will.**

ballad a narrative poem, composed of short verses to be sung or recited, usually containing elements of drama and often tragic in tone.

base word a word to which affixes may be added to create related words.

blank verse unrhymed verse, especially unrhymed iambic pentameter.

blend the joining of the sounds of two or more letters with little change in those sounds, for example, /spr/ in **spring;** also **consonant blend** or **consonant cluster.**

blending combining the sounds represented by letters or spellings to sound out or pronounce a word; contrast with **oral blending.**

breve the symbol placed above a vowel to indicate that it is a short vowel.

browse to skim through or look over in search of something of interest.

canon in literature, the body of major works that a culture considers important at a given time.

case a grammatical category that indicates the syntactic/semantic role of a noun phrase in a sentence.

cause-effect relationship a stated or implied association between an outcome and the conditions that brought it about; also the comprehension skill associated with recognizing this type of relationship as an organizing principle in text.

chapter book a book long enough to be divided into chapters, but not long or complex enough to be considered a novel.

characterization the way in which an author presents a character in a story, including describing words, actions, thoughts, and impressions of that character.

choral reading oral group reading to develop oral fluency by modeling.

cinquain a stanza of five lines, specifically one that has successive lines of two, four, six, eight, and two syllables.

cipher a system for writing in code.

clarifying a comprehension strategy in which the reader rereads text, uses a dictionary, uses decoding skills, or uses context clues to comprehend something that is unclear.

clause a group of words with a subject and a predicate used to form a part of or a whole sentence, a dependent clause modifies an independent clause, which can stand alone as a complete sentence.

collaborative learning learning by working together in small groups.

command a sentence that asks for action and usually ends with a period.

common noun in contrast to **proper noun,** a noun that denotes a class rather than a unique or specific thing such as **girl** versus **Susan.**

comprehension the understanding of what is written or said.

comprehension skill a skill that aids in understanding text, including identifying **author's purpose**, **author's point of view,** comprehending **cause-and-effect** relationships, **clarifying, comparing and contrasting** items and events, **drawing conclusions,** distinguishing **fact from opinion,** identifying **main ideas, making inferences,** distinguishing **reality from fantasy,** and understanding **sequence.**

comprehension strategy a sequence of steps for monitoring and understanding text, includes adjusting reading speed, asking questions, clarifying, making connections, predicting, summarizing, and visualizing.

conjugation the complete set of all possible inflected forms of a verb.

conjunction a part of speech used to connect words, phrases, clauses, or sentences, including the words **and, but,** and **or.**

consonant a speech sound, and the alphabet letter that represents that sound, made by partial or complete closure of part of the vocal tract, which obstructs air flow and causes audible friction.

context clue information from the immediate and surrounding text that helps identify a word.

contraction a short version of a written or spoken expression in which letters are omitted, for example, **can't.**

convention an accepted practice in spoken or written language, usually referring to spelling, mechanics, or grammar rules.

cooperative learning a classroom organization that allows students to work together to achieve their individual goals. Related term is **collaboration.**

creative writing prose and poetic forms of writing that express the writer's thoughts and feelings imaginatively.

cueing system any of the various sources of information that help identify an unrecognizable word in reading, including phonetic, semantic, and syntactical information.

cumulative tale a story, such as "The Gingerbread Man," in which details are repeated until the climax.

dangling modifier usually a participle that because of its placement in a sentence modifies the wrong object.

decodable text text materials controlled to include a majority of words whose sound/spelling relationships are known by the reader.

decode to analyze spoken or graphic symbols for meaning.

diacritical mark a mark, such as a breve or macron, added to a letter or graphic character to indicate a specific pronunciation.

dialect a regional variety of a particular language with phonological, grammatical, and lexical patterns that distinguishes it from other varieties.

dialogue a piece of writing written as conversation, usually punctuated by quotation marks.

digraph two letters that represent one speech sound, for example, /sh/ or /ch/.

diphthong a vowel sound produced when the tongue glides from one vowel sound toward another in the same syllable, for example, /oi/ or /ou/.

direct object the person or thing that receives the action of a verb in a sentence, for example, the word **cake** in this sentence: **Madeline baked a cake.**

drafting the process of writing ideas in rough form to record them.

drama a story in the form of a play, written to be performed.

edit in the writing process, to revise or correct a manuscript. Often this is part of the final step in the process with a focus on correcting grammar, spelling, and mechanics rather than content, structure, and organization.

emergent literacy the development of the association of meaning and print that continues until a child reaches the stage of conventional reading and writing.

emergent reading a child's early interaction with books and print before the ability to decode text.

encode to change a message into symbols, for example, to change speech into writing.

epic a long narrative poem, usually about a hero.

exclamatory sentence a sentence that shows strong emotion and ends with an exclamation point.

expository writing or **exposition** a composition in writing that explains an event or process.

fable a short tale that teaches a moral.

fantasy a highly imaginative story about characters, places, and events that cannot exist.

fiction imaginative narrative designed to entertain rather than to explain, persuade, or describe.

figure of speech the expressive, nonliteral use of language usually through metaphor, simile, or personification.

fluency freedom from word-identification problems that hinder comprehension in reading. Fluency involves rate, accuracy, and expression.

folktale a narrative form of genre such as an epic, myth, or fable that is well-known through repeated storytellings.

foreshadowing giving clues to upcoming events in a story.

free verse verse with irregular metrical pattern.

freewriting writing that is not limited in form, style, content, or purpose; designed to encourage students to write.

genre a classification of literary works, including tragedy, comedy, novel, essay, short story, mystery, realistic fiction, and poetry.

grammar the study of the classes of words, their inflections, and their functions and relations in sentences; includes phonological, morphological, syntactic, and semantic descriptions of a language.

grapheme a written or printed representation of a phoneme, such as **c** for /k/.

guided reading reading instruction in which the teacher provides the structure and purpose for reading and responding to the material read.

handing off a method of turning over to students the primary responsibility for controlling discussion.

indirect object in a sentence, the person or thing to or for whom an action is done, for example, the word **dog** in this sentence: **Madeline gave the dog a treat.**

inference a conclusion based on facts, data, or evidence.

infinitive the base form of a verb, usually with the infinitive marker, for example, **to go.**

inflectional ending an ending that expresses a plural or possessive form of a noun, the tense of a verb, or the comparative or superlative form of an adjective or adverb.

interrogative word a word that marks a clause or sentence as a question, including **interrogative pronouns who, what, which, where.**

intervention a strategy or program designed to supplement or substitute instruction, especially for those students who fall behind.

invented spelling the result of an attempt to spell a word based on using the sounds in the letter names to determine the sound the letter names. Gradually sounds are connected to letters, which leads to conventional spelling..

irony a figure of speech in which the literal meanings of the words is the opposite of their intended meanings.

journal a written record of daily events or responses.

juvenile book a book written for children or adolescents.

legend a traditional tale handed down from generation to generation.

leitmotif a repeated expression, event, or idea used to unify a work of art such as writing.

letter one of a set of graphic symbols that forms an alphabet and is used alone or in combination to represent a phoneme, also **grapheme.**

linguistics the study of the nature and structure of language and communication.

literary elements the elements of a story such as **setting, plot,** and **characterization** that create the structure of a narrative.

macron a diacritical mark placed above a vowel to indicate a long vowel sound.

main idea the central thought or chief topic of a passage.

making connections a reading strategy used to connect information being read to one's own experiences to other reading materials or to one's knowledge of the world. Making connections fosters engagement, while reading helps the reader make sense of the text and connect information.

mechanics the conventions of capitalization and punctuation.

metacognition awareness and knowledge of one's mental processes or thinking about what one is thinking about.

metaphor a figure of speech in which a comparison is implied but not stated; for example, **She is a jewel.**

miscue a deviation from text during oral reading in an attempt to make sense of the text.

modeling an instructional technique in which the teacher makes public the thinking needed to use critical reading and writing behaviors.

mood the literary element that conveys the emotional atmosphere of a story.

morpheme a meaningful linguistic unit that cannot be divided into smaller units, for example, **word**; **a bound morpheme** is a morpheme that cannot stand alone as an independent word, for example, the prefix **re-**; a **free morpheme** can stand alone, for example, **dog.**

myth a story designed to explain the mysteries of life.

narrative writing or **narration** a composition in writing that tells a story or gives an account of an event.

nonfiction prose designed to explain, argue, or describe rather than to entertain with a factual emphasis; includes biography and autobiography.

noun a part of speech that denotes persons, places, things, qualities, or acts.

novel an extended fictional prose narration.

onomatopoeia the use of a word whose sound suggests its meaning, for example, **purr.**

oral blending the ability to fuse discrete phonemes into recognizable words; oral blending puts sounds together to make a word, **see also segmentation.**

orthography correct or standardized spelling according to established usage in a language.

oxymoron a figure of speech in which contrasting or contradictory words are brought together for emphasis.

paragraph a subdivision of a written composition that consists of one or more sentences, deals with one point, or gives the words of one speaker, usually beginning with an indented line.

participle a verb form used as an adjective, for example, **the skating party.**

personification a figure of speech in which animals, ideas, or things take on human characteristics.

persuasive writing a composition intended to persuade the reader to adopt the writer's point of view.

phoneme the smallest sound unit of speech, for example, the /k/ in **book.**

phonemic awareness the ability to recognize that spoken words are made of discrete sounds and that those sounds can be manipulated.

phonetic spelling the respelling of entry words in a dictionary according to a pronunciation key.

phonetics the study of speech sounds.

phonics a way of teaching reading that addresses sound/symbol relationships, especially in beginning instruction.

phonogram a letter or symbol that represents a phonetic sound.

phonological awareness the ability to attend to the sound structure of language; includes sentence, word, syllable rhyme and phonological awareness.

plot the literary element that provides the structure of the action of a story, which may include rising action, climax, and falling action leading to a resolution or denouement.

plural a grammatical form of a word that refers to more than one in number; an irregular plural is one that does not follow normal patterns for inflectional endings.

poetic license the liberty taken by writers to ignore conventions.

poetry a metrical form of composition in which language is chosen and arranged to create a powerful response through meaning, sound, or rhythm.

possessive showing ownership either through the use of an adjective, an adjectival pronoun, or the possessive form of a noun.

predicate the part of the sentence that expresses something about the subject and includes the verb phrase; a **complete predicate** includes the principal verb in a sentence and all its modifiers or subordinate parts.

predicting a comprehension strategy in which the reader attempts to anticpate what will happen, using clues from the text and prior knowledge, and then confirms predictions as the text is read.

prefix an affix attached before a base word that changes the meaning of the word.

preposition a part of speech in the class of function words such as **of, on,** and **at** that precede noun phrases to create prepositional phrases.

prewriting the planning stage of the writing process in which the writer formulates ideas, gathers information, and considers ways to organize them.

print awareness in emergent literacy, a child's growing recognition of conventions and characteristics of written language, including reading from left to right and from top to bottom in English and that words are separated by spaces.

pronoun a part of speech used as a substitute for a noun or noun phrase.

proofreading the act of reading with the intent to correct, clarify, or improve text.

pseudonym an assumed name used by an author; a pen name or nom de plume.

publishing the process of preparing written material for presentation.

punctuation graphic marks such as commas, periods, quotation marks, and brackets used to clarify meaning and to give speech characteristics to written language.

question an interrogative sentence that asks a question and ends with a question mark.

realistic fiction a story that attempts to portray characters and events as they actually are.

rebus a picture or symbol that suggests a word or syllable.

revise in the writing process, to change or correct a manuscript to make its message more clear.

rhyme identical or very similar recurring final sounds in words, often at the ends of lines of poetry.

rime a vowel and any following consonants of a syllable.

segmentation the ability to break words into individual sounds; **see also oral blending.**

semantic mapping a graphic display of a group of words that are meaningfully related to support vocabulary instruction.

semantics the study of meaning in language, including the meanings of words, phrases, sentences, and texts.

sentence a grammatical unit that expresses a statement, question, or command; a **simple sentence** is a sentence with one subject and one predicate; a **compound sentence** is a sentence with two or more independent clauses usually separated by a comma and conjunction, but no dependent clause; a **complex sentence** is a sentence with one independent and one or more dependent clauses.

sentence combining a teaching technique in which complex sentence chunks and paragraphs are built from basic sentences.

sentence lifting the process of using sentences from children's writing to illustrate what is wrong or right to develop children's editing and proofreading skills.

sequence the order of elements or events.

setting the literary element that includes the time, place, and physical and psychological background in which a story takes place.

sight word a word that is taught to be read as a whole word, usually words that are phonetically irregular.

simile a figure of speech in which a comparison of two things that are unlike is directly stated, usually with the words **like** or **as**; for example, **She is like a jewel.**

spelling the process of representing language by means of a writing system.

statement a sentence that tells something and ends with a period.

study skills a general term for the techniques and strategies that help readers comprehend text with the intent to remember; includes following directions, organizing, locating, and using graphic aids.

style the characteristics of a work that reflect the author's particular way of writing.

subject the main topic of a sentence to which a predicate refers, including the principal noun; a **complete subject** includes the principal noun in a sentence and all its modifiers.

suffix an affix attached at the end of a base word that changes the meaning and the function of the word.

summarizing a comprehension strategy in which the reader constructs a brief statement that contains the essential ideas of a passage.

syllable a minimal unit of sequential speech sounds comprised of a vowel sound or a vowel-sound combination.

symbolism the use of one thing to represent something else to represent an idea in a concrete way.

synonym a word that means the same as another word.

syntax the grammatical pattern or structure of word order in sentences, clauses, and phrases.

tense the way in which verbs indicate past, present, and future time of action.

text structure the various patterns of ideas that are built into the organization of a written work.

theme a major idea or proposition that provides an organizing concept through which, by study, students gain depth of understanding.

topic sentence a sentence intended to express the main idea of a paragraph or passage.

tragedy a literary work, often a play, in which the main character suffers conflicts and which presents a serious theme and has an unfortunate ending.

usage the way in which a native language or dialect is used by the members of the community.

verb a word that expresses an action or state that occurs in a predicate of a sentence; an irregular verb is a verb that does not follow normal patterns of inflectional endings that reflect past, present, or future verb tense.

visualizing a comprehension strategy in which the reader constructs a mental picture of a character, setting, or process.

vowel a voiced speech sound and the alphabet letter that represents that sound, made without stoppage or friction of the air flow as it passes through the vocal tract.

vowel digraph a spelling pattern in which two or more letters represent a single vowel sound.

word calling proficiency in decoding with little or no attention to word meaning.

writing also **composition** the process or result of organizing ideas in writing to form a clear message; includes persuasive, expository, narrative, and descriptive forms.

writing process the many aspects of the complex act of producing a piece of writing, including prewriting, drafting, revising, editing/proofreading, and publishing.

Penmanship

SRA Imagine It! develops handwriting skills through weekly Penmanship lessons. The instruction for these lessons appears in the Language Arts part of the lesson in Levels 2 and 3. The purpose of these lessons is to develop important handwriting skills that are necessary for producing legible, properly spaced documents.

In addition to the board, the overhead projector can be a very effective device for teaching penmanship. Students can move their pencils at the same time you form letters on the transparency. It also helps to recite the descriptions or chants that go with each letter.

Penmanship in Levels K and 1

Beginning in kindergarten, the Penmanship lessons expand on the sound/letter instruction by introducing letters that students study in Sounds and Letters. Students learn that those letters are made of four basic lines: curved lines, horizontal lines, vertical lines, and slanted lines.

Next, students learn letter and number formations. Students practice letter formation by writing the letter that is being studied and then by writing words that contain that particular letter. This instruction continues in Level 1 and is tied to the letter formation instruction in Phonics and Fluency.

Cursive Handwriting Models

Penmanship is developed and practiced through Level 3, with cursive instruction beginning in the first unit of Level 2. Students are taught that most cursive letters are comprised of four strokes: undercurve, downcurve, overcurve, and slanted lines. These lessons teach students the essentials of cursive handwriting, such as proper slant; loop; joining; and spacing between letters, words, and sentences. As in the earlier levels, students practice letter formation by writing the letters and then by writing words that contain the particular letter.

The writing exercises progress with each level. Students begin writing words in kindergarten and graduate to writing sentences by the end of Level 1. Level 2 eases students into cursive by having them practice letters, words, and sentences. By Level 3, students are writing complete paragraphs in cursive.

Hand and Paper Positioning

The hand and paper positioning models are for your reference and enhance the written instruction of positioning lessons. The diagrams give you a visual aid so you may better understand and demonstrate an effective technique of positioning.

A right-handed student should hold the pencil loosely about one inch above the point, between the thumb and middle finger. A left-handed student should hold the pencil the same way, but up to one half inch farther away from the point. The index fingers of both writers should rest lightly on the top of the pencil. The wrist should be level and slightly raised from the desk.

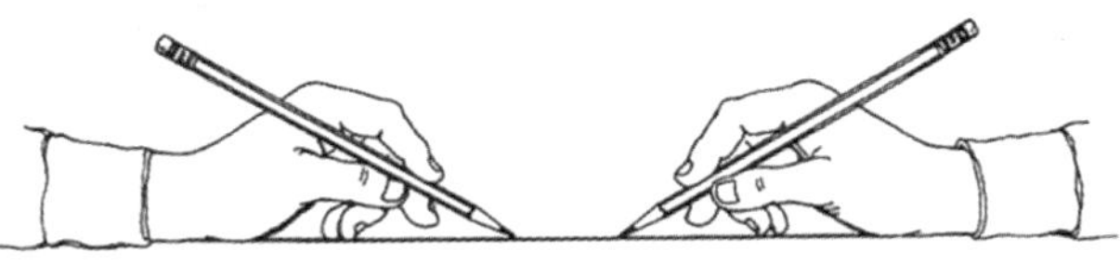

Left-handed writers Right-handed writers

For both kinds of writers, the paper should lie straight in front of the student with the edges parallel to the edges of the desk. A left-handed writer may find it easier to slant the paper slightly to the right and parallel to the left forearm. A right-handed writer's writing hand should be kept well below the writing. The left hand should hold down the paper.

Left-handed writers

Right-handed writers

Cursive Handwriting Models

The models of cursive handwriting provide you with a systematic method for teaching the formation of uppercase and lowercase letters of the alphabet. The dots on the letters indicate starting points. The numbered arrows show the order and direction the lines should go to form the particular letter. You may use the chants to give a step-by-step description of the formation of the letter as you model the formation on the board. Students may also say the chants in unison as they practice the formation, whether they are writing the letter or tracing it on the board.

The four basic cursive strokes diagram provides examples of the strokes that recur frequently in cursive handwriting. Students can form most cursive letters by using one or more of these strokes. The letters in the Penmanship lessons are grouped according to the strokes that are particular to each letter.

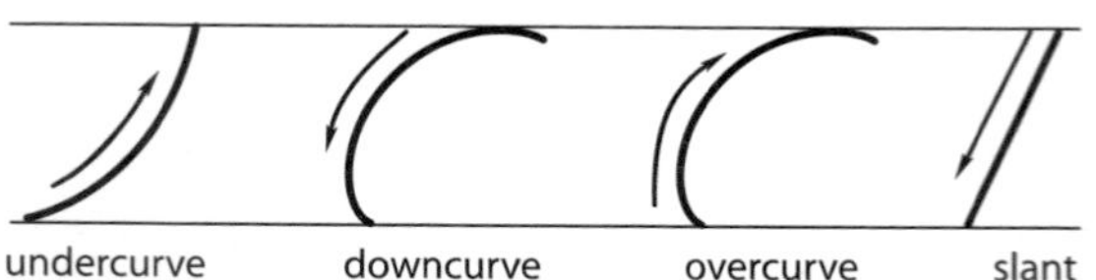

Undercurve Letters

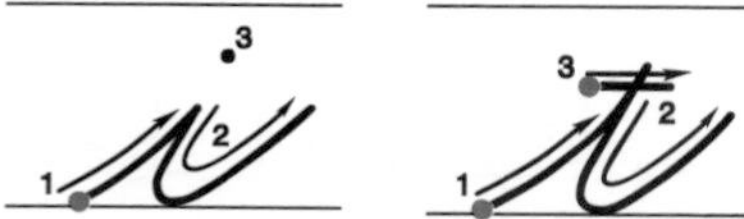

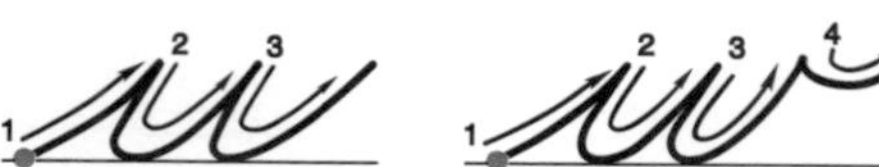

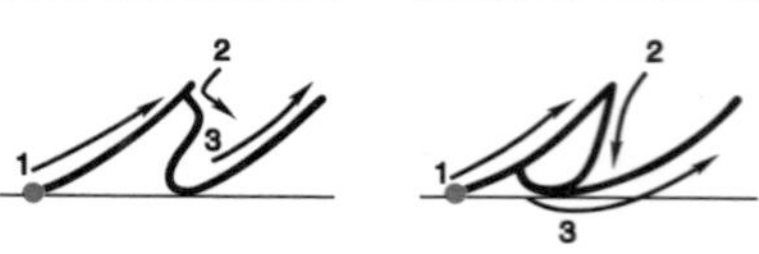

i Starting point, undercure
Slant down, undercurve to endpoint, dot exactly above: small *i*

t Starting point, undercurve
Slant down, undercurve to endpoint
Starting point, straight across: small *t*

u Starting point, undercurve
Slant down, undercurve
Slant down, undercurve: small *u*

w Starting point, undercurve
Slant down, undercurve, slant down, undercurve, small curve to right: small *w*

r Starting point, undercurve
Slant right
Slant down, undercurve: small *r*

s Starting point, undercurve
Curve down and back, undercurve: small *s*

Downcurve Letters

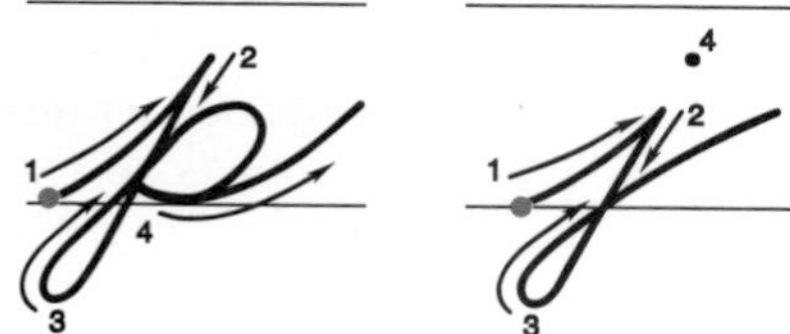

p Starting point, undercurve
Slant, loop back
Overcurve
Curve back, undercurve: small *p*

j Starting point, undercurve
Slant down
Loop back
Overcurve to endpoint
Dot exactly above: small *j*

a Starting point, undercurve
Downcurve, undercurve
Slant down, undercurve: small *a*

c Starting point, undercurve
Downcurve, undercurve: small *c*

d Starting point, undercurve
Downcurve, undercurve
Slant down, undercurve: small *d*

q Starting point, undercurve
Downcurve, undercurve
Slant down and loop forward,
Undercurve: small *q*

g Starting point, undercurve
Downcurve, undercurve
Slant down and loop back,
Overcurve: small *g*

o Starting point, undercurve
Downcurve, undercurve
Small curve to right: small *o*

Cursive Handwriting Models

Overcurve Letters

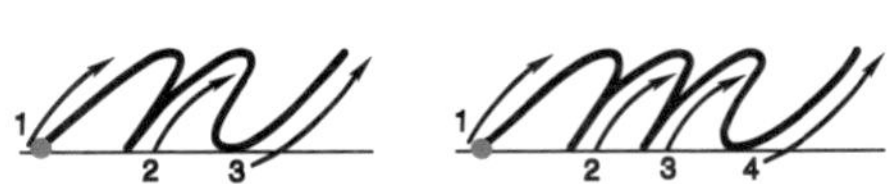

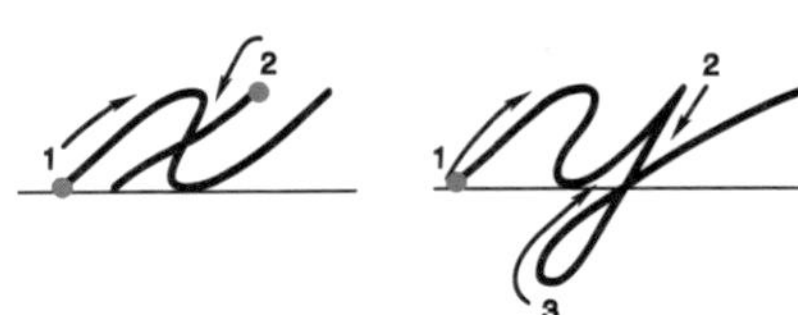

n Starting point, overcurve
Slant down, overcurve
Slant down, undercurve: small *n*

m Starting point, overcurve
Slant down, overcurve
Slant down, overcurve
Slant down, undercurve: small *m*

x Starting point, overcurve
Slant down, undercurve to endpoint
Starting point slant down: small *x*

y Starting point, overcurve
Slant down
Undercurve, slant down
Loop back into overcurve: small *y*

z Starting point, overcurve
Slant down, overcurve, down
Loop into overcurve: small *z*

v Starting point, overcurve
Slant down
Undercurve
Small curve to right: small *v*

Letters with Loops

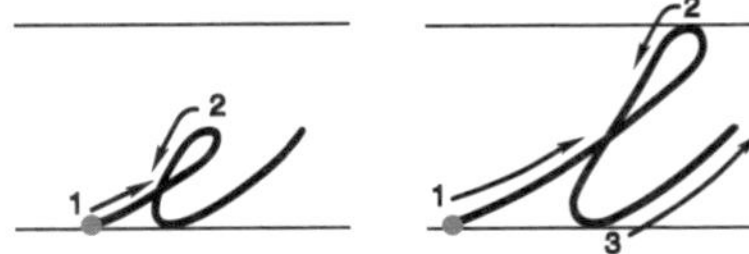

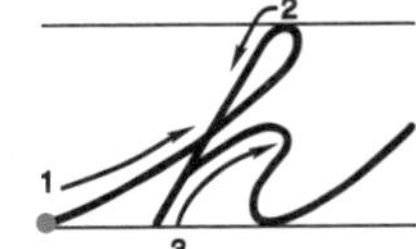

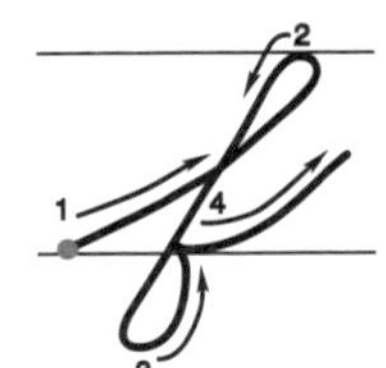

e Starting point, undercurve
Loop back, slant down
Undercurve: small *e*

l Starting point, undercurve
Loop back, slant down
Undercurve: small *l*

h Starting point, undercurve
Loop back, slant down
Overcurve, slant down
Undercurve: small *h*

k Starting point, undercurve
Loop back, slant down
Overcurve, curve forward and under
Slant down, undercurve: small *k*

f Starting point, undercurve
Loop back, slant down
Loop forward into undercurve:
small *f*

b Starting point, undercurve
Loop back, slant down
Undercurve, small curve to right:
small *b*

Cursive Handwriting Models

Downcurve Letters

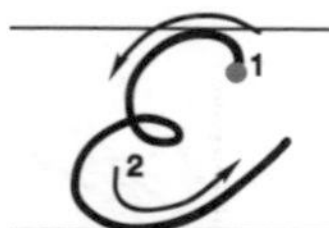
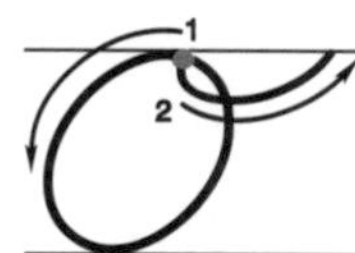
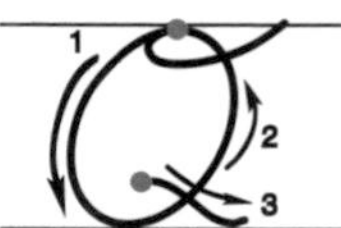

A Starting point, downcurve
Undercurve to starting point
Slant down, undercurve: capital *A*

C Starting point, downcurve
Undercurve: capital *C*

E Starting point, downcurve
Loop back, downcurve
Undercurve: capital *E*

O Starting point, downcurve
left into undercurve
Loop and curve right: capital *O*

Q Starting point, downcurve
Left into undercurve
Loop and curve right
Starting point, slant down right: capital *Q*

Overcurve Letters

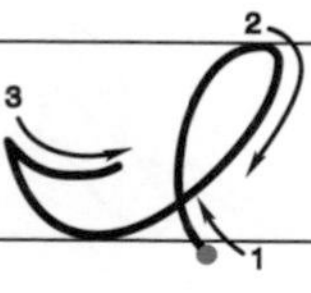
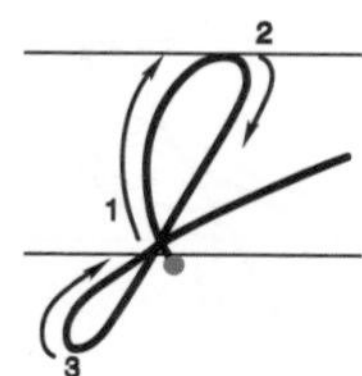

I Starting point, overcurve
Curve down and up
Curve right, capital *I*

J Starting point, overcurve
Slant down and loop back
Overcurve: capital *J*

Letters with Loops

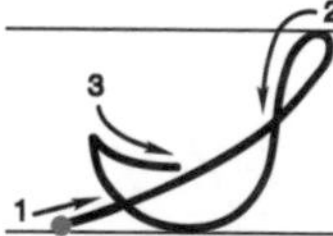
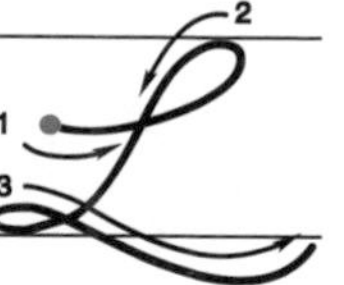
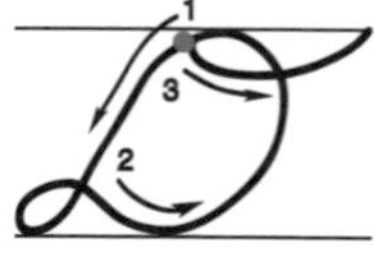

G Starting point, undercurve
Loop, curve up
Double curve, curve up
Curve right: capital *G*

S Starting point, undercurve
Loop, curve down and up
Curve right: capital *S*

L Starting point, undercurve
Loop, curve down and loop
Curve under: capital *L*

D Starting point, slant down
Loop, curve down and up
Loop and curve right: capital *D*

Cursive Handwriting Models

Undercurve-Slant Letters

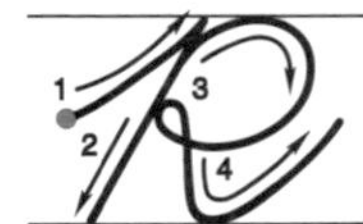

P Starting point, undercurve
Slant down, retrace up
Curve forward and back: capital *P*

R Starting point, undercurve
Slant down, retrace up
Curve forward to slant
Curve forward
Undercurve: capital *R*

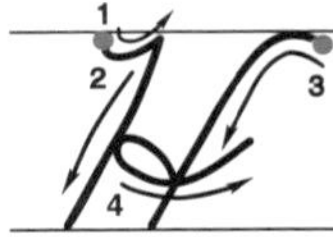

H Starting point, undercurve
Slant down to end point
Starting point
Curve back and slant down
Retrace up slant, loop left and curve right: capital *H*

K Starting point, undercurve
Slant down to end point
Starting point
Doublecurve back to slant
Curve forward
Undercurve up: capital *K*

M Starting point, undercurve
Slant down
Retrace up slant, overcurve
Slant down, retrace up slant
Overcurve down into undercurve: capital *M*

N Starting point, undercurve
Slant down
Retrace up slant
Overcurve down into undercurve: capital *N*

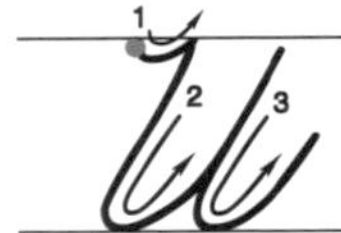

U Starting point, undercurve
Slant down into undercurve
Slant down, undercurve: capital *U*

W Starting point, undercurve
Curve forward, slant down into undercurve
Slant down into undercurve
Overcurve: capital *W*

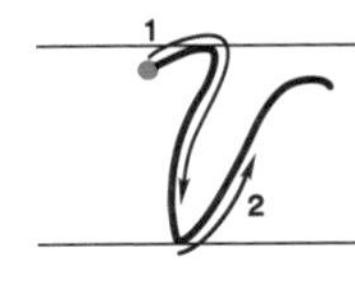
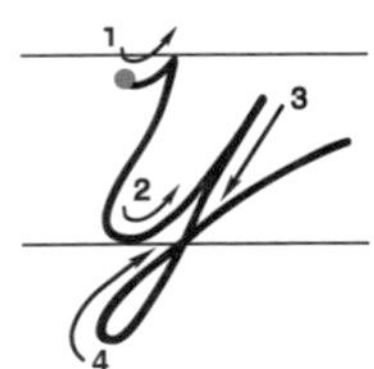

V Starting point, undercurve
Curve forward and slant down, undercurve up and overcurve: capital *V*

Y Starting point, undercurve
Slant down, undercurve up
Slant down, loop back
Overcurve: capital *Y*

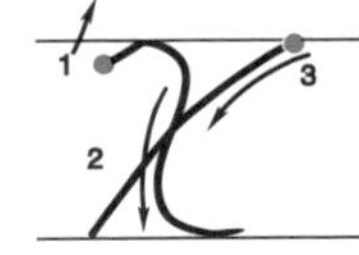

X Starting point, undercurve
Curve forward, slant down
Undercurve
Starting point, slant down: capital *X*

B Starting point, undercurve
Slant down, retrace up
Curve forward, loop
Curve forward and back
Curve right: capital *B*

Doublecurve Letters

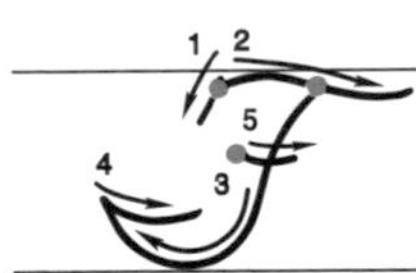

F Starting point, slant down
Curve up and right to end point
Starting point
Slant down, curve up and right
Starting point, across: capital *F*

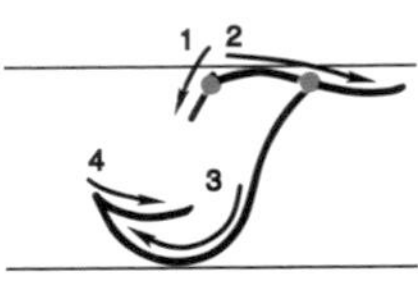

T Starting point, slant down
Curve up and right to end point
Starting point
Slant down, curve up and right: capital *T*

Curve Forward Letter

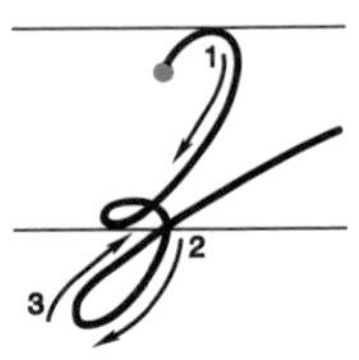

Z Starting point, curve forward
Slant down
Overcurve, curve down
Loop into overcurve: capital *Z*

Numbers

0 Starting point, curving left all the way around to starting point: *0*

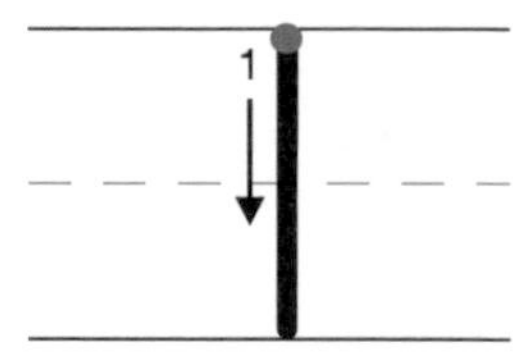

1 Starting point, straight down: *1*

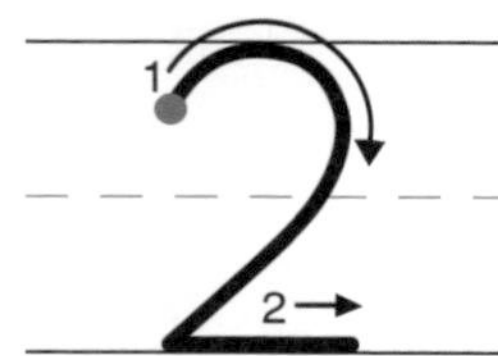

2 Starting point, around right, slanting left and straight across right: *2*

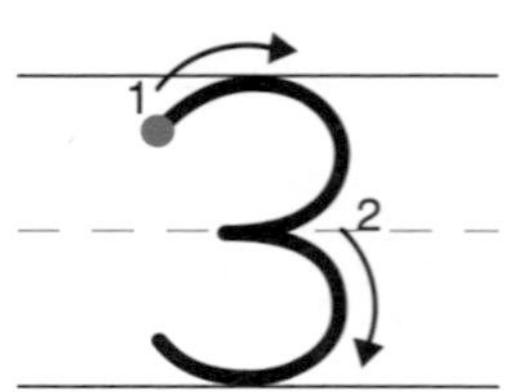

3 Starting point, around right, in at the middle, around right: *3*

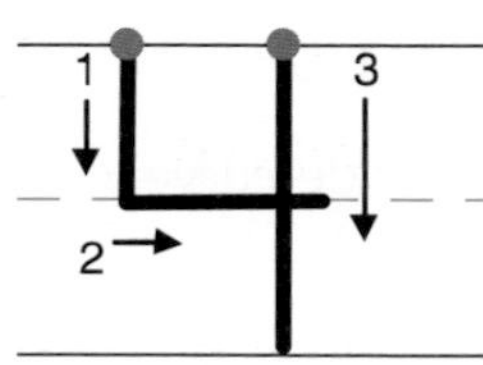

4 Starting point, straight down
Straight across right
Starting point, straight down, crossing line: *4*

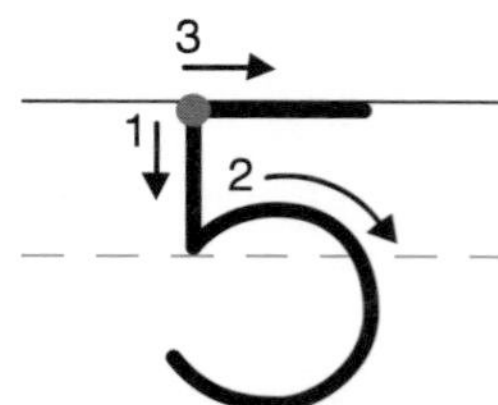

5 Starting point, straight down, curving around right and up
Starting point, straight across right: *5*

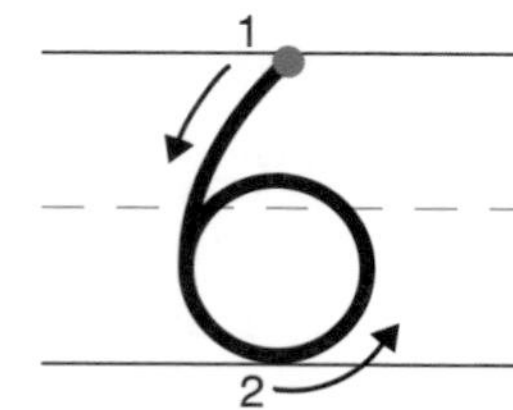

6 Starting point, slanting left, around the bottom curving up around right and into the curve: 6

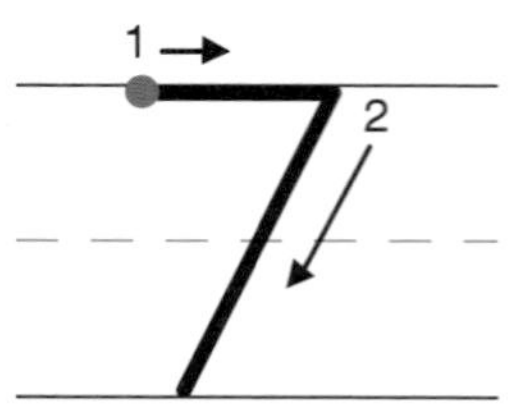

7 Starting point, straight across right, slanting down left: *7*

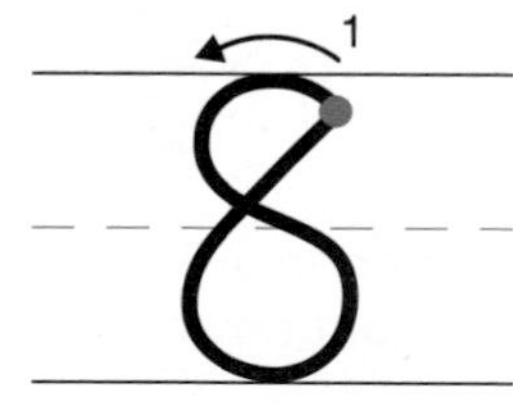

8 Starting point, curving left, curving down and around right, slanting up right to starting point: *8*

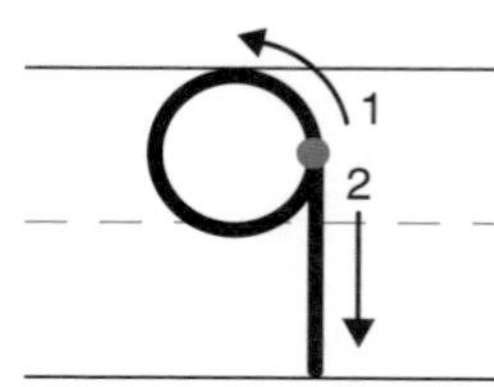

9 Starting point, curving around left all the way, straight down: *9*

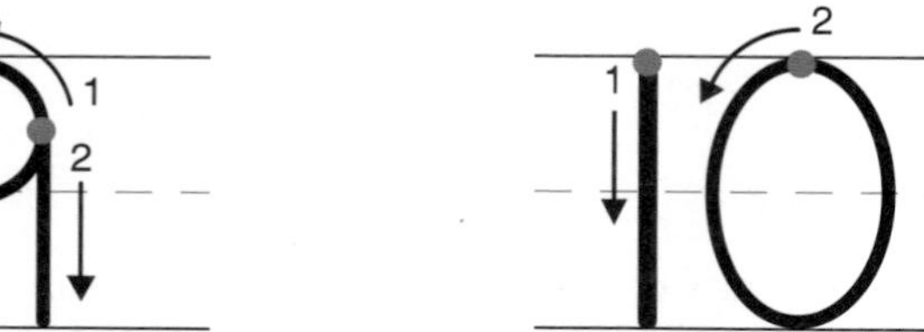

10 Starting point, straight down
Starting point, curving left all the way around to starting point: *10*

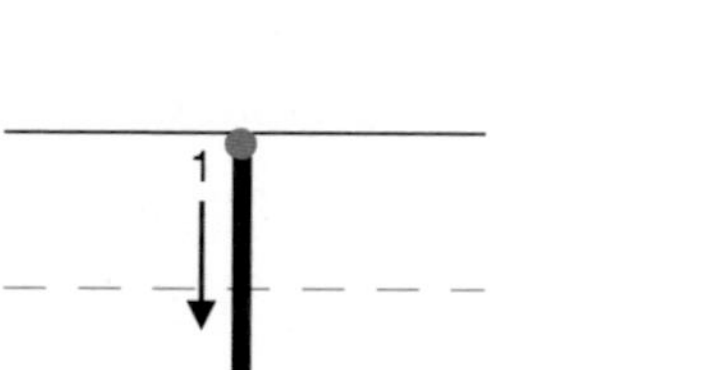

! Starting point, straight down
Dot exactly below: exclamation point

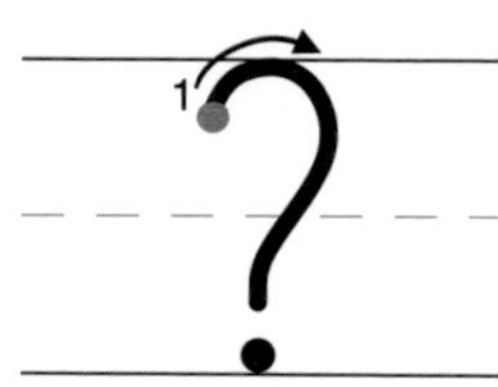

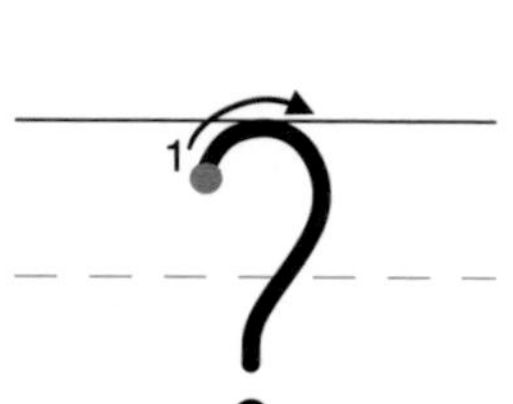

? Starting point, curving around right, straight down
Dot exactly below: question mark

High-Frequency Word List

Level 2 High-Frequency Words

again	done	grow	new	say	try
always	draw	has	off	seven	under
animal	drink	hold	once	show	upon
another	eight	hurt	only	sing	us
ate	fall	keep	open	together	use
because	far	kind	our	small	warm
been	fast	laugh	own	soon	wash
best	find	learn	people	sound	water
better	first	light	pick	start	which
black	fly	live	picture	stop	white
both	found	made	place	tell	who
bring	full	many	play	ten	why
buy	funny	may	please	thank	wish
carry	gave	much	pull	these	work
clean	give	must	read	those	write
cold	goes	myself	round	three	
does	great	never	run	today	

Level 3 High-Frequency Words

above	close	head	name	second	took
air	each	hear	near	set	trees
almost	earth	high	need	should	turned
along	end	home	next	side	until
also	enough	house	night	still	watch
answer	even	land	often	story	while
back	ever	large	other	such	without
began	eyes	last	paper	talk	words
between	face	letters	part	than	world
book	feet	might	plants	things	years
change	following	more	point	thought	
children	hand	most	same	through	
city	hard	move	school	time	

Introduction to Sounds

Lesson	Phonics and Word Structure Skills	Decodable Book/Story
Getting Started		
Day 1	/s/ spelled *s, ss;* /m/ spelled *m;* /t/ spelled *t, tt;* /d/ spelled *d;* /n/ spelled *n;* /h/ spelled *h_;* /a/ spelled *a*	1 Nat, Nan, and Sam
Day 2	/l/ spelled *l* and *ll;* /b/ spelled *b;* /p/ spelled *p;* /k/ spelled *c, k;* /r/ spelled *r;* /i/ spelled *i;* /f/ spelled *f* and *ff;* /g/ spelled *g;* /j/ spelled *j;* /ks/ spelled ■*x;* /o/ spelled *o;* /e/ spelled *e, _ea_*	2 A Pal 3 Help
Day 3	/w/ spelled *w_;* /kw/ spelled *qu_;* /v/ spelled *v;* /y/ spelled *y_;* /z/ spelled *z, zz, _s;* /u/ spelled *u;* /ch/ spelled *ch;* /th/ spelled *th;* /sh/ spelled *sh;* /hw/ spelled *wh_;* /ar/ spelled ar; closed syllables	4 Fast Sam 5 Stars
Day 4	/j/ spelled ■*dge;* /k/ spelled ■*ck;* /ch/ spelled ■*tch;* /ng/ spelled ■*ng;* /nk/ spelled ■*nk;* /ks/ spelled ■*x;* Short Vowels; Closed Syllables; /er/ spelled *er, ir,* and *ur, ear*	6 Midge 7 Fran and Ann
Day 5	/or/ spelled *or, ore;* /ar/ spelled *ar;* Syllable *-le;* ə + /l/, including words with *el, il, al;* Review	8 Tell Your Pals 9 Riddles 10 Fran's Story
Unit 1		
Lesson 1	/ā/ spelled *a* and *a_e;* /ē/ spelled *e* and *e_e;* /ī/ spelled *i* and *i_e;* /ō/ spelled *o* and *o_e;* /ū/ spelled *u* and *u_e;* Antonyms and Synonyms	11 Vic's Big Chore
Lesson 2	/s/ spelled *ce, ci_;* /j/ spelled *ge, gi_;* Compound Words	12 Gem Is Missing
Lesson 3	Review; Related Words	13 More Clover
Lesson 4	/ā/ spelled *ai_, _ay;* /ē/ spelled *ee, ea, _y, _ie_, ey;* Related words	14 On a Train
Lesson 5	/n/ spelled *kn_;* /r/ spelled *wr_;* /f/ spelled *ph;* /m/ spelled *_mb;* /s/ spelled *cy;* Review	15 Bike Races 16 Too Cold?
Unit 2		
Lesson 1	/ī/ spelled *igh, _ie, _y;* Plurals	17 Bats
Lesson 2	/ō/ spelled *oa_, _ow;* Irregular Plurals	18 More Bats
Lesson 3	/ū/ spelled *_ew , _ue;* Homographs	19 Condors
Lesson 4	Review; Homophones	20 Strange Stuff
Lesson 5	/o͞o/ spelled *oo, u, u_e, _ew, _ue;* Review	21 A Visit 22 Migrating Geese
Unit 3		
Lesson 1	/oo/ spelled *oo;* Inflectional Ending *-ing*	23 A Trade
Lesson 2	/ow/ spelled *ow, ou_;* Inflectional Ending *-ed*	24 A Brief History of Money
Lesson 3	/aw/ spelled *au_, aw, augh, ough, al, all;* Comparative and Superlative Adjectives	25 Collecting Baseball Cards
Lesson 4	/oi/ spelled *oi, _oy;* Irregular Comparative and Superlative Adjectives	26 Money Stories
Lesson 5	Contrast /ō/ spelled *_ow* and /ow/ spellings; Contrast /o͞o/ spellings and /ū/ spellings; Review	27 Seven Bank Facts 28 Dad Is Back

Lesson	Word Structure Skills
Unit 4	
Lesson 1	Suffixes *-ly*, *-y*, *-ment*, *-tion*
Lesson 2	Suffixes *-ful*, *-able;* Inflectional Endings *-ed* and *-ing*
Lesson 3	Suffixes *-ity*, *-less*, *-ness*, *-sion*
Lesson 4	Greek and Latin Roots
Lesson 5	Review
Unit 5	
Lesson 1	Prefixes *re-*, *un-*, *pre-*, *mis-*
Lesson 2	Prefixes *bi-*, *mid-*, *dis-*, *auto-*
Lesson 3	Affixes as Syllables; Affixes Used to Change Word Meaning
Lesson 4	Word Families; Multisyllabic Words and Silent Consonants
Lesson 5	Review
Unit 6	
Lesson 1	Unit 1 Review
Lesson 2	Unit 2 Review
Lesson 3	Unit 3 Review
Lesson 4	Unit 4 Review
Lesson 5	Unit 5 Review

Sound/Spelling Card Stories

Card 1: /a/ Lamb

I'm Pam the Lamb, I am.
This is how I tell my Mommy where
I am: /a/ /a/ /a/ /a/ /a/.

I'm Pam the Lamb, I am.
This is how I tell my Daddy where
I am: /a/ /a/ /a/ /a/ /a/.

I'm Pam the Lamb, I am.
That young ram is my brother Sam.
This is how I tell my brother where
I am: /a/ /a/ /a/ /a/ /a/.

I'm Pam the Lamb; I'm happy where
I am.

Can you help me tell my family where
I am?
(Have the children respond.) /a/ /a/ /a/ /a/ /a/

Card 2: /b/ Ball

Bobby loved to bounce his basketball.
He bounced it all day long.
This is the sound the ball made:
/b/ /b/ /b/ /b/ /b/.

One day, while Bobby was bouncing
his basketball,
Bonnie came by on her bike.

Bonnie said, "Hi, Bobby. I have a little
bitty ball.
May I bounce my ball with you?"

Bobby said, "Sure!" and Bonnie
bounced her little bitty ball.
What sound do you think Bonnie's ball
made?
(Encourage a very soft reply.) /b/ /b/ /b/ /b/ /b/

Soon Betsy came by. "Hi, Bobby. Hi, Bonnie," she said.
"I have a great big beach ball. May I bounce my ball with you?"

Bobby and Bonnie said, "Sure!" and Betsy bounced her
big beach ball.
What sound do you think the beach ball made?
(Encourage a louder, slower reply.) /b/ /b/ /b/ /b/ /b/

(Designate three groups, one for each ball sound.)

Now when Bobby, Bonnie, and Betsy bounce their balls
together, this is the sound you hear:
(Have all three groups make their sounds in a chorus.)
/b/ /b/ /b/ /b/ /b/

Card 3: /k/ Camera

Carlos has a new camera. When he
takes pictures, his camera makes a
clicking sound like this:
/k/ /k/ /k/ /k/ /k/.

In the garden, Carlos takes pictures of
caterpillars crawling on cabbage:
/k/ /k/ /k/ /k/ /k/.

At the zoo, Carlos takes pictures of a
camel, a duck, and a kangaroo:
/k/ /k/ /k/.

In the park, Carlos takes pictures of his
cousin flying a kite: /k/ /k/ /k/ /k/ /k/.

In his room, Carlos takes pictures of his
cute kitten, Cozy: /k/ /k/ /k/ /k/ /k/.

Can you help Carlos take pictures with his camera?
(Have the children join in.) /k/ /k/ /k/ /k/ /k/ /k/ /k/

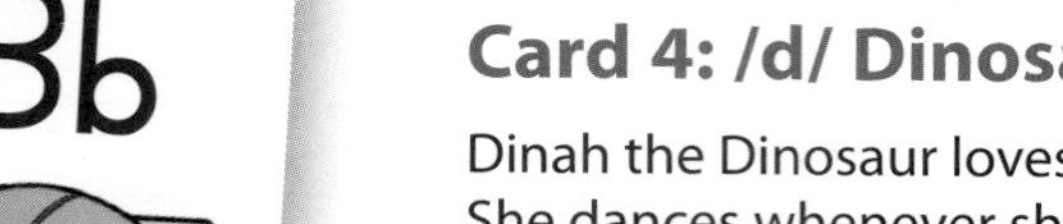

Card 4: /d/ Dinosaur

Dinah the Dinosaur loves to dance.
She dances whenever she gets the chance.
Whenever that dinosaur dips and whirls,
this is the sound of her dancing twirls:
/d/ /d/ /d/ /d/ /d/ /d/!

Dinah the Dinosaur dances all day.
From dawn to dark, she dances away.
And when Dinah dances, her dinosaur feet
make a thundering, thudding, extremely
loud beat:
(loudly, with an exaggerated rhythm)
/d/ /d/ /d/ /d/ /d/ /d/!

Now if you were a dinosaur just like Dinah,
you would certainly dance just as finely as she.
And if you were a Dino, and you had a chance,
what sound would your feet make when you did a dance?
(Have the children join in.) /d/ /d/ /d/ /d/ /d/ /d/

Card 5: /e/ Hen

Jem's pet hen likes to peck, peck, peck.
She pecks at a speck on the new red deck.
This is how her pecking sounds:
/e/ /e/ /e/ /e/ /e/.

Jem's pet hen pecks at corn in her pen.
She pecks ten kernels, then pecks again.
This is how her pecking sounds:
/e/ /e/ /e/ /e/ /e/.

Jem's hen pecks at a cracked egg shell.
She's helping a chick get out, alive and well.
This is how her pecking sounds:
/e/ /e/ /e/ /e/ /e/.

Can you help Jem's hen peck?
(Have children say:) /e/ /e/ /e/ /e/ /e/.

Card 6: /f/ Fan

/f/ /f/ /f/ /f/ /f/—What's that funny sound?
It's Franny the Fan going round and round,
and this is the sound that old fan makes:
/f/ /f/ /f/ /f/ /f/.

When it gets too hot, you see,
Franny cools the family: /f/ /f/ /f/ /f/ /f/.
She fans Father's face
and Foxy's fur
and Felicity's feet.
Hear the Fan whir: /f/ /f/ /f/ /f/ /f/.

Can you make Franny the Fan go fast?
(Have the children say quickly:)
/f/ /f/ /f/ /f/ /f/.
Faster? /f/ /f/ /f/ /f/ /f/
Fastest? /f/ /f/ /f/ /f/ /f/

Card 7: /g/ Gopher

Gary's a gopher.
He loves to gulp down food.
/g/ /g/ /g/ /g/ /g/, gulps the gopher.

Gary the Gopher gulps down grass
because it tastes so good.
/g/ /g/ /g/ /g/ /g/, gulps the gopher.

Gary the Gopher gulps down grapes—
gobs and gobs of grapes.
/g/ /g/ /g/ /g/ /g/, gulps the gopher.

Gary the Gopher gobbles green beans
and says once more,
/g/ /g/ /g/ /g/ /g/. He's such a hungry gopher!

Gary the Gopher gobbles in the garden
until everything is gone.

What sound does Gary the Gopher make?
(Ask the children to join in.) /g/ /g/ /g/ /g/ /g/

Card 8: /h/ Hound

Harry the Hound dog hurries around.
Can you hear Harry's hurrying hound-
dog sound?
This is the sound Harry's breathing
makes when he hurries:
/h/ /h/ /h/ /h/ /h/ /h/!

When Harry the Hound dog sees a
hare hop by,
he tears down the hill, and his four
feet fly.
Hurry, Harry, hurry! /h/ /h/ /h/ /h/ /h/ /h/!

How Harry the Hound dog loves to hunt
and chase!
He hurls himself from place to place.
Hurry, Harry, hurry! /h/ /h/ /h/ /h/ /h/ /h/!

When Harry the Hound dog sees a big skunk roam,
he howls for help and heads for home.

What sound does Harry make when he hurries?
(Have the children answer.) /h/ /h/ /h/ /h/ /h/ /h/

Card 9: /i/ Pig

This is Pickles the Pig.
If you tickle Pickles, she gets the giggles.
This is the sound of her giggling:
/i/ /i/ /i/ /i/ /i/.

Tickle Pickles the Pig under her chin.
Listen! She's giggling: /i/ /i/ /i/ /i/ /i/.
Wiggle a finger in Pickles' ribs.
Listen! She's giggling: /i/ /i/ /i/ /i/ /i/.

Give Pickles the Pig a wink,
and what do you think? First comes a grin.
Then listen!
She's giggling again: /i/ /i/ /i/ /i/ /i/.

Quick! Tickle Pickles the Pig. What will
she say?
(Have the children join in.) /i/ /i/ /i/ /i/ /i/

Card 10: /j/ Jump

When Jenny jumps her jump rope,
it sounds like this: /j/ /j/ /j/ /j/ /j/.
When Jackson jumps his jump rope,
it sounds like this: /j/ /j/ /j/ /j/ /j/.

The judges generally agree
that Jenny jumps most rapidly:
(quickly) /j/ /j/ /j/ /j/ /j/.

When Jenny jumps, she jumps to this jingle:
"Jump, jump, jump so quick.
Whenever I jump, I like to kick."
/j/ /j/ /j/ /j/ /j/

The judges generally agree
that Jackson jumps most quietly:
(quietly) /j/ /j/ /j/ /j/ /j/.

When Jackson jumps, he jumps to this jingle:
"Jump, jump, nice and quiet.
See what happens when you try it." /j/ /j/ /j/ /j/ /j/

(to the children) Jump rope like Jenny.
(quickly) /j/ /j/ /j/ /j/ /j/
(to the children) Jump rope like Jackson.
(quietly) /j/ /j/ /j/ /j/ /j/

Card 11: /k/ Camera

Kk
k
c
ck

Carlos has a new camera. When he
takes pictures,
His camera makes a clicking sound like this:
/k/ /k/ /k/ /k/ /k/.

In the garden, Carlos takes pictures of
caterpillars crawling on cabbage:
/k/ /k/ /k/ /k/ /k/.

At the zoo, Carlos takes pictures of a camel,
a duck, and a kangaroo:
/k/ /k/ /k/.

In the park, Carlos takes pictures of his
cousin flying a kite: /k/ /k/ /k/ /k/ /k/
In his room, Carlos takes pictures of his
cute kitten, Cozy. /k/ /k/ /k/ /k/ /k/

Can you help Carlos take pictures with his camera?
(Have the children join in.) /k/ /k/ /k/ /k/ /k/ /k/ /k/

Card 12: /l/ Lion

Look! It's Leon the Lion.
Leon loves to lap water from lakes,
and this is the sound the lapping lion
makes: /l/ /l/ /l/ /l/ /l/.

Let's join Leon. Quick!
Take a little lick: /l/ /l/ /l/ /l/ /l/.

Are you a thirsty lass or lad?
Then lap until you don't feel bad:
/l/ /l/ /l/ /l/ /l/.

What sound do you make when you lap
like Leon the Lion?
(Have the children say:) /l/ /l/ /l/ /l/ /l/.

Card 13: /m/ Monkey

For Muzzy the Monkey, bananas
are yummy.
She munches so many, they fill up
her tummy.
When she eats, she says:
/m/ /m/ /m/ /m/ /m/!

Bananas for breakfast, bananas
for lunch.
Mash them up, mush them up,
munch, munch, munch, munch!
What does Muzzy the Monkey say?
(Have the children say:) /m/ /m/ /m/ /m/ /m/.

Bananas at bedtime? I have a hunch
Muzzy will mash them up, mush them up,
munch, munch, munch, munch!
Then what will Muzzy the Monkey say?
(Have the children say:) /m/ /m/ /m/ /m/ /m/.

Card 14: /n/ Nest

Nine feet up in a neighbor's tree
is a noisy, noisy nest.
I cannot see what's in there,
but it's a noisy pest!
/n/ /n/ /n/ /n/

What is in that noisy nest?
A nervous night owl crying?
A nosy nuthatch chatting?
A nightingale that's sighing?
/n/ /n/ /n/ /n/

I think it's time we take a look,
but please, do not start yapping.
Now I see what's in that nest!
A snoring bluebird napping!
/n/ /n/ /n/ /n/

Card 15: /o/ Fox

Bob the Fox did not feel well at all.
He jogged to the doctor's office.
"Say /o/ Mr. Fox! /o/ /o/ /o/."

"My head is hot, and my throat hurts a lot,"
said the fox.
"Say /o/, Mr. Fox!
"/o/ /o/ /o/ /o/."

"Yes, you've got a rotten cold," said
the doctor.
"Say /o/, Mr. Fox!
"/o/ /o/ /o/."

"Find a spot to sit in the sun," said the doctor.
"Say /o/, Mr. Fox!
"/o/ /o/ /o/."

He sat on a rock in the sun.
Soon he felt much better.
(with a satisfied sigh) "/o/," said Mr. Fox.
/o/ /o/ /o/

Card 16: /p/ Popcorn

Ping and Pong liked to pop corn. As
it cooked, it made this sound:
/p/ /p/ /p/ /p/ /p/ /p/ /p/.

One day Ping poured a whole package of
popcorn into the pot. It made this sound:
/p/ /p/ /p/ /p/ /p/ /p/ /p/.

The popcorn popped and popped. Ping filled
two pots, and still the popcorn popped:
/p/ /p/ /p/ /p/ /p/ /p/ /p/.

Pong filled three pails with popcorn, and still
it kept popping: /p/ /p/ /p/ /p/ /p/ /p/ /p/.

"Call all your pals," said their pop. "We'll have a party."
And the popcorn kept popping.

(Have the children say the /p/ sound very fast.)

Card 17: /kw/ Quacking ducks

Quincy the Duck couldn't quite quack
like all the other quacking ducks.
Oh, he could say /kw/ /kw/ /kw/ /kw/,
but it never seemed just right.

When Quincy tried to quack quietly,
(softly) /kw/ /kw/ /kw/ /kw/
his quack came out loudly.
(loudly) /kw/ /kw/ /kw/ /kw/!

When he tried to quack slowly,
(slowly) /kw/ . . . /kw/ . . . /kw/ . . . /kw/
his quack came out quickly.
(quickly) /kw/ /kw/ /kw/ /kw/!
Quincy just couldn't quack right!

One day Quincy was practicing quacks.
His friend Quip quacked along with him.
"Repeat after me," said Quip.
(quietly) /kw/ /kw/ /kw/ /kw/
But Quincy quacked back,
(in normal voice) /kw/ /kw/ /kw/ /kw/ /kw/!

Quincy still couldn't quack quite right.
But Quincy kept quacking. He said, "I won't quit until I quack like the best quackers around."
Can you show Quincy how quacking ducks quack?
(Have the children join in.)
/kw/ /kw/ /kw/ /kw/ /kw/ /kw/ /kw/ /kw/

Card 18: /r/ Robot

Little Rosie Robot just runs and runs and runs.
She races round and round to get her chores all done.
Here's how Rosie sounds when she's working:
/r/ /r/ /r/ /r/ /r/!

Rosie can rake around your roses.
Here comes that running robot!
/r/ /r/ /r/ /r/ /r/!

Rosie can repair your wrecked radio.
Here comes that racing robot!
(softly) /r/ /r/ /r/ /r/ /r/

Rosie can mend your round red rug.
Here comes that roaring robot!
(loudly) /r/ /r/ /r/ /r/ /r/!

Rosie rarely does anything wrong.
But there are two things that Rosie can't do: rest and relax.
Here comes that roaring robot!

What does she say?

(Have the children call out the answer:)
/r/ /r/ /r/ /r/ /r/.

Card 19: /s/ Sausages

Sue and Sammy had a nice place in the city.
On Saturday, Sue and Sammy decided to have sausages for supper.
Sammy put seven sausages in a skillet. /s/ /s/ /s/ /s/ /s/ /s/ /s/

Soon the smell of sausages filled the air.
/s/ /s/ /s/ /s/ /s/, sizzled the sausages.

"Pull up a seat, Sue," said Sammy.
"The sausages are almost ready to serve."
/s/ /s/ /s/ /s/ /s/, sizzled the sausages.

Sue and Sammy ate the delicious sausages.
Soon they wanted more, so Sam put six more sausages in the frying pan.
/s/ /s/ /s/ /s/ /s/ /s/, sizzled the sausages.

If you were cooking sausages with Sammy and Sue, what sound would the sausages make as they sizzled?
(Have the children join in:) /s/ /s/ /s/ /s/ /s/ /s/

Card 20: /t/ Timer

When Tom Tuttle cooks, he uses his timer.
Tom Tuttle's timer ticks like this:
/t/ /t/ /t/ /t/ /t/ /t/ /t/

Tonight Tom Tuttle wants tomatoes on toast.
Tom turns on the oven.
Tom puts tomatoes on toast in the oven.
Tom sets the timer.
The timer will Ding! when Tom's toast and tomatoes are done.
Until the timer dings,
it ticks: /t/ /t/ /t/ /t/ /t/ /t/ /t/.

Tomatoes on toast takes ten minutes.
/t/ /t/ /t/ /t/ /t/ /t/ /t/
Tom can hardly wait. /t/ /t/ /t/ /t/ /t/ /t/ /t/
He taps out the time: /t/ /t/ /t/ /t/ /t/ /t/ /t/.

What is the sound of Tom Tuttle's ticking timer?
(Have the children join in.) /t/ /t/ /t/ /t/ /t/ /t/ /t/
Ding! Time for dinner, Tom Tuttle!

Card 21: /u/ Tug

Tubby the Tugboat can huff and puff
and push and pull to move big stuff.
/u/ /u/ /u/ /u/ /u/ /u/ /u/
That's the sound of Tubby the Tug.

If a boat is stuck and will not budge,
Tubby the Tugboat can give it a nudge.
/u/ /u/ /u/ /u/ /u/ /u/ /u/
It's Tubby the Trusty Tug.

If a ship is caught in mud and muck,
Tubby the Tugboat can get it unstuck.
/u/ /u/ /u/ /u/ /u/ /u/ /u/
It's Tubby the Trusty Tug.

Can you help Tubby push and pull?
(Have the children join in.)
/u/ /u/ /u/ /u/ /u/ /u/ /u/

Card 22: /v/ Vacuum

Vinny the Vacuum is cleaning again.
Before visitors visit, he always begins.
This is the sound of his very loud voice:
/v/ /v/ /v/ /v/ /v/!
If only that Vinny could clean without noise!

Vinny sucks up the crumbs baby Vicki dropped.
/v/ /v/ /v/ /v/ /v/!
He visits nearly everywhere except the tabletop.
/v/ /v/ /v/ /v/ /v/!
Three vine leaves, two vitamins, part of a vase—
all vanish when Vinny goes over the place!
/v/ /v/ /v/ /v/ /v/

As Vinny vacuums the velvety rug
a van full of visitors starts to drive up.
But Vinny's not done with the very last room!
Will you help Vinny the Vacuum vacuum?
(Ask groups of children to say /v/ in a round to make the continuous sound of a vacuum cleaner.)

Card 23: /w/ Washer

Willie the Washer washed white
clothes all week.
When he washed, he went:
/w/ /w/ /w/ /w/ /w/ /w/ /w/.

All winter, Willie worked well.
/w/ /w/ /w/ /w/ /w/ /w/ /w/
But last Wednesday, Willie was weak.
(softly) /w/ /w/ /w/ /w/ /w/ /w/ /w/
This week, he got worse.
(slower and slower) /w/. . . /w/. . . /w/. . .
Poor Willie was worn out.
(slowly) /w/

Then a worker came and fixed Willie's wires.
Willie felt wonderful.
(more loudly) /w/ /w/ /w/ /w/ /w/ /w/ /w/!
Now Willie can wash and wash wildly!
(quickly) /w/ /w/ /w/ /w/ /w/ /w/ /w/!

How does Willie the Washer sound now when he washes?
(Have the children join in.) /w/ /w/ /w/ /w/ /w/ /w/ /w/
Can you wash just like Willie?
(Children together:) /w/ /w/ /w/ /w/ /w/ /w/ /w/.

Card 24: /ks/ Exit

Rex is called the Exiting X;
he runs to guard the door.
To get past Rex, make the sound of X:
/ks/ /ks/ /ks/ /ks/.
That is what Rex expects!

The ox knows the sound of X,
so she says /ks/ /ks/ /ks/ /ks/
and gets past Rex.

The fox knows the sound of X,
so he says /ks/ /ks/ /ks/ /ks/
and gets past Rex.

Can you say /ks/ /ks/ /ks/ /ks/
and get past Rex the Exiting X?
(Have the children respond:) /ks/ /ks/ /ks/ /ks/!
Did we get past Rex?
(Have the children say:) Yes!

Card 25: /y/ Yaks

Yolanda and Yoshiko are yaks.
They don't yell.
They don't yelp.
They don't yodel.
They don't yawn.
These young yaks just yak.
Yakety-yak, yakety-yak!
Can you hear the sound they make?
/y/ /y/ /y/ /y/ /y/ /y/ /y/

Yolanda and Yoshiko yak in the yard.
/y/ /y/ /y/ /y/ /y/ /y/ /y/
They yak on their yellow yacht.
/y/ /y/ /y/ /y/ /y/ /y/ /y/
They yak in the yam patch.
/y/ /y/ /y/ /y/ /y/ /y/ /y/
These yaks yak all year!
/y/ /y/ /y/ /y/ /y/ /y/ /y/

Do you think these yaks like to yak?
(Have the children answer:) Yes!
(Ask the children to yak like Yolanda and Yoshiko.)

Card 26: /z/ Zipper

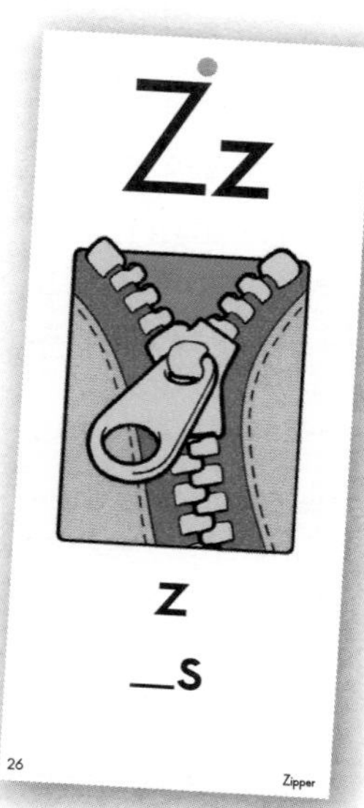

Zack's jacket has a big long zipper.
The zipper zips like this: /z/ /z/ /z/ /z/.

When little Zack goes out to play,
he zips the zipper up this way:
/z/ /z/ /z/ /z/.
Later, when he comes back in,
Zack zips the zipper down again.
/z/ /z/ /z/ /z/

Can you help Zack zip his jacket zipper?
(Have the children join in.) /z/ /z/ /z/ /z/

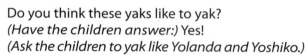

Card 32: /sh/ Shell

Sheila and Sharon went to the seashore.
They saw lots of shells.
Sheila rushed from shell to shell.
Sharon held a shell to Sheila's ear.

"Do you hear anything?" asked Sharon.
"Yes, it sounds like the ocean crashing on
the shore," shouted Sheila,
"/sh/ /sh/ /sh/ /sh/ /sh/."

"Let's try different-shaped shells," said Sharon.
She found a big shell. It made a loud
/sh/ /sh/ /sh/ /sh/.
Sheila found a small shell.
It made a soft /sh/ /sh/ /sh/ /sh/.
They found a thin shell.
It made a high /sh/ /sh/ /sh/ /sh/.
They found a fat shell. It made a deep /sh/ /sh/ /sh/ /sh/.

Sheila and Sharon listened to lots of shells. But no matter what the size and shape, what do you think Sheila and Sharon heard in every shell?
(Have the children join in.) /sh/ /sh/ /sh/ /sh/

Card 33: /th/ Thimble

Theodore Thimble is a thinker.
Theodore thinks and thinks and thinks.
And when he thinks, he rubs his head.
/th/ /th/ /th/ /th/ /th/ /th/ /th/ /th/ /th/

Theodore thinks of thumbs—
thin thumbs,
thick thumbs,
all different kinds of thumbs.
/th/ /th/ /th/ /th/ /th/ /th/ /th/ /th/ /th/

Theodore thinks of thread—
red thread,
blue thread,
all different-colored thread.
/th/ /th/ /th/ /th/ /th/ /th/ /th/ /th/ /th/

Thread and thumb,
thumb and thread.
These are the thoughts
in Theodore's head.
/th/ /th/ /th/ /th/ /th/ /th/ /th/ /th/ /th/

Card 34: /ch/ Chipmunk

Chipper the chipmunk is cheerful and chubby.
He chats and he chatters all day:
/ch/ /ch/ /ch/ /ch/ /ch/ /ch/
He sits on a chimney.
Can you hear him chat?
He chats and he chatters this way:
/ch/ /ch/ /ch/ /ch/ /ch/ /ch/.

Chipper stuffs cherries into his cheek.
Then he chatters /ch/ /ch/ /ch/ /ch/ /ch/ /ch/.
Chipper likes chestnuts and acorns to eat.
Then he chatters /ch/ /ch/ /ch/ /ch/ /ch/ /ch/.

Can you children chatter like Chipper?
(Have the children answer.)
/ch/ /ch/ /ch/ /ch/ /ch/ /ch/

Now chat with the chipmunk child beside you.
(Ask partners to have chipmunk conversations.)
/ch/ /ch/ /ch/ /ch/ /ch/ /ch/

Card 35: /hw/ Whales

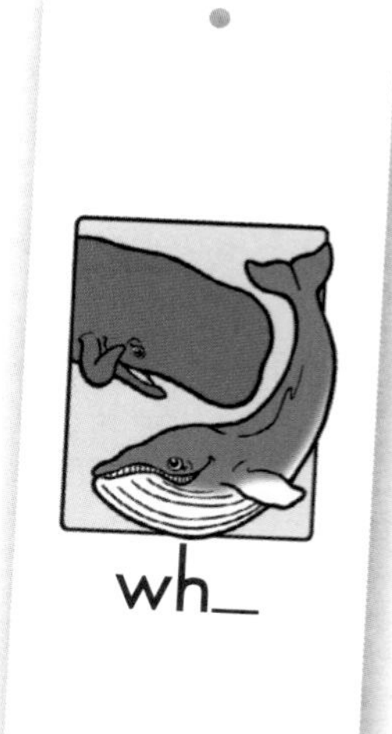

Look! It's Whitney the Whispering Whale!
Listen to her whisper: /hw/ /hw/ /hw/ /hw/ /hw/.

When Whitney meets with other whales,
she entertains them, telling tales.
She whispers: /hw/ /hw/ /hw/ /hw/ /hw/.
She's Whitney the Whispering Whale.

What ocean wonders does Whitney relate?
Does she whisper of whirlpools or whales
that are great?
We're only people, so we'll never guess.
She's Whitney the Whispering Whale!
/hw/ /hw/ /hw/.

Whatever Whitney whispers must be fun.
The other whales whistle when she's done.
They whoop and whack the white-capped waves.
They love Whitney the Whispering Whale! /hw/ /hw/ /hw/

If you were Whitney, what sounds would you whisper
to your whale friends as they gathered to listen?
(Have the children whisper:) /hw/ /hw/ /hw/ /hw/ /hw/

Card 36: /ng/ Gong

The young king has slept much
too long.
Let's go and awaken the king with
a gong.

A pinging gong? It makes a quiet song:
(softly) /ng/ /ng/ /ng/ /ng/ /ng/.

That gong is wrong.
(softly) /ng/ /ng/ /ng/ /ng/
We need a louder gong!

A dinging gong? It makes this song:
(a bit louder) /ng/ /ng/ /ng/ /ng/ /ng/ /ng/.

That, too, is wrong.
(as before) /ng/ /ng/ /ng/ /ng/
We need an even louder gong!

A clanging gong?
It makes this song:
(loudly) /ng/ /ng/ /ng/ /ng/ /ng/!

That's just the thing! /ng/ /ng/ /ng/ /ng/ /ng/!
That's the gong we needed all along!

Now, which gong should we bring to awaken the King?
(Have children make the /ng/ *sound loud enough to wake the king.)* /ng/ /ng/ /ng/ /ng/ /ng/!

Card 37: /nk/ Skunk

Sammy the Skunk
finds his skates in the trunk.
He thinks he'll go skating today.
Once at the rink,
poor Sammy does think
his pink nose feels funny some way.
/nk/ /nk/ /nk/

Home from the rink
he gets hot soup to drink.
Sammy hopes his cold slinks away.
/nk/ /nk/ /nk/ /nk/

Then the poor skunk
spends the night in his bunk.
Sammy's sneezes and honks do stay.
/nk/ /nk/ /nk/ /nk/ /nk/

Now the sun winks,
the skunk's eyes start to blink.
Sammy gets up and feels okay!
Sammy the Skunk finds his skates in the trunk.
He thinks he'll go skating today.

Can you make the sound Sammy the Skunk makes when he has a cold?

(Have the students join in.) /nk/ /nk/ /nk/ /nk/ /nk/

Card 38: /or/ Stork

Orville McCormick was quite a stork.
He liked to eat pork while holding a fork.
He also ate corn while blowing a horn:
/or/ /or/ /or/ /or/ /or/ /or/ /or/ /or/

Orville ran out of corn and needed more pork.
So he flew to the store and tore through the door
before the rain came and started to pour.
/or/ /or/ /or/ /or/ /or/ /or/ /or/

He was so happy now with his pork and his corn
that all he could say was "/or/ /or/ /or/ /or/!"

Card 39: /ar/ Armadillo

Arthur Armadillo likes to whistle,
hum, and sing.
But when he gets a head cold,
his voice won't do a thing.

To sing and still sound charming—
and not sound so alarming—
Arthur has thought up the thing
of very often gargling.

Then Arthur Armadillo sounds like this:
/ar/ /ar/ /ar/ /ar/ /ar/.
Arthur gargles in the park.
/ar/ /ar/ /ar/ /ar/ /ar/
He gargles in the dark.
/ar/ /ar/ /ar/ /ar/ /ar/
He gargles on the farm.
/ar/ /ar/ /ar/ /ar/ /ar/
He gargles in the barn.
/ar/ /ar/ /ar/ ar/ /ar/_
Arthur is great at gargling!
/ar/ /ar/ /ar/ /ar/ /ar/

What does Arthur Armadillo's gargling sound like?
(Have the children respond.) /ar/ /ar/ /ar/ /ar/ /ar/

Card 40: /er/ Bird

Bertie the Bird is the oddest bird
that anyone has ever heard.
He doesn't caw like a crow or a gull,
or tweet like a robin or a wren.
Instead, he makes a chirping sound—
over and over again!
/er/ /er/ /er/ /er/ /er/ /er/!

Bert can't fly, since his wings are too short.
He arranges his feathers in curls.
He admits, "I've short wings and I don't really sing,
but I still am an interesting bird!"
/er/ /er/ /er/ /er/ /er/ /er/

Can you chirp like Bertie the Bird?
(Have children say:) /er/ /er/ /er/ /er/ /er/ /er/!

Card 41: /o͞o/ Goo

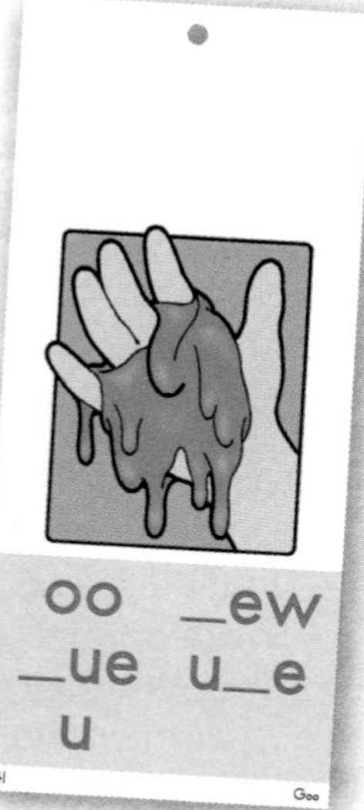

What can be making that sound?
Could it be a new flute playing a tune?
No. It's goo!
/o͞o/ /o͞o/ /o͞o/ /o͞o/

The goo is oozing all over my hand.
/o͞o/ /o͞o/ /o͞o/ /o͞o/
The goo is oozing on my boots.
/o͞o/ /o͞o/ /o͞o/ /o͞o/

The goo is oozing off the roof.
The goo is oozing everywhere!
/o͞o/ /o͞o/ /o͞o/ /o͞o/
The goo is as sticky as glue.
It is as thick as stew.
/o͞o/ /o͞o/ /o͞o/ /o͞o/

Soon the goo will fill the school!
/o͞o/ /o͞o/ /o͞o/ /o͞o/
Soon the goo will reach the moon!
/o͞o/ /o͞o/ /o͞o/ /o͞o/

What sound does the oozing goo make?
(Have the children join in.) /o͞o/ /o͞o/ /o͞o/ /o͞o/

Card 42: /o͝o/ Foot

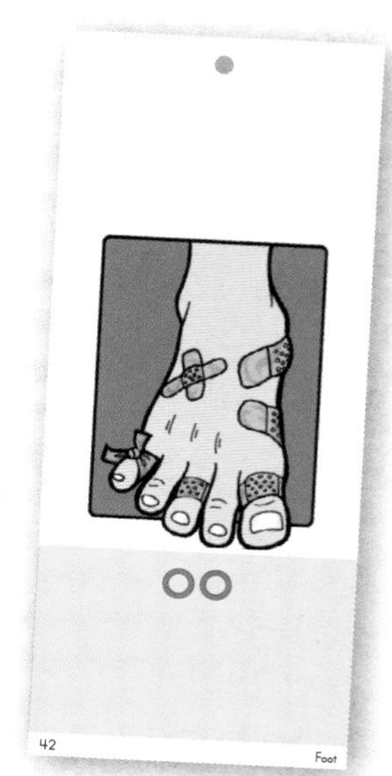

Mr. Hood took off his shoes and socks
and went out walking in the woods.
He kicked a rock and hurt his foot.
/o͝o/ /o͝o/ /o͝o/ /o͝o/

"Look, look!" said Mr. Hood. "There's a
babbling, bubbling brook. I'll walk
in the brook, so I won't hurt my foot."

So he stepped in the water, and guess what?
/o͝o/ /o͝o/ /o͝o/ /o͝o/
Mr. Hood stepped on a hook!
/o͝o/ /o͝o/ /o͝o/ /o͝o/
Mr. Hood stood. He shook his foot.
/o͝o/ /o͝o/ /o͝o/ /o͝o/

"This isn't good," said Mr. Hood.
"I think I'll go home and read a book.
At least that won't hurt my foot."
(Have the children join in.) /o͝o/ /o͝o/ /o͝o/ /o͝o/

Card 43: /ow/ Cow

Wow! Can you see poor Brownie
the Cow?
She got stung by a bee, and look at
her now!
She jumps up and down with an
/ow/ /ow/ /ow/ /ow/.

Poor Brownie found that a big
buzzing sound
meant bees all around—in the air,
on the ground.
Just one little bee gave Brownie a sting.
Now you can hear poor Brownie sing:
/ow/ /ow/ /ow/ /ow/.

Now if you were a cow and a bee found you,
you'd probably jump and shout out too!
(Have the children join in.) /ow/ /ow/ /ow/ /ow/

Card 44: /aw/ Hawk

Hazel the Hawk never cooks her food;
instead, she eats it raw.
And when she thinks of dinnertime
she caws: /aw/ /aw/ /aw/ /aw/.

Hazel the Hawk likes rabbits and mice
and catches them with her claws.
In August, she flies high above the fields
and spies them below, in the straw.
Sometimes she even snatches a snake!
And when she's caught one, she caws:
/aw/ /aw/ /aw/ /aw/.

If you were a hawk thinking of dinnertime,
what do you think you'd say?
(Have the children answer.) /aw/ /aw/ /aw/ /aw/

Card 45: /oi/ Coil

Boing! Boing! Boing! Boing!
Roy the Coil is a bouncing toy,
and this is the sound of his bounce:
/oi/ /oi/ /oi/ /oi/ /oi/.

Doing! Doing! Doing! Doing!
Roy the Coil just dances for joy.
This is the sound of his dance:
/oi/ /oi/ /oi/ /oi/ /oi/.

Ke-boing! Ke-boing!
Roy the Coil springs over a boy.
What springing sound does he make?
(Have the children join in.)
/oi/ /oi/ /oi/ /oi/ /oi/

Rubrics

Comprehension Strategy Rubrics

The following rubrics can be used to gauge students' growing knowledge of the comprehension strategies and how adept they are becoming in their use. Use the rubrics as a guide because students will probably develop strategies of their own. The important thing to consider is whether students are becoming strategic, active readers—do they employ these and other strategies, or do they continue to simply plow through text, unaware of any problems they might be having? The rubrics indicate the types of behaviors strategic readers use and will help you identify the growing facility your students can gain in dealing with text of all sorts.

Adjusting Reading Speed

- The student knows the text is not making sense and stops to reread.
- The student identifies the specific part of the text that is not making sense and rereads only that part.
- The student changes reading speed in reaction to the demands of the text.
- The student adjusts reading rate to skim or scan for specific information.

Asking Questions

- The student stops to ask questions—any question.
- The student asks questions directly related to the text.
- The student asks *who, what, why, when, where,* or *how* questions as opposed to yes or no questions.
- The student asks questions that help clarify information in the text.

Clarifying

- The student recognizes when a word or idea is not making sense.
- The student uses decoding skills to read unfamiliar words.
- The student uses structural elements in words to read them.
- The student uses structural elements, context, and questioning to clarify the meanings of unfamiliar words.

Making Connections

- The student makes connections between prior knowledge and information in the text.
- The student makes connections between or relates personal experiences to what is read in the text (text-to-self connections).
- The student makes connections across or relates information from different selections (text-to-text connections).
- The student makes connections or relates information between what is happening in the text to what is happening in the world today (text-to-world connections).

Predicting

- The student stops to make a prediction about the text.
- The student identifies the clues in the text used to make a prediction.
- The student uses clues in the text and prior knowledge to make a prediction.
- The student recognizes when a prediction is or is not confirmed by the text.

Summarizing

- The student retells information from the story.
- The student paraphrases or puts the main ideas and details in his or her own words.
- The student gives a summary that includes only the important or main ideas.
- The student recognizes when the same ideas are included more than once in a summary and deletes them.

Visualizing

- The student recognizes appropriate places in the text to stop and visualize.
- The student visualizes literal ideas or scenes described by the author.
- The student makes inferences while visualizing to show understanding of characters' feelings, mood, and setting. The visualizations go beyond the author's literal words.
- The student uses visualizing differently depending on the type of text (for example, characters, setting, and actions in narratives or a process description in nonfiction).

Inquiry Rubrics

Throughout each unit, students engage in Inquiry activities based on the unit concepts. They will present the findings of their research to the class. In this way they exhibit the wealth of knowledge and understanding they have gained about that particular concept. In addition to gaining knowledge about the concepts, students will be honing their research skills. With each unit, they will progress with their research in the same manner that professional researchers do. With each new unit of study, students should also become more sophisticated in their ability to formulate questions, make conjectures about those questions, recognize their own information needs, conduct research to find that information, reevaluate their questions and conjectures as new information is added to their knowledge base, and communicate their findings effectively. In addition, they will become more adept at working as a team and being aware of the progress being made as individuals and as a group. The Inquiry Rubrics will help you assess students' progress as researchers and as members of collaborative teams.

SRA Imagine It! provides four-point rubrics for each step in the Inquiry process. This enables you to clearly distinguish among different levels of performance.

1 Point score indicates that a student is performing below basic level.
2 Point score indicates that a student's abilities are emerging.
3 Point score indicates that a student's work is adequate and achieving expectations.
4 Point score indicates that a student is exceeding expectations.

Generating Ideas and Questions

1 With much teacher assistance, the student identifies or articulates an idea, though the idea may not be on topic.
2 With teacher assistance, the student uses some relevant background knowledge and vocabulary to identify or articulate an idea.
3 With little teacher assistance, the student identifies information and ideas to develop research questions about the topic.
4 The student independently identifies information and ideas in relation to a topic and contributes research questions.

Identifying a Question to Investigate

1 With help, the student identifies an idea or asks a question related to a particular topic.
2 With help, the student expresses curiosity about topics and translates this curiosity into a basic research question or problem.
3 With help, the student poses a problem or question for research and refines it into a researchable question.
4 The student independently identifies an interesting problem and translates it into a researchable question.

Making a Conjecture

1 The student makes a conjecture based on personal opinions or well-known facts.
2 The student makes a conjecture based on somewhat relevant background knowledge.
3 The student makes a conjecture based on relevant background knowledge and begins to address the research question.
4 The student makes a conjecture based on relevant background knowledge and addresses the research question.

Identifying Information Needs

1 The student identifies an overly broad range of information needs.
2 The student identifies information needs that are relevant but not essential to the research question.
3 The student identifies information needs that are clearly related to the specific research question.
4 The student identifies information needs that will allow for a deeper understanding of the research question.

Collecting Information

1 The student collects information that is not related to the topic.
2 The student collects information loosely related to the topic.
3 The student collects information clearly related to the topic.
4 The student collects useful information, reviews it critically, and pays attention to the reliability of sources.

Confirming and Revising Conjectures

1 Even with much teacher guidance, the student minimally participates in confirming or revising a conjecture.
2 With teacher guidance, the student recognizes whether information confirms a conjecture or requires a revision of the conjecture.
3 With some teacher guidance, the student recognizes whether new information confirms a conjecture or causes the conjecture to be revised.
4 With little teacher guidance or independently, the student revises or confirms a conjecture based on new knowledge.

Presenting Inquiry Findings

1 The student explains a key fact or idea to the teacher.
2 The student shares some new ideas with the teacher.
3 With teacher support, the student risks sharing new ideas and information with a small group of peers.
4 With teacher support or independently, the student shares new ideas and information in an organized fashion to a small group of peers or to the entire class.

Overall Research

1 With much teacher guidance, the student shows a limited understanding that research has led to new knowledge about the research question.
2 With teacher guidance, the student shows some understanding that research efforts have led to new knowledge about the research question.
3 The student understands that research efforts have led to new knowledge related to the research question.
4 The student understands that ideas change and develop and explains how (for example: *I used to think* X, *but now I know* Y).

Participation in Collaborative Inquiry

1 With much teacher prompting, the student works collaboratively with peers throughout the Inquiry process.
2 With some teacher prompting, the student works collaboratively with peers throughout the Inquiry process.
3 With little teacher prompting, the student works collaboratively with peers to share questions, ideas, and information sources.
4 With no teacher prompting, the student works collaboratively with peers to share questions, conjectures, and information. The student gains more knowledge by working with a group than by working independently.

Writing Rubrics

Rubrics are particularly effective for writing assignments, which do not have simple right or wrong answers. Different sets of rubrics cover various elements of the writing, including genre, writing process, and writing traits. They are intended to help teachers provide criteria and feedback to students.

SRA Imagine It! provides four-point rubrics for writing in each of four areas. This enables teachers to clearly distinguish among different levels of performance.

1 Point score indicates that a student is performing below basic level.
2 Point score indicates that a student's abilities are emerging.
3 Point score indicates that a student's work is adequate and achieving expectations.
4 Point score indicates that a student is exceeding expectations.

Writing Genres

Genre	1 Point	2 Points	3 Points	4 Points
Descriptive Writing	The writing includes little or no description of setting, character, or motivations.	The writing includes minimal description.	The writing includes adequate detail description.	The writing includes sensory details, motivations, and scenery details that add depth of understanding.
Narrative	The narrative has missing details or elements (characterization, plot, setting). Logical order is not apparent.	The narrative includes plot outline but does not elaborate on the details of character, plot, or setting.	The narrative adequately develops plot, character, and setting.	The narrative fully develops and elaborates on plot, character, and setting.
Personal	Personal writing is seen as an assignment rather than as an aid to the writer. Minimal effort is made, and the writing does not reflect the writer's ideas.	Some elements of personal writing reflect the writer's thoughts and ideas.	The writer uses personal writing to record or develop his or her thoughts.	The writer relies on personal writing to record, remember, develop, or express his or her thoughts.
Poetry	Little effort is made to select and arrange words to express a particular thought or idea. The main idea of the poem is not evident.	Some effort is made to work with word choice and arrangement to develop a thought in poetry form.	The writer has a clear idea and has attempted to use poetic form to express it. Poetry form may reflect established forms.	The writer has expressed an idea in an original or established poetic form. The writer has carefully selected words and arranged them for poetic effect.
Persuasive	The writer's position is absent or confusing. There is insufficient writing to show that criteria are met.	The writer's position is vague or lacks clarity. Unrelated ideas or multiple positions are included.	An opening statement identifies the writer's position. The writing may develop few or more points than delineated in the opening. The focus may be too broad.	The writer sets the scope and purpose of the paper in the introduction. The writer maintains his or her position throughout, supports his or her arguments, and includes an effective closing.
Persuasive Letter	The letter shows little audience awareness. The writer's viewpoint is not clear and/or not supported with facts, reasons, and examples.	The letter is written to a certain reader and is not likely to appeal to others. The letter begins with the writer's viewpoint but includes few facts, reasons, or examples to support that viewpoint.	The letter is written to a certain group of people and is likely to influence those readers to think, feel, or act in a certain way. The letter begins with the writer's viewpoint and includes some facts, reasons, and examples to support that viewpoint.	The letter is written to appeal to a wide audience and is likely to influence most readers to think, feel, or act in a certain way. The letter begins with the writer's viewpoint and includes concrete facts, logical reasoning, and specific examples to support that viewpoint.

Expository Writing Genres

Genre	1 Point	2 Points	3 Points	4 Points
Expository Structure	The main points and supportive details can be identified, but they are not clearly marked.	The composition is clearly organized around the main points with supportive facts or assertions.	The writer presents adequate, appropriate evidence to make a point or support a position. The positions are compared and contrasted while the main point is developed. The main points and supportive details can be identified, but they are not clearly marked.	The writer traces and constructs a line of argument, identifying part-to-whole relations. The main points are supported with logical and appropriate evidence.
Book Review (Fiction Book)	Information about the title, author, illustrator, and copyright date is missing. A sketchy description of characters, setting, and plot suggests the reviewer did not finish reading the book. The reviewer's opinion about the book is vague and unsupported.	Some basic information about the book is missing. The characters are named but not described; the time or place of the story is unclear. The plot summary is confusing. The author's main point is not mentioned. The reviewer offers an opinion about the book without supporting it.	The review includes basic information about the book and describes the main characters and setting. The plot is summarized, but parts of it may be unclear. The reviewer may not explain the author's main point. The reviewer offers an opinion about the book but may not support it strongly.	The review includes the book's title, author, illustrator, and copyright date. It briefly describes the main characters and setting and summarizes the plot. The writer explains the author's main point. The reviewer also gives an opinion about the book and supports it with examples from the story.
Compare and Contrast Essay	The subjects being compared are not clear. The writer briefly describes people, events, or objects without making connections between them. The essay lacks a summary.	The writer names the subjects being compared but does not clearly explain how they are similar and different. The essay has few clue words (such as also, like, but, although) and lacks a summary.	The writer names the subjects being compared and describes some things they have in common and some ways they are each unique. The writer uses some clue words (such as *also, like, but, although*) but mixes some comparisons with contrasts, creating confusion. The summary may not be strong	After introducing the subjects, the writer describes what they have in common using clue words such as *also, like,* and *too.* The writer also describes how each subject is unique using clue words such as *but, however,* and *although.* The essay concludes with a summary of the main points.
Explaining a Process	The process being described is not clear. The steps are sketchy, incomplete, and/or out of order. There is no awareness of the audience's needs.	The introduction names the process but lacks a needed list of materials and definition of terms. Several steps are missing, described incorrectly, or placed out of order. Too much or too little explanation is included.	The introduction names the process but lacks a needed list of materials or a definition of terms. A step may be missing, described incorrectly, or placed out of order. An explanation is included.	The introduction names the process, lists materials (if applicable), and defines the terms. Every step in the process is described accurately and in the correct order. The explanation shows an awareness of what the audience needs to know.
Informative Report	The report has no introduction or clear topic. It offers a group of loosely related facts or a series of poorly written steps. No graphic or conclusion is included.	The report has no clear introduction, but its topic is identifiable. However, it includes many facts unrelated to the topic, or it describes things in a disorganized way. No graphic or conclusion is included.	The report has an introduction and offers facts about the topic. Some facts may be irrelevant, or some ideas may be vague or out of order. A chart, diagram, or map is included. The report is fairly well-organized but doesn't have a strong conclusion.	The report begins with an introduction and offers relevant facts about the topic or describes the topic appropriately. A chart, diagram, map, or other graphic is well-integrated. The report is organized using cause/effect, comparison/contrast, or another pattern. It ends with a strong conclusion.
News Story	The topic of the story is vague. It lacks a headline and/or byline. The lead paragraph provides little accurate information.	The story describes a recent event and includes a headline and/or byline. The lead paragraph answers two or three of the five *Ws (who, what, when, where, why)* and *how* but includes many inaccuracies. The information is collected mainly by observation.	The story describes a recent event and includes a headline and byline. The lead paragraph answers four of the five *Ws* and *how* but may have slight inaccuracies. The information is collected mainly through research or observation.	The story describes a recent event or development and includes a headline and byline. The lead paragraph accurately answers the five *Ws* and *how*. Information and quotations are collected through interviews, research, or observation.

Expository Writing Genres

Genre	1 Point	2 Points	3 Points	4 Points
Summary	Sentences and phrases are taken from the original document with little attempt to identify the main ideas. The writer adds his or her own opinions.	The summary includes some of the main ideas, a few important details, and a number of minor details. Much of the wording is from the original document. The writer includes his or her own opinions.	The summary includes most main ideas and important details. Some minor details are also included. Some wording is from the original document. The writer may change the meaning of the original document slightly or add his or her own opinion.	The summary includes only the main ideas and most important details, organized by the key points. The writer uses his or her own words without changing the meaning of the original document or inserting his or her opinions or comments.

Narrative Writing Genres

Genre	1 Point	2 Points	3 Points	4 Points
Narrative: Character	The writer describes the characters in increasing detail in original stories, including the physical and mental qualities, such as *strong* or *kind.*	The writer describes the internal mental world of the story characters by explicitly describing their thoughts, feelings, and desires.	The writer creates life-like characters whose action and speech reflect unique qualities that are integral to the plot.	The writer creates complex characters, identifying psychological traits that are represented throughout the narrative.
Narrative: Plot	The plot includes a problem, failed attempts, sub-problems, and a resolution. There is evidence of coherence and cohesion, but it may depend on formulaic structure. The subject and theme are clear and maintained.	The plot is elaborated with descriptive details and elements that add excitement or color. The narrative structure is clear. The subject and theme are clear and developed throughout.	The plot is well-developed with subplots and complications that are integrated into the resolution.	The writer includes more complicated plot lines with varied time lines, flashbacks, or dual story lines.
Narrative: Setting	The writer creates settings that include simple descriptions of time, character, and place.	The writer describes the settings in ways that contribute to the mood, suspense, humor, or excitement of the story.	The writer identifies how the settings influence the story problems and their resolutions or contribute to other story elements, such as character and plot.	The writer creates settings that include metaphoric or symbolic elements that help to develop the story elements.
Narrative: Theme	No theme is apparent.	The superficial theme is included but not integrated.	A theme is expressed but not well developed.	The narrative fully develops a theme that expresses an underlying message beyond the narrative plot.
Biography/Autobiog-raphy	The events included are sketchy and do not clearly describe the life of the subject. The time line of events is not clear.	The writing describes a few events in the life of the subject but leaves unexplained gaps. Several events in the life of the subject are described out of chronological order.	The writer describes many important events in the subject's life, perhaps including family, education, early influences, and accomplishments. A few gaps remain. Most events are described chronologically.	The writer describes the most important events in the subject's life (family, education, early influences, accomplishments) and summarizes the rest. All events are described chronologically.
Play	The play does not list and describe the characters or describe all the scenes. Sketchy, confusing dialogue and stage directions do not result in life-like characters. The roles of several characters are unclear. Most stage directions are missing or confused with dialogue.	The play does not begin with a list and description of the characters and does not describe all the scenes. The dialogue and stage directions are vague and do not create unique characters. The roles of some characters in the plot are unclear. Many stage directions are missing or confused with the dialogue.	The play either does not begin with a list and description of the characters or does not describe all the scenes. The actions and speech of some characters may be inconsistent. Some of their traits are overly exaggerated. One or two characters may be superfluous to the plot. Some stage directions are confused with the dialogue.	The play begins with a list and description of its characters. The script describes the time and place of each scene or setting. The dialogue and stage directions create unique, believable characters with consistent actions and speech. All the characters are important to the plot. The stage directions are set off from the dialogue with italics, parentheses, and/or brackets.

The Writing Process

The Writing Process	1 Point	2 Points	3 Points	4 Points
Getting Ideas	The composition consists of statements that are loosely related to a topic, with no evident order or organization. Extraneous material may be present.	The statements not only relate to a topic but have an evident purpose (to describe, explain, argue, and so on).	The main points and supportive details can be identified, but they are not clearly marked.	The composition is clearly organized around the main points with supportive facts or assertions.
Prewriting—Organizing Writing	The writer makes little or no attempt to develop a plan for writing.	The writer uses a given model to plan his or her writing.	The writer elaborates on the model for planning his or her writing.	The writer develops his or her own plan based on the model.
Drafting	The writer writes without attention to a plan or is unable to write.	The writer writes a minimal amount with some attention to his or her plan.	The writer uses a plan to draft.	The writer elaborates on a plan to draft.
Revising	The writer quickly finishes his or her writing activities and does not seek feedback.	The writer pays attention as you provide feedback about his or her written work.	The writer welcomes feedback and advice from you or other students.	The writer actively seeks feedback from you or other students.
Editing	The writer demonstrates no attention to correcting grammar, usage, mechanics, or spelling errors.	Some errors in English language conventions are corrected. Many are not corrected.	The writer corrects many errors in English language conventions.	The writer corrects most errors in English language conventions and uses resources or seeks assistance to address uncertainties.
Presentation/Publishing	The writer presents his or her revised and edited draft as the final version.	The writer recopies his or her final draft with no extra presentation.	The writing includes adequate presentation efforts with illustration, format, and style.	The writer completes an impressive presentation of his or her written work with attention to format, style, illustration, and clarity.
Self-Management	The writer does not have a plan for writing and does not use graphic organizers or checklists when writing.	The writer employs an unclear plan for writing and sometimes uses graphic organizers to plan his or her writing or checklists to revise/proofread his or her writing.	The writer employs a plan for writing and often uses graphic organizers to plan his or her writing or checklists to revise/proofread his or her writing.	The writer employs a clear plan for writing and uses graphic organizers to plan his or her writing and checklists to revise/proofread his or her writing.
Time Management	The writer puts off the writing tasks to the last minute and seldom finishes his or her work on time.	The writer allows some, but often not enough, time for the writing task.	The writer allows time for writing but not enough for revising or proofreading.	The writer listens to advice about time requirements and plans accordingly.

Writing Traits

Writing Traits	1 Point	2 Points	3 Points	4 Points
Audience	The writer displays little or no sense of the audience and does not engage the audience.	The writer displays some sense of the audience	The writer writes with the audience in mind throughout.	The writer displays a strong sense of the audience and engages the audience.
Citing Sources	The writer demonstrates little commitment to the quality and significance of research and to the accuracy of the written document. There is no documentation of the sources.	The writer demonstrates limited commitment to the quality and significance of research and to the accuracy of the written document. The documentation is sometimes used to avoid plagiarism and to enable the reader to judge how believable or important a piece of information is by checking the source.	The writer demonstrates a commitment to the quality and significance of research and to the accuracy of the written document. Documentation is used to avoid plagiarism and to enable the reader to judge how believable or important a piece of information is by checking the source.	The writer demonstrates an exceptionally strong commitment to the quality and significance of research and to the accuracy of the written document. Documentation is used to avoid plagiarism and to enable the reader to judge how believable or important a piece of information is by checking the source.
Conventions Overall	Numerous errors in usage, grammar, spelling, capitalization, and punctuation repeatedly distract the reader and make the text difficult to read. The reader finds it difficult to focus on the message.	The writing demonstrates limited control of standard writing conventions (punctuation, spelling, capitalization, grammar, and usage). Errors sometimes impede readability.	The writing demonstrates control of standard writing conventions (punctuation, spelling, capitalization, grammar, and usage). Minor errors, while perhaps noticeable, do not impede readability.	The writing demonstrates exceptionally strong control of standard writing conventions (punctuation, spelling, capitalization, grammar, and usage) and uses them effectively to enhance communication. Errors are so few and so minor that the reader can easily skim over them.
Conventions: Sentence Structure	Some sentences are standard, but many are run-on sentences or sentence fragments. The writer may use repetitive sentence patterns.	The writer primarily uses simple sentences. The writing has some run-on sentences or sentence fragments. The writer may use repetitive sentence patterns.	The writer uses standard sentence construction throughout with a variety of simple and complex sentence patterns. The writing may have a few run-on sentences or sentence fragments.	The writer uses standard sentence construction throughout. The sentence pattern and length are varied, effective, and enhance what is said. The writing has no unintentional run-on sentences or sentence fragments.
Conventions: Spelling	The writer uses sound spelling as a primary strategy. Many words are misspelled.	The writer uses many correct sound spellings and some structural spelling patterns.	The writer uses mostly correct sound spellings and structural patterns.	The writer uses correct sound spelling patterns and structural patterns and understands affixes, homophones, and meaning patterns.
Conventions: Grammar and Usage	The writing shows a lack of awareness of standard usage and has many errors in subject-verb agreement.	The writing demonstrates some awareness of standard usage and proper sentence structure.	The writing includes mainly standard usage and correct sentence structures	The writer uses a variety of sentence structures appropriately for effect and demonstrates an understanding of standard usage.
Conventions: Punctuation	The writer uses periods correctly but makes little use of other punctuation.	The writer uses end punctuation correctly.	The writer uses most punctuation correctly.	The writer uses end punctuation, commas, quotation marks, parentheses, ellipses, and other forms of punctuation correctly and appropriately.
Conventions: Capitalization	The writer uses capital letters correctly at the beginnings of sentences but inconsistently in other places.	The writer consistently uses capital letters at the beginnings of sentences and for some proper nouns.	The writer uses capitalization correctly most of the time.	The writer uses capitalization correctly in sentences, proper nouns, and titles and demonstrates an awareness of capitalization rules in unique situations.
Elaboration (Supporting Details and Examples that Develop the Main Idea)	The writer states his or her ideas or points with minimal detail to support them	The writing includes sketchy, redundant, or general details; some may be irrelevant. Support for the key ideas is very uneven.	The writer includes a mix of general statements and specific details/examples. The support is mostly relevant but may be uneven and lack depth in places.	The writing includes specific details and supporting examples for each key point/idea. The writer may use compare/contrast to support those ideas.

Writing Traits

Writing Traits	1 Point	2 Points	3 Points	4 Points
Focus	The topic is unclear or wanders and must be inferred. Extraneous material may be present.	The topic/position/direction is unclear and must be inferred.	The topic/position is stated, and the direction/purpose is previewed and maintained. The writing stays mainly on topic.	The topic/position is clearly stated, previewed, and maintained throughout the paper. The topics and details are tied together with a central theme or purpose that is maintained/threaded throughout the paper.
Ideas/Content	Superficial and/or minimal content is included.	The main ideas are understandable, although they may be overly broad or simplistic, and the results may not be effective. The supporting details are limited, insubstantial, overly general, or off the topic.	The writing is clear and focused. The reader can easily understand the main ideas. Support is present, although it may be limited or rather general.	The writing is exceptionally clear, focused, and interesting. The main ideas stand out and are developed by strong support and rich details.
Organization	The writing lacks coherence; the organization seems haphazard and disjointed. The plan is not evident. Facts are presented randomly, and no transitions are included. The beginning is weak, and the ending is abrupt. There is no awareness of paragraph structure or organization.	An attempt has been made to organize the writing; however, the overall structure is inconsistent or skeletal. A plan is evident but loosely structured, or the writer overuses a particular pattern. The writing may be a listing of facts or ideas with a weak beginning or conclusion. The transitions are awkward or nonexistent. The writing includes a beginning use of paragraphs.	The organization is clear and coherent. Order and structure are present but may seem formulaic. A plan is evident. Reasons for the order of the key concepts may be unclear. A beginning or conclusion is included but may lack impact. The transitions are present. Paragraph use is appropriate.	The organization enhances the central idea and its development. The order and structure are compelling and move the reader through the text easily. The plan is evident, and the key concepts are logically sequenced. The beginning grabs the reader's attention, and the conclusion adds impact. The writing uses a variety of transitions that enhance the meaning. The writer uses paragraphs appropriately.
Sentence Fluency	The writing is difficult to follow—either choppy or rambling. The sentences are incomplete, or their awkward constructions force the reader to slow down or reread.	The writing tends to be mechanical rather than fluid. Occasional awkward constructions may force the reader to slow down.	The writing flows; however, connections between the phrases or sentences may be less than fluid. The sentence patterns are somewhat varied, contributing to an ease in oral reading.	The writing has an effective flow and rhythm. The sentences show a high degree of craftsmanship, with consistently strong and varied structure that makes expressive oral reading easy and enjoyable.
Voice	The writing provides little sense of involvement or commitment. There is no evidence that the writer has chosen a suitable voice. It does not engage the audience.	The writer's commitment to the topic seems inconsistent. A sense of the writer may emerge at times; however, the voice is either inappropriately personal or inappropriately impersonal.	A voice is present. The writer demonstrates commitment to the topic. In places, the writing is expressive, engaging, or sincere. The words and expressions are clear and precise.	The writer has chosen a voice that is appropriate for the topic, purpose, and audience. Unique style comes through. The writing is expressive, engaging, or sincere. The writer demonstrates a strong commitment to the topic.
Word Choice	The writer exhibits less than minimal word usage. The writing shows an extremely limited vocabulary and frequent misuse of words. The language is monotonous. The writing includes no interesting words. The words and expressions are simple and may be repetitive, inappropriate, or overused.	The writer exhibits minimal word usage. The language is ordinary; lacks interest, precision, and variety; or may be inappropriate to the audience and purpose in places. The writing is filled with familiar words and phrases and contains only a few interesting words. The words and expressions are clear but usually more general than specific.	The writer exhibits adequate word usage. The words effectively convey the intended message. The writer employs a variety of words that are functional and appropriate to the audience and purpose. The writing contains some interesting words and some vivid descriptive language.	The writer exhibits exceptional word usage. The words convey the intended message in an exceptionally interesting, precise, and natural way that is appropriate to the audience and purpose. The writer employs a rich, broad range of words, which have been carefully chosen and thoughtfully placed for impact. The writing contains many interesting words. The writer uses literary devices effectively.

B

C

G

M

Q

R

Rubrics

Science Inquiry

Selection Vocabulary,

Selections

Use this page to record lessons or elements that work well or need to be adjusted for future reference.

Lessons that work well.

Lessons that need adjustments.